India & World Geography

Class 6-12 (Old+New)

Authors
Vipul Kumar Tripathi
Aqsa Jamil

Series Editor
Santosh Pandey

ARIHANT PUBLICATIONS (INDIA) LIMITED

Administrative & Production Offices

Regd. Office

'Ramchhaya' 4577/15, Agarwal Road, Darya Ganj, New Delhi -110002
Tele: 011- 47630600, 43518550

Head Office

Kalindi, TP Nagar, Meerut (UP) - 250002
Tel: 0121-7156203, 7156204

Sales & Support Offices

Agra, Ahmedabad, Bengaluru, Bareilly, Chennai, Delhi, Guwahati, Hyderabad, Jaipur, Jhansi, Kolkata, Lucknow, Nagpur & Pune.

PRICE ₹275.00

PO No. : TXT-59-T071653-6-26

Published by Arihant Publications (India) Ltd.

For further information about the books published by Arihant, log on to www.arihantbooks.com or e-mail at info@arihantbooks.com

Follow us on   

Few Words

NCERTs are the Foundation in the Journey of IAS...

Civil Service Examinations are the most prestigious, tough and challenging examinations in India.

Being the toughest exam, it automatically consists of a vast and a detailed syllabus. Aspirants often find it difficult to cover the entire syllabus and lack a right direction for a proper and a systematic study for the exam.

The most important aspect of this preparation journey are the NCERT books. Every year approximately **35-40 questions** directly or indirectly asked from NCERT books.

NCERT books also play a key role in understanding the Basic Concepts; so that aspirants can easily form the basic foundation of the entire syllabus. But due to the demand for many NCERT books which are required for study, it becomes exhausting to cover each and every NCERT book.

NCERT MCQs series presented by Arihant Publications covers MCQs from Class 6th to 12th NCERT books (both Old & New) in a comprehensive manner.

Features of Revised Edition

- Each and Every Question is designed as per Latest Pattern of UPSC and State PCS.
- The chapter-wise questions given in the sequential form in the series along with the source of the questions.
- 100% Error free and detailed explanations will make the preparation easy and convenient.
- Additional coverage of Tamil Nadu Board and NIOS Books.
- 3 Practice Sets also provided for overall practice related to subject.

The book is adorned with questions prepared by a team of experts along with a vital role played by the Project Management team with members: Mona Yadav (Project Manager), Manshi Gupta (Project Coordinator), Seema Saini (Proof Reading TL), Pradeep Chaudhary (DTP TL), Bilal and Ankit Tyagi (Cover and Inner designer).

We hope this book will help the aspirants to achieve their goals of clearing UPSC as well as State PCS exams. Your valuable suggestions have always inspired us to strive for useful, authentic and more trustworthy publications.
So your inputs and suggestions are welcomed for subsequent editions.

We wish you all the very best for your preparation and journey!!

Authors

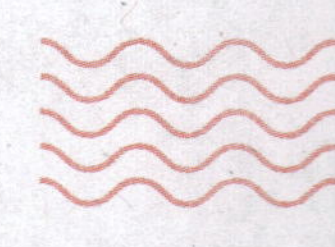

CONTENTS

WORLD GEOGRAPHY

NCERT
MCQs

ENVIRONMENT AND ECOLOGY

Geography as a Discipline

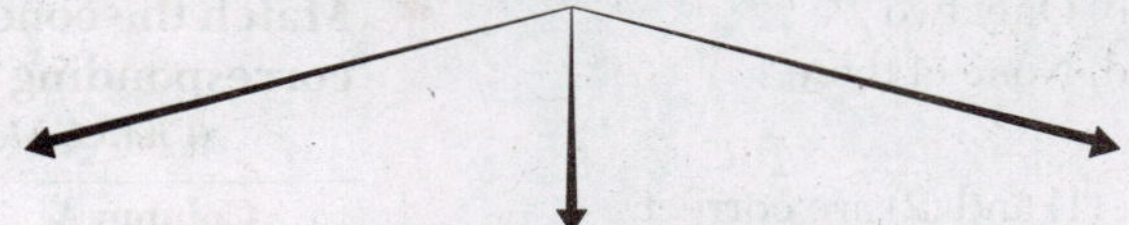

Introduction

- Term coined by **Eratosthenes** 276-194 BC
- Word derived from Greek language meaning 'description of Earth'
- Concerned with the study of nature and human interactions

Theories Propounded by Geographers

- By **Richard Hartshone,** 'Description and explanation of areal differentiation of Earth's surface'
- By **Alfred Hettner,** 'Studying the differences of phenomena in different parts of the Earth's surface'

Approaches related to Branches of Geography

- **Regional Approach** Developed by **Karl Ritter** (contemporary of Humboldt); World is divided into regions at different hierarchical levels
  - **Regional/Area Study** (Comprises micro, macro and regional studies)
  - **Regional Analysis** (Comprises of methods and techniques)
  - **Regional Development** (Concerned with geography of welfare and its evolution)
  - **Regional Planning** (Comprises Urban and Rural town planning)
- **Systematic Approach** Developed by **Alexander Von Humboldt** (1769-1859). In this, a phenomenon is studied world over as a whole i.e., study is done at world level as first step

Branches of Geography

- **Biogeography**
  - Plant Geography studies the spatial pattern of natural species
  - Zoo Geography studies the spatial patterns and characteristics of animals
  - Environmental Geography studies the spatial aspects of interaction between humans and natural world
  - Ecosystem is a scientific study of habitats
- **Physical Geography**
  - **Geomorphology** is a study of evolution of various landforms and its related processes
  - **Climatology** is a study of structure of atmosphere, elements of weather, climate, its types and regions
  - **Hydrology** studies the realm of water i.e., lakes, seas, rivers, oceans and its effect on different life forms
  - **Soils** studies the distribution and variability of soils on terrestrial landscapes
- **Human Geography**
  - **Cultural/Social Geography** is a study of society and its spatial dynamics as well as cultural elements
  - **Population and Settlement** studies population growth, sex ratio, density, migration, etc
  - **Economic Geography** studies economic activities of the people including agriculture, industry, etc
  - **Political Geography** studies political boundaries, space relations between neighbouring political units, etc

Other Important Facts

- **Comte de Buffon** was a French scientist and was the first to give a scientific explanation regarding the geological history of the Earth
- **James Hutton** is called the father of modern geology
- The term **Pangaea** was used by **Wegener**
- **Davis** had propounded the Geographical cycle
- **Ptolemy** was the first scholar to show India on the world map
- **Karl Ritter** is called the easy chair geographer. He studied the Earth's surface by keeping humans in the center

SOURCE *New NCERT Class XI* (*Geography as a Discipline*), *Old NCERT Class XI* (*Geography as a Discipline*), *New NCERT Class XII* (*Human Geography : Nature and Scope*), *Tamil Nadu Board Class XII* (*Population Geography, NIOS Chapter-1, Module 1*)

1 Consider the following statements. *(Chap 1, Module-1, NIOS) (Chap 1, Class XI, New NCERT)*

1. Geography, as a discipline, is inherently interdisciplinary.
2. It attempts to comprehend the association of phenomenon as related in sections of reality.
3. It only deals with physical features of the Earth.

How many statements given above is/are correct?

(a) Only one (b) Only two
(c) All of these (d) None of these

Ans. (b)

Exp. Only two statements i.e., (1) and (2) are correct. Geography involves the study of both physical and human aspects of the Earth, making it an interdisciplinary field. Geography seeks to understand the relationships and interactions between various phenomena on Earth.

Statement (3) is incorrect because. Geography encompasses both physical and human aspects of the Earth, so it goes beyond just physical features.

2 Consider the following statements with reference to Possibilism and Determinism. *(Chap 1, Class-XI, Old NCERT)*

1. Possibilism views humans as capable of modifying the environment and using natural resources according to their own needs.
2. Determinism propounds that human choices and needs are restricted by natural factors.
3. F Ratzel belonged to the Deterministic School.

Which of the statements given above is/are correct?

(a) 1 and 2 (b) 2 and 3 (c) 1 and 3 (d) All of these

Ans. (d)

Exp. All the statements are correct with reference to Possibilism and Determinism. The Possibilism school of thought offers many choices to human. In this approach, emphasis is based on human rather than on nature and human is seen choosing his needs according to his own culture and is also "the judge of their use". The French School of Geographers is firm supporter of Possibilism. According to Determinism thought, human is a slave of nature. There is direct dependence of human beings on nature for resources and nature is taken as a powerful force, it is worshipped, revered and conserved.

Kant, Humboldt, Ritter and German expert Ratzel belongs to the Deterministic School.

3 Which of the following pairs is/are matched correctly? *(Chap 1, Class-XII, New NCERT) (UPPSC Pre 1994)*

1. Neo Determinism – Griffith Taylor
2. Determinism – E Huntington
3. Possibilism – Vidal De La Blache

Codes

(a) 1 and 2 (b) 2 and 3 (c) Only 2 (d) All of these

Ans. (d)

Exp. All the pairs are correctly matched as Griffith Taylor gave the concept of Neo Determinism also known as 'Stop and Go Determinism'.

Determinism can be defined as naturalisation of humans. E Huntington was one of the pioneers of this approach.

Vidal De La Blache was a pioneer of possibilism along with Lucian Febre. Possibilism means humanisation of nature.

4 Match the concepts in Column A with their corresponding definitions in Column B. *(Chap 1, Module-1, NIOS) (Chap 1, Class-XI, New NCERT)*

Column A	Column B
A. Geology	1. Concerned with the movement and quality of water
B. Geomorphology	2. Studies the Earth's physical structure and substance
C. Climatology	3. Examines landforms and their evolution
D. Hydrology	4. Gathers, stores, processes and delivers geographic information of soil.
E. Soil Geography	5. Investigates the structure of the atmosphere and climates

Codes

	A	B	C	D	E		A	B	C	D	E
(a)	1	2	3	4	5	(b)	2	3	4	5	1
(c)	2	3	5	1	4	(d)	3	2	5	4	1

Ans. (c)

Exp. The correct matching is A-2, B-3, C-5, D-1, E-4.

Geology is the scientific study of the Earth's solid materials, including rocks, minerals and the processes that shape the Earth's structure.

Geomorphology is the branch of geography that deals with the study of landforms, their origin, development, and the processes that shape the Earth's surface.

Climatology is the study of climate, including the long-term patterns of temperature, humidity, wind, and precipitation. It involves examining the atmospheric conditions and variations over time and space to understand different climates.

Hydrology is the science that studies the distribution, movement, and properties of water in the Earth's atmosphere and on its surface.

Soil Geography involves the study of soils and their spatial distribution. It focuses on understanding the characteristics of soils, their formation, fertility, and how they vary across different geographical areas.

5 Consider the following statements on Systematic and Regional Approaches. *(Chap 1, Class-XI, New NCERT)*

1. The systematic approach focuses on specific themes across the globe, while the regional approach studies all facts within a defined area.

2. Both approaches exclusively deal with physical geography.
3. The regional approach is a more recent development compared to the systematic approach.

How many statements given above is/are correct?

(a) Only one (b) Only two
(c) All of these (d) None of these

Ans. (a)

Exp. Only one statement i.e., (1) is correct with respect to Systematic and Regional Approaches. The systematic approach focuses on specific themes like climate, vegetation, or population patterns, and analyses their variations and patterns across the globe. The regional approach, on the other hand, delves into all aspects of a particular region, including physical and human elements.

Statements (2) and (3) are incorrect. Both systematic and regional approaches can encompass both physical and human geography. For example, studying climate patterns globally in a systematic approach involves understanding physical elements like atmospheric circulation and temperature, while examining human settlements in a specific region (regional approach) may include factors like climate, resources and economic activities.

Both systematic and regional approaches have existed for centuries, with roots in early geographical thinking. While their emphasis and development may have evolved over time, neither can be classified as strictly more recent than the other.

6 **Match the following lists correctly and choose the correct code.** *(Chap 1, Class-XI, Old NCERT)*

	List I (Geographer)		List II (Field of Work)
A.	H Mackinder	1.	Quantitative Methods
B.	W Christaller	2.	Regional Geography
C.	Peter Haggett	3.	Settlement Hierarchy
D.	W Davis	4.	Cycle of Erosion

Codes

	A	B	C	D		A	B	C	D
(a)	1	2	3	4	(b)	2	3	1	4
(c)	3	1	4	2	(d)	4	2	1	3

Ans. (b)

Exp. The correct matching is A-2, B-3, C-1, D-4.

H Mackinder He gave his greatest contribution on Heartland Theory in the field of regional geography.

W Christaller He gave his greatest contribution on Central Place Theory in the field of settlement hierarchy.

Peter Haggett He was well-known for his work on quantitative methods as quantitative revolutionaries.

W Davis He gave the theory of cycle of erosion where he defined the three distinct stages of river erosion.

7 **Consider the following concepts in Column A with their corresponding in Column B.** *(Chap 1, Class-XII, New NCERT)*

1. Social/Cultural Geography – Social dynamics and cultural elements contributed by society
2. Population and Settlement Geography – Population growth, distribution, density and settlement characteristics
3. Economic Geography – Economic activities like agriculture, industry and trade
4. Historical Geography – Historical processes shaping spaces and geographical features
5. Political Geography – Political events, boundaries, and political behaviour analysis

How many pairs given above is/are correct?

(a) Only two (b) Only three
(c) Only four (d) All of these

Ans. (d)

Exp. All pairs are correctly matched.

Social/cultural Geography focuses on studying the spatial dynamics of societies and the cultural elements contributed by them.

Population and Settlement Geography involves the study of population-related aspects such as growth, distribution, density, as well as characteristics of settlements-whether rural or urban.

Economic Geography explores the spatial patterns and distribution of economic activities, including agriculture, industry, trade and other economic processes.

Historical Geography examines how historical processes have shaped and influenced the organisation of spaces and geographical features.

Political Geography looks at the spatial dimensions of political phenomena, including political events, the establishment of boundaries and the analysis of political behaviour.

8 **Consider the following about theme of Geography.** *(Chap 1, Class-XII, New NCERT)*

1. Location 2. Place
3. Movement 4. Technology

Which of the options given above is/are incorrect?

(a) 1 and 2 (b) 2 and 3
(c) Only 4 (d) 1 and 4

Ans. (c)

Exp. Only option (4) is incorrect with respect to the theme of geography.

Technology is not one of the five traditional themes of geography. The five themes are location, place, human-environment interaction, movement, and regions.

Chapter 02

The Universe

The Universe

Origin of Universe

Big Bang Theory

- Most popular argument, also called as expanding universe hypothesis
- Given by Georges Edouard Lemaitre
- It states all the matter existed in one place of a 'tiny ball' with small volume, infinite temperature and density
- Tiny ball exploded that lead to a huge expansion
- Energy converted to matter, expansion slowed down, temperature dropped down and give rise to atomic matter

Steady State Theory

- An alternative to Big Bang Theory Considered the universe to be roughly the same at any point of time

Pulsating Universe Theory

- A variation of Big Bang Theory
- Proposed by Allan Sandage
- According to it, universe pulsates endlessly between the Big Bang and the Big Squeeze

Age of the Universe

- Astronomers estimated that the Big Bang occurred between 12 and 14 billion years ago and the age of the universe is now accepted to be 13.7 billion years

Celestial Bodies, Galaxies & Stars

Celestial Bodies

- The Sun, Moon and all those object shining in the night sky
- Also called heavenly bodies
- They are mainly of two types
  - One which have their own heat and light; For example-stars
  - Others who do not have their own heat or light but they reflect the light; For example-planets

Galaxies

- A system of stars held together by mutual gravitation
- Contains a large number of gas clouds, some of which are quite huge
- It is of three types
  - **Elliptical galaxies** are like flattened balls of old stars and contain very little gas
  - **Spiral galaxies** have a flattened shape
  - **Irregular galaxies** have no particular shape

Stars

- Huge bodies of glowing gases which have heat and light of their own; The distances of stars are expressed in light years
- Colour of star is determined by its surface temperature
- Stars with low temperature appear red and with higher temperature appear yellow

Constellations

- Various patterns formed by different groups of stars in the night sky
- e.g. Ursa Major or Big Bear; It is one of the most easily recognisable constellation is Saptarishi

Solar System

Solar System

- A part of milky way galaxy, also known as Akash Ganga
- Our solar system contains 1 Sun, 8 planets and 293 Moons and millions of smaller bodies

Planets

- **Mercury** Nearest to the Sun, smallest planet
- **Venus** Earth's closet planetry neighbour
- **Earth** Only known planet with life in our solar system (suitable temperature, presence of water, suitable atmosphere)
- **Mars** Red planet due to reddish appearance
- **Jupiter** Largest planet in solar system
- **Saturn** Yellowish Colour and it has eight main rings
- **Uranus** Rotates from East to West
- **Neptune** Based on Sir Issac Newton's Law of Gravitation

Pluto

It was considered as ninth planet of solar system for long time, but now it is not a planet according to new definition of International Astronomical Union (IAU) in 2006

SOURCE ***New NCERT Class VI*** *(The Earth in the Solar System),* ***Old NCERT Class VI*** *(The Earth in our Solar System),* ***New NCERT Class XI*** *(Origin and Evolution of Earth),* ***Tamil Nadu Board Class XI*** *(The Solar System and the Earth)*

Study of Universe

1 In the context of the Big Bang Theory, consider the following statements. *(Chap 2 , Class-XI, New NCERT)*

1. The Big Bang Theory is the most widely accepted explanation for the origin of the universe.
2. Georges Edouard Lemaitre's observations provided evidence that galaxies are moving away from each other.
3. Scientists believe that only the space between galaxies is increasing, the galaxies themselves are not expanding.

Which of the statements given above is/are correct?

(a) 1 and 2
(b) 2 and 3
(c) 1 and 3
(d) 1, 2 and 3

***Ans.* (c)**

Exp. Statements (1) and (3) are correct.

The Big Bang Theory is the most popular argument regarding the origin of the universe. It is also called the expanding universe hypothesis.

Scientists believe that only the space between the galaxies is increasing; the galaxies themselves are not expanding. Big Bang theory considers the three stages in the development of universe.

Statement (2) is incorrect because, in 1920, Edwin Hubble provided evidence that the universe was expanding. As time passes, galaxies move farther and farther away.

2 Consider the following statements in the context of the stages in the development of the universe. *(Chap 2, Class-XI, New NCERT)*

1. The 'tiny ball' (singular atom) that existed in the beginning, according to the Big Bang Theory, had infinite temperature and infinite density.
2. The event of the Big Bang is estimated to have occurred approximately 13.7 billion years before the present.
3. The expansion of the universe has been continuous since the Big Bang, with some energy being converted into matter.

How many of the statements given above is/are correct?

(a) Only one (b) Only two
(c) All three (d) None of these

***Ans.* (c)**

Exp. All three statements i.e., (1), (2) and (3) are correct regarding the development of the universe.

According to the Big Bang Theory, in the beginning, all matter forming the universe existed in one place in the form of a 'tiny ball' (singular atom) with a small volume, infinite temperature and infinite density.

The widely accepted estimate for the age of the universe is around 13.7 billion years, based on observations such as cosmic microwave background radiation.

The universe has been expanding since the initial explosion. As it expanded, some of the initial energy was converted into matter, leading to the formation of galaxies and other cosmic structures.

3 Which of the following statements is/are not correct about the state of early universe? *(Chap 2, Class-XI, New NCERT)*

1. The distribution of matter and energy was not even.
2. Differences in the density led to differences in gravitational forces.
3. Galaxies started forming by the accumulation of a large cloud of hydrogen gas.

Select the correct answer using the codes given below.

(a) 1 and 2 (c) 1 and 3
(c) 2 and 3 (d) None of these

***Ans.* (d)**

Exp. None of these statements are correct about the state of early universe. The distribution of matter and energy was not even in the early universe. This initial density differences gave rise to differences in gravitational forces and it caused the matter to get drawn together.

Hence, galaxies started forming by the accumulation of a large cloud of hydrogen gas.

A galaxy contains a large number of stars. Galaxies spread over vast distances are measured in thousands of light years. The diameters of individual galaxies range from 80,000-1,50,000 light years.

4 Which of the following statements about the state of universe are correct? *(Chap 2, Class-XI, New NCERT)*

1. The universe is in an expanding state.
2. The distance between the galaxies is found to be increasing and thereby, the universe is considered to be expanding.
3. The formation of universe started almost 13 billion years ago.

How many statements given above is/are correct?

(a) Only one (b) Only two
(c) All three (d) None of these

***Ans.* (c)**

Exp. All three statements i.e., (1), (2) and (3) are correct about the state of universe.

According to scientist Edwin Hubble, the universe is in expanding state and with passing of time, the space between the galaxies is increasing. The Big Bang Theory is the most widely accepted theory about the genesis of the universe. According to which, the formation of universe started almost 13.7 billion years before the present and it is still expanding.

5 Which of the following statements are correct about the formation of universe? *(Chap 2, Class-XI, New NCERT)*

1. Before the Big Bang, the universe was concentrated in a singular atom.
2. The singular atom exploded violently which led to its rapid expansion.
3. The present rate of expansion of universe is more than its initial expansion.

Select the correct answer using the codes given below.

(a) 1 and 3 (b) 1 and 2 (c) 2 and 3 (d) All of these

Ans. (b)

Exp. Statements (1) and (2) are correct about the formation of universe as in the beginning, all matter forming the universe existed in one place in the form of a 'tiny ball' (singular atom) with an unimaginably small volume, infinite temperature and infinite density.

At the Big Bang, the 'tiny ball' exploded violently. This led to a huge expansion.

It is now generally accepted that the event of big bang took place 13.7 billion years before the present. The expansion continues even to the present day.

Statement (3) is incorrect because there was particularly rapid expansion within fractions of a second after the bang. But thereafter, the expansion has slowed down. Hence the present rate of expansion of universe is not more than its initial expansion.

6 In the context of Terrestrial and Jovian planets, consider the following statements. *(Chap 2, Class-XI, New NCERT)*

1. Terrestrial planets are primarily made up of gas and dust.
2. Jovian planets have thicker atmospheres mainly composed of helium and hydrogen.
3. The solar wind plays a significant role in removing gases from the terrestrial planets.

How many of the statements given above is/are correct?

(a) Only one (b) Only two
(c) All three (d) None of these

Ans. (b)

Exp. Only two statements i.e., (2) and (3) are correct regarding Terrestrial and Jovian Planets.

Jovian planets, including Jupiter, Saturn, Uranus and Neptune, have thick atmospheres composed mainly of helium and hydrogen.

Jovian planets are much larger than terrestrial planets. These planets are also referred to as 'gas giants' due to the significant presence of these gases in their atmospheres. The solar wind was most intense near the Sun so, it blew off lots of gas and dust from the terrestrial planets.

Statement (1) is incorrect. Terrestrial planets, such as Mercury, Venus, Earth, and Mars, are primarily composed of rock and metals. They have solid surfaces, and their densities are relatively high compared to the Jovian planets.

7 Given below is a list of stages of formation of planets in the universe. Arrange the list in correct sequence using the codes given below. *(Chap 2, Class-XI, New NCERT)*

1. Condensation of gas cloud around the core
2. Development of planetesimals
3. Formation of planets
4. Formation of localised gas lumps
5. Formation of core of gas cloud

Codes

(a) 1, 2, 4, 5, 3 (b) 4, 5, 1, 2, 3
(c) 2, 1, 4, 5, 3 (d) 4, 2, 1, 5, 3

Ans. (b)

Exp. The correct sequence of the stages of the formation of planets in the universe is 4, 5, 1, 2, 3.

Formation of localised gas lumps The stars are localised lumps of gas within a nebula. The gravitational force within the lumps leads to the formation of a core of the gas cloud.

Formation of core of gas cloud A huge rotating disc of gas and dust develops around the core.

Condensation of gas cloud around the core In the next stage, the gas cloud starts getting condensed and the matter around the core develops into small rounded objects.

Development of Planetesimals The small rounded objects by the process of cohesion develop into what is called planetesimals. Larger bodies start forming by the collision and gravitational attraction causes the material to stick together.

Formation of Planets In the final stage, planetesimals which are a large number of similar bodies accrete to form a fewer larger bodies in the form of planets.

8 Consider the following statements regarding the Solar System. *(Chap 1, Class-VI, Old NCERT) (CGPSC Pre 2020)*

1. Mercury is the hottest planet in the Solar System.
2. Ganymede, satellite of Saturn, is the largest satellite in the Solar System.
3. Neptune is surrounded by methane gas rings of sub-zero temperature.
4. Phobos and Deimos are two satellites of Mars.

Which of the statements given above are correct?

(a) 1 and 2 (b) 2 and 3 (c) 3 and 4 (d) 1, 2, 3 and 4

Ans. (c)

Exp. Statements (3) and (4) are correct regarding Solar System. Neptune is surrounded by methane gas rings of sub-zero temperature. Mars has two small moons: Phobos and Deimos, which were discovered by American astronomer Asaph Hall in 1877.

Statements (1) and (2) are incorrect. Venus is the hottest planet in the Solar System, not Mercury because its dense atmosphere acts as a greenhouse and heats the surface to about 880°F.

Ganymede is the satellite of Jupiter. It is the largest satellite in the Solar System.

9 **Consider the following pairs.** *(Chap 2, Class-XI, New NCERT)*

	Galaxies		Characteristics
1.	Elliptical Galaxies	–	They do not contain any newly formed stars because the majority of their member stars are very ancient.
2.	Spiral Galaxies	–	They consist of populations of old stars in the centre and the youngest stars located in the arms.
3.	Irregular Galaxies	–	Do not have a distinct regular shape, like a spiral or an elliptical galaxy.

How many of the pairs given above is/are correctly matched?

(a) Only one (b) Only two
(c) All three (d) None of these

Ans. (c)

Exp. All three pairs i.e., (1), (2) are (3) are correctly matched.

Elliptical galaxies lack newly formed stars because most of their member stars are ancient. These galaxies are characterised by their elliptical or nearly spherical shape. The absence of ongoing star formation contributes to their overall elliptical appearance.

Spiral Galaxies have a flattened shape. They have a projection in the centre composed of old stars surrounded by a disk of young stars and all arranged in spiral arms.

Irregular galaxies have no particular shape. There are billions of galaxies in the universe, the centre of the galaxy releases a huge amount of heat, radiation, radio waves and X-rays. Irregular galaxies often display a more chaotic appearance, and their members may include stars of different ages.

10 **Consider the following statements about terrestrial planets.** *(Chap 2, Class-XI, New NCERT)*

1. The terrestrial planets were formed in the close vicinity of the parent star where it was too cold for gases to condense to solid particles.
2. The terrestrial planets are larger and their lower gravity could not hold the escaping gases.

Which of the statements given above is/are incorrect?

(a) Only 1 (b) Only 2
(c) Both 1 and 2 (d) Neither 1 nor 2

Ans. (c)

Exp. Both the statements (1) and (2) are incorrect about terrestrial planets. The terrestrial planets were formed in the close vicinity of the parent star where it was too warm for gases to condense to solid particles.

The solar wind was most intense, nearer the Sun; so, it blew off lots of gases and dust from the terrestrial planets.

The terrestrial planets are smaller and their lower gravity could not hold the escaping gases.

11 **Regarding the constellations, consider the following statements.** *(Chap 1, Class-VI, New NCERT)*

1. Constellations are groups of stars that appear close together in the night sky but are vast distances apart.
2. The apparent movement of constellations is caused by the rotation of the Earth on its axis.
3. One of the most easily recognisable constellations is the Saptarishi (sapta-seven rishi stages).

How many of the statements given above is/are correct?

(a) Only one (b) Only two
(c) All three (d) None of these

Ans. (c)

Exp. All the three statements i.e., (1), (2) and (3) are correct in context of constellations.

Constellations are groups of stars that appear close together in the night sky but are vast distances apart. Constellations are not physical groupings of stars. The stars in a constellation are actually spread out in three dimensions and are all different distances from Earth.

The Earth's rotation on its axis causes the apparent movement of constellations.

The Earth rotates from West to East, carrying observers Eastward. This causes the stars to appear to move westward, creating the illusion of constellations rotating around the celestial poles.

Saptarishi, meaning 'seven sages' in Sanskrit, is a group of seven bright stars forming part of the Ursa Major constellation. It's easily recognisable from the Northern hemisphere and holds cultural significance in India.

12 **Which among the following statements can be considered as definitely true about the planets in Solar System?** *(Chap 2, Class-XI, New NCERT)*

1. The asteroids are revolving around the Sun between the orbits of terrestrial planets and Jovian planets.
2. The terrestrial planets in the Solar System are much smaller than the Jovian planets.
3. The atmosphere of Jovian planets is made up of oxygen and argon.

Codes

(a) 1 and 3 (b) 2 and 3
(c) 1 and 2 (d) All of these

Ans. (c)

Exp. Statements (1) and (2) are considered as definitely true about the planets in Solar System because out of the eight planets, Mercury, Venus, Earth and Mars are called as the inner planets as they lie between the Sun and the belt of asteroids.

The other four planets are called the outer planets. Alternatively, the first four are called terrestrial, meaning Earth-like as they are made up of rock and metals, and have relatively high densities.

The rest four are called Jovian or gas giant planets. Jovian means Jupiter-like, most of them are much larger than the terrestrial planets.
Statement (3) is false because the atmosphere of Jovian planets is made up of helium and hydrogen.

Planets

13 Which of the following statements is/are correct regarding evolution of atmosphere and hydrosphere? *(Chap 2, Class-XI, New NCERT)*

(a) During the cooling of the Earth, gases and water vapour were released from the interior solid Earth.
(b) The process through which the gases were outpoured from the interior is called degassing.
(c) Continuous volcanic eruptions contributed water vapour and gases to the atmosphere.
(d) All of the above

Ans. (d)

Exp. All of the given statements are correct regarding evolution of atmosphere and hydrosphere. During the cooling of the Earth, gases and water vapour were released from the interior of the Earth by the mode of volcanic eruptions.
This started the evolution of the present atmosphere. The early atmosphere largely contained water vapour, nitrogen, carbon dioxide, methane, ammonia and very little of free oxygen. The process through which the gases were outpoured from the interior is called degassing.
Continuous volcanic eruptions contributed water vapour and gases to the atmosphere. As the Earth cooled, the water vapour released started getting condensed.

14 Consider the following pairs. *(Chap 1, Class-VI, New NCERT)*

	Planets		Characteristics
1.	Earth	–	The fifth largest planet in the Solar System
2.	Venus	–	It is an extremely hot planet with a temperature of 480°C.
3.	Jupiter	–	Hottest planet in the solar system
4.	Uranus	–	Uranus has a highly tilted rotational axis

How many of the pairs given above is/are correctly matched?

(a) Only one (b) Only two
(c) Only three (d) All four

Ans. (c)

Exp. Only three pairs i.e., (1), (2), and (4) are correctly matched.
Earth is the fifth largest planet in our solar system. It is the third nearest planet to the Sun. The Earth is neither too hot nor too cold.
Venus has a very high surface temperature, primarily due to its thick atmosphere that traps heat. The actual temperature is even higher than 480°C. Uranus has a highly tilted rotational axis. It is the outermost planet of the solar system.
Pair (3) is incorrectly matched because Jupiter is not the hottest planet; in fact, it is a gas giant and does not have a solid surface. Jupiter is the planet with the most moons, with a total of 92. Jupiter is also the largest planet in our solar system, with a surface area that is two and a half times the size of all the other planets.

15 Regarding the characteristics of stars, consider the following statements. *(Chap 1, Class-VI, New NCERT)*

1. Stars are born within the clouds of dust and gas scattered throughout most galaxies.
2. The colour of a star is determined by its surface temperature, with low-temperature stars appearing blue and high-temperature stars appearing red.
3. Stars appear to move from West to East due to the Earth's rotation, completing one rotation in 24 hours.

How many of the statements given above is/are correct?

(a) Only one (b) Only two
(c) All three (d) None of these

Ans. (a)

Exp. Only one statement i.e., (1) is correct regarding the characteristics of stars.
Stars are born in clouds of dust and gas scattered throughout most galaxies. These clouds are called nebulae and are made up of dust and gas, primarily hydrogen atoms.
Statements (2) and (3) are incorrect because the colour of a star is determined by its surface temperature. Stars that have low temperature appear red, those with higher temperature appear yellow and those with very high temperature are blue.
With high speed, the stars appear to move from East to West. This is because the Earth rotates from West to East about an imaginary axis that passes through its center. The Earth completes one rotation in 24 hours.

16 In the context of the planets in our solar system, consider the following statements about Venus. *(Chap 1, Class-VI, New NCERT)*

1. Venus is commonly referred to as Earth's twin or sister planet due to its similar mass, size and closeness to the Sun.
2. It has the densest atmosphere of the four terrestrial planets.
3. It rotates in the opposite direction (clockwise) to most other planets.

How many of the statements given above is/are correct?

(a) Only one (b) Only two
(c) All three (d) None of these

Ans. (c)

Exp. All the three statements are correct regarding Venus.

Venus is frequently referred to as Earth's twin or sister planet due to similarities in their mass, size and proximity to the Sun as well as their shared bulk composition and physical characteristics, which include folding mountain ranges, high plateaus and an abundance of volcanoes.

Venus has the densest atmosphere among the terrestrial planets (Mercury, Venus, Earth and Mars). The atmosphere is primarily composed of carbon dioxide.

Venus rotates on its axis in the opposite direction to the majority of planets in our solar system.

17 Consider the following statements regarding light year. *(Chap 2, Class-XI, New NCERT)*

1. Light travels at a speed of 3,00,000 km/second. Therefore, the distance the light will travel in one year is taken to be one light year.
2. The mean distance between the Sun and the Earth is 149,598,000 km.
3. The diameters of individual galaxies range from 80,000-1,50,000 light years.

Which of the statements given above is/are correct?

(a) Only 1 (b) 2 and 3
(c) 1 and 3 (d) 1, 2 and 3

***Ans.* (d)**

Exp. All the given statements are correct regarding light year. A light year is a measure of distance. Light travels at a speed of 3,00,000 km/second. Considering this, the distance the light will travel in one year is taken to be one light year. This equals to 9.4611012 km. The mean distance between the Sun and the Earth is 149,598,000 km. In terms of light years, it is 8.311 minutes. The diameters of individual galaxies range from 80,000-1,50,000 light years.

18 Which of the statements is/are incorrect regarding formation of moon? *(Chap 2, Class-XI, New NCERT)*

(a) The formation of moon, as a satellite of the Earth, is an outcome of 'giant impact' or what is described as 'the big splat.'
(b) A body of the size of one to three times that of Mars collided into the Earth sometime shortly after the Earth was formed.
(c) Both a and b
(d) Neither a nor b

***Ans.* (d)**

Exp. None of the statement is incorrect regarding formation of moon. The moon's origin as a satellite of the Earth is the result of a 'giant impact,' often known as 'the big splat.' Shortly after the Earth was formed, a body, crashed with it that was the size of one to three times of Mars.

A big portion of the Earth was blown into space. About 4.44 billion years ago, a piece of the blasted material was orbiting the Earth that the current moon.

19 Arrange the planets in order based on their Period of Revolution (in Earth days), starting from the shortest to the longest. *(Chap 2, Class-XI, New NCERT)*

1. Mercury
2. Earth
3. Venus
4. Uranus
5. Jupiter

Select the correct answer using the codes given below.

(a) 1-2-3-4-5 (b) 2-4-5-3-1
(c) 1-3-2-5-4 (d) 2-4-3-5-1

***Ans.* (c)**

Exp. The correct order based on the Period of Revolution (orbital period) from the shortest to the longest is 1-3-2-5-4.

Mercury has the shortest period of revolution of 87 Earth days, followed by Venus with a period of 224 Earth days, Earth with a period of 365 Earth days, Jupiter with an orbital period of 11.9 Earth years, and Uranus with the longest period of revolution of 84 Earth years.

20 Which of the following factors have contributed to the formation of terrestrial rocky planets? *(Chap 2, Class-XI, New NCERT)*

1. Closeness to the parent star
2. Solar winds
3. Higher gravity

Select the correct answer using the codes given below.

(a) 1 and 2 (b) 2 and 3
(c) 1 and 3 (d) All of these

***Ans.* (a)**

Exp. Closeness to the parent star and solar winds have contributed to the formation of terrestrial rocky planets. The terrestrial planets were formed in the close vicinity of the parent star where it was too warm for gases to condense to solid particles.

Jovian planets were formed at quite a distant location. The solar wind was most intense, nearer the Sun; so, it blew off lots of gases and dust from the terrestrial planets.

The solar winds were not all that intense to cause similar removal of gases from the Jovian planets. The terrestrial planets are smaller and their low gravity could not hold the escaping gases.

21 Consider the following statements regarding stages in the evolution of the present atmosphere. *(Chap 2, Class-XI, New NCERT)*

1. The first stage is marked by the loss of primordial atmosphere.
2. In the second stage, the hot interior of the Earth contributed to the evolution of the atmosphere.
3. Finally, the composition of the atmosphere was modified by the living world through the process of photosynthesis.

Which of the statements given above is/are correct?
(a) Only 1
(b) Only 2
(c) 1, 2 and 3
(d) 1 and 3

***Ans.* (c)**

Exp. All the given statements regarding the stages of evolution of present atmosphere are correct. There are the three stages in the evolution of the present atmosphere. The first stage is marked by the loss of primordial atmosphere.

In the second stage, the hot interior of the Earth contributed to the evolution of the atmosphere.

Finally, the composition of the atmosphere was modified by the living world through the process of photosynthesis.

22 What is the difference between asteroids and comets? *(Chap 2, Class-XI, New NCERT) (IAS Pre 2011)*

1. Asteroids are small rocky planetoids, while comets are formed of frozen gases held together by rocky and metallic material.
2. Asteroids are found mostly between the orbits of Jupiter and Mars, while comets are found mostly between Venus and Mercury.
3. Comets show a perceptible glowing tail, while asteroids do not.

Which of the statements given above is/are correct?
(a) 1 and 2
(b) 1 and 3
(c) Only 3
(d) 1, 2 and 3

***Ans.* (b)**

Exp. Statements (1) and (3) are correct regarding asteroids and comets.

Asteroids are small, rocky bodies composed primarily of metals and minerals, whereas comets are made up of ice, dust and rocky material.

When a comet gets close to the Sun, solar radiation causes the volatile materials within the comet to vaporise and create a glowing tail that points away from the Sun. Asteroids, being made of rocky and metallic materials, do not exhibit such tails.

Statement (2) is incorrect because most asteroids are located in the asteroid belt, a region of space between the orbits of Mars and Jupiter. This region is known as the main asteroid belt, and it contains the majority of known asteroids. On the other hand, comets are found in various regions beyond the asteroid belt, such as the Kuiper Belt and Oort Cloud.

23 Consider the following statements.
(Chap 1, Class-VI, New NCERT)

Statement-I Mars is commonly known as the 'Red Planet' because of the reddish iron oxide prevalent on its surface.

Statement-II Although, the existence of life on Mars has not yet been proven, the planet is comparatively quite cold.

Which one of the following is correct in respect of the above statements?

(a) Both Statement-I and Statement-II are correct and Statement-II is the correct explanation for Statement-I.
(b) Both Statement-I and Statement-II are correct and Statement-II is not the correct explanation for Statement-I.
(c) Statement-I is correct but Statement-II is incorrect.
(d) Statement-I is incorrect but Statement-II is correct.

***Ans.* (b)**

Exp. Both Statement-I and Statement-II are correct and Statement-II is not the correct explanation for Statement-I.

"Mars is commonly known as the 'Red Planet' because of the reddish iron oxide prevalent on its surface". The surface of Mars is rich in iron, and the presence of iron oxide gives it a reddish appearance. Mars is known for its cold temperatures, but the existence of life on Mars has not been conclusively proven. Mars is also close to Earth. About 96% of Mars' atmosphere is made up of carbon dioxide, 1.93% argon and 1.89% nitrogen, with smaller amounts of oxygen, methane and water.

Chapter 03

The Earth

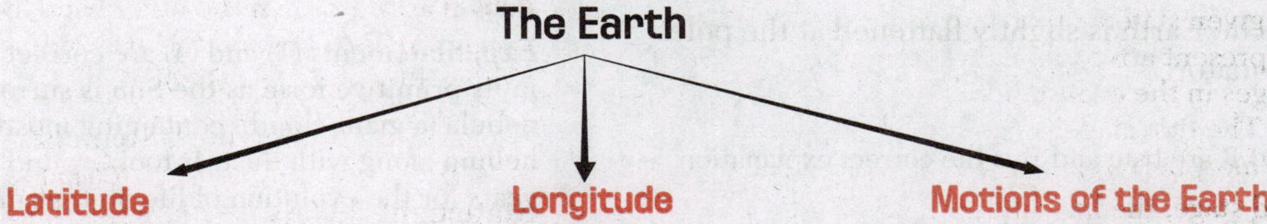

Latitude

Introduction
- A measure of angular distance of a given point from Equator
- Measured in degrees from Equator towards either poles

Important Latitudes of Earth
- **Equator** (0 degree latitude) an imaginary circular line that divides the Earth into two equal halves, i.e., Northern and Southern Hemisphere
- 90 degree of Northern Hemisphere is North Pole and Southern Hemisphere is South Pole
- **Tropic of Cancer** Important parallel of Northern Hemisphere i.e., 23° 30′ N
- **Tropic of Capricorn** Important parallel of Southern Hemisphere i.e., 23° 30′ S
- **Arctic Circle** 66° 30′ North of the Equator
- **Antarctic Circle** 66° 30′ South of the Equator

Heat Zones of Earth
- **Torrid Zone** (23° 30′ N-23° 30′ S) Mid-day Sun is exactly overhead atleast once a year on all the latitudes of the extent this area receives maximum heat
- **Temperate Zone** (23° 30′-66° 30′ N and 23° 30′-66° 30′ S) Mid-day Sun never shines overhead on any latitude

Longitude

Introduction
- Angular distance of a place from the Prime Meridian
- All meridians are of equal length unlike latitudes

Important Longitudes of Earth
- **Prime Meridian** Valued at 0° longitude which passes through Greenwich. It divides the earth into two equal halves, Eastern and Western Hemisphere
- **Standard Time** Local time of standard meridian of the country ex 82° 30′ E in India. Earth has been divided into 24 time zones of one hour each
- **International Date Line** The place where each day officially begins. The west side of date line is one day ahead of the East side

Longitude and Time
- When the Prime Meridian at Greenwich has Sun at highest point in sky, all the places along this meridian experiences noon
- As the Earth rotates from East to West, the places East of Meridian will be ahead of Greenwich time and those to West will be behind

Indian Standard Time (IST)
- In India, the longitude of 82° 30′ E is treated as the standard meridian
- The local time at this meridian is taken as the standard time for the whole country

Motions of the Earth

Rotation
- Movement of Earth on its own axis Earth takes 24 hours to complete one rotation around its axis, known as Earth Day
- Earth's axis is tilted at 23.5° at its axis to orbital plane, known as inclination of Earth's axis
- When Earth rotates, one half of it faces Sun and other half darkness

Revolution
- Movement of Earth around the Sun in a fixed path or orbit
- Earth completes one revolution in 365 days and 6 hours

Summer Solistice
- On 21st June, Northern Hemisphere is tilted towards the Sun and the rays directly fall on the Tropic of Cancer
- So, these areas receive more heat as compared to poles due to slanting nature of the sun rays. The longest day and shortest night occurs on this day

Winter Solistice
- On 22nd Dec, Southern Hemisphere is tilted towards the Sun and the rays directly fall on the Tropic of Capricorn
- The longest day and shortest night on this day in Southern Hemisphere whereas longest night and shortest day in Northern Hemisphere

Equinox
- On 21st March and 23rd September, direct sun rays fall on the Equator
- At this point, neither of the poles is tilted towards the Sun; So, Earth experiences equal days and equal nights

SOURCE **New NCERT Class VI** *(The Earth in the Solar System, Globe: Latitudes and Longitudes, Motions of the Earth)*, **Old NCERT Class VI** *(The Earth in the Solar System, Latitudes and Longitudes, Motions of the Earth)*, **New NCERT Class XI** *(The Origin and Evolution of the Earth)*, **Old NCERT Class XI** *(The Earth: Its Origin and Evolution)*, **Tamil Nadu Board Class XI** *(The Solar System and the Earth)*

Origin of Earth

1 **Consider the following Assertion (A) and Reason (R) and choose the correct code.**

(Chap 1, Class-VI, New NCERT)

Assertion (A) The shape of the Earth is Geoid.

Reason (R) The Earth is slightly flattened at the poles not at the Equator.

Codes

(a) Both A and R are true and R is the correct explanation of A.
(b) Both A and R are true, but R is not the correct explanation of A.
(c) A is true, but R is false.
(d) A is false, but R is true.

Ans. (a)

Exp. Both Assertion (A) and Reason (R) are true and Reason (R) is the correct explanation of Assertion (A). The Earth is slightly flattened at the poles not at the Equator. That is why; its shape is described as a Geoid that means an Earth-like shape.

2 **Consider the following statements about the evolution of Earth.** *(Chap 2, Class-XI, New NCERT)*

1. Initially, Earth was a barren, rocky and hot object with a thin atmosphere of hydrogen and helium.
2. Due to the gradual increase in density, the temperature inside the Earth increased.
3. There are different regions of the Earth from the surface to the inner core and each of these contains materials with similar characteristics.

How many of the statements given above is/are correct?

(a) Only one (b) Only two
(c) All three (d) None of these

Ans. (b)

Exp. Only two statements i.e., (1) and (2) are correct regarding the evolution of Earth.

The structure of the Earth is layered and divided into different layers. Initially, Earth was a barren, rocky and hot object with a thin atmosphere of hydrogen and helium.

The initial state of the Earth was unstable. Due to a gradual increase in density, the temperature inside it increased. As a result, the matter inside began to separate based on its density.

Statement (3) is incorrect because from the surface to the core, the Earth's interior has different regions and each of these contains materials with different characteristics, such as solids and liquids, varying in density.

3 **Which among the following statements are correct about the Earth in its primitive form?**

(Chap 2, Class-XI, Old NCERT)

1. It was a cloud of dust and gases in its initial stages.
2. All the gases were concentrated in the core of Earth.
3. Life was present on the land in initial stages.
4. It took 4,600 million years in formation of Earth.

Select the correct answer using the codes given below.

(a) 1, 2 and 3 (b) 2 and 4
(c) 1 and 4 (d) All of these

Ans. (c)

Exp. Statements (1) and (4) are correct about the Earth in its primitive form as the Sun is surrounded by solar nebula (a giant cloud) containing mostly, hydrogen and helium along with dust. It took around 4,600 million years for the evolution of life on the surface of the planet Earth.

Statements (2) and (3) are incorrect because planet Earth initially was a barren, rocky and hot object with a thin atmosphere of hydrogen and helium. Hence, life was not present on the land in initial stages.

The Earth was mostly in a volatile state during its primordial stage.

Due to gradual increase in density, the temperature inside the Earth increased. As a result, the material inside the Earth started getting separated depending on their densities.

4 **Regarding the origin of the Earth and the Nebular hypothesis, consider the following individuals.**

(Chap 2, Class-XI, Old NCERT)

1. Immanuel Kant 2. Otto Schmidt
3. Laplace 4. Carl Weizascar

Select the correct sequence of individuals associated with the development of the Nebular hypothesis.

(a) 1 - 2 - 3 - 4 (b) 2 - 1 - 4 - 3
(c) 1 - 3 - 2 - 4 (d) 2 - 1 - 3 - 4

Ans. (c)

Exp. The correct sequence of individuals associated with the development of the Nebular hypothesis 1-3-2-4. Regarding the Earth's genesis, numerous theories were proposed by various scientists and thinkers. One of the earlier and popular arguments was by German philosopher Immanuel Kant.

Mathematician Laplace revised it in 1796. It is known as Nebular hypothesis. According to one theory, the planets formed from a cloud of material that was connected to a young, slowly spinning Sun.

The 'Nebular hypothesis' was somewhat revised in 1950 by Otto Schmidt in Russia and Carl Weizascar in Germany, although with slight differences in specifics.

5 **Which of the following views was supported by Carl Weizascar and Otto Schmidt about the origin of Earth?**

(Chap 2, Class-XI, Old NCERT)

1. Sun was surrounded by a nebula of hydrogen and helium.
2. Collision and friction between gas particles formed the planets.
3. Planets were formed by the process of disintegration.

Select the correct answer using the codes given below.

(a) 1 and 2 (b) 2 and 3
(c) 1 and 3 (d) All of these

Ans. (a)

Exp. Statements (1) and (2) were supported by Otto Schmidt of Russia and Carl Weizascar of Germany.

Their revision of the nebular hypothesis considered that the Sun was surrounded by a solar nebula containing mostly hydrogen and helium along with dust.

The friction and collision of particles led to the creation of a disk-shaped cloud and eventually led to the formation of planet.

Statement (3) is incorrect because planets are formed through the process of accretion and not by the process of disintegration.

6 In the context of Earth's geographic features, consider the following statements. *(Unit 2, Class-XI, Tamil Nadu Board)*

1. The Equator divides the Earth into two equal halves, known as the Northern hemisphere and the Southern hemisphere.
2. The distance from the Equator to either pole measures half of a circle around the Earth, equivalent to 180°.
3. Parallels North of the Equator are called 'North latitudes' and those South of the Equator are called 'South latitudes'.

Which of the statements given above are correct?

(a) 1 and 2 (b) 2 and 3 (c) 1 and 3 (d) 1, 2 and 3

Ans. (c)

Exp. Statements (1) and (3) are correct regarding Earth's geographic features.

The Equator is an imaginary circular line that divides the Earth into two equal halves, known as the Northern hemisphere and the Southern hemisphere.

All parallels North of the Equator are called 'North latitudes' and all parallels South of the Equator are called South latitudes.

Statement (2) is incorrect because the Equator represents the zero-degree latitude. Since, the distance from the Equator to either of the poles is one-fourth of a circle round the Earth, it will measure one-fourth of 360°, i.e. 90°.

7 The stages of formation of the Earth are given in the options given below. Arrange the stages in a correct sequence and choose the correct answer using the codes given below. *(Chap 2, Class-XI, Old NCERT)*

1. Formation of ridges and basins
2. Swirling ball of dust and clouds
3. Formation of crust of the Earth
4. Floating of gases to form atmosphere
5. Formation of oceans

Codes

(a) 2, 1, 3, 5, 4 (b) 2, 3, 1, 4, 5
(c) 1, 2, 4, 5, 3 (d) 5, 1, 3, 4, 2

Ans. (b)

Exp. The correct sequence is 2, 3, 1, 4, 5. At the beginning, Earth was a giant ball of dust and cloud known as Nebula.

After that, through the process of accretion, the planet Earth started to form. This process allowed heavier materials (like iron) to sink towards the centre of the Earth and the lighter ones to move towards the surface.

The crust started to form along with ridges and basins. In the next stage, the Earth's atmosphere started to form with floating gases and at last after 500 million years from the formation of the Earth, the oceans started to form.

8 In the context of the Nebular hypothesis, consider the following statements. *(Unit 2, Class-XI, Tamil Nadu Board)*

1. It was given by philosopher Immanuel Kant.
2. As per this hypothesis, the planets were formed out of a cloud of material associated with a youthful Sun, which was slowly rotating.
3. According to Otto Schmidt and Carl Weizascar the Sun was surrounded by solar nebula containing mostly hydrogen and helium along with what may be termed as dust.'

How many of the statements given above is/are correct?

(a) Only one (b) Only two
(c) All three (d) None of these

Ans. (c)

Exp. All three statements i.e., (1), (2) and (3) are correct regarding the Nebular hypothesis.

The Nebular hypothesis was proposed by Immanuel Kant. According to the Nebular hypothesis, the Sun and planets formed from a large, diffuse and slowly rotating cloud of gas and dust known as the solar nebula. As the nebula contracted due to gravity, it started to spin faster, and a protostar (young Sun) formed at the center.

In 1950, Otto Schmidt in Russia and Carl Weizascar in Germany somewhat revised the 'Nebular hypothesis', though differing in details. They considered that the Sun was surrounded by solar nebula containing mostly hydrogen and helium along with what may be termed as dust.

9 Consider the following Assertion (A) and Reason (R) and choose the correct code. *(Chap 2, Class-XI, New NCERT) (IAS Pre 2003)*

Assertion (A) Moving from one place on Earth to another place of high latitude, the weight of an object decreases.

Reason (R) Earth is not a perfect sphere.

Codes

(a) Both A and R are true and R is the correct explanation of A.

(b) Both A and R are true, but R is not the correct explanation of A.

(c) A is true, but R is false.

(d) A is false, but R is true.

Ans. (d)

Exp. Assertion (A) is false, but Reason (R) is true.

The centrifugal force generated by the Earth's axis rotation is maximum at Equator.

As the result of this force, the weight of any object is minimum at Equator and maximum at poles and also increases towards high latitude. Earth is not perfect sphere because it is slightly flattened at the poles and not at the Equator.

10 In the context of the evolution of Earth's atmosphere, consider the following statements. *(Class-XI, Old NCERT)*

1. The early atmosphere of the Earth was primarily composed of hydrogen and helium.
2. There are four stages in the evolution of the present atmosphere.
3. In the second stage, the hot interior of the Earth contributed to the evolution of the atmosphere.

Which of the statements given above are correct?

(a) 1, and 2 (b) 2, and 3 (c) 1 and 3 (d) 1, 2 and 3

Ans. (c)

Exp. Statements (1) and (3) are correct in the context of the evolution of Earth's atmosphere.

The early atmosphere of the Earth was primarily composed of hydrogen and helium. Apart from these gases, water vapour, nitrogen, carbon dioxide, methane, and ammonia were also included in the composition of the atmosphere.

Stage-I The early atmosphere of the Earth was primarily composed of hydrogen and helium. It was stripped off from the Earth by solar winds.

Stage-II As Earth cooled down, many gases were released from inside. It contained water vapour, nitrogen, carbon dioxide, methane, ammonia and small known as Degassing.

Statement (2) is incorrect because there are three stages in the evolution of present atmosphere not four.

11 Which among the following statements about the evolution of Earth's lithosphere is correct? *(Chap 2, Class-XI, New NCERT)*

1. The materials inside the lithosphere have arranged according to density differences.
2. During its formation, the heavier materials have sink towards the centre of the Earth.
3. During its formation, the increase in density inside the Earth has resulted in increase of temperature.

Codes

(a) 1 and 2 (b) Only 2
(c) Only 3 (d) 1, 2 and 3

Ans. (d)

Exp. All the statements are correct about the evolution of Earth's lithosphere.

The Earth was mostly in a volatile state during its primordial stage.

Due to gradual increase in density, the temperature inside increased. As a result, the material inside started getting separated depending on their densities.

This allowed heavier materials (like iron) to sink towards the centre of the Earth and the lighter ones to move towards the surface.

With passage of time, it cooled further and solidified and condensed into a smaller size. This later led to the development of the outer surface in the form of a crust.

12 Consider the following pairs. *(Class-XI, Old NCERT)*

Epoch		Major Events
1. Pliocene	–	Early human ancestor
2. Miocene	–	Extinction of dinosaurs
3. Oligocene	–	Anthropoid ape
4. Palaeocene	–	Small mammals (rats-mice)

How many of the pairs given above is/are correctly matched?

(a) Only one (b) Only two
(c) Only three (d) All four

Ans. (c)

Exp. Only three pairs i.e., (1), (3) and (4) are correctly matched as the Pliocene epoch is known for the presence and evolution of early human ancestors.

The Oligocene epoch is associated with the emergence and diversification of anthropoid apes. The Palaeocene epoch is known for the evolution of small mammals, including early forms of rodents like rats and mice.

Pair (2) is incorrectly matched because the Miocene epoch was a period of great evolution for both plants and animals.

It was a time of warmer global climates and two major ecosystems made their first appearances: kelp forests and grasslands, not the extinction of dinosaurs.

13 Arrange the following geological time periods in the correct chronological order. *(Chap 2, Class-XI, Old NCERT)*

1. Oligocene 2. Pliocene
3. Palaeocene 4. Eocene

Codes

(a) 4-3-2-1 (b) 1-2-3-4
(c) 2-1-4-3 (d) 1-4-2-3

Ans. (c)

Exp. The correct chronological order is 2-1-4-3.

The Pliocene is one of the five epochs of the Tertiary period. The Pliocene epoch lasted from 5 to 2 million years ago.

The Oligocene is a geologic epoch that lasted from 37 to 24 million years ago. It was part of the Paleogene period and the Tertiary period. The Eocene epoch was a geological epoch that lasted from about 58 to 37 million years ago. It is the second epoch of the Paleogene period in the modern Cenozoic Era.

The Palaeocene is a geological epoch that lasted from about 66 to 56 million years ago. It was the first epoch of the Paleogene period and came after the Cretaceous period.

14 Which among the following were not the components of Earth's atmosphere during its origin? *(Chap 2, Class-XI, New NCERT)*

1. Carbon dioxide
2. Helium
3. Hydrogen
4. Oxygen

Codes

(a) 1, 2 and 3 (b) 1 and 4 (c) 2 and 3 (d) 1, 2 and 4

***Ans.* (b)**

Exp. Carbon dioxide and oxygen were not the components of Earth's atmosphere during its origin. Only hydrogen and helium are the gases, which were found at the primordial stage of the Earth's atmosphere.

15 Which of the following pairs are matched correctly? *(Chap 2, Class-XI, New NCERT)*

1. Origin of life on Earth – 3,800 million years ago
2. Photosynthesis begins – 2,500-3,000 million years ago
3. Release of oxygen in atmosphere – 2,000 million years ago

Codes

(a) 1 and 2 (b) 2 and 3
(c) 1 and 3 (d) All of these

***Ans.* (d)**

Exp. All of the pairs are correctly matched as the origin of life on Earth began 3,800 million years ago. It was just after the formation of ocean around 4,000 million years ago.

Around 2,500-3,000 million years ago, the process of photosynthesis evolved. Then the oceans began to have the contribution of oxygen through this process.

Eventually, oceans were saturated with oxygen and 2,000 million years ago, the oxygen began to flood the atmosphere.

Geological Time Scale

16 In the context of Earth's geological time scale, consider the following statements about the Tertiary period. *(Chap 3, Class-XI, New NCERT)*

1. The Tertiary period is the traditional name for the first period of the Cenozoic Era and includes the Paleocene, the Eocene, the Oligocene, the Miocene and the Pliocene epochs.
2. Mammals were the only group of animals that evolved during the Tertiary period.
3. The Tertiary period lasted from approximately 66 million years ago to about 2.58 million years ago.

Which of the statements given above are correct?

(a) 1 and 2 (b) 2 and 3
(c) 1 and 3 (d) 1, 2 and 3

***Ans.* (c)**

Exp. Statements (1) and (3) are correct regarding Earth's geological time scale. The Tertiary period is the traditional name for the first period of the Cenozoic Era, and it includes the Paleocene, the Eocene, the Oligocene, the Miocene and the Pliocene epochs.

The Tertiary period lasted from approximately 66 million years ago to about 2.58 million years ago.

Statement (2) is incorrect because the Tertiary period was a time when various animals, including birds, insects and mollusks, evolved dramatically, not just mammals.

17 Consider the following statements regarding dinosaurs. *(Chap 3, Class-XI, New NCERT)*

1. Dinosaurs dominated the Earth during the Cretaceous period.
2. The Sauropods group of dinosaurs were known for its large size and long neck.
3. The extinction of dinosaurs occurs in the Jurassic geological period.

Which of the statements given above are correct?

(a) 1 and 2 (b) 2 and 3 (c) 1 and 3 (d) 1, 2 and 3

***Ans.* (a)**

Exp. Statements (1) and (2) are correct as Dinosaurs dominated the Earth during the Mesozoic Era, which includes the Triassic, Jurassic and Cretaceous periods. The Cretaceous period is particularly well-known for the diverse and widespread presence of dinosaurs.

Sauropods were a group of herbivorous dinosaurs characterised by their massive size, long necks and long tails. Examples of Sauropods include Brachiosaurus and Apatosaurus.

Statement (3) is incorrect because the mass extinction event that led to the extinction of dinosaurs occurred at the end of the Cretaceous period, not the Jurassic period. The extinction of most non-avian dinosaurs actually occurred at the end of the Cretaceous period, around 66 million years ago. The Jurassic period ended about 145 million years ago, so there's a significant gap between it and the dinosaur extinction event.

18 With reference to latitude and longitude, consider the following statements. *(Chap 2, Class-VI, New NCERT)*

1. The Prime Meridian passes through Greenwich, London.
2. The Equator is an example of a line of longitude.
3. Lines of latitude are also known as parallels.
4. The International Date Line is an imaginary line located at 90° East longitude.

How many of the statements given above is/are correct?

(a) Only one (b) Only two
(c) Only three (d) All of these

Ans. (b)

Exp. Only two statements i.e., (1) and (3) are correct regarding latitude and longitude.

The Prime Meridian, also known as the Greenwich Meridian, passes through Greenwich, London. It is an imaginary line that runs between the North and South poles and indicates 0° longitude.

Lines of latitude are also known as parallels. Lines of latitude are imaginary lines that run East-West and circle the Earth's surface.

Statements (2) and (4) are incorrect because the Equator is an example of a line of latitude, not longitude. The International Date Line (IDL) is located at 180° East and 180° West longitude. It is an imaginary line that runs from the North Pole to the South Pole, passing through the Pacific Ocean.

19 Arrange the following periods in the correct sequence of the Geological Time Scale.

(Chap 2, Class-XI, New NCERT)

1. Tertiary Period 2. Carboniferous
3. Cambrian Period 4. Jurassic Period

Codes

(a) 1, 2, 3, 4 (b) 3, 2, 4, 1 (c) 2, 3, 4, 1 (d) 1, 3, 2, 4

Ans. (b)

Exp. The correct sequence of Geological Time Scale is 3, 2, 4, 1.

Cambrian period is the oldest period among the given options as it existed 505-570 million years ago.

Then, the next is Carboniferous period as it existed 286-360 million years ago.

The third is Jurassic period, which existed 286-360 million years ago.

The fourth is Tertiary period, which is the youngest among the given options as it existed 2-65 million years ago.

20 Consider the following pairs.

(Chap 2, Class-XI, New NCERT)

Periods		Major Events
1. Carboniferous	–	Early human ancestors
2. Silurian	–	Appearance of first reptiles
3. Jurassic	–	First traces of life on land

How many pairs given above is/are correct?

(a) Only one (b) Only two
(c) Only three (d) None of these

Ans. (d)

Exp. None of the given pair is correct.

Carboniferous is a part of Palaeozoic era. The age of Carboniferous period is 286-360 million years ago. The major event of this period is the appearance of first reptiles.

Silurian is also a part of Palaeozoic era. The age of Silurian period is 408-438 million years before present. The major event of this period is the first traces of life on land.

Jurassic is a part of Mesozoic era. The age of Jurassic period is 144-208 million years before present. The major event of this period is the dominance of dinosaurs.

Motions of Earth

21 Consider the following statements.

(Chap 4, Class-VI, Old NCERT) (IAS Pre 2018)

1. The Earth's magnetic field has reversed every few hundred thousand years.
2. When the Earth was created more than 4000 million years ago, there was 54% oxygen and no carbon dioxide.
3. When living organisms originated, they modified the early atmosphere of the Earth.

Which of the statements given above is/are correct?

(a) Only 1
(b) 2 and 3
(c) 1 and 3
(d) 1, 2 and 3

Ans. (c)

Exp. Statements (1) and (3) are correct as the magnetic field of Earth has reversed every few hundred thousand years. When living organisms originated, they modified the early atmosphere of the Earth.

Statement (2) is incorrect because the Earth is approximately 5 billion years old and the oxygen was completely absent at that time.

22 Which of the following statements is/are correct about the revolution of Earth around the Sun?

(Chap 3, Class-VI, New NCERT)

(a) The orbit of the Earth around the Sun is helical in shape.
(b) During its revolution, the inclination of the Earth remains constant.
(c) The shape of the Earth changes during its revolution.
(d) All of the above

Ans. (b)

Exp. Statement (b) is correct about the revolution of Earth around the Sun. The movement of the Earth around the Sun in a fixed path or orbit is called Revolution.

The axis of the Earth which is an imaginary line makes an angle of $66\frac{1}{2}^\circ$ with the orbital plane.

The orbit of the Earth around the Sun is an elliptical orbit. Throughout its orbit, the Earth is inclined in the same direction. The shape of the Earth does not change during revolution. The revolution is responsible for change in climate.

23 **Regarding Indian Standard Time (IST), consider the following statements.** *(Chap 2, Class-XI, New NCERT)*

1. IST is 5 hours and 30 minutes ahead of Greenwich Mean Time (GMT).
2. The longitude of 82° 30′ E is considered as the Standard Meridian for India.
3. India has adopted multiple standard times due to its vast longitudinal extent.
4. Each time zone covers a longitude of 20° on Earth.

How many of the statements given above is/are correct?

(a) Only one (b) Only two
(c) Only three (d) All four

Ans. (b)

Exp. Only two statements i.e., (1) and (2) are correct regarding Indian Standard Time (IST).

Indian Standard Time is 5 hours and 30 minutes ahead of Greenwich Mean Time. This means that when it is 12:00 PM (noon) GMT/UTC, it will be 5:30 PM IST. The longitude of 82°30′E is considered as the standard meridian for India. This meridian passes through Mirzapur in Uttar Pradesh. The standard meridian is a longitude that determines a standard time for the whole country.

Statement (3) and (4) are incorrect because India has a single standard time, Indian Standard Time (IST), which is based on the longitude of 82°30′E. However, India's vast longitudinal extent of about 29° of longitude means that there is a time difference of almost two hours between the Eastern and Western parts of the country.

Each time zone covers 15 degrees of longitude. There are 24 time zones in the world, so the Earth is divided into 360/24 = 15 degrees of longitude per time zone.

24 **Consider the following statements about Earth's inclined axis.** *(Chap 4, Class-VI, Old NCERT)*

1. The axis of Earth is an imaginary line.
2. The axis of Earth coincides with the circle of illumination.
3. The axis is tilted at $23\frac{1}{2}^\circ$ to the orbital plane of Earth.

Which of the statements given above is/are correct?

(a) 1 and 2 (b) Only 2
(c) Only 1 (d) All of these

Ans. (c)

Exp. Only statement (1) is correct about Earth's inclined axis. Earth's axis is an imaginary pole or line passing through the center of the Earth and makes an angle of 66½° with its orbital plane.

Statements (2) and (3) are incorrect because the circle that divides the day from night on the globe is called the circle of illumination. This circle does not coincide with the axis. Also the axis is tilted at 66 ½° to the orbital plane of Earth.

25 **Consider the following statements related to the Earth's rotation and sunlight.** *(Chap 2, Class-VI, New NCERT)*

1. The Earth takes about 24 hours to complete one rotation around its axis.
2. Aryabhatta, the ancient Indian astronomer, stated that the Earth is flat and stationary.
3. The Earth's axis is tilted at an angle of $23\frac{1}{2}^\circ$ from a perpendicular to the orbital plane.
4. If the Earth stops rotating, the portion facing the Sun would always experience day, while the other half would be in perpetual darkness.

Which of the statements given above are correct?

(a) 1, 3 and 4 (b) 1 and 2 (c) 2 and 3 (d) 1, 2, 3 and 4

Ans. (a)

Exp. Statements (1), (3) and (4) are correct in context of Earth's rotation and sunlight.

The Earth takes 23 hours, 56 minutes to complete one rotation on its axis. This is called the sidereal period. For convenience, this is rounded up to 24 hours, which is equal to one day.

The Earth's axis is tilted at an angle of $23\frac{1}{2}^\circ$ from a perpendicular to the orbital plane. In other words, the Earth's axis makes an angle of $66\frac{1}{2}^\circ$ with the plane of the Earth's orbit. Without rotation, one side of the Earth would always face the Sun, experiencing continuous daylight, while the other side would be in constant darkness.

Statement (2) is incorrect because the ancient Indian astronomer Aryabhatta had stated that 'the Earth is round and rotates on its own axis' not flat. He also stated that the Earth's rotation causes day and night and that the Sun does not orbit the Earth.

26 **Consider the following statements.** *(Chap 3, Class-XI, New NCERT)*

Statement-I The inclination of the Earth's axis, tilted at an angle of $23\frac{1}{2}^\circ$, plays a crucial role in the Earth's day and night cycle.

Statement-II The tilt of the Earth's axis causes different parts of the Earth's surface to come into the sunlight for a certain period and then turn away from it.

Codes

(a) Both Statement-I and Statement-II are correct and Statement-II is the correct explanation for Statement-I.
(b) Both Statement-I and Statement-II are correct and Statement-II is not the correct explanation for Statement-I.
(c) Statement-I is correct but Statement-II is incorrect.
(d) Statement-I is incorrect but Statement-II is correct.

Ans. (a)

Exp. Both Statement-I and Statement-II are correct and Statement-II is the correct explanation for Statement-I. The inclination of the Earth's axis, tilted at an angle of $23\frac{1^\circ}{2}$, is responsible for the changing seasons, the variation in day length, and the distribution of sunlight across different latitudes. The Earth's axis is tilted as it revolves around the Sun, which causes different parts of the Earth to receive different amounts of sunlight.

When the Earth's Northern hemisphere is tilted towards the Sun, it experiences longer days and higher temperatures. This is summer in the Northern hemisphere. At the same time, the Southern hemisphere is tilted away from the Sun, experiencing shorter days and lower temperatures.

27 Consider the following statements with respect to Earth's rotation. *(Chap 2, Class-XI, New NCERT)*

1. The Earth rotates faster at the Equator than it does at the poles.
2. The Coriolis force is minimum at the poles and it is more affected by Earth's revolution that its rotation.

Which of the statements given above is/are correct?

(a) Only 1 (b) Only 2
(c) Both 1 and 2 (d) Neither 1 nor 2

Ans. (a)

Exp. Only statement (1) is correct with respect to Earth's rotation. The Earth rotates faster at the Equator than at the poles because the Equator is wider than the poles. The Earth's rotation takes about 24 hours to complete. The Equator is the widest part of the Earth, so it has to travel a greater distance than the poles to complete a full rotation.

Statement (2) is incorrect because the invisible force that appears to deflect the wind is the Coriolis force, it applies to movement on rotating objects.

The key to the Coriolis effect lies in the Earth's rotation and not based on revolution.

28 Which of the following statements is/are correct regarding Earth's revolution around the Sun? *(Chap 4, Class-VI, Old NCERT)*

1. The Earth's movement around the Sun in its orbit is called Revolution.
2. The Earth's revolution is responsible for occurrence of leap year on Earth.

Codes

(a) Only 1 (b) Only 2
(c) Both 1 and 2 (d) Neither 1 nor 2

Ans. (c)

Exp. Both the statements (1) and (2) are correct regarding Earth's revolution around the Sun.

The Earth's movement around the Sun in its orbit is called Revolution.

It takes 365 1/4 days (one year) to revolve around the Sun. We consider it a year, as consisting of 365 days only and ignore six hours for the sake of convenience. Six hours saved every year are added to make one day (24 hours) over a span of four years.

This surplus day is added to the month of February. Thus, every fourth year, February is of 29 days instead of 28 days. Such a year with 366 days is called a Leap Year. Thus, the Earth's revolution is responsible for occurrence of leap year on Earth.

29 Consider the following statements about the revolution of Earth. *(Chap 4, Class-VI, Old NCERT)*

1. The Earth's revolution takes place in an elliptical orbit.
2. The Earth rotates from West to East.
3. Revolution of Earth on its tilted axis causes formation of seasons.

Which of the statements given above are correct?

(a) 1 and 2 (b) 2 and 3
(c) 1 and 3 (d) All of these

Ans. (d)

Exp. All the statements are correct about the revolution of Earth. The Earth revolves around the Sun in an elliptical orbit.

The Earth rotates on its own axis and it rotates in the Eastward direction and in a counter-clockwise motion. So, the direction of the Earth's rotation is considered from West to East.

The revolution of Earth on its tilted axis causes formation of seasons because change of seasons is the result of changing in the position of the Earth around the Sun.

30 Consider the following statements about the revolution of Earth and its associated effects. *(Chap 4, Class-VI, Old NCERT)*

1. When the Northern hemisphere is tilted towards the Sun, days are longer and nights are shorter in Northern hemisphere.
2. When the Southern hemisphere is tilted towards the Sun, the North Pole has 24 hours day.
3. When the Southern hemisphere is tilted towards the Sun, the North Pole has 24 hours night.

Which of the statements given above are correct?

(a) 1 and 2 (b) Only 2
(c) 2 and 3 (d) 1 and 3

Ans. (d)

Exp. Statements (1) and (3) are correct about the revolution of Earth because when the Northern hemisphere is tilted towards the Sun the rays of the Sun fall directly on the Tropic of Cancer. As a result, it is summer in the regions North of the Equator.

The longest day and the shortest night at these places occur on 21st June. On 22nd December, the Tropic of Capricorn receives direct rays of the Sun as the South Pole is tilted towards it.

Five Years' Plans

6 With reference to the 'Perspective Plan' which of the following statements is/are incorrect? *(Chap 2, Class-XI, New NCERT)*

1. It was part of Indian economic planning till 2017 and specified the objectives to be attained in the period of twenty years.
2. Contrary to the Five Year Plans, it gave equal importance to all sectors of the economy.

Codes

(a) Only 1
(b) Only 2
(c) Both 1 and 2
(d) Neither 1 nor 2

***Ans.* (b)**

Exp. Statement (2) is incorrect because in economy, different sectors are competing with each other for limited resources. Further the objectives of planning *viz* growth, modernisation, self-reliance, etc are itself contradictory. It resulted in the government giving more emphasis to some particular sector.

7 Which of the following is in the correct order in terms of its incorporation? *(Chap 2, Class XI, Old NCERT)*

(a) Bombay Plan > Gandhian Plan > People's Plan > Sarvodaya Plan
(b) People's Plan > Sarvodaya Plan > Bombay Plan > Gandhian Plan
(c) Sarvodaya Plan > Bombay Plan > Gandhian Plan > People's Plan
(d) Gandhian Plan > Sarvodaya Plan > Bombay Plan > People's Plan

***Ans.* (a)**

Exp. The correct order is Bombay Plan > Gandhian Plan > People's Plan > Sarvodaya Plan.

Bombay Plan It was presented by 8 leading industrialists of Bombay, Purshotamdas Thakurdas, JRD Tata, GD Birla, Lala Sri Ram, Kasturbhai Lalbhai, AD Shroff, Ardeshir Dalal and John Mathai in January, 1944.

Gandhian Plan Sriman Narayan Agarwal formulated 'Gandhian Plan' in 1944.

People Plan This plan was formulated by MN Roy in 1945. The plan was based on Marxist socialism and advocated the need of providing the people with the 'basic necessities of life'. Agricultural and industrial sectors, both were equally highlighted by the plan.

Jaiprakash Narayan designed the **Sarvodaya Plan** in 1950. This plan was inspired by Vinoba Bhave's Sarvodaya Idea and Gandhian Plan. Agriculture and small and cottage enterprises were highlighted in this plan.

8 Consider the following statements with respect to Gandhian plan. *(Chap 2, Class-XI, Old NCERT)*

1. The plan articulated a 'decentralised economic structure' for India with 'self-contained villages'.
2. Jayaprakash Narayan and Jawaharlal Nehru formulated the Gandhian plan.

Which of the above statements is/are incorrect?

(a) Only 1
(b) Only 2
(c) Both 1 and 2
(d) Neither 1 nor 2

***Ans.* (b)**

Exp. Statement (2) is incorrect as Gandhian plan was formulated by Acharya Shriman Narayan Agarwal in 1944.

9 Consider the following pairs. *(Chap 2, Class-XI, New NCERT)*

	Plans	Objectives
1.	First Plan	Community development projects
2.	Second Plan	Heavy industries
3.	Third Plan	Green revolution

How many of the above pairs is/are correctly matched?

(a) Only one pair
(b) Only two pairs
(c) All three pairs
(d) None of the pairs

***Ans.* (c)**

Exp. All three pairs are correctly matched.

First Five Year Plan gave preference to agriculture and related community development programme.

The main objectives of the Second Plan was an increase of 25 percent in real national income, a large expansion of employment opportunities; rapid industrialisation; and reduction of economic inequalities.

In the Third Five Year Plan, 1961-1966, the concept of the green revolution was formulated.

10 Consider the following statements. *(Chap 2, Class-XI, New NCERT)*

1. The Second Five Year Plan (FYP) was largely based on the Mahalanobis ideas and hence was called 'Mahalanobis Plan'.
2. Mahalanobis is also credited with the achievement of publishing journal 'Sankhya'?

Which of the statements given above is/are correct?

(a) Only 1
(b) Only 2
(c) Both 1 and 2
(d) Neither 1 nor 2

***Ans.* (c)**

Exp. Both the statements (1) and (2) are correct as Five-Year Plans (FYPs) are centralised and integrated national economic programs in India. The Second Five Year Plan (1956-1961) was based on the ideas of Mahalanobis. The Second Plan focused on the development of the public sector and 'Rapid Industrialisation'. Mahalanobis established the Indian Statistical Institute (ISI) in Calcutta and started a journal, Sakhya which still serves as a respective forum for statisticians to discuss their ideas.

34 **Consider the following statements.** *(Class-XI, Old NCERT)*

Statement-I Sidereal day is shorter than solar day.

Statement-II The motion of the Earth in its orbit around the Sun is termed as revolution.

Codes

(a) Both the Statements are individually true and Statement-II is the correct explanation of Statement-I.
(b) Both the Statements are individually true, but Statement-II is not the correct explanation of Statement- I.
(c) Statement-I is true, but Statement-II is false.
(d) Statement-I is false, but Statement-II is true.

Ans. (b)

Exp. Both the Statements are individually true, but Statement-II is not the correct explanation of Statement-I.

A sidereal day is about 4 minutes shorter than a solar day. A sidereal day is the time it takes for Earth to make a full rotation on its axis, while a solar day is the time it takes for Earth to rotate on its axis so that the Sun appears in the same position in the sky.

A solar day is the time it takes for Earth to rotate on its axis relative to the Sun.

The movement of the Earth around the Sun in a fixed path or orbit is called revolution. The time it takes for the Earth to revolve around the Sun is called the period of revolution. The Earth takes 365.24 days or one year to revolve around the Sun.

35 **The Winter Solstice occurs on 22nd December. During Winter Solstice, which of the following phenomenon can be observed in the Southern hemisphere?** *(Chap 3, Class-VI, New NCERT)*

1. The length of days will be longer in the Southern hemisphere.
2. Southern hemisphere experiences winter season.
3. The South Pole has 24 hours day for 6 months.

Codes

(a) 1 and 2 (b) 2 and 3 (c) 1 and 3 (d) All of these

Ans. (c)

Exp. Statements (1) and (3) can be observed in the Southern hemisphere.

During Winter Solstice, the length of days will be longer in the Southern hemisphere and the South Pole has 24 hours day for 6 months. This is because on 22nd December, the Tropic of Capricorn receives direct rays of the Sun as the South Pole tilts towards it. Therefore, it is summer in the Southern hemisphere with longer days and shorter nights. This position of the Earth is called the Winter Solstice.

Phenomenon mentioned in Statement (2) cannot be observed as during this time Southern hemisphere experiences summer season and Northern hemisphere experiences winter season.

36 **Consider the following Assertion (A) and Reason (R) and choose the correct code.** *(Chap 3, Class-VI, New NCERT)*

Assertion (A) All the places on Earth will have equal length of days and nights on 23rd September.

Reason (R) The rays of the Sun fall directly on the Equator during Equinox.

Codes

(a) Both A and R are true and R is the correct explanation of A.
(b) Both A and R are true, but R is not the correct. explanation of A.
(c) A is true, but R is false.
(d) A is false, but R is true.

Ans. (a)

Exp. Both Assertion (A) and Reason (R) are true and Reason (R) is the correct explanation of Assertion (A). Because on 21st March and 23rd September, direct rays of the Sun fall on the Equator. At this position, neither of the poles is tilted towards the Sun, so the whole Earth experiences equal days and equal nights. This is called an Equinox.

37 **Consider the following statements.** *(Class-XI, Old NCERT) (UPPSC Pre 2000)*

1. The Northern end of the Earth's axis is called 'North Pole'.
2. 45° latitude is half of the length of the Equator.
3. Earth's axis are parallel.
4. The Earth's speed of revolution is faster in Aphelion position.

How many of the statements given above is/are correct?

(a) Only one (b) Only two (c) Only three (d) All four

Ans. (b)

Exp. Only two statements i.e., (1) and (3) are correct. Northern end of the Earth's axis is called North Pole (Southern end is called South Pole). Earth's axis are parallel (parallelism). It means that the Earth's axis remain parallel to each other and the axis of rotation of the Earth is tilted with respect to the plane of its orbit. Statements (2) and (4) are incorrect because 45° latitude is not half of the length of the Equator (length of 45° latitude is around 28337 km and length of Equator is 40075 km). The Earth's speed of revolution is faster in perihelion because the Earth is closer to the Sun and feels more gravity at this position.

38 **Which among the following statements are incorrect about the rotation of Earth on its tilted axis?** *(Chap 4, Class-VI, Old NCERT)*

1. The Earth's rotation on its tilted axis is responsible for causing seasons on Earth.
2. If the Earth stops rotating, all the places will have equal days and equal nights.

3. Earth's rotates at an axial tilt of $23\frac{1}{2}^{\circ}$ from the plane of Earth's orbit.

Codes

(a) Only 1 (b) 1 and 3 (c) 2 and 3 (d) All of these

Ans. (d)

Exp. All of the statements are incorrect about the rotation of Earth on its tilted axis. The revolution of Earth around the Sun is responsible for causing seasons on Earth.

If the Earth stops rotating, the portion of the Earth facing the Sun would always experience day, thus bringing continuous warmth to the region. The other half would remain in darkness and be freezing cold all the time.

Earth's rotates at an axial tilt of $66\frac{1}{2}^{\circ}$ from the plane of Earth's orbit.

The Moon

39 Which of the following statements can be considered as certainly true about the Moon? *(Chap 1, Class-VI, Old NCERT)*

(a) The diameter of Moon is one-fifth of the Earth.
(b) A person on Earth will always see the same side of the Moon.
(c) The period of revolution of Moon is more than the period of rotation.
(d) Water and soil are present in abundant quantities on Moon.

Ans. (b)

Exp. Statement (b) can be considered as certainly true about the Moon as Earth has only one satellite, i.e., the Moon. Its diameter is only one-quarter to that of the Earth.

It appears so big because it is nearer to Earth than other celestial bodies. It is about 3,84,400 km away from us. It revolves around the Earth and rotates about its own axis in about the same time, due to, which only one side of the Moon is visible to us. Water and soil are not present on the Moon. Hence, the Moon does not have favourable conditions for life.

40 Consider the following statements about the Moon. *(Chap 1, Class-VI, Old NCERT)*

1. The Moon revolves around the Earth in a fixed path.
2. The Moon appears bright due to reflected light of the Sun.
3. The surface of Moon is characterised by unevenness.

Which of the statements given above are correct?

(a) 1 and 2 (b) 2 and 3
(c) 1 and 3 (d) All of these

Ans. (d)

Exp. All the statements are correct about the Moon because it revolves around the Earth and rotates about its own axis in about the same time. The Moon does not have its own light; it gets its light from the Sun so, the Moon appears bright due to reflected light of the Sun. The surface of Moon is characterised by unevenness as it has mountains, plains and depressions on its surface. These cast shadows on the Moon's surface.

Latitudes, Longitudes and Time

41 Consider the following statements. *(Class-XI, Old NCERT)*

1. Temperate zones lie between Arctic Circle and North Pole and Antarctic Circle and the South Pole.
2. The North Temperate zone lies between the Tropic of Cancer (23.3°N) and the Arctic Circle (66.5°N) in the Northern hemisphere.
3. Torrid zone lies within the Tropic of Cancer (23.3°N) and Tropic of Capricorn (23.3°S).

Which of the statements given above are correct?

(a) 1 and 2 (b) 2 and 3
(c) 1 and 3 (d) 1, 2 and 3

Ans. (b)

Exp. Statements (2) and (3) are correct.

The Temperate Heat Zone is the most habitable zone of the Earth. There are two temperate zones in two respective hemispheres of the Earth.

The North Temperate zone lies between the Tropic of Cancer (23.3°N) and the Arctic Circle (66.5°N) in the Northern hemisphere. The South Temperate zone lies between the Tropic of Capricorn (23.3°S) and Antarctic Circle (66.5°S) in the Southern hemisphere.

The torrid or tropical zone is the hottest zone of the Earth. This region lies within the Tropic of Cancer (23.3°N) and Tropic of Capricorn (23.3°S).

Statement (1) is incorrect because the regions enclosed by the Tropic of Cancer and the Arctic Circle in the Northern hemisphere, as well as the Tropic of Capricorn and the Antarctic Circle in the Southern hemisphere, experience moderate temperatures. These areas are designated as Temperate zones.

42 With reference to solar eclipses, consider the following statements. *(Chap 4, Class-VI, Old NCERT)*

1. A solar eclipse occurs when the Moon passes between the Earth and the Sun.
2. A total solar eclipse is visible from every location on Earth.
3. During a solar eclipse, the Moon completely covers the Sun's disk.
4 An annular solar eclipse happens when the Moon is farthest from Earth.

Which of the statements given above are correct?

(a) 1 and 2 (b) 2 and 3 (c) 1, 3 and 4 (d) 1, 2, 3 and 4

Ans. (c)

Exp. Statements (1), (3) and (4) are correct regarding solar eclipses.

A solar eclipse occurs when the Moon passes between the Sun and Earth, casting the Moon's shadow on Earth. A solar eclipse can only happen during a New Moon.

During a total solar eclipse, the Moon completely covers the Sun's disk. A solar eclipse occurs when the Moon passes between the Earth and the Sun, blocking the Sun's view from a small part of the Earth.

An annular eclipse happens when the Moon is farthest from Earth. Because the Moon is farther away, it seems smaller. It does not block the entire view of the Sun.

Statement (2) is incorrect because a total solar eclipse is only visible from a small area of the world. This is because the Moon's shadow on Earth is relatively small and the path of totality is only a few hundred kilometers wide.

43 Regarding eclipses, consider the following statements. *(Chap 4, Class- VI, Old NCERT)*

1. An eclipse is a complete or partial obscuration of light from a celestial body as it passes through the shadow of another celestial body.
2. Eclipses occur every Full Moon or New Moon positions due to the Moon's orbital plane inclination of 5° to the orbital plane of the Earth.
3. Lunar eclipses occur during the position of syzygy when the Earth comes in between the Sun and the Moon in a straight line.

Which of the statements given above are correct?

(a) 1 and 2 (b) 2 and 3 (c) 1, and 3 (d) 1, 2 and 3

Ans. (c)

Exp. Statements (1) and (3) are correct regarding eclipses.

An eclipse is a complete or partial obscuration of light from a celestial body as it passes through the shadow of another celestial body.

Syzygy is the position of alignment when Earth comes in between Sun and Moon on a straight line; in such position, lunar eclipse occurs. The conjunction is the position when Sun and Moon lie on one side of the Earth and then solar eclipse occurs.

Statement (2) is incorrect because Moon's orbital plane inclined 5° to the orbital plane of the Earth, so eclipses do not occur every Full Moon or New Moon positions.

44 Consider the following statements about the International Date Line *(Chap 3, Class-VI, Old NCERT)*

1. The International Date Line is largely based on the 180° meridian.
2. The difference in time between the places just either side of the International Date Line is almost one day.
3. The difference in time to the extent of one day on either side of the International Date Line is caused by inclined axis of the Earth.
4. The International Date Line mostly passes through the Pacific Ocean.

How many of the statements given above is/are correct?

(a) Only one (b) Only two
(c) Only three (d) All four

Ans. (c)

Exp. Only three statements i.e., (1), (2) and (4) are correct regarding International Date Line.

The International Date Line (IDL) is based on the 180° meridian. The IDL is an imaginary line that runs from the North Pole to the South Pole and marks the transition from one calendar day to the next.

The time difference between places on either side of the International Date Line (IDL) is almost one day.

The International Date Line passes through the mid-Pacific Ocean and roughly follows the 180° longitude North-South line on the Earth.

Statement (3) is not correct with respect to International Date Line because inclined axis is not at all related to difference in time on the either side of International Date Line. Difference of time is based on longitudinal positions.

45 Which of the following statements about the latitudinal heat zones is correct? *(Chap 2, Class-VI, New NCERT)*

1. The region between the Tropic of Cancer and Tropic of Capricorn is known as the Torrid Zone.
2. The region around the North Pole of the Earth is known as the Frigid Zone.

Codes

(a) Only 1
(b) Only 2
(c) Both 1 and 2
(d) None of the above

Ans. (c)

Exp. Both the statements (1) and (2) are correct about the latitudinal heat zones as the mid-day Sun is exactly overhead at least once a year on all latitudes in between the Tropic of Cancer and the Tropic of Capricorn. Therefore, this area receives the maximum heat and is called the Torrid Zone.

Areas lying between the Arctic Circle and the North Pole in the Northern hemisphere and the Antarctic Circle and the South Pole in the Southern hemisphere, are very cold.

It is because the Sun here does not rise much above the horizon. Its rays are always slanting and provide less heat. Therefore, these are called Frigid Zones (very cold).

46 Consider the following statements about the meridians of longitude on Earth. *(Chap 2, Class-VI, New NCERT)*

1. All the meridians of longitude are of same length.
2. Prime Meridian is marked by 0° longitude.
3. All the meridians are full circles.
4. Distance between longitudes becomes zero at the poles.

Which of the statements given above is/are correct?

(a) 1, 2 and 4 (b) 2, 3 and 4
(c) 2 and 4 (d) All of these

Ans. (a)

Exp. Statements (1), (2) and (4) are correct about the meridians of longitude on Earth. The line of reference running from the North Pole to the South Pole are called the Meridians of Longitude.

Unlike parallels of latitude, all meridians are of equal length. The Prime Meridian is the imaginary line used to indicate 0° longitude that passes through Greenwich.

It is also known as Greenwich Meridian because it passes through the place called Greenwich in London.

The distances between them are measured in 'degrees of longitude'. Each degree is further divided into minutes, and minutes into seconds.

Statement (3) is incorrect because the meridians are semi circles while all the latitudes are full circle.

47 Consider the following statements about the meridians on Earth. *(Chap 2, Class-VI, New NCERT)*

1. The Prime Meridian converges with all other meridians at North Pole and South Pole.
2. A meridian runs along East-West directions along the Equator.
3. The 180° meridian connects North Pole and South Pole.
4. As we move towards higher latitudes, the distance between two meridians increases.

Which of the statements given above are correct?

(a) 2 and 3 (b) 1 and 3
(c) 1, 2 and 3 (d) All of these

Ans. (b)

Exp. Statements (1) and (3) are correct about the meridians on Earth as the Prime Meridian also converges at North Pole and South Pole. The Prime Meridian value is 0° longitude and from it we count 180° Eastward as well as 180° Westward.

The Prime Meridian and 180° meridian divide the Earth into two equal halves, the Eastern hemisphere and the Western hemisphere and like other meridians. This 180° meridian connects North Pole and South Pole.

Statements (2) and (4) are incorrect because a meridian runs along North-South direction and towards the higher latitudes, the distance between two meridians decreases.

48 Which of the following statements about the longitudes on Earth is correct? *(Chap 2, Class-VI, New NCERT)*

(a) The distance between longitudes is constant from Equator to poles.
(b) All the longitudes are parallel to each other.
(c) All the longitudes converge at poles.
(d) Longitudes divide the Earth into Northern and Southern hemispheres.

Ans. (c)

Exp. Statement (c) is correct about the longitudes on Earth as the meridians or longitudes are semicircles and the distance between them decreases steadily pole wards until it becomes zero at the poles, where all the meridians meet.

49 Consider the following Assertion (A) and Reason (R) and choose the correct code. *(Chap 2, Class-VI, New NCERT)*

Assertion (A) All the places located on the East of Prime Meridian will be 2.5 hours ahead of the time at London.

Reason (R) All the places on a given meridian will have same local time.

Codes

(a) Both A and R are true and R is the correct explanation of A.
(b) Both A and R are true, but R is not the correct explanation of A.
(c) A is true, but R is false.
(d) A is false, but R is true.

Ans. (d)

Exp. Assertion (A) is false, but Reason (R) is true.
The Earth rotates from West to East, those places East of Greenwich will be ahead of Greenwich time and those to the West will be behind it. The rate of difference can be calculated as follows : The Earth rotates 360° in about 24 hours, which means 15° an hour or 1° in four minutes. Thus, when it is 12 noon at Greenwich, the time at 15° East of Greenwich will be $15 \times 4 = 60$ minutes, i.e., 1 hour ahead of Greenwich (London) time, which means 1 p.m. A local time is a time calculated on the basis of a specific meridian passing through a particular place, though the place may be included in some other time zones.

50 Consider the following statements about the longitudes and latitudes. *(Chap 2, Class-VI, New NCERT)*

1. All the longitudes are parallel to the Equator.
2. All the latitudes converge at the poles.
3. Distance between longitudes decreases from Equator to the poles.
4. All the longitudes are of same length.

Which of the statements given above are correct?

(a) 1, 2 and 3 (b) 2 and 4
(c) 3 and 4 (d) All of these

Ans. (c)

Exp. Statements (3) and (4) are correct about the longitudes and latitudes as longitudes are semicircles and the distance between them decreases steadily pole wards until it becomes zero at the poles, where all the meridians meet. All the longitudes are of same length. Each line of longitude equals to half of the circumference of the Earth because each extends from the North Pole to South Pole.

Statements (1) and (2) are incorrect because all the latitudes are parallel to the Equator and all the longitudes converge at the poles.

51 **Which of the following statements about the longitudes and latitudes is/are correct?** ***(Chap 2, Class-VI, New NCERT)***

1. To find the location of a place on Earth, both the latitude and longitude of a place must be known.
2. Distance between meridians is measured in 'degrees of longitudes'.
3. Each degree of longitude is divided into minutes and seconds.

Select the correct answer using the codes given below.

(a) Only 1 (b) 2 and 3 (c) Only 2 (d) All of these

Ans. (d)

Exp. All the statements are correct about the longitudes and latitudes. To find the location of a place on Earth, both the latitude and longitude of a place must be known.

This latitudes and longitudes help us to fix the position of a place. The distance between them is measured in 'degrees of longitude'. Each degree is further divided into minutes and minutes into seconds.

52 **Which among the following statements about the Standard Time and meridians is/are correct?** ***(Chap 2, Class-VI, New NCERT)***

(a) Places located on different meridians will have different time.

(b) The local time at Greenwich is considered as reference time for the whole world.

(c) Places on the East of Greenwich are ahead of Greenwich Time.

(d) All of the above

Ans. (d)

Exp. All the statements about the Standard Time and Meridians are correct because since the Earth rotates from West to East, the places East of Greenwich are ahead of Greenwich Mean Time (GMT) and those to the West are behind it. Areas on the East of the Prime Meridian are ahead of areas on the West. Each place crosses the Sun at different times. So, the time of sunrise also differs from place to place.

As the reference for GMT, the Prime Meridian at Greenwich therefore, became the centre of world time and the basis for the global system of time zones.

53 **Which of the following statements about time zones on Earth is incorrect?** ***(Chap 2, Class-VI, New NCERT)***

(a) The Earth has been divided into 24 time zones.

(b) Countries with a wider longitudinal extent have more time zones.

(c) Each time zone covers 30° longitude.

(d) Local time of a place depends upon its longitudinal value.

Ans. (c)

Exp. Statement (c) is incorrect about the time zones on Earth because the Earth rotates 360° in about 24 hours, which means 15° an hour or 1° in four minutes. Thus, each time zone covers 15° of longitude.

54 **Which of the following statements about the parallel of latitudes are correct?** ***(Chap 3, Class-VI, Old NCERT)***

1. The length of parallels decreases as we move away from the Equator.
2. The Tropic of Cancer is the largest parallel of latitude.
3. Latitudinal value of a place is used to determine the local time.

Select the correct answer using the codes given below.

(a) 1 and 2 (b) Only 1
(c) 1 and 3 (d) None of these

Ans. (b)

Exp. Only statement (1) is correct about the parallel of latitudes. The parallels of latitudes are always parallel to the Equator, so the length of parallels decrease as we move away from the Equator.

Statements (2) and (3) are incorrect because the Equator is the largest parallel of latitude. Longitudinal value of a place is used to determine the local time.

Chapter 04

Geomorphology

Landforms & Geomorphology & Processes

Theories About Landforms

Continental Drift Theory

- Proposed by Alfred Wegner in 1912
- Claimed that changes in appearance of Earth is due to shifting of continents
- Pangea broke into two parts - Laurasia and Gondwanaland
- Northward movement was due to gravitational force and Westward movement was due to tidal force of Moon

Sea Floor Spreading Theory

- Proposed by Harry H. Hess
- Based on the concept of age of the rocks on the sea floor is not similar
- New crust is formed in the central part of ocean and spreads towards margins
- Youngest rocks are found in the central parts of ocean whereas older ones on the margins

Plate Tectonics Theory

- Claims that Earth is divided into several big and small plates floating over the semi-molten asthenosphere
- There are 7 major and other minor plates
- Major ones are Eurasian, Antarctican, North American, South American, Pacific, African and Indo-Australian plate, with Pacific being the largest plate
- Minor ones are Cocos, Nazca, Carribean, etc

Earthquake and Tsunamis

Earthquake

- Shaking of the Earth which happens due to the release of energy generating seismic waves that travels to all directions

Types Of Earthquakes

- Tectonic Earthquake
- Collapse Earthquake
- Volcanic Earthquake
- Explosion Earthquake
- Reservoir Induced Earthquake

Earthquake Waves

- Seismograph is used to record the earthquake waves
- When waves travel through mediums with different densities, their direction changes due to reflection or refraction

Surface Waves

- Originated due to the interaction of body waves with the surface rocks
- Last to report on seismograph

Shadow Zone

- There are some specific areas where waves are not reported.
- Zone between 105°-145° is identified as shadow zone for both P-waves and S-waves

Tsunami

- Waves generated by tremors and not an earthquake itself. The effect of Tsunami will occur only if the epicentre of tremor is below the oceanic waters

Interior of the Earth

Sources of the Earth

- **Direct Sources** Underground mines, Deep Drilling Project, Volcanic Eruption
- **Indirect Sources** Meteors, Density and Temperature, Pressure, Gravity, Magnetic Field, Seismic Activity

Crust

- Outermost solid part of the Earth
- Divided into two parts - continental crust and oceanic crust
  - **Continental Crust** Thicker than oceanic crust, thicker in the areas of major mountain system
  - **Oceanic Crust** Denser and thinner than continental crust. It is composed of SiMa (Silicon and Magnesium)
- **Lithosphere** Crust and uppermost part of Mantle forms the lithosphere, nearly 100 km thick

Mantle

- Portion of interior beyond the crust, also known as Pyrosphere
- Thickness of mantle is nearly 2900km from Moho's discontinutiy

Core

- Known as Barysphere, it lies at the depth of 2900-6400 km
- It forms about 16% of the Earth's volume
- Composed of NiFe (Nickel and Iron), it is divided into inner and outer core

Geomorphic Processes

Geomorphic Processes

- The endogenic and exogenic forces causing physical stresses and chemical reactions on Earth materials and brings changes in configuration of surface of Earth
- Gravity along with a directional force, activates all downslope movements of matter causing stress on Earth's materials

Earth Movements

- Movement of lithospheric plates causes changes on the Earth surface
- Earth movements are caused due to the forces - Endogenic and Exogenic forces

Endogenic Movements

- Resultant of endogenic forces
- Leads to land subsidence, subsidence folding, fracturing and volcanic eruptions

Exogenic Movements

- Derive their energy from the atmosphere determined by the energy of Sun and also the acting tectonic forces, such as shear stress, gravitational forces, etc

Diastrophic Movements

- Vertical and horizontal movements which leads to production of primary landforms such as mountains, plateaus, plains etc Operate very slowly and are constructive forces

SOURCE **New NCERT Class VII** *(Inside Our Earth)*, **Old NCERT Class VIII** *(Inside the Earth)*, **Old NCERT Class IX** *(Our Environment)*, **New/Old NCERT Class XI** *(Interior of the Earth)*, **New NCERT Class XI** *(Land forms and their Evolution, Distribution of Continents and Oceans, Geomorphic Processes)*, **Tamil Nadu Board Class XI** *(The Solar System and the Earth)*

Earth's Internal Structure

1 Consider the following statements about the Earth's internal structure. *(Chap 2, Class-VII, New NCERT)*

1. The Earth's mantle is the thickest layer.
2. The Earth's crust is primarily composed of igneous rocks.
3. The Earth's inner core is liquid.

How many of the statements given above is/are correct?

(a) Only one (b) Only two
(c) All three (d) None of these

Ans. (a)

Exp. Only one statement i.e., (1) is correct. The Earth's mantle is the thickest layer. However, the Earth's crust is composed of all types of rocks - igneous, metamorphic, and sedimentary.

Statements (2) and (3) are incorrect. The Earth's inner core is primarily composed of iron and nickel; it is in a solid state due to immense pressure despite its high temperature.

2 Which of the following constituents form the continental crust of Earth? *(Chap 2, Class-VII, New NCERT)*

1. Silica 2. Magnesium 3. Aluminium 4. Iron

Codes

(a) 1 and 4 (b) 2, 3 and 4 (c) 1 and 3 (d) All of these

Ans. (c)

Exp. Silica and Aluminium (SiAl) form the continental crust of the Earth. Continental crust is located in the uppermost layer over the Earth's surface.

The oceanic crust mainly consists of silica and magnesium (SiMa).

The inner core of the Earth consists of nickel and iron (NiFe). Thus, aluminium and iron are not the constituent element of continental crust.

3 Consider the following statements. *(Chap 2, Class-VIII, Old NCERT)*

1. According to current technological developments, scientists have been able to drill upto 13 km inside Earth.
2. The interior structure and composition of Earth has been determined by using direct sample collected from all layers of Earth.
3. Study of seismic waves and volcanic activities can be useful in determining interior structure of Earth.

Which of the statements given above are correct?

(a) 1 and 3 (b) 1 and 2
(c) 2 and 3 (d) All of these

Ans. (a)

Exp. Statements (1) and (3) are correct. The Earth's radius is 6,370 km. According to current technological developments, scientists have been able to drill upto 13 km inside Earth.

Study of seismic waves and volcanic activities can be useful in determining interior structure of Earth.

Statement (2) is not correct as it is not possible to collect direct sample from all layers of the Earth because no one can reach the centre of Earth.

4 Consider the following pairs. *(Chap 2, Class-VIII, New NCERT)*

Discontinuity		Separates
1. Mohorovich Discontinuity	–	Mantle and Outer Core
2. Gutenberg Discontinuity	–	Crust and Mantle
3. Lehmann Discontinuity	–	Inner Core and Outer Core

How many pairs given above is/are correct?

(a) Only one (b) Only two
(c) All three (d) None of these

Ans. (a)

Exp. Only one pair i.e. (3) is correct.

Mohorovich Discontinuity (Moho) marks the abrupt change in seismic wave velocity where the Earth's crust transitions to the denser mantle. It's located around 5-70 km below the Earth's surface, varying in depth depending on the geographic location.

Gutenberg Discontinuity separates the Earth's mantle from its outer core. It's situated at a depth of about 2,900 km and is characterised by a sharp decrease in seismic wave velocity, indicating a significant change in material properties.

Lehmann Discontinuity lies within the Earth's core, dividing the solid inner core from the liquid outer core. It's positioned at a depth of around 5,150 km and is identified by a subtle difference in seismic wave velocity, suggesting a more gradual change in material composition.

5 Consider the following statements. *(Chap 2, Class-VII, New NCERT)*

1. The inner core of Earth is composed of iron and nickel.
2. It is in a solid state.
3. It has more depth than the outer core.

How many of the statements given above is/are correct?

(a) Only one (b) Only two
(c) All three (d) None of these

Ans. (c)

Exp. All three statements i.e., (1), (2) and (3) are correct. The inner core of Earth is composed of iron and nickel. Studies using seismic waves and meteorites suggest that inner core is primarily composed of an iron-nickel alloy. Though incredibly hot, the immense pressure within the inner core keeps it solid despite exceeding the melting point of iron under normal conditions.

The inner core lies within the outer core, with the boundary between them occurring at approximately 5,150 km below the Earth's surface. This means the inner core occupies the deepest part of the Earth's interior.

6 **Consider the following statements.**
(Chap 3, Class-XI, New NCERT)
(Unit 2, Class-XI, Tamil Nadu Board)

1. Radioactive decay of rocks occurs in the inner core.
2. The velocity of P waves increases inside the inner core.
3. The pressure inside the inner core increases due to overlying rock layers.
4. The inner core contains igneous rocks.

Which of the above statements is the most appropriate explanation for the phenomenon that the temperature and density inside the Earth is highest in the core and yet the inner core is in a solid state?

(a) 1 and 3 (b) 2 and 4 (c) Only 3 (d) Only 4

***Ans.* (c)**

Exp. Only statement (3) is the most appropriate explanation for the phenomenon that the temperature and density inside the Earth is highest in the core and yet the inner core is in a solid state.

The immense pressure in the Earth's core, generated by the weight of overlying rock layers, counteracts the high temperature and density, preventing the inner core from transitioning into a liquid state.

Radioactive decay is a process that releases energy. While radioactive decay does contribute to the overall heat production within the Earth, it is not the primary reason why the inner core remains solid despite high temperature and density.

The increase in P wave velocity in the inner core is due to the change in the physical state of iron under high pressure and it doesn't directly explain why the inner core remains solid despite high temperature and density.

The inner core is primarily composed of iron and nickel, and it is solid due to the high pressure, even though the temperature is extremely high.

7 **Consider the following statements.**
(Chap 3, Class-XI, New NCERT)

1. The asthenosphere is the major source of magma on the Earth's surface.
2. The core of the Earth is also known as the SiMa layer.

Which of the statements given above is/are correct?

(a) Only 1 (b) Only 2
(c) Both 1 and 2 (d) None of these

***Ans.* (a)**

Exp. Statement (1) is correct as the asthenosphere is the zone of the Earth, which lies beneath the lithosphere. The depth of this layer ranges from 100 to 700 km. It is a source of magma on the Earth's surface, which comes out in the form of lava during volcanic eruption.

Statement (2) is incorrect because the core of the Earth is known as NiFe (Nickel and Ferrous) layer.

8 **Which of the following statements is correct about the lithosphere?** *(Chap 2, Class-VIII, Old NCERT)*

1. It consists of crust and upper mantle.
2. It is in melted state.
3. It is floating over the asthenosphere.
4. Its thickness is over 100 km.

Codes

(a) 1, 2 and 4 (b) 2, 3 and 4
(c) 1, 3 and 4 (d) 1, 2 and 3

***Ans.* (c)**

Exp. Statements (1), (3) and (4) are correct about lithosphere as it is the solid crust or the hard top layer of the Earth, which floats over asthenosphere. Thickness of lithosphere is over 100 km. It includes the crust and the uppermost mantle. Lithosphere is also responsible to support the tectonic plates and the entire Earth crust lying above the fluidic asthenosphere underneath.

Statement (2) is incorrect because lithosphere is the solid crust or the hard top layer of the Earth.

9 **Consider the following statements.**
(Chap 3, Class-XI, New NCERT) (IAS Pre 2023)

1. In a seismograph, P waves are recorded earlier than S waves.
2. In P waves, the individual particles vibrate to and fro in the direction of wave propagation whereas in S waves, the particles vibrate up and down at right angles to the direction of wave propagation.

Which of the statements given above is/are correct?

(a) Only 1
(b) Only 2
(c) Both 1 and 2
(d) Neither 1 nor 2

***Ans.* (c)**

Exp. Both statements (1) and (2) are correct. In a seismograph, P waves are recorded earlier than S waves. This is because P waves are faster than S waves and so, reach the recording instrument first.

In P waves, the individual particles vibrate to and fro in the direction of wave propagation. These waves are compressional or longitudinal waves, which means the ground particles move in the same direction as the wave. On the other hand, in S waves, the particles vibrate up and down at right angles to the direction of wave propagation. S waves are transverse waves, meaning the ground particles move perpendicular to the direction of wave propagation.

10 **Consider the following statements.**
(Chap 2, Class-VII, New NCERT)

1. P waves are the first waves to hit the seismograph in the event of a disturbance.
2. Its compression waves that vibrate the rock in the direction of propagation.
3. It can travel through solids, liquids, and gases.

How many of the statements given above is/are correct?

(a) Only one (b) Only two
(c) All three (d) None of these

Ans. (c)

Exp. All three statements i.e., (1), (2) and (3) are correct. P waves, also known as primary or compressional waves, are the fastest seismic waves and are the first to be detected by a seismograph during an earthquake or any seismic event.

P waves are characterised by a compressional motion, where particles move back and forth in the same direction as the wave's propagation. This compression and rarefaction create a push-pull effect, vibrating the rock along the wave's path.

P waves have the ability to propagate through all three states of matter - solids, liquids and gases. They exhibit the ability to compress and expand material particles, allowing them to traverse through different mediums.

11 **Consider the following statements.**

(Chap 4, Module-2, NIOS) (Chap 2, Class-VII, New NCERT)

1. P waves travel faster than S waves and have a speed range of 1.5-13 km/s.
2. S waves travel slower than P waves and have a speed range of 1-8 km/s.
3. The speed of both P waves and S waves depends on the density and elasticity of the medium they travel through.

How many of the statements given above is/are correct?

(a) Only one (b) Only two
(c) All three (d) None of these

Ans. (c)

Exp. All three statements i.e., (1), (2) and (3) are correct. P waves, being primary or compressional waves, travel faster than S waves, and they typically have a speed range of 1.5-13 km/s.

S waves, also known as secondary or shear waves, travel slower than P waves and their speed range is generally in the range of 1-8 km/s. The speed of seismic waves, including both P waves and S waves, is influenced by the density and elasticity (or rigidity) of the medium through which they propagate. Different materials have different propagation speeds for seismic waves.

12 **Which of the following statements is/are correct about pressure and density inside the Earth?**

(Chap 3, Class-XI, Old NCERT)

1. The rate of increase in temperature from the surface to the depth of the Earth is constant.
2. The central core of Earth has the highest density among all the layers.

Codes

(a) Only 1 (b) Only 2
(c) Both 1 and 2 (d) Neither 1 nor 2

Ans. (a)

Exp. Only statement (2) is correct about pressure and density inside the Earth as the inner core have the highest temperature and density among all the layers. Density is used to rank the layers of the Earth's interior. The solid metal inner core is densest layer, the mantle is intermediately dense and the lithosphere particularly the continental lithosphere, is the least dense layer.

Statement (1) is incorrect because the temperature from the surface to the depth of the Earth is not constant.

13 **Consider the following pairs.**

(Chap 3, Class-XI, Old NCERT)

	Layers of Earth		**% of volume**
1.	Crust	–	15 %
2.	Mantle	–	1 %
3.	Core	–	84 %

How many of the pairs given above is/are correct?

(a) Only one (b) Only two
(c) All three (d) None of these

Ans. (d)

Exp. All the pairs given above are incorrect.

The crust forms only 1% of the volume of the Earth and is a very thin hard top layer of the Earth. 84% of the volume of the Earth is formed by mantle, which is divided into two parts i.e., upper mantle and lower mantle.

Core accounts for 15% of the Earth's volume, which is the innermost layer of the Earth. It is also divided into two parts i.e., Outer core and Inner core.

14 **Which of the following sources are used by scientists to study the interior of Earth?**

(Chap 3, Class-XI, New NCERT)

1. Samples of Earth's core 2. Gold Mines
3. Volcanic Magma 4. Meteors
5. Gravity Anomalies

Codes

(a) 1, 2, 3 and 4 (b) 2, 3, 4 and 5
(c) 1, 3, 4 and 5 (d) 2, 4 and 5

Ans. (b)

Exp. Gold mines, volcanic magma, meteors and gravity anomalies, are used by scientists to study the interior of Earth.

Gold Mines Through the mining activity, it is known that temperature and pressure increase with the increasing distance from the surface towards the interior in deeper depths.

Volcanic Magma During volcanic eruption, the molten material (magma) is thrown onto the surface of the Earth. This magma becomes an invaluable tool for laboratory analysis.

Meteors They are solid bodies developed out of materials similar to, our planet.

Gravity Anomalies They give us information about the distribution of mass of the material in the crust of the Earth. Gravity anomalies are caused due to unusual concentrations of mass in a region.

15 **Consider the following statements about the earthquake shadow zone.**
(Chap 3, Class-XI, New NCERT) (CGPSC Pre 2020)

1. The shadow zone of one earthquake is totally different from the shadow zone of another earthquake.
2. Seismometres record both 'P' and 'S' waves at any distance out of 105° from earthquake's epicentre.

Which of the statements given above is/are incorrect?
(a) Only 1 (b) Only 2
(c) Both 1 and 2 (d) None of these

Ans. (b)

Exp. Statement (2) is incorrect about the earthquake shadow zone. Seismometres record both 'P' and 'S' waves at any distance within 105° from earthquake's epicentre. Earthquake waves get recorded in seismographs. However, there exist some specific areas where the waves are not recorded, such a zone is called the 'Shadow Zone'. The study of different events reveals that for each earthquake, there exists an altogether different shadow zone.

16 **Consider the following pairs.**
(Chap 3, Class-VIII, New NCERT)

	Terms		Descriptions
1.	Lithosphere	–	Rigid outermost layer of the Earth.
2.	Asthenosphere	–	Weak, partially molten layer beneath the lithosphere.
3.	Mantle	–	Thickest layer of the Earth, made up of rocky material.

How many pairs given above is/are correct?
(a) Only one (b) Only two
(c) All three (d) None of these

Ans. (c)

Exp. All the pairs given above are correct.
The lithosphere is the rigid outermost layer of the Earth, composed of both the crust and the upper mantle.
The asthenosphere is the weak, partially molten layer beneath the lithosphere, which can flow plastically.
The mantle is the thickest layer of the Earth, making up about 84% of the Earth's volume. It is made up of rocky material that is mostly solid but can also melt and deform.
The core is the central region of the Earth, composed mainly of iron and nickel. It has an inner core that is solid and an outer core that is liquid.

Earth Movements

17 **Which of the following features on Earth are formed by tectonic movements?** *(Chap 3, Class-VIII, Old NCERT)*

1. Volcanic mountains 2. Faults
3. Folds 4. Trenches

Codes
(a) 1, 2 and 3 (b) 1, 2 and 4 (c) 2, 3 and 4 (d) All of these

Ans. (d)

Exp. All the features given above are formed by tectonic movements. These movements are movement of the plates, which results in the building up of stresses within the plates and the continental rocks. These movements of plates can make three different boundaries these are convergent, divergent and transform. In these plate boundaries, different types of Earth features are formed like folding, trenches, faulting and volcanic activity.

18 **Consider the following statements about movements of the Earth.** *(Chap 3, Class-VIII, Old NCERT)*

1. Face to face compression movements create anticlines and synclines.
2. Diverging movements are responsible for creating faults on the surface.

Which of the statements given above is/are correct?
(a) Only 1 (b) Only 2
(c) Both 1 and 2 (d) Neither 1 nor 2

Ans. (c)

Exp. Both the statements (1) and (2) are correct about the movement of the Earth. Compression is created when two plates collide during a convergent plate movement. As a result, the rock layers of the Earth's crust get folded. This process is called folding.
The folding due to face to face compression creates anticlines and synclines compression. The alternate upfolds that are formed on the rocks are called anticline and the downfolds are called syncline. Faulting occurs when two lithospheric plates move away from each other. This movement is known as divergent movement.

19 **Consider the following statements about earthquakes.**
(Chap 3, Class-VII, Old NCERT) (Chap 4, Module-2, NIOS)

1. The point inside the Earth where earthquake energy is released is called the epicenter.
2. The point on the Earth's surface where seismic waves are first experienced is called the epicenter.
3. Body waves cause the most damage on the Earth's surface.

How many of the statements given above is/are correct?
(a) Only one (b) Only two
(c) All three (d) None of these

Ans. (a)

Exp. Only one statement i.e., (2) is correct. The point on the Earth's surface directly above the focus is called the epicenter.
Statements (1) and (3) are incorrect. The point inside the Earth where earthquake energy is released is called the focus or the hypocenter.
Body waves are seismic waves that travel through the interior of the Earth, while surface waves are seismic waves that travel only at the Earth's surface. Surface waves cause the most damage on the Earth's surface, as they produce rolling motions that can topple buildings and structures.

20 **Consider the following pairs.** *(Chap 3, Class-XI, New NCERT)*

Types of Earthquake		Descriptions
1. Tectonic earthquake	–	Intense mining
2. Collapse earthquake	–	Large dams
3. Explosion earthquake	–	Nuclear detonation
4. Reservoir induced earthquake	–	Sliding of rocks along fault

How many pairs given above is/are correct?

(a) Only one (b) Only two
(c) All three (d) All four

Ans. (a)

Exp. Only one pair i.e., (3) is correct.

Ground shaking may also occur due to the explosion of chemical or nuclear devices. Such tremors are called Explosion Earthquake.

Tectonic Earthquake are generated due to sliding of rocks along a fault plane.

In the areas of intense mining activity, sometimes the roofs of underground mines collapse causing minor tremors. These are called Collapse Earthquake.

Reservoir Induced Earthquake The earthquakes that occur in the areas of large reservoirs are referred to as reservoir induced earthquake.

21 **Which of the following statements is/are correct about the earthquake measuring scales?** *(Chap 3, Class-XI, New NCERT)*

1. The Richter scale measures the magnitude of earthquake waves.
2. The Mercalli scale measures the damage of the earthquake over a region.

Codes

(a) Only 1 (b) Only 2
(c) Both 1 and 2 (d) Neither 1 and 2

Ans. (c)

Exp. Both the statements (1) and (2) are correct about the earthquake measuring scales.

The earthquake events are scaled either according to the magnitude or intensity of the shock. The magnitude scale is known as the Richter scale. The magnitude relates to the energy released during the earthquake. The magnitude is expressed in absolute numbers i.e., 0-10. The intensity scale is named after Mercalli, an Italian seismologist. The intensity scale takes into account the visible damage caused by the event. The range of intensity scale exist between 1-12.

22 **Consider the following statements about an earthquake.** *(Chap 3, Class-XI, New NCERT) (IAS Pre 2001)*

1. Intensity of earthquake is measured on Mercalli scale.
2. Earthquake's magnitude is the measurement of energy released.
3. Magnitude of earthquake depends directly upon amplitude of earthquake waves.
4. Every integer on Richter scale shows a 100 times increase in energy released.

Which of the statements given above is/are incorrect?

(a) Only 4 (b) Only 3 (c) 1 and 4 (d) 1 and 3

Ans. (a)

Exp. Statement (4) is incorrect about an earthquake because Richter scale has a shaking amplitude 10 times that of the previous integer and shows an increase of 32 times in energy. Energy equal to 6 ounces is released by an earthquake of a magnitude of 1.

23 **Consider the following statements about orogenic movements.** *(Chap 2, Class-IX, Old NCERT)*

1. Orogenic movements are large-scale vertical movements of the Earth.
2. It creates folds on the Earth's surface.
3. It is responsible for the formation of volcanic vents.

How many of the statements given above is/are correct?

(a) Only one (b) Only two (c) All three (d) None of these

Ans. (a)

Exp. Only one statement i.e., (2) is correct. Orogenic movements create folds on the Earth's surface, as the strata are compressed and uplifted to form mountain ranges.

Statements (1) and (3) are incorrect. Orogenic movements are large-scale horizontal movements of the Earth, caused by the convergence of lithospheric plates. Orogenic movements are not directly responsible for the formation of volcanic vents. Volcanic vents are formed by the eruption of magma from the mantle or the crust, which may or may not be related to Orogenic movements.

24 **Consider the following statements about the internal forces of Earth.** *(Chap 2, Class-IX, Old NCERT)*

1. Epeirogenic movements are responsible for formation of cinder cone volcanoes.
2. Epeirogenic movements are mainly vertical movements on Earth.

Which of the statements given above is/are correct?

(a) Only 1 (b) Only 2
(c) Both 1 and 2 (d) Neither 1 nor 2

Ans. (b)

Exp. Only statement (2) is correct about the internal forces of Earth as epeirogeny is a continental building process. These are mainly vertical movements of the Earth. This process involves the uplift or warping of large parts of the crust of the Earth. Through the process of epeirogeny, there may be mild deformations outside of the Earth.

Statement (1) is incorrect because epeirogenic movements are not responsible for formation of cinder cone volcanoes.

25 Which of the following statements is incorrect about the shield volcanoes on the Earth?

(Chap 3, Class-XI, New NCERT)

1. The shield volcanoes are the largest volcanoes on Earth.
2. These volcanoes are mainly made up of fluid basalt.
3. These volcanoes are characterised by highly explosive eruptions.

Codes

(a) Only 3 (b) 2 and 3 (c) 1 and 3 (d) All of these

Ans. (a)

Exp. Statement (3) is incorrect about the shield volcanoes on the Earth because the shield volcanoes become explosive if somehow water gets into the vent; otherwise, they are characterised by low-explosivity.

26 Consider the following Assertion (A) and Reason (R) and choose the correct code.

(Chap 3, Class-XI, New NCERT)

Assertion (A) Composite volcanoes are formed of many layers of volcanic materials.

Reason (R) Composite volcanoes are most explosive and tend to collapse on themselves.

Codes

(a) Both A and R are true and R is the correct explanation of A.
(b) Both A and R are true, but R is not the correct explanation of A.
(c) A is true, but R is false.
(d) A is false, but R is true.

Ans. (c)

Exp. Assertion (A) is true, but Reason (R) is false. Composite volcanoes are characterised by eruptions of cooler and more viscous lavas than basalt. These volcanoes often result in explosive eruptions. Along with lava, large quantities of pyroclastic material and ashes find their way to the ground. This material accumulates in the vicinity of the vent openings leading to formation of layers and this makes the mounts appear as composite volcanoes. Apart from that Caldera volcanoes are most explosive and tend to collapse on themselves.

27 Which of the following forces is/are responsible for driving the exogenic movements of Earth?

(Chap 6, Class-XI, New NCERT)

1. Temperature and precipitation
2. Gravitational force
3. Seismic movements

Codes

(a) Only 1 (b) Only 2 (c) 2 and 3 (d) 1 and 2

Ans. (d)

Exp. Temperature, precipitation and gravitational force are responsible for driving the exogenic movements of Earth.

The exogenic processes derive their energy from atmosphere determined by the ultimate energy from the Sun and also the gradients created by tectonic factors. Gravitational force acts upon all Earth materials having a sloping surface and tend to produce movement of matter in down slope direction. Temperature and precipitation are the two important climatic elements that control various processes while Seismic movement is a part of endogenic movement.

28 Which of the following factors affect the occurrence and intensity of exogenic movements in a region?

(Chap 6, Class-XI, New NCERT)

1. Density and type of vegetation in a region
2. Slope and altitude of a place
3. Type and structure of rocks
4. Temperature of interior of Earth

Codes

(a) 1, 2 and 4 (b) 2, 3 and 4 (c) 1, 2 and 3 (d) 1 and 3

Ans. (c)

Exp. Factors like density, distribution of vegetation, slope and altitude of a place, type and structure of rocks etc affect the exogenic movement in a region. The precipitation and temperature exert indirect influence on exogenic geomorphic processes.

29 Consider the following statements about weathering.

(Chap 4, Class-VIII, Old NCERT)

1. Weathering is the ex situ breaking of rocks into small pieces.
2. It is the transportation of rocks down a hill slope.
3. It is the in situ disintegration of rocks due to the effects of pressure, temperature and other agents.
4. It is the change in chemical composition of rocks under pressure.

How many of the statements given above is/are correct?

(a) Only one (b) Only two
(c) All three (d) None of these

Ans. (a)

Exp. Only one statement i.e., (3) is correct. Weathering is the in situ disintegration of rocks due to the effects of pressure, temperature, and other agents. Weathering is the breaking down or dissolving of rocks and minerals on the surface of the Earth by agents such as water, ice, acids, salts, plants, animals, and temperature changes. It can be mechanical, chemical, or biological. Weathering is different from erosion, which is the transport of weathered materials by water, wind, or other forces. Statements (1), (2) and (4) are incorrect, because weathering is the in situ (in place) breaking of rocks, not ex situ (out of place). Weathering is not the transportation of rocks, but the breakdown of rocks. Transportation of rocks is part of erosion, not weathering. Weathering can involve the change in chemical composition of rocks under pressure, but this is only one type of weathering called chemical weathering. There are also other types of weathering that do not involve chemical changes, such as mechanical weathering.

30 Consider the following statements about physical weathering. *(Chap 4, Class-VIII, Old NCERT)*

1. Physical weathering occurs only due to wind and water erosion.
2. Daily fluctuations in day and night temperatures can contribute to rock cracking.
3. Freezing and thawing of water within rock cracks can break them apart.
4. Production of carbonic acid inside rocks is primarily responsible for physical weathering.

Which of the statements given above are correct?

(a) 1 and 2 (b) 2 and 3
(c) 3 and 4 (d) All of these

Ans. (b)

Exp. Statements (2) and (3) are correct with respect to physical weathering. Physical weathering involves the breakdown of rocks into smaller fragments through processes such as expansion and contraction, mainly due to temperature changes. The daily fluctuations in day and night temperatures can contribute to rock cracking, as the rocks expand and contract due to thermal stress.

The freezing and thawing of water within rock cracks can break them apart, as the water expands when it freezes and exerts pressure on the surrounding rock.

Statements (1) and (4) are incorrect, because physical weathering occurs not only due to wind and water erosion, but also due to other factors such as ice wedging, plant roots, and salt crystal growth. The production of carbonic acid inside rocks is not primarily responsible for physical weathering, but for chemical weathering, as it dissolves the minerals in the rocks and alters their chemical composition.

31 Consider the following statements. *(Chap 9, Class-XI, Old NCERT)*

1. The process of mechanical weathering is faster than the process of chemical weathering.
2. Exfoliation of rock occurs due to mechanical weathering.
3. Oxidation and hydration are process of chemical weathering.

Which of the statements given above are correct?

(a) 1 and 2 (b) 2 and 3
(c) 1 and 3 (d) All of these

Ans. (b)

Exp. Statements (2) and (3) are correct.

The geological process under, which rocks break apart without losing their chemical composition is termed as mechanical or physical weathering. Exfoliation is one type of mechanical or physical weathering, which occur due to expansion and contraction induced by temperature changes.

Chemical weathering is the weakening and subsequent disintegration of rock by chemical reactions. These reactions include oxidation, hydration and carbonation.

Statement (1) is incorrect because mechanical weathering is slow but can cause great damage to the rocks because of prolonged repetition of contraction and expansion.

32 Consider the following statements about frost weathering. *(Chap 4, Class-VIII, Old NCERT)*

1. Frost weathering occurs mainly in cold climatic regions, particularly at high altitudes.
2. Desert regions are the primary locations for frost weathering.
3. Movements of animals over rocks contribute significantly to frost weathering.
4. The process of carbonation can amplify frost weathering effects in a region.

Which of the statements given above is/are correct?

(a) Only 1 (b) 1 and 4
(c) 2 and 3 (d) All of these

Ans. (b)

Exp. Statements (1) and (4) are correct as frost weathering occurs mainly in cold climatic regions, particularly at high altitudes, where water can freeze and thaw repeatedly.

The process of carbonation can amplify frost weathering effects in a region, as it involves the dissolution of carbon dioxide in water, which lowers the pH and makes the water more corrosive to rocks. Carbonation can also create cracks and pores in rocks, which increase the surface area for water infiltration and ice formation.

Statements (2) and (3) are incorrect because desert regions are not the primary locations for frost weathering, as they have low precipitation and humidity, which limit the availability of water for freezing.

The movements of animals over rocks do not contribute significantly to frost weathering, as they are not related to the formation of ice within rock outcrops.

Movements of animals may cause physical weathering by abrasion or bioturbation, but not frost weathering.

33 Consider the following statements. *(Chap 6, Class-XI, New NCERT)*

1. Mass movements usually occur under the influence of gravity of Earth.
2. Mass movements help in concentration of valuable minerals in a region.
3. Vertical cliffs and loose rock materials favour mass movements.

Which of the statements given above is/are incorrect?

(a) 1 and 2 (b) 2 and 3
(c) Only 2 (d) Only 3

Ans. (c)

Exp. Only statement (2) is incorrect because mass movements does not help in concentration of valuable minerals in a region as it relates to the downfall of rock debris.

34 Which of the following factors will aid in promoting mass movement over the surface of Earth? *(Chap 6, Class-XI, New NCERT)*

1. Torrential rain
2. Earthquake or explosion
3. Increase in gradient of slope
4. Removal of natural vegetation

Codes

(a) 1, 2 and 3 (b) 1, 2 and 4
(c) 2, 3 and 4 (d) 1, 2, 3 and 4

Ans. (d)

Exp. All the factors given above will aid in promoting mass movement over the surface of Earth. The following factors cause the mass movements

Heavy rainfall, saturation and lubrication of slope materials, which leads to indiscriminate removal of natural vegetation.

Occurrence of earthquakes, explosion or machinery.

Increase in gradient and height of slopes.

Removal of natural vegetation. Removal of material or load from the original slope surfaces. Occurrence of earthquakes, explosions or machinery.

35 Consider the following Assertion (A) and Reason (R) and choose the correct code. *(Chap 6, Class-XI, New NCERT)*

Assertion (A) Landslides are the rapid movement of dry materials over a slope.

Reason (R) Landslide is caused by slipping of rock with a backward rotation.

Codes

(a) Both A and R are true and R is the correct explanation of A.
(b) Both A and R are true, but R is not the correct explanation of A.
(c) A is true, but R is false.
(d) A is false, but R is true.

Ans. (c)

Exp. Assertion (A) is true, but Reason (R) is false. Landslides are simply defined as the mass movement of rock, debris or Earth down a slope. They often take place in conjunction with earthquakes, floods and volcanoes. These are relatively rapid and perceptible movements. The materials involved in landslides are relatively dry. Apart from that slump (not landslide) is slipping of one or several units of rock debris with a backward rotation with respect to the slope, over, which the movement takes place.

36 Consider the following options. *(Chap 4, Class-XI, New NCERT) (IAS Pre 2013)*

1. Electromagnetic radiation
2. Geothermal energy
3. Gravitational force
4. Plate movements
5. Rotation of the Earth
6. Revolution of the Earth

Which of the options given above are responsible for bringing dynamic changes on the surface of the Earth?

(a) 1, 2, 3 and 4
(b) 2, 4, 5 and 6
(c) 1, 3, 5 and 6
(d) 1, 2, 3, 4, 5 and 6

Ans. (d)

Exp. All the options mentioned above are responsible for bringing dynamic changes on the surface of the Earth. The dynamic changes on the Earth's surface are caused by endogenic forces. In general, the origin of endogenic force is due to thermal asymmetry in the inner part of the Earth and compression and expansion of rocks.

37 Which of the following statements about weathering, erosion, transportation and deposition of materials is incorrect? *(Chap 6, Class-XI, New NCERT)*

(a) Weathering and erosion of materials cause denudation of relief on Earth's surface.
(b) Erosion and transportation of Earth materials is caused by wind and water.
(c) Deposition of weathered materials mainly takes place over steep slopes.
(d) Both a and b

Ans. (c)

Exp. Statement (c) is incorrect about weathering, erosion, transportation and deposition of materials because deposition is a consequence of erosion. When the agents of erosion lose their velocity and energy on gentle slopes, the materials, which are carried by them start to settle as deposited materials.

Theories of Distribution of Continents and Oceans on Earth

38 Which of the following statements is/are correct about the early concept of Continental Drift? *(Chap 4, Class-XI, New NCERT)*

1. Abraham Ortelius was the first one to propose the concept of drift of continents.
2. Antonio Pellegrini depicted the continents of Africa, Europe and Americas joined on a map.

Codes

(a) Only 1 (b) Only 2
(c) Both 1 and 2 (d) None of these

Ans. (c)

Exp. Both the statements (1) and (2) are correct about the early concept of Continental Drift because from the known records of the history of science, it was Abraham Ortelius, a Dutch map maker, who first proposed such a possibility of the two Americas, Europe and Africa, to be once joined together in early, 1596. Antonio Pellegrini drew a map showing the three continents America, Europe and Africa together.

39 Consider the following statements.

(Chap 4, Class-XI, New NCERT)

1. Alfred Wegener, a German Meteorologist put forward a comprehensive Continental Drift Theory in 1912.
2. According to Wegener, the Pangaea broke away from Panthalassa 200 million years ago.
3. Panthalassa was a supercontinent floating over Pangaea, the mega ocean.
4. The Pangaea split into Laurasia and Gondwana.

Which of the statements given above are correct?

(a) 1, 2 and 3 (b) 2, 3 and 4
(c) 1, 2 and 4 (d) All of these

Ans. (c)

Exp. Statements (1), (2) and (4) are correct.

Alfred Wegener, a German Meteorologist put forward a comprehensive Continental Drift Theory in 1912. According to him, all the continents formed a single continental mass and mega ocean surrounded the same. 'The supercontinent was named Pangaea, which meant all Earth'. The mega-ocean was called Panthalassa, meaning 'all water'. He argued that, around 200 million years ago, the super continent, Pangaea, began to split. Pangaea first broke into two large continental masses as Laurasia and Gondwana land forming the Northern and Southern components respectively. Subsequently, Laurasia and Gondwana land continued to break into various smaller continents that exist today.

Statement (3) is incorrect because Pangaea (not Panthalassa) was a supercontinent floating over the mega ocean Panthalassa.

40 Which of the following statements can be surely stated as an evidence in support of the Continental Drift Theory of Alfred Wegener?

(Chap 4, Class-XI, New NCERT)

1. Ancient rocks (2000 million years) of Brazil coast matches with those from Western Africa.
2. Tillite deposits in Africa, Madagascar, Antarctica and Australia.
3. Gold placer deposits of Ghana Coast and gold bearing veins in Brazil.
4. Misfit of shoreline of Africa and South America.

Codes

(a) 1 and 2 (b) 1, 2 and 3
(c) 2, 3 and 4 (d) All of these

Ans. (b)

Exp. Statements (1), (2) and (3) are correct regarding the evidence that supports the Continental Drift Theory of Alfred Wegener. According to these evidences, the belt of ancient rocks of 2,000 million years from Brazil coast matches with those from Western Africa.

The Gondwana system of sediments from India is known to have its counterparts in six different landmasses of the Southern Hemisphere.

The gold bearing veins are in Brazil and it is obvious that the gold deposits of the Ghana are derived from the Brazil plateau when the two continents lay side by side.

Statement (4) is incorrect because the shorelines of Africa and South America facing each other have a remarkable and unmistakable match which is also known as jig saw fit.

41 Alfred Wegener propounded, which of the following forces to be the main reason behind drifting of continents?

(Chap 4, Class-XI, New NCERT)

1. Rotation of Earth and Polar-fleeing force.
2. Tidal force due to Moon's attraction.
3. Radioactive decay of rocks.

Codes

(a) Only 2 (b) Only 3
(c) 1 and 3 (d) 1 and 2

Ans. (d)

Exp. Alfred Wegener propounded that the movement responsible for the drifting of the continents was caused by Polar-fleeing force and tidal force.

The polar-fleeing force relates to the rotation of the Earth. Tidal force due to the attraction of the Moon and the Sun is responsible for the development of tides in oceanic waters.

42 After evidence was gathered in the 19th and 20th century about the forces driving the continental drift, the theory of Alfred Wegener was discarded. Which of the following statements is/are correct about the forces driving the drift of continents?

(Chap 4, Class-XI, New NCERT)

1. Arthur Holmes gave the theory that convection currents are responsible for driving continental drift.
2. The convection currents are generated due to radioactive elements in rocks inside Earth.
3. Convection currents operate inside the inner core of Earth.

Codes

(a) 1 and 2 (b) 2 and 3
(c) 1 and 3 (d) All of these

Ans. (a)

Exp. Statements (1) and (2) are correct about forces driving the drift of continents.

Arthur Holmes in 1930s discussed the possibility of convection currents operating in the mantle portion. These currents are generated due to radioactive elements causing thermal differences in the mantle portion. Holmes argued that there exists a system of such currents in the entire mantle portion. This was an attempt to provide an explanation to the issue of force, on the basis of, which contemporary scientists discarded the Continental Drift Theory.

Statement (3) is incorrect because convection currents operate inside the mantle portion of the Earth.

43 **Consider the following statements.** *(Chap 4, Class-XI, New NCERT)*

1. After the World War II, oceanic floor relief was mapped using modern techniques.
2. Mid-oceanic ridges with volcanic eruptions were found after the mapping of oceanic floor.
3. Paleomagnetic studies of rocks of the oceanic floor revealed that continental rocks were younger than oceanic rocks.

Which of the statements given above is/are correct?

(a) 1 and 3 (b) 2 and 3
(c) 1 and 2 (d) All of these

Ans. ***(c)***

Exp. Statements (1) and (2) are correct. Expeditions to map the oceanic floor in the Post World War II period provided a detailed picture of the ocean relief and indicated the existence of submerged mountain ranges as well as deep trenches, mostly located closer to the continental margins.

The mid-oceanic ridges were found to be most active in terms of volcanic eruptions.

Statement (3) is incorrect because the dating of the rocks from the oceanic crust revealed the fact that they are much younger than the continental rocks.

44 **Which of the following statements are correct about Seafloor Spreading?** *(Chap 4, Class-XI, New NCERT)*

1. The rocks closer to the mid-oceanic ridges are younger and have normal polarity.
2. Equidistant rocks on either sides of oceanic ridges are similar in their chemical composition.
3. The concept of Sea floor spreading was proposed by Harry Hess in 1961.

Codes

(a) 1 and 2 (b) 2 and 3 (c) 1 and 3 (d) All of these

Ans. ***(d)***

Exp. All the statements are correct about Seafloor Spreading. Hess proposed his hypothesis, known as the 'Sea Floor Spreading in 1961'. He argued that constant eruptions at the crest of oceanic ridges cause the rupture of the oceanic crust and the new lava wedges into it, pushing the oceanic crust on either side. Hence, rocks closer to the mid-oceanic ridges have normal polarity and are the youngest. The age of the rocks increases as one move away from the crest. The rocks equidistant on either sides of the crest of mid-oceanic ridges show remarkable similarities in terms of period of formation, chemical compositions and magnetic properties.

45 **Consider the following statements about the oceanic floor after seafloor spreading.** *(Chap 4, Class-XI, New NCERT)*

1. New oceanic crust forms at mid-ocean ridges and pushes older crust away.
2. When new crust forms, oceanic plates shrink in size.
3. Oceanic trenches continuously consume newly formed oceanic crust.
4. Seafloor spreading results in the continuous creation of new oceans.

Which of the statements given above is/are correct?

(a) 1 and 2
(b) 1 and 3
(c) 2 and 4
(d) Only 4

Ans. ***(b)***

Exp. Statements (1) and (3) are correct because new oceanic crust forms at mid-ocean ridges and pushes older crust away, as the plates move in opposite directions. The oceanic trenches continuously consume newly formed oceanic crust, as the plates converge and one plate subducts under another, recycling the crust back to the mantle.

Statements (2) and (4) are incorrect, because when new crust forms, oceanic plates do not shrink in size, but grow larger, as they add more material to their edges. The seafloor spreading does not result in the continuous creation of new oceans, but rather the expansion or contraction of existing oceans, depending on the balance between spreading and subduction rates.

Seafloor spreading is a geologic process in which tectonic plates split apart from each other and form new crust at mid-ocean ridges, which are divergent plate boundaries. Seafloor spreading influences sea levels, continental drift, and the age and magnetic properties of the ocean floor.

46 **Consider the following statements as Assertion (A) and Reason (R) and choose the correct code.** *(Chap 4, Class-XI, New NCERT)*

Assertion (A) The sediments on ocean floor are very thin and not much older than sediments over continents.

Reason (R) Constant eruption at the crest of oceanic ridges cause rupture of the oceanic crust and forms new crust.

Codes

(a) Both A and R are true and R is the correct explanation of A.
(b) Both A and R are true, but R is not the correct explanation of A.
(c) A is true, but R is false.
(d) A is false, but R is true.

Ans. ***(b)***

Exp. Both Assertion (A) and Reason (R) are true, but Reason (R) is not the correct explanation of Assertion (A). Scientists were expecting, if the ocean floors were as old as the continent than it must have a complete sequence of sediments for a period of much longer duration but the sediments on the ocean floor are unexpectedly very thin, which proves oceanic crust is much younger than the continental crust.

47 Consider the following statements about the major tectonic plates on Earth. *(Chap 4, Class-XI, New NCERT)*

1. There are eight major tectonic plates on Earth.
2. The Nazca plate is the largest major plate by area.
3. Major tectonic plates encompass both continental and oceanic crust.
4. All plates move with the same speed and direction.

How many of the statements given above is/are correct?

(a) Only one (b) Only two
(c) Only three (d) All of these

***Ans.* (a)**

Exp. Only one statement i.e., (3) is correct-with respect to the major tectonic plates on Earth. Major tectonic plates encompass both continental and oceanic crust, as they can consist of both types of material. For example, the North American plate contains the continent of North America as well as part of the Atlantic Ocean. Statements (1), (2) and (4) are incorrect, because there are not eight, but seven major tectonic plates on Earth, based on how they are classified: African, Antarctic, Eurasian, North American, South American, Pacific and Indo-Australian. There are also several minor and microplates that are smaller and less significant than the major plates. Nazca plate is not the largest, but one of the smallest major plates by area, covering about 15,600,000 km^2 of the Eastern Pacific Ocean. The largest major plate by area is the Pacific plate, which underlies the Pacific Ocean and covers about 103,300,000 km^2. All plates do not move with the same speed and direction, but rather with different rates and directions, depending on the forces acting on them and the boundaries they interact with.

48 Consider the following statements. *(Chap 4, Class-XI, New NCERT)*

1. The concept of Plate tectonics was given by Mckenzie, Parker and Morgan in 1967.
2. Lithospheric plates includes the crust and top mantle.
3. The concept of seafloor spreading was developed by Alfred Wegener.

Which of the statements given above is/are correct?

(a) Only 2 (b) Only 3 (c) 1 and 3 (d) 1 and 2

***Ans.* (d)**

Exp. Statements (1) and (2) are correct as in 1967, McKenzie, Parker and also Morgan, independently collected the available ideas and came out with an concept termed plate tectonics. A tectonic plate (also called lithospheric plate) is a massive, irregularly-shaped slab of solid rock, generally composed of both continental and oceanic lithosphere. Plates move horizontally over the asthenosphere as rigid units. The lithospheric plate includes both the crust and top mantle layers.
Statement (3) is incorrect because the seafloor spreading theory was developed by H. Hess.

49 Match the following lists correctly and choose the correct code. *(Chap 4, Class-XI, New NCERT)*

List I (Minor Plates)	List II (Located between)
A. Cocos Plate	1. Asiatic Plate and Pacific Plate
B. Philippine Plate	2. Central America and Pacific Plate
C. Caroline Plate	3. Philippine and Indian Plate
D. Fuji Plate	4. North-East of Australia

Codes

	A	B	C	D
(a)	4	2	1	3
(b)	3	1	2	4
(c)	2	1	3	4
(d)	4	1	3	2

***Ans.* (c)**

Exp. The correct matching is A-2, B-1, C-3, D-4.
Cocos Plate is located between Central America and Pacific plate. It is a small sized, triangular shaped oceanic plate.
Philippine Plate is located between the Asiatic and Pacific plate. It is a tectonic plate comprising oceanic lithosphere.
Caroline Plate is located between the Philippine and Indian plate (North of New Guinea). It is a minor tectonic plate.
Fuji Plate is located between North-East of Australia. These all are the examples of minor plates of the world. It is an irregular shaped plate, made of rocks.

50 Consider the following statements about the plate boundaries. *(Chap 4, Class-XI, New NCERT)*

1. The mid-Atlantic ridge in Northern hemisphere separates African Plate from Indian Plate.
2. New oceanic crust is generated at the Divergent plate boundaries.
3. The older crust is destroyed at transform plate boundaries in the subduction zone.

Which of the statements given above is/are correct?

(a) 1 and 3 (b) Only 2 (c) 1 and 2 (d) Only 3

***Ans.* (b)**

Exp. Only statement (2) is correct about plate boundaries because when both the plates moves away from each others that boundary is known as divergent plate boundary.
In this boundary new crust is generated as the plates pull away from each other like new oceanic ridge are formed in this type of boundary.
The sites where the plates move away from each other are called spreading sites. The best known example of divergent boundaries is the Mid-Atlantic ridge.
Statements (1) and (3) are incorrect as the mid-Atlantic ridge in Northern hemisphere separates African Plate from American Plate.
The subduction zone can be seen over convergent boundaries where the crust is destroyed as one plate dived under another.

51 **Consider the following statements about transform faults.** *(Chap 4, Class-XI, New NCERT)*

1. Transform faults are boundaries where plates slide past each other horizontally.
2. Earth's crust is neither created nor destroyed along transform faults.
3. Transform faults only run perpendicular to mid-ocean ridges.
4. The Earth's rotation has no influence on the movement of plates along transform faults.

How many of the statements given above is/are correct?

(a) Only one (b) Only two
(c) Only three (d) All of these

Ans. (b)

Exp. Only two statements i.e., (1) and (2) are correct with respect to transform faults.

Transform faults are specific types of plate boundaries where two plates move horizontally in opposite directions, like two pieces of ice sliding past each other on a pond. Unlike divergent boundaries where new crust is created or convergent boundaries where crust is destroyed, transform faults don't involve significant crustal creation or destruction.

Statements (3) and (4) are incorrect. Many transform faults do intersect mid-ocean ridges at roughly perpendicular angles, connecting them to other types of plate boundaries but not all of them. The Earth's rotation plays a role in influencing the overall movements of plates along all boundaries, including transform faults. The rotation's influence helps determine the direction and relative speeds of plate movement on a global scale.

52 **Consider the following Assertion (A) and Reason (R) and choose the correct code.** *(Chap 4, Class-XI, New NCERT)*

Assertion (A) Radioactive decay of rocks and residual heat forms convective cells inside the surface of Earth.

Reason (R) Different tectonic plates move at different rates over the Earth.

Codes

(a) Both A and R are true and R is the correct explanation of A.
(b) Both A and R are true, but R is not the correct explanation of A.
(c) A is true, but R is false.
(d) A is false, but R is true.

Ans. (b)

Exp. Both Assertion (A) and Reason (R) are true, but Reason (R) is not the correct explanation of Assertion (A). Heat within the Earth comes from two main sources, i.e. radioactive decay and residual heat, which makes a convective cell inside the Earth surface.

Different tectonic plates move at different rates over the Earth like the Arctic Ridge has the slowest rate (less than 2.5 cm/yr) and the East Pacific Rise near Easter Island, in the South Pacific about 3,400 km West of Chile, has the fastest rate (more than 15 cm/yr).

53 **Consider the following statements about earthquake foci and plate boundaries.** *(Chap 4, Class-XI, New NCERT)*

1. The Pacific Ring of Fire experiences frequent earthquakes with deep and shallow foci.
2. Mid-ocean ridges are known for shallow earthquakes due to plate movement and volcanic activity.
3. Oceanic trenches are associated with deep-seated earthquakes occurring where one plate subducts under another.
4. The Alpine-Himalayan belt exhibits shallow earthquakes primarily due to continental collision and mountain building.

Which of the statements given above are correct?

(a) 1 and 2 (b) 2 and 3
(c) 3 and 4 (d) All of these

Ans. (d)

Exp. All the statements is correct regarding earthquake foci and plate boundaries.

The Ring of Fire is a string of volcanoes and sites of seismic activity, or earthquakes, around the edges of the Pacific Ocean. Roughly 90% of all earthquakes occur along the Ring of Fire. Mid-ocean ridges and transform margins have shallow earthquakes (usually less than 30 km deep), in narrow bands close to plate margins.

All trenches are associated with zones of earthquake foci. Along the periphery of the Pacific Ocean, earthquakes occur close to and landward of the trenches, at depths within the Earth of 55 km (34 miles) or less.

The Alpine-Himalayan orogenic belt is a seismic and orogenic belt that includes an array of mountain ranges extending for more than 15,000 km (9,300 mil) along the Southern margin of Eurasia.

It is the second most seismically active region in the world, after the circum-Pacific belt (the Ring of Fire), with 17% of the world's largest earthquakes.

54 **Consider the following statements about rock-forming minerals and Earth's crust.** *(Chap 2, Class -VII, New NCERT)*

1. Approximately 98% of the Earth's crust is composed of eight elements, including oxygen, silicon, and aluminium.
2. Rocks are formed when two or more elements combine to create individual mineral crystals.
3. The primary source of minerals in rocks is the cooling and solidification of magma or lava from Earth's interior.
4. Rock formations generally contain only one type of mineral, and their characteristics depend solely on that mineral.

Which of the statements given above is/are incorrect?
(a) 1 and 2
(b) 2 and 3
(c) Only 4
(d) None of the above

Ans. (c)
Exp. Only statement (4) is incorrect. Rock formations generally contain only one type of mineral, and their characteristics depend solely on that mineral.

Rock formations are typically composed of multiple types of minerals. The characteristics of a rock formation depend on the combination of minerals it contains, not just one type.

Rocks

55 Which of the following pairs of minerals and their characteristics is not correctly matched?
(Chap 5, Class-XI, New NCERT)

(a) Lustre – Appearance of a mineral
(b) Streak – Particular arrangement of individual crystal
(c) Cleavage – Tendency to break in given direction
(d) Hardness – Relative resistance being scratched

Ans. (b)
Exp. Pair (b) is not correctly matched because streak is defined as the colour of the ground powder of any mineral. It may be of the same colour as the mineral or may differ—malachite is green and gives green streak, fluorite is purple or green but gives a white streak. Hence, streak is not the particular arrangement of individual crystal.

56 Consider the following statements about the sedimentary rocks. *(Chap 2, Class-VII, New NCERT) (IAS Pre 2001)*

1. Sedimentary rocks are formed at the Earth's surface by the hydrological system.
2. The formation of sedimentary rocks involves the weathering of pre-existing rocks.
3. Sedimentary rocks contain fossils.
4. Sedimentary rocks typically occur in layers.

Which of the statements given above is/are correct?
(a) 1 and 2
(b) 1 and 4
(c) 2, 3 and 4
(d) 1, 2, 3 and 4

Ans. (d)
Exp. All three statements i.e., (1), (2) and (4) are correct about sedimentary rocks. These rocks are formed by the accumulation of sediments. This sediment or debris accumulates in low lying areas like lakes.

The ocean is largely responsible for transporting sediment to locations where it accumulates. These sedimentary materials may be formed from eroded fragments of other or pre-existing rocks or even from the remains of plants, animals and fossils.

57 Consider the following statements about Rocks.
(Chap 2, Class-VII, New NCERT)

1. Sedimentary rocks are formed by transport and deposition of small fragments.
2. Sedimentary rocks contain fossil fuels.
3. Granite and marble are sedimentary rocks.
4. Sedimentary rocks are formed only above the Earth's surface.

How many of the statements given above is/are incorrect?
(a) Only one (b) Only two
(c) Only three (d) All of these

Ans. (a)
Exp. Only one statement i.e., (3) is incorrect because Granite and Marble are not a part of sedimentary rock . Granite is an igneous rock, while marble is a metamorphic rock Sedimentary rocks are the types of rock that are formed by the deposition and subsequent cementation of that material at the Earth's surface and within bodies of water.

58 Consider the following pairs.
(Chap 2, Class-VI, New NCERT) (UKPCS Pre 2005)

	Terms		Corresponding
1.	Plutonic rocks	–	Formed by the accumulation and compaction of sediments
2.	Volcanic rocks	–	Formed by the cooling and solidification of magma within the Earth's crust
3.	Metamorphic rocks	–	Formed by the transformation of existing rocks under high pressure and temperature
4.	Sedimentary rocks	–	Solidified from lava on Earth's surface

How many pairs given above is/are correct?
(a) Only one (b) Only two
(c) Only three (d) All four

Ans. (a)
Exp. Only one pair i.e., (3) is correct.

Metamorphic rocks are formed by the transformation of existing rocks under high pressure and temperature. Metamorphic rocks result from the alteration of pre-existing rocks (either sedimentary, igneous, or other metamorphic rocks) due to heat, pressure, or chemically reactive fluids.

While Plutonic rocks are formed by the cooling and solidification of magma within the Earth's crust. Plutonic rocks typically form beneath the Earth's surface through a slow cooling process, allowing large crystals to develop.

Volcanic rocks are solidified from lava on Earth's surface. Volcanic rocks are formed by the rapid cooling of lava erupted from volcanoes, resulting in smaller crystals due to the quicker cooling process.

Sedimentary rocks are formed by the accumulation and compaction of sediments. Sedimentary rocks are created through the deposition and cementation of mineral and organic particles, often in layers, over time.

59 **Consider the following statements about metamorphic rocks.** ***(Chap 2, Class-VII, New NCERT)***

1. Metamorphic rocks are formed when existing rocks are transformed by high pressure and temperature, leading to changes in their texture, mineral composition, or both.
2. Marble is an example of a metamorphic rock formed from the transformation of limestone, a sedimentary rock.
3. Metamorphic rocks always exhibit large, visible crystals due to the slow cooling process during their formation.
4. Granite, despite being hard and used in construction, is not classified as a metamorphic rock.

How many of the statements given above is/are correct?

(a) Only one (b) Only two
(c) Only three (d) All of these

Ans. (c)

Exp. Only three statements i.e., (1), (2) and (4) are correct. Metamorphic rocks are formed when existing rocks are transformed by high pressure and temperature, leading to changes in their texture, mineral composition, or both. Metamorphic rocks arise from the transformation of existing rock types in a process called metamorphism. Marble is an example of a metamorphic rock formed from the transformation of limestone, a sedimentary rock. Marble is a granular metamorphic rock derived from limestone or dolomite. Granite is classified as an intrusive igneous rock, not a metamorphic rock.

Statement (3) is incorrect. While metamorphic rocks can exhibit visible crystals, this is not always the case. The size of the crystals in metamorphic rocks can vary and is influenced by the conditions of metamorphism.

60 **Which of the following pairs is incorrectly matched?** ***(Chap 5, Class-XI, New NCERT)***

Rocks		Type
1. Gneiss, Slate	–	Igneous Rock
2. Coal, Shale	–	Sedimentary Rock
3. Marble, Diamond	–	Metamorphic Rock

Codes

(a) 1 and 2 (b) Only 2
(c) Only 1 (d) None of these

Ans. (c)

Exp. Pair (1) is incorrectly matched as the examples of igneous rocks are granite, gabbro, pegmatite, basalt, volcanic breccia and tuff, while Gneiss and slate are metamorphic rock.

61 **Which of the following rocks are intrusive igneous rock formations?** ***(Chap 3, Class-XI, New NCERT)***

1. Laccoliths 2. Batholiths
3. Dykes 4. Caldera
5. Flood Basalt

Codes

(a) 1, 2, 3 and 4 (b) 1, 2, 4 and 5
(c) 1, 2 and 3 (d) 1, 2, 3, 4 and 5

Ans. (c)

Exp. Laccoliths, batholiths and dykes are intrusive igneous rock formations. The lava that cools within the crustal portions assumes different forms. These forms are called intrusive forms. For example, Lopolith, Phacolith and Sills. Caldera and flood basalt are the examples of volcanic landforms.

62 **Consider the following statements about igneous intrusive forms.** ***(Chap 3, Class-XI, New NCERT)***

1. Laccoliths are dome shaped bodies, which are localised source of lava on Earth's surface.
2. Lopolith is a saucer shaped horizontal rock inside Earth.
3. Vertical and solidified form of lava above the Earth's surface are known as Dykes.

Which of the statements given above are correct?

(a) 1 and 2 (b) 1 and 3 (c) 2 and 3 (d) All of these

Ans. (d)

Exp. All three statements i.e., (1), (2) and (3) are correct about igneous intrusive forms because Laccoliths are large dome shaped intrusive bodies with a level base and connected by a pipe-like conduit from below.

As and when the lava moves upwards, a portion of the same may tend to move in a horizontal direction wherever it finds a weak plane. It may get rested in different forms. In case it develops into a saucer shape, concave to the sky body, it is called lopolith.

When the lava makes its way through crack sand the fissures developed in the land, it solidifies almost perpendicular to the ground. It gets cooled in the same position to develop all like structure. Such structures are called dykes.

63 **Which of the following statement is correct about batholiths?** ***(Chap 3, Class-XI, New NCERT)***

1. Batholiths are formed above the surface of Earth.
2. They are commonly found in the Western Maharashtra region.
3. Batholiths are the forms of Marble.

Codes

(a) Only 1 (b) Only 2 (c) Only 3 (d) None of these

Ans. (b)

Exp. Statement (2) is correct regarding batholiths because the Karnataka plateau (Western Maharashtra region) is spotted with domal hills of granite rocks. Most of these, now exfoliated, are examples of laccoliths or batholiths.

Statements (1) and (3) are incorrect because Batholith are large body of igneous rock formed beneath the Earth's surface by the intrusion and solidification of Magma. Batholiths are formed when magma rises into the earths crust, but does not erupt onto the surface.

64 **Consider the following statements about sedimentary rocks.** *(Chap 4, Class-XI, Old NCERT)*

1. Sedimentary rocks cover the largest area over the Earth's surface.
2. Sedimentary rocks are only derived from igneous rocks.
3. Coal and limestone are sedimentary rocks formed from organic matter.
4. Sedimentary rocks are formed by the process of lithification.

Which of the statements given above are correct?

(a) 1, 2 and 4 (b) 2 and 3 (c) 1 and 4 (d) 1, 3 and 4

***Ans.* (d)**

Exp. Statements (1), (3) and (4) are correct regarding the sedimentary rock because when big rocks break down into small fragments (or sediments), the fragments are transported and deposited by factors like water and wind. This is the reason that sedimentary rocks are found in such huge quantity. These rocks cover the largest area over Earth's surface.

Plants are lithified to become coal and when shells are cemeted together, they form limestone.

The sediment deposits through compaction turn into rocks. This process is called lithification.

Statement (2) is incorrect because sedimentary rocks are derived both from igneous as well as metamorphic rocks.

65 **Which of the following pairs is matched correctly?** *(Chap 5, Class-XI, New NCERT)*

Type of Sedimentary Rock		Rock
1. Mechanically formed	–	Conglomerate
2. Organically formed	–	Shale
3. Chemically formed	–	Gypsum

Codes

(a) 1 and 3 (b) 1 and 2 (c) Only 1 (d) All of these

***Ans.* (a)**

Exp. Pairs (1) and (3) are correctly matched. Depending upon the mode of formation, sedimentary rocks are classified into following three major groups

Mechanically formed – sandstone, conglomerate, limestone, shale, loess etc are some examples.

Organically formed – geyserite, chalk, limestone, coal etc are some examples.

Chemically formed – chert, limestone, halite, gypsum, potash etc are some examples.

66 **Match the following lists correctly and choose the correct code.** *(Chap 4, Class-XI, Old NCERT)*

	List I (Rock)		List II (Metamorphosed form)
A.	Granite	1.	Schist
B.	Clay	2.	Gneiss
C.	Limestone	3.	Quartzite
D.	Sandstone	4.	Marble

Codes

	A	B	C	D		A	B	C	D
(a)	3	4	2	1	(b)	3	2	1	4
(c)	2	1	3	4	(d)	2	1	4	3

***Ans.* (d)**

Exp. The correct matching is A-2, B-1, C- 4, D-3.

Igneous and sedimentary rocks can change into metamorphic rocks under great heat and pressure.

Schist is the metamorphic form of sedimentary rock clay. Schist is a type of rock formed of layers of different minerals, that breaks naturally into thin flat pieces.

Gneiss is a coarse to medium grained banded metamorphic rock formed from igneous or sedimentary rocks during regional metamorphism.

Quartzite is the metamorphic form of sedimentary rock sandstone.

Marble is the metamorphic form of sedimentary rock limestone.

67 **Consider the following statements.** *(Chap 4, Class-XI, Old NCERT)*

1. Arrangement of minerals in layers in the metamorphic rocks is known as lineation.
2. Arrangement of minerals in alternate dark and light bands of metamorphic rocks is known as banding.
3. Metamorphic rocks are source of minerals like sapphire and rubies.

Which of the statements given above is/are correct?

(a) Only 1 (b) Only 2
(c) 1, 2 and 3 (d) None of these

***Ans.* (c)**

Exp. All the three statements i.e., (1), (2) and (3) are correct because in the process of metamorphism, some rock grains or minerals get arranged in layers or lines. Such an arrangement of minerals or grains in metamorphic rocks is called foliation or lineation. Sometimes minerals or materials of different groups are arranged into alternating thin to thick layers appearing in light and dark shades. Such a structure in metamorphic rocks is called banding and rocks displaying banding are called banded rocks. Minerals like sapphire and rubies are found in metamorphic rocks.

68 **Consider the following statements about metamorphism.** *(Chap 5, Class-XI, New NCERT)*

1. Metamorphism occurs when crustal rocks come in contact with molten magma at high temperatures.
2. There are no chemical changes in original rocks in dynamic metamorphism.
3. Re-crystallisation of rocks due to high temperature and tectonic shearing is known as regional metamorphism.

Which of the statements given above are correct?

(a) 1 and 2 (b) 2 and 3
(c) 1 and 3 (d) All of these

***Ans.* (d)**

Exp. All the three statements i.e. (1), (2) and (3) are correct about metamorphism. It occurs when rocks are forced down to lower levels by tectonic processes or when molten magma rising through the crust comes in contact with the crustal rocks or the underlying rocks are subjected to great amounts of pressure by overlying rocks.

Mechanical disruption and re-organisation of the original minerals within rocks due to breaking and crushing without any appreciable chemical changes is called dynamic metamorphism. In regional metamorphism, rocks undergo re-crystallisation due to deformation caused by tectonic shearing together with high temperature or pressure or both.

69 Consider the following pairs. *(Chap 5, Class-XI, New NCERT)*

Rocks		Types
1. Chert, Potash	–	Metamorphic
2. Gneissoid, Slate	–	Igneous
3. Gabbro, Pegmatite	–	Sedimentary

How many of the pairs given above is/are correct?

(a) Only one (b) Only two
(c) Only three (d) None of these

Ans. (d)

Exp. None of the given pair is correct.

Sedimentary rocks are types of rock that are formed by the accumulation or deposition of mineral or organic particles at Earth's surface, followed by sedimentation. Chert, Potash, Sandstone, limestone etc., are the examples of sedimentary rocks.

Metamorphic rocks form when rocks are subjected to high heat, high pressure and hot mineral rich fluids. Gneissoid, granite, syenite, slate, schist, marble, quartzite etc., are some examples of metamorphic rocks.

Igneous rocks form when hot, molten rock crystallises and solidifies. Granite, gabbro, pegmatite, basalt, volcanic breccia, tuff etc., are some of the examples of igneous rocks.

70 Consider the following statements about mountains. *(Chap 6, Class-VI, New NCERT)*

1. Mountains are always tall, isolated peaks with sharp, pointed summits.
2. Mountains can be formed by various processes like plate tectonics, volcanic activity and erosion.
3. Flat-topped mountains like plateaus are not considered true mountains.
4. Mountains are always located above sea level, visible as landforms on Earth's surface.

Which of the statements given above are incorrect?

(a) 1 and 2
(b) 4 and 3
(c) 1, 3 and 4
(d) All of the above

Ans. (c)

Exp. Statements (1), (3) and (4) are incorrect. Mountains are always tall, isolated peaks with sharp, pointed summits. While many mountains are tall and have pointed summits, not all do. The definition of a mountain can vary, and it does not necessarily have to be an isolated peak. Flat-topped mountains like plateaus are not considered true mountains. While plateaus are different from mountains in that they are remarkably flat, they can still be considered a type of mountain especially if they are enclosed by mountains surface. While many mountains are located above sea level, not all are. For example, the base of Mauna Kea, one of the tallest mountains from base to peak, is located under the sea.

71 Consider the following mountains and their types. *(Chap 6, Class-VI, New NCERT)*

1. Himalayas	–	Fold Mountains
2. Mount Kilimanjaro	–	Volcanic Mountain
3. Table Mountain	–	Block Mountain
4. Appalachian Mountains	–	Old fold mountains

Which of the pairs given above is incorrectly matched?

(a) Only 1 (b) Only 2 (c) Only 3 (d) None of these

Ans. (d)

Exp. All pairs are correctly matched.

Himalayas - Fold Mountains. The Himalayas are indeed fold mountains, formed by the collision of the Indian and Eurasian tectonic plates.

Mount Kilimanjaro - Volcanic Mountain. Mount Kilimanjaro is a stratovolcano, a type of volcanic Mountain.

Table Mountain - Block Mountain. Table Mountain is a flat-topped mountain formed by nearly horizontal layers of sandstone exposed by vigorous wind and water erosion.

Appalachian Mountains - Old fold Mountains. This is correct. The Appalachian Mountains are old fold Mountains, formed by the collision of ancient continental plates.

Landforms

72 Which of the following statements is correct about block mountains? *(Chap 6, Class-VI, New NCERT)*

1. Block mountains are formed by vertical displacement of rocks.
2. The uplifted block of rock is known as graben.
3. Block mountains have conical peaks.

Codes

(a) 1 and 3 (b) Only 2 (c) Only 1 (d) 2 and 3

Ans. (c)

Exp. Statement (1) is correct about block mountains because block mountains are created when large areas are broken and displaced vertically. The Rhine valley and the Vosges mountains are examples of block mountains.

Statements (2) and (3) are incorrect as the uplifted blocks are termed as horsts while the lowered blocks are called graben. Block mountains have flat peaks not conical peaks.

73 Consider the following features of a plateau.
(Chap 6, Class-VI, New NCERT)

1. They have a flat top like a table.
2. Plateaus are rich in minerals like gold and diamond.
3. Tibetan plateau is the highest plateau in the World.

Which of the statements given above is/are correct?
(a) 1 and 2 (b) 1 and 3 (c) Only 3 (d) All of these

Ans. (d)

Exp. All the three statements i.e., (1), (2) and (3) are correct about a plateau because a plateau is an elevated flat land. It is a flat-topped table land standing above the surrounding area.

Plateaus are very useful because they are rich in mineral deposits. As a result, many of the mining areas in the world are located in the plateau areas.

The Tibet plateau is the highest plateau in the world with a height of 4,000 to 6,000 metres above the mean sea level.

74 Consider the following statements.
(Chap 6, Class-VI, New NCERT)

1. A stretch of flat land not more than 2000 metres above mean sea level is known as a plain.
2. Plains are formed by action of rivers and tributaries.
3. Density of population is high in plain areas as compared to mountains and plateaus.

Which of the statements given above are correct?
(a) 1 and 3 (b) 2 and 3 (c) 1 and 2 (d) All of these

Ans. (b)

Exp. Statements (2) and (3) are correct as plains are large stretches of flat land. Generally, they are not more than 200 metres above mean sea level.

Most of the plains are formed by rivers and their tributaries. Generally, plains are very fertile. Construction of transport network is easy. Thus, these plains are very thickly-populated regions of the world. Gangetic Plains of India, Bangladesh, North India and Nepal is the example of plain.

Statement (1) is incorrect as the elevations of plain areas are not more than 200 metres.

75 Which of the following statements are correct about fold mountains? *(Chap 6, Class-XI, Old NCERT)*

1. They are formed under the influence of compression tectonic forces.
2. Deep gorges and pyramidal peaks are formed in Fold mountains.
3. Igneous, sedimentary and metamorphosed rocks are found in mountain regions.

Codes
(a) 1 and 2 (b) 2 and 3
(c) 1 and 3 (d) All of these

Ans. (a)

Exp. Statements (1) and (2) are correct. Fold mountains are formed where two or more of Earth's tectonic plates are compressed together. They are formed through a process called orogeny.

Fold mountains are responsible for formation of deep gorges and pyramidal peaks. Himalayas (Asia), Aravali (Asia), Alps in Europe and Andes in South America are some of the examples of fold mountains.

Statement (3) is incorrect as the presence of fossils suggests that the sedimentary rocks of these folded mountains were formed after accumulation and consolidation of silts and sediments in a marine environment. Hence, only the sedimentary rocks are found in the fold mountains.

76 Which of the following statements is/are correct about plateaus? *(Chap 6, Class-XI, Old NCERT)*

1. An Intermontane plateau is located between two mountain ranges.
2. A plateau situated at the foot of mountains is known as Piedmont plateau.

Codes
(a) Only 1 (b) Only 2
(c) Both 1 and 2 (d) None of these

Ans. (c)

Exp. Both the statements (1) and (2) are correct about plateaus. Plateaus are classified as; Intermontane plateaus, Piedmont plateaus, Continental plateaus, Volcanic plateaus and Dissected plateaus.

Among, which the plateaus, which are bordering the mountain ranges (generally Fold mountains) or are partly or fully enclosed within them are the intermontane plateaus.

The word 'intermontane' means 'between mountains.' Intermontane plateaus are the highest in the world. Plateaus, which is situated at the foot of a mountain and is locked on the other side by a plain or a sea/ ocean is called as a Piedmont plateau. The word 'piedmont' means 'foot of a mountain'.

77 Consider the following statements about plains.
(Chap 6, Class-XI, Old NCERT)

1. Structural plains are usually found near the sea coast.
2. Erosional plains are formed by the process of deposition of river sediments.

Which of the statements given above is/are correct?
(a) Only 1 (b) Only 2
(c) Both 1 and 2 (d) None of these

Ans. (a)

Exp. Statement (1) is correct about plains as the structural plains are mainly formed by the upliftment of a part of the sea floor near sea coast. They are located on the borders of almost all the major continents. The structural plains may also be formed by the subsidence of areas.

Statement (2) is incorrect as erosional plains are formed by the continuous and longtime erosion of uplands. The surface of such plains is hardly smooth and hence, they are also called as Peneplains, which means almost plain. Hence, it is not formed because the deposition of sediments.

78 **Consider the following statements.**

(Chap 3, Class-VII, New NCERT)

1. Action of flowing water on alternate hard and soft rocks is responsible for formation of waterfalls.
2. V shaped valleys are formed by rivers in the plain areas.
3. Flood plains are formed by deposition of sediments by rivers.
4. Meanders of rivers are cutoff to form oxbow lakes.

Which of the statements given above is/are incorrect?

(a) 1 and 2 (b) 2, 3 and 4 (c) Only 2 (d) All of these

***Ans.* (c)**

Exp. Statement (2) is incorrect because V-shaped valleys are formed by rivers in the plain areas. Valleys start as small and narrow rills. These rills will progressively develop into long and wide gullies. The gullies will again deepen, widen and lengthen to give rise to valleys. These are mainly found over mountains. Depending upon dimensions and shape, many types of valleys like V-shaped valley, gorge, canyon, etc can be recognised.

79 **Which of the following is a depositional feature formed by river water?** *(Chap 4, Class-VIII, Old NCERT)*

1. Meander
2. River Delta
3. Natural Levee
4. U-shaped valley

Codes

(a) 1 and 2 (b) 3 and 4 (c) 1, 2 and 3 (d) All of these

***Ans.* (c)**

Exp. Meander, delta and natural levee are the depositional feature formed by river water. The process of erosion and deposition of river create different landforms on the surface of the Earth. When the river enters into plain it become slow and begins to deposit its load. At this point different types of depositional landforms can be formed by the river. These are alluvial fan, delta, meander, point bar natural levee and flood plains.

U-shaped valley is formed by the erosional work of glaciers, not by river water.

80 **Which of the following statements is correct about the stages of landform development in rivers?**

(Chap 2, Class-IX, Old NCERT)

(a) The path of a river is steepest in the valley stage.
(b) Volume of water in a river is highest in the mountain course.
(c) The lower course of river is characterised by gentle slope and deposition.
(d) All of the above

***Ans.* (c)**

Exp. Statement (c) is correct about the stages of landform development in rivers. The course of a river form its source to its mouth is normally divide into three sections, namely upper, middle and lower.

In the lower course of a river the valley floor has extremely gentle slope. Hence, the river is unable to transport all the sediments in its channel and starts to deposits its loads.

81 **Which of the following is incorrect about a meander?** *(Chap 7, Class-XI, New NCERT)*

1. A deep meander formed by cutting of hard rocks is known as Incised meander.
2. Meander of a river causes undercutting on the concave bank.

Codes

(a) Only 1 (b) Only 2
(c) Both 1 and 2 (d) None of these

***Ans.* (b)**

Exp. Statement (2) is incorrect about a meander because the river when enters the plain it twists and turns forming large bends known as Meanders.

Normally, in meanders of large rivers, there is active deposition along the concave bank and undercutting along the convex bank.

The concave bank is known as cut-off bank, which shows up as a steep scarp and the convex bank presents a long, gentle profile.

82 **Which of the following is a Karst topography?**

(Chap 7, Class-XI, New NCERT)

1. Sinkholes
2. Uvalas
3. Zeugens
4. Doline
5. Seif

Select the correct answer using the codes given below.

(a) 1, 2, 4 and 5 (b) 1, 2 and 4
(c) 2, 3, 4 and 5 (d) 1, 3 and 5

***Ans.* (b)**

Exp. The correct answer is option (b), i.e. 1, 2 and 4.

Sinkholes are indeed a feature of Karst topography. They are depressions that form when a portion of the lithosphere below is eroded away.

Uvalas are also a feature of Karst topography. They are typically elongated or irregularly shaped depressions with undulating floors.

Doline is another term for sinkholes, and they are a feature of Karst topography. They are closed depressions that drain underground.

Seif is not a feature of karst topography. It is a type of sand dune found in deserts, not a landform associated with the dissolution of soluble rocks.

Zeugens are not a feature of Karst topography. They are erosional landforms created by wind, not the dissolution processes that characterise Karst topography.

83 **Consider the following statements regarding the Karst topography.** *(Chap 5, Class-VIII, Old NCERT)*

1. Landscape formed by groundwater is formed mainly in the limestone regions.
2. Deposits of calcite hanging downwards in caves is known as Stalactites.
3. Deposition of calcite on the surface of a cave is known as Pillar.

Which of the statements given above is/are incorrect?

(a) 1 and 2 (b) 1 and 3 (c) 2 and 3 (d) Only 3

Ans. (d)

Exp. Statement (3) is incorrect because Pillars are formed by fusion of stalagmite and Stalactites in limestone caves.

Statements (1) and (2) are correct. Landscape formed by groundwater is formed mainly in the limestone regions. Stalactites are deposits of calcite hanging downwards. They are broad at their bases and taper towards the free ends showing up in a variety of forms.

84 **Which of the following statements is correct?** *(Chap 7, Class-XI, Old NCERT)*

1. Sinkholes can be formed either by the process of solution or by collapse.
2. The sinkholes formed by collapse is known as Doline.
3. Uvalas are formed by joining of dolines and solution sinkholes.

Codes

(a) 2 and 3 (b) Only 3
(c) 1 and 3 (d) All of these

Ans. (d)

Exp. All the three statements i.e., (1), (2) and (3) are correct because sinkhole is an opening more or less circular at the top and funnel-shaped towards the bottom with sizes varying in area from a few square metres to a hectare and with depth from a less than half a metre to thirty metres or more.

The term doline is sometimes used to refer the collapse sinks. When sink holes and dolines join together because of slumping of materials along their margins or due to roof collapse of caves, long, narrow to wide trenches called valley sinks or Uvalas form.

85 **Which of the following statements is correct?** *(Chap 5, Class-VIII, Old NCERT)*

1. Circular Depressions formed due to glacial deposition are known as Cirques.
2. Deposition of irregular rocks along the movement of glacier is known as Moraine.
3. Cirques are formed at the head of glaciers and moraines are formed at the toe of Glacier.

Codes

(a) 1 and 2 (b) 2 and 3
(c) 1 and 3 (d) All of these

Ans. (c)

Exp. Statements (1) and (3) are correct as the cirques are the most common of landforms in glaciated mountains. The cirques quite often are found at the heads of glacial valleys. They are deep, long and circular depression with very steep concave to vertically dropping high walls at its head as well as sides. A lake of water can be seen quite often within the cirques after the glacier disappears. Such lakes are called Cirque or Tarn Lakes.

Moraines are formed at the toe of Glacier.

Statement (2) is incorrect as moraine are long ridges of deposits of glacial till. Moraines can be classified in four different types depending upon their location. These are Terminal Moraines, Lateral Moraines, Ground Moraines and Medial Moraines.

86 **Which of the following is an erosional feature formed by movement of glacier?** *(Chap 7, Class-XI, New NCERT)*

1. Serrated ridge
2. Eskers
3. Drumlins
4. Glacial troughs

Codes

(a) 1, 2 and 3 (b) 1, 3 and 4
(c) 1 and 4 (d) All of these

Ans. (c)

Exp. Serrated ridge and glacial troughs are the erosional features formed by movement of glaciers. Erosion is the wearing away of the landscape by different agents like water, wind and ice. The eroded material is carried away or transported by water, wind, etc. and eventually deposited. This process of erosion and deposition create different landforms on the surface of the Earth.

Erosional landforms of glaciers are: Cirque, Horns and Serrated Ridges, Glacial Valleys/Troughs

Depositional landforms of glaciers are: Moraines, Eskers, Outwash Plains, Drumlins.

87 **Match the following lists correctly and choose the correct code.** *(Chap 7, Class-XI, New NCERT)*

List I (Glacial landform)	List II (Description)
A. Drumlins	1. Sinuous Ridges
B. Eskers	2. Long ridges of deposits at the terminal
C. Horns	3. High, sharp and steep sided peaks
D. Moraines	4. Oval shaped ridges

Codes

	A	B	C	D
(a)	4	2	1	3
(b)	3	1	2	4
(c)	2	1	3	4
(d)	4	1	3	2

Ans. (d)

Exp. The correct matching is A-4, B-1, C- 3, D- 2.

Drumlins are smooth oval shaped ridge-like features composed mainly of glacial till with some masses of gravel and sand.

Eskers form when glaciers melt in summer, the water flows on the surface of the ice or seeps down along the margins or even moves through holes in the ice. This leads to the formation of thin and meandering formation called Sinuous Ridge.

Horns form through headward erosion of the cirque walls. If three or more radiating glacier cut headward until their cirques meet, high, sharp pointed and steep sided peaks called horns form.

Moraine are long ridge debris or slit known as till deposited by the glacier. These usually comprise sand and rocks and can be large boulders or small as slits. It can be classified into four types among, which Terminal moraines are long ridges of debris deposited at the end (toe) of the glaciers.

88 Which of the following landforms is developed by deposition of sea waves and currents? *(Chap 7, Class-XI, New NCERT)*

1. Terrace 2. Dune 3. Barriers 4. Spits

Codes

(a) 1 and 2 (b) 2 and 3 (c) 3 and 4 (d) All of these

Ans. (c)

Exp. Barriers and spits are the landforms developed by deposition of sea waves and currents. There are different types of landform formed by erosional and depositional activities of sea waves.

Landform developed by deposition of sea waves and currents are Cliffs, Terraces, Caves and Stacks. Landform developed by deposition of sea waves and currents are Beaches and Dunes, Bars, Barriers and Spits.

89 Which of the following statements is correct about erosional features of sea waves? *(Chap 7, Class-XI, New NCERT)*

1. Wave cut cliffs and terraces are formed on the sea shore by erosion of sea water.
2. Isolated offshore rocks standing as small islands are known as Sea stacks.
3. Beaches are formed in shorelines by the process of wave erosion.

Codes

(a) Only 3 (b) Only 2
(c) Both 1 and 2 (d) All of these

Ans. (c)

Exp. Statements (1) and (2) are correct about erosional features of sea waves as the wave-cut cliffs and terraces are two forms usually found where erosion is the dominant shore process. Almost all sea cliffs are steep and may range from a few metres to 30 m or even more. When the roofs of caves collapse and the sea cliffs recede further inland then retreat of the cliff may leave some remnants of rock standing isolated as small islands just off the shore. Such resistant masses of rock, originally parts of a cliff or hill are called Sea stacks.

Statement (3) is incorrect because beaches are formed in shorelines by the process of wave deposition.

90 Which of the following features will act as a defence against a coastal storm? *(Chap 7, Class-XI, New NCERT)*

1. Cliffs
2. Stacks
3. Offshore bars
4. Beach dunes

Codes

(a) 1 and 2 (b) 2 and 3
(c) 3 and 4 (d) All of these

Ans. (c)

Exp. Offshore bars and beach dunes are the features that will act as a defence against a coastal storm. Coastal Offshore bars offer the first buffer or defence against storm or tsunami by absorbing most of their destructive force.

Then come the barriers, beaches, beach dunes and mangroves, if any, to absorb the destructive force of storm and Tsunami waves.

91 Consider the following pairs. *(Chap 7, Class-XI, New NCERT)*

	Terms related to Wind Erosion		Meaning
1.	Abrasion	–	Lifting and removal of dust and smaller particles
2.	Deflation	–	Erosion by sand and silt
3.	Impact	–	Sand blowing against a rock surface

How many pairs given above is/are correct?

(a) Only one (b) Only two
(c) Only three (d) None of these

Ans. (a)

Exp. Only one pair i.e. (3) is correct.

The impact is simply sheer force of momentum which occurs when sand is blown into or against a rock surface. It is similar to sandblasting operation.

Abrasion In the transportation process sand and silt act as effective tools to abrade the land surface this process is known as Abrasion.

Deflation It includes lifting and removal of dust and smaller particles from the surface of rocks.

92 Consider the following statements. *(Chap 7, Class-XI, New NCERT)*

1. Playas are shallow water bodies containing deposition of salts.
2. Shallow depressions created by movement of wind currents in one direction is known as Deflation hollow.
3. Mushroom rocks are formed by persistent deposition of sand and silt in deserts.

Which of the statements given above are correct?

(a) 1 and 2 (b) 2 and 3
(c) 1 and 3 (d) All of these

Ans. (a)

Exp. Statements (1) and (2) are correct because in times of sufficient water, the plain is covered up by a shallow water body.

Such types of shallow lakes are called as playas where water is retained only for short duration due to evaporation and quite often the playas contain good deposition of salts. Playas are found in the interior desert basin.

When the weathered materials over the rocks or bare soil, gets blown out by persistent movement of wind currents in one direction then it may create shallow depressions called deflation hollows.

Statement (3) is incorrect as mushroom rocks are formed by the erosional work of wind.

93 Which of the following are a depositional feature of wind? *(Chap 7, Class-XI, New NCERT)*

1. Barchan
2. Seif
3. Pedestal rock
4. Caldera

Codes

(a) 1, 3 and 4
(b) 1, 2 and 3
(c) 1 and 2
(d) 2 and 4

Ans. (c)

Exp. Barchan and Seif are the depositional features of wind. There are different types of sand dunes formed by the depositional work of wind like barchans, parabolic dunes, seif, longitudinal dunes and transverse dunes.

While pedestal rock is an example of erosional landform of wind and caldera is a large depression formed by Volcano.

94 Which of the following pairs is matched correctly? *(Chap 7, Class-XI, New NCERT)*

Landform		Associated with
(a) Tarn Lake	–	River Erosion
(b) Lapies	–	Groundwater
(c) Pediplain	–	Glacial Erosion
(d) Potholes	–	Wind Erosion

Ans. (b)

Exp. Only pair (b) is matched correctly as Groundwater Erosional landforms are Pools, Sinkholes, Lapies and Limestone Pavements, Caves.

While pairs (a), (c) and (d) are incorrect because River Erosional landforms are Valleys, Potholes and Plunge Pools, Incised or Entrenched Meanders, River Terraces.

Glacial Erosional landforms are Cirque, Tarn Lake, Horns and Serrated Ridges, Glacial Valleys/ Troughs

Wind Erosional landforms are Pediments and Pediplains, Playas, Deflation Hollows and Caves, Mushroom, Table and Pedestal Rocks.

95 Which of the following pairs is matched correctly? *(Chap 7, Class-XI, New NCERT)*

Landform		Associated with
(a) Alkali Flats	–	Sea Waves
(b) Inselberg	–	Groundwater
(c) Outwash plains	–	Wind
(d) Ox-bow Lake	–	River

Ans. (d)

Exp. Pair (d) is matched correctly as Ox-bow Lake is associated with river depositional landform.

Pair (a), (b) and (c) are matched incorrectly because Alkali Flats and Inselberg are associated with wind work and Outwash plains are associated with Glacio-Fluvial Erosion.

Chapter 05

Climatology

Atmosphere, Pressure & Winds

Atmosphere

Introduction

- The envelope of air consisting of gases, water vapours and dust particles that surround the Earth
- Air is essential for the survival of all the organisms

- Gases in the Atmosphere

- **Nitrogen** Most plentiful gas essential for the survival of plants
- **Oxygen** Second most abundant gas, essential for breathing and survival of humans and animals
- **Carbon Dioxide** Used by green plants to make their own food
- **Ozone** Acts as a filter that absorbs UV rays coming from Sun and prevents them from reaching the surface of Earth
- **Water Vapour** A variable gas in the atmosphere, absorbs parts of insolation and forms an immediate cause of condensation and precipitation

Air Masses

- The air with distinctive characteristics in terms of temperature and humidity is called air mass
- Classified into five categories as per the source regions

Insolation and Temperature

Insolation

- The solar energy received by Earth, it is the incoming solar radiation which is in the form of short wave radiation. As insolation enters the atmosphere, a part of it is reflected, a part is absorbed and remaining reaches the surface of Earth

Heat Budget of the Earth

- The Earth as a whole does not accumulate or lose heat but it maintains its temperature
- The amount of heat received in the form of short wave radiation insolation is equal to the amount of heat lost by the Earth through short wave terrestrial radiation

Temperature

- The standard unit of measuring is degree celsius

Distribution of Temperature

– Horizontal Distribution Represented with the help of isotherms, generally parallel to latitudes

- Vertical Distribution Temperature distribution is influenced by nature of underlying surface

- Zonal Distribution There are three heat zones namely

- Torrid zone, Temperate zone
- Frigid zone

Pressure and Winds

Atmospheric Pressure

- Weight of a column of air contained in a unit area from the mean sea level to the top of atmosphere
- In lower atmosphere, pressure decreases with increasing height

Winds

- Horizontal differences in air density leads to horizontal differences in air pressure, generating winds

Type of Winds Largely divided into three types

- Permanent Winds

- These include trade winds, Westerlies and Easterlies
- Trade winds blow from sub-tropical high pressure belt to equatorial low pressure belt
- Easterlies blow from polar high pressure belt to sub-polar low pressure belt

- Seasonal Winds

- Change their direction in different seasons, due to the shifting of regions of maximum heating, pressure and wind belts eg. Monsoon winds

- Local Winds Blow only during a particular period of the day or a year in a small region

Water in the Atmosphere

Water Atmospheric

- Water vapour is a variable gas in the atmosphere and is the immediate cause of condensation and precipitation

Clouds

A mass of minute water droplets or tiny crystals of ice formed by condensation of the water vapour in the free air at considerable elevations

- Types of Clouds

- **Cirrus** Formed at high altitudes i.e., 8000-12000m
- They are thin and detached clouds having a feathery appearance
- **Nimbus** Black or dark grey coloured clouds, extremely dense and opaque to the rays of Sun. They are so low that they seem to touch the ground
- **Stratus** Layered clouds covering large portions of the sky, generally formed due to loss of heat or mixing of air masses
- **Precipitation** Process of continuous condensation in free air helps the condensed particles to grow in size and they fall on Earth when the resistance of air to hold them fails

SOURCE **New NCERT Class VII** *(Air)*, **Old NCERT Class VII** *(The Atmosphere and Its Temperature), (Air on the Move), (Water in the Air), (Local Weather and the Sky)*, **Old NCERT Class IX** *(The Air Around Us)*, **New NCERT Class XI** *(Solar Radiation, Heat Balance and Temperature), (Composition and Structure of Atmosphere), (Water in the Atmosphere), (Atmospheric Circulation and Weather Systems), (World Climate and Climate Change)*, **Old NCERT Class XI** *(Classification of Climates, Composition and Structure of Atmosphere, Atmospheric Pressure, Winds and Airmasses, Moisture in the Atmosphere), (Insolation and Temperature),*

Atmospheric Composition and Structure

1 Consider the following pairs.

(Unit 6, Class-XI, Tamil Nadu Board)

Gas Component	Altitude Range
1. Oxygen	120 km
2. Carbon Dioxide	Up to 90 km
3. Water Vapour	Up to 120 km
4. Ozone	10-50 km

How many of the pairs given above is/are correctly represent the altitude range of the mentioned atmospheric gases?

(a) Only one
(b) Only two
(c) Only three
(d) All four

Ans. *(c)*

Exp. Only three pairs i.e., (1), (2) and (4) are correctly represent the altitude range of the mentioned atmospheric gases.

The proportion of gases varies in the upper layers of the atmosphere, at an altitude of 120 km there is almost negligible amount of oxygen. Similarly, carbon dioxide is found only at a distance of 90 km from the Earth's surface. Ozone is another important component of the atmosphere that is found between 10-50 km above the Earth's surface and acts as a filter and absorbs ultraviolet. Prevents the rays emanating from the Sun from reaching the earth's surface.

Pair (3) is incorrectly matched because water vapour is found only up to 90 km from the surface of the Earth, not 120 km.

2 Consider the following statements.

(Chap 8, Class-XI, New NCERT)

1. More than 90% of total mass of the atmosphere is confined to 32 km above the Earth's surface.
2. Nitrogen and Argon are mainly responsible for causing greenhouse effect.
3. Ozone gas is responsible for absorption of harmful ultra violet radiation.

Which of the statements given above is/are correct?

(a) 1 and 3
(b) 2 and 3
(c) Only 2
(d) All of the above

Ans. *(a)*

Exp. Statements (1) and (3) are correct as atmosphere is a mixture of different gases and it envelopes the Earth all round. The air is an integral part of the Earth's mass and 99% of the total mass of the atmosphere is confined to the height of 32 km from the Earth's surface.

Statement (2) is incorrect because Ozone gas absorbs ultraviolet rays emitting from the Sun and prevents them from reaching the surface of Earth.

3 Arrange the following atmospheric constituents in descending order based on their percentage by volume. *(Chap 8, Class-XI, Old NCERT)*

1. Helium 2. Xenon
3. Carbon dioxide 4. Argon
5. Krypton 6. Neon

Codes

(a) 1, 2, 3, 4, 5, and 6
(b) 2, 3, 5, 4,1, and 6
(c) 4, 3, 5, 2, 1, and 6
(d) 4, 3, 6, 5, 1, and 2

Ans. *(d)*

Exp. The correct arrangement in descending order 4, 3, 6, 5, 1, and 2 based on their percentage by volume is

Argon (Ar)	:	0.93%
Carbon dioxide (CO_2)	:	0.036%
Neon (Ne)	:	0.002%
Krypton (Kr)	:	0.001%
Helium (He)	:	0.0005%
Xenon (Xe)	:	0.00009%

4 Which of the following statements is correct about water vapour in the atmosphere?

(Chap 10, Class-XI, Old NCERT)

1. The amount of water vapour declines from equator towards poles.
2. The amount of water vapour decreases as the altitude increases.
3. Water vapour absorbs heat from both solar insolation as well as terrestrial radiation.
4. Atmospheric stability and instability is dependent upon water vapour.

Codes

(a) 1, 2 and 3
(b) 1, 2 and 4
(c) 2, 3 and 4
(d) 1, 2, 3 and 4

Ans. *(d)*

Exp. All the statements are correct about water vapour in the atmosphere because water vapour is also a variable gas in atmosphere, which decreases with altitude. Water vapour decreases from the equator to the poles because, the amount of rainfall is high in the equator and the wind is also calm these.

The amount of water vapour decreases with altitude. In fact, half of the total amount of water vapour in the air is found only at a height of 2 km.

The water vapour absorbs some of the insolation coming from the Sun and reduces the amount of insolation reaching the surface. The infrared radiation that goes out from the surface of the earth is called terrestrial radiation, which is absorbed by water vapour.

As water vapour condenses, latent heat is released into the air parcel. The combination of water vapour determines the stability and instability of the air and the resulting weather.

5 **Which of the following gases do not have much influence on atmospheric and weather phenomenon?** *(Chap 10, Class-XI, Old NCERT)*

1. Carbon dioxide
2. Xenon
3. Helium
4. Water vapour

Codes

(a) 1 and 2 (b) 2 and 3
(c) 1 and 3 (d) None of these

Ans. (b)

Exp. Among the given options, xenon and helium gases do not have much influence on atmospheric and weather phenomenon.

The inert gases of the atmosphere do not have much effect on the atmosphere and weather phenomena. Xenon, krypton, neon and helium are the main inert gases.

Carbon dioxide and water vapour have a wide range of effects on the atmosphere and weather events.

Structure of Atmosphere

6 **Consider the following statements about the troposphere, the lowermost layer of the Earth's atmosphere.** *(Chap 7, Class-XI, New NCERT)*

1. The troposphere is the lowermost layer of the atmosphere and extends roughly to a height of 8 km near the poles and about 18 km at the equator.
2. The troposphere at any latitude is thicker in winter than in summer.
3. The thickness of the troposphere is greatest at the equator due to the transport of heat to great heights by strong convection currents.

Which of the statements given above are correct?

(a) 1 and 2 (b) 2 and 3
(c) 1 and 3 (d) 1, 2, and 3

Ans. (c)

Exp. Statements (1) and (3) are correct regarding the troposphere.

The troposphere is the lowermost layer of the atmosphere which immediately overlies the Earth's surface. Its average height is 13 km and extends roughly to a height of 8 km near the poles and about 18 km at the equator.

The troposphere is thicker at the equator than at the poles because the equator is warmer. The heat differential on the planet's surface causes convection currents to flow from the equator to the poles. The strong convection currents transport heat to great heights, which increases the thickness of the troposphere.

Statement (2) is incorrect because the troposphere is thicker in the summer than in the winter at any latitude. The troposphere is the lowest layer of the atmosphere, extending up to 20 km. The height of the troposphere varies with latitude and seasons. It is lower in the winter and highest in the summer.

7 **Consider the following statements about the troposphere.** *(Chap 7, Class-XI, New NCERT)*

1. All changes in climate and weather take place in this layer.
2. The temperature in this layer decreases at the rate of 1° C for every 165m of height.
3. Temperature in this layer increases with altitude.
4. Troposphere is characterised by presence of strong conventional currents.

How many of the statements given above is/are correct?

(a) Only one
(b) Only two
(c) Only three
(d) All four

Ans. (c)

Exp. Only three statements (1), (2) and (4) are correct regarding the Troposphere.

All changes in climate and weather take place in this layer.

The troposphere is the lowermost layer of the atmosphere which immediately overlies the Earth's surface. This layer contains dust particles and water vapour.

The temperature in this layer decreases at the rate of 1° C for every 165m of height. This is the most important layer for all biological activity. The troposphere is characterised by strong convectionals currents. It's also known as the 'region of mixing'.

Statement (3) is incorrect because the temperature in the troposphere decreases with increasing altitude.

8 **Consider the following Assertion (A) and Reason (R) and choose the correct code.** *(Chap 8, Class-XI, New NCERT)*

Assertion (A) Most of the atmospheric and weather phenomenon takes place in the troposphere.

Reason (R) Highest concentration of gases, water vapour and dust is found in the troposphere.

Codes

(a) Both A and R are true and R is the correct explanation of A.
(b) Both A and R are true, but R is not the correct explanation of A.
(c) A is true, but R is false.
(d) A is false, but R is true.

Ans. (a)

Exp. Both Assertion (A) and Reason (R) are true and Reason (R) is the correct explanation of Assertion (A). Troposphere layer contains dust particles, gases and water vapour.

All changes in climate and weather take place in troposphere layer. This is the most important layer for all biological activity.

Exp. Among the given factors, (1), (3) and (4) determines the nature and size of the industry.

Capital Investments Capital investment helps the entrepreneur to make business grow to a big size.

Availability of Labour If the labour forces is not available in the business then business would not grow.

Power Consumption Industry uses fossil fuels and renewable energy sources.

Different industries have vastly different energy needs which determine the nature and size of the industry.

10 Consider the following statements.

(Chap 8, Class-XI, Tamil Nadu Board) (Chap 3, Module-2, NIOS)

1. The Index of Industrial Production (IIP) is an index that indicates the performance of various industrial sectors of the Indian economy.
2. It is a short term indicator of industrial growth.
3. IIP is published monthly and six weeks after the reference month ends.

How many of the above statements is/are correct?

(a) Only one (b) Only two
(c) All three (d) None of these

Ans. (c)

Exp. All three statements i.e., (1), (2) and (3) are correct as IIP is an index which helps us understand the growth of various sectors in the Indian economy such as mining, electricity and manufacturing.

It is short term indicator of industrial growth till the results from annual Survey of Industries (ASI) and National Accounts Statistics (e.g GDP) are available.

Index of Industrial production (IIP) is released by the National Statistics Office (NSO) of the Ministry of Statistics and programme implementation. It is published monthly and six weeks after the reference month ends.

11 Consider the following Assertion (A) and Reason (R) and choose the correct code.

(Chap 2, Class-XI, New NCERT)

Assertion (A) The excessive regulation of industries came to be called as the License Permit Raj, prevented certain firms from becoming more efficient.

Reason (R) More time was spent by industrialists in trying to obtain a license or lobby with the concerned ministries rather than on thinking about how to improve their products.

Codes

(a) Both A and R are true and R is the correct explanation of A.
(b) Both A and R are true, but R is not the correct explanation of A.
(c) A is true, but R is false.
(d) A is false, but R is true.

Ans. (a)

Exp. Both Assertion (A) and Reason (R) are true and Reason (R) is the correct explanation of Assertion (A).

The excessive regulation of industries came to be called as the License Permit Raj, prevented certain firms from becoming more efficient. It is because the need to obtain a license to start an industry was misused by industrial houses. A big industrialists would get license not for starting a new firm but to prevent competitors from starting new firms.

More time was spent by industrialists in trying to obtain a license or lobby with the concerned ministries rather than on thinking about how to improve their products.

12 Consider the following statements about deregulation of the industrial sector.

(Chap 3, Class-XI, New NCERT)

1. Industrial licensing was abolished for almost all except alcohols, cigarettes, hazardous chemicals, industrial explosives, electronics, aerospace, drugs and pharmaceuticals.
2. The only industries which are now reserved for the public sector are a part of atomic energy generation and some core activities in railway transport.

Which of the statement(s) given above is/are incorrect?

(a) Only 1 (b) Only 2
(c) Both 1 and 2 (d) Neither 1 nor 2

Ans. (d)

Exp. Neither statement (1) nor (2) is incorrect about deregulation of the industrial sector.

The reform policies introduced in and after 1991 removed many of the trade restrictions. Industrial licensing was abolished for almost all but for product categories like alcohols, cigarettes, hazardous chemicals, industrial explosives, electronics, aerospace, drugs and pharmaceuticals. The only industries which are now reserved for public sector are a part of atomic energy generation and some core activities in railway transport.

13 Consider the following heavy industries.

(Chap 1, Class-XI, New NCERT) (IAS Pre 2023)

1. Fertiliser plants 2. Oil refineries 3. Steel plants

Green hydrogen is expected to play a significant role in decarbonizing, how many to the above industries?

(a) Only one (b) Only two
(c) All three (d) None of these

Ans. (c)

Exp. Green hydrogen can play a significant role in decarbonizing all of the above mentioned heavy industries i.e., fertiliser plants, oil refiners and steel plants.

By using green hydrogen as a clean energy source, fertiliser plants can reduce their carbon emissions. Green hydrogen can be used to generate electricity or directly as a feedstock in the ammonia production process, which is a key component of fertiliser manufacturing.

The stratosphere is second layer of atmosphere. The ozone layer is found in the stratosphere about 15-30 km above the Earth's surface where high concentration of ozone gas is found.

The ionosphere is located between 80 and 640 km above the mesopause. The ionosphere is part of the thermosphere. It contains electrical charged particles called ions and therefore, known as the ionosphere.

Insolation and Temperature

14 Consider the following statements about insolation reaching the surface of the Earth. *(Chap 4, Class-VII, New NCERT)*

1. The distribution of temperature follows the distribution of temperature on Earth's surface.
2. Insolation is maximum over poles and reduces towards the equator.
3. Insolation received over urban areas is more as compared to rural areas.
4. About 35% of the insolation is lost by reflection.

How many of the statements given above is/are correct?

(a) Only one (b) Only two (c) Only three (d) All four

***Ans.* (b)**

Exp. Only two statements i.e., (3) and (4) are correct regarding insolation reaching the surface of the Earth.

Insolation in cities is much higher than that of villages. The concrete and metals in buildings and the asphalt of roads get heated up during the day. This heat is released during the night. About 35 percent of insolation is reflected into space before reaching the Earth's surface. The insolation received at the top of the atmosphere is 100 percent. Some amount of energy is reflected, scattered and absorbed as it passes through the atmosphere. Only the remaining part reaches the Earth's surface.

Statements (1) and (2) are incorrect because the temperature in the atmosphere does not follow the temperature of the Earth's surface. Atmospheric temperature, pressure, conduction, terrestrial radiation, less and more happens through convection, etc. The annual mean insolation at the top of the atmosphere at the poles is less than the half of that at the equator, because the Sun's rays fall obliquely near the poles. For this reason, the temperature at the poles is lower than at the equator.

15 Consider the following statements about solar insolation received over the Earth's surface. *(Chap 1, Class-VII, Old NCERT)*

1. The amount of solar insolation received in a region is directly dependent upon the angle of Sun's rays.
2. Regions receiving vertical rays of Sun have more temperature than regions receiving oblique Sun's rays.
3. In lower latitudes, amount of solar insolation received in summers exceeds the insolation received in winters.

Which of the statements given above are correct?

(a) 1 and 2 (b) 2 and 3
(c) 1 and 3 (d) 1, 2, and 3

***Ans.* (d)**

Exp. All the statements (1), (2) and (3) are correct about solar insolation received over the Earth's surface because the amount of insolation received depends on the angle of inclination of the rays.

The tropical region gets vertical rays of the Sun and receives much heat providing high temperature while the temperate and polar regions have less temperature due to slanting rays of the Sun.

In lower latitudes, the Sun's rays are vertical in summer and the Sun's rays become slightly oblique in winter, due to which the insolation in summer in lower latitudes is higher than in winter.

16 Which of the following factors cause variations in the amount of insolation received over the atmosphere of the Earth? *(Chap 9, Class-XI, New NCERT)*

1. Length of day and night
2. Transparency of atmospheric molecules
3. Land configuration

Codes

(a) 1 and 2 (b) 2 and 3
(c) 1 and 3 (d) All of these

***Ans.* (d)**

Exp. All the factors given in the question cause variations in the amount of insolation received over the atmosphere of the Earth because the amount and the intensity of insolation vary during a day, in a season and in a year. The factors that cause these variations in insolation are, the rotation of Earth on its axis; the angle of inclination of the Sun's rays; the length of the day and night; the transparency of the atmospheric molecules and the configuration of land in terms of its aspect.

17 Consider the following Assertion (A) and Reason (R) and choose the correct code. *(Chap 1, Class-VII, Old NCERT)*

Assertion (A) Torrid zone receives maximum insolation whereas Frigid zone receives minimum insolation.

Reason (R) Amount of insolation received on Earth's surface increases with increase in the latitude.

Codes

(a) Both A and R are true and R is the correct explanation of A.
(b) Both A and R are true, but R is not the correct explanation of A.
(c) A is true, but R is false.
(d) A is false, but R is true.

***Ans.* (c)**

Exp. Assertion (A) is true, but Reason (R) is false because the temperature in Torrid zone is hot and moist throughout the year.

The Sun is directly overhead at least once in a year in the tropic zone. So, this Torrid zone receives maximum insolation. The Sun does not come vertically at any time in a year in frigid or polar zones. Throughout the year, Frigid zone receives slanting Sun rays and hence experiences a very cold climate.

The amount of insolation received on Earth's surface decreases with increase in the latitude.

18 Which of the following atmospheric factors, if present, will reduce the intensity of insolation received on Earth? *(Chap 11, Class-XI, Old NCERT)*

1. Cloud cover
2. Winds
3. Dust and water vapour
4. Sea waves

Codes

(a) 1 and 3 (b) 1 and 2 (c) 2 and 4 (d) 3 and 4

Ans. (a)

Exp. Cloud cover and dust and water vapour will reduce the intensity of insolation received on Earth. Cloud cover reflects, absorbs or transmits insolation. Therefore, it reduces the intensity of insolation received on Earth. Dust particles reflect, absorb or transmit insolation. Similarly, water vapour absorbs solar radiation resulting in less amount of insolation reaching the surface.

However, winds and sea waves are not responsible for reducing the intensity of insolation received on Earth.

19 Which among the following statements about solar insolation and heating of Earth is/are incorrect? *(Chap 11, Class-XI, Old/New NCERT)*

1. Only 50% of solar insolation received at the outer atmosphere is absorbed by the surface of Earth.
2. Long wave terrestrial radiation is absorbed by atmospheric gases and heats the atmosphere.
3. Atmosphere of Earth is heated more by the solar insolation than by terrestrial radiation.
4. Earth receives insolation at a rate of two calories per m^2 per minute at the atmospheric top.

Codes

(a) 1, 3 and 4 (b) 2 and 4 (c) Only 3 (d) Only 1

Ans. (c)

Exp. Statement (3) is incorrect about solar insolation and heating of Earth because atmosphere of Earth is heated more by the terrestrial radiation than by solar insolation.

20 Consider the following statements. *(Chap 9, Class-XI, New NCERT)*

1. Subtropical desert regions receive more insolation than the equatorial and polar regions.
2. Higher latitudes receive more solar insolation in winters than in summers.

Which of the statements given above is/are correct?

(a) Only 1 (b) Only 2
(c) Both 1 and 2 (d) Neither 1 nor 2

Ans. (a)

Exp. Statement (1) is correct because maximum insolation is received over the subtropical deserts, where the cloudiness is the least. Equator and polar region receive comparatively less insolation than the tropics due to presence of clouds.

Statement (2) is incorrect because higher latitudes receive more solar insolation in summers than in winters.

21 Consider the following statements. *(Chap 8, Class-XI, New NCERT)*

Statement-1 The atmosphere receives most of the heat only indirectly from the Sun and directly from the Earth's surface.

Statement-II The conversion from shortwave solar to long wave terrestrial energy takes place at the Earth's surface.

Codes

(a) Both Statement-I and Statement-II are correct and Statement-II is the correct explanation for Statement-I.
(b) Both Statement-I and Statement-II are correct and Statement-II is not the correct explanation for Statement-I.
(c) Statement-l is correct, but Statement-II is incorrect.
(d) Statement-I is incorrect, but Statement-II is correct.

Ans. (a)

Exp. Both Statement-I and Statement-II are correct and Statement-II is the correct explanation for Statement-I. The Earth's atmosphere receives heat energy from two main sources; the Sun and the Earth's surface. Most of the heat in the atmosphere comes indirectly from the Sun (through the process of solar radiation warming the Earth's surface, which then warms the atmosphere) and directly from the Earth's surface (terrestrial radiation).

The process of conversion from shortwave solar energy (which is mostly visible light and shorter wavelengths) to longwave terrestrial energy (infrared radiation) occurs at the Earth's surface.

The Earth's surface absorbs solar radiation and then re-emits it as longer wavelength infrared radiation. This process is a fundamental aspect of the Earth's energy balance and is responsible for the warming of the atmosphere and the overall temperature regulation of the planet.

22 Consider the following statements. *(Chap 9, Class-XI, New NCERT*

1. Isotherms deviate more in the Northern hemisphere than in the Southern hemisphere.
2. In the month of January, isotherms deviate towards North over oceans and towards South over continents.
3. Isotherms are generally parallel to the latitudes in Southern hemisphere.

Which of the statements given above is/are incorrect?
(a) Only 1
(b) Only 2
(c) 1 and 3
(d) None of the above

Ans. (d)

Exp. None of the given statements are incorrect because isotherms deviate more in the Northern hemisphere than in the Southern hemisphere as in the Northern hemisphere the land surface area is much larger than in the Southern hemisphere. In January, the isotherms deviate to the North over the oceans and to the South over the continents.

The presence of warm ocean currents, Gulf Stream and North Atlantic drift, make the Northern Atlantic Ocean warmer and the isotherms bend towards the North. Over the land, the temperature decreases sharply and the isotherms bend towards South in Europe.

The effect of the ocean is well-pronounced in the Southern hemisphere. Here, the isotherms are more or less parallel to the latitudes and the variation in temperature is more gradual than in the Northern hemisphere.

23 Consider the following statements about the temperature on Earth. *(Chap 11, Class-XI, Old NCERT)*

1. Higher the angle of incidence, higher the temperature.
2. Largest temperature anomalies occur in the Northern hemisphere.
3. Temperature extremities are more over oceans as compared to continents.
4. Temperature of an inland region is moderate as compared to a coastal region.

How many of the statements given above is/are correct?
(a) Only one
(b) Only two
(c) All three
(d) None of the above

Ans. (b)

Exp. Statements (1) and (2) are correct about temperature over the Earth because when the angle of incidence is high, the area affected is small and insolation and is concentrated on a smaller area, hence the heat received per unit area is large and heated to a higher degree. The largest temperature anomalies occur in the Northern hemisphere because the amount of land in the Northern hemisphere is greater and the influence of ocean currents is greater than in the Southern hemisphere.

Statements (3) and (4) are incorrect because temperature extremities are more over continents as compared to ocean and temperature of a coastal region is moderate as compared to an inland region.

24 Which of the following conditions will be most suitable for occurrence of temperature inversion? *(Chap 11, Class-XI, Old NCERT)*

1. Cold winter night
2. Long summer days
3. Moist air
4. Calm and stable air
5. Cloudy skies

Codes
(a) 1 and 2 (b) 1, 2 and 3 (c) 1 and 4 (d) 1, 2, 3, 4 and 5

Ans. (c)

Exp. Cold winter night and calm and stable air are the conditions will be most suitable for occurrence of temperature inversion. A long cool winter night with clear sky and still air is ideal situation for inversion. Due to the slow movement of air, it does not result in heat transfer or mixing in the lower layers of the atmosphere.

25 Consider the following statements. *(Chap 8, Class-XI, New NCERT)*

1. The transfer of heat through horizontal movement of air is called advection.
2. In middle latitudes, most of diurnal (day and night) variation in daily weather is caused by advection alone.
3. Local winds called 'loo' during the summer season in Northern India are the result of the convection process.

How many of the statements given above is/are correct?
(a) Only one (b) Only two
(c) All three (d) None of these

Ans. (c)

Exp. All three statements i.e., (1), (2) and (3) are correct as the transfer of heat through horizontal movement of air is called advection. In middle latitudes, most of the diurnal (day and night) variation in daily weather is caused by advection alone. The horizontal movement of air is more significant than the vertical movement. In tropical regions particularly in Northern India during the summer season local winds called 'loo' is the outcome of advection process.

26 Consider the following Assertion (A) and Reason (R) and choose the correct code. *(Chap 11, Class-XI, Old NCERT)*

Assertion (A) Vegetation in the upper slopes of mountains is free from frost during winter nights.

Reason (R) Air above the surface of valley floor and mountain slope cools down quickly during nights in winters.

Codes
(a) Both A and R are true and R is the correct explanation of A.
(b) Both A and R are true, but R is not the correct explanation of A.
(c) A is true, but R is false.
(d) A is false, but R is true.

Ans. (a)

Exp. Both Assertion (A) and Reason (R) are true and Reason (R) is the correct explanation of Assertion (A). During night, upper slopes radiate heat and cool down quickly. The air above these slopes also cools down, becomes heavier and resulting in formation of high pressure. Thus, a wind is established from slopes to valley during night.

Due to temperature inversion, the vegetation on the lower part of the slope are affected by frost whereas the vegetation located above them are not affected by frost during winter nights.

Atmospheric Pressure, Pressure Belts and Wind Systems

27 Consider the following statements.

(Chap 9, Class-XI, New NCERT) (IAS Pre 2002)

Statement-I 60°-65° latitudes in both the hemispheres have a low pressure belt instead of high pressure.

Statement-II The low pressure areas are stable over oceans rather than on land.

Codes

(a) Both Statement-I and Statement-II are correct and Statement-II is the correct explanation for Statement-I.
(b) Both Statement-I and Statement-II are correct and Statement-II is not the correct explanation for Statement-I.
(c) Statement-l is correct, but Statement-II is incorrect.
(d) Statement-I is incorrect, but Statement-II is correct.

Ans. (c)

Exp. Statement-I is correct, but Statement-II is incorrect. 60°-65° latitudes in both the hemispheres are known as 'circum polar low pressure belts'. Due to Earth's rotation, the winds surrounding the polar region blow towards the equator.

Low atmospheric pressure builts upon land, which is not stable region. Whereas high atmospheric pressure build upon ocean, which is stable region.

28 Match List I with List II and select the correct answer by using the codes given below the list.

(Chap 9, Class-XI, New NCERT) (MPPSC Pre 2016)

List I	List II
A. Equatorial low pressure belt	1. Air in this region gets pushed upward due to the friction with the surface and the Earth's rotation.
B. Mid-latitudinal high pressure	2. The temperature is below 0°C throughout the year.
C. Sub-polar low pressure belt	3. In this area, the rays of the Sun fall mostly perpendicular.
D. Polar high pressure belt	4. Cool air descends between 25° and 35°latitude.

Codes

	A	B	C	D
(a)	1	2	4	3
(b)	4	1	2	3
(c)	3	4	1	2
(d)	2	3	4	1

Ans. (c)

Exp. The correct matching is A-3, B-4, C-1, D-2.

Equatorial low pressure belt-extends from 0° to 5° North and South of equator. In this area, the rays of the Sun fall mostly perpendicular.

Mid-latitudinal high pressure belt in this belts, the heated air becomes lighter, starts ascending and after reaching higher altitude, the air cools down and becomes heavier. This heavier air descends down in both the hemispheres in the region between 25° to 35° latitude.

Sub-polar low high pressure are formed arounds latitudes 60° to 65° North and South of the equator. The rotation of the Earth pushes up the bulk of air towards the equator. Air in this region gets pushed upward due to the friction with the surface and the Earth's rotation.

Polar high pressure belt exists between 40° North to 90° South of the equator due to extremely cold conditions that is why the temperature in below 0° throughout the year.

29 Consider the following statements about equatorial low pressure belt. *(Chap 12, Class-XI, Old NCERT)*

1. This belt is formed due to intense heating of equatorial surface due by terrestrial radiation.
2. Strong surface winds blow in the zone of this belt.
3. Calm conditions prevail in this region, which is characterised by Doldrums.

Which of the statements given above is/are incorrect?

(a) 1 and 2 (b) 2 and 3 (c) Only 2 (d) All of these

Ans. (c)

Exp. Statement (2) is incorrect about equatorial low pressure belt because strong surface winds do not blow in the region of equatorial low pressure belt. Equatorial low pressure belt is the zone of convergence of trade winds from two hemispheres of sub-tropical high pressure belts.

Equatorial low pressure belt is also called the Doldrums because of the extremely calm air movements.

30 Consider the following statements.

(Chap 12, Class-XI, Old NCERT)

1. Horse latitudes are characterised by high pressure belts.
2. High pressure in these regions is formed by the subsidence and piling up of air.
3. Coriolis force, due to rotation of Earth, blocks the air near sub-tropical latitudes which leads to its subsidence.

Which of the statements given above are correct?

(a) 1 and 2 (b) 2 and 3
(c) 1 and 3 (d) All of these

Ans. (d)

Exp. All the given statements are correct because the corresponding latitudes of sub-tropical high pressure belt are called horse latitudes. The horse latitudes are regions located at about 30° North and South of the equator. In these regions, the air coming from the equator and the temperate region descends here and starts to accumulate, due to which the horse latitude is formed. The wind descends in the middle of latitude 20 to 35 because, Coriolis force, due to rotation of Earth, blocks the air near sub-tropical latitudes which leads to its subsidence.

31 Consider the following statements about the Sub-polar low-pressure belts.

(Chap 9, Class-XI, New NCERT)

1. The sub-polar low pressure belts extend between 30 ° N and the Arctic Circle in the Northern hemisphere and between 30°S and the Antarctic Circle in the Southern hemisphere.
2. They are known as the North sub-polar low and the South sub-polar low pressure belts respectively.
3. Winds coming from the sub-tropical and the polar high belts converge here to produce cyclonic storms or low pressure conditions.

How many of the statements given above is/are correct?

(a) Only one
(b) Only two
(c) All three
(d) None of the above

Ans. (b)

Exp. Only two statements i.e., (2) and (3) are correct regarding Sub-polar low-pressure belts. In the Southern hemisphere, they extend between 45°S and the Antarctic Circle. They are known as the North sub-polar low and the South sub-polar low-pressure belts respectively. Winds coming from the sub-tropical and the polar high belts converge here to produce cyclonic storms or low-pressure conditions. This zone of convergence is also known as polar front.

Statement (1) is incorrect because the sub-polar low-pressure belts extend between 45°N and the Arctic Circle in the Northern hemisphere.

32 Which of the following pairs is correct?

(Chap 9, Class-XI, New NCERT)

(a) Equatorial Low Pressure Belt – Doldrums
(b) Sub-tropical High Pressure Belt – Polar front
(c) Sub-polar Low Pressure Belts – Horse latitude
(d) Polar High Pressure Belts – High temperature

Ans. (c)

Exp. Pair (c) is correct as due to excessive heating horizontal movement of air is absent in the Equatorial Low Pressure Belt and only conventional currents are there. Therefore this belt is called doldrums (the zone of calm) due to virtual absence of surface winds.

33 Which of the following statements about the shifting of atmospheric pressure belts is correct?

(Chap 12, Class-XI, Old NCERT)

1. Shift of pressure belts is more in Northern hemisphere than in Southern hemisphere.
2. During summers, the pressure belts shift towards South in Northern hemisphere.
3. During winters, the pressure belts shift towards South in Southern hemisphere.

Codes

(a) 1 and 3 (b) 1 and 2 (c) 2 and 3 (d) All of these

Ans. (a)

Exp. Statements (1) and (3) are correct about the shifting of atmospheric pressure belts. Due to the excess of land in the Northern hemisphere, the shifting of pressure belts is more in the Northern hemisphere than in the Southern hemisphere. Due to the predominance of water in the Southern hemisphere, during the winter, the pressure belts are shifted to the South of their annual mean locations. Due to its high heat capacity, the land takes more heat during hot times and is comparatively cooler in winters.

Statement (2) is incorrect because during summer, the pressure belts shift towards North in Northern hemisphere.

34 In the context of forces affecting wind velocity and direction, consider the following

(Unit 6, Class-XI,Tamil Nadu Board)

1. If the pressure gradient is strong, the velocity of wind is higher.
2. The velocity of the wind increases with the increase in frictional force.
3. This Coriolis force deflects the wind to the right direction in the Northern Hemisphere and the left in the Southern Hemisphere.
4. The Coriolis force is inversely proportional to the angle of latitude.

How many of the statements given above is/are correct?

(a) Only one (b) Only two
(c) Only three (d) All four

Ans. (b)

Exp. Only two statements i.e., (1) and (3) are correct regarding forces affecting wind velocity and direction. The pressure gradient is strong where the isobars are close to each other and weak where the isobars are apart. If the pressure gradient is strong, the velocity of the wind is higher.

The rotation of the Earth about its axis creates Coriolis force that affects the direction of the wind. This Coriolis force deflects the wind to the right direction in the Northern Hemisphere and the left in the Southern hemisphere. Statements (2) and (4) are incorrect because the velocity of the wind decreases with the increase in frictional force. The Coriolis force is directly proportional to the angle of latitude. This means that the Coriolis force is strongest at the poles and weakest at the equator.

35 Which of the following statements is/are incorrect? *(Chap 10, Class-XI, New NCERT)*

1. The Pressure gradient force determines the velocity of wind over the surface.
2. Winds blowing over sea surface experience lower friction than continental surface.
3. Deflection of winds due to Coriolis force is maximum at equator and negligible at the poles.

Codes

(a) Only 1
(b) 2 and 3
(c) Only 3
(d) None of the above

Ans. (c)

Exp. Statement (3) is incorrect because deflection of winds due to Coriolis force is maximum at polar region and negligible at the equator region.

36 Consider the following Assertion (A) and Reason (R) and choose the correct code. *(Chap 10, Class-XI, New NCERT)*

Assertion (A) The Coriolis force acts perpendicular to the pressure gradient force, resulting in the formation of a geostrophic wind.

Reason (R) Winds are deflected to the right in the Northern hemisphere and towards left in the Southern hemisphere.

Codes

(a) Both A and R are true and R is the correct explanation of A.
(b) Both A and R are true, but R is not the correct explanation of A.
(c) A is true, but R is false.
(d) A is false, but R is true.

Ans. (b)

Exp. Both Assertion (A) and Reason (R) are true, but Reason (R) is not the correct explanation of Assertion (A). Coriolis force deflects the wind to the right direction in the Northern hemisphere and to the left in the Southern hemisphere. The deflection is more when the wind velocity is high.

The pressure gradient force acts towards low pressure perpendicular to the lines of constant height but the Coriolis force acts to the right and perpendicular to the wind direction. A wind that results from a balance between the pressure gradient and Coriolis forces is called a geostrophic wind.

37 Consider the following statements about wind movement on the Earth. *(Chap 10, Class-XI, New NCERT)*

1. Geostrophic winds blow parallel to the isobars.
2. The speed of wind movement is influenced by friction of the surface.
3. Pressure gradient force is more when isobars are close to each other.

Which of the statements given above are correct?

(a) 1 and 2 (b) 2 and 3 (c) 1 and 3 (d) 1, 2 and 3

Ans. (d)

Exp. All the statements about wind movement on the Earth are correct. When isobars are straight and there is no friction, the pressure gradient force is balanced by the Coriolis force and the resultant wind blows parallel to the isobar. This wind is known as the geostrophic wind. Friction of the surface is greatest at the surface and its influence generally extends up to an elevation of 1-3 km. Over the sea surface, the friction is minimal. Surface friction affects the speed of the wind movement. The pressure gradient is strong where the isobars are close to each other and is weak where the isobars are apart.

38 Consider the following statements. *(Chap 12, Class-XI, Old NCERT)*

1. Trade winds converge at the Inter Tropical Convergence Zone to form a high pressure area.
2. Convergence, rise and sinking of trade winds occur in the Hadley cell.
3. Convergence of trade winds at the equator causes heavy rainfall.

Which of the statements given above are correct?

(a) 1 and 3 (b) 2 and 3 (c) 1 and 2 (d) All of these

Ans. (b)

Exp. Statements (2) and (3) are correct because Hadley cells are the low-latitude overturning circulations that have air rising at the equator and air sinking at roughly 30° latitude. The Easterlies from either side of the equator converge in Hadley cells.

Due to the convergence of the trade winds at the equator, the air becomes lighter and rises up and the air starts getting saturated after reaching the required height. This causes heavy rainfall in the equator region. Statement (1) is incorrect because trade winds converge at the Inter Tropical Convergence Zone (ITCZ) to form a low pressure area.

39 Consider the following statements. *(Chap 12, Class-XI, Old NCERT)*

1. Westerlies are stronger and more regular in the Southern hemisphere than in the Northern hemisphere.
2. Westerlies converge at the equatorial region with the trade winds.
3. Westerlies cause frontal rain in mid latitude regions.

4. Westerlies are best developed between 40° and 65° S latitudes.

How many of the statements given above is/are correct?

(a) Only one (b) Only two
(c) Only three (d) All four

Ans. (c)

Exp. Only three statements i.e., (1), (3) and (4) are correct because the Westerly winds in the Southern hemisphere are stronger and more regular because they face minimal land interference due to lack of land as compared to the Northern hemisphere. Westerly winds play an important role in carrying warm, equatorial waters and winds to the West coasts of the continents, causing rainfall along the Western coasts of the continents.

Statement (2) is incorrect because Westerlies do not converge at the equatorial region with the trade winds.

40 Arrange the following atmospheric cells in the correct sequence from equator to poles.

(Chap 10, Class-XI, New NCERT)

(a) Polar cell, Hadley cell, Ferrell cell
(b) Hadley cell, Ferrell cell, Polar cell
(c) Hadley cell, Polar cell, Ferrell cell
(d) Ferrell cell, Hadley cell, Polar cell

Ans. (b)

Exp. The correct sequence of atmospheric cells from equator to poles is Hadley cell, Farrell cell and Polar cell.

The Easterlies from either side of the equator converge in the Inter Tropical Convergence Zone (ITCZ). Such circulations from the surface upwards and vice-versa are called cells. Such a cell in the tropics is called Hadley cell.

In the middle latitudes, the circulation is that of sinking cold air that comes from the poles and the rising warm air that blows from the sub-tropical high. At the surface, these winds are called Westerlies and the cell is known as the Ferrell cell.

At polar latitudes, the cold dense air subsides near the poles and blows towards middle latitudes as the polar Easterlies. This cell is called the Polar cell.

41 Consider the following statements.

(Chap 2, Class-VII, Old NCERT)

1. Land breeze blows during the night whereas sea breeze blows during the daytime.
2. Land and sea breeze are formed due to the differential heating and cooling of land and sea surface.

Which of the statements given above is/are correct?

(a) Only 1 (b) Only 2
(c) Both 1 and 2 (d) None of these

Ans. (c)

Exp. Both the statements (1) and (2) are correct because land breeze blows during night, because at night the water cools down more slowly than the land, so the cool air moves towards the sea from land.

Sea breeze blows during day, because during the day the land gets heated faster than the water.

Land and sea breeze are formed due to the differential heating and cooling of land and sea surface. That is why, during the day, the wind blows from the sea to the land and during, the night, it moves from the land to the sea.

42 Consider the following statements.

(Chap 9, Class-XI, New NCERT) (IAS Pre 2015)

Statement-I Wind patterns are clockwise in the Northern hemisphere and anti-clockwise in the Southern hemisphere.

Statement-II The directions of wind patterns in the Northern and the Southern hemisphere are governed by the Coriolis effect.

Codes

(a) Both Statement-I and Statement-II are correct and Statement-II is the correct explanation for Statement-I.
(b) Both Statement-I and Statement-II are correct and Statement-II is not the correct explanation for Statement-I.
(c) Statement-I is correct, but Statement-II is incorrect.
(d) Statement-I is incorrect, but Statement-II is correct.

Ans. (d)

Exp. Statement-I is incorrect, but Statement-II is correct.

The direction of winds patterns in the Northern hemisphere is anti-clockwise and in the Southern hemisphere is clockwise. In the Northern Hemisphere, wind flows in an anti-clockwise direction around areas of low pressure and in a clockwise direction around areas of high pressure. This pattern is reversed in the Southern hemisphere.

The Coriolis effect, which is caused by the Earth's rotation, makes wind systems twist clockwise in the Southern hemisphere and counterclockwise in the Northern hemisphere.

43 Which of the following pairs is correct?

(Chap 12, Class-XI, Old NCERT)

Local Wind		Blows in
(a) Foehn	–	Rhone Valley in France
(b) Chinook	–	Rockies in USA and Canada
(c) Mistral	–	Northern Plains in Asia
(d) Loo	–	Alps in Europe

Ans. (a)

Exp. Pair (b) is correct as Chinook winds are warm and dry winds blowing on the Eastern slopes (leeward side) of the Rocky mountain in USA and Canada.

While pairs (a), (c) and (d) are incorrect. Foehn is a hot and dry local wind that blows over the leeward side of the Alps mountains in Europe.

Mistral is a cold and dry wind that blows in the Rhone Valley from North-West to South-East in Spain and France. Loo winds originate from the Thar desert and have North-Westerly to a Westerly direction. They dominate during early summer in the months of March to May and create heat waves in Northern plains in Asia.

44 Consider the following statements about jet streams.

(Chap 12, Class-XI, Old NCERT)

1. Jet streams blow in the stratosphere near the stratopause.
2. Sub-tropical jet streams are formed by rotation of Earth.
3. Polar jet streams are formed by thermal differences.
4. Jet streams influence cyclone formations.

Which of the statements given above are correct?

(a) 2, 3 and 4 (b) 1, 2 and 3 (c) 1, 3 and 4 (d) 1, 2 and 3

***Ans.* (a)**

Exp. Statements (2), (3) and (4) are correct about jet streams because the sub-tropical jet stream is formed by the Earth's rotation and temperature contrast between tropical and sub-tropical regions.

The polar jet streams are produced by temperature and thermal difference and it is closely related to the polar front. The polar jet streams are strong and continuous in winter. Jet streams influence the path of temperate cyclones formations. They have an influence on distribution of precipitation by the temperate cyclones.

Statement (1) is incorrect because the jet stream is a geostrophic wind blowing horizontally through the upper layers of the troposphere, generally from West to East, at an altitude of 20000 - 50000 feet.

Cyclones

45 Which of the following statements about extratropical cyclonic circulation is correct?

(Chap 10, Class-XI, New NCERT)

1. Extra Tropical Cyclonic Circulations are formed along the polar front in the Northern hemisphere.
2. Extra Tropical Cyclonic Circulations move in anti-clockwise direction in the Northern hemisphere.

Codes

(a) Only 1 (b) Only 2
(c) Both 1 and 2 (d) None of these

***Ans.* (c)**

Exp. Both the statements (1) and (2) are correct about extratropical cyclonic circulation because extra Tropical cyclones are formed along the polar front. In the Northern hemisphere, warm air blows from the South and cold air from the North of the front.

Cyclone is formed due to convergence of cold and warm airmasses. In an extra tropical cyclone, the central air pressure is lower than that of the surrounding environment, and the flow of circulation is counterclockwise in the Northern hemisphere.

46 Consider the following statements.

(Chap 4, Class-IX, Old NCERT)

1. The area covered by an extra tropical cyclone is significantly more than a tropical cyclone.
2. Extratropical cyclones can only be formed over continental surfaces.
3. These cyclones move from West to East under the influence of westerly winds.

Which of the statements given above are correct?

(a) 1 and 3 (b) 2 and 3 (c) 1 and 2 (d) All of these

***Ans.* (a)**

Exp. Statements (1) and (3) are correct because the diameter of an extra tropical cyclone can range from about 1040 to 1920 km. The average diameter of a tropical cyclone can be up to 640 km.

Hence, the area covered by an extra tropical cyclone is more than a tropical cyclone. Extra-tropical cyclones after their origin move from West to East with westerly winds.

Statement (2) is incorrect because extratropical cyclones can formed over continental or ocean surface.

47 Consider the following statements about the formation of a tropical cyclone.

(Chap 10, Class-XI, New NCERT)

1. Large sea surface with temperature higher than 27° C.
2. Small variations in the vertical wind speed.
3. A pre-existing weak low-pressure area or low-level-cyclonic circulation.
4. Upper divergence above the sea level system.

How many conditions are not necessary for the formation of a tropical cyclone?

(a) Only one
(b) Only two
(c) Only three
(d) None of the above

***Ans.* (d)**

Exp. "A cyclone is likely to form with the presence of a large sea surface featuring temperatures higher than 27°C, sufficient Coriolis force to generate a cyclonic vortex, minor fluctuations in vertical wind speed, a pre-existing weak low-pressure area or low-level-cyclonic circulation, and upper-level divergence above the sea-level system."

48 Which of the following statements is correct?

(Chap 10, Class-XI, New NCERT)

1. Tropical cyclones can originate over sea as well as land surface.
2. Wind velocity of tropical cyclones is much higher than extra tropical cyclones.
3. Tropical cyclones move from East to West.
4. Tropical cyclones can recurve beyond 20°N latitude and become more destructive.

Codes

(a) 1, 2 and 3
(b) 1, 2 and 4
(c) 1, 2, 3 and 4
(d) 2, 3 and 4

Ans. (d)

Exp. Statements (2), (3) and (4) are correct because average wind speed in tropical cyclone is more than about 100 km per hour, but in extratropical cyclone, the average wind speed is about 32 km per hour in summer and about 48 km per hour in winter.

Tropical cyclones move from East to West with the trade winds after their origin. In the 20°N latitude with continuous supply of moisture from the sea, the tropical cyclone is further strengthened.

The cyclones, which cross 20° North latitude generally, recurve and they are more destructive.

Statement (1) is incorrect because tropical cyclones can originate over sea surface.

49 Consider the following statements about tropical cyclones. *(Chap 10, Class-XI, New NCERT)*

1. The eye of a tropical cyclone is characterised by ascent of strong winds.
2. Cumulonimbus clouds cause heavy rainfall in tropical cyclones.
3. The intensity of tropical cyclones increase as they make a landfall over the continents.

Which of the statements given above is/are correct?

(a) Only 1
(b) Only 3
(c) Only 2
(d) None of these

Ans. (c)

Exp. Statement (2) is correct about tropical cyclones because Cumulonimbus clouds are associated with extreme weather in tropical cyclones. Such as heavy torrential downpours, hail storms, lightning and even tornadoes.

Statements (1) and (3) are incorrect because the eye of a tropical cyclone is characterised in a region of low atmospheric pressure, high winds and heavy rain. The intensity of tropical cyclones decreases as they make a landfall over the continents.

50 Match the following lists correctly and choose the correct code. *(Chap 10, Class-XI, New NCERT)*

List I (Tropical Cyclone Name)		List II (Region)	
A.	Cyclone	1.	Australia
B.	Willy-Willy	2.	Indian Ocean
C.	Hurricane	3.	South China Sea
D.	Typhoon	4.	Atlantic Ocean

Codes

	A	B	C	D		A	B	C	D
(a)	4	2	1	3	(b)	2	1	4	3
(c)	2	1	3	4	(d)	4	1	3	2

Ans. (b)

Exp. The correct matching is A-2, B-1, C-4, D-3.

Cyclone Tropical cyclone is a rapid rotating storm system characterised by a long-pressure centre, a closed low level strong winds and heavy rain. In Indian Ocean, tropical cyclones are also called severe cyclonic storms.

Willy-Willy It is a famons tropical cyclone in Western Australia. This tropical cyclone causes heavy rainfall.

Hurricane It is a strong tropical cyclone that occurs in the Atlantic Ocean or North-Eastern Pacific Ocean.

Typhoon It occurs in North-Western Pacific Ocean (South China Sea). It is a most dangerous natural calamity in that region.

51 Which of the following statements is incorrect about tornadoes? *(Chap 10, Class-XI, New NCERT)*

1. Tornadoes generally occur in the tropical and equatorial regions.
2. Water spouts are the tornadoes formed over sea surface.
3. Tornadoes occur for a short period as compared to cyclones.

Codes

(a) 1 and 2 (b) 2 and 3 (c) Only 2 (d) Only 1

Ans. (d)

Exp. Statement (1) is incorrect about tornadoes because tornadoes generally occur in the middle latitude between 20° and 60° N and S.

A tornado is a furiously rotating column of air that extends down to the Earth from the base of a thunderstorm.

52 Which of the following characteristics can be attributed to thunderstorms? *(Chap 10, Class-XI, New NCERT)*

1. Cumulonimbus clouds with lightning
2. Intense updraft and rising of air
3. Heavy precipitation
4. Widespread area

Codes

(a) 1, 2 and 3
(b) 2, 3 and 4
(c) 1, 3 and 4
(d) 1, 2 and 4

Ans. (a)

Exp. Among the given characteristics options (1), (2) and (3) can be attributed to thunderstorms because these are caused by intense convection on moist hot days.

A thunderstorm is a well-grown cumulonimbus cloud producing thunder and lightning. When the clouds extend to heights where sub-zero temperature prevails, hails are formed and they come down as hailstorm.

A thunderstorm is characterised by intense updraft of rising warm air, which causes the clouds to grow bigger and rise to greater height.

This causes heavy precipitation. Later, downdraft brings down to Earth the cool air and the rain. Thunderstorms are of short duration, occurring over a small area but are violent.

53 **Consider the following statements.**

(Chap 10, Class-XI, New NCERT) (IAS Pre 2020)

1. Jet streams occur in the Northern hemisphere only.
2. Only some cyclones develop an eye.
3. The temperature inside the eye of a cyclone is nearly 10°C lesser than that of the surroundings.

Which of the statements given above is/are correct?

(a) Only 1
(b) 2 and 3
(c) Only 2
(d) 1 and 3

Ans. (c)

Exp. Only statement (2) is correct as the 'eye of a cyclone' is an area of comparatively light winds and fair weather found at the centre of severe tropical cyclone that's why only some cyclones develop an eye.

Statements (1) and (3) are incorrect because jet streams are currents of air high above the surface of Earth. They occur in both hemispheres–Northern and Southern.

The temperature inside the eye of a cyclone is higher than that of the surroundings.

54 **Consider the following statements.**

(Chap 9, Class-XI, New NCERT) (CGPSC Pre 2023)

Statement-I Moving away from the sea, force of tropical cyclone decreases.

Statement-II Tropical cyclone gets its energy from release of latent heat on account of condensation of moisture that wind gathers after moving over the ocean which decreases as it moves away from sea.

Codes

(a) Both Statement-I and Statement-II are correct and Statement-II is the correct explanation for Statement-I.
(b) Both Statement-I and Statement-II are correct and Statement-II is not the correct explanation for Statement-I.
(c) Statement-I is correct, but Statement-II is incorrect.
(d) Statement-I is incorrect, but Statement-II is correct.

Ans. (a)

Exp. Both Statement-I and Statement-II are correct and Statement-II is the correct explanation for Statement-I.

When Tropical Cyclone moves away from the sea, they lose their energy source and their strength gradually diminishes. Tropical cyclones are powered by the release of latent heat during the process of moisture condensation. As moist air rises from the warm ocean surface, it cools and condenses into clouds, releasing heat into the storm system.

Tropical cyclone is also known as hurricanes or typhoons, derive their energy from warm ocean waters. As they move over the ocean, they gather heat and moisture, which fuels their intensity.

Airmass

55 **Consider the following statements regarding Air Masses.**

(Chap 9, Class-XI, New NCERT)

1. The air masses carry atmospheric moisture from oceans to continents and cause precipitation over landmasses.
2. When an air mass moves away from a source region, the upper level maintains the physical characteristics for a longer period.
3. Tropical air masses are cold and polar air masses are warm.

How many of the statements given above is/are correct?

(a) Only one
(b) Only two
(c) Only three
(d) None of these

Ans. (b)

Exp. Statements (1) and (2) are correct regarding Air Masses.

The air masses carry atmospheric moisture from oceans to continents and cause precipitation over landmasses. They transport latent heat, thus removing the latitudinal heat balance.

When an air mass moves away from a source region, the upper level maintains the physical characteristics for a longer period.

This is possible because air masses are stable with stagnant air which do not facilitate convection.

Statement (3) is incorrect because tropical air masses are warm and polar air masses are cold. Air masses are large volumes of air with uniform characteristics. They can be maritime or continental, depending on whether they form over land or water.

56 **Consider the following statements.**

(Chap 12, Class-XI, Old NCERT)

1. When a cold airmass moves over a warm airmass, it produces conditions of instability.
2. When a warm airmass moves over a cold airmass, it produces instabilities.
3. Polar airmasses usually experience the conditions of instability.

Which of the statements given above are correct?

(a) 2 and 3
(b) 1 and 3
(c) 1 and 2
(d) All of these

Ans. (b)

Exp. Statements (1) and (3) are correct because when a colder airmass moves over a warmer ground, the bottom layer of air is heated. It produces instability and that air rises, forming clouds, rain, and sometimes thunderstorm.

When the polar cold airmass reaches the region of a hot airmass, then the polar airmass becomes unstable du to heating from below and after condensation, it rains.

Statement (2) is incorrect because when a warm airmass reaches the region of a cold airmass, the warm air becomes stable due to the cooling of the hot air from below.

57 **Consider the following Assertion (A) and Reason (R) and choose the correct code.**

(Chap 12, Class-XI, Old NCERT)

Assertion (A) Convergence of warmer and colder airmass form fronts in the middle latitudes.

Reason (R) Warm front and cold front do not retain mix readily and retain their characteristics in terms of temperature and moisture.

Codes

(a) Both A and R are true and R is the correct explanation of A.
(b) Both A and R are true, but R is not the correct explanation of A.
(c) A is true, but R is false.
(d) A is false, but R is true.

Ans. (b)

Exp. Both Assertion (A) and Reason (R) are true, but Reason (R) is not the correct explanation of Assertion (A).

In the middle latitudes, there is a convergence of hot and cold airmasses. Convergence of warm and cold airmasses leads to the formation of fronts which are responsible for the origin of temperate tropical cyclones in the mid-latitudes.

Fronts are poor conductor of energy. This means that when two different bodies of air come together, they do not readily mix. Rather, each body of air will retain its individual properties, and a boundary is formed between them. When two large airmasses meet, the boundary that separates them is called a front.

Water in the Atmosphere

58 **Consider the following statements.**

(Chap 13, Class-XI, Old NCERT)

1. The amount of water vapour in the atmosphere varies from place to place.
2. The amount of water vapour determines the capacity of precipitation over a region.
3. Amount of water vapour determines the rate of humidity in a region.
4. Water vapour is added to atmosphere by only oceanic surfaces.

How many statements given above is/are correct?

(a) Only one
(b) Only two
(c) Only three
(d) All four

Ans. (c)

Exp. Only three statements i.e. (1), (2) and (3) are correct because water vapour is water in gaseous form. It can be formed either through a process of evaporation or sublimation. Water vapour is added to atmosphere by oceanic surface, land surface, lake surface and river surface, etc.

The amount of water vapour determine the capacity of precipitation and the amount of water vapour determine rate of humidity in a region.

Water vapour is basically the gaseous phase of the water. The amount of water vapour in the atmosphere varies from place to place.

59 **In context of cycle of precipitation on the Earth, consider the following statements.**

(Chap 13, Class-XI, Old NCERT)

1. Moisture is transported on Earth from one region to another through convection.
2. Cycle of precipitation over land takes more time to complete than cycle over the oceans.
3. Both evaporation and transpiration contribute moisture to the atmosphere.

How many of the statements given above is/are correct?

(a) Only one
(b) Only two
(c) All three
(d) None of these

Ans. (c)

Exp. All three statements i.e., (1), (2) and (3) are correct about the cycle of precipitation on the Earth because due to convection, the moisture on the Earth is transferred from one place to another. Convection largely occurs in the atmosphere, oceans, and mantle of planets. The movement of fluid during convection may be invisibly slow, or it may become clearer and faster, as in a storm. Ocean water warms and cools quickly and land cools and warms late.

The cycle of precipitation over land takes longer to complete than cycle over the oceans.

Sea areas, land, rivers and lakes contribute moisture to the atmosphere by evaporation. Plants also increase the moisture in the atmosphere through transpiration.

60 **Water vapour contributes to only a minute proportion of Atmospheric composition but it plays a very important role in atmospheric and weather phenomenon on Earth. Which of the following statements indicates significance of water vapour?**

(Chap 13, Class-XI, Old NCERT)

1. It regulates the rate of heat loss from Earth.
2. It decides the amount of rainfall in a region.
3. It leads to formation of storms in a region.

Codes

(a) 1 and 3
(b) 2 and 3
(c) 1 and 2
(d) All of these

Ans. (d)

Exp. All the given statements indicate significance of water vapour because water vapour plays a very important role in the occurrence of atmospheric and weather phenomenon on Earth. Water vapour controls the rate of Earth's temperature by preventing surface energy from entering the atmosphere.

Water vapour determines the amount of rainfall in an area. Where there is more water vapour, there is more condensation and there is more rainfall in that area. When water vapour condenses back into liquid water, it releases energy into the atmosphere that can originate storms.

61 **Consider the following statements.**

(Chap 10, Class-XI, New NCERT)

1. Weight of water vapour per unit volume of air determines absolute humidity.
2. Warm air can hold less moisture as compared to cold air.
3. Increase in temperature of atmosphere increases the relative humidity.
4. Relative humidity is greater over the continent and least over the oceans.

How many of the statements given above is/are correct?

(a) Only one (b) Only two
(c) Only three (d) None of these

***Ans.* (a)**

Exp. Only one statement i.e., (1) is correct.

The actual amount of water vapour present in the atmosphere is known as the absolute humidity. It is the weight of water vapour per unit volume of air and is expressed in terms of grams per cubic metre.

Statements (2), (3) and (4) are incorrect.

As the air gets warmer, its capacity to hold the water vapour increases and so it becomes more and more humid.

Increasing the temperature of the atmosphere decreases relative humidity. Temperature and humidity are inversely proportional. This means that as temperature increases, relative humidity decreases. Relative humidity is generally greater over oceans and least over continents. This is due to differences in heat capacity and evaporation rates. Oceans have a higher heat capacity than land, which means they can absorb and store more heat from the Sun.

62 **Consider the following statements.**

(Chap 10, Class-XI, New NCERT)

1. The relative humidity of a saturated air is 100%.
2. Water vapour starts changing into water and causes precipitation at the dew point.
3. Saturated air has potential to absorb large amounts of moisture.

Which of the statements given above are correct?

(a) 1 and 2 (b) 2 and 3
(c) 1 and 3 (d) All of these

***Ans.* (a)**

Exp. Statements (1) and (2) are correct because relative humidity is the water vapour content of the air relative t its content at saturation.

Saturated air, for example, has a relative humidity of 100%. When the relative humidity is 100%, the air becomes saturated and the water vapour turns into wate and causes precipitation at the dew point.

Statement (3) is incorrect because saturated air has potential to absorb less amounts of moisture.

63 **Which of the following statements is/are correct?**

(Chap 4, Class-VII, New NCER

1. Condensation of water vapour into precipitation requires cooling of atmosphere.
2. Condensation can occur around particles of dust, smoke and salt.
3. Increase in the value of relative humidity increases the chances of condensation and precipitation.

Codes

(a) Only 1 (b) Only 2
(c) 1 and 2 (d) 1, 2 and 3

***Ans.* (d)**

Exp. All the given statements are correct. Condensatior is caused by the loss of heat. When moist air is cooled. The transformation of water vapour into water is called condensation. It may reach a level when its capacity to hold water vapour ceases. Then, the excess water vapou condenses into liquid form.

In free air, condensation results from cooling around ver small particles termed as hygroscopic condensation nuclei. Particles of dust, smoke and salt from the ocean are particularly good nuclei because they absorb water. An increase in relative humidity to 100% increases the amount of condensation and increases the precipitation.

64 **Consider the following statements about frost formation.** *(Chap 9, Class-XI, New NCER*

1. Frost forms on cold surfaces when condensation takes place below freezing point.
2. The ideal conditions for the formation of white frost are the same as those for the formation of dew, except that the air temperature must be at c below the freezing point.

Which of the statements given above is/are correct?

(a) Only 1 (b) Only 2
(c) Both 1 and 2 (d) Neither 1 nor 2

***Ans.* (c)**

Exp. Statements (1) and (2) are correct regarding frost formation.

Frost forms on cold surfaces when condensation takes place below freezing point (0°C), i.e. the dew point is at or below the freezing point.The excess moisture is deposited in the form of minute ice crystals instead of water droplets.

The ideal conditions for the formation of white frost are the same as those for the formation of dew, except that the air temperature must be at or below the freezing point.

65 Consider the following statements.

(Chap 11, Class-XI, New NCERT)

1. Fog and mist are formed from air masses that are very close to the surface of Earth.
2. Mists occur frequently over mountain regions.
3. Fog has more moisture than mist.

Which of the statements given above is/are correct?

(a) Only 1 (b) Only 2
(c) 1 and 2 (d) 2 and 3

Ans. (c)

Exp. Statements (1) and (2) are correct because the fog and mist are a cloud with its base at or very near to the surface of the Earth. When the temperature of an airmass containing a large quantity of water vapour falls all of a sudden, condensation takes place within itself on fine dust particles.

Mists are frequent over mountains as the rising warm air up the slopes meets a cold surface.

Statement (3) is incorrect because mist has more moisture than the fog.

66 Consider the following pairs correctly.

(Chap 13, Class-XI, Old NCERT)

Forms of Condensation	Description
1. Dew	Deposition of water droplets over cooler surfaces
2. Frost	Formation of minute ice crystals
3. Advection Fog	Meeting of moist air mass and cooler surface

How many pairs given above is/are correctly matched?

(a) Only one
(b) Only two
(c) All three
(d) None of the above

Ans. (c)

Exp. All three pairs i.e., (1), (2) and (3) are correctly matched.

Dew When the moisture is deposited in the form of water droplets on cooler surfaces of solid objects such as grass blades and plant leaves, it is known as dew.

Frost When condensation takes place below freezing point 0°C, the excess moisture is deposited in the form of minute ice crystals instead of water droplets called frost.

Advection Fog formed by condensation of warm air when it moves horizontally over a cold surface, are known as advection fog. These fogs are thick. It is formed in the mixing areas of warm and cold water in the oceans.

67 Consider the following pairs.

(Chap 9, Class-XI, New NCERT)

Cloud Type		Characteristics
1. Cirrus	–	Formed at high altitudes (8,000 - 12,000m), thin and feathery, always white
2. Cumulus	–	They are generally formed at a height of 10,000 - 15,000 m.
3. Stratus	–	Formed due to heat loss or mixing of air masses
4. Nimbus	–	They form at middle levels or very near to the surface of the Earth.

How many of the pairs given above is/are correctly matched?

(a) Only one (b) Only two
(c) Only three (d) All four

Ans. (c)

Exp. Pairs (1), (3) and (4) are correctly matched.

Cirrus clouds are formed at high altitudes (8,000 - 12,000m). They are thin and detached clouds having a feathery appearance.

As their name implies, these are layered clouds covering large portions of the sky. These clouds are generally formed either due to loss of heat or the mixing of air masses with different temperatures.

Nimbus clouds are black or dark grey. They form at middle levels or very near to the surface of the Earth. These are extremely dense an opaque to the rays of the Sun. Sometimes, the clouds are so low that they seem to touch the ground.

Statement (2) is incorrectly matched because Cumulus clouds look like cotton wool. They are generally formed at a height of 4,000 - 7,000 m. They exist in patches and can be seen scattered here and there. They have a flat base.

68 Consider the following statements.

(Class-XI, Old NCERT) (UPPSC Pre 2007)

1. High clouds primarily reflect solar radiation and cool the surface of the Earth.
2. Low clouds have a high absorption of infrared radiation emanating from the Earth's surface and thus cause warming effect.

Select the correct answer by using the codes given below.

(a) Only 1 (b) Only 2
(c) Both 1 and 2 (d) Neither 1 nor 2

Ans. (d)

Exp. Neither statements (1) nor (2) are correct. High clouds primarily transmit incoming solar radiation; at the same time, they trap some of the outgoing infrared radiation emitted by the Earth and radiate it back downward, thereby warming the surface of the Earth. Low clouds primarily reflect solar radiation and cool the surface of Earth thus causing the cooling affect.

69 Identify the type of cloud from the information given below. *(Chap 11, Class-XI, New NCERT)*

These clouds are formed at 8-12 km above the Earth's surface. They are thin and have feathery appearance. They always appear white in colour.

(a) Cumulus clouds
(b) Cirrus clouds
(c) Nimbus clouds
(d) Stratus clouds

Ans. (b)

Exp. The information given in the question is about Cirrus clouds. These are short, detached and hair-like clouds found at high altitudes (8 – 12 km). They are thin and detached clouds having a feathery appearance. They are always white in colour.

70 Consider the following statements about clouds. *(Chap 9, Class-XI, New NCERT)*

1. Cirrus clouds are always black or dark grey in color.
2. Nimbus clouds are formed at high altitudes (above 12,000m) and are characterised by a feathery appearance.
3. Stratus clouds cover large portions of the sky and are generally formed due to the mixing of air masses with different temperatures.

How many of the statements given above is/are correct?

(a) Only one (b) Only two
(c) Only three (d) None of these

Ans. (a)

Exp. Only one statement i.e., (3) is correct.

Stratus clouds are layered clouds covering large portions of the sky. These clouds are generally formed either due to loss of heat or the mixing of air masses with different temperatures.

Statements (1) and (2) are incorrect.

Cirrus clouds are formed at high altitudes (8,000 - 12,000m). They are thin and detatched clouds having a feathery appearance. They are always white in colour. Nimbus clouds are black or dark grey. They form at middle levels or very near to the surface of the Earth. These are extremely dense and opaque to the rays of the Sun. Sometimes, the clouds are so low that they seem to touch the ground.

71 Which of the following pairs is correctly matched? *(Chap 13, Class-XI, Old NCERT)*

Clouds		Types
(a) Altostratus	–	Low Cloud
(b) Stratocumulus	–	Medium Cloud
(c) Cirrocumulus	–	High Cloud

(d) None of the above

Ans. (c)

Exp. Pair (c) is correctly matched as Cirrocumulus clouds are small rounded puffs that usually appear in long rows high in the sky. Cirrocumulus clouds are usually white, but sometimes appear grey.

While pairs (a) and (b) are incorrectly matched.

Altostratus clouds These clouds are middle-altitude, grey or blue-grey clouds that usually cover the whole sky. Altostratus clouds are belonging to the stratiform physical category.

Stratocumulus clouds These clouds are low-level patches of cloud varying in colour from bright white to dark grey. They have well-defined bases, with some parts often darker than others.

72 Consider the following statements about clouds. *(Chap 9, Class-XI, New NCERT)*

1. Clouds are caused mainly by the adiabatic cooling of air below its dew point.
2. Cirrus Clouds are thin and detached clouds having a feathery appearance.
3. Stratus Clouds are formed only due to loss of heat.

Which of the statements given above are correct?

(a) 1 and 2 (b) 2 and 3
(c) 1 and 3 (d) 1, 2 and 3

Ans. (a)

Exp. Statements (1) and (2) are correct.

Clouds are caused mainly by the adiabatic cooling of air below its dew point. Cloud is a mass of minute water droplets or tiny crystals of ice formed by the condensation of the water vapour in free air at considerable elevations. Cirrus clouds are formed at high altitudes (8,000 - 12,000m). They are thin and detatched clouds having a feathery appearance. They are always white in colour.

Statement (3) is incorrect.

Stratus clouds are generally formed either due to loss of heat or the mixing of air masses with different temperatures, not only due to loss of heat.

73 Consider the following statements. *(Chap 4, Class-VII, New NCERT)*

Statement-I The amount of moisture in the atmosphere is associated with latitude.

Statement-II The ability to keep the moisture in the form of water vapour is related to temperature.

Codes

(a) Both Statement-I and Statement-II are correct and Statement-II is the correct explanation for Statement-I.
(b) Both Statement-I and Statement-II are correct and Statement-II is not the correct explanation for Statement-I.
(c) Statement-I is correct, but Statement-II is incorrect.
(d) Statement-I is incorrect, but Statement-II is correct.

Ans. (a)

Exp. Both Statement-I and Statement-II are correct and Statement-II is the correct explanation for Statement-I. The amount of moisture in the atmosphere is associated with the latitude because with the change of latitude temperature of atmosphere changes and moisture holding capacity of atmosphere also changes. Moisture holding capacity of atmosphere depends sharply on the air's temperature (i.e., warmer the atmosphere is, the more moisture it can hold).

74 **Which of the following pairs are matched correctly?** *(Chap 3, Class-VII, Old NCERT)*

1. Precipitation below freezing point - Snowfall
2. Frozen raindrops and refrozen water - Sleet
3. Rounded solid pieces of ice - Hailstone

Codes

(a) 1 and 2 (b) 2 and 3
(c) 1 and 3 (d) All of these

Ans. (b)

Exp. Pairs (2) and (3) are correctly matched because sleet is frozen raindrops and refrozen melted snow-water. When a layer of air with the temperature above freezing point overlies a subfreezing layer near the ground, precipitation takes place in the form of sleet.

Hail is formed when drops of water freeze together in the cold upper regions of thunderstorm clouds. These chunks of rounded solid pieces of ice are called hailstones.

Pair (1) is incorrect because precipitation below freezing point is called sleet. It is basically frozen raindrops and occur when the layer of freezing air along the surface is thicker.

75 **Consider the following statements about convectional rainfall.** *(Chap 13, Class-XI, Old NCERT)*

1. It usually occurs due to excessive heating of surface of Earth in summer seasons.
2. It causes heavy rainfall in winters in the mid latitude regions.
3. It occurs in the polar regions in summer season.

How many of the statements given above is/are correct?

(a) Only one (b) Only two
(c) Only three (d) None of these

Ans. (a)

Exp. Only one statement i.e., (1) is correct about convectional rainfall because it usually occurs due to excessive heating of surface of Earth in summer season. The air on being heated, becomes light and rises up in convection currents. As it rises, it expands and loses heat and consequently, condensation takes place and cumulus clouds are formed.

With thunder and lightning, heavy rainfall takes place but this does not last long. Such rain is common in the summer or in the hotter part of the day. It is very common in the equatorial regions.

Statements (2) and (3) are incorrect because convectional rainfall causes heavy rainfall in winter in the Northern hemisphere regions and it occurs in the equatorial region in summer season.

76 **Consider the following statements about orographic rainfall is/are correct.** *(Chap 13 & 11, Class-XI, Old NCERT)*

1. Orographic rainfall occurs due to ascent and expansion of air against a mountain barrier.
2. Orographic rainfall occurs mainly in the winter seasons.
3. Windward slope of mountains receives more rainfall than leeward slope of mountains.

How many of the statements given above is/are correct?

(a) Only one (b) Only two
(c) Only three (d) None of these

Ans. (b)

Exp. Only two statements i.e., (1) and (3) are correct about orographic rainfall because orographic precipitation occurs due to ascent and expansion of air as it moves over a range of mountains.

As the air rises and cools, the orographic clouds form and serve as the precipitation source, where most falls upwind of the mountain ridge.

In Orographic rainfall, windward slope of mountains receive more rainfall than leeward slope of mountains.

Statement (2) is incorrect because orographic rainfall occurs mainly in the summer seasons.

77 **Consider the following pairs.** *(Chap 10, Class-XI, New NCERT)*

	Types of Rainfall		Related aspects
1.	Conventional Rainfall	–	It occurs mainly during summer and is common over equatorial doldrums in the Congo basin, and the Amazon basin.
2.	Orographic Rainfall	–	It is also known as the relief rain.
3.	Cyclonic Rainfall	–	It is formed when two masses of air of unlike density, temperature and humidity meet.
4.	Monsoonal Rainfall	–	Monsoon rainfall increases with increasing distance from the sea.

How many of the pairs given above is/are correctly matched?

(a) Only one (b) Only two (c) Only three (d) All four

Ans. (c)

Exp. Only three pairs i.e., (1), (2) and (3) are correct in the context of types of rainfall.

Convectional Rain is common in the summer or the hotter part of the day. It is very common in the equatorial regions and interior parts of the continents, particularly in the Northern hemisphere.

Orographic Rain is also known as the relief rain. When the saturated air mass comes across a mountain, it is forced to ascend and as it rises, it expands; the temperature falls, and the moisture is condensed. Cyclonic Rainfall is convectional rainfall on a large scale. The precipitation in a tropical cyclone is of convectional type while that in a temperate cyclone is because of frontal activity.

Pair (4) is incorrect because the monsoon rainfall has a declining trend with increasing distance from the sea. Rainfall received from the South-West monsoons is seasonal and occurs between June and September.

78 Which of the following zones are characterised by low amount of rainfall throughout the year?

(Chap 4, Class-IX, Old NCERT)

1. Kalahari Desert
2. Tibetan Plateau
3. Amazon Rainforest
4. Antarctica

Codes

(a) 1, 2 and 3 (b) 2, 3 and 4
(c) 1, 2 and 4 (d) 1, 2, 3 and 4

Ans. (c)

Exp. Kalahari Desert in Southern Africa, Tibetan Plateau in Tibet and Antarctica region are characterised by low amount of rainfall throughout the year.

In Kalahari desert, the potential evaporation rate is twice that of rainfall. That's why, it rains less here.

Due to the high altitude, the air on the Tibetan plateau is dry and thin, resulting in less rainfall.

Precipitation is also limited by the influence of polar high pressure in Antarctica region.

However, Amazon rainforest in South America is characterised by high amount of rainfall throughout the year.

79 Consider the following statements.

(Chap 4, Class-IX, Old NCERT)

1. Seasonal contrast of rainfall is very low in the equatorial regions.
2. Mediterranean regions receive rainfall in winter season and are drier in summer seasons.

Which of the statements given above is/are correct?

(a) Only 1 (b) Only 2
(c) Both 1 and 2 (d) None of these

Ans. (c)

Exp. Both the statements (1) and (2) are correct because the seasonal contrast of rainfall is minimal in the equatorial region because the Sun is almost vertically upward throughout the year. Due to this, the air on being heated, becomes light and rises up in convection currents.

Mediterranean regions experience wet winters and dry summer due to the shift of wind belts in these seasons. The Mediterranean region comes under the influence of Westerly winds in the winter and this region receives rainfall in the winter because of the shifting of the global pressure belts, and it rains in the winter by the Westerly winds.

World Climatic Classification

80 Consider the following Assertion (A) and Reason (R) and the correct code.

(Chap 12 & 14, Class-XI, New/Old NCERT, (UPPSC Pre 2010)

Assertion (A) The environment of the equatorial regions is conductive for plants but not for humans.

Reason (R) The average annual temperature difference is very low in equatorial regions.

Codes

(a) Both A and R are true and R is the correct explanation of A.
(b) Both A and R are true, but R is not the correct explanation of A.
(c) A is true, but R is false.
(d) A is false, but R is true.

Ans. (b)

Exp. Both Assertion (A) and Reason (R) are true, but Reason (R) is not correct explanation of Assertion (A). The climate is not conductive for humans but conductive for vegetation. The region between 5° to 10° latitude on North and South of the equator is known as equatorial region. In this region, there is constant high temperature and heavy rainfall occur throughout the year.

The average annual temperature difference is very low in this region.

81 Which of the following pair is correct?

(Chap 11, Class-XI, New NCERT)

Regions		Type of Climates
(a) California	–	Mediterranean
(b) West Australia	–	Tropical monsoon
(c) Bangladesh	–	Cold temperate
(d) Siberia	–	Hot desert

Ans. (b)

Exp. Pair (a) is correct as California has Mediterranean type of climate. Mediterranean climate has characterised by hot, dry, summers and cool.

While pairs (b), (c) and (d) are incorrectly matched because West Australia has the hot desert type of (climate) region. It has very hot summers, mild winters and low and variable rainfall.

Bangladesh has a tropical monsoon type of climate region with a hot and rainy summer and a dry winter.

Siberia has a cold temperature region in Russia with an average daily high temperature of only 5°C.

82 Consider the following statements about Koeppen's Scheme of Classification of Climate.

(Chap 11, Class-XI, New NCERT)

1. The capital letters A, C, D and E delineate humid climates, while B represents dry climates.
2. The small letters a, b, c and d in Koeppen's classification refer to the degree of severity of precipitation.

Which of the statements given above is/are correct?
(a) Only 1
(b) Only 2
(c) Both 1 and 2
(d) Neither 1 nor 2

Ans. (a)

Exp. Statement (1) is correct as the capital letters i.e., A, C, D and E delineate humid climates and B represents dry climates. In Koeppen's classification, w represents winter dry season and s represents summer dry season. The B-Dry Climates are subdivided using the capital letters S used for steppe or semi-arid and W represents for deserts.

Statement (2) is incorrect because the small letters a, b, c and d in Koeppen's classification refer to the degree of severity of temperature, not precipitation.

83 **Consider the following statements about Warm Temperate (Mid-Latitude) Climates.** *(Chap 11, Class-XI, New NCERT)*

1. Humid subtropical climate occurs poleward of Tropic of Cancer and Tropic of Capricorn, mainly in North Indian plains and South China interior plains.
2. Mediterranean climate (Cs) is characterised by hot, dry summers and mild, rainy winters and is found along the West coast of continents in subtropical latitudes.
3. In Humid Subtropical region, the air masses are generally unstable and cause rainfall throughout the year.

Which of the statements given above are correct?
(a) 1 and 2
(b) 2 and 3
(c) 1 and 3
(d) 1, 2 and 3

Ans. (d)

Exp. All three statements are correct regarding Warm Temperate (Mid-Latitude) Climates.

Humid subtropical climate occurs poleward of Tropic of Cancer and Capricorn, mainly in North Indian plains and South China interior plains. The climate is similar to Aw climate except that the temperature in winter is warm.

Mediterranean climates are temperate climates that occur in the lower mid-latitudes. Characteristic by hot, dry summers and mild, rainy winter. They are found along the West coast of continents between 30° and 45° latitude North and South of the Equator.

Humid subtropical climate lies on the Eastern parts of the continent in subtropical latitudes. In this region the air masses are generally unstable and cause rainfall throughout the year.

84 **Which of the following statements is/are correct about the Marine West Coastal Climate?** *(Chap 12, Class-XI, New NCERT)*

1. Marine Western coastal climate is located polewards of Mediterranean climate.
2. This type of climate is characterised by presence of seasonal rainfall.

Codes
(a) Only 1 (b) Only 2 (c) Both 1 and 2 (d) None of these

Ans. (a)

Exp. Statement (1) is correct about Marine West Coastal Climate as this type of climate is found polewards from the Mediterranean climate on the West coast of the continents.

The main areas are; North-Western Europe, West coast of North America, North of California, Southern Chile, South-Eastern Australia and New Zealand.

Statement (2) is incorrect because in Marine West coast climate, precipitation occurs throughout the year.

85 **Consider the following Assertion (A) and Reason (R) and choose the correct code.** *(Chap 12, Class-XI, New NCERT)*

Assertion (A) Polar tundra climate is characterised by short growing season and growth of lichens and mosses.

Reason (R) Polar tundra is the region of permafrost.

Codes
(a) Both A and R are true and R is the correct explanation of A.
(b) Both A and R are true, but R is not the correct explanation of A.
(c) A is true, but R is false.
(d) A is false, but R is true.

Ans. (a)

Exp. Both Assertion (A) and Reason (R) are true and Reason (R) is the correct explanation of Assertion (A). The polar tundra climate is so called after the types of vegetation, like low growing mosses, lichens and flowering plants. In polar tundra, the short growing season and water logging support only low growing plants.

Polar tundra is the region of permafrost, where the sub soil is permanently frozen.

86 **Match the following lists correctly and choose the correct code.** *(Chap 12, Class-XI, New NCERT)*

	List I (Koeppen's Climate Symbol)		List II (Climate)
A.	BWh	1.	Mediterranean Climate
B.	Cs	2.	Sub-tropical Desert Climate
C.	EF	3.	Tropical Monsoon Climate
D.	Am	4.	Polar Icecaps

Codes

	A	B	C	D			A	B	C	D
(a)	4	2	1	3		(b)	2	1	4	3
(c)	2	1	3	4		(d)	4	1	3	2

Ans. (b)

Exp. The correct matching is A-2, B-1, C-4, D-3.

Sub-tropical desert (**BWh**) located in the transition zone between humid and dry climates.

Mediterranean climate (**Cs**) occurs around Mediterranean sea, along the West coast of continents in sub-tropical latitudes between 30° - 40° latitudes.

The polar icecap climate (**EF**) occurs over interior Greenland and Antarctica.

Tropical monsoon climate (**Am**) is found over the Indian sub-continent, North-Eastern part of South America and Northern Australia.

87 **Match List I with List II.** ***(Chap 11, Class-XI, New NCERT)***

List I (Climate type in letter code)	List II (Characteristics)
A. Af	1. Winter dry season
B. Am	2. Dry hot summer
C. Aw	3. Monsoonal, short dry season
D. Cs	4. No dry season

Codes

	A	B	C	D
(a)	1	2	4	3
(b)	1	4	2	3
(c)	4	3	1	2
(d)	4	3	2	1

Ans. (c)

Exp. The correct matching is A-4, B-3, C-1, D-2.

Tropical wet climate (**Af**) is found near the equator. A significant amount of rainfall occurs in every month of the year as thunder showers in the afternoon.

Tropical monsoon climate (**Am**) is found over the Indian sub-continent, North Eastern part of South America and Northern Australia. Heavy rainfall occurs mostly in summer. Winter is dry.

Tropical wet and dry climate (**Aw**) occurs North and South of Af type climate regions. Temperature is high throughout the year and diurnal ranges of temperature are the greatest in the dry season.

Mediterranean climate (**Cs**) characteristics by hot, dry, summer and mild, rainy winter. It occurs around Mediterranean Sea, along the West coast of continents in subtropical latitudes between 30° - 40° latitudes e.g. — Central California, Central Chile, along the coast in South Eastern and South Western Australia. These areas come under the influence of sub tropical high in summer and westerly wind in winter.

88 **Consider the following statements.**

(Chap 11, Class-XI, New NCERT) (UPPSC Pre 2022)

Statement-I Rainfall occurs in the winter season in Mediterranean climate.

Statement-II In summer, these regions remain under the influence of dry terrestrial winds.

Codes

(a) Both Statement-I and Statement-II are correct and Statement-II is the correct explanation for Statement-I.

(b) Both Statement-I and Statement-II are correct and Statement-II is not the correct explanation for Statement-I.

(c) Statement-I is correct, but Statement-II is incorrect.

(d) Statement-I is incorrect, but Statement-II is correct.

Ans. (a)

Exp. Both Statement-I and Statement-II are correct and Statement-II is the correct explanation for Statement-I.

Rainfall does occur in the winter season in a Mediterranean climate. Mediterranean climates are characterised by mild, wet winters and hot, dry summers. The primary source of rainfall in these regions comes from cyclonic activity and frontal systems during the cooler months. In summer, these regions do experience the influence of dry terrestrial winds. During summer, Mediterranean climates are often affected by subtropical high-pressure systems, which lead to the dominance of dry and warm terrestrial winds.

89 **Consider the following Assertion (A) and Reason (R) and choose the correct code.**

(Chap 14, Class-XI, Old NCERT) (UPPSC Pre 2004)

Assertion (A) The Mediterranean regions have rainy winter.

Reason (R) During winter, they lie in the belt of the Westerlies.

Codes

(a) Both A and R are true and R is the correct explanation of A.

(b) Both A and R are true, but R is not the correct explanation of A.

(c) A is true, but R is false.

(d) A is false, but R is true.

Ans. (a)

Exp. Both Assertion (A) and Reason (R) are true and Reason (R) is the correct explanation of Assertion (A).

The Mediterranean regions have rainy winter. It is caused by seasonal reversal. During summer, as Sun is in summer solstice position, all pressure belts shift towards the North. This results in expansion of sub-tropical high pressure over this region. In the winter, when the Sun's position is in winter solstice, Westerly winds extend over this region which brings cyclones from mid-latitudes causing rain.

Chapter 6

Oceanography

Oceans, Lakes and Wetlands

Oceans

Oceans and its Profile

- There are 5 major oceans of the world namely, Pacific Ocean, Atlantic Ocean, Indian Ocean, Arctic Ocean and Southern Ocean
- Oceanic surface is denser and heavier than their continental counterpart

Relief Features of Ocean Floor

- **Continental Shelf** A margin of continent that is submerged under ocean water; Slope varies between 1° to 3° and is determined by coastal reliefs
- **Continental Slope** Formed due to erosion, tectonic movements and aggradations ; It has a steep slope beyond the continental shelf towards ocean
- **Continental Rise** A wide gentle decline from a deep ocean plain to a continental slope; Consists mainly of silt, mud and sand deposited by turbidity flows
- **Deep Sea Plains** A vast submarine region which collectively covers nearly three quarters of Earth's surface; It includes seismic ridges, abyssal hills, seamounts and guyots;
- **Ocean Trenches** Formed during the process of subduction, where denser tectonic plate slides under the lighter one; The subduction zone where trenches form long and deep valleys
- **Ocean Currents** A general movement of mass of water in a fairly defined direction over great distances. They are of two types, warm and cold

Salinity and Temperature

Salinity of Ocean

- Salinity means total content of dissolved salts in a sea or ocean
- Calculated as the amount of salt dissolved in 1000 gm of seawater
- A significant factors in deciding several characteristics of chemistry of natural waters and biological processes
- **Factors Affecting Salinity**
  - **Depth** Influenced by changes in depth along with latitudinal difference
  - **Current** Influenced by cold and warm currents
  - **Latitude** In high latitudes, salinity increases with depth; At Equator, surface salinity is lower
  - **Location of Sea** Influences the salinity
  - **Evaporation** Salinity of surface increases by evaporation and decreases by input of freshwater

Ocean Density

- A measure of how tightly a certain amount of matter is packed into a given volume
- Seawater is denser than pure water; Higher the salinity, higher the density
- Seawater density varies from place to place because it is affected by salinity and temperature
- **Effects of Density Changes** Dense water sinks below less dense water, thus drives the circulation of deep ocean currents around the world

Ocean Temperature

- A measure of the energy due to the motion of molecules in the ocean; It is important for marine organisms and also affects the climate of coastal lands

Tides, Lakes and Wetlands

Ocean Tides

- Periodical rise and fall of sea level , once or twice a day, mainly due to the gravitational attraction of Sun and Moon on the oceans of the Earth
- Surges are non-regular and non-periodic movement of water caused by meteorological effects

Lakes

- An inland body of water, not a part of ocean that is larger and deeper than a pond and is localised at the bottom of the basin on two basis
- Classified on two basis, namely
  - **On the basis of geography** Consists of polar lakes and lakes in temperate regions
  - **On the basis of Temperature Cycles** Consists of amictic lakes, cold monomictic lakes, dimictic lakes, warm monomictic lakes, etc

Wetlands

- A place where the land is covered by water, either salt, fresh or somewhere in between
- **Types of Wetlands**
  - **Marshes** That are always inundated rather than being submerged under water. They can be freshwater or saltwater
  - **Swamps** Differ from marshes as they are dominated by woody plants rather than soft-stemmed plants. They are of two types, forested and shrub
  - **Bogs** Characterised by more acidic waters and spongy peaty deposits. They tend to get their wetness from precipitation rather than waterways
  - **Fens** Usually get their wetness from groundwater rather than precipitation so they are slightly less acidic

SOURCE **New NCERT Class VII** *(Water)*, **Old NCERT Class VII** *(Ocean Waters and Their Circulation)*, **Old NCERT Class IX** *(Realms of Water)*, **New NCERT Class XI** *(Oceans)*, **New NCERT Class XI** *(Movements of Ocean Water)*, **Old NCERT Class XI** *(The Profile of the Ocean Floor)*, **Old NCERT Class XI** *(Ocean Waters and Their Circulation)*, **Old NCERT Class XI** *(Marine Life and Deposits)* **Tamil Nadu Board Class XI** *(Hydrosphere)*

Distribution of Water on the Earth

1 With reference to the water on the planet Earth, consider the following statements. *(Chap 5, Class-XI, New NCERT) (IAS Pre 2011)*

1. The amount of water in the rivers and lakes is more than the amount of groundwater.
2. The amount of water in polar ice caps and glaciers is more than the amount of groundwater.

Which of the statements given above is/are correct?

(a) Only 1
(b) Only 2
(c) Both 1 and 2
(d) Neither 1 nor 2

Ans. (b)

Exp. Statement (2) is correct with respect to water on Earth.

The total freshwater, 69% resides in glaciers and 30% underground. Polar ice caps and glaciers has more water than groundwater.

Statement (1) is incorrect because the total freshwater, 69% resides in glaciers, 30% underground, and less than 1% is located in lakes, rivers and swamps. Thus, the amount of water in rivers and lakes is less than amount of groundwater.

2 Arrange the following sources of water on the Earth in increasing order and choose the correct answer using the codes given below. *(Chap 5, Class-VII, New NCERT)*

1. Freshwater lakes 2. Atmosphere
3. Rivers 4. Groundwater

Codes

(a) 1, 2, 4, 3 (b) 3, 2, 4, 1
(c) 3, 2, 1, 4 (d) 1, 4, 3, 2

Ans. (c)

Exp. The correct sequence of sources of water on the Earth in increasing order is rivers, atmosphere, freshwater lakes and groundwater.

Three-fourths of the Earth's surface is covered with water, but the distribution of water on the Earth is not uniform. Most of the water on the Earth is found in the groundwater, which accounts to about 0.68% and about 0.009% water is found in freshwater lakes and about 0.0019% water is found in the atmosphere.

The lowest amount of water is found in rivers, which is about 0.0001%.

3 Consider the following statements about water sources on Earth. *(Chap 3, Class-XI, Old NCERT)*

1. Oceanic water is primarily circulated in the water cycle through the process of evaporation.
2. Groundwater remains largely unaffected by the process of evaporation.
3. The majority of surface water on Earth is stored in ice caps and glaciers.

How many of the statements given above is/are correct?

(a) Only 1 (b) Only 2
(c) All three (d) None of these

Ans. (c)

Exp. All the three statements i.e., (1), (2) and (3) are correct as in marine areas where evaporation is high, the water level decreases. Due to this, the oceanic current flows from high water level to low water level.

Evaporation decreases rapidly with depth of groundwater. That's why groundwater is not affected by the process of evaporation. More than 68% of the freshwater on the Earth is found in glaciers and only over 30% is found in groundwater. Only about 0.3% of our freshwater is found in the surface waters of lakes, rivers and marshes.

4 Consider the following statements about the water cycle. *(Chap 3, Class-IX, Old NCERT)*

1. The water cycle over oceans is shorter compared to that over land.
2. The total amount of water on Earth remains constant.
3. Evaporation of water over oceans is balanced by surface runoff.

How many of the statements given above is/are incorrect?

(a) Only one (b) Only two
(c) All three (d) None of these

Ans. (a)

Exp. Only one statement i.e., (1) is incorrect because the water cycle is longer over ocean than over the land, because it takes longer time for evaporation and precipitation to occur on ocean, whereas in the land, precipitation and evaporation occur at a faster rate.

5 Consider the following statements about the continental shelf. *(Chap 13, Class-IX, New NCERT)*

1. It has an average gradient of 1° or less.
2. It is the shallowest part of the ocean, characterised by shallow seas and gulfs.
3. The depth and width of the continental shelf remain constant across all oceans.

How many of the statements given above is/are correct?

(a) Only one (b) Only two
(c) All three (d) None of these

Ans. (b)

Exp. Only two statements i.e. (1) and (2) are correct regarding the continental shelf. The continental shelf is a gently sloping oceanic extension of the continental plate. The continental shelf of all the oceans together covers 7.5% of the total area of the oceans. The continental slope is 1° or less. The shelf usually ends at a very steep slope, which is called a shelf break. These extended margins of each continent are occupied by relatively shallow seas and gulfs.

Statement (3) is incorrect because the depth and width of continental shelf is not constant over the entire ocean. The depth and width of the continental shelf is influenced by terrestrial relief. Where there are high mountains, the depth of the continental shelf is more and less in width.

6 Consider the following Assertion (A) and Reason (R) and choose the correct code. *(Chap 13, Class-XI, New NCERT)*

Assertion (A) Fossil fuels are obtained from the continental shelves.

Reason (R) Sedimentary deposits over the continental shelf is deposited by rivers, glaciers and winds.

Codes

(a) Both A and R are true and R is the correct explanation of A.
(b) Both A and R are true, but R is not the correct explanation of A.
(c) A is true, but R is false.
(d) A is false, but R is true.

Ans. (a)

Exp. Both Assertion (A) and Reason (R) are true and Reason (R) is the correct explanation of Assertion (A). The continental shelves are covered by terrigenous sediments. Continental shelves are covered with variable thickness of sediment brought down by rivers, glaciers and winds, etc.

Massive sedimentary deposits received over a long time by the continental shelves, become the source of fossil fuels such as petroleum, coal, etc.

7 Which of the following statements is correct? *(Chap 13, Class-XI, New NCERT)*

1. Continental slopes are steeper than continental shelves.
2. Canyons are trenches that can be observed in the continental slopes.
3. Deep sea plains have low gradient than continental slopes.

Codes

(a) 1 and 2 (b) Only 2 (c) 1 and 3 (d) All of these

Ans. (d)

Exp. All the three statements i.e., (1), (2) and (3) are correct. Floor or the bottom of the sea can be divided into major divisions i.e., (i) Continental shelf, (ii) Continental slope, (iii) Deep sea plain, (iv) Ocean depths.

The Continental slope connects the continental shelf and oceanic basins where it starts the lower part of the continental shelf rapidly collapses locked in a steep slope.

The Continental slope is much steeper than that of the shelf. The angle of the continental slope is 5° while the angle of the shelf is less than 1°. Due to tectonic and wave erosion on the continental slope, continental canyons and trenches are formed.

Deep sea plains are areas of slow slope ocean basins. Their slope is less than continental slope. These are the flattest and smoothest areas in the world.

8 With reference to oceanic relief, consider the following statements. *(Chap 13, Class-XI, New NCERT)*

1. Oceanic trenches are located at the base of continental slope.
2. Deep earthquakes and volcanoes occur in the Oceanic trenches.
3. Largest number of trenches are found in the Atlantic Ocean.

Which of the statements given above is/are correct?

(a) Only 1
(b) 2 and 3
(c) 1 and 2
(d) All of the above

Ans. (c)

Exp. Statements (1) and (2) are correct with reference to oceanic relief.

Oceanic trenches areas are the deepest parts of the oceans. The trenches are relatively steep sided in narrow basins. They occur at the bases of continental slopes along island arcs.

Deep earthquakes and volcanoes occur due to the energy generated by the convergence of continental plates and oceanic plates on oceanic trenches.

Statement (3) is incorrect because largest number of trenches are found in Pacific Ocean not in Atlantic Ocean.

9 Consider the following statements about the relief features found over the oceanic surface. *(Chap 13, Class-XI, New NCERT)*

1. Mid oceanic ridges can be rise even above the oceanic surface.
2. Sea mounts are features of volcanic origin, which do not rise above the oceanic surface.

Which of the statements given above is/are correct?

(a) Only 1
(b) Only 2
(c) Both 1 and 2
(d) Neither 1 nor 2

Ans. (c)

Exp. Both the statements (1) and (2) are correct about the relief features found over the oceanic surface.

A mid ocean ridge is a seafloor mountain system which is formed by plate tectonics. A mid oceanic ridge is composed of two chains of mountains separated by a large depression. The mountain ranges can have peaks as high as 3000 m and some even reach above the ocean's surface.

A sea mount is a large geologic landform that rises from the ocean floor but that does not reach to the water's surface. Sea mounts are typically formed from extinct volcanoes that rise abruptly and are usually found rising from the seafloor to 1,000-4,000 m in height.

10 Which of the following statements is correct about the Atlantic Ocean? *(Chap 15, Class-XI, Old NCERT)*

1. The floor of Atlantic has more trenches than the Pacific Ocean.
2. The longest mid-oceanic ridge is found in the Atlantic Ocean.
3. The size of Atlantic Ocean is about 1/3rd of the Pacific Ocean.

Codes

(a) 1 and 2 (b) 2 and 3 (c) Only 2 (d) All of these

Ans. (c)

Exp. Statement (2) is correct about the Atlantic Ocean. The Mid-Atlantic Ridge is a mid-ocean ridge (an isolated or compositional plate boundary) located along the floor of the Atlantic Ocean. It is the longest mid-oceanic ridge in the ocean. Its length is about 14,400 km.

Statements (1) and (3) are incorrect because the floor of Pacific Ocean has more trenches than the Atlantic Ocean. Also, the size of Atlantic Ocean is about half of the Pacific Ocean.

11 Consider the following statements about the Indian Ocean. *(Chap 15, Class -XI, Old NCERT)*

1. The Indian Ocean connects to the Arctic Ocean in the North.
2. The Indian Ocean floor is smoother and more regular compared to the Pacific Ocean.
3. The Lakshadweep Chagos Ridge divides the Indian Ocean into two distinct basins.

How many of the statements given above is/are incorrect?

(a) Only one (b) Only two (c) All three (d) None of these

Ans. (a)

Exp. Only one statement i.e., (1) is incorrect regarding the Indian Ocean, because it is bounded by Asia to the North, Africa to the West and Australia to the East. To the South, it is bounded by the Southern Ocean or Antarctica. The Indian Ocean is the third-largest of the world's oceanic divisions, covering 19.8% of the water on Earth's surface.

12 Consider the following statements about the Indian Ocean. *(Chap 15, Class-XI, Old NCERT)*

1. Most of the Indian Ocean's islands are concentrated in the Eastern parts.
2. The Central Indian ridge, a major underwater mountain range, is subdivided into several smaller ridges.
3. The Madagascar Ridge splits the Arabian Sea into two distinct halves.

How many of the statements given above is/are correct?

(a) Only one (b) Only two
(c) All three (d) None of these

Ans. (a)

Exp. Only one statement i.e., (2) is correct regarding the Indian Ocean, the Central ridge of the Indian Ocean is divided into several smaller ridges.

The ridge to the South of Peninsular India is called the Lakshadweep ridge. The ridge between 30° latitudes from the Equator is called the St. Paul Ridge; to the South is the Amsterdam Ridge.

Statements (1) and (3) are incorrect because most of the islands of the ocean are located in the Western parts and the Madagascar ridge does not divide its Arabian Sea int two parts.

13 Consider the following pairs. *(Chap 15, Class-XI, Old NCERT)*

Trenches		Located in
1. Mindanao Trench	–	Atlantic Ocean
2. Sunda Trench	–	Pacific Ocean
3. Romanche Trench	–	Indian Ocean

Which of the pairs given above is correctly matched.

(a) Only 1
(b) Only 3
(c) Only 2
(d) None of the above

Ans. (d)

Exp. None of the given pair is correct.

Mindanao Trench (Philippine Trench) It is a submarine trench in the East of the Philippines. The trench is located in the Philippine Sea of the Western-North Pacific Ocean.

Sunda Trench It is formerly known as the Java Trench, is an oceanic trench located in the Indian Ocean near Sumatra.

Romanche Trench It is the third deepest trench in the Atlantic Ocean after the Puerto Rico Trench and the South Sandwich Trench.

Temperature and Salinity of Oceans

14 Consider the following statements. *(Chap 5, Class-XI, NCERT) (IAS Pre 202*

Statement-I The temperature contrast between continents and oceans is greater during summer than in winter.

Statement-II The specific heat of water is more than that of land surface.

Which one of the following is correct in respect of th above statements?

(a) Both Statement-I and Statement-II are correct and Satement-II is the correct explanation for Statement-I.
(b) Both Statement-I and Statement-II are correct and Statement-I is not the correct explanation for Statement-I.
(c) Statement-I is correct, but Statement-II is incorrect.
(d) Statement-I is incorrect, but Statement-II is correct.

Ans. (d)

Exp. Statement-I is incorrect, but Statement-II is correct.

The temperature contrast between the continents and oceans is more during summer rather than winter.

However, specific heat is the amount of heat energy required to raise the temperature of a substance by a certain amount. Water has a relatively high specific heat compared to land surfaces. This means that it takes a larger amount of heat energy to raise the temperature of water compared to an equal mass of land surface material by the same amount. The high specific heat of water is due to its molecular structure and the presence of hydrogen bonding, which allows water to absorb and store a significant amount of heat energy.

15 **Consider the following statements about the thermocline.** *(Chap 15, Class-XI, Old NCERT)*

1. It is the boundary where oceanic waters completely freeze.
2. It is the boundary where there is a rapid decrease in ocean temperature.
3. It is the boundary where the temperature of oceanic water increases.
4. It is the boundary where oceanic water becomes denser.

How many of the statements given above is/are correct?

(a) Only one (b) Only two
(c) Only three (d) None of these

Ans. (b)

Exp. Only two statements i.e., (2) and (4) are correct as a thermocline is the transition layer between warmer mixed water at the ocean's surface and cooler deep water below it. This second layer lies below the first layer and is characterised by rapid decrease in temperature with increasing depth. The thermocline is 500-1000 m thick. The thermocline separates the less dense warmer water at the surface from the denser cooler water below.

Statements (1) and (3) are incorrect because, the thermocline is not where oceanic waters freeze. It is a transition layer between the warmer mixed water at the surface and the cooler deep water below.

It is the boundary where the temperature of oceanic water increases. In the thermocline, the temperature decreases rapidly from the mixed layer temperature to the much colder deep water temperature.

16 **Consider the following statements.** *(Chap 13, Class-XI, New NCERT)*

1. Heat is distributed in oceans from the surface to the bottom layers through the process of conduction.
2. The temperature-depth profile for the ocean water shows how the temperature decreases with the increasing depth.
3. The Antarctic region is characterised by only one layer of uniform temperature from surface to the bottom.

Which of the statements given above is/are correct?

(a) 1 and 2 (b) 1 and 3
(c) 2 and 3 (d) Only 3

Ans. (c)

Exp. Statements (2) and (3) are correct as the temperature-depth profile for the ocean water shows how the temperature decreases with the increasing depth. In the Arctic and Antarctic circles, the surface water temperatures are close to 10° C and so the temperature change with the depth is very slight. Here, only one layer of cold water exists, which extends from surface to deep ocean floor.

Statement (1) is not correct because heat is distributed in oceans from the surface to the bottom layers through the process of convection.

17 **Consider the following statements about the salinity of oceans.** *(Chap 15, Class- XI, Old NCERT)*

1. Open seas generally have higher salinity than inland seas.
2. There is no seasonal fluctuation in salinity in the Arctic region.
3. Salinity in coastal regions is typically very similar to salinity in open oceans.

How many of the statements given above is/are correct?

(a) Only one (b) Only two
(c) All three (d) None of these

Ans. (a)

Exp. Only one statement i.e., (2) is correct about salinity of oceans because in the Arctic region, the salinity is low in the summer due to the melting of snow and the arrival of river water also reduces the salinity in summer. But in winter, due to the freezing of show, the salinity increases slightly in hot and dry regions, where evaporation is high, the salinity sometimes reaches to 70%.

Statements (1) and (3) are incorrect because ocean salinity in inland seas is higher than in open ocean. Salinity in coastal areas is same as salinity in oceans. Sometimes, it is more than oceans while sometimes it is less.

18 **Which of the following factors will change the salinity of a water body?** *(Chap 13, Class-XI, New NCERT)*

1. Freshwater inflow
2. Increase in temperature
3. Decline in density
4. Wind movement

Codes

(a) 1, 2 and 3 (b) 1, 2 and 4
(c) 2, 3 and 4 (d) 1, 2, 3 and 4

Ans. (d)

Exp. All the given factors, freshwater inflow, increase in temperature, decline in density and wind movement have the property to change the salinity of water body.

Salinity is the term used to define the total content of dissolved salts in sea water. Factors affecting ocean salinity are, the salinity of water in the surface layer of oceans depend mainly on evaporation and precipitation. Surface salinity is greatly influenced in coastal regions by the freshwater flow from rivers, and in Polar regions by the processes of freezing and thawing of ice.

Wind, also influences salinity of an area by transferring water to other areas. The ocean currents contribute to the salinity variations. Salinity, temperature and density of water are interrelated. Hence, any change in the temperature or density influences the salinity of an area.

19 Arrange the salts given below in increasing order of their percentage composition in the sea water. *(Chap 16, Class-XI, Old NCERT) (UPPSC Pre 2000)*

1. Sodium chloride
2. Magnesium chloride
3. Magnesium sulphate
4. Calcium sulphate

Codes

(a) 1, 2, 4, 3 (b) 2, 3, 4, 1
(c) 1, 2, 3, 4 (d) 4, 3, 2, 1

Ans. (d)

Exp. The correct increasing order of salts according to percentage composition is Calcium sulphate (3.6%), Magnesium sulphate (4.7%), Magnesium chloride (10.9%) and Sodium chloride (77.7%). Salinity means the total amount of dissolved salts in the ocean. Salinity is calculated as the amount of salt dissolved in 1,000 grams of seawater.

20 Consider the following Assertion (A) and Reason (R) and choose the correct code. *(Chap 13, Class-XI, New NCERT)*

Assertion (A) The layer at which salinity of ocean records a sharp decline is known as Halocline.

Reason (R) The salinity of layer in deep oceans do not change much as compared to salinity at the surface.

Codes

(a) Both A and R are true and R is the correct explanation of A.
(b) Both A and R are true, but R is not the correct explanation of A.
(c) A is true, but R is false.
(d) A is false, but R is true.

Ans. (b)

Exp. Both Assertion (A) and Reason (R) are true, but Reason (R) is not the correct explanation of Assertion (A). Halocline is a vertical zone in the oceanic water column in which salinity changes rapidly with depth. It located below the well mixed, uniformly saline surface water layer. Salinity at the surface increases by the loss of water to ice or evaporation, or decreased by the input of fresh waters, such as from the rivers.

Salinity at depth is very much fixed because there is no way that water is lost, or the salt is added.

21 Which of the following factors is/are responsible for maintaining low salinity in equatorial regions than the Polar areas? *(Chap 16, Class-XI, Old NCERT)*

1. Calm winds at the equator
2. Clouds and convective rainfall throughout the year
3. Lesser sunshine and lesser precipitation in polar regions

Codes

(a) 1 and 2 (b) 1 and 3
(c) Only 3 (d) All of these

Ans. (d)

Exp. All the three statements (1), (2) and (3) are correct because the amount of salinity at the equator is found to be 34% and in the Northern and Southern hemispheres, the salinity ranges from about 32 % to 34%.

In the equatorial regions, the salinity is low due to calm winds and the availability of pure water due to cloud and convective rainfall throughout the year reduces the amount of salinity.

Also in the polar regions, the salinity is low due to less sunlight, less rainfall and melting of snow.

Oceanic Movements : Waves, Tides, Currents

22 Consider the following statements. *(Chap 14, Class- XI, New NCERT) (IAS Pre 2021)*

1. In the tropical zone, the Western sections of the oceans are warmer than the Eastern sections owing to the influence of trade winds.
2. In the temperate zone, Westerlies make the Eastern sections of oceans warmer than the Western sections.

Which of the statements given above is/are correct?

(a) Only 1 (b) Only 2
(c) Both 1 and 2 d) Neither 1 nor 2

Ans. (c)

Exp. Both statements (1) and (2) are correct. The North-East trade winds blow from the North-East to the South-West in the Northern hemisphere of the tropical zone. These winds push the surface water of the ocean towards the West, creating a warmer water layer on the Western side of the ocean basin. The tropical zone is the region of Earth between the Tropic of Cancer and the Tropic of Capricorn, where the Sun is directly overhead at least once a year.

The Westerlies are winds that blow from the West to the East in the middle latitudes, between 30 and 60 degrees latitude. They steer the Warm, equatorial water and air currents towards the Eastern coasts of continents, making the Eastern side of the ocean basin warmer than the Western side. The Westerlies are stronger and more consistent in the Southern hemisphere, where there is less land to disrupt their flow.

23 **With reference to Ocean Mean Temperature (OMT), which of the following statements is/are correct?** *(Chap 13, Class-XI, New NCERT) (IAS Pre 2020)*

1. OMT is measured up to a depth of 26°C isotherm which is 129 meters in the South-Western Indian Ocean during January-March.
2. OMT collected during January-March can be used in assessing whether the amount of rainfall in monsoon will be less or more than a certain long-term mean.

Select the correct answer using the codes given below.

(a) Only 1 (b) Only 2
(c) Both 1 and 2 (d) Neither 1 nor 2

Ans. (b)

Exp. Only statement (2) is correct as OMT data can be employed to predict variations in monsoon rainfall. Indeed, ocean temperatures have a substantial impact on climate and weather patterns, including monsoons. Thus, OMT measurements, along with other factors, could potentially be used to determine whether monsoon rainfall will deviate from the long-term average.

Statement (1) is incorrect because the depth of the 26°C isotherm can fluctuate significantly depending on the region and time, and it's not always 129 meters deep in the specified area.

24 **Consider the following pairs.** *(Chap 16, Class-XI, Old NCERT)*

	Type of Sea Waves		Descriptions
1.	Catastrophic Wave	–	Waves caused due to difference in density of layers of water
2.	Storm Wave	–	Sudden waves caused due to tectonic movements
3.	Seiche	–	Waves with not much movement, stationary waves

How many pairs given above is/are correctly matched?

(a) Only one (b) Only two (c) All three (d) None of these

Ans. (a)

Exp. Only one pair i.e., (3) is correct.

Seiche is a standing or stationary wave in an enclosed body of water. Seiche related phenomena have been observed on lakes, reservoirs, bays, harbours and seas.

While pairs (1) and (2) are incorrectly matched Catastrophic sea wave is a sudden wave usually caused by a submarine earthquake, an underwater or coastal landslide, or a volcanic eruption.

Storm wave is primarily caused by strong winds in a hurricane or tropical storm. The high winds associated with tropical and extra tropical storms can cause extreme waves and storm surges. Waves and storm surges are responsible for severe flooding and property damage.

25 **Tides occur in oceans and seas due to which of the following?** *(Chap 14, Class- XI, NCERT) (IAS Pre 2015)*

1. Gravitational force of the Sun
2. Gravitational force of the Moon
3. Gravitational force of the Earth

Codes

(a) Only 1 (b) 2 and 3
(c) 1 and 3 (d) 1, 2 and 3

Ans. (d)

Exp. All the given factors i.e. the gravitational forces of the Sun, the Moon and the Earth can play a role in the occurrence of tides.

Tides in oceans and seas are primarily caused by the gravitational forces of the Moon and the Sun and the rotation of the Earth. The Moon's gravitational pull is the major contributor to the tides because it is much closer to the Earth than the Sun. The Sun also exerts a gravitational force on the Earth, contributing to the tides. The Earth's rotation creates a centrifugal force that interacts with the gravitational pulls of the Moon and the Sun to create high and low tides.

26 **The annual range of temperature in the interior of the continents is high as compared to coastal areas. What is/are the reason/ reasons?** *(Chap 9, Class-XI , Old NCERT)*

1. Thermal difference between land and water.
2. Variation in altitude between continents and oceans.
3. Presence of strong winds in the interior.
4. Heavy rains in the interior as compared to coasts.

Select the correct answer using the codes given below.

(a) Only 1 (b) 1 and 2
(c) 2 and 3 (d) All of these

Ans. (a)

Exp. Only statement (1) is correct.

The primary reason for the high annual range of temperature in the interior of the continents compared to coastal areas is the thermal difference between land and water. Land heats and cools more quickly than water, leading to a larger temperature difference between day and night and between summer and winter. This phenomenon is known as the continental effect.

The other options listed—variation in altitude between continents and oceans, presence of strong winds in the interior, and heavy rains in the interior as compared to coasts-do not significantly contribute to the high annual range of temperature in the interior of continents.

27 **Consider the following benefits of occurrence of tides.** *(Chap 5, Class-VII, Old NCERT)*

1. Tides makes navigation of large ships easier.
2. Fishing becomes easier with the occurrence of tides.
3. Tides help in bringing rainfall in dry regions.

Which of the statements given above is/are correct?

(a) 1 and 3 (b) 1 and 2
(c) Only 2 (d) Only 3

Ans. (b)

Exp. Benefits of occurrence of tides mentioned in statements (1) and (2) are correct because tidal heights are very important, especially harbours near rivers and within estuaries having shallow at the entrance, which prevent ships and boats from entering into the harbour. High tides help in navigation.

They raise the water level close to the shores. This helps the ships to arrive at the harbour more easily.

Tides generally help in making some of the rivers navigable for ocean-going vessels.

The high tides also help in fishing. Many more fish come closer to the shore during the high tide. This enables fishermen to get a plentiful catch.

While tide cannot help in bringing rainfall in dry regions.

28 **Which among the following statements about tide is/are correct?** *(Chap 5, Class-VII, New NCERT)* *(UPPSC Pre 1999)*

1. The highest tides are known as Spring tides.
2. The lowest tides are known as Neap tides.
3. Spring tides occur when Moon is in first quarter.

Codes

(a) 1 and 3 (b) 2 and 3 (c) 1 and 2 (d) All of these

Ans. (c)

Exp. Statements (1) and (2) are correct because the positions of both the Sun and the Moon with respect to the Earth have a direct effect on the height of the tides. When the Sun, Moon and Earth are in a straight line, the height of the tide is high. These types of tides are also called Spring tides or High tides. They occur twice a month, one during the full Moon period and the other during the new Moon.

There is a gap of seven days between Spring tide and Neap tide. At this time, the Sun and the Moon are at right angles to each other and the forces of the Sun and the Moon oppose each other. The attraction of the Moon is less than the repulsive force of the Sun's gravitational pull like spring tides; these tides also come twice a month.

Statement (3) is incorrect because Spring tide occurs when the Moon is either new or full and closest to Earth.

29 **Which of the following statements is true about the neap and spring tides?** *(Chap 14, Class-XI, New NCERT)*

1. There are usually two spring tides in a month.
2. There is a gap of 21 days between a spring tide and a neap tide.

Codes

(a) Only 1 (b) Only 2
(c) Both 1 and 2 (d) None of these

Ans. (a)

Exp. Statement (1) is correct about spring tides because spring tides occur twice a month, one during the full Moon period and the other during the new Moon. Spring tides are the highest tides, they are formed when the Earth, Sun and Moon are lined up in a row.

Statement (2) is incorrect because there is a gap of 7 days between a spring tide and a neap tide.

30 **Consider the following Assertion (A) and Reason (R) and choose the correct code.** *(Chap 16, Class-XI, Old NCERT)*

Assertion (A) The height of tide varies at different places on Earth.

Reason (R) The position of Earth continuously changes with respect to Moon and Sun.

Codes

(a) Both A and R are true and R is the correct explanation of A.
(b) Both A and R are true, but R is not the correct explanation of A.
(c) A is true, but R is false.
(d) A is false, but R is true.

Ans. (a)

Exp. Both Assertion (A) and Reason (R) is true and Reason (R) is the correct explanation of Assertion (A). The periodical rise and fall of the sea level, once or twice a day, is called a periodic tide.

Coastal tidal range vary globally and can vary anywhere from zero to more than 16 metres. Tides also differ in height on a daily basis because of coastal topography.

The daily differences between tidal heights due to the gravitational pull of the Moon and the Sun on the ocean water and the position of Earth that continuously changes with respect to Moon and Sun.

31 **Consider the following statements about the occurrence of tides on Earth.** *(Chap 14, Class-XI, NCERT)*

1. Tidal height and depth are identical in all water bodies on Earth.
2. Tides are primarily caused by the gravitational pull of the Sun.
3. The highest tides occur when the Moon is in its first quarter phase.
4. Tides happen at consistent intervals.

How many of the statements given above is/are correct?

(a) Only one
(b) Only two
(c) Only three
(d) All four

Ans. (a)

Exp. Only one statement i.e., (4) is correct about the occurrence of tides because the Earth rotates through two tidal bulges on each lunar day, coastal areas experience two high and two low tides every 24 hours and 50 minutes.

High tides occur at intervals of 12 hours 25 minutes. Statements (1), (2) and (3) are incorrect because tidal depth and height is different in all water bodies on Earth. Tides are mainly caused due to Sun and Moon's attraction and are greatest when Moon is either new or full and closest to Earth.

32 Consider the following statements about tides.
(Chap 16, Class-XI, Old NCERT)

1. On the side of Earth facing the Moon, tides are caused due to Moon's attraction.
2. On the side of the Earth which is away from the Moon, tides are caused by Sun's attraction.
3. Force of attraction of Moon is much greater than force of attraction of Sun.

Which of the statements given above are correct?

(a) 1 and 2 (b) 1 and 3 (c) 2 and 3 (d) All of these

Ans. (b)

Exp. Statements (1) and (3) are correct because the closest part of the Earth in front of the Moon is most affected by the Moon's attraction, which is responsible for causing tides.

Even though the Sun is much more massive and therefore has a stronger gravity than the Moon, the Moon is closer to the Earth so the Moon's gravitational gradient is stronger than that of the Sun.

Statement (2) is incorrect because Sun has lower attraction power than Moon in context of Earth.

Sun's tide generating force is about half of the Moon because Sun is 390 times further from the Earth than is the Moon.

33 Consider the following statements about tidal bores.
(Chap 14 Class- XI, NCERT)

1. They are rises in water level in an estuary caused by seismic activity.
2. They are walls of water rushing upstream in an estuary.
3. They are the inward and outward movements of water in a gulf.
4. They are the tides with the highest altitude in a water body.

Which of the statements given above is/are correct?

(a) Only 1 (b) Only 2
(c) Only 3 (d) All of these

Ans. (b)

Exp. Only statement (2) correctly defines a tidal bore because tidal bores are walls of water rushing upstream in an estuary. A tidal bore occurs along a coast where a river empties into the sea. A tidal bore is a strong tide that pushes the river upstream. It has a narrow outlet to the sea. However, the estuary, or the place where the river meets the sea, must be wide and flat.

34 The occurrence of tides forms tidal currents in gulfs. Which among the following conditions must be fulfilled for the occurrence of tidal currents in a gulf? *(Chap 16, Class-XI, Old NCERT)*

1. The gulf must have steep slope.
2. The gulf must have shallow water.
3. The gulf must be connected to the sea by a narrow channel.

Codes

(a) 1 and 2 (b) Only 2
(c) Only 3 (d) 2 and 3

Ans. (c)

Exp. Statement (3) must be fulfilled for the occurrence of tidal currents in a gulf. When a gulf is connected with the open sea by a narrow channel, water flows into the gulf at the time of high tide and comes out of the gulf at low tide.

Statements (1) and (2) are incorrect because there is no need for slope in the gulf for the tides to arise and it is not necessary to have shallow water in the gulf.

35 Consider the following statements about tidal bulge.
(Chap 14, Class-XI, Old NCERT)

1. Centrifugal force and gravitational force work together to create tidal bulges.
2. On Earth's surface, horizontal tide generating forces are more prominent than vertical forces.
3. On wide continental bulges, tidal bulges are low in height.

Which of the statements given above are correct?

(a) 1 and 2 (b) 1 and 3
(c) 2 and 3 (d) None of these

Ans. (a)

Exp. Statements (1) and (2) are correct about tidal bulge because the part of the Earth that is closest to the Moon produces tidal waves due to the force of gravity. The other side of the Earth, which is farthest from the Moon, is generated by the centrifugal force. This is due to the origin of the tidal bulge. On the surface of the Earth, the horizontal tide generating forces are more important than the vertical forces in generating the tidal bulges.

Statement (3) is incorrect because the tidal bulges on wide continental shelves have greater height. When tidal bulges hit the mid-oceanic islands they become low.

36 Consider the following pairs.
(Chap 14, Class-XI, New NCERT)

	Type of Tide		Description
1.	Diurnal Tide	–	Variations in height
2.	Semidiurnal Tide	–	One high tide, one low tide
3.	Mixed Tide	–	Sun, Moon and Earth are at right angles
4.	Neap Tide	–	Two high tides, two low tides

How many pairs given above is/are incorrectly matched?

(a) Only one (b) Only two
(c) Only three (d) All four

Ans. (d)

Exp. All the pairs given above are incorrectly matched. A diurnal tidal cycle is a cycle with only one high and low tide each lunar day. Diurnal tidal cycles can be found in the Gulf of Mexico.

A semidiurnal tidal cycle is a cycle with two nearly equal high tides and two low tides every lunar day. They have a period of 12 hours and 25 min, and a wavelength of more than half the circumference of Earth.

Tides having variations in height are known as mixed tides. These tides generally occur along the West coast of North America and along the coasts of many islands of the Pacific Ocean.

There is a gap of seven days between spring tide and Neap Tide. At this time, the Sun, Earth and the Moon are at right angles to each other and the powers of the Sun and the Moon act opposite to each other.

37 Consider the following Assertion (A) and Reason (R) and choose the correct code.

(Chap 14, Class-XI, New NCERT) (IAS Pre 1998)

Assertion (A) During the times of neap tide, high tide is below normal and low tide is above normal.

Reason (R) Neap tides occur during the new moon instead of full Moon.

Codes

(a) Both A and R are true and R is the correct explanation of A.
(b) Both A and R are true, but R is not the correct explanation of A.
(c) A is true, but R is false.
(d) A is false, but R is true.

Ans. (c)

Exp. Assertion (A) is true, but Reason (R) is false. During the neap tides, high tide remains to be 20% less than the normal and low tide at this time remains to be higher than the normal.

Neap tide opposite to the spring-tide does not occur at new Moon or full Moon but on 7th or 8th days from these two extremes.

38 Consider the following statements.

(Chap 14, Class-XI, New NCERT)

1. When Moon is at the Perigee, there is unusually low and high tides.
2. When Moon is at the Apogee, the tidal range is greatest.
3. When Earth is at the Aphelion, the tidal range is less than the average.

Which of the statements given above are correct?

(a) 1 and 2 (b) 2 and 3
(c) 1 and 3 (d) All of these

Ans. (c)

Exp. Statements (1) and (3) are correct because the periodical rise and fall of the sea level, once or twice a day, mainly due to the attraction of the Sun and the Moon, is called a tide. Once in a month, when the Moon's orbit is closest to the Earth called Perigee unusually high and low tides occur. During this time, the tidal range is greater than normal.

When the Earth is farthest from the Sun called Aphelion, around 5th July each year, tidal ranges are much less than average.

Statement (2) is incorrect because when the Moon is farthest from Earth called apogee, the Moon's gravitational force is limited and the tidal ranges are less than their average heights.

39 What explains the Eastward flow of the equatorial counter-current?

(Chap 14 ,Class-XI, New NCERT) (IAS Pre 2015)

(a) The Earth's rotation on its axis.
(b) Convergence of the two equatorial currents.
(c) Difference in salinity of water.
(d) Occurrence of the belt of calm near equator.

Ans. (b)

Exp. Convergence of the two equatorial currents explains the Eastward flow of the equatorial counter-current. The Earth's rotation does play a role in the formation of the counter-current, but it is the convergence of the two equatorial currents that primarily explains the Eastward flow. The equatorial counter-current is an Eastward flowing current found in the Atlantic, Indian and Pacific Oceans, located near the equator. This Eastward flow is primarily driven by the convergence of the two equatorial currents (North and South Equatorial Currents) that flow from East to West. The convergence of these currents piles up water in certain areas, such as near Brazil. This piled-up water then flows Eastward under the influence of the Earth's rotation, giving rise to the equatorial counter-current.

40 Which of the following statements is/are incorrect?

(Chap 14, Class-XI, New NCERT)

(a) Oceanic currents move at a greater speed deep inside the oceans than on the surface.
(b) Coriolis force results in formation of Gyres over the surface of the ocean.
(c) The less the speed of a current, the more is its strength.
(d) Both a and c

Ans. (d)

Exp. Statements (a) and (c) are incorrect because currents are referred according to their drift (speed). Usually, the currents are strongest near the surface. At depths, currents are generally slow. The strength of a current refers to the speed of the current. A fast current is considered strong. A current is usually strongest at the surface and decreases in strength (speed) with depth. The greater the speed of the ocean current, the greater will be its power because with the increase in the speed of the current, its power increases.

41 Which of the following factors/forces are responsible for providing initial movement to the oceanic currents? *(Chap 14, Class-XI, New NCERT)*

1. Solar insolation
2. Salinity of water
3. Coriolis force
4. Gravity of Earth

Codes

(a) 1, 2 and 3
(b) 1, 3 and 4
(c) 2, 3 and 4
(d) All of these

Ans. (b)

Exp. Solar insolation, Coriolis force and Gravity of Earth are the factors/forces responsible for providing initial movement to the oceanic currents because oceanic currents are like river flow in oceans. They represent a regular volume of water in a definite path and direction.

Ocean currents are influenced by primary forces that initiate the movement of water and secondary forces that influence the currents to flow.

The primary forces that influence the currents are heating by solar energy, wind, gravity of earth and coriolis force.

42 **Consider the following statements about oceanic currents.** *(Chap 14, Class-XI, New NCERT)*

1. More than 90% of oceanic currents occur on the surface of the oceans.
2. Movement of deep water current is mainly influenced by density and gravity.
3. Surface current move from equator to poles whereas deep current move from poles to equator.

Which of the statements given above are correct?

(a) 1 and 2
(b) 2 and 3
(c) 1 and 3
(d) 1, 2 and 3

Ans. (b)

Exp. Statements (2) and (3) are correct about oceanic currents because deep water currents make up the other 90% of the ocean water currents. These water currents move around the oceanic basins due to variations in the density and gravity.

Deep water sink into the deep ocean basins at high latitudes, where the temperatures are cold enough to cause the density to increase. Cold-water oceanic currents occur when the cold water at the poles sinks and slowly moves towards the equator. Warm-water currents travel out from the equator along the surface, flowing towards the poles to replace the sinking cold water.

Statement (1) is incorrect because more than 90% of oceanic currents occur in the deep ocean.

43 **Which of the following factors can modify the movement and direction of oceanic currents?** *(Chap 16, Class-XI, Old NCERT)*

1. Melting of ice in polar areas
2. Bottom topography of oceans
3. Orientation and configuration of the coast
4. Seasonal winds

Codes

(a) 1, 2 and 3
(b) 2, 3 and 4
(c) 1, 3 and 4
(d) 1, 2, 3 and 4

Ans. (d)

Exp. All the four factors i.e., (1) (2), (3) and (4) can modify the movement and direction of oceanic currents because many factors affect the speed and direction of ocean currents.

The melting of ice in the polar regions increases the amount of water, which causes the current to flow from the polar region towards the equator.

Topography has a profound effect on the direction of currents, especially near the bottom. For this reason, the equator current in the Atlantic Ocean collides with the mid-Atlantic ridge and turns North and South.

The coastline plays an important role in controlling the direction of the ocean current. For example, the equatorial current splits into two branches after being interrupted off the coast of Brazil.

Winds are responsible for both magnitude and direction of the ocean currents. For example, Monsoon winds are responsible for the seasonal reversal of ocean currents in the Indian Ocean.

44 **Consider the following Assertion (A) and Reason (R) and choose the correct code.** *(Chap 14, Class-XI, New NCERT)*

Assertion (A) The best fishing grounds are found in the regions of mixing of cold and warm oceanic waters.

Reason (R) Mixing of warm and cold currents replenishes levels of oxygen and favours the growth of Planktons.

Codes

(a) Both A and R are true and R is the correct explanation of A.
(b) Both A and R are true, but R is not the correct explanation of A.
(c) A is true, but R is false.
(d) A is false, but R is true.

Ans. (a)

Exp. Both Assertion (A) and Reason (R) are true and Reason (R) is the correct explanation of Assertion (A). The mixing of warm and cold currents help to replenish the oxygen and favour the growth of planktons, the primary food for fish population.

The best fishing grounds of the world exist mainly in these mixing zones. e.g., Grand Banks around Newfoundland, Canada and North-Eastern Coast of Japan.

45 **The most important fishing grounds of the world are found in the regions where** *(Chap 14, Class-XI, New NCERT) (IAS Pre 2013)*

(a) warm and cold atmospheric currents meet
(b) rivers drain out large amounts of freshwater into the sea
(c) warm and cold oceanic currents meet
(d) continental shelf is undulating

Ans. (c)

Exp. The most important fishing grounds of the world are found in the regions where warm and cold oceanic currents meet.

The most productive fishing grounds in the world are found in regions where warm and cold oceanic currents meet. This convergence of currents leads to upwelling, a process that brings nutrient-rich water from the ocean's depths to the surface. These nutrients support the growth of phytoplankton, which forms the base of the marine food web and attracts a diverse array of marine life, including commercially valuable fish species.

46 Consider the following factors. *(Chap 14, Class- XI, New NCERT)*

1. Rotation of the Earth
2. Air pressure and wind
3. Density of ocean water
4. Revolution of the Earth

Which of the above factors influence the ocean currents?

(a) 1 and 2
(b) 1, 2 and 3
(c) 1 and 4
(d) 2, 3 and 4

Ans. (b)

Exp. The rotation of the Earth, air pressure and wind and the density of ocean water all influence the ocean currents.

Ocean currents are influenced by a variety of factors

1. Rotation of the Earth (Coriolis Effect) The rotation of the Earth causes the Coriolis effect, which deflects the path of the ocean currents.
2. Air Pressure and Wind Wind blowing on the surface of the ocean pushes the water to move.
3. Density of Ocean Water Differences in water density, resulting from variations in temperature and salinity, also cause ocean currents.

The revolution of the Earth (Option 4) does not directly influence ocean currents.

47 Which of the following is a warm oceanic current? *(Chap 14, Class-XI, New NCERT)*

1. Falkland Current
2. Florida Current
3. East Australian Current

Codes

(a) 1 and 2
(b) 1 and 3
(c) 2 and 3
(d) All of these

Ans. (c)

Exp. Florida Current and East Australian Currents are warm oceanic currents while Falkland Current is cold oceanic current. Ocean currents can also be classified on the basic of temperature. Warm oceanic currents bring warm water into cold water areas and are usually observed on the East coast of continents in the low and middle latitudes.

48 Which of the following are cold oceanic current? *(Chap 16, Class-XI, Old NCERT)*

1. Antilles Current
2. Benguela Current
3. West Wind Drift
4. Counter Equatorial Current

Codes

(a) 1 and 2
(b) 2 and 3
(c) 1 and 3
(d) All of the above

Ans. (b)

Exp. Benguela Current and West Wind Drift are cold oceanic currents while Antilles and Counter Equatorial are warm currents.

Cold currents bring cold water into warm water areas. These currents are usually found on the West coast of the continents in the low and middle latitudes and on the East coast in the higher latitudes in the Northern hemisphere.

49 Match the following lists correctly and choose the correct code. *(Chap 16, Class-XI, Old NCERT)*

	List I (Oceanic Currents)	List II (Cold /Warm)	List III (Flows in)
A.	Kuroshio Current	1. Warm	i. North Atlantic Ocean
B.	Gulf Stream	2. Cold	ii. North Pacific Ocean
C.	West Australian Current	3. Warm	iii. Indian Ocean
D.	Humboldt Current	4. Cold	iv. South Pacific Ocean

Codes

(a) A-1-ii, B-3-i, C-4-iii, D-2-iv
(b) A-2-iii, B-1-i, C-3-ii, D-4-iv
(c) A-4-ii, B-2-i, C-3-iv, D-1-iii
(d) A-3-iv, B-1-i, C-4-ii, D-2-iii

Ans. (a)

Exp. The correct matching is A-1-ii, B-3-i, C-4-iii, D-2-iv.

Kuroshio Current, is a warm type of current, also called Japan Current, strong surface oceanic current of the Pacific Ocean.

The **Gulf Stream**, North Atlantic Drift, is a warm and strong Atlantic Ocean current that originates from the Gulf of Mexico and extends to the tip of Florida.

The **West Australian Current** is a cold surface current of the Southern Ocean and Southern Indian Ocean.

The **Humboldt Current**, also called the Peru Current, is a cold ocean current that flows North along the Western coast of South America in Pacific Ocean.

50 **Which of the following pairs given above is correct?**
(Chap 14, Class-XI, New NCERT)

(a)	Agulhas Current	–	Flows Southward along the Eastern coast of Africa.
(b)	Monsoon Currents	–	Reverses direction with the changing monsoon winds.
(c)	Somali Current	–	Influenced by the South-West Monsoon, flows from the Arabian Sea to the Bay of Bengal.

Ans. (c)
Exp. Only pair (c) is correct as Somali Current is influenced by the South-West Monsoon and flows from the Arabian Sea to the Bay of Bengal along the Western coast of India.

While Agulhas Current flows Southward along the Eastern coast of Africa and is known for its strong and warm currents in the South-Western Indian Ocean.

Monsoon Currents in the Indian Ocean are influenced by the changing monsoon winds. They typically reverse direction with the changing seasons, flowing from the South-West during the South-West Monsoon and from the North-East during the Northeast Monsoon.

West Australian Current flows Southward along the Western coast of Australia, influenced by the complex circulation patterns in the South-Eastern Indian Ocean.

51 **Consider the following statements about the Equatorial Counter Current (ECC).**
(Chap 14, Class-XI, New NCERT)

1. The ECC flows Eastward across the tropical Indian Ocean, opposing the Westward-flowing Equatorial Currents.
2. The ECC is primarily driven by the strong trade winds at the equator.
3. The ECC is warm and carries tropical surface water rich in nutrients and marine life.
4. The depth of the ECC is typically less than 200 meters.

How many of the statements given above is/are correct?

(a) Only one (b) Only two
(c) Only three (d) All of these

Ans. (d)
Exp. Only three statements i.e., (1), (3) and (4) are correct. The Equatorial Counter Current is an Eastward flowing, wind-driven current in the Atlantic, Indian, and Pacific Oceans which opposes the Equatorial ocean current which flows Westward near the equator, predominantly controlled by the winds.

Equatorial Counter Current are warm and it carries tropical surface water. ECC is rich in nutrients and supports marine life because of upwelling. The deep ocean currents tend to be nutrient-poor, the ECC is a shallow current that carries surface water from areas where nutrients have been upwelled. This upwelled water is rich in nutrients like nitrates, phosphates, and silicates, which are essential for marine life.

The depth of ECC is typically less than 100-150 meters in the Atlantic, Indian, and Pacific Oceans.

Statement (2) is incorrect as the ECC is primarily not driven by strong trade winds but it is more due to pilled up water under the influence of Equatorial currents.This excess water starts moving in opposite direction of Equatorial currents.i.e. west to east in the region of doldrum.

Oceanic Deposits

52 **Consider the following statements.**
(Chap 16, Class-XI, NCERT)

1. Most of the world's coral reefs are in tropical waters.
2. More than one-third of the world's coral reefs are located in the territories of Australia, Indonesia and Philippines.
3. Coral reefs host far more number of animal phyla than those hosted by tropical rainforests.

How many of the statements given above is/are correct?

(a) Only one (b) Only two
(c) Only three (d) All of these

Ans. (c)
Exp. All three statements i.e., (1), (2) and (3) are correct.

Most coral reefs grow in shallow, clean ocean waters on either side of the Equator, because they need sunlight and warm temperatures all year to survive.

The Indo-Pacific region has 91.9% of all the world's coral reefs, and Australia, Indonesia and Philippines are among the top five countries with the largest coral reef area.

Coral reefs are sometimes known as the "rainforests of the sea." Nearly a quarter of all the fish in the sea rely on healthy coral reefs. Corals provide habitats for fish and other organisms in the ocean. Coral reefs host more than 800 different types of hard coral and thousands of animal species.

53 **Consider the following statements.**
(Chap 13, Class-XI, New NCERT) (IAS Pre 2012)

1. The Global Ocean Commission grants licenses for seabed exploration and mining in international waters.
2. India has received licenses for seabed mineral exploration in international waters.
3. 'Rare earth minerals' are present on seafloor in international waters.

Which of the statements given above are correct?

(a) 1 and 2 (b) 2 and 3
(c) 1 and 3 (d) 1, 2 and 3

Ans. (b)
Exp. Statements (2) and (3) are correct. In 1987, India became the first country to attain the status of a 'Pioneer Investor' and was granted a region of approximately 1.5 lakh sq km in the Central Indian Ocean Basin (CIOB) for nodule exploration.

India's exclusive rights to explore polymetallic nodules in the Central Indian Ocean Basin have been extended by five years, covering an area of over 75,000 sq. km in international waters as allocated by the International Seabed Authority for developmental activities related to polymetallic nodules. The ocean floor in various oceans holds one of the largest untapped reservoirs of rare-earth elements.

For instance, scientists have identified an extensive reserve of rare Earth elements on the Japan side of the Pacific Ocean.

Statement (1) is incorrect because the International Seabed Authority (ISA) is responsible for reviewing applications for the exploration and exploitation of deep-sea resources, conducting environmental impact assessments, and overseeing mining operations..

54 Which of the following statements is/are correct about the terrigenous deposits?

(Chap 13, Class-XI, New NCERT)

1. Terrigeneous deposits are mostly deposited on the continental slope.
2. Quartz is a terrigenous deposit found in the oceans.

Codes

(a) Only 1
(b) Only 2
(c) Both 1 and 2
(d) None of the above

Ans. (c)

Exp. Statements (1) and (2) are correct about terrigenous deposits because these deposits are found on the continental shelves and slopes. They mainly consist of the rock material derived because of wear and tear.

Terrigenous sediments are derived from the erosion of rocks on land. Quartz and volcanic ash are terrigenus deposits found in the ocean.

55 Consider the following statements about red clay.

(Chap 13, Class-XI, New NCERT)

1. Red clay is the most widespread pelagic deposit.
2. Red clay is an organic deposit.
3. More than 50% of Pacific Ocean is covered with Red clay.

Which of the statements given above is/are correct?

(a) Only 2 (b) 1 and 3 (c) 2 and 3 (d) All of these

Ans. (b)

Exp. Statements (1) and (3) are correct about red clay because the inorganic material that makes up pelagic deposits consists mainly of red clay that usually results from volcanic activity. Red clay is primarily composed of silicon and aluminum dioxide, while other components may include phosphorus manganese and iron. Red clay comprises the most widely distributed typical pelagic deposits and covers more than half of the total ocean floor in the Pacific Ocean.

Statement (2) is incorrect because red clay is an inorganic deposit.

56 Which of the following are organic deposit in the oceans? *(Chap 13, Class-XI, New NCERT)*

1. Volcanic dust
2. Calcareous ooze
3. Sand
4. Siliceous ooze

Codes

(a) 1 and 2 (b) 2 and 3 (c) 1 and 4 (d) 2 and 4

Ans. (d)

Exp. Calcareous and Siliceous ooze are organic deposits mainly found in deep sea. The organic matter in the form of liquid clay is called ooze, which contains the shells and skeletons of various marine organisms. The pelagic deposits are those which are found over deep sea plains and the deeps.

These deposits mainly consist of organic remains of plants and animals. While volcanic dust and sand are inorganic deposits mainly found in continental shelves and slopes.

Chapter 07

Soils and Natural Vegetation

Soils and Natural Vegetation

Soil

Introduction

- Mixture of many solid, liquid and gaseous substances
- Top most layer of Earth's crust and contains minerals as well as organic matter

Classification of Soils

On the Basis of Parent Rock

- **Azonal soils** Soils of recent origin and are immature soils
- **Intrazonal soils** Formed within definite climatic belt are different from normal due to the dominance of any local factor
- **Zonal soils** Formed at the site of parent rocks and the influence of climate and parent rock is clearly visible

On the Basis of Chemical Compositions

- **Pedalfer** Have abundance of iron and aluminium
- **Pedocals** Have abundance of calcium

Soil Forming Process

- **Translocation** Movement of soil constitutents within the soil profile
- **Leaching** Removal of soluble components from soil
- **Eluviation** Removal of finer grained particles like clay from top soil
- **Illuviation** Deposition or accumulaiton of materials washed down from upper layer to lower horizon through eluviation
- **Calcification** Formation and accumulation of calcium carbonate and gypsum in arid and semi-arid regions
- **Alkalisation** When temporary excess of water and extreme evaporation bring the underground salts to the surface
- **Podzolisation** Occurs in cool and humid climates where bacterial acitivity is low through the influence of organic agents
- **Organic changes** Accumulation of decaying plants and organic matter on ground surface
- **Gleying** Occurs in waterlogged, anaerobic conditions, when iron compounds are reduced or removed from soil
- **Desilication** Common in hot, wet tropical and equatorial climates, a process of removal of silicon from soil

Natural Vegetation

Equatorial Vegetation

- The natural vegetation includes tall trees, shrubs, grasses and bushes which live in association with one another in a given environment

Deciduous Vegetation

- Classified as Temperate and Tropical forests
- Also known as monsoon forests, tropical forests are found in the belt along the Equator. They carry both broad leaved forests and deciduous trees

Tundra Vegetation

- Vast lowlands along the Arctic oceanic shores where the ground is frozen for the majority of year
- Devoid of trees, mosses, lichens and other low level vegetation can be found

Taiga Vegetation

- Also known as Sub-arctic climate, accounts for lowest annual average temperatures
- Found only in Northern hemispheres due to great East-West extent. Found in the regions just below the Arctic circle

Mangroves Vegetation

- A group of broad-leaved trees, that grow in muddy creeks and tidal estuaries, located on a transition zone between land and sea

Desert Vegetation

- Region witnesses high temperature and less rainfall
- Vegetation here is xerophytic and drought resistant scrubs
- Major hot deserts are located on the Western coasts of continents. e.g., Sahara desert, Great Australian, etc

Grassland Vegetation

- Grass dominated areas, account for roughly 20% of the earth surface
- Occur in both tropical and temperate regions where rainfall is insufficient to support tree growth

SOURCE **Old NCERT Class VI** *(Africa Land, Climate, Resources and their Utilisations)*, **New NCERT Class VII** *(Human Environment Interactions: The Tropical and Subtropical Regions, Life in the Deserts)*, **Old NCERT Class VII** *(North America Land and Climate)* **New NCERT Class VIII** *(Land, Soil, Water, Natural Vegetation and Wildlife Resources)*, **Old NCERT Class VIII** *(Indonesia and Malaysia)* **Old NCERT Class IX** *(Human Life in the Natural Regions of the World)*, **New NCERT Class XI** *(Geomorphic Processes, Life on the Earth)* **Old NCERT Class XI** *(Soils)*, **Tamil Nadu Board Class XI** *(Lithosphere-Exogenic Processes)*, **Tamil Nadu Board Class XII** *(The Biosphere)*

Soils

1 **Consider the following statements about soil formation.** *(Chap 6, Class-XI, New NCERT)*

1. Weathered material of rocks is the most important input for soil formation.
2. Humus is formed in the soil by dead remains of plants and animals.
3. Bacteria, lichens and mosses are responsible for the formation of soil.

Which of the statements given above is/are correct?

(a) Only 1
(b) 1 and 2
(c) 2 and 3
(d) All of the above

Ans. (d)

Exp. All the given statements are correct about soil formation. Soil formation depends first on weathering. Due to weathering, basic inputs are obtained for the formation of soil.

Humus is the dark organic matter that forms in soil when dead plant and animal matter break down further, specifically through the action of anaerobic organisms. Humus is formed in the soil by dead remains of plants and animals, which is most important for soil formation.

In soil, bacteria, lichens and mosses are responsible for the formation of soil. Weathered material or transported deposits are colonised by bacteria and other inferior plant bodies like mosses and lichens. Decomposition of organic matter and accumulation of substances is done by bacteria.

2 **With reference to agricultural soils, consider the following statements.** *(Chap 9, Class-VII, New NCERT) (IAS Pre 2021)*

1. High content of organic matter in soil drastically reduces its water holding capacity.
2. Soil does not play any role in the sulphur cycle.
3. Irrigation over a period of time can contribute to the salinisation of some agricultural lands.

Which of the statements given above is/are incorrect?

(a) 1 and 2 (b) Only 3
(c) 1 and 3 (d) 1, 2 and 3

Ans. (a)

Exp. Statements (1) and (2) are incorrect with reference to agricultural soils. Organic matter helps improving water retention capacity. The process of decay, added by bacterial action, transforms organic matter into humus. Humus enhances water retention capacity of the soil. The sulphur reservoir is in the soil and sediments where it is locked in organic and inorganic deposits. Sulphur bound in living organisms is carried back to the soil, through excretion and decomposition. Thus, the soil plays an important role in the sulphur cycle.

3 **Consider the following statements about soil formation.** *(Chap 6, Class-XI, New NCERT)*

1. Residual soils are formed by in-situ disintegration of parent material.
2. Mineral and chemical composition of the parent material influences the type of soil formed.
3. Texture and structure of parent material have no influence on the type of soil formed.

Which of the statements given above is/are incorrect?

(a) Only 1 (b) Only 2 (c) Only 3 (d) Both 1 and 2

Ans. (c)

Exp. Only statement (3) is incorrect because parent material is a passive control factor in soil formation. Parent materials can be any in-situ or on-site weathered rock debris or transported deposits. Soil formation depends upon the texture and structure as well as the mineral and chemical composition of the rock debris and deposits.

4 **Consider the following statements.** *(Chap 6, Class-XI, New NCERT)*

1. The content of organic matter in a soil is dependent upon the type of slope.
2. In regions with wet climate components such as calcium, sodium, magnesium and silica are removed from the soil.
3. In dry climates, soils usually forms hardpans.

Which of the statements given above are correct?

(a) 1 and 2 (b) 2 and 3
(c) 1 and 3 (d) All of these

Ans. (d)

Exp. All the statements given above are correct.
The content of organic matter in a soil is dependent upon the type of slope. Soils on a steep slope will tend to have low amounts of organic matter because the topsoil is continually eroded. Also if elevation increase, the soil organic matter content also increases.

In climates like wet equatorial rainy areas with high rainfall, not only calcium, sodium, magnesium, potassium etc but also a major part of silica is removed from the soil. Removal of silica from the soil is known as desilication. In dry climates, soils usually forms hardpan. Hardpans include calcic horizons (commonly called caliche), in which calcium carbonate cements the soil particles.

5 **Consider the following Assertion (A) and Reason (R) and choose the correct code.** *(Chap 6, Class-XI, New NCERT)*

Assertion (A) Soil in the tundra regions contains largely mechanically broken materials whereas soils in tropical regions have deep profiles.

Reason (R) Regions with high temperature have higher chemical activity and regions with very low temperatures have very low chemical activity.

Codes

(a) Both A and R are true and R is the correct explanation of A.
(b) Both A and R are true, but R is not the correct explanation of A.
(c) A is true, but R is false.
(d) A is false, but R is true.

***Ans.* (a)**

Exp. Both Assertion (A) and Reason (R) are true and Reason (R) is the correct explanation of Assertion (A). Tropical soils with higher temperatures show deeper profiles and in the tundra regions, soils contain largely mechanically broken materials. Temperature affects the rate of chemical, physical and biological reactions in the soil.

With the increase in soil temperature, the rate of decomposition of organic matter by chemical reactions and decomposing organisms increases. With the decrease in soil temperature, the rate of decomposition of organic matter by chemical reactions and decomposing organisms decreases.

6 Which of the following statements is/are correct? *(Chap 6, Class-XI, New NCERT)*

1. Eluviation is the downward transportation of soil components with the help of water.
2. Illuviation is the deposition of components in the lower layers of soil.

Codes

(a) Only 1
(b) Only 2
(c) Both 1 and 2
(d) Neither 1 nor 2

***Ans.* (c)**

Exp. Both the statements (1) and (2) are correct. Excess of water helps in the downward transportation of soil components through the soil called eluviation and deposits the same down below from water called illuviation. Precipitation gives soil its moisture content which makes the chemical and biological activities possible.

7 Consider the following statements about soil formation. *(Chap 6, Class-XI, New NCERT)*

1. Accumulation of humus is higher in the cold Polar regions.
2. In tropical regions, intense bacterial activity oxidizes dead vegetation.
3. Humification helps in decomposing the minerals present in the parent material.

How many of the statements given above is/are correct?

(a) Only one
(b) Only two
(c) All three
(d) None of the above

***Ans.* (c)**

Exp. All the three statements i.e., (1), (2) and (3) are correct about soil formation. Humus accumulates in cold climates as bacterial growth is slow. Intensity of bacterial activity is responsible for differences between soils of cold and warm climates.

With undecomposed organic matter because of low bacterial activity, layers of peat develop in subarctic and tundra climates.

In humid, tropical and equatorial climates, bacterial growth and action is intense and dead vegetation is rapidly oxidised leaving very low humus content in the soil.

Humification helps in decomposing the minerals present in the parent material. In the process of humification, organic matters are transformed into organic polymers, which are stable and cannot be decomposed further by organisms and remain as humus.

8 Consider the following statements. *(Chap 6, Class-XI, New NCERT)*

1. Parent materials influence soil formation through their mineralogical composition, their texture and their stratification.
2. The length of time the soil forming processes operate, determines maturation of soils and profile development.
3. Climate and temperature affect the rate of chemical, physical and biological reactions in the soil.

Which of the statements given above are incorrect?

(a) 1 and 2
(b) 2 and 3
(c) 1, 2 and 3
(d) None of these

***Ans.* (d)**

Exp. None of the given statements are incorrect.

Parent material is a passive control factor in soil formation. Parent materials influence soil formation through their mineralogical composition, their texture and their stratification.

Time is the important controlling factor in soil formation. The length of time the soil forming processes operate, determines maturation of soils and profile development. A soil becomes mature and thick when all soil-forming processes act for a sufficiently long time developing a profile.

Climate and temperature affects the rate of chemical, physical and biological reactions in the soil. With the increase in soil temperature, the rate of decomposition of organic matter or humus formation by chemical reactions and decomposing organisms increases.

9 The black cotton soil of India has been formed due to the weathering of *(Chap 6, Class-XI, New NCERT)* *(IAS Pre 2021)*

(a) brown forest soil
(b) fissure volcanic rock
(c) granite and schist
(d) shale and limestone

***Ans.* (b)**

Exp. Black soil in India is formed by the weathering of fissure volcanic rock.

Climatic condition along with the parent rock material is the important factors for the formation of black soil. Black soils are spread mostly across interior Gujarat, Maharashtra, Karnataka and Madhya Pradesh on the Deccan lava plateau and the Malwa plateau, where there is both moderate rainfall and underlying basaltic rock.

10 **Consider the following Assertion (A) and Reason (R) and choose the correct code.** *(Chap 6, Class-XI, New NCERT) (IAS Pre 2003)*

Assertion (A) Unlike temperate forests, tropical forests if cleared can yield productive farmlands that can support intensive agriculture for several years even without chemical fertilisers.

Reason (R) The primary productivity of the tropical rain forest is very high when compared to that of temperate forests.

Codes

(a) Both A and R are true and R is the correct explanation of A.
(b) Both A and R are true, but R is not the correct explanation of A.
(c) A is true, but R is false.
(d) A is false, but R is true.

Ans. (d)

Exp. Assertion (A) is false, but Reason (R) is true.

In tropical rainforest areas, heavy rainfall occurs throughout the year and there is a lot of leaching of minerals. These areas also have high temperature and bacterial activity is enormous which leads to decrease in humus content. Thus the fertility of soil is reduced and no intensive cultivation is possible without application of chemical fertilisers. The production of tropical evergreen forests is roughly double that of temperate forests.

11 **Consider the following statements about pedalfers.** *(Chap 7, Class-XI, Old NCERT)*

1. Pedalfers are usually formed in arid climates.
2. Podsol soils are characterised by accumulation of salts.
3. The colour of red pedalfers of low latitudes is due to the presence of aluminium.
4. Pedalfers are neutral to slightly acidic soils.

How many of the statements given above is/are incorrect?

(a) Only one (b) Only two (c) Only three (d) All four

Ans. (a)

Exp. Only one statement i.e., (4) is incorrect because pedalfers are acidic type of soil and not alkaline. Pedalfer is the dark brown or black fertile type of soil that will form in a deciduous forested region. They are rich in aluminium clays and iron oxides. It lacks humus and calcium.

12 **Which of the following statements are correct about the pedocal soil?** *(Chap 7, Class-XI, Old NCERT)*

1. These soils are rich in minerals and calcium salts.
2. They can be found in the Steppes grasslands.
3. These soils develop in arid and semi-arid regions.

Codes

(a) 1 and 2 (b) 2 and 3
(c) 1 and 3 (d) All of these

Ans. (d)

Exp. All the given statements are correct about padocal soil.

Pedocal soil is a class of soil which forms in semi-arid and arid regions. Calcium carbonate and mineral salts are high in pedocal soil. Pedocal soil has low soil organic matter.

Pedocal soils are formed and developed on grasslands such as Steppes and Prairies in the temperate regions. Pedocal soils are formed in arid, semi-arid and sub-temperate regions of the world where grasslands and brush are common vegetation types.

13 **Consider the following statements about chernozem soil.** *(Chap 7, Class-XI, Old NCERT)*

1. Chernozem soil is characterised by very low levels of humus content.
2. These soils have high moisture retention capacity.
3. The soil fertility of chernozem is very high.

Which of the statements given above is/are correct?

(a) Only 1 (b) 2 and 3
(c) 1 and 2 (d) All of these

Ans. (b)

Exp. Statements (2) and (3) are correct about chernozem soil.

Chernozem soil has a great capacity to hold moisture. The clay of the chernozem soil has an ability to expand and contract. When the soil comes in contact with water, the clay present in the soil absorbs the water and the moisture content available.

Chernozem soil contains a very high quantities, ammonia and phosphoric acids. Chernozem soil is very fertile and can produce high agricultural yields with its high moisture storage capacity.

Statement (1) is incorrect because chernozem soil contains a very high percentage of humus.

14 **Which of the following statements is/are correct?** *(Chap 7, Class-XI, Old NCERT)*

1. Desert soils are poor in humus content.
2. Desert soils are mostly alkaline in nature.
3. Barren soils of arid regions is known as usar soil.
4. Salts are generally accumulated in the desert soils.

Codes

(a) 1, 2 and 3 (b) 2, 3 and 4
(c) 1, 3 and 4 (d) All of these

Ans. (d)

Exp. All the given statements are correct.
Desert soil has a low content of nitrogen, organic matter and poor humus content with very high calcium carbonate and phosphate, thus making it infertile and it is mostly alkaline in nature.
In arid regions, barren soil is known as usar soil. Salts are generally accumulated in the desert soils because of excess heat in the desert region.

15 **Which of the following measures is/are used for preventing soil erosion?** *(Chap 2, Class-VIII, New NCERT)*

1. Terrace farming
2. Shelterbelt plantation
3. Inter-cropping
4. Mulching

Codes
(a) 1, 2 and 3
(b) 2, 3 and 4
(c) 1, 2 and 4
(d) 1, 2, 3 and 4

Ans. (d)

Exp. All the given measures can be used for preventing soil erosion.
Terrace farming break the slope, splitting one big slope into several smaller ones, making it less steep, and the force of water due to gravitation is less destructive.
Shelterbelt plantation reduces soil erosion by wind, conserve soil moisture and reduces wind damage to crops.
Inter-cropping is the cultivation of two or more crops simultaneously on the same field.
Inter-cropping averts soil runoff and can prevent the growth of weeds.
Basically, mulching conserves soil water by reducing soil evaporation and regulating soil temperature which decreases irrigation demand during crop cultivation periods.
Some other factors to prevent soil erosion are prevention of deforestation, excessive grazing, etc.

Major Biomes

16 **Consider the following definitions of a biome.** *(Chap 15, Class-XI, New NCERT)*

1. A plant and animal community covering a large geographical area.
2. An ecosystem in the equatorial regions.
3. A distinct natural region with the presence of life.

How many of the definitions given above is/are correct?
(a) Only one
(b) Only two
(c) All three
(d) None of these

Ans. (a)

Exp. Only one statement i.e. (1) is correctly defines a biome. A biome is a plant and animal community that covers a large geographical area. The boundaries of different biomes on land are determined mainly by climate. Therefore, a biome can be defined as the total assemblage of plant and animal species interacting within specific conditions.
Biome does not necessarily limited to the equatorial region.
Biome is not only vegetation but also include animal.

17 **Consider the following statements about biomes.** *(Chap 10, Class-IX, Old NCERT)*

1. Major biomes of the world are formed due to the variations in climatic conditions.
2. The boundaries between two biomes are transitional regions.
3. One biome mostly contains uniform conditions in terms of soil, vegetation and climate.

How many of the statements given above is/are correct?
(a) Only one
(b) Only two
(c) All three
(d) None of these

Ans. (c)

Exp. All the three statements i.e., (1), (2) and (3) are correct about biomes.
The revolution of our planet around the Sun and the tilt of axis cause annual variations in the intensity and duration of temperature, resulting in distinct seasons. These variations together with annual variation in precipitation account for the formation of major biomes such as desert, rainforest and tundra.
An ecotone is a zone of junction or a transitional area between two biomes. In other words, it is the zone where two communities meet and integrate.
One biome mostly contains uniform conditions in terms of soil, vegetation and climate because, a biome is a large area characterised by its vegetation, soil, climate and wildlife.

18 **Consider the following statements.** *(Chap 15, Class-XI, New NCERT) (IAS Pre 2021)*

1. Moringa (drumstick tree) is a leguminous evergreen tree.
2. Tamarind tree is endemic to South Asia.
3. In India, most of the tamarind is collected as minor forest produce.
4. India exports tamarind and seeds of moringa.
5. Seeds of moringa and tamarind can be used in the production of biofuels.

Which of the statements given above are correct?
(a) 1, 2, 4 and 5
(b) 3, 4 and 5
(c) 1, 3 and 4
(d) 1,2, 3 and 5

Ans. (b)

Exp. Statements (3), (4) and (5) are correct. Minor forest produce refers to non-timber forest products including fruits, nuts, seeds, and other biological materials collected from forests. Tamarind trees grow in the wild in many parts of India, and the fruit is collected by local communities as a source of food and income.

India is a major producer of both tamarind and moringa, and these products are exported to various countries around the world.

The seeds of both moringa and tamarind contain oil that can be extracted and converted into biodiesel, a type of biofuel. This is part of a broader effort to find sustainable alternatives to fossil fuels.

Statements (1) and (2) are incorrect because Moringa, also known as the drumstick tree, is not a leguminous tree. Leguminous trees are part of the Fabaceae family, which includes peas, beans, and lentils. Moringa belongs to the Moringaceae family, which is a separate family of flowering plants.

Tamarind (Tamarindusindica) is a leguminous tree bearing edible fruit that is indigenous to tropical Africa. The term "endemic" means that a species is native or restricted to a certain place. While tamarind trees are now found throughout South Asia, they are not endemic to this region as they originated in Africa.

19 **"Leaf litter decomposes faster than in any other biome and as a result, the soil surface is often almost bare. Apart from trees, the vegetation is largely composed of plant forms that reach up into the canopy vicariously, by climbing the trees or growing as epiphytes, rooted on the upper branches of trees."**

This is the most likely description of

(Chap 10, Class-VIII, Old NCERT) (IAS Pre 2021)

(a) Coniferous forest
(b) Dry deciduous forest
(c) Mangrove forest
(d) Tropical rainforest

Ans. (d)

Exp. The above description is of tropical rainforest.

In tropical rainforest biome, hot, moist atmosphere and all the dead plant material create the perfect conditions in which bacteria and other microorganisms can thrive. This leads to rapid decomposition of leaf litter material. The tropical rainforest is a hot, moist biome where it rains all year long. It is known for its dense canopies of vegetation. The top layer or canopy contains giant trees that grow to heights of 75 m or more. They are known to climb trees in the canopy to reach for sunlight.

20 **Consider the following statements about the equatorial biome.** *(Chap 10, Class-IX, Old NCERT)*

1. The seasonal contrast is maximum in equatorial regions.
2. It is characterised by absence of a dry season.
3. There is high level of leaching in the soils of this region.

Which of the statements given above are correct?

(a) 1 and 2 (b) 2 and 3
(c) 1 and 3 (d) All of these

Ans. (b)

Exp. Statements (2) and (3) are correct about the equatorial biome. The annual rainfall in the equatorial biome is more than 200 cm and it rains daily, due to which there is absence of a dry season. The amount of leaching is high due to the daily rainfall and temperature exceeding 25°C, and the frequency of rainfall in which the soil minerals move into the soil, so this soil is not very fertile.

Statement (1) is incorrect because the seasonal contrast is very low (not maximum) in equatorial regions.

21 **'Climate is extreme, rainfall is scanty and the people used to be nomadic herders.'**

(Chap 10, Class-VIII, Old NCERT) (IAS Pre 2013)

The above statement best describes which of the following regions?

(a) African Savanna (b) Central Asian Steppe
(c) North American Prairie (d) Siberian Tundra

Ans. (b)

Exp. The given statement best describes the climate of Central Asian Steppe. Nomadic herding is the controlled movement of livestock. It is a primitive subsistence activity, in which the herders rely on animals for food, clothing, shelter and transport.

Savanna doesn't have extreme climate. In North American Prairies, there is no nomadic life and Tundra does not have herders because climate is not suitable for herding.

22 **Which of the following crops is/are generally found in the equatorial rainforests of Central Africa?**

(Chap 6, Class-VI, Old NCERT)

1. Ebony
2. Mahogany
3. Rubber
4. Palm

Codes

(a) 1, 2 and 3 (b) 1, 2 and 4
(c) 2, 3 and 4 (d) All of these

Ans. (d)

Exp. All the given crops i.e., ebony, mahogany, rubber and palm trees are found in the equatorial rainforests of Central Africa. These forests cover most of the central part of the continent of Africa.

Evergreen forests are found in this region due to high temperature, high rainfall and high humidity.

23 **Which of the following is/are the characteristics associated with Amazon rainforests?**

(Chap 8, Class-VII, New NCERT)

1. There are hot and humid days and nights.
2. The Sunlight does not reach the floor of the forest due to dense roof of trees.
3. Presence of hunting and slash and burn agriculture.

Codes

(a) 1 and 2 (b) 2 and 3 (c) 1 and 3 (d) All of these

Ans. (d)

Exp. All the given statements (1), (2) and (3) are the characteristic associated with Amazon rainforests. The atmosphere in the Amazon tropical rainforest is hot and humid because of high temperature and abundance of water. The top layer or canopy in this forest contains giant trees that grow to heights of 75 m or more. This layer of vegetation prevents much of the sunlight from reaching the ground.

Natives cut down the trees at the end of the dry season and then burn them just before the rains begin. Slash and burn is a common practice here during the dry season. Due to the dense forest here, the number of animals is high and that's why the native people hunt the animals for their needs.

24 **Which of the following crops is/are grown in the Amazon rainforest region?**

(Chap 8, Class-VII, New NCERT)

1. Coffee and cocoa
2. Tapioca
3. Wheat
4. Cassava

Codes

(a) 1, 2 and 3 (b) 2, 3 and 4 (c) 1, 3 and 4 (d) 1, 2 and 4

Ans. *(d)*

Exp. Among the given options, coffee and cocoa, tapioca and cassava are grown in the Amazon rainforest region. In Amazon forest, the staple food is cassava that grows under the ground like the potato. Cash crops like coffee, maize, tapioca and cocoa are also grown.

Wheat is not grown in Amazon rainforest. Wheat is grown in temperate and sub-tropical regions like India, China, USA, Russia, etc.

25 **Consider the following Assertion (A) and Reason (R) and choose the correct code.**

(Chap 10, Class-IX, Old NCERT)

Assertion (A) The equatorial biome is mostly inhabited by tribal groups with low density of population.

Reason (R) Shifting cultivation, subsistence farming and plantation agriculture are practised in the equatorial regions.

Codes

(a) Both A and R are true and R is the correct explanation of A.
(b) Both A and R are true, but R is not the correct explanation of A.
(c) A is true, but R is false.
(d) A is false, but R is true.

Ans. *(b)*

Exp. Both Assertion (A) and Reason (R) are true, but Reason (R) is not the correct explanation of Assertion (A). Due to the high rainfall, high temperature, high humidity, low fertility of the land and habitat of the native people in the equatorial regions, shifting farming, subsistence farming and plantation agriculture are practised here.

26 **Consider the following statements.**

(Chap 10, Class-IX, Old NCERT)

1. The tropical Eastern margins of continents between 10° to 30° N are characterised by tropical deciduous vegetation.
2. There is seasonal reversal of winds in the tropical Eastern continental margins.
3. Tropical Eastern continental margins are characterised by the presence of lateritic soils.

Which of the statements given above are incorrect?

(a) 1 and 2 (b) 2 and 3
(c) 1 and 2 (d) None of these

Ans. *(d)*

Exp. None of the given statements are incorrect. Between 10° to 30° North, the tropical Eastern edge of the continents has a humid and dry season. Due to this, the forest becomes green during the rainy season and the plant sheds its leaves in the dry season. That's why tropical deciduous vegetation is found along the tropical Eastern edge of the continents between 10° to 30° North. The seasonal reversal of winds occurs along the tropical Eastern continental margin. The tropical Eastern continental marginal is characterised by the presence of lateral soils.

27 **Consider the following trees.**

(Chap 15, Class-XI, New NCERT)
(IAS Pre 2023)

1. Jackfruit (Artocarpusheterophyllus)
2. Mahua (Madhucaindica)
3. Teak (Tectonagrandis)

How many of the above is/are deciduous trees?

(a) Only one
(b) Only two
(c) All three
(d) None of the above

Ans. *(b)*

Exp. The correct answer is (b) Only two (Mahua and Teak are deciduous trees).

Mahua (Madhucaindica) Mahua is found in the dry deciduous type of forests like the Forests of Chhattisgarh and Jharkhand. So, it is a deciduous tree.

Jackfruit (Artocarpusheterophyllus) Jackfruit is an evergreen tree, which means it retains its leaves throughout the year and does not shed them seasonally.

Teak (Tectonagrandis) Teak is a large deciduous tree that occurs in mixed hardwood forest.

28 **Consider the following characteristics of tropical savannas.** *(Unit 7, Class-XI, Tamil Nadu Board)*

1. Dominated by tall grasses and scattered trees.
2. Distinct wet and dry seasons with intense summer heat.
3. Home to large herbivores like zebras and giraffes.
4. Located primarily near the equator.

How many of the characteristics given above is/are correct for tropical savannas?

(a) Only one (b) Only two
(c) Only three (d) All four

Ans. (d)

Exp. All the four statements regarding tropical savannas are correct.

Tropical savannas are characterised by a continuous cover of perennial grasses, often tall, with scattered trees and shrubs. This vegetation pattern is a result of the savanna's climate, which is characterised by a long dry season followed by a wet season. It has a distinct wet and dry season. The wet season is characterised by heavy rainfall, while the dry season is characterised by high temperatures and little to no rainfall. This cycle of wet and dry seasons influences the types of plants and animals that can survive in the savanna.

It also has, particularly in Africa, are home to a variety of large herbivores, including zebras and giraffes. These animals are well-adapted to the savanna's climate and vegetation. For example, giraffes can reach the leaves of tall trees that other herbivores can't, and zebras can travel long distances to find water during the dry season.

Tropical savannas are found in regions near the equator, between the Tropic of Cancer and the Tropic of Capricorn. This location near the equator results in a warm climate with high annual temperatures.

29 Tropical savanna regions mostly occur in which of the following regions? *(Chap 10, Class-IX, Old NCERT)*

1. Amazon basin
2. Brazilian plateau
3. Orinoco basin

Select the correct answer using the codes given below.

(a) 1 and 2 (b) 2 and 3
(c) 1 and 3 (d) All of these

Ans. (b)

Exp. In South America, savanna regions are found in the Orinoco basin and the Brazilian plateau or highlands. Some of the other regions which include tropical savanna are Serengeti plains of Tanzania, the vast Acacia plains of East Africa and savannas of Venezuela.

In Amazon basin, tropical rainforests (not savanna regions) are found.

30 Which of the following statements is/are correct? *(Chap 10, Class-IX, Old NCERT)*

1. The deserts are formed under the influence of Westerly winds on the Western margins of continents.
2. Diurnal range of temperature is high in desert regions.
3. There is total absence of cultivation in desert regions.

Select the correct answer using the codes given below.

(a) Only 2
(b) Only 3
(c) 1 and 2
(d) 2 and 3

Ans. (c)

Exp. Statements (1) and (2) are correct. Most of the world's deserts are located in the Eastern margins of continents in the subtropics because of prevailing winds in the tropics i.e., tropical Easterly winds. The tropical Easterly winds become dry by the time they reach the Western margins of the continents and so they bring no rainfall. That's why deserts are formed in Western margin of continents.

Diurnal range of temperature is more in desert areas because of the property of sand to heat and cool very quickly. Hence, in the morning, it is very hot and at night it is very cold in deserts.

Statement (3) is incorrect because there is not total absence of cultivation in desert regions as heat-loving plants are best suited for summer production in desert climates. Crops grown in the desert include watermelons, green onions, apple, cucumbers, etc.

31 Consider the following statements about human habitations in the desert regions of the world. *(Chap 10, Class-IX, Old NCERT)*

1. The Bushmen tribe of Kalahari desert practise settled agriculture in South Africa.
2. Bedouin tribe of Sahara desert are Nomadic herdsmen that rear sheep and camels.
3. Settled agriculture has been developed in the region of Indus Valley in Asia.

Which of the statements given above is/are correct?

(a) Only 1
(b) Only 2
(c) 2 and 3
(d) All of the above

Ans. (c)

Exp. Statements (2) and (3) are correct about human habitations in the desert regions of the world.

The Sahara Desert experiences harsh climate. Despite that various groups of people such as the Bedouins live here. These are nomadic tribes who pursue different activities. They rear animals such as goats, sheep, camels and horses.

Agriculture in the Indus Valley in Asia was completely dependent on good quality soil and advances in agricultural techniques. That is why settled agriculture developed here. The main crops produced here barley, wheat grown in winter and rice in summer.

Statement (1) is incorrect because, Bushmen tribes of South Africa are engaged in food gathering, hunting, fishing, primitive agriculture, etc.

32 Which of the following statements are correct about the human habitations in Sahara desert?

(Chap 9, Class-VII, New NCERT)

1. Tuareg are settled agricultural communities in the region.
2. Crops such as rice and wheat are grown in the oasis regions in Sahara.
3. Important minerals such as uranium are mined in the Sahara region.

Codes

(a) 1 and 2
(b) 2 and 3
(c) 1 and 3
(d) All of these

***Ans.* (b)**

Exp. Statements (2) and (3) are correct about the human habitations in Sahara desert. People live around the oasis region in the Sahara where water is available, and they grow date palms. Crops such as wheat, rice, barley and beans are also grown in the Sahara oasis. Uranium is abundant in the Sahara and has historically been important in Niger. The main minerals found in the Sahara desert are iron, phosphorus, manganese and uranium.

Statement (1) is incorrect because Tuareg are nomadic agricultural communities in the Sahara Desert region.

33 Which of the following statements is/are correct about the characteristics of Mediterranean region?

(Chap 10, Class-IX, Old NCERT)

1. Warm and dry summers and cool and moist winters
2. Occurrence of cyclones in winter season
3. Fruits and grape cultivation
4. Presence of coniferous trees

Codes

(a) 1, 2 and 3
(b) 2, 3 and 4
(c) 1, 3 and 4
(d) All of the above

***Ans.* (d)**

Exp. All the given statements are correct about the characteristics of Mediterranean region.

Mediterranean region has hot, dry summers and cool, wet winters.

In the Mediterranean region, in winter, the convergence of cold air from the North and warm air from the South is the cause of cyclones.

Mediterranean regions are famous for their fruit cultivation. The trees in this region adapt themselves to the dry summers with the help of their thick barks and wax coated leaves which reduce transpiration. Traditional Mediterranean fruit and nut crops include grapes, olives, figs and almonds. The Mediterranean vegetation is dominated by evergreen shrubs and presence of coniferous trees.

34 Which of the following regions is characterised by mid-latitude desert vegetation?

(Chap 10, Class-IX, Old NCERT)

1. Tibetan Plateau
2. Sahara Desert
3. Patagonia Plateau
4. Savanna Region

Codes

(a) 1 and 3
(b) 2, 3 and 4
(c) 1 and 4
(d) 1, 2, 3 and 4

***Ans.* (a)**

Exp. Tibetan plateau and Patagonia plateau are characterised by mid-latitude desert. These mid-latitude desert basins lay hundreds of miles from the sea, and are sheltered by the high mountains all around them. The mid-latitude desert is an excessively dry region with an arid climate. Sahara desert and Savanna region are low latitude arid desert.

35 The vegetation of savanna consists of grassland with scattered small trees. The forest development in such areas is generally kept in check by one or more or a combination of some conditions.

(Chap 10, Class-VIII, Old NCERT) (IAS Pre 2021)

Which of the following are such conditions?

1. Borrowing animals and termites
2. Fire
3. Grazing herbivores
4. Seasonal rainfall
5. Soil properties

Codes

(a) 1 and 2
(b) 4 and 5
(c) 2, 3 and 4
(d) 1, 3 and 5

***Ans.* (c)**

Exp. The correct options are (2), (3) and (4) because Fire, Grazing herbivores and seasonal rainfall are conditions for savanna vegetation.

Fire or lightning is a natural ignition source and savanna vegetation that is flammable during the dry winter period. Thus, it is prone to fire during the dormant season of the year.

Grazing herbivores play a major role in maintaining savanna landscapes. Smaller herbivores graze on lower seedling and saplings, preventing them to growing into larger things, while larger herbivores like elephants fell down trees, stop them growing as much and prevent them from dominating.

Savannas grow in tropical regions 8° to 20° from the equator. Conditions are warm to hot in all seasons but significant rainfall occurs for only a few months each year about October to March in Southern Hemisphere and April to September in Northern Hemisphere.

Options (1) and (5) are not correct because Borrowing animals and termites and soil properties are not controllable conditions for vegetation landscape in Savannas.

36 Consider the following statements about the Ladakh cold desert region. *(Chap 9, Class-VII, New NCERT)*

1. Ladakh experiences large temperature variations between day and night during summers.
2. Poplars and Willows are characteristic trees of the region.
3. Crops like wheat and barley are primarily cultivated in the winter season.
4. Animal husbandry involving sheep, goats and yaks plays a significant role alongside agriculture.

How many of the statements given above is/are incorrect?

(a) Only one (b) Only two
(c) Only three (d) All four

Ans. (a)

Exp. Only one statement i.e., (2) is incorrect about the Ladakh cold desert region because poplars and willows are not characteristic trees of Ladakh's cold desert region, due to the harsh climate and extreme dryness, vegetation in Ladakh is sparse.

37 Consider the following statements about mid-latitude grasslands (temperate grasslands). *(Chap 10, Class-IX, Old NCERT)*

1. Rainfall in this region is mostly convective in nature.
2. Trees are absent in these regions.
3. It is characterised by occurrence of black soil containing high organic matter.

Which of the statements given above is/are correct?

(a) Only 1 (b) 1 and 2
(c) 2 and 3 (d) All of these

Ans. (d)

Exp. All the statements are correct about mid-latitude grasslands.

Temperate grasslands are characterised as having grasses as the dominant vegetation. Trees and large shrubs are absent.

Temperatures vary more from summer to winter and rainfall in this region is mostly convective in nature. Black soil is humus-rich or high organic matter, mid- latitude grassland soil that is extensively used for growing grain or raising livestock. Mid-latitude grasslands are found in the middle latitudes of both the hemispheres.

38 Match the following lists correctly and choose the correct code. *(Chap 10, Class-IX, Old NCERT)*

List I (Temperate Grasslands)	List II (Region)
A. Velds	1. Argentina
B. Downs	2. South Africa
C. Pampas	3. Central Asia
D. Steppes	4. Australia

Codes

	A	B	C	D		A	B	C	D
(a)	3	1	2	4	(b)	4	1	3	2
(c)	4	2	3	1	(d)	2	4	1	3

Ans. (d)

Exp. The correct matching is A-2, B-4, C-1, D- 3.

The temperate grasslands of South Africa are called the **Veld** grasslands. It is a flat open land, with grass and no trees.

Downs are temperate, grasslands in Australia located to the West of South-East Queensland. It is mostly treeless grasslands; covered with black agricultural soil.

Pampas are temperate grasslands found in Argentina in South America. They are flat, fertile plains, covered with grass.

Steppes are temperate grasslands found in Eastern Europe and Central Asia. They are characterised by dry and grassy plain.

39 Which of the following statements are correct regarding grasslands? *(Chap 6, Class-VII, Old NCERT)*

1. The grassland located in interior of North America is called Prairies.
2. Prairies are bound by rocky mountains in the West and the Great lakes in the East.

Codes

(a) Only 1
(b) Only 2
(c) Both 1 and 2
(d) Neither 1 nor 2

Ans. (c)

Exp. Both the statements (1) and (2) are correct regarding grasslands.

The Prairies grasslands are temperate grasslands of North America. Prairies grasslands are located in the interior region of North America. Prairies have rich biodiversity, with a temperate climate. The prairies are bound by the Rocky Mountains in the West and the Great Lakes in the East. It is very famous for wheat cultivation.

40 Which of the following characteristics are associated with mid-latitude grassland regions? *(Chap 10, Class-IX, Old NCERT)*

1. In USA and Canada, this region is characterised by extensive mechanised agriculture.
2. The wheat and maize grown in USA and Canada region is mostly consumed in domestic markets.
3. In Australia and New Zealand, this region has commercialised pastoral industry.

Codes

(a) 1 and 2 (b) Only 3 (c) 2 and 3 (d) 1 and 3

Ans. (d)

Exp. Statements (1) and (3) are associated with mid-latitude grassland regions.

Prairies are ecosystems considered part of the temperate grasslands which is found in USA and Canada. Extensive mechanised commercial grain farming is practiced in Prairie grassland. In Australia and New Zealand, this region has commercialised pastoral industry due to fair and suitable climatic conditions and better mechanisation.

Statement (2) is not a characteristic associated with mid-latitude grassland region because the wheat and maize grown in USA and Canada region is mostly exported in international market.

41 Consider the following characteristics of commercial pastoral agriculture in the mid-latitude grasslands. *(Chap 10, Class-IX, Old NCERT)*

1. Large-scale processing and packaging rely heavily on automated machines.
2. The industry primarily focuses on domestic consumption of meat and dairy products.
3. Raising livestock involves extensive grazing practices with minimal manual labour.
4. Exports of meat and dairy products are a significant economic activity.

How many of the statements given above is/are correct?

(a) Only one (b) Only two
(c) Only three (d) All four

***Ans.* (c)**

Exp. Characteristics of commercial pastoral agriculture given in statements (1), (3) and (4) are practiced in the mid-latitude grasslands region.

Extensive mechanised commercial grain farming is practiced in mid-latitude grasslands. There is a shortage of labour in these areas and the production of food grains is excessive, due to which machines are used on a large scale in processing and packaging in these areas.

Livestock are reared on large farms in these areas, of which cows and sheep are important. The milk or dairy product and meat of these animals are exported to international markets.

Statement (2) is incorrect. The industry does not primarily focuses on domestic consumption of meat and dairy products.

42 Which of the following is/are the characteristics of cool mid-latitude Western margin regions? *(Chap 10, Class-IX, Old NCERT)*

1. Westerly winds influence the climate of this region throughout the year.
2. Rainfall is mainly cyclonic and maximum rain occurs in winters.
3. Evergreen vegetation is found in this region.

Codes

(a) 1 and 3 (b) 2 and 3
(c) 1 and 2 (d) All of these

***Ans.* (c)**

Exp. Characteristics given in statements (1) and (2) are of cool mid-latitude Western margin regions because regions of this type are found on the Western margins of the continents in the permanent zone of Westerlies. This region is under the influence of Westerly winds throughout the year.

The winters are warmer and annual rainfall is higher than in cool East margin region.

Rainfall is of mainly cyclonic origin and occurs throughout the year with a maximum in winter.

Statement (3) is not a characteristic of cool mid-latitude Western margin region because Deciduous forest are found in this region. Coniferous forests are found on hill slopes.

43 Consider the following statements about the agriculture of the warm mid-latitude East margin region. *(Chap 10, Class-IX, Old NCERT)*

1. Both types of agriculture heavily rely on advanced technology and mechanisation.
2. Traditional farming practices using manual labour are dominant in this region.

Which of the statements given above is/are incorrect?

(a) Only 1
(b) Only 2
(c) Both 1 and 2
(d) Neither 1 nor 2

***Ans.* (b)**

Exp. Statement (2) is incorrect. Traditional farming practices with manual labour are not dominant in this region; instead, there is a trend towards modern and mechanised farming methods.

44 Consider the following locations. *(Chap 10, Class-IX, Old NCERT)*

1. Northern regions of Japan
2. North-Eastern region of USA and Canada
3. Korea region in Asia

In how many of these locations is the cool mid-latitude Eastern margin region mainly found?

(a) Only one
(b) Only two
(c) All three
(d) None of the above

***Ans.* (c)**

Exp. All the given locations are correct regarding cool mid-latitude Eastern margin region is mainly found in North-Eastern United States and adjoining parts of Canada, Korea and Northern Japan.

This region lies pole ward of the warm East margin region. The region has warm wet summer and cold dry winter. It has laurentian type of climate. Annual range of temperature is high as the summers are hot and winters are very cold.

45 **Which of the following is/are the characteristics of Taiga coniferous forest region?**

(Chap 10, Class-IX, Old NCERT)

1. Nomadic herding and subsistence agriculture.
2. Short and warm summer and long and cold winter.
3. Lumbering in the winters and fishing in the summers.

Codes

(a) 1 and 2 (b) 1 and 3 (c) Only 2 (d) 2 and 3

Ans. (d)

Exp. Statements (2) and (3) are correct characteristics of Taiga coniferous forest region.

In Taiga coniferous forest region, the climate is cold and moist. The region has short warm summer and long cold winter. Coniferous forests are found here and contain softwood trees like oak, birch and maple. Lumbering is the main occupation of the people. While lumbering is common during winter, fishing is practised in the short summer season, when the snow cover melts.

Statement (1) is not the characteristic of this region because people here do not practice nomadic herding and subsistence agriculture.

46 **Consider the following pairs.**

(Chap 10, Class-IX, Old NCERT)

Nomadic Tribes		Region
1. Inuits	–	Scandinavia
2. Lapps	–	Siberia
3. Samoyeds	–	Canada and Alaska
4. Bushmen	–	Nigeria

Which among the above pairs is/are correctly matched?

(a) 1 and 4 (b) 2 and 4 (c) Only 3 (d) None of these

Ans. (d)

Exp. None of the given pair is correctly matched.

The Inuits are a group of culturally similar indigenous people inhabiting the Arctic regions of Greenland, Canada and Alaska (United States).

The Lapps of Scandinavia constitute a small indigenous ethnic community. Lapps people used to depend on reindeer farming.

The Samoyedic people are a group of closely related people who speak Samoyedic languages.

They are a linguistic, ethnic and cultural grouping. The name derives from the obsolete term 'Samoyed' used in Russia for some indigenous people of Siberia.

The Bushmen people of South Africa lived in Kalahari Desert. They were part of the Khosian group. They are popularly known as San, Khwe, or Basarwa.

47 **Consider the following statements about the Polar biome.**

(Chap 10, Class-IX, Old NCERT)

1. The sub-soil in the Polar regions remain permanently frozen throughout the year.
2. Generally-mosses, lichens and sedges grow in patches.
3. Mining of minerals such as oil, iron ore, and nickel.
4. Cultivation of vegetables in glass houses.

Which of the statements given above are correct?

(a) 1 and 2 (b) 2 and 3
(c) 1, 2 and 3 (d) 1, 2, 3 and 4

Ans. (d)

Exp. All the given statements (1), (2), (3) and (4) are correct about the Polar biome. Polar biome region has long cold winters, with annual temperatures mostly below freezing. Here, the ground remains frozen for most of the year.

The climate of Arctic region is so cold that trees and plants do not grow, there, only mosses, sedges and lichen are found there.

The most popular minerals found in the Polar regions include oil, coal, iron ore, zinc, lead, nickel, etc. That's why minerals like oil, iron ore and nickel are mined here.

The temperature here is always below 0° Celsius, so farming is most difficult here but here vegetables are cultivated in glass houses.

Chapter 08

Agriculture and Animal Husbandry

Agriculture and Animal Husbandry

Agriculture

Introduction

- Most fundamental form of economic activities in any nation
- Earliest agriculture was practised in South-East Asia; Land suitable for agricultural activities is known as cultivable land
- Divided into two types - Commercial and Subsistence

Major Crops of the World

- **Food Grains** Rice, wheat, maize, etc
- **Millets** Jowar, bajra, etc
- **Oil Seeds** Mustard, groundnut, coconut, etc
- **Fibrous Crops** Cotton and jute
- **Beverages** Tea and coffee
- **Commercial Crops** Sugarcane and rubber

Subsistence Agriculture

- Practised to meet the needs of farmer's family;
- Low levels of technology and household labour are used to produce on small output
- **Primitive Subsistence Farming**
    - **Shifting Cultivation** Practised in thickly forested areas of Amazon Basin, tropical Africa, etc
    - **Nomadic Herding** Herdsmen move from one place to another with their animals for fodder and water
- **Intensive Subsistence Farming** Largely found in densely populated regions of monsoon Asia

Commercial Agriculture

- Crops and livestock are raised to sell products in order to make money
- Involves huge amount of capital investment
- **Commercial Grain Farming** Farms are large and important crop grown is wheat
- **Plantation Agriculture** Holdings are of variable size, farms have individual family ownership and are operated by family labour

Animal Husbandry

Introduction

- Science of caring and breeding of domestic animals
- Animal husbandry involves breeding and raising livestock like buffaloes, cows, goats, camels, horses, sheep, etc and even extended to poultry farming and fisheries

Management of Farms and Farm Animals

- **Dairy Farm Management** This is the management of the animals that provide milk (milch animals) The goal is to enhance the quantity and quality of the milk produced
- **Poultry Farm Management** Poultry farming refers to the rearing of domesticated fowl (birds) for their meat and eggs. These birds include chicken, ducks, turkey, geese, etc

Animal Breeding

- Breeding of animals aiming to develop high yielding animals and improve the desirable qualities of produce
- **Inbreeding** It refers to the practice of mating closely related superior males to superior females within the same breed for 4-6 generations
- **Out-breeding** It is the breeding of the unrelated animals that can be carried out in three different fashions.
- When two unrelated individuals of the same breed, which do not have a common ancestor for the past 4-6 generations are mated, it is called out-crossing

Apiculture

- Maintenance of hives of honeybees for the production of honey and beeswax is known as beekeeping or apiculture beekeeping
- Honey is an age old food of high nutritional value and is also used in traditional medicines across various cultures
- It is not a labour intensive practice

Fishing

- Fishes found in saline marine ecosystem, fresh water, in tropical as well as freezed zones. Major fishing zones of the world are North-West Pacific region, North-East Pacific region, South-East Pacific, etc
- **Fish Conservation**
    - Factors which are hindering the development of fishing in tropical latitudes are, a large variety of species all mixed up
    - High temperature does not support plankton population

SOURCE **Old NCERT Class VII** *(North America Resources and their Utilisation)*, **New NCERT Class VIII** *(Agriculture)*, **Old NCERT Class VIII** *(Asia : People and Natural Resources)*, **New NCERT Class X** *(Agriculture)*, **Old NCERT Class XI** *(Renewable Resources 'Forest and Fisheries')*, **Old NCERT Class XI** *(Grasslands and Pastoralism)*, **Old NCERT Class XI** *(Utilisation of Natural Resources)*, **Old NCERT Class XI** *(Major Crops of the World)*, **New NCERT Class XII** *(Primary Activities)*, **Tamil Nadu Board Class XII** *(Economic Activities)*

Agriculture

1 **In the context of India, which of the following is/are considered to be of practices of eco-friendly agriculture?** *(Chap 5, Class-XII, New NCERT) (IAS Pre 2020)*

1. Crop diversification
2. Legume intensification
3. Use of Tensiometer
4. Vertical farming

Codes

(a) 1, 2 and 3 (b) Only 3
(c) Only 4 (d) 1, 2, 3 and 4

Ans. (d)

Exp. All the four options i.e. (1), (2), (3) and (4) are the practices of eco-friendly agriculture in India.

Crop variety on a land surface and crop rotation practices can help farmers reduce the risk of plant and vegetable diseases. Pesticides and chemical fertilisers may be used less frequently as a result of these methods.

Farmer preferences and legume intensification are preferred for low nutrient environments.

Tensiometer is used for the timing of field irrigations.

Vertical farming is the process of cultivating crops in layers that are piled vertically. It frequently integrates soilless farming techniques such as hydroponics, aquaponics and aeroponics, as well as controlled environment agriculture, which tries to optimise plant development.

2 **Which of the following statements highlight advantage of fertigation in agriculture?** *(Chap 5, Class-VIII, New NCERT) (IAS Pre 2020)*

1. Controlling the alkalinity of irrigation water is possible.
2. Efficient application of rock phosphate and all other phosphatic fertilisers is possible.
3. Increased availability of nutrients to plants is possible.
4. Reduction in the leaching of chemical nutrients is possible.

Codes

(a) 1, 2 and 3 (b) 1, 2 and 4
(c) 1, 3 and 4 (d) 2, 3 and 4

Ans. (c)

Exp. Statements (1), (3) and (4) are correctly highlight advantage of fertigation in agriculture.

Fertigation controls the alkalinity of irrigation water, it also increased the availability of nutrients and reduce the leaching of chemical nutrients from the soil.

Fertigation increases efficiency by delivering water and nutrients directly into the root zone, where they are most needed. This results in the need for less fertiliser and water. Other potential advantages of fertigation include flexibility, saving on labour and energy costs, and the ability to add nutrients that may be otherwise difficult to apply.

Statement (2) do not highlight advantage of fertigation because efficient application of all phosphatic fertilisers is not possible.

3 **Consider the following statements regarding primitive subsistence agriculture.** *(Chap 5, Class-XII, New NCERT)*

1. Primitive subsistence agriculture is widely practised by almost all the tribes in the tropics, especially in Africa, South and Central America and South-East Asia.
2. This type of cultivation is also known as slash and burn agriculture.
3. Cultivation is done with relatively primitive instruments such as sticks and hoes and the cultivated patches are very small.

Which of the statements given above is/are correct?

(a) 1 and 2 (b) 2 and 3
(c) Only 3 (d) 1 and 3

Ans. (b)

Exp. Statements (2) and (3) are correct regarding primitive subsistence agriculture.

Primitive subsistence agriculture is also known as slash and burn agriculture. This type of cultivation is done with relatively primitive instruments such as sticks and hoes, and the cultivated patches are very small. After sometime (3 to 5 years) the soil loses its fertility and the farmer shifts to another parts and clears other patch of the forest for cultivation.

Statement (1) is incorrect because primitive subsistence agriculture or shifting cultivation is widely practised by many tribes (not all) in the tropics, especially in Africa, South and Central America and South-East Asia.

4 **Consider the following pairs.** *(Chap 4, Class-X, New NCERT)*

Shifting cultivation		Practised in the region
1. Milpa	-	Indonesia
2. Ladang	-	Central America
3. Jhuming	-	North-Eastern India
4. Taungya	-	Sri Lanka

How many of the pairs given above is/are correctly matched?

(a) Only one (b) Only two (c) Only three (d) All four

Ans. (a)

Exp. Only one pair i.e., (3) is correctly matched.

Shifting cultivation is prevalent in tropical region in different names

Jhuming in North-Eastern states of India

Milpa in Central America and Mexico

Ladang in Indonesia and Malaysia

Taungya in Myanmar

Chena in Sri Lanka

Caigin in the Philippines

One of the major problems of shifting cultivation is that the cycle of jhum becomes less and less due to loss of fertility in different parcels.

5 Consider the following statements. *(Chap 3, Class-VIII, New NCERT)*

Statement-I Subsistence agriculture is done for consumption purpose.

Statement-II Shifting cultivation or slash and burn agriculture is not same.

Codes

(a) Both Statement-I and Statement-II are correct and Statement-II is the correct explanation for Statement-I.
(b) Both Statement-I and Statement-II are correct, but Statement-II is not the correct explanation for Statement-I.
(c) Statement-I is correct, but Statement-II is incorrect.
(d) Statement-I is incorrect, but Statement-II is correct.

Ans. (c)

Exp. Statement-I is correct, but Statement-II is incorrect. Subsistence agriculture is primarily practiced for the purpose of self-sufficiency and consumption within the farming community. In subsistence agriculture, farmers focus on growing crops and raising livestock to meet the basic needs of their own families or local communities. The goal is to produce enough food to sustain the household and ensure food security. Shifting cultivation, also known as slash and burn agriculture, is a specific type of subsistence agriculture. In this practice, farmers clear a piece of land, burn the vegetation, and use the ash as fertiliser. They then cultivate the land for a few years until soil fertility declines, after which they move to a new plot of land.

6 Match the following lists correctly and choose the correct code. *(Chap 7, Class-XI, Old NCERT)*

List I (Type of Shifting Cultivation)	List II (Regions)
A. Ladang	1. Zaire basin
B. Chengin	2. Central America
C. Milpa	3. Philippines
D. Konuko	4. Venezuela
E. Masole	5. Malaysia

Codes

	A	B	C	D	E		A	B	C	D	E
(a)	3	2	5	1	4	(b)	5	1	4	3	2
(c)	1	2	3	4	5	(d)	5	3	2	4	1

Ans. (d)

Exp. The correct matching is A-5, B-3, C-2, D-4, E-1. Shifting cultivation is known as **Ladang** in Malaysia, **Chengin** in Philippines, **Milpa** in Central America and Mexico, **Konuko** in Venezuela, Roca in Brazil and **Masole** in Zaire Basin Central Africa.

7 Which of the following statements with reference to transhumance is/are incorrect? *(Chap 5, Class-XII, New NCERT)*

(a) Transhumance involves movement of pastoral communities from mountains to plains and vice-versa.
(b) Transhumance is a seasonal activity practised across regions.
(c) Transhumance mainly involves movement of nomads horizontally across regions.
(d) Both a and c

Ans. (c)

Exp. Statement (c) is incorrect with reference to transhumance because movement or transhumance in search of pastures is undertaken either over vast horizontal distances or vertically from one elevation to another in the mountainous regions.

8 Which of the following is the most plausible explanation for the declining numbers of pastoral nomads across the world? *(Chap 3, Class-XI, Old NCERT)*

1. Emergence of political boundaries
2. Expansion in settled agriculture
3. Competition from industry

Codes

(a) Only 1 (b) Only 2
(c) 2 and 3 (d) 1 and 2

Ans. (d)

Exp. Statements (1) and (2) are most plausible explanation for declining numbers of pastoral nomads because emergence of political boundaries and expansion in settled agriculture are the most plausible explanation for declining numbers pastoral nomads across the world. With the emergence of political boundaries, the movement of pastoral nomads from one place to another almost stopped, as can be seen in the region of Tibet. Due to the expansion of agriculture in the areas of these people, there was a gradual shortage of useful space for their residence and living. For this reason, their numbers are decreasing.

9 Which among the following are types of intensive subsistence agriculture? *(Chap 5, Class-XII, New NCERT)*

1. Intensive subsistence agriculture dominated by wet paddy cultivation.
2. Intensive subsistence agriculture dominated by crops other than paddy.
3. Intensive subsistence agriculture dominated by plantation agriculture.
4. Intensive subsistence agriculture dominated by mixed farming.

Codes

(a) 1 and 2 (b) 3 and 4
(c) 2 and 4 (d) 1 and 4

Ans. (a)

Exp. Statements (1) and (2) are types of intensive subsistence agriculture.

Intensive subsistence agriculture dominated by wet paddy cultivation is characterised by dominance of the rice crop. Land holdings are very small due to the high density of population.

Intensive subsistence agriculture dominated by crops other than paddy prevail in those areas where due to the difference in relief, climate, soil and some of the other geographical factors, it is not practical to grow paddy.

10 In the context of shifting cultivation, consider the following statements. *(Chap 4, Class-X, New NCERT)*

1. It involves clearing a small patch of land and burning the vegetation.
2. Crops are grown for a few years until soil fertility declines.
3. Farmers then move on to a new patch of land, leaving the previous one fallow.
4. This method relies heavily on external inputs like fertilisers and machinery.

How many of the statements given above is/are incorrect?

(a) Only one
(b) Only two
(c) Only three
(d) All four

Ans. (a)

Exp. Only one statement i.e., (4) is incorrect regarding shifting cultivation. Shifting cultivation, also known as slash-and-burn agriculture, is traditionally characterised by its reliance on natural processes and minimal external inputs such as fertilisers and machinery. This agricultural practice involves clearing a piece of land, burning the vegetation, and using the ash as a form of natural fertiliser. After cultivation for a few years, farmers move on to a new plot of land, allowing the previously used area to regenerate.

11 Consider the following statements about intensive subsistence agriculture. *(Chap 5, Class-XII, New NCERT)*

1. Family labour is used for agricultural operations and manual labour.
2. It is practised in regions with large landholdings and moderate density of population.
3. Farm yard manure is mainly used in this type of agriculture.

Which of the statements given above are correct?

(a) 1 and 2
(b) 2 and 3
(c) 1 and 3
(d) All of these

Ans. (c)

Exp. Statements (1) and (3) are correct about intensive subsistence agriculture because, in intensive subsistence agriculture, farmers work with the help of family labour leading to intensive use of land.

Farm yard manure is used to maintain the fertility of the soil. In this type of agriculture, the yield per unit area is high but per labour it is low.

Statement (2) is incorrect because in this type of agriculture, landholdings are very small due to the high density of population.

12 Consider the following statements in respect of intensive and extensive farming. *(Chap 12, Module-2, NIOS)*

1. Intensive farming records high production per unit of land.
2. Extensive farming is characterised by using large patches of land for cultivation.
3. India extensively practices cultivation in comparison to temperate areas of the USA, Canada, and the former USSR.
4. Japan is an example of a country where extensive farming is predominant.

Which of the statements given above are correct?

(a) 1 and 2
(b) 2 and 3
(c) 3 and 4
(d) 1, 2, 3 and 4

Ans. (a)

Exp. Statements (1) and (2) are correct regarding intensive and extensive farming.

Intensive farming records high production per unit of land. It is characterised by high inputs of labour, capital, and technology per unit area, resulting in high productivity. Extensive farming involves using a large amount of land for cultivation with lower inputs per unit area. This leads to lower productivity per unit of land.

Statements (3) and (4) are incorrect because India does not practice extensive cultivation compared to temperate areas. Extensive cultivation is more characteristic of temperate regions like the USA, Canada, and the former USSR. Japan is an example of a country where intensive cultivation is predominant due to limited availability of land.

13 Consider the following statements about extensive commercial grain farming. *(Chap 7, Class-XI, Old NCERT)*

1. Extensive grain farming is practised in regions with low population density.
2. Very high production levels, for export markets.
3. Mechanisation of farms and crop specialisation.

How many of the statements given above is/are correct?

(a) Only one
(b) Only two
(c) All three
(d) None of these

Ans. (c)

Exp. All the three statements i.e., (1), (2) and (3) are correct regarding extensive commercial grain farming because this agriculture is adopted in those areas where the density of population is low.

Here, machines are used on a large scale in agricultural work. This farming yield very high production, for export market.
The main purpose of this type of agriculture is to produce agricultural products to be sold in the market.
Crop specialisation is the main feature of production in this agriculture.

14 **Which of the following are the crops commonly grown in extensive commercial grain farming?** *(Chap 5, Class-XII, New NCERT)*

1. Wheat
2. Corn
3. Barley
4. Lentils

Codes

(a) 1, 2 and 4 (b) 2, 3 and 4
(c) 1, 2 and 3 (d) All of these

Ans. (c)

Exp. Wheat, corn and barley are commonly grown in extensive commercial grain farming. Commercial grain cultivation is practised in the interior parts of semi-arid lands of the mid-latitudes. Wheat is the principal crop, though other crops like corn, barley and oats are also grown.
Lentils are not grown in extensive commercial grain farming as they Lentils are not a grain.

15 **Consider the following statements regarding extensive commercial grain cultivation.** *(Chap 5, Class-XII, New NCERT)*

1. Commercial grain cultivation is practised in the interior parts of semi-arid lands of the mid-latitudes.
2. The size of the farm is very small, therefore entire operations of cultivation from ploughing to harvesting are mechanised.
3. Wheat is the principal crop, though other crops like corn, barley, oats and rye are also grown.
4. There is low yield per acre but high yield per person.

How many of the statements given above is/are incorrect?

(a) Only one (b) Only two
(c) Only three (d) All of these

Ans. (a)

Exp. Only one statement i.e., (2) is incorrect regarding extensive commercial grain cultivation because the size of the farm is very large (not small).
Therefore, entire operations of cultivation from ploughing to harvesting are mechanised.
Extensive commercial grain cultivation type of agriculture is best developed in Eurasian steppes, the Canadian and American Prairies, the Pampas of Argentina, the Velds of South Africa, the Australian Downs and the Canterbury Plains of New Zealand.

16 **In the context of commercial farming, consider the following statements.** *(Chap 4, Class-X, New NCERT)*

1. Commercial farming involves the cultivation of crops and rearing of animals for sale in the market.
2. The area cultivated in commercial farming is generally small, and minimal capital is used.
3. Most of the work in commercial farming is carried out using machines.
4. Commercial grain farming primarily focuses on growing crops for personal consumption.

How many of the statements given above is/are correct?

(a) Only one (b) Only two
(c) Only three (d) All four

Ans. (b)

Exp. Only two statements i.e., (1) and (3) are correct regarding commercial farming.
In commercial farming crops are grown and animals are reared for sale in market. 'Most of the work in commercial farming is carried out using machines'. Commercial farming is characterised by extensive mechanisation to increase efficiency and productivity.
Statements (2) and (4) are incorrect because commercial farming typically involves large areas of cultivation, and a significant amount of capital is invested in machinery, technology, and other resource. Commercial grain farming is undertaken for commercial purposes, i.e., for sale in the market, rather than for personal consumption.

17 **Consider the following statements regarding commercial farming.** *(Chap 5, Class-XII, New NCERT)*

1. It is a type of Agricultural practised in 'Fazendas of Brazil'.
2. In commercial farming, crops are grown and animals are reared for sale in market.

Which of the statements given above is/are correct?

(a) Only 1
(b) Only 2
(c) Both 1 and 2
(d) Neither 1 nor 2

Ans. (c)

Exp. Both the statements (1) and (2) are correct regarding commercial farming.
Large coffee plantations in Brazil are called Fazendas.
A Fazenda is a plantation found throughout Brazil, during the colonial period. Fazendas agriculture is related to commercial agriculture.

18 **Which of the following is a feature of plantation agriculture practised in different parts of the world?** *(Chap 5, Class-XII, New NCERT)*

1. Single crop specialisation
2. Well-developed transportation system
3. Scientific techniques of cultivation
4. Manual labour

Codes

(a) 1, 2 and 3 (b) 2 and 3
(c) 1 and 2 (d) All of these

Ans. (d)

Exp. All the features mentioned in the question are of plantation agriculture practised in different parts of the world. Plantation agriculture was introduced by the Europeans in colonies situated in the tropics. Some of the important plantation crops are tea, coffee, cocoa, rubber, oil palm, sugarcane and pineapples.

The characteristic features of this type of farming are large estates or plantations, managerial and technical support, scientific methods of cultivation, single crop specialisation, cheap labour and manual labour, and a good system of transportation which links the estates to the factories and markets for the export of the products.

19 Match the following lists correctly and choose the correct code. *(Chap 5, Class-XII, New NCERT)*

List I (Regions)	List II (Plantations)
A. West Africa	1. Sugarcane
B. Malaysia	2. Coconut and sugar
C. Philippines	3. Cocoa and coffee
D. Indonesia	4. Rubber plantations

Codes

	A	B	C	D		A	B	C	D
(a)	1	3	4	2	(b)	3	4	2	1
(c)	4	2	3	1	(d)	3	1	4	2

Ans. (b)

Exp. The correct matching is A-3, B-4, C-2, D-1.

Plantation agriculture was introduced by the Europeans in colonies situated in the tropic.

The French established cocoa and coffee plantations in **West Africa**. The British set up large tea gardens in India and Sri Lanka.

The British set up large rubber plantations in **Malaysia**.

Sugarcane and banana plantations in West Indies.

Spanish invested heavily in coconut and sugarcane plantations in the **Philippines**.

The Dutch once had monopoly over sugarcane plantation in **Indonesia**.

20 Which of the following statements correctly defines mixed farming? *(Chap 5, Class-XII, New NCERT)*

(a) Cultivation of crops in alternate rows and columns.
(b) Cultivation of commercial crops with plantation crops.
(c) Cultivation of citrus fruits and grains.
(d) Cultivation of crops and rearing of animals.

Ans. (d)

Exp. Statement (d) is correctly defines mixed farming. It is a type of farming which involves both the growing of crops and the raising of livestock.

Mixed farms are moderate in size and usually the crops associated with it are wheat, barley, maize, fodder and root crops. Fodder crops are an important component of mixed farming.

Equal emphasis is laid on crop cultivation and animal husbandry. Animals like cattle, sheep, pigs and poultry provide the main income along with crops.

21 With reference to mixed farming, consider the following statements. *(Chap 5, Class-XII, New NCERT)*

1. It involves primitive form of tools, techniques and traditional methods of cultivation.
2. Mixed Farming is practised in Europe, Eastern USA, Argentina, South-East Australia, New Zealand.
3. Crop rotation and mixed cropping practises are also used in Mixed farming.

Which of the statements given above are correct?

(a) 1 and 2 (b) 2 and 3
(c) 1 and 3 (d) All of these

Ans. (b)

Exp. Statements (2) and (3) are correct with reference to mixed farming. It is practised in Europe, Eastern USA, Argentina, South-East Australia, New Zealand and South Africa.

In mixed agriculture, crop rotation and intercropping play an important role in maintaining soil fertility.

Statement (1) is incorrect because mixed farming is characterised by high capital expenditure on farm machinery and building, extensive use of chemical fertilisers and green manure and also by the skill and expertise of the farmers.

22 Consider the following about features of sedentary agriculture. *(Chap 7, Class-XI, Old NCERT)*

1. Crop rotation to maintain fertility of soil.
2. Livestock farming to supplement agriculture.
3. Use of animals for obtaining manure for the field.

Which of the statements given above are correct?

(a) 1 and 2
(b) 2 and 3
(c) 1 and 3
(d) 1, 2 and 3

Ans. (d)

Exp. All the given statements are the features of sedentary agriculture. Sedentary agriculture is a farming method in which the farmer lives in a particular area of his choice.

The special feature of such agriculture is that the farmers adopt the method of soil conservation and adopt a cropping model. Fertilisation of the soil increases through crop rotation.

To help in agricultural work and to increase their income, they do livestock farming from which they get manure. The farmers use this manure in agriculture.

23 Consider the following statements about lumbering.
(Chap 2, Class-XI, Old NCERT)

1. Lumbering is practised on a commercial scale in the temperate regions.
2. Lumbering requires a good transport and communications network.
3. Lumbering is mostly carried out in the developed countries with the help of manual tools and labour.

Which of the statements given above are correct?

(a) 1 and 2 (b) 2 and 3 (a) 1 and 3 (d) 1, 2 and 3

Ans. (a)

Exp. Statements (1) and (2) are correct about lumbering. Lumbering is the economic activity involving felling, hauling, logging of timber is known as lumbering.

It is well developed in the coniferous forest belt of the cool temperate lands. Lumbering requires a good transport and communication network, because good transport and communication is needed to transport the cut wood from one place to another.

Statement (3) is incorrect because, lumbering is mostly carried out in the developed countries with the help of big machine, motorised saws, tractor and good transportation system.

24 Which of the following pairs is/are incorrectly matched? *(Chap 4, Class-VIII, New NCERT)*

(a) Sericulture – Commercial rearing of silk worms
(b) Pisciculture – Breeding of fish in specially constructed tanks and ponds
(c) Viticulture – Cultivation of grapes
(d) Apiculture – Artificial rearing of worms (Earthworms)

Ans. (d)

Exp. Only pair (d) incorrectly matched.

Apiculture is the act of rearing honeybees. The bees are taken care of and managed to produce wax and honey.

Sericulture is commercial rearing of silk worms. It may supplement the income of the farmer.

Pisciculture It is breeding of fish in specially constructed tanks and ponds. It involves raising fish commercially in tanks or enclosures, usually for food.

Viticulture It is cultivation of grapes. It is a branch of the science of horticulture (Cultivation of high value crops).

Major Crops of the World

25 Which of the following is/are correct about viticulture? *(Chap 5, Class-XII, New NCERT)*

(a) It is mostly practised in tropical regions.
(b) It involves cultivation of grapes for commercial purposes.
(c) Products obtained from viticulture are used for making wines, raisins and currants.
(d) Both b and c

Ans. (d)

Exp. Statements (b) and (c) are correct about viticulture because high quality grapes are produced for commercial purpose under viticulture. Here, the inferior grapes are dried into raisins and currants. Here, wine is made by keeping the grapes for many years.

Statement (a) is incorrect because, viticulture or grape cultivation is a specialty of the Mediterranean region.

26 Which of the following statements is correctly defines cooperative farming?
(Chap 7, Class-XI, Old NCERT)

(a) Private ownership of farmlands for maximising farm output.
(b) Family ownership of agricultural land for developing farmland.
(c) Collective ownership of all factors of production by the members of the society.
(d) Government ownership of all the factors of production for betterment of agriculture.

Ans. (c)

Exp. Statement (c) is correctly defines cooperative farming. Group of farmers forms a cooperative society by pooling in their resources voluntarily for more efficient and profitable farming.

In the cooperative society, the collective ownership of all factors of production is done by the members of the society. Cooperative societies help farmers, to procure all important inputs of farming, sell the products at the most favourable terms.

Statements (a), (b) and (d) are incorrect because, cooperative society farming based on collective ownership.

27 Match the following lists correctly and choose the correct code.
(Chap 4 , Class-X, New NCERT) (MPPSC Pre 2021)

List I (Economic activities)	List II (Countries)
A. Commercial dairy farming	1. Argentina
B. Commercial grain farming	2. France
C. Commercial plantation farming	3. Denmark
D. Commercial fruits production	4. Malaysia

Codes

	A	B	C	D
(a)	1	2	4	3
(b)	4	1	2	3
(c)	1	3	2	4
(d)	3	1	4	2

Ans. (d)

Exp. The correct matching is A-3, B-1, C-4, D-2.

Commercial dairy farming is a practiced in Denmark. It is the most advanced and efficient type of rearing of milch animals. It is highly capital intensive.

Commercial grain farming is practiced in Argentina. In this type of farming, wheat is the principal crop, though other crops like corn, barley, oats and rye are also grown.

Commercial plantation farming is a practiced in Malaysia. The characteristic features of this type of farming are; large estates or plantations, large capital investment, managerial and technical support, scientific methods of cultivation, single crop specialisation, cheap labour and a good system of transportation.

Commercial fruits production (mainly apple, pears and peaches) is practiced in France.

28 Consider the following statements about the cultivation of rice. *(Chap 8, Class-XI, Old NCERT)*

1. The transplantation method of rice cultivation gives more yield than the broadcast method.
2. Rice is grown in plains as well as highlands.
3. Rice is mostly grown in Asian countries.

How many of the statements given above is/are correct?

(a) Only one
(b) Only two
(c) All three
(d) None of the above

Ans. (c)

Exp. All the three statements i.e., (1), (2) and (3) are correct about the cultivation of rice because transplanting method of rice cultivation ensures a uniform plant stands and gives the rice crop a head start over emerging weeds.

It is helpful in achieving an economical use of water and a highest yield. The cultivation of rice requires proper water and alluvial soil.

This type of situation is found in flat and plain areas. Rice is grown in places where flat land is found in hilly areas. Rice is mostly grown in Asian countries because of good and favourable climate, monsoon regions and found alluvial soil.

29 Which of the following are the major producers of tea in Asia? *(Chap 7, Class-VIII, Old NCERT)*

1. China
2. Kazakhstan
3. India
4. Sri Lanka

Codes

(a) 1 and 3
(b) 2, 3 and 4
(c) 1, 3 and 4
(d) All of these

Ans. (c)

Exp. Among the given options, China, India and Sri Lanka are the major producers of Tea in Asia.

China is the biggest tea producer in the world, with India and Sri Lanka following closely behind. Tea is grown in those regions of Asia that have a hot, humid climate with at least 100 cm of rainfall a year.

While Kazakhstan is not a major producer of tea as the temperature is high in Kazakhstan and there is a lack of rainfall.

30 Consider the following statements. *(Chap 8, Class-XI, Old NCERT)*

1. Wheat can only be grown in the tropical regions.
2. Wheat can be cultivated in both winter and spring seasons in different parts of the world.
3. Soft wheat is grown in dry regions and hard wheat is grown in humid regions.

Which of the statements given above is/are correct?

(a) Only 3
(b) Only 2
(c) Only 1
(d) All of these

Ans. (b)

Exp. Statement (2) is correct because most of the world's wheat is grown in the temperate areas of the Northern Hemisphere. Wheat in string are grown in the mild winters of North Africa, Pakistan, India and Australia. Wheat in winter most of the United States, Europe and China.

Statements (1) and (3) are incorrect because wheat can be grown in tropical, subtropical and temperate zone regions in the world. Soft wheat is grown in humid region and hard wheat is grown in dry region.

31 Consider of the following statements about wheat crop. *(Chap 8, Class-XI, Old NCERT)*

1. China is the largest wheat producer in the world.
2. Russia is the largest exporter of wheat in the world.

Which of the statements given above is/are incorrect?

(a) Only 1
(b) Only 2
(c) Both 1 and 2
(d) Neither 1 nor 2

Ans. (c)

Exp. Both the statements (1) and (2) are incorrect about wheat crop.

China is the largest wheat producer in the world. As of 2023, wheat production in China was 136.6 million metric tonnes. That accounts for 20.66% of the world's wheat production.

Russia is the largest wheat exporter in the world followed by Canada in the United States.

32 Wheat is most extensively cultivated in which of the following regions? *(Chap 8, Class-XI, Old NCERT)*

(a) Huang Ho basin of China
(b) Temperate grasslands of USA
(c) Central Asian States
(d) North Australia

Ans. (b)

Exp. Most extensively wheat is cultivated in temperate grasslands of USA under extensive cultivation. Wheat is cultivated under intensive and extensive cultivation. In China, Central Asian countries and North Australia, extensive cultivation of wheat is not grown.

33 Consider the following statements regarding oilseeds. *(Chap 8, Class-XI, Old NCERT)*

1. Sugar beet is an example of oilseed plant.
2. Oilseeds are main crop cultivated under intensive subsistence agriculture.

Which of the statements given above is/are correct?

(a) Only 1 (b) Only 2
(c) Both 1 and 2 (d) Neither 1 nor 2

Ans. (d)

Exp. None of the statements are correct regarding oilseeds. Sugar beet is a plant whose root contains a high concentration of sucrose and which is grown commercially for sugar production. Sugar beet is not an oilseed plant. Rice is the main crop cultivated under intensive subsistence agriculture.

34 Consider the following statements about the plantation of tea crop. *(Chap 8, Class-XI, Old NCERT)*

1. The most successful condition for the cultivation of tea is uniform distribution of rainfall.
2. Tea plantations are generally located on the hill slopes in tropical regions.
3. Tea plant best grows in acidic soils with high humus content.

How many of the statements given above is/are correct?

(a) Only one (b) Only two (c) All three (d) None of these

Ans. (c)

Exp. All the three statements i.e. (1), (2) and (3) are correct about the plantation of tea crop. Tea plant requires warm and humid climatic condition. It thrives well in a region between 48 North to 27 South latitude and maybe planted up to an altitude of 2,450 meters above sea level.

Evenly distributed rainfall is an important condition for its successful growth. It is generally grown in a zone having 125 to 750 cm rainfall. Therefore, tea gardens are located on hill slops.

Its plants grow well in fertile soil with high humus content. Acidic soil with low calcium and higher iron content are better suited.

35 Which of the following pair is correct? *(Chap 4, Class-X, New NCERT)*

Crops		Largest producer
(a) Wheat	–	Brazil
(b) Cotton	–	China
(c) Tea	–	India
(d) Sugarcane	–	USA

Ans. (c)

Exp. Only pair (c) is correct as India stands as the top producer of tea.

While China leads globally in wheat production, with around two-thirds of the total output originating from the North China plain and an additional one-third from the central provinces.

The United States holds the top position as the largest cotton producer.

Brazil is the largest producer of sugarcane in the world followed by India which accounts for about 21% and 18% respectively.

36 Consider the following statements regarding coffee plantations in the world. *(Chap 8, Class-XI, Old NCERT)*

1. Brazil is the largest coffee producer in the world.
2. Coffee requires warm and wet climate and will drained loamy soil.

Which of the statements given above is/are correct?

(a) Only 1 (b) Only 2
(c) Both 1 and 2 (d) Neither 1 nor 2

Ans. (c)

Exp. Both the statements (1) and (2) are correct regarding coffee plantations in the world.

Brazil is the largest and top coffee producer in the World. Annual output of Brazil is 3,009 metric tonnes. Vietnam is the second largest producer of coffee.

Coffee requires warm and wet climate and well drained loamy soil. Hill slopes are more suitable for growth of this crop.

37 Consider the following statements. *(Chap 8, Class-XI, Old NCERT)*

1. Coffee is grown under shade in highly humid conditions.
2. Coffee is grown as a plantation crop in tropical regions of the world.
3. Arabica and Robusta are high quality varieties of coffee.

Which of the statements given above is/are correct?

(a) Only 1 (b) 2 and 3 (c) 1 and 2 (d) All of these

Ans. (d)

Exp. All the three statements i.e., (1), (2) and (3) are correct as coffee needs hot and humid climate with temperature varying between 15°C and 28°C. It is generally grown under shady trees. Coffee is grown as plantation crop in tropical region in the world.

Like Brazil, Columbia and Vietnam large coffee plantations are Brazil known as Fazendas. Arabica coffee and Robusta coffee are high quality varieties of coffee in the world.

38 Consider the following statements regarding Sugarcane. *(Chap 12, Module-2 NIOS)*

1. It is the least water intensive crop.
2. It can be grown on all varieties of soils ranging from sandy loam to clay loam.
3. Punjab is the top sugar producing state in India.

How many of the statements given above is/are correct?

(a) Only one (b) Only two
(c) All three (d) None of these

Ans. (b)

Exp. Only two statements i.e., (1) and (2) are correct regarding sugarcane in India.

Sugarcane is the least water-intensive crop. It is also the least water-efficient crop, requiring 1800-2200 mm of water per season. This is due to its high sensitivity to drought. Sugarcane is grown in tropical and subtropical regions, where the climate is hot and humid.

Sugarcane can be grown in all types of soils, from sandy loam to clay loam. However, it grows best in well-drained soils. It can also grow in lighter soils if there is adequate irrigation, and in heavy clays with proper drainage and organic matter.

Statement (3) is incorrect because Uttar Pradesh (not Punjab) is the India's largest producer of sugar, accounting for 38.6% of the country's total production. Other major producers include Maharashtra and Karnataka.

39 Consider the following statements regarding sugarcane production. *(Chap 8, Class-XI, Old NCERT)*

1. It is a tropical as well as a subtropical crop that grows well in hot and humid climate.
2. It requires temperature of 21°C to 27°C and an annual rainfall between 75 cm and 100 cm.
3. India is the second largest producer of sugarcane only after Brazil.

Which of the statements given above are correct?

(a) 1 and 2 (b) 2 and 3
(c) 1 and 3 (d) 1, 2 and 3

Ans. (d)

Exp. All the three statements i.e. (1), (2) and (3) are correct regarding sugarcane production. Sugarcane is a tropical as well as a subtropical crop that grows well in hot and humid climate. It requires temperature of 21°C to 27°C and an annual rainfall between 75 cm and 100 cm. Irrigation is required in the regions of low rainfall. India is the second largest producer of sugarcane only after Brazil.

40 Consider the following statements about the cultivation of cotton. *(Chap 8, Class-XI, Old NCERT)*

1. It is mostly grown in tropical regions.
2. It requires low rainfall of about 50 cm.
3. It requires intensive utilisation of fertilisers.

How many of the statements given above is/are correct?

(a) Only one (b) Only two
(c) All three (d) None of these

Ans. (c)

Exp. All the three statements i.e. (1), (2) and (3) are correct about the cultivation of cotton because cotton plant is a shrub native to tropical and subtropical regions around the world. It is mainly grown in tropical regions as well as subtropical regions like Egypt, India, China and USA. Cotton essentially is a plant of dry climate.

A rainfall of 50 cm is a enough for cotton cultivation but it should be evenly distributed during the entire growth period. Cotton plant requires intensive fertiliser application to increase productivity.

41 Which of these regions is/are known for cultivation of cotton? *(Chap 8, Class-XI, Old NCERT)*

1. Nile Delta
2. Northern China Plains
3. South-Eastern USA

Codes

(a) 1 and 2 (b) 2 and 3
(c) 1 and 3 (d) All of the above

Ans. (d)

Exp. All the given regions are known for the cultivation of cotton. Cotton is grown in the Nile delta of Egypt. Nile delta produces good quality of Egyptian cotton. In China, cotton is produced in North China Plain.

Wei ho Valley and lower Yangtze Valley are major cotton producing regions in China. Cotton is grown in the cotton belt of USA, which is located in its Southern part.

42 Consider the following Assertion (A) and Reason (R) and choose the correct code. *(Chap 8, Class-XI, Old NCERT)*

Assertion (A) Rubber plant was found as a wild plant in Amazon Rainforest.

Reason (R) The latex of Rubber tree was used by local natives for water proofing their shoes.

Codes

(a) Both A and R are true and R is the correct explanation of A.
(b) Both A and R are true, but R is not the correct explanation of A.
(c) A is true, but R is false.
(d) A is false, but R is true.

Ans. (b)

Exp. Both Assertion (A) and Reason (R) are true, but Reason (R) is not the correct explanation of Assertion (A).

Rubber is latex of a tree widely found in the tropical forest of Amazon and Zaire basin. The latex of this tree was used by the local natives for water proofing their shoes.

43 Consider the following statements about rubber cultivation. *(Chap 8, Class-XI, Old NCERT)*

1. It generally grows in equatorial climate.
2. It is planted on gentle sloping highlands.
3. Thailand is the largest producer of rubber in the world.

Which of the statements given above are correct?

(a) 1 and 2 (b) 2 and 3
(c) 1 and 3 (d) All of these

Ans. (d)

Exp. All the three statements i.e. (1), (2) and (3) are correct about rubber cultivation because rubber is latex of a tree widely found in the equatorial climatic condition because it requires high temperature of about 27°C and rainfall of 150 cm.

Its plantations are generally located on undulating or gently sloping highlands so that the water is drained efficiently.

Thailand produced 4.37 million metric tonnes of natural rubber in 2020, making it the leading producer of natural rubber Worldwide.

44 Which of the following statements are correct regarding jute crop? *(Chap 4, Class-X, New NCERT)*

1. Jute is also known as golden fibre.
2. Jute grows well on well-drained fertile soils in the flood plains where soils are renewed every year.

Codes

(a) Only 1 (b) Only 2
(c) Both 1 and 2 (d) Neither 1 nor 2

Ans. (c)

Exp. Both the statements (1) and (2) are correct regarding jute crop. It is known as the golden fibre. In the flood plains, where soils are regenerated every year, jute grows successfully on well-drained fertile soils. During the growing period, a high temperature is required. Gunny bags, mats, ropes, yarn, carpets and other artefacts are made from it. It is losing market share to synthetic fibres and packing materials, mainly nylon, due to its expensive cost.

45 Consider the following statements about food security. *(Chap 4, Class-X, New NCERT)*

1. India's food security policy has a primary objective to ensure availability of foodgrains to the common people at an affordable price.
2. The focus of the policy is on growth in agriculture production and on fixing the support price for procurement of wheat and rice, to maintain their stocks.
3. Public Distribution System (PDS) is responsible for procuring and stocking foodgrains, whereas distribution is ensured by Food Corporation of India (FCI).

Which of the statements given above are correct?

(a) 1 and 2 (b) 2 and 3 (c) 2 and 3 (d) 1, 2 and 3

Ans. (a)

Exp. Statements (1) and (2) are correct regarding food security. The fundamental goal of India's food security strategy is to ensure that foodgrains are available to the general public at a reasonable cost. It has made it possible for the destitute to obtain food. The strategy focuses on increasing agricultural production and maintaining stock levels by establishing the support price for wheat and rice procurement.

Statement (3) is incorrect because Food Corporation of India (FCI) is responsible for procuring and stocking foodgrains, whereas distribution is ensured by Public Distribution System (PDS).

Animal Husbandry

46 Consider the following statements about dairy farming practised in New Zealand. *(Chap 3, Class-XI, Old NCERT)*

1. Refrigeration and transport has enabled the export of milk products from New Zealand.
2. Milk products are marketed and sold through co-operatives.
3. Dairy farms are spread over large areas in New Zealand.
4. Milk is converted into high value products for export to Europe.

How many of the statements given above is/are incorrect?

(a) Only one (b) Only two
(c) Only three (d) All four

Ans. (a)

Exp. Only one statement i.e. (3) is incorrect about dairy farming practised in New Zealand because the Taranaki region of the Northern Island of New Zealand has the highest density of milch cows of all regions in the World. The people here have gained proficiency in the milk business from their experiences. Due to the good weather here grass grows throughout the year and it rains throughout the year.

Dairy farmers are not spread over large areas in New Zealand.

47 Consider the following statements about dairy farming. *(Chap 3, Class-XI, Old NCERT)*

1. Dairy farmers grow fodder crops like corn and oats.
2. Large scale refrigeration and storage infrastructure are needed for dairy farming.
3. High yielding milch cows are used in dairy farms.

Which of the statements given above are correct?

(a) 1 and 2 (b) 2 and 3 (c) 1 and 3 (d) 1, 2 and 3

Ans. (d)

Exp. All the three statements i.e. (1), (2) and (3) are correct about dairy farming. In addition to milk production in dairy agriculture, it also produces fodder crops, sorghum, maize, oats and wheat, which are used as fodder. Like labour, capital is also needed in this industry. The management and infrastructure of milk refrigeration and storage require more capital. The high yielding milch cows in the world are reared in dairy farming.

Dairy is the most advanced and efficient type of rearing of milch animals. It is highly capital intensive farming.

48 Consider the following statements with reference to dairy farming in the developed regions of the world.

(Chap 7, Class-XI, Old NCERT)

1. It is a highly capital intensive occupation.
2. It involves labour intensive activities.
3. It is practised far away from the urban and industrial centres.
4. It is extensively practised in New Zealand and Tasmania in Australia.

How many of the statements given above is/are correct?

(a) Only one (b) Only two
(c) Only three (d) All four

***Ans.* (c)**

Exp. Only three statements i.e., (1), (2) and (4) are correct with reference to dairy farming. It is highly capital intensive farming. Dairy farming is highly labour intensive as it involves rigorous care in feeding and milching. There is no off season during the year as in the case of crop raising. It is widely practiced in Tasmania, New Zealand and Australia because of the high number of milch cows and the use of mechanisation here. Due to the good weather, grass grows throughout the year and it rains throughout the year.

Statement (3) is incorrect because, dairy farming is practised mainly near urban and industrial centres which provide neighbourhood market for fresh milk and dairy products.

49 Consider the following Assertion (A) and Reason (R) and choose the correct code.

(Chap 3, Class-XI, Old NCERT)

Assertion (A) Commercial grazing is organised on scientific basis and special emphasis is put upon genetic improvements and disease control.

Reason (R) Commercial grazing is practised in ranches which are divided into different parcels according to their carrying capacity.

Codes

(a) Both A and R are true and R is the correct explanation of A.
(b) Both A and R are true, but R is not the correct explanation of A.
(c) A is true, but R is false.
(d) A is false, but R is true.

***Ans.* (b)**

Exp. Both Assertion (A) and Reason (R) are true, but Reason (R) is not the correct explanation of Assertion (A). Commercial grazing is essentially associated with Western cultures and is practiced on permanent ranches. These ranches cover large areas and are divided into a number of parcels, which are fenced to regulate the grazing. The number of animals in a pasture is kept according to the carrying capacity of the pasture.

Grazing of animals in ranching is organised on a scientific basis. The main emphasis is on breeding, genetic improvement, disease control and health care of the animals.

50 In the context of features of market gardening, Consider the following statements.

(Chap 5, Class-XII, New NCERT)

1. It involves cultivation of crops for the purpose of selling in urban markets.
2. Vegetables and fruits are cultivated using high yielding seeds and assured irrigation methods.
3. It is practised in North-Western Europe and North-Eastern USA.

Which of the statements given above are correct?

(a) 1 and 2 (b) 2 and 3
(c) 1 and 3 (d) All of these

***Ans.* (d)**

Exp. All the given statements i.e. (1), (2) and (3) are the features of market gardening because market gardening specialises in the cultivation of high value crops such as vegetables, fruits and flowers, solely for the urban markets. It is labour and capital intensive and lays emphasis on the use of irrigation, high yielding seeds, fertilisers, insecticides, greenhouses and artificial heating in colder regions. This type of agriculture is well-developed in North-Western Europe, North-Eastern United States of America and the Mediterranean regions.

51 Consider the following pairs.

(Chap 5, Class-XII, New NCERT)

	Types of farming	Description
1.	Truck farming	– Cultivation of vegetables
2.	Factory farming	– Poultry and cattle rearing
3.	Horticulture	– Cultivation of high value crops

How many of the pairs given above is/are correctly matched?

(a) Only one (b) Only two
(c) All three (d) None of these

***Ans.* (c)**

Exp. All the given pairs are correctly matched because the regions where farmers specialise in vegetables only, the farming is known as truck farming.

In factory farming, livestock, particularly poultry and cattle rearing, is done in stalls and pens, fed on manufactured feedstuff and carefully supervised against diseases. Horticulture specialises in the cultivation of high value crops such as vegetables, fruits and flowers, solely for the urban markets.

52 Which of the following are the conditions required for optimal growth of rice?

(Chap 8, Class-XI, Old NCERT)

1. Warm and humid climate
2. 100 cm of rainfall
3. Deltaic soil

Codes

(a) 1 and 2
(b) 2 and 3
(c) 1 and 3
(d) All of these

***Ans.* (d)**

Exp. All the given options i.e. (1), (2) and (3) are the conditions required for optimal growth of rice because rice crop requires hot and humid climate. It is best suited for areas with high humidity, prolonged sunlight and an assured supply of water.

The average temperature required for the entire life span of the crop is between 21° and 37°C. The production of rice requires deltaic soil and alluvial soil. Rice is more in those areas where the rainfall is more than 100 cm.

53 **Consider the following statements.** *(Unit 4, Class-XII, Tamil Nadu Board)*

1. Coffee cultivation requires temperatures between 15°C to 28 °C.
2. Assam is the highest coffee producing state in India.
3. Arabica and Robusta are two types of coffee produced in India.

Which of the statements given above is/are correct?

(a) 1 and 2
(b) Only 2
(c) 1 and 3
(d) 1, 2 and 3

***Ans.* (c)**

Exp. Statements (1) and (3) are correct regarding coffee in India.

Coffee plants require a hot and humid climate with temperatures between 15°C and 28°C. They also need rainfall between 150 and 250 cm.

Indian coffee is one of the best coffees in the world due to its high quality and gets a high premium in the international markets. India produces two types of coffee. Arabica and Robusta. Arabica has high market value than Robusta coffee due to its mild aromatic flavour.

Statement (2) is incorrect because Karnataka is the largest coffee-producing state in India, accounting for over 70% of the country's total production.

54 **Consider the following pairs.** *(Class-XII, Old NCERT)*

Crops	Regions/countries
1. Rubber	Mauritius
2. Coffee	Italy
3. Olive	Columbia
4. Sugarcane	Malaysia

How many of the pairs given above is/are correctly matched?

(a) Only 1 (b) Only 2
(c) Only 3 (d) None of these

***Ans.* (d)**

Exp. None of the given pair is correct.

Malaysia is the third largest producer of natural rubber. Thailand is the largest producer of rubber.

Columbia is one of the leading producers of coffee in the world. Brazil is the largest producer of coffee.

Italy is the second largest producer of olive in the world. Spain is the largest producer of olive.

Mauritius is one of the main producers of sugarcane. Brazil holds first position in sugarcane production in the world.

55 **Consider the following statements.** *(Chap 4, Class-VIII, New NCERT)*

1. India is the second-largest producer of fruits and vegetables globally.
2. Horticulture contributes more than 33 percent to the agricultural GVA.

Which of the statements given above is/are correct?

(a) Only 1 (b) Only 2
(c) Both 1 and 2 (d) Neither 1 nor 2

***Ans.* (c)**

Exp. Both the statements (1) and (2) are correct.

India is the second-largest producer of fruits and vegetables in the world, after China. In 2021-2022, India produced 107.24 million metric tonnes of fruits and 204.84 million metric tonnes of vegetables.

Indian horticulture sector contributes about 33% to the agricultural Gross Value Added (GVA)-making a very significant contribution to the Indian economy.

Productivity of horticulture crops is much higher compared to the productivity of foodgrains (12.49 tonnes/ha against 2.23 tonnes/ha.).

Chapter 9

Mineral Resources

Mineral Resources

Mineral

Introduction
- A naturally occurring organic and inorganic substance having a definite chemical composition and physical properties
- Composed of two or more elements but single elements may also be found

Physical Features of Minerals
- **External Crystal Form** Determined by internal arrangement of molecules
- **Cleavage** Tendency to break in given directions producing relatively plane surfaces
- **Fracture** Breaking along random directions
- **Lustre** Appearance of the mineral irrespective of its colour
- **Colour** Characteristic colour determined by their molecular structure
- **Transparency** Can be transparent, translucent and opaque
- **Structure** Particular arrangement of individual crystals
- **Specific Gravity** Ratio of weight of volume of substance to the weight of an equal volume of reference substance

Conservation of Minerals
- A non-renewable resource so takes thousand of years for formation and concentration
- Rate of formation is much slower than rate of consumption
- It is necessary to reduce wastage in the process of mining
- Rise in prices due to increase in commercial uses

Types and Distribution of Mineral

Iron Ore
- Metallic mineral not found in pure form in nature
- Different types of iron ore are haemetite, magnetite, limonite and siderite
- Most widely used metal in the world
- Leading producers are China, Australia, Brazil, etc

Copper
- Largely used in electrical industry due to its quality of electrical conductivity
- Malleable and ductile along with corrosion resistant
- Leading producers are Chile, Peru, China, etc

Bauxite
- An ore of aluminium, light and versatile metal
- Has wide industrial uses such as aeroplane industry, machine tools, automobiles, etc
- Leading producers are China, India, Russia, etc

Manganese
- An important raw material for smelting iron ore and manufacturing ferro alloys
- Deposits are found in almost all geological formations, however mainly associated with Dharwar system
- Leading producers are South Africa, Australia, China, etc

Chromium
- Used for making high quality alloy steel
- Largest producers are South Africa and Russia

Zinc
- Occurs in association of lead, hence both are mined together
- Leading producers are China, Australia, Peru, etc

Mica
- Lustrous mineral
- Bad conductor of heat and electricity
- Largest producer being India

Tin
- One of the important metals used for making alloys
- found in placer deposit
- Leading producers are China, Indonesia, Myanmar, etc

Gold
- Occurs in the form of Alluvial placer depositor as reefs
- Used for making ornaments, electronics, pharmaceuticals, etc
- Leading producers are China, Australia, Russia, etc

Silver
- Occurs in pure state as well as combination with gold, lead and copper
- Used for making coins, ornaments, crafts, etc
- Leading producers are Mexico, Peru, China, etc

Diamond
- Purest form of carbon and also the hardest substance
- Used for cutting glasses, drilling in rocks, making ornaments, etc
- Leading producer is Republic of Congo

Platinum
- Rare mineral, also called white gold
- Used for making ornaments, laboratory instruments, etc
- Leading producers are Canada and South Africa
- The melting point of platinum is 1550°C to 2700°C

SOURCE ***New NCERT Class VIII*** *(Mineral and Power Resources),* ***Old NCERT Class VIII*** *(Our Eastern and Southern Neighbours),* ***Old NCERT Class IX*** *(Our Resources),* ***New NCERT Class XI*** *(Minerals and Rocks)* ***Old NCERT Class XI*** *(Non-renewable Resources (Minerals),* ***Old NCERT Class XI*** *(Energy Resources),* ***Tamil Nadu Board Class XII*** *(Resources)* ***Chap 18, Module-8 NIOS*** *(Mineral and Energy Resources)*

Mineral Resources

1 **Consider the following sentences about minerals.** *(Chap 3, Class-VIII, New NCERT)*

1. A useful substance distributed uniformly over the Earth.
2. A complex substance which can be extracted by special machines.
3. A naturally formed substance which has a definite chemical composition.
4. A natural substance formed by chemical reaction inside the Earth.

Which of the statements above is most appropriate definition of minerals?

(a) Only 1 (b) Only 2 (c) Only 3 (d) All four

***Ans.* (c)**

Exp. Statement (3) shows the most appropriate definition of a mineral resource. A naturally formed inorganic substance which has a definite chemical composition is known as Mineral Resources. Minerals are not evenly distributed over the Earth, they are concentrated in a particular area or rock formations.

2 **Consider the following statements about mineral resources in India.** *(Chap 3, Class-VIII, New NCERT)*

1. The vast alluvial plain tract of North India is devoid of minerals of economic use.
2. The majority of valuable minerals are associated with metamorphic and igneous rocks of the peninsular India.
3. Non-metallic minerals like coal and petroleum are formed from buried animal and plant life.

How many of the statements given above is/are correct?

(a) Only one (b) Only two
(c) All three (d) None of these

***Ans.* (b)**

Exp. Only two statements i.e. (2) and (3) are correct regarding mineral resources in India. The peninsular region of India, which is composed of ancient igneous and metamorphic rocks, is rich in valuable minerals such as iron ore, magnesium, bauxite, mica, coal, and more. Coal and petroleum are organic minerals formed from the remains of ancient plant and animal life.

Statement (1) is incorrect because the alluvial plains of North India are not as mineral-rich as the peninsular region, they are not devoid of minerals of economic use.

3 **Consider the following sentences about iron.** *(Chap 4, Class-XI, Old NCERT)*

1. Iron can be extracted from the ores of haematite, magnetite and limonite.
2. Impurities can be removed from iron ores by the process of smelting.
3. Alloys of iron can be obtained by mixing metals such as manganese and vanadium.

How many of the statements given above is/are correct?

(a) Only one (b) Only two
(c) All three (d) None of these

***Ans.* (c)**

Exp. All three statements i.e. (1), (2) and (3) are correct as the percentage of pure iron varies in different forms of iron ore. Some of the iron ores are magnetite, haematite, limonite and siderite. Iron is obtained from ores of magnetite, haematite and limonite.

There are many types of impurities present in iron ore. These impurities can be removed by the process of smelting to improve the quality of iron.

Alloy, metallic substance composed of two or more elements. Iron alloys can be obtained by mixing metals like manganese, nickel and vanadium.

4 **Match the iron ore regions with their respective countries.** *(Chap 4, Class-XI, Old NCERT)*

(Iron ore)		(Region/country)
1. Karaganda	–	Kazakhstan
2. Mesabi	–	USA
3. Schefferville	–	Canada
4. Kiruna	–	Germany

Which of the following pairs given above is/are not matched correctly?

(a) Only 1 (b) Only 2 (c) Only 3 (d) All of these

***Ans.* (a)**

Exp. Only one pair i.e., (4) is not matched correctly because the Kiruna mine is the largest and most modern underground iron ore mine in the world. The mine is located in Kiruna in Norrbotten County, Lapland, Sweden. Kiruna mine has been in operation since 1900.

5 **Consider the following statements about mineral formations in India.** *(Chap 5, Class- X, New NCERT)*

1. Minerals in igneous and metamorphic rocks may occur in cracks, crevices, faults, or joints, forming veins and lodes.
2. Sedimentary rocks can contain minerals in beds or layers, and some, like coal and certain iron ores, result from long periods of heat and pressure.
3. Alluvial deposits in sands of valley floors and base of hills are known as placer deposits, containing minerals like gold, silver, tin, and platinum.

How many of the statements given above is/are correct?

(a) Only one (b) Only two (c) All three (d) None of these

***Ans.* (c)**

Exp. All three statements i.e. (1), (2) and (3) are correct about mineral formation in India.

Minerals of great economic value found in igneous rocks are magnetic iron, nickel, copper, lead, zinc, chromite, manganese, gold, diamond, and platinum. They occur in lodes in igneous and metamorphic rocks.

Sedimentary rocks are formed by the deposition of fragments of rocks by exogenous processes. They contain minerals in beds or layers.

Sedimentary rocks can contain minerals like limestone, dolomite, and phosphate. Placer deposits are the natural concentrations of heavy minerals of economic importance. Important placer deposits occur in various parts of India, including Kerala, Tamil Nadu, Odisha, and Andhra Pradesh. These deposits contain minerals like ilmenite, rutile, garnet, zircon, sillimanite, and others.

6 Which of the following pair is correct? *(Chap 4, Class-XI, Old NCERT)*

Iron Ore mining		Country
(a) Pilbara	–	Brazil
(b) Carajas	–	China
(c) Siegen	–	Germany
(d) Bailadila	–	Australia

***Ans.* (c)**

Exp. Only pair (c) is correct as Siegen in Germany, iron ore deposits are found in the Siegen regions. iron mining is also done here.

While pairs (a), (b) and (d) are incorrect. Pilbara is the important iron ore mining regions located in Australia. Australia is an important producer and exporter of iron ore. Iron ore deposits in Australia are found in the Western region.

Carajas mine is the largest iron ore mine in the world. It is located in the Carajas mountains of the Para district of Northern Brazil. The mine is operated as an open-pit mine. Germany is the important producer of iron.

Bailadila is the iron ore mine located in Chhattisgarh, India. Hematite is the major ore produced in the Bailadila mines.

7 Consider the following statements about the distribution of minerals in India. *(Chap 5, Class- X, New NCERT)*

1. Ferrous minerals account for about three-fourths of the total value of the production of metallic minerals in India.
2. Iron ore, a basic mineral for industrial development, is primarily found in abundance in Southern states like Kerala and Tamil Nadu.
3. Rajasthan, with its rock systems similar to the peninsular region, has significant reserves of non-ferrous minerals.

How many of the statements given above is/are correct?

(a) Only one (b) Only two
(c) All three (d) None of these

***Ans.* (b)**

Exp. Only two statements i.e. (1) and (3) are correct. Ferrous minerals, primarily iron ore, contribute significantly to the total value of mineral production in India.

Rajasthan shares geological similarities with the peninsular region, making it rich in minerals like copper, lead, and zinc, which fall under the category of non-ferrous minerals.

Statement (2) is incorrect while India has iron ore deposits across the country, the major ones are located in Eastern states like Odisha, Jharkhand, and Chhattisgarh, not in the South. Kerala and Tamil Nadu have limited iron ore deposits.

8 Consider the following minerals. *(Chap 4, Class-XI, Old NCERT)*

1. Cuprite 2. Malachite
3. Chalcocite 4. Lignite

How many of these minerals are ores of copper?

(a) Only one (b) Only two
(c) Only three (d) All four

***Ans.* (c)**

Exp. Three of the given minerals (Cuprite, Malachite, and Chalcocite) are ores of copper. Cuprite is a mineral composed of copper (I) oxide, Cu^2O. It is an important ore of copper and has a characteristic red colour.

Malachite is a green carbonate mineral, and it is a secondary copper mineral. It is often associated with copper deposits and is an important ore of copper.

Chalcocite is a sulfide mineral and an important secondary ore of copper. It typically forms in the oxidation zones of copper ore bodies.

However, lignite is not a mineral associated with copper, it is a soft, brown, combustible sedimentary rock that is often considered the lowest rank of coal.

9 Match the copper mining regions with their respective countries. *(Chap 4, Class-XI, Old NCERT)*

Copper Mine		Country
1. Sudbury	–	Canada
2. Katanga	–	Zaire (Democratic Republic of Congo)
3. Montana	–	USA

Which of the pairs given above is/are matched correctly?

(a) Only 1 (b) Only 2
(c) All of these (d) None of these

***Ans.* (c)**

Exp. All of these given pairs are correctly matched. Canada has an important place in the production of copper. Copper mines in Canada are located at Sudbury in the district of Ontario and at Quebec.

Zaire and Zambia are the main producers of copper in Africa. The Katanga copper deposit area is the main copper producing district of Zaire.

The copper mining area in USA is towards the West. Arizona is the main producing state in the USA. In the USA, in addition to Montana, copper is also mined in state of Arizona.

10 **Which of the following statements is/are incorrect regarding natural gas?** *(Chap 5, Class-XI, Old NCERT)*

1. Natural gas is used as a source of energy as well as an industrial raw material in the petrochemical industry.
2. Natural gas is not an environment friendly.
3. The power and fertiliser industries are the key users of natural gas.

Codes

(a) 1 and 2 (b) 2 and 3
(c) Only 2 (d) All of these

***Ans.* (c)**

Exp. Statement (2) is incorrect regarding natural gas because it is considered as environment friendly fuel due to low carbon dioxide emissions.

Natural gas is used as a source of energy as well as industrial raw material in the petrochemical industry. The power and fertiliser industries are the key users of natural gas.

11 **Consider the following statements regarding petroleum oil.** *(Chap 5, Class-XI, Old NCERT)*

1. Most of the petroleum occurrences in India are associated with anticlines and fault traps in the rock formations of the tertiary age.
2. It provides fuel for heat and lighting, lubricants for machinery and raw materials for a number of manufacturing industries.
3. Petroleum refineries act as a 'nodal industry' for synthetic textile, fertiliser and numerous chemical industries.

Which of the statements given above are correct?

(a) 1 and 2 (b) 2 and 3 (c) 3 and 1 (d) 1, 2 and 3

***Ans.* (d)**

Exp. All the statements (1), (2) and (3) are correct regarding petroleum oil. Petroleum, (often known as mineral oil), is India's second most important energy source. It offers heat and illumination, as well as lubricants for machinery and raw materials for a variety of businesses.

Petrochemical refineries serve as a 'nodal industry' for the synthetic textile, fertiliser and chemical sectors. Most of the petroleum occurrences in India are associated with anticlines and fault traps in the rock formations of the tertiary age.

12 **Which of the following statements is/are correct?** *(Chap 4, Class-XI, Old NCERT) (UPPSC Pre 2015)*

1. USA is the largest producer of bauxite.
2. Bauxite is an ore of aluminium.

Codes

(a) Only 1 (b) Only 2
(c) Both 1 and 2 (d) Neither 1 nor 2

***Ans.* (b)**

Exp. Only statement (2) is correct because bauxite is the principal ore of aluminium. It is a rock largely composed of a mixture of hydrogen aluminium oxide.

Australia is the world's largest producer of bauxite. Australia produced the largest amount of bauxite in the world in 2020. Australia produced 110 million metric tonnes of bauxite in 2020.

13 **Which of the following statements is/are correct regarding tin?** *(Chap 3, Class-VIII, New NCERT) (UPPSC Pre 2010)*

1. China is the largest tin producing country in the world.
2. Tin ore is also known as Cassiterite.

Codes

(a) Only 1 (b) Only 2
(c) Both 1 and 2 (d) Neither 1 nor 2

***Ans.* (c)**

Exp. Both the statements (1) and (2) are correct regarding tin. China is the largest tin producing country in the world. China is by far the world's largest market for tin.

The production of refined tin in China in 2020 was about 2,03,000 metric tonnes. The ore of tin is known as Cassiterite.

14 **Match the iron ore producing regions with their respective countries.** *(Chap 3, Class-VIII, Old NCERT)*

(Iron ore)	(Region/country)
1. Liberia	1. Africa
2. Shenyang	2. China
3. Brazil	3. South America
4. Great Lakes area	4. South America

How many of the pairs given above is/are matched correctly?

(a) Only one
(b) Only two
(c) Only three
(d) All of the above

***Ans.* (c)**

Exp. Only three pairs i.e., (1), (2) and (3) are correctly matched.

Liberia in Africa is major iron producing region.
Shenyang in China is famous for iron production.
Brazil is major iron producing region in South America.
Pair (4) is not correctly matched because Great Lakes area is in North America, not South America.

15 **With reference to India, consider the following statements.** *(Chap 7, Class-XII, NCERT) (IAS Pre 2022)*

1. Monazite is a source of rare earths.
2. Monazite contains thorium.
3. Monazite occurs naturally in the entire Indian coastal sands in India.
4. In India, government bodies only can process or export monazite.

Which of the statements given above are correct?
(a) 1, 2 and 3
(b) 1, 2 and 4
(c) 3 and 4
(d) 1, 2, 3 and 4

Ans. (b)

Exp. Statements (1), (2) and (4) are correct. monazite is a major source of rare earths and it contains Thorium. It yields a number of rare-earth elements, such as neodymium and praseodymium. Both of these are in demand internationally for making high-performance rare-earth magnets (components of power wind turbines, electric vehicles and robotics). Government of India (GOI) under DAE, is the only entity which has been permitted to produce and process monazite, and handle it for domestic use as well as for export.

Statement (3) is incorrect because the main mines of menazite of monazite are found along the coasts of Southern India in Kerala, Tamil Nadu and in Odisha. Monazite is a brown crystalline mineral consisting of cerium, lanthanum, other rare Earth elements, and thorium. Monazite usually occurs in small, isolated crystals or grains that are resistant to weathering and become concentrated in soils.

16 Which of the given pairs is/are incorrectly matched? *(Chap 4, Class-XI, Old NCERT)*

Bauxite mining		Region
1. Arkansas	–	USA
2. Weipa	–	Australia
3. Guinea	–	Africa
4. Henan	–	Oman

Codes
(a) Only 4
(b) Only 2
(c) Only 3
(d) All of the above

Ans. (a)

Exp. Pair (4) is incorrectly matched because Henan is a bauxite mining region located in Norway.

17 Match the following lists correctly and choose the correct code. *(Chap 9, Class-VIII, Old NCERT)*

List I (Minerals)	List II (Found in)
A. Precious stones	1. Tanintharyi
B. Tungsten	2. Irrawaddy valley
C. Coal	3. Kalewa
D. Mineral oil	4. Shan plateau

Codes

	A	B	C	D
(a)	1	2	3	4
(b)	4	1	3	2
(c)	3	1	2	4
(d)	1	2	4	3

Ans. (b)

Exp. The correct matching is A-4, B-1, C-3, D-2.
The **Shan plateau** lies in the Eastern part of Myanmar and is a part of the Indo Malayan mountain system. The plateau is the country's main source of lead, zinc, precious stones and silver and is home to major teak forests.

Myanmar is rich in mineral resources. Tungsten, chromium and nickel minerals found in **Tanintharyi** region in Myanmar.

Kalewa Township is a township of Kale district in Sagaing Division of Myanmar. Coal mines is located in Kalewa region in Myanmar.

Myanmar is rich in minerals including metal ores, petroleum and natural gas. Mineral oil is found in the **Irrawaddy** river valley in Myanmar.

18 Which of the following do not contains silver? *(Chap 5, Class-XI, New NCERT) (IAS Pre 2007)*

(a) Horn silver
(b) German silver
(c) Ruby silver
(d) Lunar caustic

Ans. (b)

Exp. German silver does not contains silver. It is also known as Nickel silver, New silver, Alpacca, etc. It is a copper alloy with nickel and often zinc..The usual formulation is 60% copper, 20% nickel and 20% zinc. It is named for its silvery appearance but contains no silver element.

Chapter 10

Energy Resources

Energy Resources

Non-Renewable Energy Sources

Coal

- Most abundantly found fossil fuel, used as domestic fuel as well as in industries too; Found in the seams of sedimentary rocks. It is of four types, namely
  - **Anthracite** Very hard, shiny and free of impurities; Contains 90% of carbon and they left little ash after burning
  - **Bituminous** Contains 70-90% of carbon; It is black, shiny and gives smoky flame
  - **Lignite** Contains 45-70% of carbon and burns with high smoky flames; It is of recent origin and contains higher proportion of vegetal matter
  - **Peat** First stage in formation of coal from vegetation, light brown in colour with high humidity content

Petroleum

- Found between the layers of rocks and is drilled from oil fields located in off-shore and coastal areas. The oil extracted is sent to refineries for processing
- They are labelled as black gold

Natural Gas

- Found with Petroleum deposits and is released when crude oil is brought to surface; Can be used as domestic and industrial fuel; It is a source of energy as well as raw material for petrochemical industry; Considered as environment friendly fuel

Thermal Power

- Generated by using coal, petroleum and natural gas i.e., usage of non-renewable fossil fuels for generation of electricity

Hydel Power

- Rain water or stored water in dams is made to fall from a height over turbine blades, which then move and generate hydroelectricity; It is the cleanest mode since it does not pollute environment

Nuclear Energy

- Obtained from the energy stored in nuclei of atoms of naturally occuring radioactive elements like uranium or thorium; These fuels undergo nuclear fission in nuclear reactors and emit power

Renewable Energy Sources

Solar Energy

- Most widely available and non-exhaustible source of energy
- Solar energy can be directly converted into electricity with the help of PV cells

Wind Energy

- An inexhaustible source of energy where wind mills have been used for grinding grain and lift waters since ancient times Presently, they are used to generate electricity

Biogas

- Organic waste such as dead plants, animals, kitchen waste can be converted to biogas An excellent fuel for cooking, lighting and produces huge amounts of organic manure every year
- It prevents loss of trees and manure due to burning of fuel wood

Geothermal Energy

- Heat energy obtained from the Earth is called Geothermal energy
- Geothermal energy in the form of hot springs has been used for cooking, heating and bathing for several years

Tidal Energy

- Energy generated from tides and can be harnessed by building dams at narrow openings of sea

SOURCE New NCERT Class VIII *(Mineral and Power Resources)*, Old NCERT Class VIII *(Our Eastern and Southern Neighbours)*, Old NCERT Class IX *(Our Resources)*, New NCERT Class XI *(Minerals and Rocks)* Old NCERT Class XI *(Non-renewable Resources (Minerals)*, Old NCERT Class XI *(Energy Resources)*, Tamil Nadu Board Class XII *(Resources)* NIOS Module 8 Chap 18 *(Mineral and Energy Resources)*

Energy Resources

1 **Consider the following statements about coal quality.** *(Chap 5, Class- X, New NCERT)*

1. Higher calorific value indicates lower carbon content and less efficient burning.
2. Moisture content in coal has negligible impact on its energy output.
3. Ash content in coal decreases its heating value and increases environmental pollution.

How many of the statements given above is/are correct?

(a) Only one (b) Only two
(c) All three (d) None of these

***Ans.* (a)**

Exp. Only one statement i.e., (3) is correct regarding quality of coal.

Higher amounts of ash content reduce the calorific value of coal, causes health and environmental damages and lowers the boiler efficiency. Thus, ash content is an important parameter to determine the coal price as coal's purity and efficiency greatly depend on ash content.

Statements (1) and (2) are incorrect.

An increase in the percentage of fixed carbon in coal will be followed by an increase of calorific value. This shows a very strong correlation between fixed carbon content and calorific value in coal. Moisture absorbs heat, so high moisture content in coal reduces the relative efficiency of heating when a coal is combusted. This is why low-rank, high-moisture coals have lower calorific values than high-rank, low-moisture coals.

2 **Match List I (Minerals) with List II (Location) and select the correct answer using the codes given below.** *(Chap 5, Class-X, New NCERT) (IAS Pre 2004)*

List I	List II
A. Coal	1. Giridih
B. Copper	2. Jayamkondam
C. Manganese	3. Alwar
D. Lignite	4. Dharwar

Codes

	A	B	C	D		A	B	C	D
(a)	1	4	3	2	(b)	1	3	4	2
(c)	2	3	4	1	(d)	2	4	3	1

***Ans.* (b)**

Exp. The correct matching is A-1, B-3, C-4, D-2.

Giridih is a district in Jharkhand famous for coal production.

Alwar city is located in Rajasthan famous for copper production.

Dharwar region is in Karnataka famous for manganese production.

Jayamkondam is located in Tamil Nadu is famous for the production of lignite.

3 **Arrange the following types of coal in increasing order of their quality in terms of carbon content, with the help of codes given below.** *(Chap 5, Class-XI, Old NCERT)*

1. Peat
2. Lignite
3. Anthracite
4. Bituminous

Codes

(a) 1-4-3-2 (b) 2-1-4-3 (c) 1-4-3-2 (d) 1-2-4-3

***Ans.* (d)**

Exp. The increasing order of coal of their quality in terms of carbon content is 1-2-3-4 i.e., peat coal, lignite coal, bituminous coal and anthracite coal.

Anthracite contains 86% to 97% carbon. Anthracite coal has the highest heating value of all ranks of coal.

Bituminous coal contains 70% to 90% carbon. It has a lower heating value than anthracite coal.

Lignite coal typically contains 45% to 70% carbon, and it has a lower heating value than bituminous coal.

Peat coal contains 25% to 35% carbon and it has the lowest energy content of all coal ranks.

4 **Match items in the List I with List II and select the correct answer using the codes given below the lists.** *(Chap 5, Class XII, New NCERT) (IAS Pre 2005)*

List I (Power Station)	List II (State)
A. Kothagudem	1. Andhra Pradesh
B. Raichur	2. Gujarat
C. Mettur	3. Karnataka
D. Wanakbori	4. Tamil Nadu

Codes

	A	B	C	D		A	B	C	D
(a)	4	2	1	3	(b)	1	3	4	2
(c)	4	3	1	2	(d)	1	2	4	3

***Ans.* (b)**

Exp. The correct matching is A-1, B-3, C-4, D-2.

Kothagudem power station has installed capacity of 1680 MW in Andhra Pradesh.

Raichur thermal power station is coal fired electric power station in Karnataka.

Mettur thermal and Nuclear plant with 840 MW capacity in Tamil Nadu.

Wanakbori power station is located on Mahi river in Gujarat.

5 **Despite having large reserves of coal, why does India import millions of tonnes of coal?** *(Chap 5, Class-XI, Old NCERT) (IAS Pre 2012)*

1. It is the policy of India to save its own coal reserves for the future, and import it from other countries for the present use.
2. Most of the power plants in India are coal based and they are not able to get sufficient supplies of coal from within the country.

3. Steel companies need a large quantity of coking coal which has to be imported.

Codes

(a) Only 1 (b) 2 and 3
(c) 1 and 3 (d) 1, 2 and 3

Ans. (b)

Exp. Statements (2) and (3) are the reasons due to which India imports millions of tonnes of coal despite having large reserves. India imports around 300-400 million tonnes of coal primarily from Indonesia, Australia and South Africa.

The lack of coking coal reserves that are used as a row material in power plant, steel plants and other allied industries is the main reason that India imports coal.

Statement (1) is not the reason because the imports are mainly to compensate for the lack of good quality coal, its not the policy of India to save its own coal reserves for the future.

6 Which of the following pairs is correct?

(Chap 5, Class-XI, Old NCERT)

	List I (Coal Mining Region)		List II (Country)
1.	Jiangsu and Kailuan	–	China
2.	Wyoming and Colorado	–	Russia
3.	Kuznetsk Basin	–	USA

How many pairs given above is/are correct?

(a) Only one (b) Only two
(c) Only three (d) None of these

Ans. (a)

Exp. Only one pair i.e. (1) is correct.

Jiangsu and Kailuan mining regions are located in China. Here, coal is also mined from Datang, Shatang and Manchuria regions.

While pairs (2) and (3) are incorrect Wyoming and Colorado are major coal mining regions located in USA. In USA, coal is mined mainly from illinois, Utah and Arizona regions.

Kuznetsk Basin is the main coal-producing regions in Russia. Here, the layer of coal is close to surface that is why open mining is done here.

7 Consider the following statements about mineral oil.

(Chap 5, Class-XI, Old NCERT)

1. Mineral oil is a more versatile source of energy than coal.
2. It can be used in the manufacturing of chemical fertilisers and insecticides.
3. Mineral oil is found together with the deposits of natural gas.

How many of the statements given above is/are correct?

(a) Only one (b) Only two
(c) All three (d) None of these

Ans. (c)

Exp. All three statements i.e., (1), (2) and (3) are correct about mineral oil. In the present time, the importance of mineral oil is huge. Mineral oil has more energy providing capacity than coal.

Mineral oil is a more versatile source of energy than coal. Mineral oil is used to run the means of transport, to make chemical fertilisers and insecticides. Generally, deposit of natural gas is also found in the area where mineral oil is found.

8 Consider the following statements.

(Chap 5, Class XI, Old NCERT)

1. In India, State Governments do not have the power to auction non-coal mines.
2. Andhra Pradesh and Jharkhand do not have gold mines.
3. Rajasthan has iron ore mines.

Which of the statements given above is/are correct?

(a) 1 and 2 (b) Only 2
(c) 1 and 3 (d) Only 3

Ans. (d)

Exp. Only statement (3) is correct. Hematite, and magnetite are the most important iron ores in India it spread in Rajasthan, Uttar Pradesh, Bihar etc.

Statements (2) and (3) are incorrect. According to MMDR Amendment Act 2015 the State Governments will conduct auction for grant of minerals concessions but Central Government have only advisory power.

Rajasthan, Andhra Pradesh and Jharkhand have trace of Gold.

9 Consider the following statements.

(Chap 7, Class-XII, NCERT) (IAS Pre 2020)

1. Coal ash contains arsenic, lead and mercury.
2. Coal-fired power plants release sulphur dioxide and oxides of nitrogen into the environment.
3. High ash content is observed in Indian coal.

Which of the statements given above is/are correct?

(a) Only 1 (b) 2 and 3
(c) Only 3 (d) 1, 2 and 3

Ans. (d)

Exp. Statements (1), (2) and (3) are correct.

Coal ash, also referred to as coal combustion residuals or CCRs, contains contaminants like mercury, cadmium, and arsenic. Coal-fired power plants are one of the largest sources of health-harming air pollutants being emitted into the atmosphere. This includes sulphur dioxide (SO_2), nitrogen oxide (NOx), and particulate matter (PM). The ash content of coal produced in India is generally 25% to 45%, which is higher compared to the ash content of imported coal that varies from 10% to 20%.

10 Consider the following minerals.

(Chap 7, Class-XII, NCERT) (IAS Pre 2020)

1. Bentonite 2. Chromite
3. Kyanite 4. Sillimanite

In India, which of the above is/are officially designated as major minerals?

(a) 1 and 2 (b) Only 4
(c) 1 and 3 (d) 2, 3 and 4

Ans. (d)

Exp. The minerals that are officially designated as major minerals in India are Chromite, Kyanite and Sillimanite.

11 Which of the following statements is/are correct regarding thorium? *(Chap 5, Class-XI, Old NCERT)*

1. Main mineral sources of thorium are thorianite, allanite and monazite.
2. Chalcocite is an important thorium ore.

Codes

(a) Only 1 (b) Only 2
(c) Both 1 and 2 (d) Neither 1 nor 2

Ans. (a)

Exp. Statement (1) is correct regarding thorium as the main mineral sources of thorium are thorianite, allanite and monazite. Allanite is a brown and black mineral found in granite rocks. Monazite is the main source of thorium in the world. It is a yellowish brown mineral, a composite of granite and pegmatite.

Statement (2) is incorrect because Chalcocite is an important copper ore mineral.

12 In which of the following regions of India are shale gas resources found? *(Chap 8, Class-VIII, New NCERT) (IAS Pre 2016)*

1. Cambay Basin 2. Cauvery Basin
3. Krishna-Godavari Basin

Codes

(a) 1 and 2 (b) Only 3
(c) 2 and 3 (d) All of these

Ans. (d)

Exp. All of these options are correct regarding shale gas resources found in India. Shale gas presence have been found by researcher in Cambay basin at Meshsana, Ahmedabad and Basuch district of Gujarat, Canvery basin at Nagapattinam in Tamil Nadu and in KG (Krishna-Godavari) Basin of Andhra Pradesh.

13 Consider the following statements about solar energy. *(Chap 5, Class-XI, Old NCERT)*

1. USA is the top solar energy producing country in the world.
2. The installed solar energy capacity of India is 44.3 GW.

Which of the statements given above is/are incorrect?

(a) Only 1
(b) Only 2
(c) Both 1 and 2
(d) Neither 1 nor 2

Ans. (a)

Exp. Statement (1) is incorrect about solar energy because China is the top solar energy producing country in the world.

China leads the world as top producer of solar power by installing over 30.1 GW of photovoltaic capacity in 2019. USA is the second largest solar energy producing country in the world.

14 Consider the following statements. *(Chap 6, Class-X, New NCERT)*

1. National Thermal Power Corporation has diversified into hydropower sector.
2. Power Grid Corporation of India has diversified into telecom sector.

Which of the statements given above is/are correct?

(a) Only 1 (b) Only 2
(c) Both 1 and 2 (d) Neither 1 nor 2

Ans. (a)

Exp. Statement (1) is correct as National Thermal Power Corporation has diversified into hydropower sector.

Statement (2) is incorrect because Power Grid Corporation of India Limited have main functions are transmission of electricity across India.

15 Consider the following statements. *(Chap 5, Class-XII, New NCERT) (IAS Pre 2004)*

1. Damodar, Valley Corporation is the first multi-purpose river valley project of independent India.
2. Damodar Valley Corporation includes thermal and gas power stations.

Which of the statements given above is/are correct?

(a) Only 1 (b) Only 2
(c) Both 1 and 2 (d) Neither 1 nor 2

Ans. (a)

Exp. Only statement (1) is correct as Damodar Valley Corporation is first multi-purpose river valley project of independent India. It was setup in 1954.

Statement (2) is incorrect because the DVC has four coal based thermal power stations, three hydro power stations and one gas turbine station with the most of operational airports.

16 Consider the following statements about geothermal energy. *(Chap 3, Class-VIII, New NCERT)*

1. It can be harnessed naturally in the form of hot springs.
2. It is a non-polluting source of energy.
3. It can be used to generate electrical power.

How many of the statements given above is/are correct?

(a) Only one (b) Only two
(c) All three (d) None of these

Ans. (c)

Exp. All three statements i.e., (1), (2) and (3) are correct about geothermal energy as this type of energy itself can come to the surface in the form of hot springs.
Geothermal energy captures the heat from two to three kilometres under the Earth's surface.
It is a non-polluting and environment friendly renewable energy source. Geothermal energy can be used to generate electricity power.

17 Which of the following techniques can be most helpful in conservation of mineral resources on the Earth? *(Chap 5, Class-XI, Old NCERT)*

1. Recycling of metallic minerals
2. Efficient utilisation transport infrastructure
3. Shifting to non-conventional energy resources
4. Plantation of trees on barren lands

Codes

(a) 2, 3 and 4 (b) 1, 3 and 4
(c) 1 and 3 (d) All of these

***Ans.* (c)**

Exp. Techniques mentioned in statements (1) and (3) can be most helpful in conservation of mineral resources on the Earth because mineral resources are exhaustible resources. Therefore, it is necessary to protect them.
It is also possible to conserve minerals by re-using metals. Recycling of some metals can also save their reserves.
Mineral resources can also be conserving by promoting the use of non-conventional energy resources like bio gas, tidal energy, wind or solar power, etc.
Techniques mentioned in statements (2) and (4) will not be helpful because efficient utilisation transport infrastructure and plantation of trees on barren lands are not helpful for conservation of mineral resources.

18 Which of the following statements is/are correct regarding bio-energy?

(Chap 7, Class-XI, New NCERT)

1. Energy obtained from biological products, such as agricultural residues, municipal, industrial, and other wastes, is referred to as bio-energy.
2. Bio-energy is a potential source of energy conversion. It can be converted into electrical energy, heat energy or gas for cooking. It will also process the waste and garbage and produce energy.

Codes

(a) Only 1 (b) Only 2
(c) Both 1 and 2 (d) Neither 1 nor 2

***Ans.* (c)**

Exp. Both the statements (1) and (2) are correct regarding bio-energy. Energy obtained from biological products, such as agricultural residues, municipal, industrial, and other wastes, is referred to as bio-energy. It can be used to generate electricity, heat, or gas for cooking.
It will also process and generate electricity from waste and garbage. This would improve the economic well-being of rural communities in developing countries, reduce pollution, increase self-sufficiency and reduce the demand for fuel wood.

Chapter 11

Industries

Industries

Classification

Introduction

- An economic activity concerned with production of goods, extraction of minerals and provision of services

Classification of Manufacturing Industries

- **Based on Size**
  - **Cottage Industry** Smallest manufacturing unit, local raw materials and simple tools are used to produce everyday goods. Capital and transportation do not weild much influence
  - **Small scale Industry** Uses local raw material, simple power driven machines and semi skilled labour. It provides employment and raises local purchasing power
  - **Large scale Industry** Involves large market, enormous raw materials, vast energy, specialised workers, etc
- **Based on Raw Materials**
  - **Agro Based** Involves processing of raw materials from field to finished products such as fruit juices, spices, tea, coffee, etc
  - **Mineral Based** Uses minerals as raw material such as iron and steel industry
  - **Chemical Based** Uses natural chemical minerals such as mineral oils, salt, sulphur, potash, etc
  - **Forest Based** Uses major and minor products obtained from forests as raw material such as timber, wood, paper, lac etc
  - **Animal Based** Leather for leather industry and wool for woollen textiles are some examples
- **Based on Output** Whose products are used to make other goods by using them as raw materials such as products from iron and steel industry are used to make machine tools
- **Based on Ownership**
  - **Public Sector** Owned and managed by governments
  - **Private Sector** Owned by individual investors and managed by private organisations
  - **Joint Sector** Managed by joint stock companies
  - **Cooperative Sector** Owned and operated by producers or suppliers by raw materials

Industrial Regions

Introduction

- Emerge when a number of industries are located close to each other and share the benefits of their closeness
- Major industrial regions tend to be located in the temperate areas, near sea ports and especially near coal fields

World Industrial Regions

- **North America** Concentrated in North-Eastern quadrant of United States
- **Mid-Rhine Belt** Second most important industrial region in Western Europe and lies at the center of Europe's most important consumer market
- **Europe** Developed as major industrial region due to location of manufacturing in a North-South linear pattern, Rhine river being the main waterway, etc
- **Northern Italy Region** Lies in Po river basin of Northern Italy Eastern Europe and Russia; Major manufacturing centers are clustered here

Major Types of Industries

- **Iron and Steel Industry** Forms the base of all other industries, also called a basic industry. Largely setup close to the source of raw materials, the trend for setting up such industries is also changing with improved connectivity and reach of raw materials. It is also called a heavy industry as it uses large quantities of bulky raw material and produces heavy products
- **Cotton Textile Industry** It has 3 sub-sectors, handloom, powerloom and mills starting from more labour intensive to less one. Cotton textile mill sector is however highly capital intensive and produces goods in bulk. Industry requires good quality cotton as raw material
- **Woollen Textile Industry** Older than cotton textile industry and has been developed at local and cottage industry level. Most of the highly productive woollen industries are developed near the market
- **Information Technology** Deals in the storage, processing and distribution of information. Main factors guiding the location of these industries are resource availability, cost and infrastructure
- **Transport Equipment Industry** Includes ship building, automobiles, aircraft and railway equipment making industries
- **Fertiliser Industry** Nitrogen, phosphate and potash are prominent fertiliser industries
- Among these fertiliser Nitrogen being the prominent. These fertilisers have been crucial to the success of green revolution across the globe

SOURCE *New NCERT Class VIII (Industries), Old NCERT Class XI (Location of Industries and Major Industries of the World), New NCERT Class XII (Secondary Activities, Tertiary and Quaternary Activities), NIOS Module 8 Chap 24 (Industrial Development)*

Manufacturing Sector

1 **Consider the following statements about cottage industry.** *(Chap 9, Class-XI, Old NCERT)*

1. It relies on large industrial machinery and specialised processes.
2. It utilises local raw materials primarily for selling in local markets.
3. Production typically involves hired professional labour.
4. Craftsmen are often hired from outside to design products.

How many of the statements given above is/are correct?

(a) Only one (b) Only two
(c) Only three (d) All of these

Ans. (a)

Exp. Only one statement i.e., (2) is correct with reference to cottage industry. Local raw materials are used under this industry. Here the manufactured goods are sold in the local market. Under this industry, the handicraftsman makes things at home with the help of his family members on the basis of his parental skills.

Statements (1), (3) and (4) are incorrect because in cottage industry, production is done with the help of very simple tools and equipment. Production takes place with the help of family members and the craftsmen are not hired outside to design products.

2 **Consider the following statements about modern large-scale industries.** *(Chap 9, Class-XI, Old NCERT)*

1. They produce large quantities of standardised products, often involving the repetition of a single task.
2. They utilise machinery extensively to achieve high levels of production and efficiency.
3. They employ a hierarchical management structure to oversee various production tasks and personnel.

How many of the above statements accurately describe a modern large-scale industry?

(a) Only one (b) Only two
(c) All three (d) None of these

Ans. (c)

Exp. All three statements i.e., (1), (2) and (3) correctly describes a modern large scale industry. Large scale industries produce large quantities of standardised products with the repetition of only one task. Product specialisation is done on a large scale in this industry. Machinery for the production of specialised products is extensively used in this industry. By using large-scale mechanisation, the commodity is produced quickly and easily.

Management is also complex in this industry because the entire management is divided into hierarchical order of masters, managers and labourers etc.

3 **Basic industries are characterised by which of the following features?** *(Chap 9, Class-XI, Old NCERT)*

1. It uses specialised machines and processes for production.
2. Its products are used as raw material for other industries.
3. The forward and backward linkages of such industries are strong.

Select the correct answer by using the codes given below.

(a) 1 and 2 (b) 2 and 3
(c) 1 and 3 (d) All of these

Ans. (d)

Exp. All of the above statements are correct. Basic industries are characterised by all given features because special machines and processes are used for production in basic industries.

Its products are used as raw material for other industries. These include some industries whose products are used to obtain other types of production. Machines are made from iron and steel industry.

This machine is used to make other products. In this type of industries, the forward and backward linkages are clear. For example, the mining of iron-ore is the backward link of iron steel industry and manufacturing of machines for the textile industry is forward link.

4 **Which of the following industry is a type of consumer goods industry?** *(Chap 9, Class-XI, Old NCERT)*

1. Television manufacturing
2. Steel manufacturing
3. Tea and coffee processing

Select the correct answer by using the codes given below.

(a) 1 and 2 (b) 2 and 3 (c) 1 and 3 (d) All of these

Ans. (c)

Exp. Options (1) and (3) are correct. Television manufacturing and tea and coffee processing are types of consumer goods industry.

Some industries manufacture products that are used for direct consumption. Cooking oil, tea, coffee, radio and television are all products of consumption. These are called consumption goods manufacturing industries.

5 **Match the following lists correctly and choose the correct code.** *(Chap 9, Class-XI, Old NCERT)*

Industries		Types
(a) Agricultural tools industry	–	Ferrous based industry
(b) Fertiliser industry	–	Chemicals based industry
(c) Pulp and paper industry	–	Forest based industry
(d) All the above		

Ans. (d)

Exp. All the given pair are correctly matched.

Agricultural tools industry In the agricultural tools industry, raw materials are obtained from the iron and steel industry in the production of agricultural machines. Agriculture tools industry is a Ferrous based industry.

In the present industrial age, the chemical industry is responsible for the development of petrochemical industry based on petroleum.

Fertiliser industry is a chemical based industry. Forests are the source of many such products which are used as raw material in the industry.

Pulp and Paper industry is important in the forest based raw material industry. Furniture industry is also a forest produce based industry.

6 Consider the following statements about the distribution of manufacturing industries across the world. *(Chap 6, Class-XII, New NCERT)*

1. Major regions of modern manufacturing industries occupy more than 20% of the world's land area.
2. Modern manufacturing typically requires more land for operations than agriculture.
3. Industries tend to locate in areas where maximising production costs and minimising profits is the primary objective.

How many of the statements given above is/are incorrect?

(a) Only one (b) Only two
(c) All three (d) None of these

Ans (c)

Exp. All three statements i.e., (1), (2) and (3) are incorrect about distribution of manufacturing industries across the world.

Major concentrations of modern manufacturing have flourished in a few numbers of places. These cover less than 10% of the world's land area. In terms of the total area covered, manufacturing sites are much less conspicuous and concentrated on much smaller areas than that of agriculture due to greater intensity of processes. Industries maximise profits by minimising cost. Therefore, manufacturing industries should be set up at the points where production costs the minimum.

7 Consider the following Assertion (A) and Reason (R) and choose the correct code. *(Chap 8, Class-XII, New NCERT)*

Assertion (A) Agro and dairy processing industry is located closer to the sources of farm produce and milk supply.

Reason (R) Industries using weight losing materials are located closer to the sources of raw materials.

Codes

(a) Both A and R are true and R is the correct explanation of A.
(b) Both A and R are true, but R is not the correct explanation of A.
(c) A is true, but R is false.
(d) A is false, but R is true.

Ans. (a)

Exp. Both Assertion (A) and Reason (R) are true and Reason (R) is the correct explanation of Assertion (A) because industries based on cheap, bulky and weight-losing material are located closer to the sources of raw material such as steel, sugar and cement industries. Raw material used by industries should be cheap and easy to transport.

The agricultural and dairy processing industries are located closer to the sources of supply of agricultural produce and milk, as the raw material gradually deteriorates due to the establishment of the industry away from the raw material. That is why these industries are set up near raw materials.

8 Consider the following factors influencing the dependence of industries on labour. *(Chap 6, Class-XII, New NCERT)*

1. Expanding access to markets for manufactured goods.
2. Advancement in technologies and adoption of mechanisation.
3. Increased focus on producing perishable goods in manufacturing.
4. Implementation of government policies promoting balanced development.

Which of these factors has primarily contributed to the reduction of industries dependence on labour?

(a) Only 1 (b) 1 and 2
(c) 2 and 3 (d) All of these

Ans. (b)

Exp. Only statements (1) and (2) are correct.

The factor that has primarily contributed to the reduction of industries dependence on labour is the advancement in technologies and adoption of mechanisation. This is because technological advancements and mechanisation have led to automation, which reduces the need for manual labour in industries.

Statements (3) and (4) are incorrect because Government policies for market access for manufactured goods, perishability of manufactured products and balanced growth factors do not reduce the dependence of industries on labour.

9 Consider the following factors influencing the location of industries. *(Chap 6, Class-XII, New NCERT)*

1. Proximity to sources of raw materials.
2. Presence of a nearby established industry serving as a leader or supplier.
3. Easy access to a pool of available labour.
4. Convenient connection to transportation and communication networks.

Which of these factors primarily contributes to the phenomenon of agglomeration economies?

(a) Only 1 (b) 2 and 3
(c) 3 and 4 (d) All of these

Ans. (d)

Exp. All the statements are correct regarding factors primarily contributes to the phenomenon of agglomeration economies. The phenomenon of agglomeration economies primarily refers to the benefits that companies obtain by locating near each other ('agglomerating'). This is because businesses, by locating close to one another, can have a better access to.

10 Which of the following factors do not influence the location of an industry? *(Chap 6, Class-XII, New NCERT)*

1. Access to sources of energy
2. Market access
3. Government policy
4. Industrial disaster

Codes

(a) 1 and 2 (b) Only 3
(c) Only 4 (d) None of these

Ans. (c)

Exp. Among the given factors, industrial disaster does not influence the location of an industry.

Some of the factors influencing industrial locations are access to market, access to raw material, access to labour supply, access to agglomeration economies and links between industries, access to sources of energy, access to transportation and communication facilities and government policy.

11 Which of the following statements is/are correct about traditional large scale industrial regions? *(Chap 6, Class-XII, New NCERT)*

1. These are located near sea ports.
2. They are characterised by congested spaces and pollution.
3. Poor quality of services inside the industrial region.

Codes

(a) 1 and 2 (b) 2 and 3
(c) 1 and 3 (d) All of these

Ans. (b)

Exp. Statements (2) and (3) are correct about traditional large scale industrial regions because these regions are based on heavy industry.

Traditional large-scale industrial areas provide high-density housing and often poor services. This area is very congested. Unattractive environment here. e.g., pollution, heaps of garbage, etc.

Statement (1) is incorrect because these are located near coal-fields and engaged in metal smelting, heavy engineering, chemical manufacture or textile production.

12 With reference to iron and steel industries in the world, consider the following statements. *(Chap 6, Class-XII, New NCERT)*

1. Integrated iron and steel plants are located closer to the sources of coal.
2. Iron and steel plants can also be located near sea ports.
3. Iron and steel industry is highly capital intensive industry.

Which of the statements given above is/are correct?

(a) 1 and 2 (b) 2 and 3
(c) Only 3 (d) All of these

Ans. (d)

Exp. All the given statements are correct with reference to iron and steel industries in the world because the large integrated iron-ore steel industry is traditionally located closer to the sources of raw materials iron-ore, coal, manganese and limestone or at places where these could be easily brought.

Iron and steel plants may also be located near sea ports to facilitate the import and export of raw materials and manufactured iron-ore steel goods.

The iron and steel industry is one of the most complex and capital intensive industries and is concentrated in the advanced countries of North America, USA, Europe and Asia.

13 Consider the following pairs. *(Chap 6, Class-XII, New NCERT)*

Country		Iron and Steel Centre
1. UK	–	Sparrows Point and Pittsburgh
2. Germany	–	Dortmund and Dusseldorf
3. USA	–	Krivoi Rog and Donetsk

How many pairs given above is/are correct?

(a) Only one (b) Only two
(c) All three (d) None of these

Ans. (a)

Exp. Only one pair i.e. (2) is correct. In Germany, the important iron and steel industry centres are located in Duisburg, Dortmund, Dusseldorf and Essen.

While pairs (1) and (3) are incorrect. In UK, the important iron and steel industry centres are Scun Thorpe, Port Talbot, Birmingham and Sheffield in the UK.

In USA, most of the production comes from the North Appalachian region (Pittsburgh), Great Lake region and the Atlantic Coast (Sparrows Point and Morrisville).

14 Consider the following statements about the cotton textile industry. *(Chap 6, Class-XII, New NCERT)*

1. After World War II, the cotton textile industry has largely shifted to less developed countries.
2. Cotton textile mills typically require high capital investment for setting up and operation.
3. The emergence of synthetic fibers has led to a significant decline in the cotton textile industry.

How many of the statements given above is/are correct?

(a) Only one (b) Only two
(c) All three (d) None of these

Ans. (c)

Exp. All three statements i.e., (1), (2) and (3) are correct about cotton textile industry because Germany and UK recorded constant growth in cotton textile industry, after World War II it has shifted to less developed countries.

Cotton textile mills sector is highly capital intensive and manufactures fine clothes in bulk. The cotton industry requires working capital to overcome price volatility. The cotton industry has to face very stiff competition with synthetic fibres and now shown a declining trend in many countries.

15 Consider the following statements about synthetic fibers industry. *(Chap 10, Class-XI, Old NCERT)*

1. The first Rayon factory of the world was started by HB de Chardonnet.
2. The synthetic textiles obtain their raw materials from chemicals based industries.
3. Natural fibers are stronger and versatile than synthetic fibres.

How many statements given above is/are correct?

(a) Only one (b) Only two
(c) All of three (d) None of these

***Ans.* (b)**

Exp. Only two statements i.e., (1) and (2) are correct about synthetic fibres industry. The synthetic fibers industry originated in France. In 1884, a French chemist, HB de Chardonnet, made synthetic fibers from the nitro-cellulose process. Synthetic textiles get their raw material from chemical based industries. Synthesised polymers are obtained from coal and petroleum by chemical technology.

Statement (3) is incorrect because natural fibers are less strong and versatile then synthetic fibers.

16 Which of the following statements are correct regarding petrochemicals? *(Chap 5, Class-VIII, New NCERT)*

1. Chemicals which are obtained from petroleum and natural gas are called Petrochemicals.
2. Hydrogen gas is obtained as a petrochemical from natural gas.

Codes

(a) Only 1 (b) Only 2
(c) Both 1 and 2 (d) Neither 1 nor 2

***Ans.* (c)**

Exp. Both the statements (1) and (2) are correct regarding petrochemicals. These are chemicals obtained from petroleum and natural gas. Hydrogen gas is obtained as a petrochemical from natural gas. It is used in manufacture of fertilisers. Petroleum is not only a source of fuels but also provides raw materials for manufacture of large number of useful substances.

17 Which of the following pairs is/are incorrect? *(Chap 9, Class-XI, Old NCERT)*

Petrochemicals Industry		Country
(a) Philadelphia and Delaware	–	USA
(b) Antwerp	–	Belgium
(c) Ras Tanura	–	Saudi Arabia
(d) None of the above		

***Ans.* (d)**

Exp. None of the given pair is incorrect.
Petrochemical Industry is located in Philadelphia and the Great Lakes region of Delaware and Chicago, USA.
The concentration of the petrochemical industry in Europe is closer to those areas where the demand is high. The petrochemical industry in Belgium is located in the Antwerp region.
The Petrochemical industry is located in Ras Tanura in Saudi Arabia and Mina Al Ahmadi in Kuwait.
The Petrochemical industry in Canada is located in Montreal. Here oil is brought by pipeline from Portland. The second petrochemical industry in Canada is located in Sarnia.

18 Consider the following statements about footloose industries. *(Chap 6, Class-XII, New NCERT)*

1. Footloose industries are highly dependent on raw material sources.
2. Footloose industries have a high degree of geographical mobility.
3. Footloose industries are likely to heavy industries like steel and iron.

How many of the statements given above is/are correct?

(a) Only one (b) Only two
(c) All three (d) None of these

***Ans.* (a)**

Exp. Only one statement i.e., (2) is correct. One of the key characteristics of footloose industries is their flexibility in location. They are highly mobile and able to relocate based on factors like skilled labour availability, government incentives, or changing market conditions. They are not constrained by factors like bulky raw materials, heavy infrastructure needs, or proximity to specific markets.

Statements (1) and (3) are incorrect because Footloose industries, by definition, are less dependent on specific raw material sources because they can be easily transported or obtained from multiple locations. Their production process is not tied to a particular geographical location for resource availability.
Footloose industries are generally not heavy industries. They are often involved in high-value, low volume production with lightweight and easily transportable inputs and outputs.

Service Sector

19 With reference to the usefulness of the by products of the sugar industry, which of the following statements is/are correct? *(Chap 6, Class-XII, New NCERT) (IAS Pre 2013)*

1. Bagasse can be used as biomass fuel for the generation of energy.
2. Molasses can be used as one of the feedstocks for the production of synthetic chemical fertilisers.

3. Molasses can be used for the production of ethanol.

Codes

(a) Only 1 (b) 2 and 3 (c) 1 and 3 (d) 1, 2 and 3

Ans. (c)

Exp. Both the statements (1) and (3) are correct about usefulness of the byproducts of the sugar industry. Bagasse is the dry pulpy fibrous material that remains after crushing sugarcane or sorghum stalks to extract their juice. It is used as a biofuel for the production of heat, energy, and electricity and in the manufacture of pulp and building materials.

Molasses is a thick syrup that results from refining of sugarcane. It can be used for the production of ethanol. Statement (2) is incorrect because molasses are used in production of organic product not synthetic production.

Which of the given techniques is/are used in high technology industry? *(Chap 6, Class-XII, New NCERT)*

1. Robotics and assembly lines
2. Computer aided design
3. Electronic control of manufacturing processes

Codes

(a) 1 and 3 (b) 1 and 2
(c) 2 and 3 (d) All of these

Ans. (d)

Exp. All the given techniques are used in high technology industry which includes latest generation of manufacturing activities. Some of the technologies used in the high technology industry include robotics on the assembly line, computer aided design and manufacturing, electronic control of smelting and refining processes, and the continuous development of new chemical and pharmaceutical products.

21 Consider the following statements about the features of high technology industry. *(Chap 6, Class-XII, New NCERT)*

1. Blue collar workers are mostly employed in these industries.
2. Research and development facilities are located in these industries.
3. These are characterised by massive assembly structures.

How many of the statements given above is/are correct?

(a) Only one (b) Only two
(c) All three (d) None of these

Ans. (a)

Exp. Only one statement i.e., (2) is the feature of high technology industry because high technology industry is the latest generation of manufacturing activities. It is best understood as the application of intensive research and development efforts leading to the manufacture of products of an advanced scientific and engineering character.

Statements (1) and (3) are not its feature because white collar workers are mostly employed in high technology industry. These are characterised by neatly spaced, low, modern, dispersed, office-plant-lab buildings rather than massive assembly structures.

22 Consider the following statements. *(Chap 6, Class-XII, New NCERT)*

1. Industries which employs high-tech machinery.
2. Industries which uses research and development techniques.
3. Regional concentration of highly specialised high-tech industries.
4. Industrial cluster of similar industries over a large area.

Which of the given statements is the most comprehensive definition of technopolis?

(a) Only 2 (b) 2 and 3
(c) Only 3 (d) 4 and 2

Ans. (c)

Exp. Statement (3) is the most comprehensive definition of technopolis because high-technology industry which are regionally concentrated, self-sustained and highly specialised are called Technopolis. The Silicon Valley and Silicon Forest near Settle are examples of technopolis.

23 Which of the following is/are correct regarding high technology industry? *(Chap 6, Class-XII, Old NCERT)*

1. High technology industry is best understood as the application of intensive research and development efforts leading to the manufacture of products of an advanced scientific and engineering character.
2. Professional (white collar) workers make up a large share of the total workforce. These highly skilled specialists greatly outnumber the actual production (blue collar) workers.

Codes

(a) Only 1
(b) Only 2
(c) Both 1 and 2
(d) Neither 1 nor 2

Ans. (c)

Exp. Both the statements (1) and (2) are correct regarding high technology industry.

The high-tech sector represents the most recent generation of manufacturing operations. It's best defined as the application of rigorous research and development activities that result in the creation of advanced scientific and engineering products.

Professional (white collar) employees account for a sizable portion of the workforce. The real production (blue collar) workers are vastly outnumbered by these highly skilled specialists.

24 **Consider the following statements.**
(Chap 7, Class-XII, New NCERT)

1. There has been a rapid growth in demand for the consumption of knowledge based services in the modern economy.
2. Knowledge industry is not tied to resources or affected by markets.
3. Most of the knowledge sector companies operate in the localised markets.

How many of the statements given above is/are correct about knowledge industry?

(a) Only one (b) Only two
(c) All three (d) None of these

***Ans.* (b)**

Exp. Statements (1) and (2) are correct about knowledge industry because the knowledge economy is a system of consumption and production based on intellectual capital. This sector is growing rapidly.

Currently more than half of all workers developed economies are in knowledge sector and has grown much more in demand and consumption of information based services from mutual fund managers tax consultants, software developers and statistician. Like some of the tertiary functions, knowledge economy activities can also be outsourced. They are not tied to resources, affected by the environment or necessarily localised by market.

Statement (3) is incorrect because most of the knowledge sector companies operate in the world markets.

25 **People, materials, and manufactured commodities are physically transported from one area to another through transportation. Which among the following is/are the factors affecting transport systems?**
(Chap 6, Class-XII, New NCERT)

1. Demand for transport is influenced by the size of population. The larger the population size, the greater is the demand for transport.
2. Routes depend on location of cities, towns, villages, industrial centres and raw materials, pattern of trade between them, nature of the landscape between them, type of climate, and funds available for overcoming obstacles along the length of the route.

Select the correct answer by using the codes given below.

(a) Only 1 (b) Only 2
(c) Both 1 and 2 (d) Neither 1 nor 2

***Ans.* (c)**

Exp. Both the statements (1) and (2) are correct regarding transport system. Demand for transport is influenced by the size of population. The larger the population size, the greater is the demand for transport. The transport industry is created to satify the need of mobility.

Transportation routes depends on location of cities, towns, villages, industrial centres and raw materials, pattern of trade between them, nature of the landscape between them, type of climate and fund available for over coming obstacles along the length of the route. Modern society requires speedy and efficient transport system to assist in the production, distribution and consumption of goods.

26 **Consider the following statements about services as an alternative to outsourcing.**
(Chap 7, Class-XII, New NCERT

1. Services can be more cost-effective than outsourcing.
2. Services can provide more control over business processes than outsourcing.
3. Services always lead to job losses in the home country.

How many of the statements given above is/are correct?

(a) Only one (b) Only two
(c) All of these (d) None of these

***Ans.* (b)**

Exp. Statements (1) and (2) are correct. Services, especially when they involve hiring freelancers or remot employees, can be more cost-effective than outsourcing. Services, such as adopting an extended team model, can provide more control over business processes than outsourcing.

Statement (3) is incorrect. While it's true that outsourcing can sometimes lead to job losses in the hom country, it's not always the case with services. For example, hiring freelancers or remote employees doesn' necessarily lead to job losses.

Industrial Regions

27 **Which of the following pairs is correct?**
(Chap 9, Class-XI, Old NCER

	Industrial centre		Famous for
(a)	New Jersey	–	Automobile manufacturing
(b)	Buffalo	–	Garment industry
(c)	Texas	–	Food processing
(d)	All of the above		

***Ans.* (b)**

Exp. Only pair (c) is correct. There is an industrial complex extending from Carolina to Louisiana and Texa in the Southern USA, in which Dallas and Atlanta are large industrial cities. The food processing industries exist in Texas, Oklahoma and Arkansas.

While pairs (a), (b) are incorrect the present New Jersey region in the North-East region of USA is known as the garment industry due to the favourable climate.

Iron-ore smelting started in Buffalo about 1860. Buffalo region is famous for iron and steel industry in the world.

28 **Match the following lists correctly and choose the correct code.** *(Chap 9, Class-XI, Old NCERT)*

List I (Industrial centre)	List II (Famous for)
A. London	1. Glass industry
B. Birmingham	2. Heavy machinery
C. Charleroi	3. Paper and pulp industry
D. Sweden	4. Textiles

Codes

	A	B	C	D		A	B	C	D
(a)	4	1	3	2	(b)	2	3	1	4
(c)	3	1	2	4	(d)	4	2	1	3

Ans. (d)

Exp. The correct matching is A-4, B-2, C-1, D-3.
The UK is the birthplace of the Industrial Revolution. Due to the favourable climate and location in **London**, the textile industry is located around the River Thames.

Birmingham in the Midland region of Britain is the center of iron and steel and heavy machinery.

Charleroi is a Belgian city in the Walloon province of Hainaut.

The Charleroi municipality contains an industrial area for electrical engineering and the production of iron, steel, glass and chemicals.

In the Southern part of **Sweden** from Stockholm to the Southern shores of Lake Ven there is a pulp and paper and wood industry based on forest resources.

29 **Which of the given factors is/are responsible for the development of Rhine valley as an industrial region?** *(Chap 9, Class-XI, Old NCERT)*

1. Presence of rich uranium resources
2. Well-connected railways network
3. High density of population
4. Presence of well-built canal system

Codes

(a) 1 and 3
(b) 1, 2 and 4
(c) 2, 3 and 4
(d) All of these

Ans. (c)

Exp. Statements (2), (3) and (4) are the factors responsible for the development of Rhine valley as an industrial region because this region is connected by railway network, waterways of the Rhine and canals. This area is the densely populated area of Europe. There is also a big local market here. The Rhine valley is known as an industrial area. The Ruhr coalfield is located in the lower Rhine valley.

Statement (1) is not a factor responsible for the development of Rhine valley as an industrial region because there is no presence of rich uranium resources in the industrial area of the Rhine valley.

30 **Which of the given factors is/are responsible for development of the New England region as an industrial complex in North America?** *(Chap 9, Class-XI, Old NCERT)*

1. Development of hydroelectric power
2. Presence of densely forested region
3. Presence of large reserves of limestone

Codes

(a) 1 and 2 (b) 2 and 3 (c) Only 2 (d) Only 3

Ans. (a)

Exp. Options (1) and (2) are the factors responsible for development of the New England region as an industrial complex in North America. Many factors are responsible for the industrial development of New England. Immigrants from Europe first settled in this area. The density of population here was high. Being a mountainous area, hydroelectric power was available from small rivers. New England region is also known as industrial region. However, Option (3) is not a factor because there is no presence of large reserves of limestone in the industrial area of the New England region on North America.

31 **Which of the given factors has aided in the development of Central Volga industrial region?** *(Chap 9, Class-XI, New NCERT)*

1. Hydroelectric power 2. Mineral oil exploration
3. Inland waterways

How many statements given above is/are correct?

(a) Only one (b) Only two
(c) All three (d) None of these

Ans. (c)

Exp. All the given factors have aided in the development of central Volga industrial region. The Middle Volga region is an agricultural region. But after the discovery of oil, the area became an industrial area.

Hydroelectricity is obtained by building a dam on the Volga river. The Moscow Volga Canal and the Volga Don Canal being a ferry vehicle provides waterways in the region. Mining of coal, iron-ore etc. is done here.

32 **Which of the given pairs is/are correctly matched?** *(Chap 9, Class-XI, Old NCERT)*

	Industrial Centre in Russia	Famous for
(a)	Ivanovo	Textiles
(b)	Nizhny Novgorod	Machinery
(c)	Vladivostok	Shipbuilding
(d)	All of the above	

Ans. (d)

Exp. All the given pairs are correctly matched.
The city of Ivanovo is located on the banks of the Uvod river in Western Russia.

The Nizhny **Novgorod** region is one of the largest industrial centers of the Russian Federation with a great potential in machinery.

Vladivostok region is famous for steel industry and shipbuilding.

Chapter 12

Transport and Communication

Transport and Communication

Land Transport

Land Transport

- Most movement of goods and services takes place through land *via* rail, road, etc

Roadways

- Most economical for short distances compared to railways
- Offers door-to-door services
- Roads often face traffic congestion due to the inability of roads to meet the demands of traffic
- An important road, highways are metalled roads connecting distant places, e.g.
  - Trans-Canadian Highway links British Columbia to Newfound city
  - Alaskan Highway links Canada to Alaska
  - Moscow-Vladivostok Highway connects Russia from West to East

Railways

- A mode of land transport for bulky goods and passengers over long distances
- Europe has the most dense rail networks in the world with important rail heads as London, Brussels, Paris, Milan, etc
- Most dense rail network of North America is found in highly industrialised and urbanised region of East Central USA
- Rail network is dense in two regions of South America, i.e., Pampas of Argentina and coffee growing region of Brazil

Pipelines

- Used to transport liquids and gases such as water, petroleum, natural gas, etc
- Through pipeline network, cooking gas, liquid petroleum is transported to many parts of world. Important pipelines are Trans-Afghanistan pipeline also called Tapi pipeline i.e., Turkmenistan-Afghanistan-Pakistan-India pipeline

Water Transport

Water Transport

- Does not require route construction but needs port facilities at two ends; Divided into sea routes and inland waterways
- **Sea Routes** Offers a smooth traversable highway in all directions with no maintenance costs
  - Compared to land and air, ocean transport is much cheaper for transport of bulky materials over long distances
  - A few important sea routes are the North Atlantic sea route, the North Pacific sea route, etc
- **Inland Waterways** Development of inland waterways depends on the navigable depth and width of the channel
  - Important waterways are rivers, canals, lakes, etc
  - A few of inland waterways are the Danube waterway, the Rhine waterway, the Volga waterway, etc

Ports

- The chief gateways of world of international trade are ports and harbours, which provides facilities Certain types of ports are
- **On the Basis of Cargo Handled** Industrial ports, commercial ports and comprehensive ports
- **On the Basis of Location** Inland ports and out ports
- **On the Basis of Specialised Functions** Oil ports, ports of call, entrepot ports and naval ports

Air Transport and Communication

Air Transport

- Fastest means of transport and only means to reach inaccessible areas; Favoured for long distance trade as well as movement of valuable goods
- Services performed by air transport are
  - **Inter-continental Air Route** Like New York-London-Paris-Rome-Cairo-Delhi-Kolkata-Hong Kong-Tokyo, etc
  - **Continental Air Route** Like New York-Chicago-Montreal Route, etc
  - **National Air Route** Like Delhi-Mumbai-Chennai, etc

Communications

- A process of conveying messages to others *via* telephone, telegraphs, etc
- Satellite communication emerged as a new area where satellites are deployed in Earth's orbit to connect even the remote areas
- Cyber space and internet are also a new emerging area in the field of communication which is the electronic digital world for connecting and accessing the information over computer networks
- Global Positioning System (GPS) is a space-based satellite navigation system that provides location and time information about the earth in all weather conditions

SOURCE *NIOS Chapter-13, Module-2, Old NCERT Class X (Transport and Communication and International Trade), Old NCERT Class XII (Transport Systems), New NCERT Class XII (Transport and Communication)*

Transport

1 **Consider the following statements about various forms of road (land) transport.** *(Chap 8, Class-XII, New NCERT)*

1. Road transport is used for short distance door to door services.
2. Railways transport is most suitable for bulky materials over longer distances.
3. Road and railways transport can complement each other for improving the transport efficiency.

How many of the statements given above is/are incorrect?

(a) Only one (b) Only two
(c) All three (d) None of these

Ans. (d)

Exp. None of the statements is incorrect about various forms of road transport.

Road transport is cheaper and faster over short distances and for door to door services.

Railways are most suited for large volumes of bulky materials over long distances within a country.

Road and railway transport can complement each other to improve transport efficiency and a well-managed transport system.

Transport is a service or facility for the carriage of persons and goods from one place to the other using humans, animals and different kinds of vehicles.

2 **Consider the following statements regarding highways in North America.** *(Chap 7, Class-XII, New NCERT)*

1. The Trans-Canadian Highway links Vancouver in British Columbia (West coast) to St. John's City in Newfoundland (East coast).
2. The Alaskan Highway connects Edmonton (Canada) to Anchorage (Alaska).
3. The Pan-American Highway connects only the countries of South America.

How many of the statements given above is/are correct?

(a) Only one (b) Only two
(c) All three (d) None of these

Ans. (b)

Exp. Only two statements i.e., (1) and (2) are correct regarding highways in North America.

The Trans-Canadian Highways links Vancouver in British Columbia(West coast) to St. John's City in Newfoundland (East coast).

The Alaskan Highway links Edmonton (Canada) to Anchorage (Alaska). The Alaska Highway was constructed during World War II to connect the contiguous United States to Alaska across Canada.

Statement (3) is incorrect because the Pan-American Highway, a larger portion of which has been constructed, will connect the countries of South America, Central America, and USA, Canada. Originally, conceived in 1923 as a single route, the road grew to include a great number of designated highways in participating countries.

3 **Which of the following statements is/are correct about 'Golden Quadrilateral'?** *(Chap 13, Module-2, NIOS)*

1. It is a network of highways connecting India's top metropolitan cities, namely Delhi, Mumbai, Bengaluru, Chennai, and Kolkata, thereby, forming a quadrilateral.
2. It was launched in 2001 as part of the National Highways Development Project (NHDP).

Select the correct answer using the codes given below.

(a) Only 1
(b) Only 2
(c) Both 1 and 2
(d) Neither 1 nor 2

Ans. (b)

Exp. Only statement (2) is correct about golden Quadrilateral. The Golden Quadrilateral project was planned in 1999, and launched in 2001 as part of National Highways Development Project (NHDP).

Statements (1) is incorrect because Golden Quadrilateral is a network of four or six-lane highways which connects top four metropolitan cities of India, namely Delhi, Mumbai, Chennai, and Kolkata, thereby, forming a quadrilateral. It is the largest highway project in India.

4 **Consider the following pairs.** *(Chap 7, Class-XII, New NCERT)*

	Highways		Connecting Cities/Regions
1.	Alaskan Highway	–	Edmonton (Canada) to Anchorage (Alaska)
2.	National Highway No 44 (NH 44)	–	Kashmir to Kanyakumari
3.	Trans-continental Stuart Highway	–	Darwin to Melbourne

How many of the pairs given above is/are correctly matched?

(a) Only one (b) Only two
(c) All three (d) None of these

Ans. (c)

Exp. All three pairs are correctly matched.

The Alaskan Highway links Edmonton (Canada) to Anchorage (Alaska). It was previously called the Alaskan International Highway, the Alaska Military Highway, and the Alcan (Alaska-Canadian) Highway.

NH 44 is the longest national highway in India that stretches from Srinagar in the North to Kanyakumari in the South.

It passes through the Union Territory from Srinagar, Jammu and Kashmir, in the North to Kanyakumari, Tamil Nadu, in the country's South.

The Trans-continental Stuart Highway connects Darwin (North Coast) and Melbourne *via* Tennant creak and Alice springs in Australia.

5 Consider the following statements regarding National Highway Authority of India.
(Chap 8, Class-XII, New NCERT)

1. The National Highway Authority of India (NHAI) is an autonomous body under the Ministry of Surface Transport, established in 1995.
2. It acts as an apex body to improve the quality of the roads designated as National Highways.

Which of the statements given above is/are correct?

(a) Only 1 (b) Only 2
(c) Both 1 and 2 (d) Neither 1 nor 2

Ans. (c)

Exp. Both the statements (1) and (2) are correct about the National Highways Authority of India (NHAI) as it was operationalised in 1995. It is an autonomous body under the Ministry of Surface Transport.

It is entrusted with the responsibility of development, maintenance and operation of National Highways. This is also the apex body to improve the quality of the roads designated as National Highways.

6 Consider the following statements regarding Bharatmala Scheme. *(Chap 7, Class-XII, New NCERT)*

1. Development of state roads along coastal border areas, including connectivity of non-major ports.
2. Backward areas religious and tourist places connectivity programme.

Which of the statements given above is/are correct?

(a) Only 1 (b) Only 2
(c) Both 1 and 2 (d) Neither 1 nor 2

Ans. (c)

Exp. Both the statements (1) and (2) are correct regarding the Bharatmala Scheme because it provides for development of state roads along coastal border areas, including connectivity of non-major ports. It is an umbrella programme for highways sector. It connects backward area dreligious and tourist places.

Railways

7 Consider the following statements.
(Chap 4, Class-XII, Old NCERT)

1. The first public railways line was opened in 1825 between Stockton and Darlington.
2. Africa has the most dense railways network in the world.
3. North America has the largest rail network in the world.

Which of the statements given above is/are incorrect?

(a) 1 and 2 (b) Only 2
(c) 1 and 3 (d) All of the above

Ans. (b)

Exp. Statement (2) is incorrect because Europe has one of the most dense rail networks in the world.

The US boasts the world's largest rail network, while China and Russia holds the second and third position respectively.

8 Which of the following is the most plausible reason for the declining significance of Trans-continental railways? *(Chap 8, Class-X, Old NCERT)*

(a) Degrading infrastructure due to older tracks.
(b) Establishment of closed borders in countries.
(c) Competition from road transport and airways.
(d) All of the above

Ans. (c)

Exp. Competition from road transport and airways is the most plausible reason for the declining significance of Trans-continental railways.

Road transport is cheaper and faster over short distances and for door to door services and High-value, light and perishable goods are best moved by airways.

However, degrading infrastructure due to older tracks and establishment of closed borders in countries are not plausible reasons for the declining significance of Trans-continental railways.

9 Consider the following statements.
(Chap 8, Class-XII, New NCERT)

1. Railways in New Zealand are mostly concentrated in the North island for serving the farming regions.
2. East Asia has high density of railways and West Asia has lower density of railways.

Which of the statements given above is/are correct?

(a) Only 1
(b) Only 2
(c) Both 1 and 2
(d) Neither 1 nor 2

Ans. (c)

Exp. Both the statements (1) and (2) are correct.

New Zealand railways are mainly in the North island to serve the farming areas.

In East Asia, rail network is the most dense in the thickly populated areas of Japan, China and India. West Asia is the least developed in rail facilities because of vast desert and sparsely populated region.

10 Which of the following is the longest Trans-continental railways in the world?
(Chap 8, Class-XII, New NCERT)

(a) Trans-Canadian Railways
(b) Australian Trans Pacific Railways
(c) Pacific Railways
(d) Trans-Siberian Railways

Ans. (d)

Exp. The Trans-Siberian Railways is the longest Trans-continental railways in the world. It is a network of railways connecting Western Russia to the Russian Far East.

It is the most important route in Asia and the longest 9,332 km double tracked and electrified trans-continental railway in the world. It has helped in opening up its Asian region to West European markets.

11 **Consider the following statements regarding the Trans-continental railways.**

(Chap 7, Class-XII, New NCERT)

1. The Trans-Siberian Railway is the longest double-tracked and electrified trans-continental railway in the world.
2. The Union Pacific Railway connects New York on the Atlantic Coast to San Francisco on the Pacific Coast.
3. The Australian Trans-continental railway passes through Kalgoorlie, Broken Hill, and Port Augusta.

Which of the statements given above are correct?

(a) 2 and 3 (b) 1 and 3
(c) 1, 2 and 3 (d) None of the above

Ans. (c)

Exp. Statements (1), (2) and (3) are correct.

The Trans-Siberian Railway is the world's first double-tracked and electrified trans-continental railway. It is also the longest railway in the world, spanning 9,289 kilometers (5,772 miles).

The Union Pacific Railway connects New York on the Atlantic Coast to San Francisco on the Pacific Coast passing through Cleveland, Chicago, Omaha, Evans, Ogden and Sacramento. The most valuable exports on this route are ores, grain, paper, chemicals and machinery.

The Australian Trans-continental Railway passes through Kalgoorlie, Broken Hill, and Port Augusta. The railway runs West-East across the Southern part of Australia, from Perth to Sydney.

12 **Arrange the given set of regions on the Trans-Siberian rail route in a correct sequence from East to West.** *(Chap 8, Class-XII, New NCERT)*

1. St. Petersburg 2. Krasnoyarsk
3. Vladivostok 4. Khabarovsk

Codes

(a) 1-3-2-4 (b) 3-4-2-1 (c) 2-1-3-4 (d) 1-2-4-3

Ans. (b)

Exp. The correct sequence of Trans-Siberian rail route from East to West is 3-4-2-1 i.e., Vladivostok, Khabarovsk, Krasnoyarsk and St.Petersburg.

Trans-Siberian railway major rail route of Russia runs from St. Petersburg in the West to Vladivostok on the Pacific Coast in the East passing through Moscow, Ufa, Novosibirsk, Irkutsk, Chita and Khabarovsk.

13 **Which of the following statements is/are correct about the railway network of Russia?**

(Chap 7, Class-XII, New NCERT)

1. Moscow is the most important rail head with major lines radiating to different parts of the country's vast geographical area.
2. Railways account for about 60% of the country's total transport.

Codes

(a) Only 1 (b) Only 2
(c) Both 1 and 2 (d) Neither 1 nor 2

Ans. (a)

Exp. Only statement (1) is correct Moscow is Russia's most important railhead, with major lines that extend to various parts of the country. Underground railways and commuter trains are also important in Moscow. In Russia, a dense highway network is developed in the industrialised region West of the Urals with Moscow as the hub.

Statement (2) is incorrect because in Russia, railways account for about 90% of the country's total transport with a very dense network West of the Urals.

Waterways

14 **Consider the following statements.**

(Chap 7, Class-XII, New NCERT)

Statement-I The Northern Atlantic Sea Route is also referred as Big Trunk Route and one-fourth of the world's foreign trade moves on this route.

Statement-II The Southern Atlantic Sea Route connects West European and West African countries with Brazil, Argentina and Uruguay in South America.

Codes

(a) Both Statement-I and Statement-II are correct and Statement-II is the correct explanation for Statement-I.
(b) Both Statement-I and Statement-II are correct and Statement-II is not the correct explanation for Statement-I.
(c) Statement-I is correct, but Statement-II is incorrect.
(d) Statement-I is incorrect, but Statement-II is correct.

Ans. (b)

Exp. Both Statement-I and Statement-II are correct and Statement-II is not the correct explanation for Statement-I.

The Northern Atlantic Sea Route links North-Eastern USA and North-Western Europe, the two industrially developed regions of the world. It is the busiest waterway and is also referred as Big Trunk Route. One fourth of the world's foreign trade moves on this route.

The Southern Atlantic Sea Route connects West European and West African countries with Brazil, Argentina and Uruguay in South America. The traffic is far less on this route because of the limited development and availability of similar products and resources in Africa and South America.

15 **Which of the following sea routes connects the industrialised countries of Western Europe with West Africa and Southern Africa?**

(Chap 8, Class-X, Old NCERT)

(a) Southern Atlantic Sea Route
(b) Cape of Good Hope Sea Route
(c) North Pacific Sea Route
(d) South Pacific Sea Route

Ans. (b)

Exp. Cape of Good Hope Sea Trade Route connects the industrialised countries like Western European region with West Africa, Southern Africa, South-East Asia and the commercial agriculture and livestock economies of Australia and New Zealand.

16 Consider the following pairs. *(Chap 8, Class-XII, New NCERT)*

Sea Port		Country
1. Auckland	–	USA
2. Rio de Janeiro	–	Brazil
3. New Orleans	–	New Zealand
4. Japan	–	Yokohama

How many pairs given above is/are incorrect?

(a) Only one (b) Only two
(c) Only three (d) All four

Ans. (b)

Exp. Only two pairs i.e., (1) and (3) are incorrect.

The Port of Auckland is a large container and international trade port on the Waitemata Harbour, lying on the Central and Eastern Auckland waterfront in New Zealand.

The Port of New Orleans is an embarkation port for cruise passengers located in USA. It is also Louisiana's only international container port.

17 Consider the following statements about the Panama Canal. *(Chap 7, Class-XII, New NCERT)*

1. It connects the Atlantic Ocean in the East to the Pacific ocean in the West.
2. It shortens the distance between New York and San Francisco by 13,000 km by sea.
3. The economic significance of this canal is relatively more than that of the Suez.

How many of the statements given above is/are correct?

(a) Only one (b) Only two
(c) Only three (d) None of these

Ans. (b)

Exp. Only two statements i.e., (1) and (2) are correct regarding the Panama Canal.

The Panama Canal connects the Atlantic Ocean in the East to the Pacific ocean in the West. It has been constructed across the Panama Isthmus between Panama City and Colon by the US Government which purchased 8 km of area on either side and named it the Canal Zone. It shortens the distance between New York and San Francisco by 13,000 km by sea. Likewise the distance between Western Europe and the West-Coast of USA; and North-Eastern and Central USA and East and South-East Asia is shortened.

Statement (3) is incorrect because the economic significance of this canal is relatively less than that of the Suez. However, it is vital to the economies of Latin America.

18 Consider the following statements. *(Chap 7, Class-XII, New NCERT)*

1. The Suez Canal is an artificial sea-level waterway that connects the Mediterranean sea and the Red sea.
2. The canal is owned and maintained by the Suez Canal Authority (SCA), which is under the Government of Egypt.

Which of the statements given above is/are correct?

(a) Only 1 (b) Only 2 (c) Both 1 and 2 (d) Neither 1 nor

Ans. (c)

Exp. Both the statements (1) and (2) are corrects as the Suez Canal is a man-made (artificial) canal that connect the Mediterranean sea to the Red sea, providing a crucia shortcut for shipping between Europe and Asia. It gives Europe a new gateway to the Indian ocean and reduces the direct sea route distance between Liverpool and Colombo compared to the Cape of Good Hope route.

The canal is owned and maintained by the Suez Canal Authority (SCA), which is under the Government of Egypt. The canal was nationalised by Egyptian Presider Gamal Abdel Nasser in July 1956, which led to the Suez Crisis in October-November 1956.

19 Consider the following statements about the Panam Canal. *(Chap 8, Class-XII, New NCER*

1. It is significant for the economies of the countries in Latin America.
2. It is a direct link between the Pacific ocean and the Atlantic ocean.
3. It has shortened the distance between Western Europe and Northern America.

How many of the statements given above is/are correct?

(a) Only one (b) Only two (c) Only three (d) None of thes

Ans. (b)

Exp. Only two statements i.e., (1) and (2) are correct about the Panama Canal because this canal is located near Latin American countries, so this canal is importan for the economic interests of Latin countries. Panama Canal connects the Atlantic ocean in the East to the Pacific ocean in the West. It is a direct link between the Pacific ocean and the Atlantic ocean.

Statement (3) is incorrect because Panama Canal has shortened the distance between Western Europe and West coast of America.

20 Which of the following factors determines the development of inland waterways in a region? *(Chap 8, Class-XII, New NCER*

1. Width and depth of the channel of water.
2. Continuity in the flow of water in the river.
3. Competition from railways and roadways.

Codes

(a) Only 1 (b) Only 2 (c) Only 3 (d) All of the

Ans. (d)

Exp. All the given factors determine the development of inland waterways in a region because the development of inland waterways is dependent on the width and depth of the channel of water, continuity in the flow of water in the river, transport technology in use and competition from railways and roadways. Rivers, canals, lakes and coastal areas have been important waterways since time immemorial.

21 **Consider the following pairs.** *(Chap 7, Class-XII, New NCERT)*

Inland Waterways		Related Aspects
1. The Rhine Waterway	–	It flows through Germany and the Netherlands.
2. The Danube Waterway	–	The Danube river rises in the Black Forest and flows Eastwards through many countries.
3. The Volga Waterway	–	It connects the industrial areas of Switzerland, Germany and France.
4. The Mississippi Waterway	–	It connects the interior part of USA with the Gulf of Mexico in the South.

How many of the pairs given above is/are correctly matched?

(a) Only one (b) Only two
(c) Only three (d) All four

Ans. (c)

Exp. Only three pairs i.e., (1), (2) and (4) are correctly matched as the Rhine Waterway flow through Germany and the Netherlands. It is navigable for 700 km from Rotterdam (Netherland) to Basel (Switzerland).

The Danube river is a waterway in Central and Eastern Europe that flows through 10 countries. The river originates in Germany's Black Forest and flows South-East for 1,780 miles (2,860 km). It passes through Austria, Slovakia, Hungary, Croatia, Serbia, Romania, Bulgaria, Moldova and Ukraine before draining into the Black sea.

The Mississippi Waterway connects the interior part of USA with the Gulf of Mexico in the South.

Pair (3) is incorrectly matched because the Volga Waterway is the most important waterways of Russia. It provides a navigable waterway of 11,200 km and drains into the Caspian Sea. The Volga-Moscow Canal connects it with the Moscow region and the Volga-Don Canal with the Black sea.

22 **Consider the following pairs.** *(Chap 7, Class-XII, New NCERT)*

Port		Country
1. Auckland	–	New Zealand
2. Chicago	–	United Kingdom
3. Hamburg	–	Germany
4. Marseilles	–	France

How many of the pairs given above is/are incorrectly matched?

(a) Only one (b) Only two
(c) Only three (d) All four

Ans. (a)

Exp. Only one pair i.e., (2) is incorrectly matched because the port of Chicago is located in the USA. The Uinais International Port district, also known as the Chicago regional port district, operates the port.

23 **Match the following lists correctly and choose the correct code.** *(Chap 8, Class-XII, New NCERT)*

List I (Waterway)	List II (Located in)
A. Volga Waterway	1. Russia
B. Mississippi Waterway	2. Eastern Europe
C. Danube Waterway	3. USA
D. Rhine Waterway	3. Germany

Codes

	A	B	C	D		A	B	C	D
(a)	1	2	3	4	(b)	2	1	3	4
(c)	3	2	1	4	(d)	1	3	2	4

Ans. (d)

Exp. The correct matching is A-1, B-3, C-2, D-4.

Volga Waterways are one of the most important waterways in Russia. The Volga-Moscow Canal connects it with the Moscow region and the Volga-Don Canal with the Black sea.

Mississippi Waterways are one of the most important waterways in USA.

Danube Waterway are one of the most important waterways in Eastern Europe. Danube waterways are important inland waterway serves Eastern Europe.

The **Rhine Waterway** flows through Germany and Netherlands. It is navigable for 700 km from Rotterdam.

24 **Consider the following Assertion (A) and Reason (R) and choose the correct code.** *(Chap 8, Class-XII, New NCERT) (UPPSC Pre 2003)*

Assertion (A) North Atlantic Sea Route is the busiest sea route in the world.

Reason (R) It connects two major industrial zones of the world.

Codes

(a) Both A and R are true and R is the correct explanation of A.
(b) Both A and R are true, but R is not the correct explanation of A.
(c) A is true, but R is false.
(d) A is false, but R is true.

Ans. (a)

Exp. Both Assertion (A) and Reason (R) are true and Reason (R) is the correct explanation of Assertion (A).

North Atlantic Sea Route connects two major industrial zones of Europe and North America. It includes Suez Canal, which connects Europe to the Mediterranean Sea. It is the busiest sea route in the world.

25 With reference to Rhine river in Europe, which of the following statements is/are correct?

(Chap 8, Class-XII, New NCERT)

1 Rhine river is an important pathway for industrial activity in Northern Germany.

2. Port of Rotterdam is located at the mouth of Rhine river.

Select the correct answer using the code given below

(a) Only 1 (b) Only 2
(c) Both 1 and 2 (d) Neither 1 nor 2

Ans. (c)

Exp. Both the statements (1) and (2) are correct with reference to Rhine river in Europe. Rhine river is an important pathway for industrial activity in Northern Germany. It is the second longest river in Central and Western Europe after the Danube. It runs for over 1,232 km from its source in the Swiss Alps (in Switzerland). Port of Rotterdam is located at the mouth of Rhine river. The Rhine flows through six countries; Switzerland, Principality of Liechtenstein, Austria, Germany, France and the Netherland before flowing into the North sea at Roterrdam.

26 Assertion (A) North Atlantic sea route is the busiest sea route in the world.

Reason (R) It connects two major industrial zones of the world. *(Chap 8, Class-XII, New NCERT)*

Codes

(a) Both (A) and (R) are true and (R) is correct explanation of (A).
(b) Both (A) and (R) are true, but (R) is not the correct explanation of (A).
(c) (A) is true, but (R) is false.
(d) (R) is true, but (A) is false.

Ans. (a)

Exp. Both Assertion (A) and Reason (R) are true and Reason (R) is the correct explanation of Assertion (A). North Atlantic sea route is the busiest sea route in the world, because it connects with two major industrial zones (North America to Europe) of the world. One-fourth of the world foreign trades moves through this route.

Airways

27 Consider the following statements with reference to air transport. *(Chap 8, Class-XII, New NCERT)*

1. It is possible to reach areas hit by natural disasters.
2. It is cheaper than ocean transport.
3. It can be used for both cargo and strategic purposes.

Which of the statements given above are correct?

(a) 1 and 2 (b) 2 and 3 (c) 1 and 3 (d) None

Ans. (c)

Exp. Statements (1) and (3) are correct with reference to air transport.

In the Himalayan region or any other region, the routes are often obstructed due to landslides, avalanches or heavy snow fall. At such times, air travel is the only alternative to reach these places.

Valuable cargo can be moved rapidly on a world wide scale and the remote and strategic areas are easily accessible due to air transport.

Statement (2) is incorrect because ocean transport system is cheaper than air transport system.

28 Which of the following pairs is correct? *(Chap 8, Class-XII, New NCERT)*

Airport		Located in
(a) Buenos Aires	–	Australia
(b) Darwin	–	Argentina
(c) Santiago	–	Chile
(d) Cairo	–	South Africa

Ans. (c)

Exp. Pair (c) is correct as Santiago International Airport is located in Pudahuel, which is 15 km North-West of Downtown Santiago. This is Chile's largest aviation facility and busiest international airport.

While pairs (a), (b) and (d) are incorrect Buenos Aires is the capital of Argentina. Buenos Aires airport is the biggest airport in Argentina is located in Ezeiza, 32 km from the centre of Buenos Aires city.

Darwin International Airport is the busiest airport serving the Northern Territory in Australia.

Cairo international airport is in Egypt.

Pipelines

29 Which of the following statements is/are correct? *(Chap 8, Class-XII, New NCERT)*

1. Pipelines can be used to transfer both liquid and gases over long distances.
2. Big Inch pipeline is used for supplying milk in New Zealand.
3. Pipeline transport is used for supplying petroleum from Gulf of Mexico to USA.

Codes

(a) Only 1 (b) Only 3
(c) 1 and 3 (d) All of these

Ans. (c)

Exp. Statements (1) and (3) are correct as pipelines are used extensively to transport liquids and gases such as water, petroleum and natural gas for an uninterrupted flow. Pipelines can also be used to transport liquefied coal over long distances.

In USA, there is a dense network of oil pipelines from the producing areas to the consuming areas.

Statement (2) is incorrect because Big Inch is one such famous pipeline, which carries petroleum from the oil wells of the Gulf of Mexico to the North-Eastern States.

Communication

30 **Consider the following statements Assertion (A) and Reason (R) and choose the correct code.**

(Chap 8, Class-XII, New NCERT)

Assertion (A) Development of telecommunication services has made communication dependent upon the means of transportation.

Reason (R) Optical fibre cables allow large quantities of data to be transmitted as compared to copper cables.

Codes

(a) Both A and R are true and R is the correct explanation of A.
(b) Both A and R are true, but R is not the correct explanation of A.
(c) A is true, but R is false.
(d) A is false, but R is true.

Ans. *(d)*

Exp. Assertion (A) is false, but Reason (R) is true. The development of telecommunication services allows the transmission of large amounts of data rapidly, securely and for error- free communication of services. Due to the development of communication, it did not depend on the means of transport.

Optical fibre cables allow large quantities of data to be transmitted as compared to copper cables because these allow large quantities of data to be transmitted rapidly, securely, and are virtually error-free.

31 **Which of the following statements is/are correct with reference to satellite communication?**

(Chap 8, Class-XII, New NCERT)

(a) The per unit cost of transmission of data has declined with the advent of satellites.
(b) Satellite communication can be used for mass media.
(c) Satellite communication can be used to connect remote places on Earth.
(d) All of the above

Ans. *(d)*

Exp. All the given statements are correct with reference to satellite communication as the satellites have rendered the unit cost and time of communication invariant in terms of distance.

This means it costs the same to communicate over 500 km as it does over 5,000 km *via* satellite.
Satellite communication can be used for mass media. Today weather forecasting through television is a boon. Satellite communication can also be used to connect remote places on Earth.

32 **Which of the following statements most appropriately defines cyber space?**

(Chap 8, Class-XII, New NCERT)

(a) A modern communication system which uses satellites for multi-purpose communication.
(b) A virtual link between all the computer and electronic devices operating in the world.
(c) A modern telecommunication technique which is used for transmitting data.
(d) A network of electronic computerised space interconnected by the World Wide Web.

Ans. *(d)*

Exp. Statement (d) most appropriately defines cyber space. Cyber space is the world of electronic computerised space.

It is encompassed by the Internet such as the World Wide Web.

It is the electronic digital world for communicating or accessing information over computer networks without physical movement of the sender and the receiver.

Chapter 13

Population and Settlement

Population and Settlement

Population

Introduction

- The pattern of population distribution refers to how people are distributed across the Earth surface. The world's population distribution is highly unequal

Factors Affecting Population Distribution

- **Geographical Factors**
  - **Climate** People prefer to live in pleasent climates compared to extreme ones like cold deserts etc
  - **Topography** People prefer to live on plains rather than mountains or plateaus
  - **Fertility of soil** Higher the fertility, higher the population density
  - **Availability of water** River valleys are the densely populated ones due to availability of water
  - **Landforms** People prefer flat plains and gentle slopes for living
- **Socio-cultural and Economic Factors**
  - **Urbanisation** Cities provide better employment opportunities, educational and medical facilities with enhanced modes of transport
  - **Industrialisation** Creates jobs and attracts large numbers of people
  - **Social factors** Some places draw visitors due to their cultural or religious significance

Population Density

- Finite capacity of people supported by each block of land. It is calculated by dividing number of persons of a region by the total land area
- According to density, regions can be divided into high density, medium density and low density areas

Population Change

- Change in number of people over a specific period of time
- Components of population change are
  - **Migration** When people move from their place of origin to the place of destination
  - **Crude Birth Rate** Expressed as number of live births in a Year Per Thousand population
  - **Crude Death Rate** Expressed as number of deaths in a year per thousand of population

Demographic Transition

Introduction

- Refers to change that population undergoes from high rates of births and deaths to low rates of births and deaths
- Many populations not only failed to grow but instead died when birth rates did not compensate for high death rates
- **Stages of Demographic Transition**
  - Stage 1 - High birth rates and highly fluctuating death rates
  - Stage 2 - Birth rate remains high and death rates begin to fall
  - Stage 3 - Birth rate starts to decline, rate of population growth decelerates
  - Stage 4 - Low birth rates and low death rates. Population growth is negligible
- **Age Pyramids** Useful for analysing a population's age composition. It can be of three types
  - **Expanding** Triangular in shape with a wide base, showing high birth rate
  - **Constant** Bell shaped and tapered towards the top, has birth rates and death rates almost the same
  - **Declining** Narrow base and tapered top, showing low birth rate and death rate
- **Sex Composition** Ratio of number of women and men in a population is called as sex ratio. It is an important information about the status of women in a country

Urban and Rural Settlement

Rural Settlement

- Site is the important aspect as needs of village folks lie around basic requirements of food, clothing and shelter
  - **Rural Settlement Patterns** Reflects the way houses are sited in relation to each other may be classified as
  - **On the Basis of Setting** Main types are plain villages, plateau villages, coastal villages etc
  - **On the Basis of Functions** May be farming villages, fisherman's villages, pastoral villages etc
  - **On the Basis of Shape of Settlements** Can be linear, rectangular, circular, star-like, T-shaped etc

Urban Settlement

A recent phenomenon observed due to increase in urban areas and urban population

- **Urban Settlement Pattern**
  - **Town** Basic unit of urban settlement
  - **City** Regarded as leading town, are much larger than towns and offers a great number of economic functions
  - **Conurbation** A large area of urban development that resulted from merging of originally separate towns
  - **Million City** When population of a city crosses one million mark
  - **Megapolis** A union of conurbations

SOURCE *Tamil Nadu Board Class XII* (*Population Geography*), ***New NCERT Class VIII*** (*Human Resources*), ***Old NCERT Class IX*** (*Our Growing Numbers, Human Life in the Natural Regions of the World*), ***New NCERT Class XII*** (*The World Population Distribution, Density and Growth, Population Composition, Human Development, Human Settlements*)

Population Distribution and Growth

1 Consider the following statements.

(Chap 6, Class-VIII, New NCERT)

1. Africa is the most densely populated continent of the world.
2. More than 50% of world's population is concentrated in Europe.
3. 90% of world's population is concentrated only in 10% of land area.
4. The population of Southern hemisphere is more than the population of Northern hemisphere.

Which of the statements given above is/are correct?

(a) Only 1 (b) Only 2
(c) Only 3 (d) Only 4

***Ans.* (c)**

Exp. Only statement (3) is correct as 90% of the world's population lives in about 10% of its land area. The 10 most populous countries of the world contribute about 60% of the world's population.

Statements (1), (2) and (4) are incorrect because Asia is the most densely populated continent of the world. More than 50% of world's population is concentrated in Asia. The population of Northern hemisphere is more than the population of Southern hemisphere.

2 Consider the following statements with reference to factors influencing the distribution of population.

(Chap 2, Class-XII, New NCERT)

1. Regions with large mineral deposits force people to migrate to other areas.
2. The rural areas have more population density as compared to urban areas.
3. Places with religious and cultural significance attract migrants from other regions.
4. Areas with social conflict and political unrest are densely populated.

Which of the statements given above is/are correct?

(a) Only 1 (b) Only 2 (c) Only 3 (d) Only 4

***Ans.* (c)**

Exp. Only statement (3) is correct with reference to factors influencing the distribution of population. Places of religious and cultural importance attract migrants from other regions, as people prefer to stay at their religious places.

Statements (1), (2) and (3) are incorrect because areas with mineral deposits attract industries. Mining and industrial activities generate employment. So, skilled and semi-skilled workers move to these areas and make them densely populated.

The urban areas have more population density as compared to rural areas and the areas with social conflict and political unrest tend to be less populated.

3 Consider the following statements regarding the percentage of world population.

(Chap 2, Class-XII, New NCERT)

1. Approximately around 60% of the world's population lives in the Asia continent.
2. About 10% of the world's population lives in the Europe continent.
3. More than 5% of the world's population lives in the North America continent.

Which of the statements given above is/are correct?

(a) Only 1 (b) 2 and 3
(c) 1, 2 and 3 (d) 1 and 3

***Ans.* (c)**

Exp. All the statements (1), (2) and (3) are correct regarding the percentage of world population.

About 60% of the world's population lives in the Asia continent. Asia is the highly populated continent in the world and 17% of the world's population lives in the Africa continent. Africa continent is the second largest populated continent in the world.

About 10% of the world's population lives in the Europe continent. Europe is the third largest populated continent in the world.

About 5% of the world's population lives in the North America continent. North America is the fifth largest populated continent in the world.

4 Consider the following statements with reference to natural growth of population.

(Chap 2, Class-XII, New NCERT)

1. Natural growth of population occurs when birth rate is less than the death rate.
2. Natural growth of population is the difference between births and deaths in a given region.
3. Natural growth of a population is the difference between in migration and out migration in a region.
4. Natural growth of population is the positive growth in the number of males in a region.

Which of the statements given above is/are correct?

(a) Only 1 (b) Only 2
(c) Only 3 (d) Only 4

***Ans.* (b)**

Exp. Only statement (2) is correct with reference to natural growth of population. Natural growth of population is defined as the population increased by difference between births and deaths in a particular region between two points of time.

Statements (1), (3) and (4) are incorrect because natural growth of population occurs when birth rate is higher than the death rate. Negative growth of a population is the difference between in migration and out migration in a region. Natural growth of population is the positive growth in the number of males and females in a region.

5 Consider the following statements about the population density of world regions. *(Chap 3, Class-XI, New NCERT)*

1. South Asia has the highest population density among all world regions.
2. Australia and Oceania have a higher population density than North America.
3. Africa has a lower population density than Europe.

How many of the statements given above is/are correct?

(a) Only one (b) Only two
(c) All three (d) None of these

***Ans.* (c)**

Exp. All three statements i.e., (1), (2) and (3) are correct. While South Asia has a high population density, it's actually surpassed by East Asia as the region with the highest global density. Australia and Oceania have a considerably lower population density compared to North America. In fact, it's among the lowest globally. Even though Europe has a relatively high population density, Africa actually surpasses it as the continent with the highest average density overall.

6 With reference to high density of population in the Eastern coastal regions of America, which of the following is/are incorrect? *(Chap 3, Class-XII, New NCERT)*

1. Immigrations from Europe has led to increased concentration of population in Eastern USA and Canada.
2. Early industrial development and industrialisation led to increase in population of these regions.
3. Eastern coastal plains had highly fertile alluvial soil, which increased the level of agricultural development, leading to increase in population.

Codes

(a) Only 1 (b) Only 3
(c) 1 and 3 (d) 1 and 2

***Ans.* (b)**

Exp. Statement (3) is incorrect with reference to high density of population in Eastern coastal regions of America because due to industrial development and industrialisation in Eastern USA, economic development took place in this area and urbanisation started increasing. For this reason, the population is more in Eastern USA.

7 Which of the following physical factors is/are responsible for high density of population in a region? *(Chap 3, Class-XII, New NCERT)*

1. High and rugged mountains
2. Dense forests
3. Mineral concentration
4. Harsh climate

Codes

(a) 1 and 2 (b) Only 3
(c) 1 and 4 (d) Only 4

***Ans.* (b)**

Exp. Mineral concentration is responsible for high density of population in a region because areas with mineral deposits is key factor for industrial areas activities.

Mining and industrial activities generate employment. So, skilled and semi-skilled workers move to these areas and make them densely populated.

High and rugged mountains, dense forest and harsh climate are not responsible for high density of population in a region.

8 Consider the following statements about the Crude Death Rate. *(Chap 2, Class-XII, New NCERT)*

1. The Crude Death Rate is the total number of deaths per year per 1,000 people.
2. A high crude death rate indicates a high standard of living.
3. The crude death rate can be influenced by factors such as healthcare, sanitation and nutrition.

How many of the statements given above is/are correct?

(a) Only one (b) Only two
(c) All three (d) None of these

***Ans.* (b)**

Exp. Only two statements i.e., (1) and (3) are correct about the crude death Rate.

The Crude Death Rate is indeed calculated as the total number of deaths in a given year divided by the mid-year population, expressed per 1,000 people. Factors like healthcare, sanitation, and nutrition significantly influence the Crude Death Rate. Better healthcare and sanitary conditions lead to lower death rates, while malnutrition can contribute to higher death rates.

Statement (2) is incorrect because a high crude death rate actually indicates a low standard of living. It suggests poorer healthcare, sanitation, nutrition and overall socio-economic conditions.

9 Which one of the following are a push factors for migration? *(Chap 2, Class-XII, New NCERT)*

1. Peace and stability
2. Socio-economic backwardness
3. Moderate and pleasant climate
4. Political turmoil
5. Unemployment

Codes

(a) 1, 2, 3
(b) 2, 4, 5
(c) 1, 3, 5
(d) 2, 3, 4

***Ans.* (b)**

Exp. The push factors for migration are unemployment, poor living conditions, political turmoil, unpleasant climate, natural disasters, epidemics and socio-economic backwardness.

Push factors are the factors, which make the place of origin seem less attractive and people want to move to a new area. It is classified as a negative factor.

10 Which of the following pairs is/are not correctly matched? *(Chap 2, Class-XII, New NCERT)*

	Stages of Demographic Transition		Characteristics
1.	Stage I	–	Decline in mortality, high growth of population
2.	Stage II	–	Urbanised and literate society
3.	Stage III	–	High fertility, high mortality, illiterate society
4.	Stage IV	–	Near zero growth rate

Codes

(a) 1 and 2 (b) 3 and 4
(c) Only 2 (d) 1, 2 and 3

Ans. (d)

Exp. Pairs (1), (2) and (3) are not correctly matched. The first stage, has high fertility and high mortality because people reproduce more to compensate for the deaths due to epidemics and variable food supply. The population growth is slow and most of the people are engaged in agriculture where large families are an asset.

In the second stage, fertility remains high but it declines with time. This is accompanied by reduced mortality rate. Improvements in sanitation and health conditions lead to decline in mortality.

In the third stage, both fertility and mortality decline considerably. The population is either stable or grows slowly.

11 With reference to Malthus' ideas about the growth of population, which of the following statements is/are correct? *(Chap 2, Class-XII, New NCERT)*

1. The growth of population is more than that of the food supply.
2. Preventive checks are better than physical checks in controlling the growth of population.
3. Rapid increase in population growth may lead to population crash due to famines and diseases.

Codes

(a) 1 and 2 (b) Only 1
(c) 1 and 3 (d) All of these

Ans. (d)

Exp. All the statements (1), (2) and (3) are correct with reference to Malthus's ideas about growth of population. Thomas Malthus in his theory, 'Malthusian Growth Model' (1798) stated that the number of people would increase faster than the food supply.

The preventive checks are better than the physical checks. For the sustainability of our resources, the world will have to control the rapid population increase. Any further rapid population increase would result in a population crash caused by famines, diseases and war.

12 Which of the following factors, will reduce natural growth rate of population of a country? *(Chap 7, Class-IX, Old NCERT)*

1. Economic development
2. Increase in female education
3. Increase in land under agriculture
4. Rise in famines

Codes

(a) 1, 2 and 3
(b) 1 and 2
(c) 1, 2 and 4
(d) All of these

Ans. (a)

Exp. Among the given factors i.e., (1), (2) and (3) will reduce natural growth rate of population of a country because with the increase of economic development, people get employment and there is increase in education, urbanisation and industrialisation. This can reduce the natural growth rate of the population.

Women empowerment will be promoted through female literacy. This will give employment to women and women will be able to educate their children. All these reasons reduce the natural growth rate of the population.

By increasing the land under agriculture, employment is encouraged in the rural area and there is economic and social development of the rural people. This reduces the natural growth rate of the population.

Statement (4) is incorrect because rise in famines will not reduce natural growth rate of population.

Population Composition

13 Consider the following pairs. *(Chap 2, Class-XII, New NCERT)*

	Stages of Demographic Transition		Characteristics
1.	Pre-transition	–	High birth rates and high fluctuating death rates
2.	Early transition	–	Death rate begins to fall
3.	Late transition	–	Rate of population growth decelerates
4.	Post-transition	–	Low birth and High death rates

How many pairs given above is/are not correctly matched?

(a) Only one (b) Only two
(c) Only three (d) All four

Ans. (a)

Exp. Only one pair i.e., (4) is not correctly matched because societies are characterised by low birth and low death rates. Population growth is negligible or even enters a decline. The demographic transition model argues that economic development can help reduce crude death rates.

14 With reference to age structure of population, consider the following statements. *(Chap 3, Class-XII, New NCERT)*

1. The greater is the proportion of population above 60 years, the less is the health expenditure of the region.
2. Higher proportion of population below 15 years indicates a higher birth rate.
3. Greater the number of people in the age group 15-59 years, more is the working age population.

How many statements given above is/are incorrect?

(a) Only one (b) Only two
(c) All three (d) None of these

Ans. (a)

Exp. Only one statement i.e., (1) is incorrect with reference to age structure of population because a greater proportion of population above 60 years represents an ageing population which requires more expenditure on health care facilities.

15 Consider the following statements regarding age-sex pyramid. *(Chap 3, Class-XII, New NCERT)*

1. The age-sex structure of a population refers to the number of females and males in different age groups.
2. A population pyramid is used to show the age-sex structure of the population.

Which of the statements given above is/are correct?

(a) Only 1 (b) Only 2
(c) Both 1 and 2 (d) Neither 1 nor 2

Ans. (c)

Exp. Both the statements (1) and (2) are correct regarding age-sex pyramid. The age-sex structure of a population refers to the number of females and males in different age groups. A population pyramid is used to show the age-sex structure of the population.

The shape of the population pyramid reflects the characteristics of the population.

16 With reference to the structure and composition of the population of a country 'X', consider the following statements. *(Chap 3, Class-XII, New NCERT)*

1. The population pyramid of this country has narrow base and a tapered top.
2. Population growth in this country is nearly zero.
3. It is located in Asia.

Which of the following is country 'X'?

(a) China (b) Indonesia (c) Japan (d) Myanmar

Ans. (c)

Exp. According to the given statements, country X is identified as Japan.

The pyramid of Japan has a narrow base and a tapered top showing low birth and death rates. The population growth in developed countries is usually zero or negative.

17 Which of the following is/are most probable factors that leads to higher sex ratio for women in urban areas and higher sex ratio of men in rural areas in the Western countries? *(Chap 3, Class-XII, New NCERT)*

1. Female migration to urban areas for job opportunities.
2. Highly mechanised male dominated farming.
3. Shortage of housing in rural regions.

Codes

(a) 1 and 3 (b) 2 and 3
(c) Only 2 (d) 1 and 2

Ans. (d)

Exp. Among the given factors i.e., (1) and (2) will be the most probable reason for the higher sex ratio of women in urban areas and higher sex ratio of men in rural areas in the Western countries. The excess of females in urban areas of USA, Canada and Europe is the result of influx of females from rural areas to avail of the vast job opportunities. Farming in these highly developed countries is also highly mechanised and remains largely a male occupation.

Statement (3) is not a factor because the lack of homes in rural areas is not the most likely factor in the high sex ratio for women in urban areas and the high sex ratio for men in rural areas in Western countries.

18 Consider the following statements about age composition and population growth. *(Chap 3, Class-XII, New NCERT)*

1. The age composition is important for understanding the natality and mortality of a community.
2. Expanding/growing population pyramids are characterised by a narrow base.
3. The bell-shaped pyramid has birth and death rates almost the same leading to a constant population.
4. Under normal circumstances, the number of people in each age group tends to increase each year.

How many of the statements given above is/are correct?

(a) Only one (b) Only two
(c) Only three (d) All four

Ans. (b)

Exp. Only two statements i.e., (1) and (3) are correct regarding age composition and population growth.

The age composition is important for understanding the natality and mortality of a community. Age differences may create social and economic differences.

Constant/Stationary population is shown in bell-shaped and tapered towards the top. The bell-shaped pyramid has birth and death rates almost the same and leading to a constant population. e.g., Australia.

Statements (2) and (4) are incorrect because expanding/growing population type of population pyramid is triangular with a wide base. e.g., Nigeria, Bangladesh, Mexico. It is generally in less developed countries. A large base shows a high birth rate.

Under normal circumstances, the number of people at each age group will be lower than the previous year. As a result, the age structure of the population tends to take.

19 Consider the following statements about the occupational structure of a population. *(Chap 3, Class-XII, New NCERT)*

1. In a developed country, more number of people are engaged in secondary and tertiary sector.
2. In a developing economy, large number of people are engaged in the extraction of natural resources.
3. Skilled and young population in a country increases the productivity of a nation.

How many of the statements given above is/are correct?

(a) Only one (b) Only two
(c) All of these (d) None of these

Ans. (c)

Exp. All the statements i.e., (1), (2) and (3) are correct about the occupational structure of a population. In a developed country, the literacy rate is high and people are more aware. For this reason, most of the people in developed countries are engaged in secondary and tertiary sectors.

If the economy is still in the primitive stages or developing economy, then the proportion of people engaged in primary activities would be high. Due to skilled and young population in a country, employment and savings increase. It increases the economic productivity of a nation.

Human Development

20 Consider the following statements about human development. *(Chap 9, Class-XII, New NCERT)*

1. Human development is solely determined by a country's Gross Domestic Product (GDP).
2. The Human Development Index (HDI) is a measure that includes indicators of life expectancy, education and per capita income.
3. The concept of human development considers people as passive recipients of benefits.

How many of the statements given above is/are correct?

(a) Only one (b) Only two
(c) All three (d) None of these

Ans. (a)

Exp. Only one statements i.e., (2) is correct with regarding to human development. The Human Development Index (HDI) is indeed a measure that includes indicators of life expectancy, education, and per capita income.

Statements (1) and (3) are incorrect because Human development is not solely determined by a country's Gross Domestic Product (GDP). While economic factors are important, human development is a broader concept that includes aspects like education, health and overall well-being.

The concept of human development does not consider people as passive recipients of benefits. Instead, it emphasises the active involvement of individuals and communities in their own development.

21 Sustainability is one of the four pillars of human development. Which of the following statements given below correctly defines sustainability? *(Chap 4, Class-XII, New NCERT)*

(a) Equal access of opportunities for everyone.
(b) Improving the access to knowledge for the marginalised sections.
(c) Continuity in the availability of opportunities for present and future generations.
(d) Improvement in human choices.

Ans. (c)

Exp. Statement (c) correctly defines sustainability because it means continuity in the availability of opportunities. To have sustainable human development, each generation must have the same opportunities. All environmental, financial and human resources must be used keeping in mind the future.

22 With reference to welfare approach of measuring human development, consider the following statements. *(Chap 4, Class-XII, New NCERT)*

1. It argues for higher government expenditure on education, health and social sector.
2. It emphasises on basic needs of certain sections.
3. It links human development to income.

How many of the statements given above is/are correct?

(a) Only one (b) Only two
(c) All three (d) None of these

Ans. (a)

Exp. Only one statement i.e., (1) is correct with reference to welfare approach of measuring human development as this approach looks at human beings as beneficiaries or targets of all development activities. The approach argues for higher government expenditure on education, health, social secondary and amenities. People are not participants in development but only passive recipients. The government is responsible for increasing levels of human development by maximising expenditure on welfare.

Statements (2) and (3) are incorrect because welfare approach emphasises on the basic needs of all sections. Welfare approach links human development with social development.

23 Which of the following is among the six basic needs as per the International Labour Organisation's Basic Needs Approach for measuring human development? *(Chap 4, Class-XII, New NCERT)*

1. Health
2. Child welfare
3. Sanitation
4. Housing
5. Labour
6. Food

Codes

(a) 1, 2, 3, 4, 5 (b) 2, 4, 5, 6
(c) 1, 3, 4, 6 (d) 3, 4, 5, 6

Ans. (c)

Exp. As per International Labour Organisation's (ILO's) Basic Needs Approach, six basic needs are health, education, food, water supply, sanitation and housing were identified. The emphasis is given on the provision of basic needs of defined sections.

Basic needs approach was initially proposed by International Labour Organisation. It is one of the major approaches to the measurement of absolute poverty in developing countries.

It attempts to define the absolute minimum resources necessary for long term physical well-being, usually in terms of consumption of goods.

24 Which of the following indicators are used to measure shortfall in human development in the Human Poverty Index? *(Chap 4, Class-XII, New NCERT)*

1. Number of underweight children
2. Number of people not having access to clean water
3. Lack of technological development

Codes

(a) 1 and 3
(b) 2 and 3
(c) 1 and 2
(d) All of the above

Ans. (c)

Exp. Among the given indicators i.e., (1) and (2) are used to measure shortfall in human development in the Human Poverty Index.

This index basically used to measures the shortfall in human development. It is a non-income measure. The probability of not surviving till the age of 40, the adult illiteracy rate, the number of people who do not have access to clean water, and the number of small children who are underweight are all taken into account to show the shortfall in human development in any region.

While lack of technological development indicators ia not used to measure shortfall in human development in the Human Poverty Index.

25 With reference to Gross National Happiness (GNH) Index, consider the following statements. *(Chap 4, Class-XII, New NCERT)*

1. The concept of GNH was started in Bhutan.
2. It takes into account the harmful effects of technology on the environment.
3. It focuses on non-material and spiritual development.

Which of the statements given above are correct?

(a) 1 and 3 (b) 1 and 2
(c) 2 and 3 (d) All of these

Ans. (d)

Exp. All the statements (1), (2) and (3) are correct with reference to Gross National Happiness (GNH). This index was started in Bhutan to takes into account the harmful effects of technology on the environment. This index encourages us to think of the spiritual, non-material and qualitative aspects of development.

26 Which of the following statements are correct regarding measuring Human Development? *(Chap 4, Class-XII, New NCERT)*

1. The human development index assesses progress in human development. It highlights progress made in crucial areas of human development.
2. Human development index is not the reliable source to measure because it lacks distribution factor.

Codes

(a) Only 1 (b) Only 2
(c) Both 1 and 2 (d) Neither 1 nor 2

Ans. (c)

Exp. Both the statements (1) and (2) are correct regarding measuring Human Development. The Human Development Index (HDI) assesses progress in human development. It highlights progress made in crucial areas of human development. Yet, it is not the most reliable measure. This is because it does not say anything about the distribution.

Human Development Index (HDI) is published by United Nations Development Programme (UNDP), every year.

Human Settlements

27 Consider the following statements about temporary human settlements. *(Chap 10, Class-XII, New NCERT)*

1. Temporary human settlements can be found in cold desert regions due to seasonal migration.
2. Deep forested areas are unsuitable for temporary human settlements due to lack of resources.
3. Rugged mountainous regions often see temporary human settlements due to mountaineering expeditions.

How many of the statements given above is/are correct?

(a) Only one (b) Only two
(c) All three (d) None of these

Ans. (b)

Exp. Only two statements i.e., (1) and (3) are correct. Temporary human settlements are usually built in cold desert regions, deep forested areas and rugged mountain slopes. Settlements which are occupied for a short time are called temporary settlements. The people living in deep forests, hot and cold deserts and mountains often dwell in such temporary settlements. They practice hunting, gathering, shifting cultivation and transhumance.

Statement (2) is incorrect because deep forests can provide ample resources for temporary settlements, including food, water, and materials for shelter. Hunter-gatherer communities have thrived in such environments for centuries.

28 Consider the following statements about sub-urbanisation. *(Chap 10, Class-XII, New NCERT)*

1. It is the movement of people from one region to another in search of jobs.
2. It is the movement of people from the city to cleaner areas outside the city.
3. It is the movement of women in search of safe places and employment.
4. It is the movement of people towards environmentally sustainable regions.

Which statements given above is/are correct?

(a) 1 and 2
(b) Only 2
(c) 2 and 4
(d) Only 4

Ans. (b)

Exp. Statement (2) is correct with reference to sub-urbanisation. It is a new trend of people moving away from congested urban areas to cleaner areas outside the city in search of a better quality of living.

Important suburbs develop around major cities and everyday thousands of people commute from their homes in the suburbs to their work places in the city.

29 Consider the following statements about rural settlements. *(Chap 10, Class-XII, New NCERT)*

1. People in rural settlements are occupied in primary activities.
2. Rural settlements cannot be built over hills and islands.
3. Rural settlements can be situated near a lowland coastal region.

Which of the statements given above is incorrect?

(a) Only 1 (b) Only 2
(c) Only 3 (d) All of these

Ans. (b)

Exp. Statement (2) is incorrect about rural settlements because rural settlements can be built over hills and islands. Rural settlements are found in the Himalayan region of India and Lakshadweep and Andaman and Nicobar islands.

30 Consider the following Assertion (A) and Reason (R) and choose the correct code. *(Chap 10, Class-XII, New NCERT)*

Assertion (A) Dry point settlements are generally found in low lying river basins.

Reason (R) Most of the fortified settlements are located in the higher grounds and hills.

Codes

(a) Both A and R are true and R is the correct explanation of A.
(b) Both A and R are true, but R is not the correct explanation of A.
(c) A is true, but R is false.
(d) A is false, but R is true.

Ans. (b)

Exp. Both Assertion (A) and Reason (R) are true, but Reason (R) is not the correct explanation of Assertion (A). Most of the fortified settlements are located in high plains and hills as the high plains and mountains protect them from floods.

Dry point settlements are generally found in low lying river basins because many advantages such as water for drinking, cooking and washing. Rivers and lakes can be used to irrigate farm land. Water bodies also have fish which can be caught for diet and navigable rivers and lakes can be used for transportation.

31 Which of the following statements is/are correct with reference to patterns of rural settlements? *(Chap 10, Class-XII, New NCERT)*

1. Linear rural settlements are formed along roads and railways.
2. Rectangular patterns of rural settlements are found in wide intermontane valleys.
3. Cruciform settlements are developed around a river.

Codes

(a) 1 and 3 (b) 2 and 3
(c) 1 and 2 (d) All of these

Ans. (c)

Exp. Statements (1) and (2) are correct with reference to patterns of rural settlements. Linear pattern settlements houses are located along a road, railway line, and river, canal edge of a valley or along a levee. Rectangular patterns of rural settlements are found in plain areas or wide intermontane valleys. The roads are rectangular and cut each other at right angles.

Statement (3) is incorrect because cruciform settlements develop on the crossroads and houses extend in all the four directions.

32 **Which of the following is/are the problems generally faced by the rural settlements?** *(Chap 10, Class-XII, New NCERT)*

1. Vulnerability to natural disasters
2. Floods and droughts
3. Over congestion
4. Lack of modern communication infrastructure

Codes

(a) 1, 2 and 3
(b) 1, 2 and 4
(c) 2, 3 and 4
(d) 1 and 2

Ans. (b)

Exp. Among the given problems i.e., (1), (2) and (4) are generally faced by the rural settlements.

The construction of houses in rural settlements is made of mud, thatch and wood. That is why, the houses in the rural region are vulnerable to the disaster that comes during heavy rains and floods.

Natural disasters like drought and flood are faced by rural settlements.

The countries of South Asia face conditions of drought and flood very often. Unmetalled roads and lack of modern communication network create a unique problem in rural settlements.

Statement (3) is incorrect because the problem of over congestion occurs in urban settlements and not in rural settlements.

33 **Consider the following pairs.** *(Chap 10, Class-XII, New NCERT)*

	Pattern of rural settlement		Formed around
1.	Star shaped pattern	–	Convergence of several roads
2.	T shaped pattern	–	Tanks and lakes
3.	Circular pattern	–	Tri-junctions of roads
4.	Rectangular pattern	–	Intermontane valley

How many pairs given above is/are correct?

(a) Only one
(b) Only two
(c) Only three
(d) All four

Ans. (b)

Exp. Only two pairs i.e., (1) and (4) are correct.

The place where several roads converge, Star shaped settlements are developed by the houses built along the roads.

Rectangular pattern are found in plain areas or wide Intermontane valleys.

While pairs (2) and (3) are incorrect. T shaped settlements are developed at tri-junctions of the roads.

Circular villages developed around lakes, tanks and sometimes the village is planned in such a way that the central part remains open and is used for keeping the animals to protect them from wild animals.

34 **Which of the following statements is/are correct about urban settlements?** *(Chap 10, Class-XII, New NCERT)*

(a) Trade routes are significant in deciding the growth of urban settlements.
(b) Uniform international criteria are used by all the countries of the world to classify urban settlements.
(c) Majority of the population in urban areas is involved in non-agricultural activities.
(d) Both a and c

Ans. (d)

Exp. Statements (a) and (c) are correct about urban settlements or centres because these are located close to an important trade route have experienced rapid development. Majority of the population in urban areas is involved in non-agricultural activities. In India, if more than 75% of the productive population engaged in non-agricultural activities then it is an urban region.

Statement (b) is incorrect because different international criteria are used by all the countries of the world to classify urban settlements. In Italy, a settlement is called urban, if more than 50 % of its economically productive population is engaged in non-agricultural pursuits. India has set this criterion at 75 %.

35 **Consider the following Assertion (A) and Reason (R) and choose the correct code.** *(Chap 10, Class-XII, New NCERT)*

Assertion (A) Modern technological development plays a very important role in determining the location of urban settlements.

Reason (R) The location of earliest urban settlements was dependent upon water, building material and fertile land.

Codes

(a) Both A and R are true and R is the correct explanation of A.
(b) Both A and R are true, but R is not the correct explanation of A.
(c) A is true, but R is false.
(d) A is false, but R is true.

Ans. (b)

Exp. Both Assertion (A) and Reason (R) are true, but Reason (R) is not the correct explanation of Assertion (A). Locations of the earliest urban settlements were based on the availability of water, building materials and fertile land.

Today's modern technological development plays a significant role in locating urban settlements. Like, piped water can be supplied to a distant settlement, building material can be transported from long distances etc.

36 **Which of the following can be considered as an administrative town?** *(Chap 10, Class-XII, New NCERT)*

1. Beijing
2. Canberra
3. Jamshedpur
4. Addis Ababa

Codes

(a) 1, 2 and 3 (b) 2, 3 and 4
(c) 1, 2 and 4 (d) 1, 2, 3 and 4

Ans. (c)

Exp. Among the given options, Beijing, Canberra and Addis Ababa are considered as administrative town. An administrative town is a town that support to the administration headquarters of higher order. e.g., In India, Chandigarh, New Delhi etc are the administrative towns.

37 **Which of the following pairs are correct?**

(Chap 14, Class-XI, Old NCERT)

Towns		Functions
1. Amsterdam	–	Commercial town
2. Jerusalem	–	Cultural town
3. Jodhpur	–	Defence town
4. Guangzhou	–	China

Chose the correct code

(a) 1 and 2 (b) 2 and 3
(c) 3 and 4 (d) All of these

Ans. (d)

Exp. All the given pairs are correct.

Amsterdam It is known as trading and commercial town. A commercial town or commercial zone is any part of a city or town in which the primary land use in commercial activities.

Jerusalem It is considered as cultural town and famous for great religious importance.

Jodhpur This city of Rajasthan is a defence city. Defence cities are those cities that provide natural protection.

Guangzhou is in the South-Eastern part of China. It is famous for trade.

38 **Which of the following statements is/are correct with reference to planned cities?**

(Chap 10, Class-XII, New NCERT)

1. Planned cities are mostly developed by the governments of the country.
2. Canberra in Australia is an example of planned city designed by Walter Griffin.

Codes

(a) Only 1 (b) Only 2
(c) Both 1 and 2 (d) Neither 1 nor 2

Ans. (c)

Exp. Both the statements (1) and (2) are correct as planned cities are mostly developed by the governments of the country. Chandigarh city comes under a planned city in India. It was built by Britishers in his time.

Canberra was planned as the capital of Australia in 1912 by American landscape architect, Walter Burley Griffin.

Consider the following statements about large cities.

(Chap 10, Class-XII, New NCERT)

1. The first city to reach one million plus population in the world was London.
2. New York city was the first mega city of the world.
3. Any city with a population greater than one million is considered as a mega city.

Which of the statements given above are correct?

(a) 1 and 2 (b) 2 and 3 (c) 1 and 3 (d) All of these

Ans. (a)

Exp. Statements (1) and (2) are correct about large cities because the city whose population is more than one million is called million city. London was the first million city in the world.

London reached the million marks in 1800, followed by Paris in 1850 and New York in 1860. A mega city is a general term for cities together with their suburbs with a population of more than 10 million people.

New York was the first to attain the status of a mega city by 1950 with a total population of about 12.5 million.

Statement (3) is incorrect because any city with a population greater than 10 million is considered as a mega city.

40 **With reference to the types of urban settlements, which of the following groups have been arranged in a correct sequence from smaller to larger?**

(Chap 10, Class-XII, New NCERT)

(a) Megalopolis, Million City, Conurbation
(b) Megalopolis, Conurbation, Million City
(c) Million City, Megalopolis, Conurbation
(d) Conurbation, Million City, Megalopolis

Ans. (d)

Exp. The correct sequence from smaller to larger of urban settlements is Conurbation, Million City and Megalopolis.

The term 'Conurbation' was coined by Patrick Geddes in 1915 and applied to a large area of urban development that resulted from the merging of originally separate towns or cities.

The city whose population is more than one million is called million cities. London was the first million cities in the world. London reached the million marks in 1800.

The Megalopolis popularised by Jean Guttmann in 1957, and signifies 'super-metropolitan' region extending, as union of conurbations.

Boston in USA is the best known example of a megalopolis.

41 **With reference to the rural-urban linkages, which of the following statements is/are correct?**

(Chap 10, Class-XII, New NCERT)

1. Rural and urban regions are often in competition with each other.
2. Rural and urban regions are complementary to each other.
3. There is a continuous exchange of commodities between rural and urban areas through trade ties.

Codes

(a) 1 and 3 (b) 1 and 2 (c) 2 and 3 (d) All of these

Ans. (d)

Exp. All the statements (1), (2) and (3) are correct with reference to the rural-urban linkages as rural and urban areas are often in competition with each other. Rural and urban areas complement each other because the city provides employment and education to the rural people and the rural region provides food. There is a continuous exchange of goods between rural and urban areas through trade relations.

Major Tribes

42 Match the following lists correctly and choose the correct code. *(Chap 10, Class-IX, Old NCERT)*

List I (Nomadic tribes)	List II (Regions)
A. Bedouin	1. Kalahari desert
B. Bushman	2. Sahara desert
C. Pygmies	3. Zaire basin

Codes

	A	B	C
(a)	3	2	1
(b)	2	1	3
(c)	3	1	2
(d)	2	3	1

***Ans.* (b)**

Exp. The correct matching is A-2, B-1, C-3.

Bedouin The Bedouin tribes are nomadic people who live in the desert. They mainly live in the Sahara desert, Arabian and Syrian deserts and the Sinai in Egypt.

Bushman The Bushman tribe is found in Kalahari desert. They are native to Southern Africa, and have lived there for thousands of years. In Southern Africa, the Bushman tribe is found mainly in Botswana, Namibia, South Africa and Zambia.

Pygmies The African Pygmy is a group of ethnicities native to Central Africa, mostly the Congo/Zaire Basin, traditionally subsistence on a forest dweller and hunter-gatherer lifestyle.

43 Consider the following pairs. *(Chap 10, Class-IX, Old NCERT)*

Nomadic Tribes		Regions
1. Inuits		Scandinavia
2. Lapps	–	Siberia
3. Samoyeds	–	Canada and Alaska
4. Altai	–	Turkey

How many of the pairs given above is/are correct?

(a) Only one (b) Only two
(c) Only three (d) All four

***Ans.* (a)**

Exp. Only one pair i.e., (1) is correct.

Inuits tribes refer broadly to the Arctic indigenous population of Alaska, Canada and Greenland. Inuit means people, and the language they speak is called Inuktitut.

While, pairs (2), (3) and (4) are incorrect the Lapps people are an indigenous Finno Ugric speaking people inhabiting Sapmi, which today encompasses large Northern parts of Norway, Sweden, Finland and Scandinavia, the Kola Peninsula within the Murmansk Oblast of Russia.

The Samoyeds are the indigenous people of the Northern Eurasia and Siberia who speak a systematically related set of languages.

Altia, Balkar, Dolgan are tribes of Turkey.

44 Consider the following statements. *(Chap 10, Class-IX, Old NCERT)*

1. The Maasais are mainly involved in plantation agriculture.
2. Maasais live in temporary settlements in Eastern African Grasslands.

Which of the statements given above is/are correct?

(a) Only 1
(b) Only 2
(c) Both 1 and 2
(d) Neither 1 nor 2

***Ans.* (b)**

Exp. Statement (2) is correct as the Maasai tribes belongs to the Nilotic ethnic group inhabiting in temporary settlements in Eastern African Grasslands. The Maasai tribes are famous for herders and warriors.

Statement (1) is incorrect because Maasai tribes are mainly involved in cattle grazing. Maasai tribes speak Maa language and the official languages of Kenya and Tanzania.

45 Which of the following pairs is correct? *(Chap 10, Class-IX, Old NCERT)*

Nomadic Tribes		Occupation
1. Hausa tribe	–	Hunting and fishing
2. Bedouins	–	Nomadic herding
3. Yakuts	–	Settled agriculture

How many of the above pairs is/are correctly matched?

(a) Only one (b) Only two
(c) All three (d) None of these

***Ans.* (b)**

Exp. Only two pairs i.e. (1) and (2) are correctly matched.

Hausa tribes are an ethnic designation scattered throughout West Africa with smaller population in other African regions. The Hausa tribes specialised in settled agriculture, fishing, hunting and salt-mining.

Bedouin tribes are Arabic speaking nomadic people of the Middle Eastern deserts. Most Bedouins are animal herders who migrate into the desert during the rainy winter season and move back toward the cultivated land in the dry summer months.

While pair (3) is incorrect because Yakuts tribes are one of the major people of Eastern Siberia. The Yakut tribes are largely hunters, fishermen and reindeer herders, raised cattle and horses.

Chapter 14

Continents

Continents

Asia and Africa

Asia

- Largest continent of the world and contains 59.22% of world's population as of 2024.
- It is surrounded by oceans from three sides
- **Climate** It has a great range of climate due to large area. It not only experiences winters but also summers, monsoons, etc
- **Soil** With the continent possessing varied terrains, variety of soils like podzolic soils, black prairie soils, alluvial soils, etc are found
- **Agriculture** Shifting agriculture is practised in wide areas. Intensive as well as Extensive agriculture can also be found
- **Crops** Rice is the main crop grown in this continent

Africa

- Second largest continent both in size and population
- Hottest continent on the earth and has shortest coastline
- Most centrally located continent and is also known as Dark continent
- **Climate** Continent not only faces equatorial climate but also sudan type, desert type, mediterranean type etc
- **Soil** Only 10% of soil is suitable for crops, including volcanic soils, alluvial soils, etc
- **Forest** Shifting agriculture is practised in wide areas. Intensive as well as Extensive agriculture can also be found
- **Industry** Cotton clothes industry, cement industry, iron, steel, machinery, etc are found here

North and South America

North America

- Third largest continent of the world and has rich farmlands, extensive forests, abundant minerals, huge water power resources and extensive coastal fishing grounds
- **Climate** It has varied climate extending between tropical zone in South to frigid zone in North
- **Vegetation** Tundra, Taiga, Mediterranean types of vegetation is seen here
- **Crops** Maize, wheat, barley are important cereals
- **Transport** Panama canal connecting two oceans, superways and large navigational rivers exist here

South America

- Fourth largest continent and is connected to North America through the Isthmus of Panama
- **Climate** Large part of continent lies in tropical zone, thus equatorial type of climate
- **Vegetation** Equatorial rain forests called Selvas are found here. Along with it, Savanna grasslands, temperate grasslands called Pampas, desert type and mediterranean type vegetations are also found here
- **Crops** Only 10% of soil is suitable for farming. Wheat and maize are important crops along with coffee, cocoa, sugarcane, etc. Animal rearing is also done here
- **Population** People here belong to 3 main racial groups i.e., American Indians, Blacks and Europeans

Europe and Australia

Europe

- A peninsula of Eurasian continent and is the most densely populated one
- **Climate** Majority of Europe lies in temperate zone but climate here is mild. Continental climate, Tundra climate, Mediterranean climate, etc can be found here
- **Vegetation** Olives, figs, grapes, oranges are some of the important fruits found in Mediterranean region along with Tundra type vegetation and steppes
- **Crops** Wheat is an important crop with barley and oats being the staple crop. Sugar beet and potatoes are also gr here along with flax, large varieties fruits, etc
- **People** Population here is unevenly distributed with industrial regions being densely populated, Eastern and Southern Europe with moderate density and Northern Europe with thin density

Australia

- Smallest continent and the only country in the world that covers the entire continent
- **Climate** Most of the continent is dry The Eastern, North-East and South-West parts come in way of winds and receive heavy rainfall. Very large part of Central and Western part of continent has no rain at all, thus a hot desert type of climate is found
- **Forests And Grasslands** Tropical grasslands called Savannas and temperate grasslands called Downs are also found
- **Minerals** Good amount of fold is produced here along with large reserves of coal, iron-ore, bauxite, etc

Antarctica It is also known as White continent and lies completely in Southern hemisphere. About 99% of the continent remains permanently covered with ice. Some amount of coal, iron and copper have been found but their commercial utilisation is not possible

SOURCE *Old NCERT Class VI* (Africa), *Old NCERT Class VI* (South America), *Old NCERT Class VI* (Australia), *Old NCERT Class VI* (Australia), *Old NCERT Class VI* (Antarctica), *Old NCERT Class VII* (North America), *Old NCERT Class VII* (Europe), *Old NCERT Class VIII* (Asia)

Asia

1 Consider the following statements about Asia. *(Chap 6, Class-VIII, Old NCERT)*

1. Four-fifth of the world's population resides in Asia.
2. No part of Asia lies below the Equator.
3. Asia constitutes about one-third of the land surface area of the world.
4. The whole of the Asian landmass lies entirely in the western hemisphere.

How many of the statements given above is/are correct?

(a) Only one (b) Only two
(c) Only three (d) All four

Ans. (a)

Exp. Only one statement i.e., (3) is correct with respect to Asia. It is the largest continent in the world and it constitutes about one-third of the land surface area of the world. Its latitudinal range is between 10° South latitude to 80° North latitude.

Statements (1), (2) and (4) are incorrect because 59% of world's population resides in Asia. The entire part of the mainland of Asia is North of the Equator. The whole of the Asian landmass lies entirely in the Eastern Hemisphere.

2 The Eastern and Western boundary of Siberian Plain region in Northern Asia is marked by, which of the following rivers? *(Chap 6, Class-VIII, Old NCERT)*

(a) Brahmaputra river (b) Mekong river
(c) Lena river (d) None of these

Ans. (c)

Exp. The Eastern and Western boundary of Siberian Plain region in Northern Asia is marked by Lena river. Lena river is located in Russia.

Brahmaputra river flows in China and India and Mekong river flows in Vietnam, Laos, Thailand, etc.

3 Consider the following statements about Lake Baikal. *(Chap 6, Class-VIII, Old NCERT)*

1. Lake Baikal is located in China.
2. It is a saline water lake in Asia.
3. It is the deepest lake in Asia.
4. It holds more than 50% of freshwater in the world.

How many of the statements given above is/are correct?

(a) Only one (b) Only two
(c) Only three (d) All four

Ans. (a)

Exp. Only one statement i.e., (3) is correct as Lake Baikal is the deepest lake in Asia.

Statements (1), (2) and (4) are incorrect because Lake Baikal is a freshwater lake in Asia located in Siberia. It holds more than 20% of freshwater in the world.

4 Consider the following statements about highlands in Asia. *(Chap 6, Class-VIII, Old NCERT)*

1. A chain of mountain ranges converges at the Pamir Knot.
2. The Zagros mountains extend in Iran along the Arabian Sea.
3. The Karakoram range extends in a South-East direction from the Pamir.

How many of the statements given above is/are correct?

(a) Only one (b) Only two
(c) All three (d) None of these

Ans. (c)

Exp. All the three statements i.e., (1), (2) and (3) are correct with reference to highlands in Asia as many mountain ranges come together on the Pamir Plateau and form the Pamir Knot. This plateau is also called the 'Roof of the world' because it is the highest plateau in the world.

The Zagros mountains are a long mountain range in Iran, Northern Iraq and South-Eastern Turkey. The Zagros mountains extends in Iran along the Arabian Sea.

5 Arrange the given mountains in a correct sequence from North to South using the codes given below. *(Chap 6, Class-VIII, Old NCERT)*

1. Kunlun
2. Yablonovy
3. Tian Shan
4. Altai

Codes

(a) 1-2-4-3 (b) 2-1-3-4
(c) 1-4-3-2 (d) 2-4-3-1

Ans. (d)

Exp. The correct sequence of mountains from North to South is 2-4-3-1 i.e., Yablonovy mountains, Altai mountains, Tian Shan mountains and Kunlun mountains.

The Yablonovy mountains is a mountain range in Siberia.

The Altai mountains are a mountain range in Central and East Asia, where Russia, China, Mongolia, and Kazakhstan converge.

Tian Shan is a great mountain system of Central Asia. The Tian Shan extend 2,500 km East to West across Central Asia.

The Kunlun mountains is one of the longest mountain chains in Asia, extending for more than 3,000 km. In the broadest sense, the chain forms the northern edge of the Tibetan Plateau in the South of the Tarim Basin.

6 The Pontic and Taurus mountains in West Asia encloses, which of the following plateau within it? *(Chap 6, Class-VIII, Old NCERT)*

(a) Tibet plateau (b) Pamir plateau
(c) Arabian plateau (d) Anatolian plateau

Ans. (d)

Exp The Pontic and Taurus mountains in West Asia encloses within Anatolian plateau. The Anatolian plateau is a plateau that occupies most of Turkey's surface area. The elevation of the plateau ranges from 600 to 1,200 metres. The Anatolian plateau, bounded by the Pontic mountains in the North and the Taurus mountains in the South, is an ancient rock-formed plateau.

7 **Consider the following statements with reference to physical features in Asia.** *(Chap 6, Class-VIII, Old NCERT)*

1. Kunlun mountain range forms the Northern boundary of Tibetan highlands.
2. Altai range is located on the Southern border of Gobi desert.

Which of the statements given above is/are correct?

(a) Only 1
(b) Only 2
(c) Both 1 and 2
(d) Neither 1 nor 2

Ans. (a)

Exp. Statement (1) is correct with reference to physical features in Asia as Kunlun mountain range forms the Northern boundary of Tibetan highlands. The Kunlun mountains is one of the longest mountain chains in Asia, extending for more than 3,000 km.

Statement (2) is incorrect because the Altai mountains are a mountain range in Central and East Asia, it covers Russia, China, Mongolia and Kazakhstan.

8 **Consider the following statements with reference to the river system in Asia.** *(Chap 6, Class-VIII, Old NCERT)*

1. The rivers such as Tigris, Euphrates, Mekong are older than the highlands on, which they flow.
2. These rivers form deep gorges in the mountain ranges through, which they pass
3. These rivers are trans-continental rivers flowing through both Asia and Europe.

Which of the statements given above is/are correct?

(a) 2 and 3 (b) 1 and 2
(c) 1 and 3 (d) All of these

Ans. (b)

Exp. Statements (1) and (2) are correct with reference to the river system in Asia. The rivers such as Tigris, Euphrates, Indus, Irrawaddy and Mekong are older than the highlands on, which they flow.

Tigris-Euphrates river system, great river system of South-Western Asia. It comprises the Tigris and Euphrates rivers, which follow roughly parallel courses through the heart of the Middle East. The Mekong River is a trans-boundary river in East Asia and South-East Asia. These rivers form deep gorges in the mountain ranges through, which they pass.

Statement (3) is incorrect because rivers like Tigris, Euphrates and Indus, Irrawaddy and Mekong flow only in the Asia and thus, they not trans-continental.

9 **Consider the following statements about the climate of Asia.** *(Chap 6, Class-VIII, Old NCERT)*

1. Most of the rainfall in Asia is received in the summer season.
2. There is heavy rainfall in winters in the interior regions of Asia.
3. Mountain barriers play an important role in influencing the climate pattern in Asia.

How many of the statements given above is/are correct?

(a) Only one
(b) Only two
(c) All three
(d) None of the above

Ans. (b)

Exp. Only two statements i.e., (1) and (3) are correct about the climate of Asia. In summer, most parts of Asia receive rainfall due to monsoon winds. The climate of Asia is influenced by many factors. Factors such as the sheer size of Asia, wide latitudinal extension, large mountain barriers, etc. affect the climate in Asia.

Statement (2) is incorrect because, due to the low temperature in the winter season, high air pressure is formed in the interior region of Asia. That is why, there is no rain in the interior region of Asia during the winter season.

10 **Consider the following statements with reference to the various types of natural vegetation found in Asia.** *(Chap 6, Class-VIII, Old NCERT)*

1. Northern coast of Asia is marked by Tundra Vegetation.
2. Pine, fir and spruce are found in Taiga region of Asia.
3. Temperate grasslands known as steppes are located on the coastal regions of Asia.
4. Desert vegetation is found mostly in Central Asia.

Which of the statements given above is/are correct?

(a) 1, 2 and 3 (b) 2, 3 and 4
(c) 1, 2 and 4 (d) 1, 3 and 4

Ans. (c)

Exp. Statements (1), (2) and (4) are correct with reference to the various types of natural vegetation found in Asia.

Tundra vegetation is found on the Northern coast in Asia. Due to the lack of temperature in the Northern region of Asia, this region remains below zero degrees for most of the time.

To the South of the tundra is a wide belt of coniferous forests called Taiga. Soft wood trees like pine, fir and spruce are found in this region. Deserts are found over vast land in South-West and Central Asia.

Statement (3) is incorrect because Temperate grasslands known as steppe are located on the Central regions of Asia.

11 **Match the following lists correctly and choose the correct codes.** *(Chap 7, Class-VIII, Old NCERT)*

List I (Crops)	List II (Mainly grown in)
A. Sugarcane	1. Tajikistan
B. Cotton	2. Malaysia
C. Rubber	3. China
D. Tea	4. India

Codes

	A	B	C	D		A	B	C	D
(a)	1	2	3	4	(b)	2	1	3	4
(c)	3	1	2	4	(d)	3	2	1	4

***Ans.* (c)**

Exp. The correct matching is A-3, B-1, C-2, D-4.

Sugarcane It requires hot and humid climate and fertile soil with good drainage system. In Asia, sugarcane is mainly produced in countries like China, Thailand, etc.

Cotton It is grown in dry climate. In Asia, cotton is mainly produced in Tajikistan, Turkmenistan, and Pakistan, etc.

Rubber It is an important commercial crop of Asia. Rubber is mainly grown in Malaysia and Sri Lanka, etc.

Tea It is mainly grown in Asia. The Tea producing countries are India, Kenya and Sri Lanka, etc.

12 **Consider the following statements about tropical rainforests.** *(Chap 7, Class-VIII, Old NCERT)*

1. Tropical rainforests are mainly located between the latitudes of 23.5° N and 23.5°S, the tropics.
2. Tropical rainforests in Asia are mainly found in the region of Malaysia and Indonesia.

Which of the statements given above is/are correct?

(a) Only 1 (b) Only 2
(c) Both 1 and 2 (d) Neither 1 nor 2

***Ans.* (c)**

Exp. Both the statements (1) and (2) are correct. Tropical rainforests are mainly located between the latitudes of 23.5°N and 23.5°S, the tropics. Here the temperature is more than 25° Celsius and the annual rainfall is more than 200 cm. Tropical rainforests in Asia are mainly found in the region of Malaysia and Indonesia.

13 **Consider the following pairs of minerals and countries.** *(Chap 7, Class-VIII, Old NCERT)*

1. Tin – Malaysia
2. Mineral oil – Central Asia, South-West Asia
3. Iron ore – Russia, China
4. Coal – Greenland

How many pairs given above is/are matched incorrectly?

(a) Only one (b) Only two
(c) Only three (d) All four

***Ans.* (a)**

Exp. Only one pair i. e., (4) is incorrectly matched because coal is absent in some areas like Greenland and much of Northern Canada.

14 **Match the following lists.** *(Chap 8, Class-VIII, Old NCERT) (IAS Pre 2007)*

List I (City)	List II (River)
A. Bangkok	1. Irrawaddy
B. Phnom-Penh	2. Mekong
C. Hanoi	3. Menam (Chao Phraya)
D. Yangon	4. Red River

Codes

	A	B	C	D		A	B	C	D
(a)	3	2	4	1	(b)	4	1	3	2
(c)	3	1	4	2	(d)	4	2	3	1

***Ans.* (a)**

Exp. The correct matching is A-3, B-2, C-4, D-1.

Bangkok It is located on the Menam (Chao Phraya) river.

Phnom-Penh It is located on the Mekong river.

Hanoi It is located on the Red river.

Yangon It is located on the Irrawaddy river.

15 **Arrange the given mountains ranges in correct sequence from North to South using the codes given below.** *(Chap 8, Class-VIII, Old NCERT)*

1. Sulaiman 2. Kirthar
3. Hindu Kush

Codes

(a) 2-1-3 (b) 3-1-2
(c) 2-3-1 (d) 1-3-2

***Ans.* (b)**

Exp. The correct sequence of mountains ranges from North to South is 3-1-2 i.e., Hindu Kush mountain range, Sulaiman mountain and Kirthar mountain.

Hindu Kush is a great mountain system of Central Asia. It is some 800 km long and as much as 240 km wide.

The Sulaiman mountains are a North-South extension of the Southern Hindu Kush mountain system in Afghanistan and Pakistan.

The Kirthar mountains are a mountain range that marks the boundary between the Pakistan provinces of Baluchistan and Sindh.

16 **Arrange the following mountain ranges from East to West in correct order using the codes given below.** *(Chap 8, Class-VIII, Old NCERT)*

1. Dhaulagiri 2. Makalu
3. Annapurna 4. Gaurishankar

Codes

(a) 1-2-4-3 (b) 2-1-4-3
(c) 2-4-3-1 (d) 1-4-3-2

***Ans.* (c)**

Exp. The correct sequence of mountain ranges from East to West is 2-4-3-1 i.e., Makalu mountain, Gaurishankar mountain, Annapurna mountain and Dhaulagiri mountain.

Makalu Mountain is the fifth highest mountain in the world. It has height of 8485 m. It is situated on the border between Nepal and China, about 19 km South-East of Mount Everest.

Gaurishankar mountain is a mountain in the Nepal Himalayas, the second highest peak of the Rolwaling Himal.

Annapurna mountain is a massif of the Himalayas in North-Central Nepal.

Dhaulagiri mountain is situated in Western Nepal. It has height of 8000 m. It is the seventh highest mountain in the world.

17 Consider the following statements about the Indus river basin. *(Chap 8, Class-VIII, Old NCERT)*

1. The Indus flows through the Potwar plateau located in Iran.
2. The Indus makes a large delta on the coast before draining into the sea.
3. Indus river is a seasonal river, which is useful for agriculture in the summer season in the drier regions of Asia.

How many of the statements given above is/are correct?

(a) Only one (b) Only two
(c) All three (d) None of these

Ans. (a)

Exp. Only one statement i.e., (2) is correct with reference to the Indus river basin. The Indus river forms a fertile delta at its mouth before joining the Arabian Sea.

Indus river originates from Tibet and flows from North to South. The Indus river flows through the Thar desert in its lower course.

Statements (1) and (3) are incorrect because the Indus river flows through the Potwar plateau located in Pakistan. Indus river is an evergreen river, which is useful for agriculture in summer or winter season in the drier regions of Pakistan.

18 Match the following lists correctly and choose the correct codes. *(Chap 7, Class-VIII, Old NCERT)*

List I (Minerals)	List II (Found in)
A. Coal	1. Yenangyaung (Myanmar)
B. Natural gas	2. Shengli, Dagang (China)
C. Mineral oil	3. Potwar (Pakistan)

Codes

	A	B	C		A	B	C
(a)	1	2	3	(b)	2	1	3
(c)	3	1	2	(d)	3	2	1

Ans. (c)

Exp. The correct matching is A-3, B-1, C-2.

Coal It is found in Potwar plateau. The Potwar plateau is a plateau in North-Eastern Pakistan, which forms the Northern part of Punjab.

Natural gas It is found in Yenangyaung of Myanmar. Yenangyaung is a region in the Magway region of Central Myanmar, located on the Irrawaddy river.

Mineral oil It is found in Shengli, Dagang region of China. The Shengli and Dagang regions are famous and largest oil field in the China.

19 Consider the following statements about the mineral resources in Bhutan. *(Chap 8, Class-VIII, Old NCERT)*

1. Bhutan's main mineral export is calcium carbide.
2. The country's mining activities primarily produce limestone, dolomite, gypsum, coal, marble, quartzite, and talc.
3. The Chunailkhola spur in Bhutan is famous for dolomite.

How many of the statements given above is/are correct?

(a) Only one (b) Only two
(c) All three (d) None of these

Ans. (c)

Exp. All three statements i.e., (1), (2) and (3) are correct with respect to mineral resources of Bhutan.

Bhutan's main minerals export is calcium carbide.

Bhutan is endowed with abundant deposits of limestone minerals.

The most lucarative mineral mine is dolomite mine in Chunailkhola spur.

20 Which of the following pairs of rivers and their characteristics is/are correctly matched? *(Chap 8, Class-VIII, Old NCERT) (IAS Pre 2020)*

1. Irrawaddy river – Flows from South to North
2. Chindwin river – Flows through the plains of Southern Myanmar
3. Salween river – Forms the border between Myanmar and Laos
4. Sittang river – Joins the Gulf of Martaban

Codes

(a) Pair 1 (b) Pair 2
(c) Pair 3 (d) Pair 4

Ans. (d)

Exp. Pair (4) is correctly matched as the Sittang river flows through Central Myanmar, joining the Gulf of Martaban. It has historical importance, especially during World War II.

Pairs (1), (2) and (3) are not correctly matched because Irrawaddy river is the longest river in Myanmar, flowing from North to South. It is a crucial waterway for transportation and plays a significant role in Myanmar's agriculture.

Chindwin river is one of the major tributaries of the Irrawaddy river. It flows through the mountainous regions of Northern Myanmar.
Salween river is one of the longest free-flowing rivers in the world. It forms the border between Myanmar and Thailand and is significant for its biodiversity.

21 Consider the following statements. *(Chap 9, Class-VIII, Old NCERT)*

1. Shan plateau is mainly located in East of Myanmar.
2. It is crossed by deep trench of the Salween river in the East.

Which of the statements given above is/are correct?
(a) Only 1 (b) Only 2
(c) Both 1 and 2 (d) Neither 1 nor 2
Ans. (c)

Exp. Both the statements (1) and (2) are correct.
Shan plateau is mainly located in East side of Myanmar. The plateau is crossed by the deep trench of the Salween river in the East and is bordered by the upper course of the Irrawaddy river to the West.

22 Which of the following is the longest sand beach in the world? *(Chap 9, Class-VIII, Old NCERT)*
(a) Ninety Mile Beach (b) South Padre Island
(c) Cox's Bazar Beach (d) Virginia Beach
Ans. (c)

Exp. Cox's Bazar beach is the longest sand beach in the world located on the Eastern coast of Bangladesh. It is also the longest natural sea beach in the world. It is about 120 km long.

23 Which of the following rivers of Bangladesh forms the Padma river after merging with the Ganga? *(Chap 9, Class-VIII, Old NCERT)*
(a) Tista (b) Jamuna (c) Sibsa (d) Meghna
Ans. (b)

Exp. Among the given options, Jamuna river forms the Padma river after merging with the Ganga. Brahmaputra river is known as Jamuna in Bangladesh. In Bangladesh, after the Jamuna river joins the Ganges, its combined stream is called Padma river. Jamuna river is one of the three main rivers of Bangladesh.

24 Consider the following statements about the geography of South Asia. *(Chap 9, Class-VIII, Old NCERT)*

1. Sri Lanka is located in the South-Western direction from the Indian mainland.
2. Gulf of Mannar and Palk Strait separates the Southern tip of India from Sri Lanka.
3. Colombo is a strategic airport and the largest city in Sri Lanka.

How many of the statements given above is/are correct?
(a) Only one (b) Only two (c) All three (d) None
Ans. (c)

Exp. All the three statements i.e., (1), (2) and (3) are correct.
Sri Lanka is an island country, which is a large island and has many small islands. It is located in South-Western direction from the Indian mainland. Gulf of Mannar and Palk Strait separate the Southern tip of India from Sri Lanka. Colombo is the largest city of Sri Lanka. There is also an international airport in Colombo. Colombo airport is also a strategically important airport.

25 Which of the following islands do not belong to Indonesia? *(Chap 10, Class-VIII, Old NCERT)*
(a) Bali (b) Sumatra
(c) Cocos (d) Borneo
Ans. (c)

Exp. Cocos island do not belongs to Indonesia. The Cocos islands are a remote territory of Australia in the Indian ocean.
It is a coral atolls comprising 27 tiny islands with white sand beaches, palm trees and lagoon.
Some of the islands in Indonesia are Bali, Borneo, Sumatra, New Guinea, etc.

26 The island of Sumatra is separated from Malaysia by which of the following strait? *(Chap 10, Class-VIII, Old NCERT)*
(a) Malaya Strait (b) Strait of Panama
(c) Malacca Strait (d) Strait of Kerch
Ans. (c)

Exp. The island of Sumatra is separated from Malaysia by Malacca Strait. The Strait of Malacca is a narrow stretch of water between the Malay Peninsula and the Indonesian island of Sumatra.
The island of Sumatra is the main shipping channel between the Indian ocean and the Pacific ocean. It is also one of the most important shipping lanes in the world.

27 The islands of Celebes and Borneo are separated by which of the following straits? *(Chap 10, Class-VIII, Old NCERT)*
(a) Makassar Strait (b) Malacca Strait
(c) Bosporus Strait (d) Gibraltar Strait
Ans. (a)

Exp. The islands of Celebes and Borneo are separated by Makassar Strait. Makassar Strait is a strait between the islands of Borneo and Sulawesi in Indonesia and it is situated within a complex tectonic region at the edge of the Eurasian plate. To the North, it joins the Celebes sea, while to the South it meets the Java sea.

28 Match the following lists correctly and choose the correct codes. *(Chap 10, Class-VIII, Old NCERT)*

List I (City)	List II (Island)
A. Palembang	1. Java
B. Jakarta	2. Sumatra
C. Palu	3. Sulawesi

Codes

	A	B	C
(a)	1	2	3
(b)	2	1	3
(c)	3	1	2
(d)	3	2	1

Ans. (b)

Exp. The correct matching is A-2, B-1, C-3.

Palembang It is a capital of Indonesian an province South Sumatra. It is a port city on the Musi river. The city covers land on both the banks of Musi river on the Eastern lowland of Southern Sumatra.

Jakarta It is the capital of Indonesia. It lies on the North-West coast of Java (the world's most populous island).

Palu It is located on the Indonesian island of Sulawesi, at the mouth of the Palu river. It is the capital of the province of Central Sulawesi, situated on a long, narrow bay.

29 Arrange the following islands of Indonesia from West to East using the codes given below. *(Chap 10, Class-VIII, Old NCERT)*

1. Sumatra
2. Bali
3. Java
4. Lombok

Codes

(a) 2-3-4-1 (b) 1-2-4-3
(c) 1-3-2-4 (d) 2-4-1-3

Ans. (c)

Exp. The correct sequence of island of Indonesia from West to East is 1-3-2-4 i.e., is Sumatra, Java, Bali and Lombok island.

Sumatra is a large Indonesian island lies in West of Java and South of the Malay Peninsula, is known for its rugged tropical terrain, wildlife and smoldering volcanoes.

Java island is lying between Sumatra and Bali; it is a volcano-dotted island that's is the geographic and economic center of Indonesia.

Bali island is a province of Indonesia and the Westernmost of the Lesser Sunda Islands. It is part of the Coral Triangle, the area with the highest biodiversity of marine species.

Lombok is an Indonesian island lies in East of Bali and West of Sumbawa, part of the Lesser Sunda Islands chain. It is known for beaches and surfing spots, particularly at Kuta and Banko Banko.

30 Which of the following seas separates the island of Borneo from Philippines? *(Chap 10, Class-VIII, Old NCERT)*

(a) Banda Sea (b) Celebes Sea
(c) Java Sea (d) South China Sea

Ans. (b)

Exp. Celebes Sea separates the island of Borneo from Philippines. The Celebes Sea of Western Pacific Ocean is borderd on the North by Sulu Archipelago and Sulu Sea and Mindanao Island of Philippines and on the West by Northern Kalimantan in Indonesia.

31 Loess Plateau Tarim Basin and Sichuan Basin are located in, which of the following countries? *(Chap 11, Class-VIII, Old NCERT)*

(a) Japan (b) China
(c) Indonesia (d) India

Ans. (b)

Exp. Loess Plateau, Tarim Basin and Sichuan Basin are located in China. Loess Plateau is a highland area in North-Central China. The Tarim Basin is an endorheic basin in North-West China and it is one of the largest basins in North-West China. The Sichuan Basin is a lowland region in South-Western China. It is surrounded by mountains on all sides and is drained by the upper Yangtze river and its tributaries.

32 Consider the following statements about cold deserts in Asia. *(Chap 11, Class-VIII, Old NCERT)*

1. The Ladakh region in India is part of a cold desert in Asia.
2. The Gobi desert, located in Northern China and Southern Mongolia, is a cold desert.
3. The Taklamakan desert, situated in the Uygur autonomous region of Xinjiang, China is a cold desert.
4. The Kyzylkum desert, primarily in Uzbekistan, is a cold desert in Central Asia.

How many of the statements given above is/are correct?

(a) Only one (b) Only two (c) Only three (d) All four

Ans. (d)

Exp. All four statements i.e. (1), (2), (3) and (4) are correct.

The Ladakh region in India is a part of a cold desert in Asia.

The Gobi Desert, located in Northern China and Southern Mongolia, is a cold desert.

The Taklamakan Desert, situated in the Uygur Autonomous Region of Xinjiang, China, is a cold desert.

The Kyzylkum Desert, primarily in Uzbekistan, is a cold desert in Central Asia.

Cold deserts are located at higher latitudes than deserts situated in tropical and subtropical climates, and thus they experience colder temperatures, especially in the winter. They are found in Central Asia, Western North America, Southeastern South America, Antarctica, and the Arctic.

33 Which of the following statements are correct regarding Loess Plateau? *(Chap 11, Class-VIII, Old NCERT)*

1. Loess plateau is a highland area in North-Central China.
2. Loess plateau is made up of five sediments.

Select the correct answer using the code given below.

(a) Only 1 (b) Only 2
(c) Both 1 and 2 (d) Neither 1 nor 2

Ans. (c)

Exp. Both the statements (1) and (2) are correct regarding Loess plateau.

It is a highland area in North-Central China. The Loess plateau is made up five sediments. These sediments have been deposited in this region through winds. This Loess soil has been brought here continuously by the winds coming from the inner desert part in winter.

34 The Xi Jiang, Huang He and Chang Jiang rivers drain in, which of the following water bodies?

(Chap 11, Class-VIII, Old NCERT)

(a) Yellow Sea (b) Pacific Ocean
(c) Indian Ocean (d) North Sea

Ans. (b)

Exp. The Xi Jiang, Huang He and Chang Jiang rivers drain in Pacific ocean. The Xi Jiang, Huang He and Chang Jiang rivers flow Eastwards through China to join the Pacific ocean. Xi Jiang's valley is the largest valley.

35 Arrange the following islands of Japan according to their size in increasing order by using the codes given below.

(Chap 11, Class-VIII, Old NCERT) (APSC Pre 2013)

1. Shikoku 2. Hokkaido
3. Kyushu 4. Honshu

Codes

(a) 1-2-3-4 (b) 4-3-2-1 (c) 1-4-3-2 (d) 1-3-2-4

Ans. (d)

Exp. The correct sequence of increasing order of Japan's islands according to their size is Shikoku, Kyushu, Hokkaido and Honshu.

Japan is located in the Pacific Ocean to the East of the mainland of Asia. It is a country of about 3900 islands. Of these, there are only four main islands.

Shikoku is the smallest island among them.

Kyushu island size is smaller than Hokkaidu.

Hokkaido Island size is smaller than Honshu. Honshu is the largest island in size.

36 Consider the following statements about the South-East Monsoon in Asia. *(Chap 4, Class-IX, NCERT)*

1. The South-East Monsoon is the prevailing wind system during the summer in South Asia, bringing moist air from the Indian Ocean.
2. The South-East Monsoon is characterised by dry conditions and a lack of rainfall in the Indian subcontinent.
3. The South-East Monsoon plays a crucial role in the agriculture of countries like India, as it brings the majority of the annual rainfall.

How many of the statements given above is/are correct?

(a) Only one (b) Only two
(c) All three (d) None of these

Ans. (b)

Exp. Only two statements i.e., (1) and (3) are correct. The South-East Monsoon is indeed the prevailing wind system during the summer in South Asia, bringing moist air from the Indian Ocean. The South-East Monsoon does play a crucial role in the agriculture of countries like India, as it brings the majority of the annual rainfall.

Statement (2) is incorrect. South-East Monsoon is not characterised by dry conditions and a lack of rainfall in the Indian subcontinent. In fact, the monsoon season brings substantial rainfall to the region.

37 Arrange the following cities of Japan from North to South using the codes given below.

(Chap 11, Class-VIII, Old NCERT)

1. Yokohama 2. Nagoya
3. Hiroshima 4. Nagasaki

Codes

(a) 1-2-4-3 (b) 1-2-3-4 (c) 1-4-3-2 (d) 2-1-4-3

Ans. (b)

Exp. The correct sequence of cities of Japan from North to South is 1-2-3-4 i.e., Yokohama, Nagoya, Hiroshima and Nagasaki.

Yokohama city also known as 'Port City' is located on the island of Honshu. It is located in the South of Tokyo.

Nagoya city is also located on the island of Honshu. It is the largest city in the Chubu region, the fourth most populous city and third most populous urban area in Japan.

Hiroshima city is also located on the island of Honshu. It is located in the South of Honshu Island.

Nagasaki is a Japanese city on the North-West coast of the island of Kyushu. It is set on a large natural harbour.

Africa

38 Consider the following statements about Africa.

(Chap 2, Class-VI, Old NCERT)

1. Africa constitutes 20% of the land area of Earth.
2. Both tropical and temperate climates are found in Africa.
3. Africa has the second-largest population in the world.

How many of the statements given above is/are correct?

(a) Only one (b) Only two
(c) All three (d) None of these

Ans. (c)

Exp. All three statements i.e., (1), (2) and (3) are correct about Africa. It is the largest continent after Asia. About 20% of the entire land area of the Earth is in Africa.

Africa is a continent of plateaus. Africa is the warmest of all the continents. It is located in the tropics and temperate zone. Here tropical and temperate climate is found. The world's second largest population is found in Africa.

39 Which of the following water bodies separates African landmass from Asia? *(Chap 6, Class-VI, Old NCERT)*

(a) Caribbean Sea (b) Red Sea
(c) Caspian Sea (d) Sea of Azov

Ans. (b)

Exp. Red Sea separates African landmass from Asia. The Red Sea is a sea water inlet of the Indian Ocean, lying between Africa and Asia continent. Its connection to the ocean is in the South, through the Bab el Mandeb strait and the Gulf of Aden.

40 Which of the following strait separates the landmass of Africa and Europe in the North-West? *(Chap 6, Class-VI, Old NCERT)*

(a) Strait of Kerch
(b) Strait of Panama
(c) Strait of Gibraltar
(d) Strait of Bab-el-mandeb

Ans. (c)

Exp. Strait of Gibraltar separates the landmass of Africa and Europe in the North-West. Straits of Gibraltar are a narrow strait that connects the Atlantic Ocean to the Mediterranean Sea and separates the Iberian Peninsula in Europe from Morocco in Africa.

41 Which of the following countries is not located in the continent of Africa? *(Chap 6, Class-VI, Old NCERT) (UPPSC Pre 2017)*

(a) Gabon (b) Guinea
(c) Guinea Bissau (d) Guyana

Ans. (d)

Exp. Among the given options, Guyana is not located in the continent of Africa. It is located in South America.

Gabon is a country located on the West coast of Central Africa. Guinea and Guinea Bissau are also located in Africa.

42 The Great Rift Valley of Africa is found in, which of the following regions? *(Chap 6, Class-VI, Old NCERT)*

(a) North-West Africa (b) West Africa
(c) South-West Africa (d) East Africa

Ans. (d)

Exp. The Great Rift Valley of Africa found in East Africa. This valley is a series of contiguous geographic trenches, approximately 7,000 kilometers in total length that runs from the Beqaa Valley in Lebanon, which is in Asia to Mozambique in South-East Africa.

43 Consider the following statements about the river Nile. *(Chap 6, Class-VI, Old NCERT)*

1. Nile is the largest river in the world in terms of volume.
2. Nile drains into the Red Sea.
3. The source of river Nile is Lake Victoria in Africa.

How many of the statements given above is/are correct?

(a) Only one (b) Only two
(c) Only three (d) None of these

Ans. (a)

Exp. Only one statement i.e., (3) is correct about river Nile. The Nile river originates from Lake Victoria. Lake Victoria is the largest lake in Africa. Nile is the longest river in the world.

Statements (1) and (2) are incorrect because Amazon river is the largest river in the world in terms of volume.

The Nile river flows from South to North through Eastern Africa. It begins in the rivers that flow into Lake Victoria (located in modern-day , Tanzania, and Kenya), and empties into the Mediterranean Sea more than 6,600 kilometers (4,100 miles) to the North, making it one of the longest river in the world.

44 Consider the following pairs. *(Chap 6, Class-VI, Old NCERT)*

Physical Feature in Africa	Name
1. Highest Mountain peak	– Mt. Kilimanjaro
2. Largest River of Africa	– Congo or Zaire
3. Largest Lake of Africa	– Lake Victoria

How many of the pairs given above is/are matched correctly?

(a) Only one (b) Only two
(c) All three (d) None of these

Ans. (c)

Exp. All three pairs i.e., (1), (2) and (3) are matched correctly.

Mount Kilimanjaro is a dormant volcano in Tanzania. Mount Kilimanjaro is the highest mountain peak in Africa. Its height is 5895 metres above sea level. It is covered with snow throughout the year.

The Congo or Zaire river flows into Central Africa, this river is known as the Congo in its last part. This river is the largest river of Africa. This river flows towards the West and joins the Atlantic Ocean.

Lake Victoria is the largest lake in Africa. The Nile river originates from Lake Victoria. Victoria lake is situated in East Africa.

45 The Victoria falls are located on, which of the following rivers of Africa? *(Chap 6, Class-VI, Old NCERT)*

(a) Congo river
(b) Nile river
(c) Zambezi river
(d) Orange river

Ans. (c)

Exp. Victoria falls is a waterfall on the Zambezi river in southern Africa. It is located on the border between Zambia and Zimbabwe and is one of the world's largest waterfalls.

46 Consider the following statements with reference to major latitudes and physical features intersected by them. *(Chap 6, Class-VI, Old NCERT)*

1. Kalahari desert is intersected by Tropic of Cancer in Africa.
2. The Limpopo river is intersected by the Equator in Africa.

Which of the statements given above is/are incorrect?

(a) Only 1 (b) Only 2
(c) Both 1 and 2 (d) Neither 1 nor 2

***Ans.* (c)**

Exp. Both the statements (1) and (2) are incorrect with reference to major latitudes and physical features intersected by them because, Kalahari desert is intersected by Tropic of Capricorn in Africa. The Kalahari desert is a large semi-arid sandy savannah in southern Africa extending for covering much of Botswana, and parts of Namibia and South Africa.

The Limpopo river is intersected by the Tropic of Capricorn in Africa. The Limpopo river rises in South Africa and flows Eastwards through Mozambique to the Indian Ocean. The Limpopo river cuts through the Tropic of Capricorn twice.

47 African mainland and the island of Madagascar are separated by, which of the following water bodies? *(Chap 6, Class-VI, Old NCERT)*

(a) Bering Strait (b) English Channel
(c) Mozambique Channel (d) Gulf of Guinea

***Ans.* (c)**

Exp. African mainland and the island of Madagascar are separated by Mozambique Channel. The Mozambique Channel is an arm of the Indian Ocean located between the South-East African countries of Madagascar and Mozambique. The channel is about 1,600 km long and 419 km across at its narrowest point.

48 The Aswan dam, located on river Nile in Africa, is located in, which of the following country? *(Chap 6, Class-VI, Old NCERT)*

(a) Democratic Republic of Congo
(b) South Africa
(c) Egypt
(d) Libya

***Ans.* (c)**

Exp. The Aswan dam, located on river Nile in Africa, is located in Egypt. It is world's largest embankment. The Egyptian economy benefits heavily from the Aswan High Dam. Due to this, the floods due to the Nile river have been controlled.

49 Which of the given minerals is/are mainly mined in Africa? *(Chap 6, Class-VI, Old NCERT)*

1. Gold 2. Platinum 3. Diamond 4. Talcum

Codes

(a) 1 and 3 (b) 2 and 4 (c) 1, 2 and 3 (d) All of these

***Ans.* (c)**

Exp. Africa is the leader in the production of gold, diamond and platinum. Africa is the largest producer of platinum in the world by a significant margin.

Africa accounts for more than 95% of the world's diamond production. More than half of the world's gold comes from Africa.

50 Arrange the given countries in Africa from West to East in a correct sequence using the codes given below. *(Chap 6, Class-VI, Old NCERT)*

1. Ghana 2. Chad
3. Sudan 4. Nigeria

Codes

(a) 1-2-4-3 (b) 1-4-2-3
(c) 2-1-4-3 (d) 2-4-1-3

***Ans.* (b)**

Exp. The correct sequence of African countries from West to East is 1-4-2-3 i.e., Ghana, Nigeria, Chad and Sudan.

Ghana is located in the West of Africa, North of the Gulf of Guinea. Its capital is Accra.

Nigeria is located in the West of Africa. It is bordered by the Atlantic Ocean. Its capital is Abuja.

Chad is a landlocked country is located in the middle of Africa. Its border is with the countries of Niger, Libya, Sudan, Central African Republic, Nigeria and Cameroon. Its capital is N'Djamena.

The country of Sudan is located in the North-East of Africa. Its border is with the Red Sea. The Nile river flows through Sudan. Its capital is Khartoum.

51 The Cape of Good Hope lies on the southern tip of which of the following country? *(Chap 6, Class-VI, Old NCERT)*

(a) Angola (b) Nigeria
(c) Namibia (d) South Africa

***Ans.* (d)**

Exp. The Cape of Good Hope is lies on the Southern tip of South Africa. The Cape of Good Hope is a rocky headland on the Atlantic coast of the Cape Peninsula in South Africa.

52 Which one of the following is a part of the Congo Basin? *(Chap 8, Class-VII, New NCERT) (IAS Pre 2023)*

(a) Cameroon (b) Nigeria
(c) South Sudan (d) Uganda

***Ans.* (a)**

Exp. Cameroon is a part of the Congo Basin.

The Congo Basin is a vast region in Central Africa, encompassing multiple countries. It is primarily characterised by the Congo Rainforest, the second-largest rainforest in the world. The Congo Basin spans across six countries-Cameroon, Central African republic, Democratic Republic of the Congo, Republic of the Congo, Equatorial Guinea and Gabon.

53 **Consider the following statements about cloves.**

(Chap 6, Class-VI, Old NCERT)

1. Zanzibar islands on the coast of Africa is one of the largest producers and exporters of clove in the world.
2. Zanzibar produces almost 60% of the world's clove production.

Which of the statements given above is/are not correct?

(a) Only 1 (b) Only 2
(c) Both 1 and 2 (d) Neither 1 nor 2

Ans. (b)

Exp. Statement (2) is not correct about cloves because about 90% of the world's clove production comes from the island of Zanzibar.

The tree of clove grows up to a height of about 12 metres. Due to the tropical climate found in the island of Zanzibar, clove production is high here.

54 **About three-fourths of world's cobalt, a metal required for the manufacture of batteries for electric motor vehicles, is produced by**

(Chap 7, Class-VI, New NCERT) (IAS Pre 2023)

(a) Argentina
(b) Botswana
(c) the Democratic Republic of the Congo
(d) Kazakhstan

Ans. (c)

Exp. The Democratic Republic of the Congo (DRC) is the world's largest producer of cobalt, accounting for about three-fourths (75%) of the global production. The country has been the top producer of the metal for some time, and reported output of 130,000 MT in 2022. Cobalt is a crucial component in the manufacture of batteries for electric vehicles, as well as for various electronic devices such as smartphones and laptops.

55 **Arrange the following physical features of Africa correctly from North to South according to the codes given below.** *(Chap 6, Class-VI, Old NCERT)*

1. Libyan desert 2. Zaire basin
3. Ethiopian highlands 4. Kalahari desert

Codes

(a) 1-2-3-4 (b) 3-4-1-2 (c) 4-3-1-2 (d) 1-3-2-4

Ans. (d)

Exp. The correct sequence of physical features of Africa from North to South is 1-3-2-4 i.e., Libyan desert, Ethiopian highlands, Zaire basin and Kalahari desert.

Libyan desert is a geographic region that extends from eastern Libya to the western desert of Egypt and far North-western Sudan. Libyan desert is located in North Africa.

Ethiopian plateau is a highland covering much of Ethiopia and Central Eritrea.

The Zaire river basin is the largest river basin of Africa, covering over 12% of the continent. It is one of the most humid basins of Africa as it is located in Equator region.

Kalahari desert is a large basin like plain of the interior plateau of southern Africa.

56 **Assertion** (A) Egypt is the gift of the Nile.

Reason (R) It is an oasis of the Sahara desert.

Codes *(Chap-11, Class-XII, New NCERT)*

(a) Both A and R are true and R is the correct explanation of A.
(b) Both A and R are true, but R is not the correct explanation of A.
(c) A is true, but R is false.
(d) A is false, but R is true.

Ans. (a)

Exp. Both Assertion (A) and Reason (R) are true and Reason (R) is the correct explanation of Assertion (A).

Most of the population of the Egypt benefitted from fertile land and water sources of the Nile river.

River Nile is the lifeline of Egypt. Therefore, Egypt is called the gift of the Nile.

The region is seem to be oasis of the Sahara desert because the presence of water and fertile land in Egypt. An Oasis is an small patch of vegetation surrounded by desert.

57 **Match the following ports with their respective countries.** *(Chap 11, Class-XII, New NCERT)*

List I (Ports)	List II (Countries)
A. Port of Mombasa	1. South Africa
B. Port of Suez	2. Nigeria
C. Port of Durban	3. Egypt
D. Port of Lagos	4. Kenya
E. Dar-es-Salaam Port	5. Tanzania

Codes

	A	B	C	D	E
(a)	1	2	3	4	5
(b)	2	3	4	1	5
(c)	4	3	1	2	5
(d)	3	2	1	4	5

Ans. (c)

Exp. The correct matching is A-4, B-3, C-1, D-2, E-5.

Mombasa port is in Kenya, it is the one of the busiest port along the East coast of Africa.

Port Suez is an Egypt port located an Suez canal on Read Sea.

Port Durban is in South Africa.

Port Lagoas is in Nigeria and **Port Dar-es-Salaam port** is located in Tanzania.

58 The Jos plateau of Nigeria is covered with which of the following type of vegetation?

(Chap 8, Class-VI, Old NCERT)

(a) Equatorial rainforests (b) Grasslands
(c) Alpine vegetation (d) Dry scrubland

Ans. (b)

Exp. The Jos plateau of Nigeria is covered with grasslands type of vegetation. Jos plateau is located in the North of Nigeria. Here, the density of the forest area in the South gradually decreases and the land turns into grasslands. Hence, grasslands are found here.

59 Which of the following statements is/are correct?

(Chap 10, Class-VI, Old NCERT)

1. Kainji Dam is a 7.2 km long gravity dam situated on the river Niger.
2. Kainji Dam is used for flood control, power generation and irrigation.
3. The Niger river is the main river flowing in Nigeria.

Codes

(a) Only 1 (b) 1 and 3
(c) 1, 2 and 3 (d) 2 and 3

Ans. (c)

Exp. All the given statements (1), (2) and (3) are correct. Kainji Dam is a 7.2 km long gravity dam situated on the river Niger. Kainji Dam is used for flood control, power generation and irrigation. Nigeria is a rich country in terms of hydropower. The Niger river is the main river here. This river falls into the Gulf of Guinea.

60 Which of the following statements are not correct regarding the Orange river?

(Chap 10, Class-VI, Old NCERT)

1. Orange river originates from the Drakensberg Mountains.
2. Orange river is longest river in North Africa.

Codes

(a) Only 1 (b) Only 2
(c) Both 1 and 2 (d) Neither 1 nor 2

Ans. (b)

Exp. Statement (2) is not correct regarding the Orange river because Orange river is longest river in South Africa and not in North Africa. The Orange river originates from the Drakensberg Mountains. The Orange river flows West and falls into the Atlantic Ocean. The Vaal river is the major tributary of the Orange river.

61 Consider the following pairs of lakes and countries in Africa.

(Chap 4, Class-XI, NCERT)

1. Lake Victoria - Kenya
2. Lake Tanganyika - South Africa
3. Lake Malawi - Malawi
4. Lake Turkana - Ethiopia
5. Lake Kivu - Rwanda

Which of the pairs given above is/are correctly matched?

(a) 1 and 3
(b) 2 and 4
(c) 1, 3 and 5
(d) All of the above

Ans. (c)

Exp. Pairs (1), (3) and (5) are correctly matched. Lake Victoria is in Kenya, Lake Malawi is in Malawi, and Lake Kivu is in Rwanda.

62 Consider the following statements regarding the city of Kimberley in Africa.

(Chap 10, Class-VI, Old NCERT)

1. Kimberley is the most important of mining of diamond in South Africa.
2. The city of Kimberley is surrounded by seven of South Africa's big rivers.

Which of the statements given above is/are incorrect?

(a) Only 1 (b) Only 2
(c) Both 1 and 2 (d) Neither 1 nor 2

Ans. (b)

Exp. Statement (2) is incorrect regarding the city of Kimberley in Africa because this city is surrounded by five of South Africa's big rivers. Kimberley is the most important centre of mining of diamond in South Africa. Kimberley is a prospecting city famous for its quality diamonds, the largest man made excavation in the world. It is the capital city of the Northern Cape.

63 Which of the given pairs is/are correctly matched ?

(Chap 10, Class-VI, Old NCERT)

List I (River)	List II (Drains into)
1. Niger river	Gulf of Guinea
2. Zambezi river	Indian Ocean
3. Congo river	Pacific

Codes

(a) 1 and 2 (b) Only 3 (c) 1 and 3 (d) Only 2

Ans. (a)

Exp. Pairs (1) and (2) are correctly matched as the Niger river originates in the Guinea Highlands and flows Southward into Nigeria and drains into the Gulf of Guinea. Niger river is the prominent river of Nigeria in Western Africa, with a length of 4,200 km. It is the third longest river in Africa.

The Zambezi river is the fourth longest river in Africa and the largest river drains into the Indian Ocean from Africa The Zambezi river originates in the Mwinilunga district in North-West Zambia.

Pair (3) is not correctly matched because Congo river drains into Atlantic Ocean. The Congo river is the world's eighth longest river. It begins at the junction of the Lualaba and Luvua rivers, in the Altai mountains and flows South-West to the Atlantic Ocean.

Australia

64 Which of the given statements is/are not correct about Australia? *(Chap 14, Class-VI, Old NCERT)*

(a) Tropic of Cancer passes through middle of the continent.
(b) The entire landmass of Australia is located to the South of Equator.
(c) It was discovered by James Cook in 1770.
(d) It is located in South-East direction from Asia.

Ans. (a)

Exp. Statement (a) is not correct about Australia because Tropic of Capricorn passes through the middle of the continent. The Australian continent is located completely in South of the Equator.

65 Consider the following statements about Western Plateau of Australia. *(Chap 14, Class-VI, Old NCERT)*

1. The Western Plateau of Australia occupies nearly two-third of the continent.
2. It is rich in minerals such as gold and iron ore.

Which of the statements given above is/are correct?

(a) Only 1 (b) Only 2
(c) Both 1 and 2 (d) Neither 1 nor 2

Ans. (c)

Exp. Both the statements (1) and (2) are correct about the Western Plateau of Australia.

The Western Plateau occupies nearly two-thirds of the Australian continent. It covers approximately 2,700,000 square kilometers, encompassing large parts of Western Australia, South Australia and the Northern Territory. The Western Plateau is rich in minerals. It's known for its deposits of gold, iron ore, diamonds, nickel and other valuable resources. The Pilbara region, especially, is a hotspot for mineral extraction.

66 The rivers flowing through the Central Lowland Basin of Australia forms, which of the following type of drainage in Lake Eyre? *(Chap 14, Class-VI, Old NCERT)*

(a) Trellis drainage (b) Centripetal drainage
(c) Inland drainage (d) None of these

Ans. (c)

Exp. The rivers flowing through Australia's Central Lowland Basin create inland drainage type drainage in Lake Eyre.

The rivers flowing through the Central Lowland Basin of Australia do not reach the sea. Most of these rivers drain into inland lakes and most of the river drains into Lake Eyre.

67 Consider the following statements about Lake Eyre *(Chap 14, Class-VI, Old NCERT)*

1. Lake Eyre is a great salt lake in central South Australia.
2. It lies in the South-Western corner of the Great Artesian Basin.

Which of the statements given above is/are correct?

(a) Only 1 (b) Only 2
(c) Both 1 and 2 (d) Neither 1 nor 2

Ans. (c)

Exp. Both the statements (1) and (2) are correct about the Lake Eyre.

Lake Eyre, also known as Kati Thanda-Lake Eyre, is a salt lake in central South Australia. It's Australia's largest salt lake and is located 647 kilometers North-East of Adelaide.

Lake Eyre is located in the South-Western corner of the Great Artesian Basin. The Lake Eyre basin is the largest drainage division in Australia, covering almost one-sixth of the country.

68 Which of the following statements about physical features of Australia is/are correct? *(Chap 14, Class-VI, Old NCERT)*

1. The Great Dividing Range is the longest mountain chain in Australia.
2. The Great Dividing Range runs parallel to the Southern Coast of Australia.
3. The Great Barrier Reef runs in the North-Eastern direction to Australia.

Select the correct answer by using the codes given below.

(a) 1 and 2 (b) 2 and 3
(c) 1 and 3 (d) All of these

Ans. (c)

Exp. Statements (1) and (3) are correct about physical features of Australia as, the Great Dividing Range is the longest mountain chain in Australia. The Great Dividing Range is located on the East coast of Australia. Kosciuszko is the highest peak of the Great Dividing Range. The altitude of Kosciuszko is 2,234 m above sea level. The Great Barrier Reef runs in the North-Eastern direction to Australia. The length of the Great Barrier Reef is more than 1,900 km. It is the world's largest coral reef in the world.

Statement (2) is incorrect because the Great Dividing Range is located on the East coast of Australia.

69 Jarrah and Karri varieties of trees are commonly grown in Australia for timber. These species belongs to, which of the following tree? *(Chap 15, Class-VI, Old NCERT)*

(a) Teak
(b) Eucalyptus
(c) Pine
(d) Spruce

Ans. (b)

Exp. Jarrah and Karri varieties of trees are commonly grown in Australia for timber. These species belong to Eucalyptus trees.

Eucalyptus is a common tree native to Australia. It is an evergreen tree and is often known as a gum tree.

70 **Consider the following statements.**

(Chap 15, Class-VI, Old NCERT)

1. Australia is renowned for its high-quality wool and superior sheep breeds.
2. Merino sheep is the most influential breed and much prized for its wool.
3. The North Australia region is very suitable for sheep farming.

How many of the statements given above is/are correct?

(a) Only one (b) Only two
(c) Only three (d) None of these

Ans. (b)

Exp. Only two statements i.e., (1) and (2) are correct as Australia is known for its high-quality wool. The Merino is the most popular sheep breed in Australia, known for its soft, fine wool that's in high demand for clothing and textiles. Merino wool is also dense, soft to the touch, and finely crimped. In regions like southern Australia, Tasmania, Victoria and New South Wales, people rear a special breed of sheep named Merino.

Statement (3) is incorrect because Australia's temperate South is more suitable for raising sheep than the tropical North. The Murray-Darling Basin is very suitable for sheep farming in Australia. Queensland and New South Wales are two famous states for sheep farming. Sheep production occurs mainly in the agricultural zone in the South-West of Western Australia.

71 **Consider the following pairs.**

(Chap 15, Class-VI, Old NCERT)

Desert		Country
1. Great Basin	–	Turkmenistan
2. Patagonian	–	Arabian Peninsula
3. Gibson	–	Australia
4. Atacama	–	Chile

How many pairs given above is/are correctly matched?

(a) Only one (b) Only two (c) Only three (d) All four

Ans. (b)

Exp. Only two pairs i.e., (3) and (4) are correctly matched.

The Gibson Desert is located in Western Australia. It's bordered by the Great Sandy Desert to the North, the Great Victoria Desert to the South, the northern territory border to the East, and Lake Disappointment to the West.

The Atacama Desert is located in Chile. The Atacama Desert is bordered by the Andes Mountains to the East and the Pacific Ocean to the West. The Atacama Desert is known as the driest place on Earth, with an annual rainfall of only 0.03 inches.

Pairs (1) and (2) are not correctly matched.

The Great Basin Desert is located in the United States. It's the largest desert in the country, covering most of Nevada and parts of Utah, California, Oregon and Idaho. The Patagonian Desert is located in Argentina and parts of Chile. It's a cold and dry desert that covers about 200,000 square miles.

72 **Which of the following is not a capital city of a country?** *(Chap 15, Class-VI, Old NCERT)*

(a) Canberra (b) Sydney
(c) Welligton (d) Riyadh

Ans. (b)

Sydney is the capital city of the state of New South Wales and the most populous city in Australia. It is not a capital city of a country. The city's nicknames include the Emerald city and the Harbour city.

73 **Match List I with List II.**

(Chap 15, Class-VI, Old NCERT) (RAS/RTS 2016)

List I (Mountain Peak)	List II (Continent)
A. Kosciuszko	1. Europe
B. Mckinley	2. Africa
C. Elbrus	3. Australia
D. Kilimanjaro	4. North America

Codes

	A	B	C	D		A	B	C	D
(a)	3	4	1	2	(b)	2	4	3	1
(c)	4	3	2	1	(d)	3	1	2	4

Ans. (a)

Exp. The correct matching is A-3, B-4, C-1, D-2.

Mount **Kosciuszko** is mainland Australia's tallest mountain at 2228m above sea level. Puneak Jaya in New Guinea, Indonesia which stands at 4884m. It is the tallest mountain in the Australian continent and as well as Oceania.

Mount **McKinley** also known as Denali is the highest mountain peak in North America with 20310 ft (6,190 m) above sea level. It is located in interior of the US State of Alaska.

Mount **Elbrus** is the highest mountain in Europe (Russia). Its height is 5,642m above sea level.

Mount **Kilimanjaro** is located in Tanzania. It is the tallest mountain in the Africa.

North America

74 **Which of the following statements are correct regarding North America?**

(Chap 6, Class-VII, Old NCERT

(a) North America is the third largest continent by area.
(b) North America lies entirely within the Western Hemisphere.
(c) Both a and b
(d) Neither a nor b

Ans. (c)

Exp. Both the statements (a) and (b) are correct regarding North America.
North America is the third largest continent by area, following Asia and Africa and the fourth by population after Asia, Africa and Europe. North America is a continent in the Northern Hemisphere and almost entirely within the Western Hemisphere.

75 Arrange the Great Lakes in chronological order from West to East. *(Chap 6, Class-VII, Old NCERT)*

1. Lake Superior 2. Lake Ontario
3. Lake Erie 4. Lake Huron
5. Lake Michigan

Select the correct answer using the codes given below.

(a) 1, 5, 3, 4, 2 (b) 2, 1, 3, 4, 5
(c) 1, 5, 4, 3, 2 (d) 2, 3, 1, 5, 4

Ans. (c)

Exp. The correct chronological order from West to East is 1-5-4-3-2.
Lake superior is the Western most river than joined by Lake Michigan, then comes lake Huron. Erie and ontaria and this is the order of West to East of Great lakes.

76 The Niagara Falls is located between, which of the following lakes? *(Chap 6, Class-VII, Old NCERT)*

(a) Lake Erie and Lake Ontario
(b) Lake Huron and Lake Michigan
(c) Lake Michigan and Lake Superior
(d) Lake Ontario and Lake Huron

Ans. (a)

Exp. The Niagara Falls is located between Erie lake and Ontario lake. Niagara Falls is a group of three waterfalls at the Southern end of Niagara Gorge, spanning the border between the province of Ontario in Canada and the state of New York in the United States.

77 Which among the following minerals is/are commonly found in the Canadian Shield region? *(Chap 6, Class-VII, Old NCERT)*

1. Iron ore 2. Copper 3. Uranium 4. Cobalt

Select the correct answer by using the codes given below.

(a) 1, 2 and 3 (b) 2, 3 and 4 (c) 1, 3 and 4 (d) 1, 2, 3 and 4

Ans. (d)

Exp. All the given minerals (1), (2), (3) and (4) are commonly found in Canadian Shield region. It is formed from ancient hard rocks. Its height is less than 300 to 400 metres. The Canadian Shield is a storehouse of valuable mineral resources. Here gold, silver, nickel, iron ore, copper, uranium, radium, cobalt, etc are found.

78 Consider the following statements regarding North America's mineral production. *(Chap 7, Class-VII, Old NCERT)*

1. The Canadian Shield contains deposits of nickel, iron, lead, gold, platinum and copper.
2. The Appalachian highlands produce a large amount of anthracite and high-grade bituminous coal.
3. The Gulf Coast and the Atlantic coastal plain produce much of the world's petroleum and natural gas.
4. The Western Cordilleras have vast deposits of lead and zinc.

How many of the statements given above is/are correct?

(a) Only one (b) Only two (c) Only three (d) All four

Ans. (c)

Exp. Only three statements i.e., (1), (2) and (3) are correct regarding North America's mineral production.
The Canadian Shield is one of the world's richest areas for mineral ores, including nickel, gold, silver and copper. It also contains other metals, such as iron, copper, zinc, uranium and niobium. The Appalachian highlands produce a large amount of anthracite and high-grade bituminous coal. They have the largest soft coal field in the world. The Gulf Coast is the primary source of oil and gas for the United States, generating about 97% of all oil and gas production. The Gulf Coast is also home to one-fifth of the country's crude oil production, 45% of its petroleum refining capacity, and 51% of its natural gas processing plant capacity.
Statement (4) is incorrect because Western Cordilleras have vast deposits of copper. This region also possesses mineral oil, natural gas, coal and rock phosphate.

79 Consider the following statements regarding the Appalachian Mountains. *(Chap 6, Class-VII, Old NCERT)*

1. The Appalachian mountain is a young fold mountain.
2. The Hudson river flows through the Appalachian mountain.
3. Mount Mitchell is the highest peak of the Appalachian mountain range.

How many of the statements given above is/are correct?

(a) Only one (b) Only two
(c) Only three (d) None of these

Ans. (b)

Exp. Only two statements i.e., (2) and (3) are correct regarding the Appalachian Mountain.
The Hudson river flows through the Appalachian mountains. The Hudson river originates in the Adirondack mountains of upstate New York and flows southward through the Hudson Valley to New York Harbour. Mt. Mitchell.
Mount Mitchell's summit is located in the Black Mountain range of the Blue Ridge Mountains in Western North Carolina. It is the highest point East of the Mississippi river.
Statement (1) is incorrect because Appalachian mountain range is an old fold mountain range located in the eastern region of North America. The Appalachians first formed roughly during the Ordovician Period.

80 Which of the following pairs of region in North America and minerals is not matched correctly?

(Chap 7, Class-VII, Old NCERT)

Region		Minerals
(a) Canadian Shield	–	Nickel, Iron
(b) Appalachian	–	Coal
(c) Lake Superior	–	Limestone
(d) Pennsylvania	–	Petroleum

Ans. (c)

Exp. Pair (c) is not matched correctly.
The Lake Superior region in North America is the leading producer of high quality iron ore not limestone. The Lake Superior iron ore deposits were the largest ever discovered in the United States.

81 Consider the following statements.

(Chap 6, Class-VII, Old NCERT)

1. The Himalayan mountains and the Alps are young fold mountains.
2. The Appalachians in North America and the Ural mountains in Russia are old fold mountains.
3. The Rhine Valley and the Vosges mountain in Europe are examples of Block mountains systems.

How many of the statements given above is/are correct?

(a) Only one (b) Only two
(c) All three (d) None of these

Ans. (c)

Exp. All three statements i.e., (1), (2) and (3) are correct.
The Himalayan mountains and the Alps are young fold mountains with rugged relief and high conical peaks. Fold mountains are formed when two or more tectonic plates collide and the debris and boundaries are folded into hills, rocky terrain, and mountain ranges.
The Appalachians and the Ural mountains are both old fold mountains. Old fold mountains are mountains that are over 200 million years old. The Appalachians in North America and the Ural mountains in Russia have rounded features and low elevation.
The Rhine Valley and the Vosges mountains in Europe are examples of block mountains. Block mountains are created when large areas are broken and displaced vertically. The uplifted blocks are termed as horsts and the lowered blocks are called Graben.

82 Which of the following statements is/are correct?

(Chap 6, Class-VII, Old NCERT)

1. Mt McKinley (Denali) is the highest point in North America.
2. The Colorado Plateau is the largest plateau in North America.

Select the correct answer by using the codes given below.

(a) Only 1 (b) Only 2
(c) Both 1 and 2 (d) Neither 1 nor 2

Ans. (c)

Exp. Both the statements (1) and (2) are correct.
Mt McKinley also called Denali is the highest point or peak in North America. It is located near the centre of the Alaska range.
The height of Mt McKinley is about 6,187 metres above sea level. The Colorado Plateau is the largest plateau in North America. It covers nearly 337,000 km^2 of area. It is a huge, structurally unchanged, high elevated and tectonically impenetrable region.

83 Which river is known for sculpturing deep and steel canyons in North America?

(Chap 6, Class-VII, Old NCERT

(a) Columbia river (b) Mississippi river
(c) Colorado river (d) Missouri river

Ans. (c)

Exp. Colorado river is known for sculpturing deep and steel canyons in North America.
Colorado river is a major river of North America, rising in the Rocky mountains of Colorado in USA and flowing West and South for 2,330 kilometres into the Gulf of California in North-Western Mexico.

84 The Mackenzie river of North America drains into which of the following water bodies?

(Chap 6, Class-VII, Old NCERT

(a) Pacific Ocean (b) Atlantic Ocean
(c) Gulf of Mexico (d) Arctic Ocean

Ans. (d)

Exp. The Mackenzie river of North America drains into Arctic Ocean. Mackenzie river is the longest river in Canada, which spills out of Great Slave lake. This river flows through very sparsely populated areas.

85 Match the following rivers with their destination falling water body. *(Unit 5, Class-XI, Old NCERT*

List I (Rivers)	List II (Oceans)
A. River St. Lawrence	1. Gulf of Mexico
B. River Mackenzie	2. Atlantic Ocean
C. Mississippi	3. Pacific Ocean
D. Colorado river	4. Arctic Ocean

Codes

	A	B	C	D		A	B	C	D
(a)	3	4	1	3	(b)	2	4	1	3
(c)	4	3	2	1	(d)	3	1	2	4

Ans. (b)

Exp. The correct matching is A-2, B-4, C-1, D-3.
The **St. Lawrence** river flows into the Atlantic Ocean. The St. Lawrence river is part of the Great Lakes-St. The Mackenzie river flows into the Arctic Ocean through the Beaufort Sea.
The **Mackenzie river** is the largest river in North America that flows northward. The **Mississippi river** flows into the Gulf of Mexico, which is part of the Atlantic Ocean.

The river enters the Gulf about 100 miles South of New Orleans, Louisiana. The Colorado river flows into the Gulf of California, which is part of the Pacific Ocean. The river originates in the rocky mountains of Colorado.

86 Consider the following statements about the Mississippi river. ***(Chap 8, Class-VII, Old NCERT)***

1. It is the second-longest river in North America.
2. The Missouri river is the longest tributary of the Mississippi river.
3. The Mississippi river flows into the Arctic Ocean.

How many of the statements given above is/are correct?

(a) Only one (b) Only two
(c) Only three (d) None of these

Ans. (b)

Exp. Only two statements i.e., (1) and (2) are correct regarding the Mississippi river.

The Mississippi river is the second longest river in North America, flowing 2,350 miles from its source at Lake Itasca through the center of the continental United States to the Gulf of Mexico. The Missouri river is the longest tributary of the Mississippi river. It originates from the rocky mountains of western Montana, USA, and meets with the Mississippi river at St. Louis, USA.

Statement (3) is incorrect. The Mississippi river flows into the Gulf of Mexico, which is connected to the Atlantic Ocean. As the river approaches the ocean, it creates a rich estuary in the state of Louisiana where many types of wildlife thrive.

87 Consider the following statements regarding North American vegetation and animals. ***(Chap 6, Class-VII, Old NCERT)***

1. Taiga, a belt of coniferous forests, stretches from the Atlantic to the Pacific across Canada.
2. Deciduous forests in South-East Canada and North-East United States are characterised by trees like beech, birch, maple and oak.
3. Tropical forests in North America are primarily found in the central region, including Eastern Mexico and West Indies.

How many of the statements given above is/are not correct?

(a) Only one (b) Only two
(c) All three (d) None of these

Ans. (c)

Exp. All three statements i.e., (1), (2) and (3) are correct regarding North American vegetation and animals.

The taiga is a belt of coniferous forests that stretches from the Atlantic to the Pacific across North America and Eurasia. The taiga, also known as the boreal forest or snow forest, is the world's largest land biome.

Deciduous forests in the North-Eastern United States and South-Eastern Canada are characterised by trees like beech, birch, maple and oak.

Tropical forests are found in central America, Eastern Mexico and West Indies. Palm, mahogany and logwood are common trees found in North America.

88 Consider the following statements. ***(Chap 7, Class-VII, Old NCERT)***

1. The white pine tree is used for obtaining Newsprint in North America.
2. Wood for furniture is obtained from oak and willow trees.

Which of the statements given above is/are correct?

(a) Only 1 (b) Only 2
(c) Both 1 and 2 (d) Neither 1 nor 2

Ans. (c)

Exp. Both the statements (1) and (2) are correct as the white pine and spruce tree are used for obtaining Newsprint in North America. This paper is of thick and cheap type. The soft wood found in the taiga forests is used to make furniture. Wood from oak and willow trees is used to make furniture.

89 The Grand Bank, a famous region for fishing, is found near, which of the following islands? ***(Chap 7, Class-VII, Old NCERT)***

(a) Greenland (b) Victoria
(c) Newfoundland (d) Baffin

Ans. (c)

Exp. The Grand Bank, a famous region for fishing, is found near Newfoundland. There is a shallow sea around the North-Eastern coast of North America, in which an abundance of fishes are found. Tuna and salmon fish are caught from here.

90 Cotton and tobacco are found in, which of the following regions in North America? ***(Chap 7, Class-VII, Old NCERT)***

(a) Colorado plateau (b) Mississippi basin
(c) Great basin (d) None of these

Ans. (b)

Exp. Cotton and tobacco are found in Mississippi basin regions in North America. The soil and climate are very suitable for the cultivation of cotton in the Mississippi region.

The summers in this region are warm and rainfall is normal. Clear skies and strong sunlight are ideal for the ripening and picking of the cotton crop.

91 Consider the following statements. ***(Chap 7, Class-VII, Old NCERT)***

1. Mediterranean-type climate is found on the West coast of California.
2. Prairies, found in the interior plains of North America, are known for tall and nutritious grasses.

Which of the statements given above is/are correct?

(a) Only 1 (b) Only 2
(c) Both 1 and 2 (d) Neither 1 nor 2

Ans. (c)

Exp. Both the statements (1) and (2) are correct.

The Mediterranean type of climate is found on the West coast of California. Olive, pine, orange and cork oak trees are found here. Prairies are found in the interior plains of North America and these grasslands are known for their tall and nutritious grasses. Prairies are part of the temperate grasslands, savannas and shrublands biome. They are made up of grasses, herbs, and shrubs, rather than trees.

92 Arrange the following physical features of USA in a correct sequence from West to East using the codes given below. *(Chap 8, Class-VII, Old NCERT)*

1. Sierra Nevada
2. Great Plains
3. Rockies
4. Appalachian

Codes

(a) 2-3-4-1 (b) 1-3-2-4 (c) 1-2-3-4 (d) 4-3-2-1

Ans. (b)

Exp. The correct sequence of physical features of USA from West to East is 1-3-2-4 i.e., Sierra Nevada, Rockies mountains, Great Plains and Appalachian mountains.

The Sierra Nevada is a mountain range in the Western United States, between the central valley of California and the Great basin.

The Rocky mountains stretch more than 4,800 kilometres from British Columbia, in Canada to New Mexico in North America.

The Great plains is a broad expanse of flatland located West of the Mississippi river and East of the Rocky mountains, much of it covered in prairie, steppe and grassland.

The Appalachian mountains are a system of mountains in Eastern to North-Eastern North America. The Appalachian first formed roughly 480 million years ago during the Ordovician Period.

93 The North-Western part of USA receives rainfall by, which of the following wind systems? *(Chap 8, Class-VII, Old NCERT)*

(a) Trade winds (b) Tropical cyclones
(c) Westerly winds (d) None of these

Ans. (c)

Exp. North-Western part of USA receives rainfall because of Westerly winds. It rains here almost all the time. The main reason for this is the mountain ranges, which obstructs the passage of air. Due to Westerly winds, more rainfall occurs in the Western region of the mountain and the amount of rainfall is less in the Eastern part of mountain.

94 Consider the following Assertion (A) and Reason (R) and choose the correct code. *(Chap 8, Class-VII, Old NCERT)*

Assertion (A) Desert vegetation is generally found in Colorado basin in region of North America.

Reason (R) Colorado basin comprises of high temperature and lack of rainfall.

Codes

(a) Both A and R are correct and R is the correct explanation of A.
(b) Both A and R are correct, but R is not the correct explanation of A.
(c) A is true, but R is false.
(d) A is false, but R is true.

Ans. (a)

Exp. Both Assertion (A) and Reason (R) are correct and Reason (R) is the correct explanation of Assertion (A). Desert vegetation is generally found in Colorado basin in region of North America.

Due to the high temperature and lack of rainfall in the Colorado region of North America, desert vegetation is found here. Different types of cactus and different types of thorny shrubs are found in the Colorado basin.

95 Consider the following statements regarding the climate of North America. *(Chap 8, Class-VII, Old NCERT)*

1. North America has a varied climate extending between the tropical zone in the South and frigid zone in the North.
2. Winter temperature is much below the freezing point in the northern and central parts.
3. Temperature increases from South to North.

Which of the statements given above are correct?

(a) 1 and 2 (b) 2 and 3
(c) 1 and 3 (d) 1, 2 and 3

Ans. (a)

Exp. Statements (1) and (2) are correct regarding the climate of North America.

North America is a large continent that extends from the tropical zone in the South to the frigid zone in the North. It has a continental climate, which means it's generally dry with cold winters and hot summers.

Winters are cold over much of the North America. Winter temperature is much below the freezing point in the northern and central parts.

Statement (3) is incorrect. In North America, the average temperature decreases from South to North. This is due to the influence of latitude.

96 Which of the following type of vegetation grown in North America for obtaining furniture? *(Chap 8, Class-VII, Old NCERT)*

(a) Tropical Deciduous Trees
(b) Temperate Hardwood Forests
(c) Alpine Forests
(d) Montane Forests

Ans. (b)

Exp. In North America, furniture is obtained from temperate hardwood forests. North America is ahead of all countries in the production of temperate hardwood. In North America, temperate forests are found in the Northern region.

97 Arrange the following lakes in the correct descending order of their area using the codes given below. *(Chap 8, Class-VII, Old NCERT) (UPPSC Pre 2016)*

1. Great Bear 2. Baikal 3. Victoria 4. Superior

Codes

(a) 4, 3, 2, 1 (b) 3, 2, 1, 4 (c) 4, 2, 1, 3 (d) 3, 1, 4, 2

Ans. (a)

Exp. The correct sequence is 4, 3, 2, 1.

Superior, Victoria, Baikal and Great Bear lakes is correct descending order of their area.

Lake Superior is the largest freshwater lake in the world by surface area and the third largest by volume, located in Central North America. It has a surface area of 31,700 sq miles (82,103 sq km). It drains into Lake Huron via St. Marys river.

Lake Victoria is one of the African Great lakes with a surface area of approximately 59,947 sq km (23,146 sq miles). It is Africa's largest lake by area, the world's largest tropical lake and the world's second largest freshwater lake by surface area after Lake Superior in North America.

Lake Baikal is the world's largest freshwater lake by volume. It is also the world's deepest lake and the world's oldest lake. It is the world's seventh largest lake by surface area with 31,722 sq km (12,248 sq miles). It is included in UNESCO World Heritage Site in 1996.

Great Bear is located in the boreal forest of Canada and eight largest lake in the world. It is largest lake in Canada with surface area of 31,153 sq km.

98 Which of the following statements is/are correct? *(Chap 8, Class-VII, Old NCERT)*

(a) USA has the third largest population in the world.
(b) More than 70% of the people of USA live in Urban areas.
(c) New York is the largest city of USA.
(d) All of the above

Ans. (d)

Exp. All the above statements are correct as USA is the fourth largest country in terms of area after Russia, Canada and China. USA has the third largest population in the world.

The distribution of population in the United States is very uneven. Here about third-fourth population lives in the eastern half of the country. About 70% of the population of the USA lives in cities. New York is the largest city of USA. Its population is more than 10 million.

99 Which one of the following is the correct sequence of the given continents in the decreasing order of their percentage of Earth's land? *(Chap 9, Class-VII, Old NCERT) (UPPSC Pre 2005)*

(a) North America -Africa -South America-Europe
(b) Africa-North America-South America-Europe
(c) North America-Africa-Europe-South America
(d) Africa-North America-Europe-South America

Ans. (b)

Exp. The correct sequence of continents in decreasing order based on the percentage of Earth's land is as follows: Africa-North America-South America-Europe. Africa holds the largest land area with 29,800,000 sq km, followed by North America with 21,510,000 sq km, South America with 17,598,000 sq km and Europe with 9,699,550 sq km.

100 Match the following mineral deposits with their respective regions in North America. *(Chap 9, Class-VII, Old NCERT)*

List I (Regions)	List II (Mineral Deposits)
A. Canadian Shield Region	1. Iron ore, nickel, gold, uranium and copper
B. Appalachians region	2. Copper, lead, zinc, gold, and silver
C. Western Cordilleras	3. Coal

Codes

	A	B	C
(a)	1	2	3
(b)	1	3	2
(c)	3	2	1
(d)	2	3	1

Ans. (b)

Exp. The correct matching is A-1, B-3, C-2.

The mineral deposits in North America are located in three zones: the **Canadian region** North of the Great Lakes, the Appalachians region and the mountain ranges of the West.

Iron ore, nickel, gold, uranium and copper are mined in the Canadian Shield Region, coal in the **Appalachians region**. **Western Cordilleras** have vast deposits of copper, lead, zinc, gold and silver.

101 Which of the following statements is/are correct regarding St. Lawrence river? *(Chap 9, Class-VII, Old NCERT)*

1. St. Lawrence river of Canada drains into the Pacific Ocean.
2. St. Lawrence river starts at the outflow of Lake Ontario.

Codes

(a) Only 1 (b) Only 2
(c) Both 1 and 2 (d) Neither 1 nor 2

Ans. (b)

Exp. Statement (2) is correct regarding St. Lawrence river.

St. Lawrence river starts at the outflow of Lake Ontario and leads into the Atlantic Ocean in the extreme East of Canada. It is important river for seaway.

Statement (1) is incorrect because St. Lawrence river of Canada drains into Atlantic Ocean.

102 **Which of the following type of vegetation covers the largest area of Canada in North America?**
(Chap 9, Class-VII, Old NCERT)

(a) Evergreen forests
(b) Coniferous Taiga forests
(c) Polar tundra
(d) Deciduous forests

Ans. (b)

Exp. Coniferous Taiga type of vegetation covers the largest area of Canada in North America. A wide belt of coniferous forests is found in the South of the Tundra region. This belt is called Taiga forest. This belt covers 40% of the total area of Canada. The wood of Taiga forests is very soft, which is used to make paper.

103 **Consider the following statements about the transport system in North America.**
(Chap 9, Class-VII, Old NCERT)

1. The Panama Canal connects the Atlantic and Pacific Oceans.
2. In North America, highways are known as Freeways or Superways.
3. Mississippi and St. Lawrence are large navigational rivers.

Which of the statements given above are correct?

(a) 1 and 2 (b) 2 and 3
(c) 1 and 3 (d) 1, 2 and 3

Ans. (d)

Exp. All the statements (1), (2) and (3) are correct regarding the transport system in North America.
The Panama Canal connects the Atlantic Ocean with the Pacific Ocean through the narrow Isthmus of Panama. It also divides North America and South America.
In North America, large highways that connect major cities are known as Superways or Freeways. Superhighways are large, fast highways or freeways with multiple lanes.
The Saint Lawrence river and the Mississippi river system are both large rivers that can be used for navigation. The Saint Lawrence river is part of a larger system that begins in Minnesota and stretches for about 2,500 miles.

104 **Which of the following pairs is not correctly matched?** *(Chap 9, Class-VII, Old NCERT)*

(a) Quebec – Industrial area in Canada
(b) Toronto – Largest city of Canada
(c) Montreal – Capital of Canada
(d) Both (a) and (b)

Ans. (c)

Exp. Pair (c) is not correctly matched because Ottawa is the capital of Canada not Montreal.
Pairs (a) and (b) are correctly matched.
Ottawa is situated on the South bank of the Ottawa river, across from Gatineau, Quebec.

South America

105 **Consider the following statements about South America.** *(Chap 11, Class-VI, Old NCERT)*

1. Most of the South American landmass is located South of the Equator.
2. South America is the third largest continent in the world.
3. South America is a part of Latin America.
4. South America and North America are separated by the Panama Canal.

Which of the statements given above is/are not correct?

(a) Only 1 (b) Only 2
(c) Only 3 (d) Only 4

Ans. (b)

Exp. Statement (2) is not correct about South America. South America is the fourth (not third) largest continent in the world after Asia, Africa and North America.

106 **Which of the given statements is/are incorrect?**
(Chap 11, Class-VI, Old NCERT)

1. Bolivia is the only landlocked country in South America.
2. Brazil is the largest country in South America.
3. Cotopaxi is an extinct volcano located in Ecuador.
4. Equator passes through Venezuela in Africa.

Codes

(a) 1 and 2 (b) 2, 4 and 3
(c) 1, 3 and 4 (d) 1 and 4

Ans. (c)

Exp. Statements (1), (3) and (4) are incorrect.
Paraguay and Bolivia are two landlocked countries in South America. Cotopaxi located in Andes mountain range, Ecuador is the tallest active volcano in the world. Equator passes through Venezuela, Colombia and Brazil in South America.

107 **Consider the following statements about the Andes Mountains in South America.**
(Chap 11, Class-VI, Old NCERT)

1. The Andes is the longest mountain range in the world.
2. The Andes run through several South American countries including Peru, Chile and Ecuador.
3. Aconcagua, the highest peak in the Andes, is located in Argentina.

How many of the statements given above is/are correct?

(a) Only one
(b) Only two
(c) All three
(d) None of the above

Ans. (b)

Exp. Only two statements i.e., (2) and (3) are correct. The Andes run through several South American countries, including Peru, Chile and Ecuador. The Andes run along the western edge of South America, gracing seven countries: Venezuela, Colombia, Ecuador, Peru, Bolivia, Chile and Argentina.

Aconcagua, the highest peak in the Andes, is located in Argentina. Aconcagua, reaching a height of 6,961 meters, is the highest point in the Andes and the entire Western Hemisphere.

Statement (1) is incorrect because the Andes is not the longest mountain range in the world. While the Andes are indeed impressive, stretching for over 7,000 kilometers, the Himalayas in Asia hold the title of the longest mountain range globally.

108 Consider the following statements about the Amazon River. *(Chap 11, Class-VI, Old NCERT)*

1. The Amazon river is the longest river in the world.
2. The Amazon river basin is home to the largest rainforest on Earth.
3. The Amazon river flows through Brazil, Colombia and Peru.

How many of the statements given above is/are correct?

(a) Only one (b) Only two
(c) Only three (d) None of these

Ans. (a)

Exp. Only one statement i.e., (2) is correct about the Amazon river.

The Amazon river basin is home to the largest rainforest on Earth. The Amazon rainforest, blanketing much of the Amazon basin, is indeed the largest rainforest on Earth, boasting unparalleled biodiversity and ecological importance.

Statements (1) and (3) are incorrect because the Nile river is the longest river in the world," While the Amazon is incredibly vast, the Nile river in Africa holds the title of the world's longest river by some 400 kilometers.

The Amazon does flow through Brazil, Columbia and Peru. But it also grazes Bolivia, Ecuador, Venezuela, and Guyana.

109 Consider the following statements about the Gran Chaco region in South America. *(Chap 11, Class-VI, Old NCERT)*

1. The Gran Chaco is a vast plain covering parts of Argentina, Paraguay and Bolivia.
2. It is characterised by dry and arid conditions.
3. The Gran Chaco is a major agricultural region in South America.

How many of the statements given above is/are correct?

(a) Only one (b) Only two
(c) All three (d) None of these

Ans. (a)

Exp. Only one statement i.e., (1) is correct.

The Gran Chaco is a vast plain covering parts of Argentina, Paraguay and Bolivia,. The Gran Chaco is indeed a vast lowland plain stretching across these three countries.

Statements (2) and (3) are incorrect. The Gran Chaco can be hot and dry, it's more accurately described as semi-arid, with seasonal variations in rainfall and pockets of humidity. Agriculture does exist in the Gran Chaco, primarily cattle ranching, it's not considered a major agricultural region compared to other areas in South America.

110 Consider the following statements about Amazon river. *(Chap 11, Class-VI, Old NCERT)*

1. Amazon river originates from the Andes mountains and flows East and drains into the Atlantic Ocean.
2. Amazon river has the largest drainage system in the world.

Which of the statements given above is/are correct?

(a) Only 1 (b) Only 2
(c) Both 1 and 2 (d) Neither 1 nor 2

Ans. (c)

Exp. Both the statements (1) and (2) are correct about Amazon river.

Amazon river originates from the Andes mountains and flows East and drains into the Atlantic Ocean is the largest river in the world.

Its length of 6,992 km is the largest drainage system in the world in terms of the volume of its flow and the area of its basin.

111 Angel Falls, the highest waterfall in the world, is located in, which of the following country? *(Chap 11, Class-VI, Old NCERT)*

(a) Venezuela (b) Ecuador
(c) Suriname (d) Colombia

Ans. (a)

Exp. Angel Falls, the highest waterfall in the world is located in Venezuela. The height of this waterfall is about 979 meters. It is situated on the Churun river.

112 Consider the following statements. *(Chap 11, Class-VI, Old NCERT)*

1. The Amazon basin in South America is covered by tropical deciduous forests.
2. The Orinoco river basin is covered by Savanna vegetation known as Llanos.

Which of the statements given above is/are correct?

(a) Only 1 (b) Only 2
(c) Both 1 and 2 (d) Neither 1 nor 2

Ans. (b)

Exp. Statement (2) is correct as the North of South America, grasslands are found in the Orinoco river basin. This area is covered with savanna vegetation.

These grasslands are bounded on the West and North-West by the Andes and on the North by the Venezuelan coastal range.
Statement (1) is incorrect because the Amazon basin in South America is covered by tropical rainforest.

113 Which of the following statement(s) is/are correct regarding Atacama desert? *(Chap 11, Class-VI, Old NCERT)*

(a) Atacama desert is the driest desert in the world.
(b) It is located in the Western regions of South America.
(c) It is located in parts of Southern Peru and Northern Chile.
(d) All of the above

Ans. (c)

Exp. All of the above statements are correct regarding Atacama desert.

The Atacama desert, the driest desert in the world, is located in the western regions of South America. It is located in parts of Southern Peru and Northern Chile. It covers a land of 1,600 km. Hawthorn and thorny shrubs are the natural vegetation found in this area.

114 Consider the following statements about the Guiana Highlands. *(Chap 11, Class-VI, Old NCERT)*

1. The Guiana Highlands are located in the northern part of South America.
2. The highlands are known for their rich mineral resources.
3. The Angel Falls, the world's highest uninterrupted waterfall, is situated in the Guiana Highlands.

How many of the statements given above is/are correct?

(a) Only one (b) Only two
(c) All three (d) None of these

Ans. (c)

Exp. All three statements i.e., (1), (2) and (3) are correct about the Guiana Highlands.

The Guiana Highlands are indeed located in the northern part of South America, spanning across Venezuela, Guyana, Suriname, French Guiana, and parts of northern Brazil and South-Eastern Colombia.The region is known for its abundance of mineral resources, including gold, diamond, bauxite and manganese. These resources have been a major economic driver for the countries within the region. Angel Falls, with a plunge of 979 meters (3,212 feet), is the world's highest uninterrupted waterfall and is located in Venezuela's Canaima National Park, part of the Guiana Highlands.

115 Consider the following statements. *(Chap 11, Class-VI, Old NCERT)*

1. The interior regions of Argentina are covered by temperate grasslands known as Steppes.
2. The Gran Chaco in Argentina is covered with temperate forests.

Which of the statements given above is/are correct?

(a) Only 1
(b) Only 2
(c) Both 1 and 2
(d) Neither 1 nor 2

Ans. (b)

Exp. Statement (2) is correct as the Gran Chaco in Argentina is covered with temperate forests. In the Gran Chaco region, rainfall occurs in summer and winter is dry. This region is covered with dense or temperate forests and grasses.

Statement (1) is incorrect because the interior regions of Argentina are covered by temperate grasslands known as Pampas. Winters in this area are mild to cold and summers are hot and humid. Rainfall is fairly uniform throughout the year but is slightly heavier during the summer.

116 Match the following lists correctly and choose the correct codes. *(Chap 11, Class-VI, Old NCERT)*

List I (Forest Products)	List II (Used for)
A. Balsa	1. Medicine
B. Carnauba Palm	2. Wax
C. Cinchona	3. Wood

Codes

	A	B	C		A	B	C
(a)	1	2	3	(b)	2	1	3
(c)	3	2	1	(d)	1	3	2

Ans. (c)

Exp. The correct matching is A-3,B-2,C-1.

Balsa It is a medicinal plant found in the tropical rainforests of the Amazon river basin. Balsa is the world's lightest wood.

Carnauba Palm It is found in the Amazon rainforest. Wax is obtained from this tree which is used to polish shoes and to polish furniture.

Cinchona It tree is found in the rainforests of the Amazon. The bark of cinchona is used to make quinine medicine.

117 Which of the following is a variety of nutritious grass that is mainly grown in the grasslands of South America? *(Chap 11, Class-VI, Old NCERT)*

(a) Alfalfa
(b) Zoysia
(c) Sporobolus
(d) None of these

Ans. (a)

Exp. Alfalfa is a variety of nutritious grass mainly grown in grasslands of South America. It is also called lucerne. It is a perennial flowering plant in the legume family Fabaceae.

It is cultivated as an important forage crop in many countries around the world. It is used for grazing, hay and silage, as well as a green manure and cover crop.

118 Consider the following statements about the Pampas region in South America. *(Chap 11, Class-VI, Old NCERT)*

1. The Pampas are extensive grasslands located in Argentina.
2. The region is known for its fertile soils and is a major agricultural area.
3. The Pampas are characterised by a humid subtropical climate.

How many of the statements given above is/are correct?

(a) Only one (b) Only two
(c) All three (d) None of these

Ans. (b)

Exp. Only two statements i.e., (1) and (2) are correct. The Pampas cover a vast area, encompassing parts of Argentina, Uruguay, and southern Brazil, but Argentina holds the majority of the region.The Pampas are famous for their rich fertile soil, making them a major producer of agricultural products like soyabeans, wheat and corn. Statement (3) is incorrect because the climate of the Pampas is more accurately described as temperate humid, with warm summers and mild winters. It can vary across the region, with drier conditions in the West and more humid areas in the East.

119 Which of the following country of South America is a landlocked country? *(Chap 11, Class-VI, Old NCERT) (IAS Pre 2003)*

(a) Brazil (b) Peru (c) Bolivia (d) Argentina

Ans. (c)

Exp. Bolivia is the landlocked country of South America. The capital of Bolivia is La Paz. Lake Titicaca is located on the border of Bolivia and Peru. Apart from Bolivia, Paraguay is also a landlocked country.

120 Which of the following country do not share its border with the largest country of South America? *(Chap 12, Class-VI, Old NCERT)*

(a) Peru (b) Bolivia (c) Chile (d) Colombia

Ans. (c)

Exp. Chile do not share its border with the Brazil. Brazil is the largest country of South America. Brazil does not share its borders with Chile and Ecuador. Chile is located in the West of South America. It shares borders with Peru, Bolivia and Argentina. Santiago is the capital of Chile.

121 Which of the following statements is/are correct? *(Chap 12, Class-VI, Old NCERT)*

(a) Brazil is known for growing cash crops such as coffee and cocoa.
(b) Large plantations of coffee are known as Fazendas in Brazil.
(c) Coffee is grown on the slopes of highlands in Brazil.
(d) All of the above

Ans. (d)

Exp. All of the above statements are correct as coffee, cotton, sugarcane, cocoa and tobacco are the main cash crops of Brazil. Here cocoa and coffee are grown in large plantations. Due to the fertile soil and warm climate in Brazil, different types of cash crops are grown here. Coffee and cocoa are the main crops of Brazil.

122 The wide treeless grassy plain in South America are called *(Chap 11, Class-VI, Old NCERT) (UPPSC Pre 2005)*

(a) Selvas (b) Pampas (c) Prairies (d) Steppes

Ans. (b)

Exp. The wide treeless grassy plain in South America are called Pampas. These plains are very fertile. These grass fields spread from the Atlantic Ocean to Andes mountain upto Argentina and Uruguay.

Europe

123 Which of the given pairs is/are matched incorrectly? *(Chap 10, Class-VII, Old NCERT)*

	Boundary of Surrounded by	Europe
(a)	North	Arctic Ocean
(b)	East	Ural Mountains and Asia
(c)	West	Pacific Ocean
(d)	South	Mediterranean Sea

Ans. (c)

Exp. Pair (c) is matched incorrectly because West side boundary of Europe is surrounded by Atlantic Ocean.

124 Which of the following countries together are known as Scandinavian countries? *(Chap 10, Class-VII, Old NCERT)*

1. Denmark 2. Norway
3. Germany 4. Sweden
5. France

Codes

(a) 1, 2 and 4 (b) 2, 3 and 4
(c) 1, 3 and 5 (d) 2, 3 and 5

Ans. (a)

Exp. Denmark, Norway, Sweden, Finland and Iceland are known as Scandinavian countries. Scandinavian is a sub-region in Northern Europe, with strong historical, cultural and linguistic ties.

125 Consider the following statements about the Europe continent. *(Chap 10, Class-VII, Old NCERT)*

1. Iceland, Norway, Sweden and Denmark are collectively known as Scandinavia.
2. Belgium, Netherlands and Luxemburg are together known as the Baltic States.

Which of the statements given above is/are correct?

(a) Only 1 (b) Only 2
(c) Both 1 and 2 (d) Neither 1 nor 2

Ans. (a)

Exp. Statement (1) is correct about the Europe Continent.

Iceland, Norway, Sweden, and Denmark are collectively known as Scandinavia. The name Scandinavia comes from the region of southern Sweden called Skane or Scania.

Statement (2) is incorrect because Estonia, Lithuania, and Latvia are together known as the Baltic States while Belgium, Netherlands, and Luxemburg are called Low countries.

126 Which of the following country is one of the Balkan states? *(Chap 10, Class-VII, Old NCERT)*

(a) Portugal (b) France (c) Italy (d) Bulgaria

Ans. (d)

Exp. Among the given options, Bulgaria is one of the Balkan states. Bulgaria, Bosnia, Croatia, Kosovo, Montenegro, North Macedonia, Romania, Serbia, Slovenia, etc. are the Balkan states. The Balkans states is a group of geographic area in South-East Europe. The 11 countries lying on the Balkan peninsula are called the Balkan states.

127 Which of the following statements is/are correct about the North-Western highlands of Europe? *(Chap 10, Class-VII, Old NCERT)*

(a) The Fennoscandian shield is located in the North-Western highlands.

(b) This region is rich in metallic minerals such as iron and copper.

(c) Coal and Petroleum are found in abundant quantities in this region.

(d) Both a and b

Ans. (d)

Exp. Statements (a) and (b) are correct about the North-Western highlands of Europe. North-Western highlands of Europe is a region of highlands. It extends from Finland to Iceland, through Sweden, Norway and the British Islands. The Northern part of this highland is called the Fennoscandian shield. This region is rich in metallic minerals such as iron and copper. The rocks of this shield are the oldest exposed rocks in Europe.

Statement (c) is incorrect because fossil fuels such as coal, petroleum and natural gas are almost not found in this region.

128 Consider the following statements about the Rhine river. *(Chap 10, Class-VII, Old NCERT)*

1. The Rhine river is the second-longest river in Central and Western Europe.
2. It rises in two headstreams high in the Swiss Alps.
3. It flows through four countries.

How many of the statements given above is/are correct?

(a) Only one (b) Only two
(c) All three (d) None of these

Ans. (b)

Exp. Only two statements i.e., (1) and (2) are correct regarding the Rhine river.

The Rhine river is the second-longest river in Central and Western Europe, at about 1,230 km (760 miles) long. The Rhine river's name varies depending on the country it's in. In France, it's called the Rhine, in Germany it's called Rhein, and in the Netherlands it's called Rijn.

The Rhine river begins in the Swiss Alps, where two headstreams, the Vorderrhein and the Hinterrhein, merge. The two streams merge to form the Alpen Rhine, which then flows northward out of the Alps and into Lake Konstanz.

Statement (3) is incorrect because the Rhine flows through six countries -Switzerland, Principality of Liechtenstein, Austria, Germany, France and the Netherlands before flowing into the North Sea at Rotterdam.

129 Which of the following statements is/are correct regarding North Sea? *(Chap 10, Class-VII, Old NCERT)*

1. Finland does not share its border with the North Sea.
2. North Sea is located in Western Europe.

Codes

(a) Only 1
(b) Only 2
(c) Both 1 and 2
(d) Neither 1 nor 2

Ans. (c)

Exp. Both the statements (1) and (2) are correct regarding North Sea. Finland does not share its border with the North Sea. Finland is a Scandinavian country. North Sea is located in Western Europe. The North Sea is bordered by countries like Norway, UK, Netherlands, Belgium, Germany, Denmark, etc.

130 The Mediterranean Sea shares borders with which of the following countries? *(Chap 10, Class-VII, Old NCERT) (IAS 2017)*

1. Jordan 2. Iraq
3. Lebanon 4. Syria

Codes

(a) 1, 2 and 3 (b) 2 and 3
(c) 3 and 4 (d) 1, 3 and 4

Ans. (c)

Exp. Among the given options, Lebanon and Syria shares border with Mediterranean Sea.

The Mediterranean Sea is bordered by 21 countries. They are Albania, Algeria, Bosnia and Herzegovina, Croatia, Cyprus, Egypt, France, Greece, Israel, Italy, Lebanon, Libya, Malta, Morocco, Monaco, Montenegro, Slovenia, Spain, Syria, Tunisia and Turkey. In addition, the Gaza Strip and the British Overseas Territories of Gibraltar and Akrotiri and Dhekelia have coastlines on the sea. On the eastern shore, Turkey, Syria, Lebanon and Israel have their coastline on the Mediterranean Sea.

131 **Which of the given statements is/are incorrect?** *(Chap 10, Class-VII, Old NCERT)*

(a) France shares longest border with the Adriatic Sea.
(b) The Black Sea is located between Europe and Asia.
(c) The North Sea separates United Kingdom from mainland Europe.
(d) None of the above

Ans. (a)

Exp. Statement (a) is incorrect because Italy shares longest border with the Adriatic Sea. France does not share border with the Adriatic Sea, it as borders with the Mediterranean Sea.

132 **Match the following lists correctly and choose the correct code.** *(Chap 10, Class-VII, Old NCERT)*

List I (Physical Feature)	List II (Found in)
A. Meseta	1. Germany
B. Massif Central	2. Spain and Portugal
C. Black Forest	3. France
D. Vidda	4. Norway

Codes

	A	B	C	D		A	B	C	D
(a)	1	2	3	4	(b)	2	3	1	4
(c)	3	1	2	4	(d)	3	2	1	4

Ans. (b)

Exp. The correct matching is A-2, B-3, C-1, D-4.

The **Meseta** plateau is one of the basic geographical units of the Iberian Peninsula. The Meseta plateau is located in Spain and Portugal.

The **Massif Central** is a highland region in the middle of southern France, consisting of mountains and plateaus.

The **Black Forest** is located in South-West Germany, bordering France. The Black Forest is a block mountain.

Vidda also known as Hardanger plateau is located in South-Western Europe.

133 **Consider the following statements about the Alps mountains.** *(Chap 10, Class-VII, Old NCERT)*

1. The Alps are young fold mountains with rugged relief and high conical peaks.
2. Monte Rosa is the highest peak in the Alps.
3. Only Switzerland and Austria can be considered true Alpine countries.

How many of the statements given above is/are correct?

(a) Only one (b) Only two
(c) Only three (d) None of these

Ans. (b)

Exp. Only two statements i.e., (1) and (3) are correct regarding the Alps mountains.

The Alps are young fold mountains with rugged relief and high conical peaks.

Young fold mountains are mountains that have rugged relief and high conical peaks and are generally formed between 10 and 25 million years ago.

The Alps form part of France, Italy, Switzerland, Germany, Austria, Slovenia, Croatia, Bosnia and Herzegovina, Montenegro, Serbia, and Albania. Only Switzerland and Austria can be considered true Alpine countries.

Statement (2) is incorrect because Monte Rosa is a mountain massif in the Alps that contains several peaks, including the Dufourspitze. The Dufourspitze is the highest peak in the Monte Rosa massif and Switzerland, at 4,634 meters (15,203 ft).

134 **Mount Elbrus, the highest peak of Europe, is located on, which of the following mountain range?** *(Chap 10, Class-VII, Old NCERT)*

(a) Ural mountains (b) Caucasus mountains
(c) Black Forest mountain (d) Pyrenees range

Ans. (b)

Exp. Mount Elbrus is the highest peak of Europe is located on Caucasus mountain range. The height of Mount Elbrus is about 5,633 metres. The Caucasus mountain is located between Asia and Europe.

135 **Consider the following statements with reference to climate of Europe.** *(Chap 10, Class-VII, Old NCERT)*

1. Southern Europe region experiences Mediterranean climate.
2. Western Europe experiences dry continental climate.

Which of the statements given above is/are incorrect?

(a) Only 1 (b) Only 2
(c) Both 1 and 2 (d) Neither 1 nor 2

Ans. (b)

Exp. Statement (2) is incorrect with reference to climate of Europe.

In Western Europe, due to the proximity to the westerly winds and the sea, the summers are warm and the winters are cool. The temperature remains almost the same throughout the year. Rainfall also occurs almost throughout the year.

136 **Which of the following statements is are correct?** *(Chap 10, Class-VII, Old NCERT)*

(a) Steppes are temperate Grassland of Europe.
(b) Steppes grasslands extend from the valley of Danube River in Romania to Ukraine.
(c) Both a and b
(d) Neither a nor b

Ans. (c)

Exp. Both the statements (a) and (b) are correct.

In Europe and Asia, temperate grasslands are called Steppes. In the South-East of Europe, there are extensive grasslands called temperate grasslands. This grassland extends from the valley of the Danube river in Romania to Ukraine.

137 **Which of the following countries of Europe is/are landlocked?** *(Chap 10, Class-VII, Old NCERT)*

1. Austria 2. Germany 3. Italy
4. Belarus 5. Luxembourg

Codes

(a) 1 and 2 (b) 2, 3, and 4
(c) 1, 4 and 5 (d) 1, 2, 3, 4 and 5

***Ans.* (c)**

Exp. Among the given options, Austria, Belarus and Luxemburg countries of Europe are Landlocked.

There are 15 landlocked countries in Europe: Andorra, Austria, Belarus, Czech Republic, Hungary, Liechtenstein, Luxembourg, Macedonia, Moldova, San Marino, Serbia, Slovakia, Switzerland and Vatican City. A landlocked country is a country which has no connection to a sea or ocean.

138 **Which of the following statements are correct?** *(Chap 11, Class-VII, Old NCERT)*

1. Wheat is a main crop in Europe.
2. Flax is a fibre crop grown in Europe.
3. Flax crop is used to make linen cloth.

Codes

(a) 1 and 2 (b) 2 and 3 (c) 1 and 3 (d) 1, 2 and 3

***Ans.* (d)**

Exp. Statements (1), (2) and (3) are correct.

Wheat is the main crop grown in Europe. Wheat is produced in the Ukraine basin, the Paris basin. Flax is a fibrous crop, which is used to make linen cloth. The main producers of Flax and Belgium and Baltic states.

139 **Which of the following countries of Europe have developed food processing and agro-based industries?** *(Chap 11, Class-VII, Old NCERT)*

(a) Bulgaria (b) Belgium
(c) Netherlands (d) All of these

***Ans.* (d)**

Exp. In Eastern Europe, countries such as Bulgaria, Hungary, Belgium and Poland industries have developed food processing and agro-processing. An agro-based and food processing industry also exists in the Netherlands of Western Europe.

140 **Which of the following country is not a major centre of iron and steel industry in Europe?** *(Chap 11, Class-VII, Old NCERT)*

(a) United Kingdom (b) Germany
(c) France (d) Italy

***Ans.* (d)**

Exp. Italy is not a major centre of iron and steel industry in Europe. Countries like Italy and Poland make steel by importing iron ore from other countries. The major centers of iron and steel industry in Europe are established in the United Kingdom, France, Germany, Ukraine and Russia.

141 **Match List I with List II.** *(Chap 11, Class-VII, Old NCERT)*

List I (Fishing Bank)	List II (Country)
A. Agulhas Bank	1. England
B. Georges Bank	2. USA
C. Dogger Bank	3. South Africa
D. Grand Banks	4. Canada

Codes

	A	B	C	D		A	B	C	D
(a)	3	4	1	3	(b)	2	4	1	3
(c)	4	3	2	1	(d)	3	2	1	4

***Ans.* (d)**

Exp. The correct matching is A-3, B-2, C-1, D-4.

The **Agulhas Bank** is located in South Africa. It is a 116,000 square kilometer (45,000 square mile) continental shelf that extends 250 kilometers offshore. **Georges Bank** is located in United State of America (USA). The **Dogger Bank** is a large sandbank in the North Sea, located about 100 kilometers off the East coast of England.

The **Grand Banks** are located in Canada, South-East of Newfoundland Island.

142 **Which of the following statement(s) is/are correct?** *(Chap 11, Class-VII, Old NCERT)*

(a) The Danube river in Europe drains into Black Sea.
(b) The Volga and Thames river are important waterways in Europe.
(c) Ural river forms an important waterway in Eastern Europe.
(d) Both a and b

***Ans.* (d)**

Exp. Both the statements (a) and (b) are correct as Danube river rises from the Black Forest and travels through much of Central and South-Eastern Europe, eventually drains into Black Sea. The Danube river is the second longest river in Europe after the Volga in Russia.

The Thames, Seine, Danube and Volga are the major waterways in Europe. The Rhine is the busiest waterway in Europe.

Statement (c) is incorrect because the Ural river does not form an important waterway in Eastern Europe. Ural river originates in the Southern Ural mountains and discharges into the Caspian Sea.

143 **Which of the following statements are correct regarding the density of population in Europe?** *(Chap 11, Class-VII, Old NCERT)*

(a) Density of population is high in the coalfields and industrial regions of United kingdom, France, Germany and Italy.
(b) The density of population is high in the plains of Europe.
(c) Both a and b
(d) Neither a nor b

***Ans.* (c)**

Exp. Both the statements (a) and (b) are correct regarding the density of population in Europe.
The density of population is high in the coalfields and industrial regions of United Kingdom, France, Germany and Italy.
The density of population is high in the plains of Europe. The density of population is medium in Eastern and Southern Europe and low in Northern Europe.

144 Which of the given activities is/are mainly practised in United Kingdom? *(Chap 12, Class-VII, Old NCERT)*

(a) Dairy Farming (b) Cattle and sheep rearing
(c) Mixed Farming (d) All of these

Ans. (d)

Exp. All the above given activities are practised in United Kingdom.
Nearly half of the land in the United Kingdom is pasture. Little rain and mild temperature throughout the year are favourable for the grass to grow.
Sheep rearing and animal husbandry are the main agricultural activities here. Meat and dairy industry is established here.
Most farmers in the United Kingdom practice mixed farming. Under mixed farming, animal husbandry and agriculture are done together.

145 Which among the following industrial region is located in United Kingdom? *(Chap 12, Class-VII, Old NCERT)*

1. Liverpool 2. Sheffield
3. Newcastle 4. Moore
5. Victoria

Codes

(a) 1, 2 and 4 (b) 2, 3 and 4
(c) 1, 4 and 5 (d) 1, 2 and 3

Ans. (d)

Exp. Liverpool, Glasgow, Sheffield and Newcastle are the main industrial centres located in United Kingdom. Birmingham and Manchester are the other main industrial regions of the United Kingdom. Moore and Victoria region are located in Australia.

146 Match List I with List II. *(Chap 12, Class-VII, Old NCERT)*

List I (Range)	List II (Highest Peak)
A. Pyrenees Range	1. Kebnekaise
B. Scandinavian Range	2. Elbrus
C. Ural Range	3. Aneto
D. Caucasus Range	4. Narodnaya

Codes

	A	B	C	D		A	B	C	D
(a)	3	1	4	2	(b)	2	4	1	3
(c)	4	3	2	1	(d)	3	2	1	4

Ans. (a)

Exp. The correct matching is A-3, B-1, C-4, D-2.
The highest peak in the **Pyrenees** is Aneto Peak. It's located in the Maladeta massif of the Central Pyrenees. Kebnekaise is the highest peak in the **Scandinavian** mountains.
Mount Narodnaya is the highest peak in the Ural mountains. The mountain is also known as Naroda and Poenurr. The **Ural** mountains are some of the oldest in the world, dating back 250-300 million years.
Mount Elbrus is the highest peak in the **Caucasus** mountains, standing at 18,510 feet (5,642 meters) above sea level. It's located in southern Russia, just North of the Georgian border.

147 Consider the following statements. *(Chap 12, Class-VII, Old NCERT)*

1. Loraine field in Europe is known for deposits of Iron Ore.
2. The Rhone Valley of France is known for the concentration of silk manufacturing industry.

Which of the statements given above is/are correct?

(a) Only 1 (b) Only 2
(c) Both 1 and 2 (d) Neither 1 and 2

Ans. (c)

Exp. Both the statements (1) and (2) are correct as the Loraine region in Europe is known for its iron ore deposits. More than 90% of iron ore is extracted from the Loraine region itself. Industrial centre is established in this region due to iron ore. The Rhone Valley of France is known for its concentration of silk manufacturing industry due to its favourable climate.

148 Grape Cultivation is mostly practised in, which of the following region of France? *(Chap 12, Class-VII, Old NCERT)*

(a) Lowlands of France (b) Terraced slopes
(c) Eastern France (d) Southern France

Ans. (b)

Exp. In France, grape cultivation is mostly practised in terraced slopes and shielded slopes of the valleys. This is especially done in Southern France.

149 Which one of the following pairs is not correctly matched? *(Chap 12, Class-VII, Old NCERT)*

City		River
1. Berlin	–	Rhine
2. London	–	Thames
3. New York	–	Hudson
4. Vienna	–	Danube

Codes

(a) Only 1 (b) Only 2
(c) Only 3 (d) Only 4

Ans. (a)

Exp. Pair (1) is not correctly matched.
Berlin is located on the banks of the Spree River, which runs through the center of the city.

150 **Which of the following coal producing region is located in Germany?** *(Chap 12, Class-VII, Old NCERT)*
(a) Ural (b) Pennines
(c) Pyrenees (d) Ruhr
Ans. (d)
Exp. Ruhr is the largest and most prosperous region of coal production in Europe and Germany. Especially Bituminous coal is found in Germany.

151 **The Kiel canal in Europe connects, which of the following water bodies?** *(Chap 12, Class-VII, Old NCERT)*
(a) North Sea and Scandinavian Sea
(b) North Sea and Baltic Sea
(c) Baltic Sea and Scandinavian Sea
(d) Black Sea and Aral Sea
Ans. (b)
Exp. The Kiel canal connects the Baltic Sea to the North Sea. It is a 99 km long canal. This canal is of great importance in trade with the Scandinavian countries. In addition to rivers in Germany, there are canals to reach the interior of the country. The canal also encourages trade.

152 **Which of the following cities is/are located in the Rhine river valley?** *(Chap 12, Class-VII, Old NCERT)*
1. Frankfurt 2. Cologne 3. Hamburg 4. Berlin
Codes
(a) 2 and 3 (b) 1 and 4 (c) 1 and 2 (d) All of these
Ans. (c)
Exp. Frankfurt and Cologne cities in Germany are located in the Rhine river valley. The Rhine river originates from the Alps mountains and falls in the North Sea in the West.
While Hamburg city of Germany is located in Elbe river valley and Berlin city located in Spree river valley.

153 **Consider the following statements about Ural Mountain.** *(Chap 13, Class-VII, Old NCERT)*
1. The Ural mountains are also known as the Urals or Russian Uralskie Gory.
2. Mount Narodnaya is the highest peak of this mountain range.
3. The Eastern part of this mountain is considered the boundary between Europe and Asia.

Which of the statements given above are correct?
(a) 1 and 2 (b) 2 and 3 (c) 1 and 3 (d) 1, 2 and 3
Ans. (d)
Exp. All the given statements (1), (2) and (3) are correct regarding Ural Mountain.
The Ural Mountains, also called the Urals, Russian Uralskie Gory or Ural, mountain range form a rugged spine in West-Central Russia and the major part of the traditional physiographic boundary between Europe and Asia. Mount Narodnaya is the highest peak in the Ural Mountains, reaching 1,895 meters (6,217 feet). It's located in the Nether-Polar section of the Urals, on the border between the Khanty-Mansi Autonomous Okrug and the Komi Republic. The Eastern part of this mountain is considered the boundary between Europe and Asia.

154 **Which of the following rivers flow through the Western Siberian Plains?** *(Chap 13, Class-VII, Old NCERT)*
1. Ob river 2. Yenisei river
3. Ural river 4. Rhine river
Codes
(a) 2 and 4 (b) 1 and 3 (c) 1 and 2 (d) 1 and 4
Ans. (c)
Exp. West Siberian Plains extends between the Ural mountains and the Yenisei river in the East. The Irtysh, Ob and Yenisei rivers flow through the Western Siberia plains and fall into the North Pole Ocean.
While Ural river, originates from Russia's Ural mountains and flows through Russia and Kazakhstan into the Caspian Sea. The Rhine river originates from the Alps mountains and falls in the North Sea in the West.

155 **The Central Siberian Plateau lies between, which of the following rivers?** *(Chap 13, Class-VII, Old NCERT)*
(a) Rhine and Volga (b) Lena and Yenisei
(c) Danube and Elbe (d) Rhone and Seine
Ans. (b)
Exp. The Central Siberian Plateau lies between the Yenisei in the West and the Lena river in the East.
The height of this plateau is upto 500 metres.

156 **The Kamchatka peninsula belongs to, which of the following country?** *(Chap 13, Class-VII, Old NCERT)*
(a) Germany (b) France
(c) Russia (d) United Kingdom
Ans. (c)
Exp. The Kamchatka peninsula belongs to Russia.
The Kamchatka peninsula is a 1,250 km long peninsula in the Russian far East. Kamchatka peninsula is lying between the Sea of Okhotsk on the West and the Pacific Ocean and Bering Sea on the East.

157 **Which of the following statements is/are correct?** *(Chap 13, Class-VII, Old NCERT)*
1. Moscow is known as the port of five seas.
2. St. Petersburg is an important port city of Finland.

Codes
(a) Only 1 (b) Only 2
(c) Both 1 and 2 (d) Neither 1 nor 2
Ans. (a)
Exp. Statement (1) is correct as Moscow is known as the port of five seas because of the Moscow Canal. The length of the Moscow Canal is 128 kilometres. This canal completed in 1937, connects the five seas, the White Sea, the Baltic Sea, the Caspian Sea, the Sea of Azov and the Black Sea.
Statement (2) is incorrect because St. Petersburg is an important port city of Russia.

158 **The Kuznetsk Basin is known for, which of the following minerals?** *(Chap 13, Class-VII, Old NCERT)*

(a) Uranium (b) Thorium
(c) Coal (d) None of these

Ans. (c)

Exp. The Kuznetsk Basin is known for coal. Coal is the most important source of power in Russia. In Russia coal is found in the Kuznetsk Basin, Eastern Siberia, the Ural region and the Moscow sub-basin.

Antarctica

159 **Which of the following statements is/are not correct regarding Antarctica?** *(Chap 16, Class-VI, Old NCERT)*

1. Antarctica is the world's Southernmost and fifth largest continent.
2. It is coldest, windiest and driest continent.
3. It is completely covered with ice that is why it is known as White continent.

Codes

(a) 1 and 2 (b) 2 and 3
(c) 1, 2 and 3 (d) None of these

Ans. (c)

Exp. All the given statements (1), (2) and (3) are correct regarding Antarctica.

Antarctica is the world's Southernmost and fifth largest continent. Its landmass is almost wholly covered by a vast ice sheet. It is the world's Southernmost continent as well as the world's highest, driest, windiest, coldest and iciest continent.

This continent is known as White continent because it is completely covered with ice.

160 **Consider the following statements.** *(Chap 16, Class-VI, Old NCERT)*

1. Antarctica is the sixth largest continent of the world.
2. Mount Erebus is the second highest volcano in Antarctica.

Which of the statements given above is/are correct?

(a) Only 1 (b) Only 2
(c) Both 1 and 2 (d) Neither 1 nor 2

Ans. (b)

Exp. Statement (2) is correct regarding Antarctica.

Mount Erebus is the second highest volcano in Antarctica, after Mount Sidley. It is also the southernmost active volcano on Earth. Its summit temperature averages between -20°C during the summer and -50°C in winter, for this reason, despite the volcanic activity, it remains covered by glaciers.

Statement (1) is incorrect because antarctica is the fifth largest continent in the world, covering an area of 14.2 million square kilometers
(5.5 million square miles). Antarctica is mostly uninhabitable and is the coldest, driest, and windiest continent. About 98% of Antarctica is covered by ice that averages about 1.6 kilometers in thickness.

161 **Consider the following statements about Antarctica.** *(Chap 15, Class-VI, Old NCERT)*

1. Antarctica lies completely in Southern Hemisphere with South Pole almost in its centre.
2. The mainland of Antarctica was first discovered in 1820.
3. About 99% of the continent remains covered permanently with ice.

How many statements given above is/are not correct?

(a) Only one (b) Only two
(c) Only three (d) None of these

Ans. (b)

Exp. Only two statements i.e., (1) and (2) are correct regarding Antarctica.

Antarctica is located entirely in the Southern Hemisphere, with the South Pole almost at its center. Antarctica is the southernmost continent and is covered by thick ice sheets. It is larger than the combined area of Europe and Australia, and has no permanent human settlements.

The mainland of Antarctica was first sighted by European explorers in 1820. The first person to actually see the Antarctic mainland has been debated: in the last week of January, Thaddeus von Bellingshausen reported seeing 'an ice shore of extreme height' during a Russian expedition to the Antarctic.

Statement (3) is are incorrect because about 98% of Antarctica is covered by the Antarctic ice sheet, which is the largest single mass of ice on Earth.

162 **Consider the following pairs of lakes and countries in Africa.** *(Unit 5, Class-XI, Tamil Nadu Board)*

1. Lake Victoria-Kenya
2. Lake Tanganyika-South Africa
3. Lake Malawi-Malawi
4. Lake Turkana-Ethiopia
5. Lake Kivu-Rwanda

Which of the pairs given above is/are correctly matched?

(a) 1 and 3 (b) 2 and 4 (c) 1, 3 and 5 (d) All of these

Ans. (c)

Exp. Pairs (1), (3) and (5) are correctly matched.

Lake Victoria is in Kenya, Lake Malawi is in Malawi and Lake Kivu is in Rwanda.

However, Lake Tanganyika is not in South Africa, it forms the boundary between Tanzania and the Democratic Republic of the congo (DRC) and part of the boundary between Burundi and the DRC as well as part of the boundary between Tanzania and Zambia. It occupies the Southern end of the Western Rift Valley and for most of its length the land rises steeply from its shores. Its waters tend to be frackish and Lake Turkana is not in Ethiopia, Lake Turkana, formely known as Lake Rudolf, is a lake in the Great Rift Valley in North-West Kenya. Its far Northern end crosses into Ethiopia.

Chapter 15

Map Studies

Map Studies

Map and its type

Map

- A selective, symbolised and generalised representation of the whole or part of the Earth at a reduced scale is called a map
- A two-dimensional form of three-dimensional Earth
- They can be used to measure distances, directions and area

Classification of Maps

- **Political Maps** Represent political divisions or human created boundaries of the world
- **Physical Maps** Represent natural features of the Earth such as mountains, plateaus, plains, rivers etc.
- **Thematic Maps** Portray the geographic pattern of a particular subject matter

Types of Maps

- **Based on Scale** Can be classified into two types,
  - large scale maps drawn to show small areas at a relatively large scale. They can be of two types, cadastral and topographical maps
  - Small scale maps drawn to show large areas. They can be of two types, wall maps and atlas map
- **Based on Function** Can be classified into two types
  - Physical maps show natural features such as relief, geology, soils, drainage etc
  - Cultural maps show man-made features. There are variety of maps showing population distribution and growth, location of settlements, occupational structure etc

Essentials of Map Making and Component of Maps

Essentials of Map Making

- **Scale** The scale of a map sets the limits of information content and the degree of reality with which it can be delineated on the map
- **Projection** It is a system of transformation of spherical surface to the plane surface
- **Generalisation** Generalising the map contents is important task while drawing it on a reduced scale
- **Map Design** It involves the planning of graphic characteristics of maps including selection of appropriate symbols, style of lettering, etc
- Map construction and production

Component of Maps

- **Direction** A measurement between two points initial and final. It tells about the time indirectly in the terms of reaching a particular place
- **Distance** maps are always drawn with North orientation. Direction is usually indicated by a North-South line with North direction represented by an arrow head
- **Symbols** Since it is impossible to draw exact size of different features like buildings, roads, bridges, trees etc, so they are shown by using certain symbols

SOURCE *New NCERT Class VI (Maps), Old NCERT Class IX (Maps as Aid to Understanding Environment)*

1 **Physical or terrain maps can be used to depict which of the following features of Earth's surface?** *(Chap 4, Class-VI, New NCERT)*

1. Mountains 2. Plateaus 3. Plains
4. Oceans 5. Lakes

Codes

(a) 1, 2, 3 (b) 2, 4, 5
(c) 1, 3, 5 (d) 1, 2, 3, 4, 5

Ans. (d)

Exp. Physical or terrain maps can be used to depict natural features of the Earth such as mountains, plateaus, plains, rivers, oceans, etc.

2 **Which of the following pairs is correctly matched?** *(Chap 4, Class-VI, New NCERT)*

	Types of Maps		Descriptions
(a)	Physical Maps	–	Maps showing cities, towns, villages, and different countries and states of the world with their boundaries.
(b)	Political Maps	–	Maps showing natural features of the Earth such as mountains, plateaus, plains, rivers, oceans, etc.
(c)	Thematic Maps	–	Some maps focus on specific information, such as road maps, rainfall maps and maps showing distribution of forests, industries, etc.
(d)	All of the above		

Ans. (c)

Exp. Pair (c) is correctly matched.

Maps showing natural features of the Earth such as mountains, plateaus, plains, rivers, oceans, etc., are called physical or relief maps.

Maps showing cities, towns villages, and different countries and states of the world with their boundaries are called political maps.

Some maps focus on specific information; such as road maps, rainfall maps and maps showing distribution of forests, industries, etc. are known as thematic maps.

3 **Consider the following statements regarding contour maps.** *(Chap 5, Class-XI, New NCERT)*

1. Contours are imaginary lines joining places having the same elevation above mean sea level.
2. The vertical interval between the two successive contour lines varies from place to place.
3. The horizontal distance between two successive contour lines decreases with increasing slope gradient.

How many of the statements given above is/are correct?

(a) Only one (b) Only two
(c) All three (d) None of these

Ans. (b)

Exp. Only two statements i.e., (1) and (3) are correct regarding contour.

Contours are imaginary lines joining places having the same elevation above mean sea level. A map showing the landform of an area by contours is called a contour map. The method of showing relief features through contour is very useful and versatile. The horizontal distance, also known as the Horizontal Equivalent is large when the slope is gentler and decreases with increasing slope gradient.

Statement (2) is incorrect because the vertical interval between the two successive contour lines remains constant. Contours are drawn at different vertical intervals (VI), like 20, 50 and 100 m above the mean sea level. It is known as a contour interval.

4 **Consider the following statements.** *(Chap 6, Class-IX, Old NCERT)*

1. Signs and symbols are often used in the maps to provide necessary information.
2. A sketch is a map which provides great details for a smaller area on a large scale.
3. On large scale maps, relief features can be shown with the help of contour lines.

Which of the statements given above are correct?

(a) 1 and 2 (b) 2 and 3 (c) 1 and 3 (d) All of these

Ans. (c)

Exp. Statements (1) and (3) are correct as one cannot draw on a map the actual shape and size of different features and natural features such as buildings, roads, etc. Hence, they are represented by using certain letters, shades, colours, pictures and lines. These symbols provide a lot of information in a limited space. They show the height of ground above Mean Sea Level (MSL) either in metres or feet, and can because drawn at any desired interval.

Statement (2) is incorrect because a sketch map is drawn without a scale, based on memory and observation, and represents the main features of an area.

5 **Consider the following statements regarding distance on maps.** *(Chap 4, Class-VI, New NCERT)*

1. The scale is the ratio between the actual distance on the ground and the distance shown on the map.
2. Large scale maps are used to show large areas like continents or countries on paper.

Which of the statements given above is/are correct?

(a) Only 1 (b) Only 2
(c) Both 1 and 2 (d) Neither 1 nor 2

Ans. (a)

Exp. Statement (1) is correct regarding distance on maps. The Scale is the ratio between the actual distance on the ground and the distance shown on the map.

Statement (2) is incorrect because when large areas like continents or countries are to be shown on paper, then we use a small scale. For example, 5 cm on the map shows 500 km of the ground. When a small area like your village or town is to be shown on paper, then we use a large scale that is 5 cm. On the map shows 500 m only on the ground.

Location and Structure of India

Location and Structure of India

Geographical Location

Geographical Location
- India is located latitudinally in Northern Hemisphere and longitudinally in Southern hemisphere
- Accounts for 2.4% of world's land surface area
- North-South extent is 3214 km and East-West extent is 2933 km
- Standard Meridian of country is 82° 30'E passing through Mirzapur
- Divided into 6 physiographic divisions i.e., Northern and North-Eastern mountains, Northern plains, Peninsular plateau, Indian desert, coastal plains and islands
- Tropic of Cancer passes through 8 states in India

Important Facts About India

Important Facts about India
- There are two major island groups in India, one in Arabian Sea and other in Bay of Bengal
- Largest district is Kutch (Gujarat) and smallest is Mahe (Pondicherry)
- Barren Island is India's only active volcano Narcondam Insland is a volcanic island situated in North Andaman

Extreme Points of India
- Southernmost point of country - Indira point
- Southernmost point of mainland Cape Comorin - (Kanyakumari)
- Northernmost point - Indira Col (Ladakh)
- Westernmost point - Guhar Mothi (Rann of Kutch)
- Easternmost point - Kibithu (Arunachal Pradesh)

India and Its Neighbourhood

India and its Neighbourhood
- Part of Asian Continent
- Towards its NW is Afghanistan and Pakistan
- Towards its North is China, Bhutan, Tibet and Nepal
- Towards its East is Bangladesh and Myanmar
- Towards its South is Maldives and Sri Lanka

Important Straits and Channels
- Indira Point and Indonesia - Great Channel
- Little Andaman and Nicobar - 10° channel Minicoy and Lakshadweep - 9° channel
- Maldives and Minicoy - 8° channel
- India and Sri Lanka - Gulf of Mannar and Palk Strait

SOURCE *NIOS Chap 16, Module 6,* ***New NCERT Class VI*** *(Our Country : India),* ***New NCERT Class IX*** *(India : Size and Location),* ***New NCERT Class XI*** *(India : Location)*

1 Consider the following statements about location setting of India. *(Chap 1, Class-IX, New NCERT)*

1. The longitudinal and latitudinal extent of India are roughly 30°.
2. The actual distance from East to West is less than the distance between North to South.

Which of the statements given above is/are correct?

(a) Only 1 (b) Only 2
(c) Both 1 and 2 (d) Neither 1 nor 2

Ans. (c)

Exp. Both the given statements (1) and (2) are correct regarding the location setting of India as the longitudinal extent of India from West end Gujarat to East end Arunachal Pradesh is 68°7′E to 97°25′E.On calculating both of these extents, we get to know that these are roughly of 30°.

India lies to the North of the Equator between 6°44′ N and 35°30′ N (North) latitute, this extent is also roughly 30°.

The actual distance measured from North to South extremity is 3,214 km and from East to West is only 2,933 km. Thus, the actual distance from East to West is less than the distance between North to South.

2 Consider of the following statements. *(Chap 1, Class-IX, New NCERT) (JPSC Pre 2016)*

1. The Indian mainland begins to taper at about 30° N latitude.
2. The total length of coastline of India is 15,200 km.
3. The mainland of India extends between 8°4′ N and 37° 6′ N latitudes.

How many of the statements given above is/are correct?

(a) Only one (b) Only two (c) All three (d) None of these

Ans. (a)

Exp. Only one statement i.e., (3) is correct as the mainland of India extends from Kashmir in the North to Kanyakumari in the South and Arunachal Pradesh in the East to Gujarat in the West.

India's territorial limit further extends towards the sea upto 12 nautical miles (about 21.9 km) from the coast.

Statements (1) and (2) are incorrect because Indian mainland begins to taper at about 22° N latitude not 30° N latitude. The total length of coastline in India is 7516.6 km not 15,200 km.

3 The Tropic of Cancer (23°30′ N latitude) divides India into almost two equal parts. It passes through, which of the following group of states? *(Chap 1, Class-XI, New NCERT) (UPPSC Pre 2017)*

(a) Tripura, West Bengal, Odisha, Uttar Pradesh
(b) Mizoram, West Bengal, Rajasthan, Jharkhand
(c) Tripura, Odisha, Jharkhand, Rajasthan
(d) Maharashtra, Meghalaya, Jharkhand, Chhattisgarh

Ans. (b)

Exp. The Tropic of Cancer (23° 30′ N latitude) divides the country into almost two equal parts. It passes through 8 Indian states including Gujarat, Rajasthan, Madhya Pradesh, Chhattisgarh, Jharkhand, West Bengal, Tripura and Mizoram.

4 With reference to India, which of the following statements is/are correct? *(Chap 1, Class-IX, New NCERT)*

1. India is the sixth largest country of the world.
2. India occupies about 2.4% of the total area of the world.
3. Tropic of Cancer passes through the middle of the country dividing into two latitudinal halves.
4. India lies completely in tropic zone.

Select the correct answer by using the codes given below.

(a) 1 and 2 (b) 2 and 4 (c) 3 and 4 (d) 2 and 3

Ans. (d)

Exp. Statements (2) and (3) are correct with reference to India. India occupies 2.4% of the world's land area with its 3.28 million sq km area. However, it holds 17.5% of the world's population.

Tropic of Cancer divides India into almost two equal parts. Tropic of Cancer is the most Northerly circle of the latitude on the Earth at an angle of 23.43° North to the Equator.

Statements (1) and (4) are incorrect because India is the seventh largest country in the world, with a total area of 32,87,263 sq km.

India lies entirely in the tropical and sub-tropical regions of the Northern Hemisphere.

5 Consider the following statements about Indian Standard Meridian. *(Chap 1, Class-IX, New NCERT) (UPPSC Pre 2013)*

1. 82°30' E has been designated as the standard Meridian of India.
2. Indian Standard Meridian passes through Mirzapur in Uttar Pradesh.
3. Indian Standard Time is ahead of Greenwich Mean Time by 8 hours.

Which of the statements given above is/are correct?

(a) 1 and 3 (b) 1 and 2
(c) 2 and 3 (d) All of these

Ans. (b)

Exp. Statements (1) and (2) are correct regarding the Indian Standard Meridian as the Standard Meridian of India (82°30′E) passing through Mirzapur (in Uttar Pradesh) is taken as the standard time for the whole country.

The latitudinal extent influences the duration of day and night, as one moves from South to North.

Statement (3) is incorrect because IST (Indian Standard Time) is 5:30 hours ahead of GMT (Greenwich Mean Time).

6 Consider the following statements about the size of India. *(Chap 1, Class-IX, New NCERT)*

1. India accounts for 4.2% of the world's total land surface area.
2. It is the seventh largest country in the world.
3. The landmass of India has an area of 3.28 million sq km.
4. India is usually considered as the Southward extension of Asia.

How many of the statements given above is/are incorrect?

(a) Only one (b) Only two
(c) All three (d) None of these

Ans. (a)

Exp. Only one statement i.e., (1) is incorrect regarding the size of India because the landmass of India has an area of 3.28 million square km. India's total area accounts for about 2.4% of the total geographical area of the world.

7 Consider the following statements with reference to the location of India. *(Chap 1, Class-XI, New NCERT)*

1. All the territories of India, including the island groups are entirely located in the Northern Hemisphere.
2. The Andaman and Nicobar islands, located in the Bay of Bengal, are intersected by the Equator.

Which of the statements given above is/are incorrect?

(a) Only 1
(b) Only 2
(c) Both 1 and 2
(d) Neither 1 nor 2

Ans (b)

Exp. Statement (2) is incorrect with reference to the location of India because the entire country is in the Northern Hemisphere so the Andaman and Nicobar islands, located in the Bay of Bengal, are not intersected by the Equator.

8 With reference to land boundaries of India, consider the following statements. *(Chap 1, Class-IX, New NCERT)*

1. Assam shares land boundary with six North-Eastern states except Sikkim.
2. Uttar Pradesh shares its boundary with the maximum number of Indian states.
3. Telangana is the Southernmost landlocked state of India.

Which of the statements given above are correct?

(a) 1 and 3 (b) Only 1 and 2
(c) 2 and 3 (d) All of these

Ans (d)

Exp. All the statements are correct with reference to the land boundaries of India. Assam shares land boundary with Arunachal Pradesh, Meghalaya, Nagaland, Manipur, Mizoram and Tripura. However, it does not share the boundary with Sikkim.

Uttar Pradesh shares its boundaries with maximum number of Indian states. In the North, Uttar Pradesh shares its border with Uttarakhand and Himachal Pradesh, in the West with Haryana, Delhi, and Rajasthan, in the South with Madhya Pradesh and Chhattisgarh and in the East with Jharkhand and Bihar. Telangana is the Southernmost landlocked state in India situated on the South-Central stretch of the Indian Peninsula on the high Deccan Plateau.

9 With reference to states and Union Territories of India, consider the following statements. *(Chap 1, Class-XI, New NCERT)*

1. After reorganisation of Jammu and Kashmir, Ladakh became the Northernmost landlocked Union Territory of India.
2. Lakshadweep Islands are located in the Arabian Sea nearest to the coast of Karnataka.
3. In North-East India, only Mizoram, Manipur and Nagaland shares its border with Myanmar.

How many of the statements given above is/are incorrect?

(a) Only one (b) Only two (c) All three (d) None of these

Ans. (a)

Exp. Only one statement i.e., (3) is incorrect because four North-Eastern states *viz.* Arunachal Pradesh, Nagaland, Manipur and Mizoram share international boundary with Myanmar.

10 Which one of the following groups of states are the Northernmost, Southernmost, Easternmost and Westernmost landlocked states of India (excluding UTs) having no International Boundaries? *(Chap 1, Class-IX, New NCERT)*

(a) Punjab, Andhra Pradesh, Manipur, Gujarat
(b) Haryana, Telangana, Jharkhand, Madhya Pradesh
(c) Himachal Pradesh, Kerala, Tripura, Rajasthan
(d) Haryana, Andhra Pradesh, Assam, Madhya Pradesh

Ans. (b)

Exp. Haryana, Telangana, Jharkhand, Madhya Pradesh are the landlocked states having no International Boundaries. Among, which Haryana is Northernmost, Telangana is Southernmost, Jharkhand is Easternmost and Madhya Pradesh is Westernmost landlocked states of India. A landlocked state is a state entirely enclosed by land or whose coastlines lie on closed seas.

11 Consider the following statements regarding India's Neighbours. *(Chap 1, Class-IX, New NCERT)*

1. Bangladesh shares 4096 km long International Border with India.
2. The Indian states that shares border with Bangladesh are West Bengal, Assam, Meghalaya and Mizoram.
3. Union Territory Ladakh, shares border with China and Pakistan.

How many of the statements given above is/are correct?

(a) Only one (b) Only two
(c) All three (d) None of these

Ans. (a)

Exp. Only one statement i.e., (1) is correct regarding India's Neighbours.

Bangladesh and India share a 4096 km International Border, which is the fifth-longest land border in the world.

Statements (2) and (3) are incorrect because Bangladesh shares a border with five Indian states Assam, West Bengal, Meghalaya, Mizoram and Tripura.

Ladakh shares its boundaries with Pakistan, Afghanistan and China. Ladakh was administered as part of Jammu and Kashmir state from 1947 until 2019, when it became a separate administrative unit.

12 **Consider the following statements about India's neighbouring countries.** *(Chap 7, Class-VI, New NCERT)*

1. India's shares its international land boundary with seven countries.
2. India's marine border extends with three countries in the Indian Ocean.

Which of the statements given above is/are incorrect?

(a) Only 1 (b) Only 2
(c) Both 1 and 2 (d) Neither 1 nor 2

Ans. (b)

Exp. Statement (2) is incorrect about the India's neighbouring countries because India's marine border extends with two countries in the Indian Ocean. These are Sri Lanka and Maldives. Sri Lanka is separated from India by the Palk Strait.

13 **Consider the following statements.** *(Chap 16, Module-6, NIOS)*

1. A subcontinent is a part of a continent that has distinct geographical, political and cultural identity.
2. The Indian subcontinent consists of seven countries, namely India, Pakistan, Nepal, Bhutan, Bangladesh, Sri Lanka and the Maldives.

Which of the statements given above is/are correct?

(a) Only 1 (b) Only 2
(c) Both 1 and 2 (d) Neither 1 nor 2

Ans. (c)

Exp. Both the statements (1) and (2) are correct. India is called a subcontinent due to its distinct geographical, geological, cultural, historical and socio-economic characteristics that set it apart from the rest of the Asian continent. The term 'subcontinent' refers to a large, separate landmass that is part of a larger continent. The Indian subcontinent consists of India, Bhutan, Maldives, Sri Lanka, Nepal, Bangladesh, and Pakistan. The Indian subcontinent is part of the Asia continent, which is the largest continent in the world.

14 **Which of the following pairs are incorrectly matched?** *(Chap 1, Class-IX, New NCERT)*

States		International Boundary
1. Tripura	–	Myanmar
2. Assam	–	Nepal
3. West Bengal	–	Bhutan

Codes

(a) 1 and 3 (b) 1 and 2
(c) Only 3 (d) All of these

Ans. (b)

Exp. Pairs (1) and (2) are incorrectly matched because Tripura shares its boundary only with Bangladesh and Assam shares its boundary with Bangladesh and Bhutan.

15 **Consider the following statements with reference to the marine borders of India.** *(Chap 1, Class-IX, New NCERT)*

1. The territories of India and Sri Lanka are separated by Palk Strait.
2. The territories of India and Maldives are separated by 10° Channel.

Which of the statements given above is/are incorrect?

(a) Only 1
(b) Only 2
(c) Both 1 and 2
(d) Neither 1 nor 2

Ans. (b)

Exp. Statement (2) is incorrect with reference to the marine borders of India because the maritime boundary between the Maldives and India runs through the 8° Channel. It separates the islands of Minicoy and Maldives.

16 **Which of the following states do not share its border with Myanmar?** *(Chap 1, Class-VI, New NCERT)*

1. Arunachal Pradesh 2. Nagaland
3. Assam 4. Mizoram

Codes

(a) 2 and 3 (b) 1 and 3 (c) Only 3 (d) 1 and 4

Ans. (c)

Exp. Assam does not shares its border with Myanmar. There are four North-Eastern Indian states that share the border with Myanmar i.e., Arunachal Pradesh, Nagaland, Mizoram and Manipur.

17 **Extension of the international boundaries of India along with their neighbouring countries in ascending order are** *(Chap 1, Class-IX, New NCERT) (MPPSC Pre 2016)*

(a) China, Bangladesh, Pakistan, Nepal
(b) Nepal, Pakistan, China, Bangladesh
(c) Nepal, Pakistan, Bangladesh, China
(d) Pakistan, Nepal, China, Bangladesh

Ans. (b)

Exp. Extension of the international boundaries of India along with their neighbouring countries in ascending order are Nepal (1752 km), Pakistan (3310 km), China (3488 km) and Bangladesh (4096 km).

18 Consider the following statements.

(Chap 1, Class-IX, New NCERT) (IAS Pre 2006)

1. Assam shares border with Bhutan and Bangladesh.
2. West Bengal shares border with Bhutan and Nepal.
3. Mizoram shares border with Bangladesh and Myanmar.

Which of the statements given above is/are correct?

(a) 1 and 2
(b) 1 and 3
(c) 2 and 3
(d) All of the above

Ans. (d)

Exp. All the given statements (1), (2) and (3) are correct Assam shares boundary with two countries, Bhutan and Bangladesh. West Bengal shares border with Bangladesh, Bhutan and Nepal. Mizoram shares border with two countries Myanmar and Bangladesh. Mizoram is a landlocked state in North Eastern India. Mizoram's Northern part shares domestic borders with the states of Manipur, Assam and Tripura.

19 Among the following cities, which one lies on a longitude closest to that of Delhi?

(Chap 1, Class-IX, New NCERT)

(a) Bengaluru (b) Hyderabad (c) Nagpur (d) Pune

Ans. (a)

Exp. Bengaluru is lie on a longitude closest to Delhi.
Bengaluru 12 °58′ N, 77 °38′ E.
Hyderabad 17°20′ N, 78°30′ E
Nagpur 21°09′ N, 79°09′ E
Pune 18°31′ N, 73°55′ E

20 The Tropic of Cancer passes through which of the following states? ***(Chap 1, Class-IX, New NCERT)***

1. Gujarat
2. Chhattisgarh
3. Uttar Pradesh
4. Jharkhand

Codes

(a) 1, 2 and 4 (b) 1, 2, 3 and 4 (c) 1, 3 and 4 (d) 2, 3 and 4

Ans. (a)

Exp. The Tropic of Cancer is an imaginary line that passes through eight states in India i.e., Gujarat, Rajasthan, Madhya Pradesh, Chhattisgarh, Jharkhand, West Bengal, Tripura and Mizoram. The Tropic of Cancer's counterpart in the Southern Hemisphere is the Tropic of Capricorn, which is located approximately 23.5° South of the Equator. The area between the Tropic of Cancer and the Tropic of Capricorn is known as the Torrid Zone.

Chapter 17

Geological History and Physiography of India

Geological History and Physiography

Geological History of India

Introduction

- There was a supercontinent Pangea that existed during Paleozoic and mesozoic era, Pangea broke up into two parts - Northern Laurasia and Gondwana land, both of which drifted apart
- Gondwanal and included the Indian subcontinent, which moved entirely into Northern hemisphere whereas Himalayan Mountain chain came from

Geological Structure of India

- India has an assemblage of rocks belonging to different ages ranging from Pre-Cambrian era to recent times. So, geological formations of India are divide into four parts
- **The Archaen Rock System** Rock structure prior to Cambrian system, do not contain fossils thereby depicting the absence of life forms. It includes two rock groups
  - Gneiss and Schist
  - Dharwar system
- **The Purana Rock System** Includes two divisions
  - **Cuddapah System** A thick layer of unfossiliferous clay, slate, sandstone, limestone deposited and first studied in Cuddapah district of Andhra Pradesh
  - **Vindhyan System** Ancient sedimentary rock system standing over Cuddapah rocks, do not have any recognisable fossils. Found in large areas of Madhya Pradesh, Bihar, Rajasthan, etc
- **The Dravidian Rock System** Do not occur in Peninsular plateau but are found in continuous sequence in Himalayas. These rocks contain abundant fossils
- **The Aryan Rock System** Marine sedimentary rocks belonging to late Paleozoic to tertiary periods, occurs in places like Rajasthan, Gujarat, Tamil Nadu, etc

Physical Divisions of India

Introduction

- On the basis of physical features, India is divided into 6 divisions

The Northern Mountains or Himalayas

- Himalayas are the highest mountain range in the world and located between South of Himalayas and North of Peninsular natural barrier
- There are 3 parallel ranges of Himalayas
  - The Greater Himalayas
  - The Lesser Himalayas
  - The Outer Himalayas

The Northern Plains

- These are located between South of Himalayas and North of Peninsular plateau, formed by the deposition of sediments brought by Indus, Ganga and Brahmaputra river systems, making it very fertile
- Major crops like wheat, rice, sugarcane, pulses, etc are grown here

The Peninsular Plateau

- Part of Gondwana land, spread over the states of Gujarat, Maharashtra, Bihar, Karnataka and Andhra Pradesh. It is divided into 2 parts
  - The Central Highlands
  - The Deccan Plateau

The Coastal Plains

- Run parallel to the Arabian Sea and Bay of Bengal along with Peninsular plateau.
- These plains are center for trade and commerce, fishing areas, etc

The Indian Desert

- Lies towards Western margins of Aravalli ranges, a land with undulating topography dotted with barchans. Spread over the states of Gujarat and Rajasthan, region has semi-arid and arid weather conditions

The Islands

- Bay of Bengal Island groups consists of about 572 islands, divided into two broad categories, Andaman and Nicobar
- Arabian sea Island group includes Lakshadweep and Minicoy

SOURCE *Old NCERT Class VIII (India : The Land),* ***New NCERT Class IX*** *(Physical Features of India),* *Old NCERT Class X (Physical Features),* ***New NCERT Class XI*** *(Structure and Physiography),* *Old NCERT Class XII (Natural Resources of India)*

Evolution of India's Geological Structure

1 Consider the following statements with reference to evolution of physiographical structure of India.
(Chap 1, Class-XII, Old NCERT)

1. The Peninsular plateau of India was submerged below the ocean during the Cambrian period.
2. Renewed erosional activity over the Peninsular block has resulted in appearance of youthful features.

Which of the statements given above is/are correct?

(a) Only 1 (b) Only 2
(c) Both 1 and 2 (d) Neither 1 nor 2

Ans. (b)

Exp. Only statement (2) is correct with reference to evolution of physiographical structure of India. Peninsular mountains are young, weak and flexible in their geological structure unlike the rigid and stable Peninsular block. These mountains are tectonic in origin, dissected by fast-flowing rivers, which are in their youthful stage.

Statement (1) is incorrect because since, the Cambrian period, the Peninsula has been standing like a rigid block with the exception of some of its Western coast, which is submerged below the ocean.

2 With reference to geological evolution of various features in India. Consider the following statements.
(Chap 1, Class-XII, Old NCERT)

1. The Himalayan mountains in the North and North-Western India are relatively young as compared to Peninsular block.
2. The region currently occupied by Great plains was originally covered with the Tethys sea.
3. The sediments deposited in the Tethys sea has resulted in uplift of Vindhya mountains in the Peninsula.
4. Himalayas have been formed due to the collision of Indian plate with Eurasian plate.

How many statements given above is/are incorrect?

(a) Only one (b) Only two (c) Only three (c) All four

Ans. (a)

Exp. Statement (3) is incorrect with reference to the geological evolution of various features in India because the sediments deposited in the Tethys sea has resulted in uplift of Himalayan mountains.

The Gondwana land included India, Australia, South Africa, South America and Antarctica as one single landmass.

3 Which of the following forces has led to the evolution and development of various physiographic and geological features of India?
(Chap 1, Class-XII, Old NCERT)

1. Endogenetic forces acting inside Earth's surface.
2. Exogenetic forces over the surface of Earth.
3. Movement of tectonic plates.

Codes

(a) Only 1 (b) Only 2
(c) 1 and 2 (d) 1, 2 and 3

Ans. (d)

Exp. All the given forces led to the evolution and development of various physiographic and geological features of India. The interplay of the endogenic forces acting inside Earth's surface, exogenic forces over the surface of Earth and lateral movements of the plates are responsible for the present physiographic conditions of India.

4 On the basis of physiographical divisions, India has been divided into, which of the following divisions?
(Chap 2, Class-XI, New NCERT)

1. Northern and North-Eastern Mountain chain
2. Northern Plains of India
3. Peninsular Plateau of India
4. Great Indian Desert
5. Islands of India

Codes

(a) 1, 2, 3, 4 (b) 2, 4, 5
(c) 1, 3, 4, 5 (d) 1, 2, 3, 4, 5

Ans. (d)

Exp. All the given options form the basis of physiographical division in India. On the basis of physiographical divisions, India can be divided into the following

1. The Northern and North-Eastern Mountains
2. The Northern Plains
3. The Peninsular Plateau
4. The Indian Desert
5. The Coastal Plains
6. The Islands

Himalayan Mountains

5 If you travel through the Himalayas, you are likely to see which of the following plants naturally growing there?
(Chap 1, Class-XII, Old NCERT), (IAS Pre 2014)

1. Oak
2. Rhododendron
3. Sandalwood

Codes

(a) 1 and 2 (b) 1 and 3
(c) Only 3 (d) 1, 2 and 3

Ans. (a)

Exp. Among the given plants, Oak and Rhododendron are characteristic plants of the Temperate forest.Temperate forests are mainly found in the middle altitudes of the Himalayas.

Oak is a hardwood that is heavy, long-lasting and expensive. Oak is also known for its strength and durability, as well as its high moisture and humidity resistance.Rhododendron is a genus of flowering plants that includes about 1,000 species, primarily native to the temperate regions of Asia, North America, and Europe, as well as to the tropical regions of South-East

Asia and Northern Australia.In India, Pink Rhododendron is the state flower of Himachal Pradesh, while Rhododendron arboreum is the state flower of Nagaland and the official State Tree of Uttarakhand

Statement (3) is incorrect. Sandalwoods are found in tropical deciduous forests or monsoon forests which are found in Western ghats, Deccan plateau, Northern plains and along the foothills of the Himalayas but the presence is 'negligible' and/or confined only to North-Eastern states.

6 Consider the statements with reference to Himalayan mountain ranges. *(Chap 1, Class-XII, Old NCERT)*

1. Himalayas young fold mountains, which extend from Indus in West to Brahmaputra in the East.
2. V shaped valleys and waterfalls are common features found in Himalayas.
3. Volcanic activity is most prominent in Northern Himalayan ranges.
4. Himalayas are geologically unstable as compared to Indian Peninsula.

How many of the statements given above is/are incorrect?

(a) Only one (b) Only two
(c) Only three (d) None of these

Ans. (a)

Exp. Only one statement i.e., (3) is incorrect with reference to Himalayan mountain ranges because volcanic activity is not prominent in Northern Himalayan ranges. Volcanoes are most common in these geologically active boundaries.

The two types of plate boundaries that are most likely to produce volcanic activity are divergent plate boundaries and convergent plate boundaries.

But in India, only active volcano is located in Barren island of Andaman, which is also the only confirmed active volcano in South Asia.

7 Which of the following statements about the geological structure of Himalayan mountain ranges is/are correct? *(Chap 2, Class-XI, New NCERT)*

1. Geological structure of Himalayan mountains is weaker than the structure of the Peninsular block.
2. These mountains have evolved due to tectonic processes, which are still active.

Codes

(a) Only 1 (b) Only 2
(c) Both 1 and 2 (d) Neither 1 nor 2

Ans. (c)

Exp. Both the statements (1) and (2) are correct regarding geological structure of Himalayan mountain ranges because the Himalayas are young, weak and flexible in their geological structure unlike the rigid and stable Peninsular block.

Consequently, these are still subjected to the interplay of exogenic and endogenic forces, resulting in the development of faults, folds and thrust plains. These mountains are tectonic in origins, which are still active.

8 Consider the following statements with reference to North and North-Eastern mountains of India. *(Chap 2, Class-XI, New NCERT)*

1. The Great Himalayan range constitutes the Central Axial range of Northern mountains.
2. The Shiwalik range is the Northernmost range of the Northern mountain chain.
3. The North-South extension of Great Himalaya is lesser than East-West extension.
4. Northern mountain chain separates India from Central and East Asian countries.

How many of the statements given above is/are incorrect?

(a) Only one (b) Only two
(c) Only three (d) All four

Ans. (a)

Exp. Statement (2) is incorrect with reference to North and North-Eastern mountains of India. The Shiwalik range is the outermost range of the Himalayas and the Shiwalik hills. It is also known as Churia hills. This range is stretched from the Indus river to the Brahmaputra river, which spans across the Northern part of the Indian subcontinent. The Northernmost range is the oldest range and it is known as Great Himalayas.

9 Consider the following peaks. *(Chap 1, Class-X, Old NCERT)*

1. Saramati 2. Nokrek
3. Makalu 4. Annapurna
5. Kamet 6. Nanda Devi

Which of the following is the correct sequence of the above peaks in the East to West direction?

(a) 2-1-4-3-5-6 (b) 1-2-3-4-6-5
(c) 2-1-4-3-6-5 (d) 1-2-4-3-6-5

Ans. (b)

Exp. The correct sequence is 1-2-3-4-6-5.

Saramati Peak is situated in the state of Nagaland whereas Nokrek is situated in the state of Meghalaya. Annapurna and Makalu are a part of Nepal, where Makalu is to the East of Annapurna. Kamet peak and Nanda Devi lie in the state of Uttarakhand with Nanda Devi to the East of Kamet. Hence, the correct order from the East to West direction is Saramati, Nokrek, Makalu, Annapurna, Nanda Devi, and Kamet.

10 Consider the following pairs. *(Chap 1, Class-IX, New NCERT)*

	Mountain range		Located between
1	Kumaon Himalayas	–	Sutlej and Kali
2.	Nepal Himalayas	–	Kali and Teesta
3.	Assam Himalayas	–	Teesta and Dihang

How many pairs given above is/are correctly matched?

(a) Only one (b) Only two
(c) Only three (d) None of these

Ans. (c)

Exp. All the given pairs are correctly matched as Kumaon Himalayas, West-Central section of the Himalayas in Northern India, extending 200 miles (320 km) from the Sutlej river in East to the Kali river. The Kali and Teesta rivers divide the Nepal Himalayas and the part lying between Teesta and Dihang rivers is known as Assam Himalayas.

11 **Consider the following relief features.**

(Chap 12, Class-XI, Old NCERT) (JPSC Pre 2013)

1. Zaskar range 2. Dhauladhar range
3. Ladakh range 4. Karakoram range

The correct South to the Northward sequence of the above relief features is

(a) 2, 1, 3, 4 (b) 2, 3, 4, 1
(c) 4, 3, 2, 1 (d) 4, 2, 1, 3

Ans. (a)

Exp. From South to Northward, the correct sequence of given options is Dhauladhar range, Zaskar (Zanskar) range, Ladakh range and Karakoram range. Karakoram, Ladakh and Zaskar ranges are related to trans Himalayas while Dhauladhar range is situated in Lesser or Middle Himalayas.

12 **Consider the following statements with reference to Kashmir Himalayas.** *(Chap 2, Class-XI, New NCERT)*

1. North-Eastern part of Kashmir Himalayas is a cold desert.
2. Valley of Kashmir lies between Pir Panjal and Ladakh range.
3. Karewa formations are found in various parts of Kashmir Himalayas.
4. Baltoro is an important glacier found in Kashmir Himalayas.

How many of the statements given above is/are incorrect?

(a) Only one (b) Only Two
(c) Only three (d) All four

Ans. (a)

Exp. Only one statement i.e., (2) is incorrect with reference to Kashmir Himalayas because Kashmir Valley is located between Pir Panjal and Zaskar range (not Ladakh range).

13 **Consider the following Assertion (A) and Reason (R) and choose the correct code.**

(Chap 2, Class-XI, New NCERT)

Assertion (A) The North-Eastern part of Kashmir Himalayas forms a cold desert region.

Reason (R) Jhelum river in Kashmir valley is in its youthful stage still forms meanders.

Codes

(a) Both A and R are true, and R is the correct explanation of A.
(b) Both A and R are true, but R is not the correct explanation of A.
(c) A is correct, R is incorrect.
(d) Both A and R are incorrect.

Ans. (b)

Exp. Both Assertion (A) and Reason (R) are true but Reason (R) is not the correct explanation of Assertion (A).

The North-Eastern part of the Kashmir Himalayas is a cold desert, which lies between the Greater Himalayas and the Karakoram ranges. It comprises a series of ranges such as the Karakoram, Ladakh, Zaskar and Pir Panjal. Jhelum is in youth stage and yet it forms meanders – a typical feature associated with the mature stage in the evolution of fluvial landform. In Kashmir valley, the meanders in Jhelum river are caused by the local base level provided by the erstwhile larger lake of, which the present Dal lake is a small part.

14 **Consider the following statements with reference to Greater Himalayan mountain range.**

(Chap 12, Class-XII, Old NCERT)

1. The average altitude of this range is over 6000 m.
2. World's highest peaks are found on this mountain range, which form many glaciers.
3. The core of this range is made up of granite.

How many of the statements given above is/are incorrect?

(a) One only (b) Two only
(c) All three (d) None of these

Ans. (c)

Exp. All the given statements are correct with reference to Greater Himalayan mountain range.

Great Himalayas, also called Higher Himalayas or Great Himalaya Range, are the highest and Northernmost section of the Himalayan mountain ranges. The range's total length is some 1,400 miles (2,300 km), and it has an average elevation of more than 20,000 feet (6,100 m). The Great Himalayas contain many of the world's tallest peaks, including (from West to East) Nanga Parbat, Annapurna, Mount Everest and Kanchenjunga. The core of the Himalayan mountain range is made up of granite.

15 **Consider the following statements with reference to Himalayan mountain ranges.**

(Chap 5, Class-XII, Old NCERT)

1. Baltoro and Siachen glaciers are located in the Greater Himalayan region.
2. Kashmir Valley is located between Ladakh range and Greater Himalayan range.

Which of the statements given above is/are correct?

(a) Only 1 (b) Only 2
(c) Both 1 and 2 (d) Neither 1 nor 2

Ans. (a)

Exp. Statement (1) is correct with reference to the Himalayan mountain ranges because glaciers, which are present in Greater Himalaya are Baltoro, Gangotri, Yamunotri, Siachen, etc.

Statement (2) is incorrect because Kashmir valley is located between Pir Panjal and Zaskar range.

16 Which of the following pairs is/are correctly matched? *(Chap 2, Class-XI, New NCERT)*

Mountain Pass		Located on
1. Banihal Pass	–	Pir Panjal range
2. Photu La	–	Dhauladhar range
3. Khardung La	–	Ladakh range

Codes

(a) Only 1 (b) Only 3 (c) 1 and 2 (d) 1 and 3

Ans. ***(d)***

Exp. Pairs (1) and (3) are correctly matched because Banihal Pass is located in Pir Panjal range. It connects the Kashmir valley in the Union Territory of Jammu and Kashmir to the outer Himalaya and the plains to the South.

Khardung La pass is present in Ladakh range. It connects Leh and Nubra valley and also serves as a gateway to the famous Siachen Glacier.

Pair (2) is not correctly matched because Photu La is located in Zaskar range (not Dhauladhar range). It connects Leh with Kargil of Ladakh.

17 Consider the following statements about Karewa formations. *(Chap 2, Class-XI, New NCERT)*

1. Karewas are thick deposits of glacial clay and other materials, which are embedded in moraines.
2. Karewa formations are famous for cultivation of apple in Kashmir.

Which of the statements given above is/are incorrect?

(a) Only 1 (b) Only 2
(c) Both 1 and 2 (d) Neither 1 nor 2

Ans. ***(b)***

Exp. Statement (2) is incorrect about the Karewa formations as these are famous for variety of saffron, which is locally known as Zafron. These are composed of sand, silt, clay, shale, mud, lignite, gravel and loessic sediments.

Therefore, it is extremely important for agricultural and horticultural practices in the valley. It also helps in the cultivation of almond, walnut, apple and orchards.

18 Which one of the following geographical regions is the oldest in the country? *(Chap 1, Class-XI, New NCERT) (CGPSC Pre 2017)*

(a) Himalayan Mountainous Region
(b) Great Plains of North India
(c) Indian Peninsular Plateau
(d) Eastern Coastal Plains

Ans. ***(c)***

Exp. Among the given options, Indian Peninsular Plateau is the oldest geographical region in the country. Himalayas are newly developed folded mountain. Eastern crustal plains are a wide stretch of landmass of India, lying between the Eastern ghats and Bay of Bengal.

19 Which one of the following is the youngest mountain range of India? *(Chap 2, Class-XI, New NCERT) (UPPSC Pre 2020)*

(a) Himadri range (b) Aravalli range
(c) Western ghat (d) Vindhya range

Ans. ***(a)***

Exp. Among the given options, Himadri range is the youngest mountain range of India. It is also an example of new folded mountain. Himadri range is located in the physiography of Uttarakhand. Aravalli range is the old mountain range in India. Vindhya range is a block mountain range in India. Western ghats also known as Sahyadri. They are Block mountains.

20 Valley of Kashmir is situated between *(Chap 1, Class-XI, Old NCERT) (UPPSC Pre 2020)*

(a) Kangra and Dhauladhar ranges
(b) Pir Panjal and Himadri ranges
(c) Mahabharat and Dhauladhar ranges
(d) Pir Panjal and Mahabharat ranges

Ans. ***(b)***

Exp. Valley of Kashmir is situated between Pir Panjal and Himadri ranges. It is bounded on South-west by Pir Panjal range and on the North-East by Great Himalayan range. Pir Panjal range is located in Middle Himalayas. It is spread in Himachal Pradesh and Jammu and Kashmir. Kangra valley extends from foot of Dhauladhar range to the South of river Beas. Mahabharat range is the inner mountain range of Himalayas.

21 Consider the following statements with reference to Lesser Himalayan mountain range. *(Chap 2, Class-XI, New NCERT)*

1. They are known as Dhauladhar in Himachal Pradesh and Nagtibha in Uttarakhand.
2. Most of the hill stations have been developed on the lesser Himalayan Range.
3. Lesser Himalayas are characterised by average altitude of 1200 m.

How many of the statements given above is/are correct?

(a) One only (b) Only two
(c) All three (d) None of these

Ans. ***(c)***

Exp. All the given statements are correct regarding the Lesser Himalayan mountain range. The Lesser Himalayas (average altitude of 1200 m) are also known as Lower Himalayas or the Himachal. It lies between the Greater Himalayas or Himadri and the Outer Himalayas or the Shiwaliks. Most of the hill stations have been developed on the Lesser Himalayan Range.

The Lesser Himalayas run approximately parallel to both of these ranges. Lesser Himalayas are characterised by average altitude of 1200m.

22 Consider the following statements.

(Chap 2, Class-XI, New NCERT)

1. Duar formations in Eastern Himalayas have led to the development of tea gardens.
2. Dehradun is the largest of all Dun formations in the Himalayan region.
3. Duns and Duar formations are the most prominent in the Karakoram range.

How many of the statements given above is/are incorrect?

(a) Only one (b) Only two
(c) All three (d) None of these

Ans. (a)

Exp. Only one statement i.e., (3) is incorrect because the Duns or Duars are the valleys found in the Shiwalik range (not Karakoram range). These are open valleys between the Shiwalik and the higher Himalayan foothills.

These Duns are longitudinal valleys, which are formed due to folding, which occurs when the Eurasian and the Indian plate collide with each other.

These valleys have deposits of coarse alluvium, which is brought down by the Himalayan rivers.

23 Consider the following statements regarding the Middle Himalayas. *(Chap 5, Class-XII, Old NCERT)*

1. The Middle Himalayas have been formed by consolidation and compaction of sediments brought down by the rivers in Greater Himalayas.
2. The average altitude of Middle Himalayas is 1000 m above the sea level.

Which of the statements given above is/are incorrect?

(a) Only 1 (b) Only 2
(c) Both 1 and 2 (d) Neither 1 nor 2

Ans. (b)

Exp. Statement (2) is incorrect regarding the Middle Himalayas. The Middle Himalayas lies in between the Shiwaliks in the South and the Greater Himalayas in the North. It runs almost parallel to both the ranges. It is also called the Himachal or Lower Himalayas. Lower Himalayan ranges are 60-80 km wide and about 2400 km in length. Elevations vary from 3,500 to 4,500 m above sea level.

24 Consider the following statements with reference to Darjeeling and Sikkim Himalayas.

(Chap 2, Class-XI, New NCERT)

1. The higher regions of this region is inhabited by Lepcha tribes.
2. They are flanked by Bhutan Himalayas in the East.
3. Kangchenjunga mountain peak is in Himalayas.

How many of the statements given above is/are correct?

(a) Only one (b) Only two
(c) All three (d) None of these

Ans. (c)

Exp. All the given statements are correct regarding the Darjeeling and Sikkim Himalayas as the higher regions of this region are inhabited by Lepcha tribes while the Southern part, particularly the Darjeeling Himalayas, has a mixed population of Nepalis, Bengalis and tribals from Central India.

They are flanked by Nepal Himalayas in the West and Bhutan Himalayas in the East. It is relatively small but it is a most significant part of the Himalayas known for its fast-flowing rivers such as Teesta. It is a region of high mountain peaks like Kangchenjunga (Kanchengiri) and deep valleys.

25 Consider the following statements regarding International borders. *(Chap 1, Class-X, Old NCERT)*

1. Mizoram and Nagaland share a border with Myanmar only.
2. Sikkim is the only state forming an international boundary on the three sides.
3. Tripura forms the longest boundary with Bangladesh.

Which of the statements given above is/are incorrect?

(a) Only 3 (b) 2 and 3 (c) Only 2 (d) All of these

Ans. (d)

Exp. All the statements are incorrect.

Manipur and Nagaland are the states that share borders with Myanmar only while Mizoram shares borders with both Myanmar and Bangladesh.

Sikkim, Tripura and Mizoram are the states that form international boundaries on the three sides. Sikkim is bordered by Tibet, Nepal and Bhutan whereas Tripura is surrounded by Bangladesh from three sides.

West Bengal forms the longest international boundary with Bangladesh. Besides, West Bengal, Meghalaya, Assam, Tripura and Mizoram also share a boundary with Bangladesh.

26 Consider the following statements regarding Hill Ranges. *(Chap 1, Class-X, Old NCERT) (Chap 2, Module-2, NIOS)*

1. The Himalayas in the North-East India are continuously aligned in the North to South direction.
2. Meghalaya and the Karbi Anglong hills are the extension of Deccan Plateau.
3. Duar formations in the Sikkim region is an extension of the Shiwalik.

How many of the statements given above is/are correct?

(a) Only one (b) Only two
(c) All three (d) None of these

Ans. (d)

Exp. All the given statements are incorrect.

The Himalayas in the North-Western region are aligned in the North-West to South-East direction while the Himalayas in the North-Eastern region are not continuous and aligned in various directions. Darjeeling and Sikkim in the North-East direction. Arunachal Pradesh in the South-West to North-East direction. Nagaland, Manipur and Mizoram in the North south direction.

Meghalaya and the Karbi Anglong hills in Assam are an extension of the Peninsular Plateau. They are a part of the North-Eastern Plateau and not the Deccan Plateau.

Darjeeling, Sikkim and the Arunachal Himalayas are different from the rest as there is an absence of Shiwalik in these areas. In place of Shiwalik, duar formations are found in these areas which are used for the cultivation of the plantation crops. Hence, Duar are different from Shiwaliks and not an extension of it.

27 Which of the following pairs is/are not matched correctly? *(Chap 1, Class-XI, New NCERT)*

Mountain Peaks		Mountain Ranges
1. Kanchenjunga	–	Sikkim Himalayas
2. Namcha Barwa	–	Kashmir Himalayas
3. Badrinath	–	Uttarakhand Himalayas

Codes

(a) 1, 2 and 3 (b) 1 and 3 (c) Only 2 (d) 1 and 2

Ans. (c)

Exp. Pair (2) is not matched correctly because Namcha Barwa is located in Arunachal Himalayas (not Kashmir Himalayas).

28 Mizoram is also known as 'molasse basin'. Consider the following statements. *(Chap 2, Class-XI, New NCERT)*

1. It is made up of ancient granitic rocks over millions of years.
2. It is made up of basaltic rocks deposited due to cooling of magma on Earth's surface during ancient times.
3. It is made up of soft and unconsolidated deposits brought down by various rivers and their tributaries.
4. It is made up of hard igneous rocks, which consists of huge mineral reserves.

How many of the statements given above is/are correct?

(a) Only one (b) Only two
(c) All three (d) All four

Ans. (a)

Exp. Only one statement i.e., (3) is correct with reference to the fact that Mizoram is known as molasse basin because it is made up of soft and unconsolidated deposits brought down by various rivers and their tributaries. It is also known Land of Rolling Mountains. They are not made up of granite rocks, they made up of sandstones and conglomerates.

29 Arrange the following hills of Purvanchal Himalaya in correct order from South to North and choose the correct answer using the codes given below. *(Chap 2, Class-XI, New NCERT)*

1. Manipur hills 2. Naga hills
3. Patkai bum hills 4. Mizo hills

Codes

(a) 2, 3, 1, 4 (b) 3, 2, 1, 4 (c) 2, 1, 3, 4 (d) 3, 1, 2, 4

Ans. (b)

Exp. The arrangement of Purvanchal hills from South to North is Patkai Bum hills, Naga hills, Manipur hills and Mizo hills.

Purvanchal mountain range is also called Eastern highlands in Eastern India. They extend over an area of about 37,900 square miles (98,000 square km) in Arunachal Pradesh, Nagaland, Manipur, Mizoram, Tripura and Eastern Assam states.

30 Match the following lists correctly and choose the correct code. *(Chap 2, Class-IX, New NCERT)*

List I (Peaks)	List II (Altitude)
A. Kangchenjunga	1. 8586 m
B. Dhaulagiri	2. 8167 m
C. Nanga Parbat	3. 8126 m
D. Namcha Barwa	4. 7782 m

Codes

	A	B	C	D		A	B	C	D
(a)	1	2	3	4	(b)	1	4	2	3
(c)	2	1	4	3	(d)	3	1	2	4

Ans. (a)

Exp. The correct matching is A-1, B-2, C-3, D-4.

Kangchenjunga is the third highest mountain in the world. It rises with an elevation of 8586 m.

Dhaulagiri is the seventh highest mountain in the world at elevation of 8,167 m.

Nanga Parbat is also known locally as Diamer. It is the ninth highest mountain in the world at the height of 8,126 m.

Namcha Barwa with height of 7,782 m is an Easternmost syntaxis of Himalaya.

31 Match the following lists correctly and choose the correct code. *(Chap 2, Class-XI, New NCERT)*

List I (Mountain Ranges)	List II (States)
A. Dafla hills	1. Arunachal Pradesh
B. Khasi hills	2. Meghalaya
C. Lushai hills	3. Mizoram
D. Barail range	4. Assam

Codes

	A	B	C	D		A	B	C	D
(a)	1	2	3	4	(b)	1	4	2	3
(c)	2	1	4	3	(d)	3	1	2	4

Ans. (a)

Exp. The correct matching is A-1, B-2, C-3, D-4.

Dafla or Daphla hills is a tract of hilly country on the border of Western Arunachal and Assam occupied by an independent tribe called Daphla.

Khasi hills is a low mountain formation on the Shillong Plateau in Meghalaya state of India.

Lushai hills are a mountain range in Mizoram and Manipur, India.

Barail range is a tertiary mountain range in North-East India located in Dima Hasao district of Assam.

Northern Plains

32 Consider the following statements with reference to Ganga-Brahmaputra plains. *(Chap 1, Class-X, Old NCERT)*

1. It was formed out of Tethys Geosynclinal depression, which was formed 64 million years ago.
2. The maximum depth of Northern plains of India is 1000-2000 m.

Which of the statements given above is/are correct?

(a) Both 1 and 2
(b) Only 2
(c) Only 1
(d) None of these

Ans. (a)

Exp. Both the statements (1) and (2) are correct with reference to the Ganga-Brahmaputra plains.

The formation of Indo-Gangetic plain is closely related to the formation of Himalayas. The rivers, which were previously flowing into Tethys sea deposited huge amount of sediments in the Tethys Geosyncline. From these sediment deposits, the Himalayan mountains and the Ganga-Brahmaputra Plains formed around 64 million years ago.

Indo-Gangetic-Brahmaputra Plain is the largest alluvial tract of the world. The maximum depth of Northern plains of India is 1000-2000 m.

33 Consider the following statements with reference to North Indian plains. *(Chap 8, Class-XII, Old NCERT)*

1. Rivers flow at a faster rate in the lower regions of the Northern Plains of India.
2. These plains are made up of red and yellow soil.
3. These plains are highly fertile and most densely populated regions of India.
4. Rivers draining the Northern plains form cataracts and rapids in this region.

How many of the statements given above is/are correct?

(a) Only one (b) Only two (c) Only three (d) All four

Ans. (a)

Exp. Only one statement i.e., (3) is correct with reference to North Indian plains. These plains lie in the South of Himalayas mountains and North of Deccan plateau. They are are highly fertile and most densely populated region in India. These are drained by many other rivers like Yamuna, Ghaghara, Gandak etc.

These are perennial rivers, which flow throughout the year, which helps plains to maintain their fertility. Thus, soil of these plains is highly fertile.

Statements (1), (2) and (4) are incorrect because rivers in the lower regions of the Northern plains flow at a slow rate. In mountainous areas, rivers flow at the faster rate. In these plains, alluvial soil is found not red and yellow soil. It has the largest tract of 2400 km of alluvial soil in the world. Also cataracts and rapids are formed in mountainous regions not in Northern plains.

34 Consider the following statements with reference to the Great Plains of India. *(Chap 2, Class-XI, New NCERT)*

1. Bhabhar zone runs along the foothills of Himadri and consists of marshy and swampy soil.
2. Khadar plains are characterised by deposition of new alluvium every year.
3. Bhangar plains are characterised by deposition of calcereous deposits, known as Kankars.

Which of statements given above is/are incorrect?

(a) Only 1
(b) 2 and 3
(c) 1 and 3
(d) 1, 2 and 3

Ans. (a)

Exp. Statement (1) is incorrect with reference to the Great Plains in India because Bhabhar zone lies along the foothills of the Shiwaliks from the Indus to the Teesta. It is about 8-16 km wide. The rivers descending from the Himalayas deposit their loads along the foothills in the form of alluvial fans.

35 Consider the following statements regarding alluvial plains. *(Chap 2, Class-XI, New NCERT)* *(Unit 3, Class-XI Tamil Nadu Board)*

1. Bhabar areas are more suitable for crop cultivation than Terai.
2. Khadar sediments are deposited near the flood plains.

Which of the statements given above is/are correct?

(a) Only 1
(b) Only 2
(c) Both 1 and 2
(d) Neither 1 nor 2

Ans. (b)

Exp. Statement (2) is correct. The alluvial plains are subdivided into Khadar and Bhangar. Bhangar are the older alluvium and are deposited away from the flood plains of the rivers. Khadar are the new alluvium deposits which are subjected to frequent flooding and deposited near the flood plains. Hence, they are more fertile with finer silt deposition.

Statement (1) is incorrect because Bhabar is a narrow area running parallel to the foothills of the Shiwalik. It is located at the end of its slope and hence river deposits are associated with this area. The streams or rivers usually disappear in this area. Terai areas are found South of the Bhabar areas and the streams or rivers emerge in these areas. Hence, Terai areas are more suitable for the cultivation of crops as compared to Bhabar.

36 **Which of the given pairs is not matched correctly?** *(Chap 5, Class-XII, Old NCERT)*

(a) Bari Doab-between Beas and Ravi
(b) Bisht Doab-between Beas and Chenab
(c) Rachna Doab-between Ravi and Chenab
(d) Jech Doab-between Chenab and Jhelum

Ans. (b)

Exp. Pair (b) is not correctly matched because the Bisht Doab is a triangular region and covers an area of 9060 sq km. Bisht Doab lies between Beas and Sutlej.

37 **Consider the following statements about Sunderban delta.** *(Chap 2, Class-XI, New NCERT)*

1. The Sunderban delta is a featureless plain, formed by the Northern rivers, with an average elevation of 50-150 metres.
2. The Majuli Island is the largest riverine island located in the Sunderban delta.

Which of the statements given above is/are correct?

(a) Both 1 and 2 (b) Only 1
(c) Only 2 (d) Neither 1 nor 2

Ans. (b)

Exp. Statement (1) is correct about Sunderban delta. Sunderban delta or Bengal delta is the world's largest delta with an average elevation of 50-150 metres. It is also known as Ganga-Brahmaputra delta as it is formed by these two major rivers of India. It is formed in the region of Bangladesh and West Bengal, India.

The Delta stretches from the Hooghly river on the West to the Meghna river on the East. The Sunderban delta got its name from the Sundari tree, which fills well in bogland. It is the world's biggest and quickest developing delta.

Statement (2) is not correct because Majuli Island is the largest riverine island in the world, located on the Brahmaputra river in Assam.

Peninsular Plateau

38 **Consider the following statements with reference to Indian Peninsular block.** *(Chap 2, Class-XI, New NCERT)*

1. Geologically, the Karbi Anglong Plateau and Meghalaya Plateau do not form a part of the Indian Peninsular block.
2. The Peninsular block is made up of a great complex of ancient gneisses and granites and its North Western part is made up of volcanic rocks.
3. The North-Eastern parts are separated by Koyna fault from the Chhota Nagpur plateau.
4. There have been no faulting activities in the Peninsular block since its rifting from the Australian plate.

Which of the statements given above is the most appropriate option?

(a) Only 1 (b) Only 2 (c) Only 3 (d) Only 4

Ans. (b)

Exp. Statement (2) is correct with reference to the Peninsular block in India. The Peninsula is formed essentially by a great complex of very ancient gneisses and granites, which constitutes a major part of it and its North-Western part is made up of volcanic rocks.

Statements (1), (3) and (4) are incorrect because geologically, the Karbi Anglong Plateau and Meghalaya Plateau form a part of the Indian Peninsular block.

The North-Eastern parts are separated by Koyna fault from the Peninsular plateau. Continuously, there have been faulting activities in the Peninsular block since its rifting from the Australian plate.

39 **Consider the following statements about Peninsular block of India.** *(Chap 1, Class-X, Old NCERT)*

1. Karbi Anglong Plateau and Meghalaya Plateau in North-East India are extensions of Peninsular block.
2. The North-Eastern extension of this block is separated by Koyna Fault.

Which of the statements given above is/are correct?

(a) Only 1 (b) Only 2
(c) Both 1 and 2 (d) Neither 1 and 2

Ans. (a)

Exp. Statement (1) is correct about Peninsular block of India.

Karbi-Meghalaya plateau is an extension of the main Indian peninsular plateau.

The Meghalaya plateau is traditionally divided into Garo, Khasi and Jaintia hills.

Statement (2) is incorrect because the North-Eastern parts of India are separated by the Malda fault in West Bengal from the Chhota Nagpur plateau.

40 **Consider the following statements with reference to Indian Peninsula.** *(Chap 2, Class-XI, New NCERT)*

1. The Delhi ridge forms North-Western boundary of the Indian Peninsula whereas the Malwa plateau forms the Eastern boundary.
2. Seismic activities are completely absent from the Indian Peninsula.
3. The Patland plateaus are geologically the parts of the Indian Peninsular region.
4. The Indian Peninsula was once a part of the Angara land, which split up due to plate tectonics.

How many of the statements given above is/are correct?

(a) Only one (b) Only two
(c) Only three (d) All four

Ans. (a)

Exp. Only one statement i.e., (3) is correct about Indian Peninsula, as The patland plateau are geology the parts of the This plateau consists of series of step like sub-plateaus (locally called patlands – high-level plateau). It is thus famous as the Patland plateau and known as Ruhr of India. Chhota Nagpur plateau – the

North-East part of Peninsular plateau includes Jharkhand, parts of Chhattisgarh and West Bengal. Rajmahal hills are the North-Eastern projection of Chota Nagpur Plateau. It is a mineral rich plateau.

41 Consider the following physiographic features. *(Chap 2, Class-XI, New NCERT)*

1. Tors
2. Spurs
3. Block Mountains

Which of the feature/features given above is/are found in Peninsular plateau of India?

(a) 1 and 3 (b) Only 3
(c) 2 and 3 (d) 1, 2 and 3

Ans. (d)

Exp. All the given physiographic features are found in the Peninsular plateau. It is composed of the oldest rocks because it was formed from the drifted part of the Gondwana land.

42 Consider the given statements with reference to Peninsular plateau. *(Chap 5, Class-XII, Old NCERT)*

1. It has been subjected to various faulting and vertical movements.
2. It consists of deep gorges in its North-Western part.
3. Black soil has developed in this division due to denudation of volcanic lava.
4. The Deccan plateau in this region is also known as central highlands.

How many of the statements given above is/are incorrect?

(a) Only one (b) Only two
(c) Only three (d) All four

Ans. (a)

Exp. Only one statement i.e., (2) is incorrect regarding the Peninsular plateau as it is made up of various faulting and vertical movements and a series of patland plateaus such as the Hazaribagh plateau, the Palamu plateau, the Ranchi plateau, the Malwa plateau, the Coimbatore plateau and the Karnataka plateau, etc. This is one of the oldest and the most stable landmass of India.

The Western and North-Western part of the plateau has an emphatic presence of black soil.

43 Consider the following statements with reference to Deccan plateau. *(Chap 1, Class-X, Old NCERT)*

1. The Deccan plateau is separated from the Northern Plains by the Satpuras, Maikal range and Mahadeo hills.
2. The Deccan plateau is highest in the Western part, and slopes towards the Bay of Bengal in the East.

Which of the statements given above is/are correct?

(a) Only 1 (b) Only 2
(c) Both 1 and 2 (d) Neither 1 nor 2

Ans. (c)

Exp. Both the statements (1) and (2) are correct with reference to Deccan plateau. The Deccan plateau is separated from the Northern plains by the Satpuras, Maikal and Mahadeo Hills.

The Deccan plateau is a high plateau in Western and Southern India. The plateau is divided into two parts called Malnad and Maidan. The Malnad in Kannada means hill country, It is dissected into deep valleys covered with dense forests.

The Maidan on the other hand is formed of rolling plain with low granite hills. It is separated from the Gangetic plain to the North by the Satpura and Vindhya ranges, which form its Northern boundary.

The Deccan plateau is highest in the Western part, and slopes towards the Bay of Bengal in the East because the Deccan plateau is higher in the West and slopes gently Eastwards.

44 With reference to hill ranges of Peninsular India. Consider the following statements. *(Chap 2, Class-XI, New NCERT)*

1. The Eastern Ghats are higher and more continuous than the Western Ghats.
2. The highest peak of Peninsular mountains is located in the Western Ghats.
3. The Eastern and Western Ghats meet at the Palni hills.
4. Most of the rivers of Peninsular region originate in the Eastern Ghats.

How many of the statements given above is/are correct?

(a) Only one (b) Only two
(c) Only three (d) All four

Ans. (a)

Exp. Only one statement i.e., (2) is correct with reference to the hill ranges of Peninsular India because the highest peak of Peninsular mountains is Anaimudi located in the Western ghats.

Statements i.e., (1), (3) and (4) are incorrect because Eastern ghats are discontinuous and low-height mountain ranges. Western Ghats are higher and more continuous than the Western Ghats. The Eastern and Western Ghats meet at Nilgiri hills (not Palni hills).

The meeting point of the Eastern Ghats and the Western Ghats is the Nilgiri plateau and most of the rivers of Peninsular region originate in the Western Ghats.

Most of the rivers (such as Mahanadi, Godavari, Krishna, Kaveri, etc) of Peninsular region originate in Western Ghats.

45 Consider the following ranges/mountains: *(Chap 2, Class-XI, New NCERT)*

1. Harishchandra
2. Nallamala
3. Dandakaranya
4. Ramgarh
5. Malya giri
6. Garhjat

Arrange the above ranges in the South-North direction.

(a) 2-3-1-6-5-4 (b) 2-1-3-4-6-5
(c) 2-1-3-5-6-4 (d) 1-2-4-3-6-5

Ans. (c)

Exp. The correct arranging of ranges from South-North direction is 2-1-3-5-6-4 i.e., Nallamala<Harishchandra range<Dandakaranya<Malyagiri hills<Garhjat range<Ramgarh hills.

Harishchandra range is located in the state of Maharashtra.

Nallamala hills form a part of the Eastern Ghats in Andhra Pradesh,

Dandakaranya is associated with Odisha, Chhattisgarh, Telangana and Andhra Pradesh, Ramgarh hills are found in the state of Jharkhand.

Malyagiri hills are located in the state of Odisha, and Garhjat range are the mountain ranges stretching across Odisha, Jharkhand and Chhattisgarh.

46 **The Peninsular plateau of India consists of, which of the following plateaus?** *(Chap 3, Class-XII, Old NCERT)*

1. Malwa plateau
2. Hazaribagh plateau
3. Palamu plateau
4. Karnataka plateau

Codes

(a) 1, 2 and 3 (b) 2 and 4
(c) 1 and 4 (d) 1, 2, 3 and 4

Ans. (d)

Exp. The Peninsular plateau in India consists of a series of patland plateaus such as the Hazaribagh plateau, the Palamu plateau, the Ranchi plateau, the Malwa plateau, the Coimbatore plateau and the Karnataka plateau, etc.

47 **Match the following lists correctly and choose the correct code.** *(Chap 2, Class-XI, New NCERT)*

List I (Peninsular Hills)	List II (States)
A. Nilgiri hills	1. Karnataka
B. Anaimalai hills	2. Maharashtra
C. Sahyadri	3. Kerala

Codes

	A	B	C		A	B	C
(a)	1	2	3	(b)	1	3	2
(c)	2	1	3	(d)	3	1	2

Ans. (b)

Exp. The correct matching is A-1, B-3, C-2.

Nilgiri hills, one of the oldest mountain ranges, located at the tri-junction of Tamil Nadu, Kerala and Karnataka.

Anaimalai hills is located in both Tamil Nadu and Kerala state. Anaimudi Peak is the highest peak in Southern India.

Sahyadri is located in Maharashtra. The Western Ghats, also called the Sahyadri, are a North-South chain of mountains or hills that mark the Western edge of the Deccan plateau region.

48 **Consider the following statements regarding mountain ranges and faults.** *(Chap 2, Class-XI, New NCERT)*

1. All the rivers of the Central Highlands originate in the Vindhya and Satpura ranges.
2. Malda fault exists between the Malwa plateau and the Shillong plateau.

Which of the statements given above is/are incorrect?

(a) Only 1 (b) Only 2
(c) Both 1 and 2 (d) Neither 1 nor 2

Ans. (c)

Exp. Both the statements are incorrect. Vindhya and Kaimur range are the source of origin of several rivers. Most of the tributaries of Yamuna originate from here. However, Banas river originates from the Aravallis and is an exception here.

Malda fault exists between the Rajmahal Hills/Chhota Nagpur plateau and the Meghalaya/Shillong plateau. It is responsible for the detachment of the North-Eastern plateau from the Deccan plateau. The North-Eastern plateau consists of Garo, Khasi, Jaintia hills in Meghalaya and the Karbi Anglong hills of Assam.

49 **Consider the following statements about Central Highlands.** *(Chap 2, Class-XI, New NCERT)*

1. Satpura range is formed by series of scarped plateaus in the South of Central highlands.
2. The Western margins are covered with crescent shaped sand dunes known as Barchans.
3. This region has remained untouched from the metamorphic proces< s.

Which of the statements given above is/are correct?

(a) 1 and 2 (b) 1 and 3
(c) 2 and 3 (d) 1, 2 and 3

Ans. (a)

Exp. Statements (1) and (2) are correct regarding the Central Highlands. The Central Highlands are bounded to the West by the Aravalli range.

The Satpura range is formed by a series of scarped plateaus on the South, generally at an elevation varying between 600-900 m above the mean sea level.

The extension of the Peninsular plateau can be seen as far as Jaisalmer in the West, where it has been covered by the longitudinal sand ridges and crescent-shaped sand dunes called barchans.

Statement (3) is incorrect because this region has undergone metamorphic processes in its geological history, which can be corroborated by the presence of metamorphic rocks such as marble, slate, gneiss, etc.

50 **Consider the following statements regarding Ghats and Plateaus.** *(Chap 1, Class-IX, NCERT)*

1. The elevation of Western ghats increases southwards.
2. Eastern ghats are continuous with lower elevation.

3. Bundelkhand forms the upper part of the Deccan Plateau.

How many of the statements given above is/are correct?

(a) Only one (b) Only two
(c) Only three (d) None of these

Ans. (a)

Exp. Only one statement i.e., (1) is correct. Western ghats are continuous with higher elevation as compared to Eastern ghats. The height of the Western ghats increases southwards with the highest peak Anamudi (Kerala) located on the Annamalai hills of the Western Ghats.
Statements (2) and (3) are incorrect. Eastern ghats are discontinuous and lower in elevation as compared to the Western ghats. It is highly eroded and eastwards flowing rivers like Mahanadi, Godavari, Krishna, Kaveri forms delta.
Bundelkhand region forms a part of the Central Highlands of the Peninsular plateau and not the Deccan plateau.The region is associated with the states of Uttar Pradesh and Madhya Pradesh.

51 Consider the following statements with reference to Meghalaya plateau. *(Chap 2, Class-XI, Old NCERT)* *(BPSC Pre 2018)*

1. Meghalaya plateau is sub-divided into - Garo, Khasi and Jaintia hills.
2. Rajmahal hills are eastward extension of the Meghalaya plateau.
3. Meghalaya plateau is a highly eroded landmass, which occurs due to fluvial erosion.

Which of the statements given above is/are correct?

(a) 1 and 2 (b) 2 and 3 (c) 1 and 3 (d) 1, 2 and 3

Ans. (c)

Exp. Statements (1) and (3) are correct with reference to Meghalaya plateau.
The Meghalaya plateau is subdivided into Garo, Khasi and Jaintia hills, which are named after the tribal groups inhabiting this region. Meghalaya plateau is a highly eroded landmass, which occurs due to fluvial erosion.
Statement (2) is incorrect because a huge fault was created between the Rajmahal hills and the Meghalaya plateau. Hence, Rajmahal hills are not the eastward extension of the Meghalaya plateau.

52. Which of the given pairs is/are not correctly matched? *(Chap 5, Class-XII, Old NCERT)*

1.	Thalghat gap	–	Maharashtra
2.	Bhorghat gap	–	Madhya Pradesh
3.	Palghat gap	–	Kerala
4.	Shencotta gap	–	Karnataka

Codes

(a) 1 and 2 (b) 2 and 4 (c) 1, 2 and 4 (d) 2, 3 and 4

Ans. (b)

Exp. Pairs (2) and (4) are not correctly matched because Bhorghat is a mountain passage located between Palasdari and Khandala for railway and between Khopoli and Khandala on the road route in Maharashtra, India, situated on the crest of the Western Ghats and Shencotta gap located between the Nagercoil and the Cardamom hills in Tamil Nadu, links Thiruvananthapuram and Madurai.

Great Indian Desert

53 Consider the following statements about the Great Indian desert. *(Chap 2, Class-XI, New NCERT*

1. It is an extension of the Shiwalik mountain range towards South.
2. It is a land of undulating topography covered with longitudinal dunes and barchans.
3. Marine deposits have been found from this region during excavations.
4. Brackish water lakes and playas are found in abundance in this region.

How many of the statements given above is/are incorrect?

(a) Only one (b) Only two
(c) Only three (d) All of these

Ans. (a)

Exp. Only one statement i.e., (1) is incorrect about the Great Indian Desert because Great Indian desert lies to the North- West of Aravalli hills. It is a land of undulating topography dotted with longitudinal dunes and barchans. This region receives low rainfall below 15[illegible] mm per year; hence, it has arid climate with low vegetation cover.

54 Consider the following statements with reference to Great Indian desert. *(Chap 2, Class-IX & XII, New NCERT*

1. Most of the rivers in this region do not drain into the ocean and form inland drainage.
2. Playa lakes are commonly found in the Great Indian desert.

Which of the statements given above is/are correct?

(a) Only 1 (b) Only 2
(c) Both 1 and 2 (d) Neither 1 nor 2

Ans. (c)

Exp. Both the statements (1) and (2) are correct about the Great Indian desert because in the Great Indian Desert, most of the rivers in this region do not drain into the ocean and form inland drainage.
The Luni river flowing in the Southern part of the deser is of some significance. Low precipitation and high evaporation makes it a water deficit region.
There are some streams, which disappear after flowing for some distance and present a typical case of inland drainage by joining a lake or playa. The lakes and the playas have brackish water, which is the main source of obtaining salt.

Coastal Plains

55 Consider the following statements about India's Western coast. *(Chap 2, Class-XI, New NCERT)*

1. The Western coast of India is a submergent coast.
2. It is narrower than the East coast and suitable for development of natural harbours.

Which of the statements given above is/are correct?

(a) Only 1 (b) Only 2
(c) Both 1 and 2 (d) Neither 1 nor 2

Ans. (c)

Exp. Both the statements (1) and (2) are correct regarding India's Western coasts. The Western coast of India is a submergent coast because of its submergence, it is narrow belt and provides natural conditions for development of ports.

Western coast are narrower in comparison with the Eastern coast of India. The Eastern coast has gentle slope when compared with Western coast.

56 Arrange the following coastal plains in correct order from North to South and choose the correct option using the codes given below. *(Chap 2, Class-XI, New NCERT)*

1. Kathiawar Coast 2. Goa Coast
3. Malabar Coast 4. Konkan Coast

Codes

(a) 1, 2, 3, 4 (b) 1, 4, 2, 3 (c) 4, 1, 2, 3 (d) 4, 1, 3, 2

Ans. (b)

Exp. The correct order of Coastal Plains from North to South 1, 4, 2, 3 i.e., Kathiawar coast, Konkan coast, Goa coast and Malabar coast. The Kachchh and Kathiawar coast in Gujarat, Konkan coast is in Maharashtra, Goa coast and Malabar coast in Karnataka and Kerala respectively.

57 Consider the following statements with reference to India's East coast. *(Chap 2, Class-XI, New NCERT)*

1. Eastern coast is broader and gentle sloping than the Western coast.
2. Eastern coast is emergent in the nature unlike Western coast.
3. Rivers in this region form well developed estuaries.

Which of the statements given above is/are correct?

(a) 1, 2 and 3 (b) 1 and 3
(c) 1 and 2 (d) 2 and 3

Ans. (a)

Exp. All the given statements are correct about India's East coast because as compared to the Western coastal plain, the Eastern coastal plain is broader and it is an example of an emergent coast. Rivers in this region form well developed estuaries.

These include the deltas of the Mahanadi, the Godavari, the Krishna and the Kaveri. Because of its emergent nature.

58 With reference to coastal plains of India. Consider the following statements. *(Chap 2, Class-XI, New NCERT)*

1. The continental shelf of Eastern coast extends up to 5000 km into the sea.
2. Rivers form great deltas on the East coast of India due to its gentler slope.

Which of the statements given above is/are correct?

(a) Only 1 (b) Only 2
(c) Both 1 and 2 (d) Neither 1 nor 2

Ans. (b)

Exp. Only statement (2) is correct about coastal plains of India, because due to the presence of gentle slope there are well developed deltas in Eastern coasts, formed by the rivers flowing eastward into the Bay of Bengal. These include the deltas of the Mahanadi, the Godavari, the Krishna and the Kaveri.

Statement (1) is not correct because the continental shelf extends up to 500 km into the sea, which makes it difficult for the development of good ports and harbours.

59 Consider the following statements regarding the Indian coasts. *(Chap 2, Class-XI, New NCERT)*

1. Natural harbours and ports are a characteristic feature of the emergent coasts.
2. Gujarat has the maximum coastline amongst all the States/UTs of India.
3. Northern Circars are the region lying between Mahanadi and Krishna.

How many of the statements given above is/are correct?

(a) Only one (b) Only two
(c) Only three (d) None of these

Ans. (a)

Exp. Only one statement i.e., (3) is correct. Northern Circars formed a part of the former British territory in the Madras presidency. They are found along the states of Andhra Pradesh and Odisha. It is a region lying between Mahanadi and Krishna rivers.

Statements (1) and (2) are incorrect. Western coasts of India are an example of submergent coasts. Natural ports and harbours are formed along the submergent coasts. Kandla, Mangalore, Cochin, Mormugao, JLN port, etc. are some of the examples of natural ports.

Gujarat has the maximum coastline among the mainland states. If the all states and Union territories are also considered together, then Andaman and Nicobar Islands have the maximum coastline.

Islands

60 Consider the following statements. *(Chap 2, Class-XI, New NCERT)*

1. The entire Island of Lakshadweep lies below the 12-degree Channel.
2. Duncan Passage is situated between Swarajdweep and the Shaheed dweep.

3. Agatti Island is situated to the North of the capital Kavaratti.
4. The highest peak of Andaman, Saddle Peak is located in the South Andaman.

Which of the statements is most appropriate regarding the Islands of India?

(a) Only 1 (b) Only 2
(c) Only 3 (d) Only 4

Ans. (c)

Exp. Only statement (3) is correct. Agatti Islands of Lakshadweep is situated to the North of the capital Kavaratti.

Statements (1), (2) and (4) are incorrect. Some parts of Lakshadweep Island lie above the 12-degree Channel. Duncan Passage in the Andaman is situated between South Andaman and the Little Andaman. Saddle peak is the highest peak of Andaman and is situated in the North Andaman.

61 Which of the following pairs is/are correctly matched? *(Chap 2, Class-XI, New NCERT)*

Peaks	Islands
1. Saddle Peak	Little Andaman
2. Mount Thullier	Great Nicobar
3. Mount Koyob	Middle Andaman

Codes

(a) 2 and 3 (b) Only 2
(c) Only 1 (d) None of these

Ans. (b)

Exp. Pair (2) is correctly matched. Mount Thullier is a mountain on Great Nicobar Island, located in the Indian Ocean and bordering on the Andaman Sea.

Pairs (1) and (3) are not correctly matched because Saddle Peak or Saddle hill is located on North Andaman Island whereas Mount Koyob is the highest point of the South Andaman Island.

62 Consider the following statements regarding Andaman and Nicobar Islands. *(Chap 2, Class-XI, New NCERT)*

1. These islands are an extension of the ArakanYoma range.
2. Narcondam Island in the Andaman is a dormant volcano.
3. Mt. Thullier is the highest peak of the Andaman group of Islands.

Which of the statements given above are correct?

(a) 1 and 3
(b) 1 and 2
(c) 2 and 3
(d) 1, 2 and 3

Ans. (b)

Exp. Statements (1) and (2) are correct as the Andaman and Nicobar group of Islands are an extension of Arakan Yoma range which passes through Myanmar and the Indian states of Assam, Nagaland, Manipur, and Mizoram. Narcondam Island is situated in the North Andaman is an example of a dormant volcano.

Statement (3) is incorrect because Mt. Thullier is the highest peak of the Nicobar group of Islands. It is located in the Great Nicobar group of Islands.

63 Consider the following statements about Lakshadweep Island group. *(Chap 2, Class-XI, New NCERT)*

1. The entire island group is formed of coral deposits.
2. Shaheed Dweep is the largest island of Lakshadweep Islands.
3. 10° Channel divides the island group into Aminidivi Island and Cannanore Island.

Which of the statements given above is/are correct?

(a) 1 and 2 (b) 2 and 3
(c) 1 and 3 (d) 1, 2 and 3

Ans. (c)

Exp. Statements (1) and (3) are correct about the Lakshadweep Island group as the islands of the Arabian sea include Lakshadweep and Minicoy.

These are scattered between 8°N-12°N and 71°E -74°E longitude. These islands are located at a distance of 280 km-480 km off the Kerala coast.

The entire island group is built of coral deposits. There are approximately 36 islands of, which 11 are inhabited. The entire group of islands is broadly divided by the 10° Channel, North of, which is the Aminidivi Island and to the South of the Cannanore Island.

Statement (2) is incorrect because Minicoy is the largest island with an area of 453 sq. km of Lakshadweep Islands

64 Storm beaches are found near the Lakshadweep Island group. Which of the following is the feature of storm beaches? *(Chap 2, Class-XI, New NCERT)*

(a) Rich deposits of Guano and small rocks.
(b) Granular deposits of sand and silt deposited due to sea waves.
(c) Unconsolidated deposits of pebbles, shingles, cobbles and boulders.
(d) Diverse coral deposits of varying shapes and sizes.

Ans. (c)

Exp. Statement (c) describes the feature of storm beaches. The Lakshadweep Island group has storm beaches consisting of unconsolidated pebbles, shingles, cobbles and boulders on the Eastern seaboard. A storm beach is a beach affected by particularly fierce waves, usually with a very long fetch. They are often very steep beaches.

Chapter 18

Drainage System of India

Drainage System of India

Types

Introduction

System of flow of surface water mainly through the forms of rivers and basins. It is an outcome of topography, nature and structure of rocks, slope, periodicity, etc can be broadly classified into three categories

(i) **Based on the size of catchment** area-divided as major river, medium river and small river

(ii) **Based on the type of drainage** rivers draining into sea, inland drainage and seasonal streams

(iii) **Based on orientation to the sea** divided into Bay of Bengal drainage and Arabian Sea drainage

Types of Drainage Pattern

- **Antecedent Drainage** Pattern present before the upliftment of land and post upliftment, rivers were able to maintain the same course
- **Superimposed Drainage** Pattern developed on the rock strata removed by erosion
- **Discordant Drainage** Pattern that bears no relation to the structure of underlying rocks
- **Concordant Drainage** Pattern which closely follows the trend of underlying strata
- **Dendritic Drainage** Pattern resembles the branching pattern of tree roots, it develops where river channel follows the slope of terrain
- **Parallel Drainage** Develops in regions of parallel, elongated landforms and tributaries stretch out in a parallel pattern following the slope of surface

Himalayan Drainage System

Introduction

- The Himalayan drainage system comprises all the international rivers of India, i.e., the Indus, the Ganga and the Brahmaputra
- Most of these rivers and their major tributaries are perennial in character, obtaining their water from the glaciers, springs and rains
- Most of the rivers, which rise in the Himalayas are antecedent in nature

Indus River System

- One of the largest river basins of the world
- Originates in Tibet and flows in India through Leh district
- Some of its tributaries are Jhelum, Chenab, Ravi, Beas, Sutlej, Shyok, Gilgit, Nubra, etc

Ganga River System

- Largest river system of India
- Originates as Bhagirathi from Gangotri glacier in Uttarkashi district of Uttarakhand,merges with Alaknanda at Devprayag and forms Ganga
- Flows from the States of Uttarakhand, Uttar Pradesh, Bihar and West Bengal
- Some of its tributaries are Chambal, Ken, Yamuna, Tons, Ghaghra, Gandak, Kosi, etc

Brahmaputra River System

- Originates from Chemayungdung glacier in Tibet as Tsangpo and enters India as Dihang
- One of the largest rivers of the world; Major tributaries are Lohit, Dihang, Dibang, Dhansiri, Kameng, Manas, etc

Peninsular Drainage System

Introduction

Peninsular rivers are characterised by fixed course, absence of meanders and non-perennial flow of water

Narmada River System

- Rises in Amarkantak hills and forms traditional outline between North and South India; Flowing from East to West, its major tributaries are Barna, Kolar, etc

Tapi River System

- Originates in Satpura ranges an flows from East to West; Its important tributaries are Arunavati, Gomai, Girna, etc

Krishna River System

- Originates from Mahabaleshwar, its major tributaries are Ghatprabha, Malprabha, Tungabhadra, Bhima, etc

Godavari River System

- Second longest river course in India, often referred as Dakshin Ganga
- Originating from Triambakeshwar, its major tributaries are Pranhita, Indravati, Manjira, etc

Kaveri River System

- Originates from Talkaveri, supports irrigation activities and is considered as means of support of ancient kingdoms; Its major tributaries are Arkavati, Amravati, Kabani, etc

Mahanadi River System

- Originates from Satpura ranges, flows to the East and drains in Bay of Bengal; Hirakud dam is built on this river

SOURCE **Old NCERT Class IX** *(Drainage)*, **New NCERT Class X** *(Water Resources)*, **New NCERT Class XI** *(Drainage System)*

Indian Drainage

1 **Consider the following pairs.** *(Chap 3, Class-XI, New NCERT)*

	Drainage pattern		Description
1.	Radial	–	The rivers originate from a hill and flow in all directions
2.	Dendritic	–	Rivers discharge their waters from all directions into a lake or depression.
3.	Trellis	–	The drainage pattern resembles the branches of a tree.
4.	Centripetal	–	Primary tributaries flow parallel with secondary tributaries joining them at right angles.

How many pairs given above is/are correct?

(a) Only one (b) Only two
(c) Only three (d) All four

Ans. (a)

Exp. Only one pair i.e., (1) is correct. When the rivers originate from a hill and flow in all directions, the drainage pattern is known as radial. The rivers originating from the Amarkantak range present a good example of it.

While pairs (2), (3) and (4) are incorrect. The drainage pattern resembling the branches of a tree is known as **dendritic** the examples of which are the rivers of Northern plain.

When the primary tributaries of rivers flow parallel to each other and secondary tributaries join them at right angles, the pattern is known as trellis.

When the rivers discharge their waters from all directions in a lake or depression, the pattern is known as centripetal.

2 **Consider the following pairs.** *(Chap 3, Class-X, New NCERT)*

1. Catchment area – An area drained by a river and its tributaries
2. Drainage basin – Water collected by the river from a specific area
3. Watershed – A boundary separating two river basins

How many of the pairs given above is/are not correctly matched?

(a) Only one
(b) Only two
(c) All three
(d) None of the above

Ans. (b)

Exp. Only two pairs i.e., (1) and (2) are not correctly matched because when a river drains the collected water from a specific area, then it is called as its 'catchment area'.

A drainage basin is an area drained by a river and its tributaries.

3 **Consider the following statements.** *(Chap 3, Class-XI, New NCERT)*

1. The catchments of large rivers are called river basins.
2. Small rivulets and rills are often referred to as watersheds.
3. Watersheds are large in area while the basins cover small areas.

How many of the statements given above is/are correct?

(a) Only one (b) Only two
(c) All three (d) None of these

Ans. (b)

Exp. Only two statements i.e., (1) and (2) are correct. The catchments of large rivers are called river basins while those of small rivulets and rills are often referred to as watersheds. The boundary line separating one drainage basin from the other is known as the watershed.

Statement (3) is incorrect because there is, a slight difference between a river basin and a watershed. Watersheds are small in area while the basins cover larger areas.

4 **Which of the following statements is/are correct with reference to the drainage system of India?** *(Chap 3, Class-XI, New NCERT)*

1. The area of Bay of Bengal drainage system is more than that of the Arabian Sea drainage.
2. Any river basin with an area more than 20,000km^2 is considered as a major river basin.
3. The Ganga basin is the largest river basin in India.

Codes

(a) 1 and 2 (b) 2 and 3
(c) 1 and 3 (d) All of these

Ans. (d)

Exp. All the statements (1), (2) and (3) are correct with reference to drainage system of India. The area of Bay of Bengal drainage system is more than that of Arabian Sea drainage. Nearly 77% of the drainage area is oriented towards the Bay of Bengal while 23% of the drainage area discharge their water in the Arabian Sea.

Any river basin with an area more than 20,000 km^2 is considered as major river basin. It includes river basins, such as the Ganga, Brahmaputra, Krishna, etc.

Ganga river basin is the largest river basin in India. It originates from the Gangotri glacier near Gaumukh (Uttarkashi, Uttarakhand). It has a length of 2525 km and its rivers basin is 8.6 lakh km^2 area in India.

5 **Consider the following statements regarding drainage pattern.** *(Chap 3, Class-XI, New NCERT)*

1. Rivers originating from the Amarkantak range are an example of centripetal drainage.
2. Rivers Narmada and Son flow in different directions despite the same source of origin.

Which of the statements given above is/are correct?
(a) Only 1 (b) Only 2
(c) Both 1 and 2 (d) Neither 1 nor 2

Ans. (b)

Exp. Statement (2) is correct regarding drainage pattern Both river Narmada and Son originate from the Amarkantak plateau. Narmada flows to the Arabian Sea while Son river joins Ganga as its tributary, which eventually drains at the Bay of Bengal.

Statement (1) is incorrect because rivers originating in the Amarkantak plateau are an example of the radial drainage system. The radial drainage system is formed when a river originating from a hill discharges its water in all directions.

Himalayan Drainage System

6 Which of the following is not correctly matched?

(Chap 9, Module-2, NIOS)

River		Origin
(a) Bhagirathi	–	Gaumukh glacier
(b) Alaknanda	–	Satopanth glacier
(c) Pindar	–	Badrinath
(d) Mandakini	–	Kedarnathh

Ans. (c)

Exp. Pair (c) is not correctly matched because Pindar river also known as Pindari river is a Himalayan river, which emerges from Pindari glacier in Bageshwar district of Uttarakhand.

7 Consider the following statements with reference to Himalayan Drainage System.

(Chap 3, Class-IX, New NCERT)

1. These rivers form deep gorges and V-shaped valleys in the Himalayas.
2. These rivers are fed by melting of ice caps, which make them perennial.
3. Large dams cannot be constructed on these rivers.

Which of the statements given above is/are correct?
(a) 2 and 3 (b) 1 and 3
(c) 1 and 2 (d) All of these

Ans. (c)

Exp. Statements (1) and (2) are correct with reference to Himalayan Drainage System.

The Himalayan rivers pass through the giant gorges carved out by the erosional activity carried on simultaneously with the uplift of Himalayas.

Besides deep gorges, these rivers also form V-shaped valleys, rapids and waterfalls in their mountainous course. Himalayan rivers are fed both by melting of snow and precipitation that's why they are perennial.

Statement (3) is incorrect because several large dams have been constructed on these rivers. For instance, Bhakra Nangal dam has been constructed on Sutlej river.

8 Consider the following statements regarding the Himalayan Drainage System.

(Chap 3, Class-XI, New NCERT)

1. The Ganga, the Indus, and the Brahmaputra are the main river basins of the Himalayan drainage.
2. The rivers in this system are mainly fed by precipitation and not by the melting of snow.
3. Rivers in the Himalayan system form V-shaped valleys, rapids and waterfalls during their mountainous course.
4. The rivers in the Himalayan drainage system do not form any depositional features in the plains.

How many of the statements given above is/are correct?
(a) Only one
(b) Only two
(c) Only three
(d) All of the above

Ans. (b)

Exp. Only two statements i.e., (1) and (3) are correct regarding the Himalayan Drainage System.

The Himalayan drainage system has evolved through a long geological history. It mainly includes the Ganga, the Indus and the Brahmaputra river basins. These rivers pass through the giant gorges carved out by the erosional activity carried on simultaneously with the uplift of the Himalayas. Besides deep gorges, these rivers also form V-shaped valleys, rapids and waterfalls in their mountainous course.

Statements (2) and (4) are incorrect because these rivers are fed both by the melting of snow and precipitation, rivers of this system are perennial. While entering the plains, Himalayan rivers form depositional features like flat valleys, ox-bow lakes, flood plains, braided channels, and deltas near the river mouth.

9 Which of the following events is/are responsible for the dismemberment of the mighty Shiwalik river into the Himalayan drainage basin in its present form?

(Chap 3, Class-XI, New NCERT)

(a) Uplift of Potwar plateau
(b) Down thrusting of Malda gap
(c) Upheaval of Western Himalayas in Pleistocene period
(d) All of the above

Ans. (d)

Exp. All the given options are responsible for the dismemberment of the mighty Shiwalik river into the Himalayan drainage basin in its present form.

The Pleistocene upheaval in the Western Himalayas, including the uplift of the Potwar plateau (Delhi ridge). Down thrusting to the Malda gap area between Rajmahal hills and the Meghalaya plateau during the Mid-Pleistocene period.

The Indus

10 Consider the following statements with reference to Indus river system in India. *(Chap 3, Class-IX, New NCERT)*

1. Indus originates from the Bokhar Chu glacier in Himalayas.
2. Indus is known as Yarlung Tsangpo in the Tibetan region.
3. It forms a deep and steep gorge in the Gilgit region.

Which of the statements given above is/are incorrect?

(a) 1 and 3 (b) Only 2
(c) 1 and 2 (d) Only 3

Ans. (b)

Exp. Statement (2) is incorrect with reference to Indus river system in India. Brahmaputra river is known as Yarlung Tsangpo river in Tibetan region. In Tibetan region, Indus river is known as Singi Khamban or Lion's mouth. This river cuts across the Ladakh range, forms a spectacular gorge near Gilgit in Jammu and Kashmir.

11 Which of the following is/are the right bank tributaries of Indus? *(Chap 3, Class-XI, New NCERT)*

1. Nubra 2. Zaskar
3. Khurram 4. Shigar

Codes

(a) 1, 2 and 3 (b) 2, 3 and 4
(c) 1, 3 and 4 (d) 1, 2, 3 and 4

Ans. (c)

Exp. Nubra, Khurram and Shigar rivers are the right bank tributaries of Indus. The other right bank tributaries of Indus river are Tochi, Gomal, Viboa, Shyok, Gilgit and Hunza river that originate in Sulaiman range. Zanskar river is the left bank tributary of Indus river. The other left bank tributaries of Indus river are Jhelum, Chenab, Ravi, Beas and Sutlej.

12 Which of the given pairs is/are matched correctly? *(Chap 3, Class-XI, New NCERT)*

Rivers		Sources
1. Jhelum	–	Verinag
2. Ravi	–	Kullu Hills
3. Sutlej	–	Rakas Lake

Codes

(a) 1 and 2 (b) 2 and 3
(c) 3 and 3 (d) 1, 2 and 3

Ans. (d)

Exp. All of the given pairs (1), (2) and (3) are matched correctly.

The Jhelum, an important tributary of the Indus, originates from a spring at Verinag situated at the foot of the Pir Panjal in the South-Eastern part of the Kashmir valley. It flows through Srinagar and the Wular lake before entering Pakistan through a deep narrow gorge.

The Ravi is the tributary of the Indus, which rises West of the Rohtang pass in Kullu hills of Himachal Pradesh and flows through the Chamba Valley of the state.

The Sutlej river in the tributary of the Indus, originates in the Rakas Tal near Mansarovar at an altitude of 4,555 m in Tibet, where it is known as Langchen Khambab.

13 Consider the following statements regarding Sutlej river. *(Chap 3, Class-XI, New NCERT)*

1. The Sutlej river is a Trans-Himalayan river.
2. It originates from the Manasarovar-Rakas lakes in Western Tibet and flows through the Indian States of Himachal Pradesh and Punjab.
3. The Sutlej is the longest tributary of the Indus river.

How many of the statements given above is/are correctly matched?

(a) Only one (b) Only two
(c) All three (d) None of these

Ans. (c)

Exp. All three statements i.e., (1), (2) and (3) are correct regarding the Sutlej river. The Sutlej river is a Trans-Himalayan river. This means it originates beyond the Greater Himalayas. It originates from Manasarovar-Rakas lakes in Western Tibet and flows through the Indian States of Himachal Pradesh and Punjab before entering Pakistan. Sutlej is the longest of the five tributaries of the river Indus. It crosses Himachal Pradesh before entering Punjab. It receives the Beas river before entering Pakistan and merging with Indus.

14 With reference to Indus and its tributaries, consider the following statements. *(Chap 3, Class-XI, New NCERT)*

1. The Jhelum river joins the Indus river in Pakistan.
2. The Chenab is the largest tributary of Indus formed by Chandra and Bhaga rivers.
3. The Beas and Sutlej river meets at Harike in Punjab.

How many of the statements given above is/are correct?

(a) Only one (b) Only two
(c) All three (d) None of these

Ans. (c)

Exp. All three statements i.e., (1), (2) and (3) are correct with reference to Indus and its tributaries.

The Jhelum river joins the Indus river in Pakistan.

The Chenab is the largest tributary of the Indus. It is formed by two streams, the Chandra and the Bhaga, which join at Tandi near Keylong in Himachal Pradesh. Hence, it is known as Chandrabhaga.

The Beas river, tributary of the Indus (originates from Beas kund near Rohtang Pass) flows through the Kullu valley. It enters the Punjab Plains where it meets Sutlej river near Harike.

The Ganga

15 With reference to Ganga river system, consider the following statements. *(Chap 3, Class-XI, New NCERT)*

1. The Satopanth glacier is the main source of Alaknanda river.
2. Bhagirathi and Alaknanda meet at Devprayag to form Ganga.
3. The Ganga descends on the plains at Dehradun.
4. The Son is a right bank tributary of Ganga.

How many of the statements given above is/are not correct?

(a) Only one
(b) Only two
(c) Only three
(d) None of the above

Ans. (a)

Exp. Only one statement i.e., (3) is not correct with reference to Ganga river system. The Ganga descends on the plains at Haridwar and not Dehradun. It rises in the Gangotri Glacier near Gaumukh (Uttarkashi district, Uttarakhand). Here, it is known as the Bhagirathi.

16 Match the following lists correctly and choose the correct code. *(Chap 3, Class-IX, New NCERT)*

	List I (Confluence)		List II (Tributaries of Alaknanda)
A.	Rudraprayag	1.	Dhauli Ganga
B.	Vishnuprayag	2.	Pindar
C.	Karnaprayag	3.	Mandakini

Codes

	A	B	C		A	B	C
(a)	1	2	3	(b)	1	3	2
(c)	3	1	2	(d)	3	2	1

Ans. (c)

Exp. The correct matching is A-3, B-1, C-2.

Rudraprayag is the confluence of Alaknanda and Mandakini rivers.

Vishnuprayag is the confluence of Alaknanda and Dhauli Ganga .

Karnaprayag is the confluence of Alaknanda and Pindar river.

17 Arrange the following left bank tributaries of Ganga from West to East. *(Chap 3, Class-XI, New NCERT)*

1. Gandak
2. Gomti
3. Ramganga
4. Ghaghara

Codes

(a) 2-3-1-4
(b) 2-4-1-3
(c) 3-2-4-1
(d) 3-4-2-1

Ans. (c)

Exp. The order of the left bank tributaries of the Ganga from West to East is 3-2-4-1.

Ganga river basin has the largest basin area in India. It is a Himalayan river with a comprehensive network of tributaries and distributaries. It is formed by two head streams, Alaknanda and Bhagirathi which joins at Devprayag. Its left bank tributaries from West to East are: Ramganga – Gomti– Ghaghara– Gandak.

18 Consider the following statements with reference to Ganga river basin in India. *(Chap 3, Class-XI, New NCERT)*

1. It is the second largest river basin in India in terms of its area.
2. Ganga river flows through only seven states of India.
3. Ganga rises in the Gangotri glacier where it is known as Bhagirathi.

Which of the statements given above is/are correct?

(a) 1 and 2
(b) Only 2
(c) Only 1
(d) Only 3

Ans. (d)

Exp. Statement (3) is correct with reference to Ganga river basin in India.

The Ganga rises in the Gangotri glacier near Gaumukh (3900 m) in the Uttarkashi district of Uttarakhand. Here, it is known as Bhagirathi.

Statements (1) and (2) are incorrect. The Ganga river has a length of 2525 km and it covers about 8.6 lakh km^2 area India. Hence, it is the largest river basin in India in terms of its area.

The Ganga river flows through states of Uttarakhand, Uttar Pradesh, Bihar and West Bengal. Besides these, it flows through Jharkhand state also.

19 Consider the following statements with reference to river Yamuna? *(Chap 3, Class-IX, New NCERT)*

1. It rises near the Kailash Mansarovar lake, near Tibet.
2. Chambal, Sind and Betwa are the left bank tributaries of Yamuna.
3. Yamuna is the second longest tributary of Ganga.
4. Yamuna basin is larger than the basin of Chambal.

How many of the statements given above is/are not correct?

(a) Only one
(b) Only two
(c) Only three
(d) All of these

Ans. (c)

Exp. Only three statements i.e., (1), (2) and (3) are not correct because Yamuna has its source in the Yamunotri glacier on the Western slopes of Banderpunch range (6316 km). It joins the Ganga at Prayagraj. Chambal, Sind, Betwa and Ken are its right bank tributaries. Yamuna is the longest tributary of the river Ganga.

20 Which of the following statements is/are incorrect? *(Chap 3, Class-XI, New NCERT)*

1. The Chambal river originates in the Malwa Plateau in Madhya Pradesh.
2. Chambal forms badlands known as Ravines in this region.

Codes

(a) Only 1 (b) Only 2
(c) 1 and 2 (d) Neither 1 nor 2

Ans. (d)

Exp. Neither statements (1) nor (2) are incorrect.

The Chambal rises near Mhow in the Malwa plateau of Madhya Pradesh. It flows Northwards through a gorge upwards of Kota in Rajasthan, where the Gandhisagar dam has been constructed from Kota, it traverses down to Sawai Madhopur and Dholpur and finally joins the Yamuna.

The Chambal is famous for its badland topography called the Chambal ravines.

21 Consider the statements regarding Ghaghara river system. *(Chap 3, Class-XI, New NCERT)*

1. Ghaghara river originates in the Banderpunch Glacier.
2. It meets the Ganga river near Sonpur in Bihar.
3. Tila, Seti and Beri are the tributaries of Ghaghara.

How many of the statements given above is/are incorrect?

(a) Only one (b) Only two
(c) All three (d) None of these

Ans. (b)

Exp. Only two statements i.e., (1) and (2) are incorrect regarding Ghaghara river system. The Ghaghara originates in the glaciers of Mapchachungo.

The river Sarda (Kali or Kali Ganga) joins it in the plain before it finally meets the Ganga at Chhapra.

22 Consider the following Assertion (A) and Reason (R) and choose the correct code. *(Chap 3, Class-XI, New NCERT) (UPPSC Pre 2005)*

Assertion (A) The Ganga is a highly polluted river.

Reason (R) The holier the river, the more polluted it is.

Codes

(a) Both A and R are true, and R is correct explanation of A.
(b) Both A and R are true, but R is not explanation of A.
(c) A is true, but R is false.
(d) A is false, but R is true.

Ans. (c)

Exp. Assertion (A) is true, but Reason (R) is false.

The Ganga is a highly polluted river but it is polluted because higher organic load of urban areas is dumped in the Ganga, which is the root cause of pollution in Ganga.

23 With reference to river Teesta, consider the following statements. *(Chap 3, Class-XI, New NCERT) (IAS Pre 2017)*

1. The source of river Teesta is the same as that of Brahmaputra but it flows through Sikkim.
2. River Rangeet originates in Sikkim and it is a tributary of river Teesta.
3. River Teesta flows into Bay of Bengal on the border of India and Bangladesh.

Which of the statements given above is/are correct?

(a) 1 and 3 (b) Only 2
(c) 2 and 3 (d) All of these

Ans. (b)

Exp. Statement (2) is correct as the Rangeet river originates in the Zemu glacier in the North Sikkim district. It flows through the States of Sikkim and West Bengal before joining the Teesta river at Sevoke. The Rangeet river is a tributary of the Teesta river.

Statements (1) and (3) are incorrect because the source of the Teesta river is the Teesta Khangtse glacier, West of Pahunri (or Teesta Kangtse) glacier above 5,400 m (17,700 ft) and flows Southward through gorges and rapids in the Sikkim Himalaya.

The Teesta river does not originate from the same source as the Brahmaputra river. The Teesta river does not flow into the Bay of Bengal. It flows into the Brahmaputra river in Bangladesh.

24 Consider the following statements with reference to Ganga and its tributaries. *(Chap 3, Class-XI, New NCERT)*

1. The Sarda river originates in Nepal in the Milam Glacier.
2. The Saryu river is also known as Sorrow of Bengal.
3. The Son river originates from Amarkantak Plateau.

Which of the statements given above is/are correct?

(a) 1 and 2
(b) 2 and 3
(c) 1 and 3
(d) All of the above

Ans. (c)

Exp. Statements (1) and (3) are correct with reference to Ganga and its tributaries.

The Sarda river or Saryu river originates from the Milam Glacier in the Nepal Himalayas where it is known as the Goriganga. Along the Indo-Nepal border, it is called Kali or Chauk, where it joins the Ghaghara.

The Son river is a large South bank tributary of the Ganga and it originates in the Amarkantak Plateau. After forming a series of waterfalls, it reaches Arrah, West of Patna, to join the Ganga.

Statement (2) is incorrect because the Damodar river, not the Saryu river, is known as 'Sorrow of Bengal.'

The Brahmaputra

25 Match List I with List II.

(Chap 3, Class-XI, New NCERT), (UPPSC Pre 2022)

	List I (Rivers)		List II (Places on their banks)
A.	Barak	1.	Sivasagar
B.	Brahmaputra	2.	Golaghat
C.	Dikhow	3.	Silchar
D.	Dhansiri	4.	Goalpara

Codes

	A	B	C	D		A	B	C	D
(a)	3	4	1	2	(b)	2	4	3	1
(c)	4	3	2	1	(d)	1	2	3	4

Ans. (a)

Exp. The correct matching is A-3, B-4, C-1, D-2.

Silchar is situated on the Surma (**Barak**) river near the Bangladesh border.

Goalpara is located on the bank of the river **Brahmaputra**. It is located at 134 km to the West of Guwahati.

Sivasagar lies on the **Dikhow** river, a tributary of the Brahmaputra river about 30 miles (50 km) North-East of Jorhat.

Golaghat city is located on the banks of **Dhansiri**.

26 Which of the following statements is/are correct with reference to Brahmaputra river system?

(Chap 3, Class-XI, New NCERT)

1. The Brahmaputra river originates in Kailash range near Mansarovar Lake.
2. It is known as Tsangpo in Tibetan region.
3. It enters in India flowing through Assam at Namcha Barwa.

Codes

(a) 1 and 3 (b) 2 and 3 (c) Only 3 (d) 1 and 2

Ans. (d)

Exp. Statements (1) and (2) are correct with reference to Brahmaputra river system.

The Brahmaputra river originates in Kailash range near Mansarovar Lake. It traverses Eastward longitudinally for a distance of nearly 1200 km in a dry and flat region of the Southern Tibet, where it is known as the Tsangpo which means the purifier.

Statement (3) is incorrect because it enters in India, through Arunachal Pradesh. Following Southwards, it receives its main left bank tributaries, *viz* Dibang or Sikang and Lohit, thereafter it is known as the 'Brahmaputra'.

27 Which of the following river is a tributary of Brahmaputra in India? *(Chap 3, Class-XI, New NCERT)*

1. Chindwin
2. Dhansari
3. Teesta
4. Dibang

Codes

(a) 1, 2, 3 and 4 (b) 2, 3 and 4
(c) 1, 2 and 3 (d) 1, 3 and 4

Ans. (b)

Exp. Dhansari, Teesta and Dibang are the tributaries of Brahmaputra river in India. The Brahmaputra receives a numerous tributaries in its 750 km long journey through the Assam valley.

Dhamiri is its major left bank tributary. Dibang or Sikang is also its left bank tributary. The other left bank tributaries of Brahmaputra river are Lohit, Burhi-Dihing, etc.

Teesta is its right bank tributary. In Bangladesh, Teesta joins the Brahmaputra on its right bank, from where it is known as 'Jamuna'. The other right bank tributaries of Brahmaputra rivers are Subansiri, Kameng, Manas and Sankosh.

28 The Brahmaputra, Irrawady and Mekong rivers originate in Tibet and flow through narrow and parallel mountain ranges in their upper reaches. Of these rivers, Brahmaputra makes a 'U' turn in its course to flow into India. This 'U' turn is due to

(Chap 3, Class-XI, New NCERT), (UPSC Pre 2011)

(a) Uplift of folded Himalayan series
(b) Syntaxial bending of geologically young Himalayas
(c) Geo-Tectonic disturbance in the tertiary folded mountain chains
(d) Both a and b

Ans. (d)

Exp. The Brahmaputra river's 'U' turn to flow into India is due to the uplift of folded Himalayan series and the syntaxial bending of geologically young Himalayas. The Brahmaputra, Irrawady and Mekong rivers originate in Tibet and flow through narrow and parallel mountain ranges in their upper reaches. The western syntaxial bend occurs near the Nanga Parbat and the eastern syntaxial bend occurs near the Namche Barwa.

29 Consider the following statements with reference to flow of Brahmaputra in India.

(Chap 3, Class-XI, New NCERT)

1. Brahmaputra flows for almost 800 km in the Assam valley.
2. It is known as river Jamuna as it enters plains of Assam.
3. It is responsible for channel shifting and bank erosion in the Assam plains.

How many of the statements given above is/are correct?

(a) Only one (b) Only two
(c) all three (d) None of these

Ans. (b)

Exp. Only two statements i.e., (1) and (3) are correct with reference to flow of Brahmaputra in India. The Brahmaputra receives numerous tributaries in its 800 km long journey through the Assam valley.

The Brahmaputra enters into Bangladesh near Dhuleri and flows Southward. In Bangladesh, the Teesta joins it on its right bank from where the river is known as the Jamuna. It finally merges with the river Padma, which falls in the Bay of Bengal. The Brahmaputra is well-known for floods, channel shifting and bank erosion. This is due to the fact that most of its tributaries are large and bring large quantity of sediments owing to heavy rainfall in its catchment area.

Statement (2) is incorrect because it known as river Jamuna in Bangladesh not in Assam.

Peninsular Drainage

30 With reference to the peninsular drainage system, which of the statements are correct?

(Chap 3, Class-XI, New NCERT)

1. The Godavari is one of the largest peninsular river systems.
2. Its tributaries run through Maharashtra, Madhya Pradesh, Orissa, etc.
3. It's important tributaries are Penganga, Indravati and Koyna.

Select the correct answer from the codes given below.

(a) 1 and 2 (b) 1 and 3
(c) 2 and 3 (d) All of these

Ans. (a)

Exp. Statements (1) and (2) are correct.

Godavari, also known as 'Dakshin Ganga' – the South Ganges, is the longest river in peninsular India, and the second longest river of India after the Ganges, it drains about 10% of India's total geographical area. Its tributaries run through the state of Maharashtra, Madhya Pradesh, Chhattisgarh, Orissa and Andhra Pradesh.

Statement (3) is incorrect because Koyna river is a tributary of the river Krishna, not Godavari. Important tributaries of the Godavari river are the Penganga, the Indravati, Pranhita and Manjra.

31 Arrange the following river basins of India from lowest to highest in relation to area.

(Chap 3, Class-XI, New NCERT), (Telangana PCS Pre 2023)

1. Pennar
2. Tapi
3. Cauvery
4. Narmada

Codes

(a) 1-2-3-4 (b) 2-4-3-1 (c) 4-3-2-1 (d) 1-3-2-4

Ans. (a)

Exp. The correct order of the river basins of India from lowest to highest in terms of area is 1, 2, 3, 4.

The Pennar river has a drainage basin of 55,213 sq km. The basin covers part of the States of Andhra Pradesh and Karnataka in India.

The Tapi river drain an area of 65145 sq km out of which nearly 80% lies in Maharashtra.

The Cauvery basin extends over the states of Tamil Nadu. Karnataka, Kerala and Union Territory of Puducherry draining an area of 81155 sq km which is nearly 2.7% of the total geographical area of the country.

The Narmada river basin has a drainage area of 88000 sq km upto the dam site. The total basin area is 97410 sq km.

32 Match List I with List II.

(Chap 3, Class-XI, New NCERT), (UKPSC Pre 2016)

List I (Region)	List II (River)
A. Brahmagiri hills	1. Cauvery
B. Verinag spring	2. Jhelum
C. Mahabaleshwar	3. Krishna
D. Chota Nagpur plateau	4. Subarnarekha

Codes

	A	B	C	D		A	B	C	D
(a)	3	4	1	2	(b)	2	4	3	1
(c)	4	3	2	1	(d)	1	2	3	4

Ans. (d)

Exp. The correct matching is A-1, B-2, C-3, D-4.

The Cauvery river is the longest river in South India. It originates in the **Brahmagiri hills** in Karnataka and flows through Karnataka, Tamil Nadu and Kerala.

The Jhelum river is a tributary of the Indus river. It originates from the **Verinag spring** in Kashmir and flows through Kashmir, Pakistan and Punjab, India.

The Krishna river is the third longest river in India. It originates from the **Mahabaleshwar hills** in Maharashtra and flows through Maharashtra, Telangana, Andhra Pradesh and Karnataka.

The Subarnarekha river is a river in Jharkhand and Odisha. It originates from the **Chhota Nagpur plateau** in Jharkhand and flows through Jharkhand and Odisha.

33 Which of the given pairs is/are matched correctly?

(Chap 3, Class-XI, New NCERT)

Rivers		Sources
1. Mahanadi	–	Raipur, Chhattisgarh
2. Krishna	–	Mahabaleshwar, Maharashtra
3. Cauvery	–	Brahmagiri Hills, Karnataka

Codes

(a) 1 and 3 (b) Only 2 (c) Olny 1 (d) 1, 2 and 3

Ans. (d)

Exp. All the given pairs (1), (2) and (3) are matched correctly.

The Mahanadi river rises near Sihawa in Raipur district of Chhattisgarh and runs through Odisha to discharge water into Bay of Bengal. It is 851 km long and its catchment area spreads over 1.42 lakh sq km.

The Krishna river is the second largest East flowing Peninsular river, which rises near Mahabaleshwar in Sahyadri (Maharashtra). It's total length is 1,401 km.

The Cauvery river rises in Brahmagiri hills of Kogadu district in Karnataka. Its length is 800 km and it drains an area of 81,155 sq km.

34 The drainage basin of Mahanadi river is located in, which of the following states?

(Chap 3, Class-XI, New NCERT)

1. Madhya Pradesh
2. Odisha
3. Chhattisgarh
4. Maharashtra

Codes

(a) 1, 2 and 4 (b) 2, 3 and 4
(c) 1, 3 and 2 (d) All of these

Ans. (c)

Exp. The drainage basin of Mahanadi river is located in Madhya Pradesh, Chhattisgarh and Odisha. 53% of the drainage basin of this river lies in Madhya Pradesh and Chhattisgarh, while 47% lies Odisha.

35 Which of the following statements is/are incorrect with reference to river Godavari?

(Chap 3, Class-XI, New NCERT)

1. It is the largest river of the Peninsular region.
2. It has the second largest basin in India in terms of its area.
3. It forms estuary on the East coast of India.

Codes

(a) 1 and 3 (b) 2 and 3
(c) Only 3 (d) All of these

Ans. (c)

Exp. Statement (3) is incorrect with reference to river Godavari because this river forms delta and not estuary. It forms delta along the coast of the Bay of Bengal. After Rajahmundry, this river splits into several branches forming a large delta.

36 Consider the following pairs.

(Chap 3, Class-XI, New NCERT)

	Peninsular Rivers		**Origin**
1.	Narmada	-	Amarkantak Plateau
2.	Godavari	-	Sahyadri Hills
3.	Krishna	-	Trimbakeshwar Plateau
4.	Cauvery	-	Brahmagiri Hills

How many of the pairs given above is/are incorrectly matched?

(a) Only one (b) Only two
(c) Only three (d) All of these

Ans. (b)

Exp. Only two pairs i.e., (2) and (3) are incorrectly matched.

The Godavari rises from Trimbakeshwar plateau in the Nashik district of Maharashtra and discharges its water into the Bay of Bengal. The Godavari is India's second-longest river after the Ganga and third largest in India. The Krishna is the second largest East flowing peninsular river which rises near Mahabaleshwar in Sahyadri hills. The Krishna river is the fourth-largest river in terms of water inflows and river basin area in India, after the Ganges, Godavari and Brahmaputra.

37 Consider the following rivers.

(Chap 3, Class-XI, New NCERT) (IAS Pre 2015)

1. Vansadhara
2. Indravati
3. Pranahita
4. Pennar

Which of the river given above is/are the tributaries of Godavari?

(a) 1, 2 and 3 (b) 2, 3 and 4 (c) 1, 2 and 4 (d) 2 and 3

Ans. (d)

Exp. Among the given options, Indravati and Pranahita are the tributaries of Godavari. The other major tributaries of Godavari are : Purna, Sabari, Pravara, Manjra, Manair.

38 Which of the following statements is/are incorrect?

(Chap 3, Class-XI, New NCERT)

1. Krishna is the third largest Peninsular river in India.
2. River Narmada forms a gorge in the marble rocks.

Codes

(a) Only 1 (b) Only 2
(c) Both 1 and 2 (d) Neither 1 nor 2

Ans. (a)

Exp. Statement (1) is incorrect because the Krishna river is the second largest East flowing Peninsular river, which rises near Mahabaleshwar in Sahyadri. Its total length is 1,401 km. The Koyana, the Tungabhadra and the Bhima are its major tributaries.

39 Which of the following are the tributaries of river Mahanadi?

(Chap 3, Class-XI, New NCERT)

1. Seonath
2. Ib
3. Indravati
4. Sabari
5. Mand

Codes

(a) 1, 2 and 4 (b) 1, 2 and 5
(c) 2, 3 and 4 (d) All of these

Ans. (b)

Exp. Among the given options, Seonath, Ib and Mand are the tributaries of river Mahanadi.

Mahanadi rises from the Raipur district of Chhatisgarh and flows for about 851 km before its outfall into the Bay of Bengal. Its main tributaries are the Seonath, the Jonk, the Hasdeo, the Mand, the Ib, the Ong and the Tel. The Hirakud Dam, the world's longest earthen dam, is located on the Mahanadi river.

Indravati and Sabari are the major left-bank tributaries of Godavari.

40 Consider the following statements.

(Chap 3, Class-XI, New NCERT) (IAS Pre 2009)

1. There are no East flowing rivers in Kerala.
2. There is no West flowing river in Madhya Pradesh.

Which of the statements given above is/are correct?

(a) Only 1 (b) Only 2
(c) Both 1 and 2 (d) Neither 1 nor 2

Ans. (d)

Exp. Neither statements (1) nor (2) is correct. There are three East flowing rivers in Kerala i.e. Kabani river, Bhavani river and Pambar river.

The Tapti, Mahi and Narmada rivers originate in Madhya Pradesh and flow from East to West and empty into the Arabian Sea.

41 **Consider the following statements related to the Peninsular rivers.** *(Chap 3, Class-XI, New NCERT)*

1. Krishna river rises near Mahabaleshwar.
2. Saraswati and Sabarmati join to form Luni river.
3. Godavari river is the second longest river in India rises in Maharashtra.

How many of the statements given above is/are correct?

(a) Only one (b) Only two
(c) All three (d) None of these

Ans. (c)

Exp. All three statements i.e., (1), (2) and (3) are correct about Peninsular rivers.

The Krishna river originates in the Western Ghats near Mahabaleshwar, Maharashtra. The Luni river originates from the Aravalli range and is formed by the confluence of the Saraswati and Sabarmati rivers. The Saraswati river's mouth is the Alaknanda river.

The Sabarmati river originates from Dhebar Lake. The Godavari is India's second-longest river after the Ganga. The Godavari rises from Triambakeshwar, Maharashtra. It flows across the states of Maharashtra, Telangana, Andhra Pradesh, Chhattisgarh and Odisha.

42 **Which of the following rivers are not East flowing rivers?** *(Chap 3, Class-XI, New NCERT)*

1. Bharatpuzha
2. Sharavati
3. Subarnarekha
4. Palar

Codes

(a) 1, 2 and 3 (b) 2, 3 and 4
(c) 1 and 2 (d) All of these

Ans. (c)

Exp. Bharatpuzha and Sharavati are not East flowing rivers. They are West flowing rivers. Bharatpuzha, the longest river of Kerala, rises near Annamalai hilly, it is also known as Ponnari.

It drains an area of 5,397 sq km. The Sharavati river originates in Shimoga district of Karnataka and drains a catchment area of 2,209 sq km.

The Subarnarekha and the Palar are the East flowing small rivers in India. The Subarnarekha has the catchment area of 19,296 sq km and the Palar has the catchment area of 17,870 sq km. Baitarani, Brahmani, Pennar, etc are some of the important East flowing rivers.

Lakes

43 **Consider the following statements with reference to Wular lake.** *(Chap 3, Class-XI, New NCERT)*

1. Wular lake has been formed due to tectonic activities.
2. Wular lake is the largest fresh water lake in India.
3. It has one of the largest deposits of rare the Earth minerals in India.

Which of the statements given above are correct?

(a) 1 and 2 (b) 2 and 3
(c) 1 and 3 (d) 1, 2 and 3

Ans. (a)

Exp. Statements (1) and (2) are correct with reference to Wular lake.

Wular lake has been formed due to tectonic activities. It is the fresh water lake in the Himalayan region. It is also the largest fresh water lake in India. The Dal Lake, Bhimtal, Nainital, Loktak and Barapani are some of the important fresh water lakes.

44 **Match List I with List II.** *(Chap 3, Class-XI, New NCERT), (UPPSC Pre 2020)*

	List I (Lakes)		List II (Locations)
A.	Sela lake	1.	Arunachal Pradesh
B.	Badkhal lake	2.	Haryana
C.	Loktak lake	3.	Manipur
D.	Kaliveli lake	4.	Tamil Nadu

Codes

	A	B	C	D
(a)	3	4	1	2
(b)	2	4	3	1
(c)	4	3	2	1
(d)	1	2	3	4

Ans. (d)

Exp. The correct matching is A-1, B-2, C-3, D-4.

The **Sela lake** or a Sela pass is in the Northern State of Arunachal Pradesh is located on the border between Tawang and West Kameng district of Arunachal Pradesh in India.

Badkhal lake is a natural lake situated in Badkhal village near Faridabad, in the Indian State of Haryana, fringed by the hills of the Aravalli range, this was a man-made embankment.

The largest freshwater lake in North-East India, the **Loktak lake** is one of the most popular tourist attractions in Manipur. Known for its floating circular swamps, which are called Phumdis.

Kaliveli lake is a coastal lake and lagoon with wetlands in the Viluppuram district of Tamil Nadu. This lake is on the Coromandel coast, near the Bay of Bengal. It lies approximately 16 km North of Puducherry city and 10 km North of Auroville.

45 **Which of the following pairs of lake is example of freshwater lake?** *(Chap 2, Class-XI, New NCERT)*

(a) Dal Lake and Pangong Tso
(b) Wular lake and Pangong Tso
(c) Dal lake and Tso Moriri
(d) Dal lake and Wular lake

Ans. (d)

Exp. Dal lake and Wular lake are the examples of freshwater lake. The Wular lake in Jammu and Kashmir is the largest freshwater lake in India. It is formed as a result of tectonic activity. Dal lake is a freshwater lake in Jammu and Kashmir. Pangong and Tso Moriri and the salt water lakes in Himalayan region.

46 **Match the following lists correctly and choose the correct codes.** *(Chap 3, Class-XI, New NCERT) (MPPSC Pre 2014)*

List I (Lake)	List II (State)
A. Chilka lake	1. Rajasthan
B. Kolleru lake	2. Andhra Pradesh
C. Sambar lake	3. Odisha

Codes

	A	B	C		A	B	C
(a)	1	2	3	(b)	1	3	2
(c)	2	3	1	(d)	3	2	1

Ans. (d)

Exp. The correct matching is A-3, B-2, C-1.

Chilka lake is a water lagoon formed in the coastal area of Odisha.

Kolleru lake is a water lagoon formed in the coastal area of Andhra Pradesh.

Sambar lake in Rajasthan is a salt water lake. Its water is used for producing salt.

47 **Consider the following pairs.** *(Chap 3, Class-XI, New NCERT)*

Lakes		State
1. Haflong Lake	-	Assam
2. Udai Sagar	-	Rajasthan
3. Deedana	-	Haryana
4. Kolleru	-	Odisha

How many of the pairs given above is/are correctly matched?

(a) Only one
(b) Only two
(c) Only three
(d) All four

Ans. (c)

Exp. Only three pairs i.e., (1), (2) and (3) are correctly matched.

Haflong lake is located in the State of Assam. It's a major tourist destination in the downtown area of Haflong, a hill station in the Dima Hasao district of Assam.

Udai Sagar lake is located in Udaipur, Rajasthan, India.

Damdama lake is located in the Indian State of Haryana. It's situated in the Gurugram district, a few kilometers South of Gurgaon.

Pair (4) is incorrectly matched because Kolleru lake is located in the State of Andhra Pradesh, India. It's one of the largest freshwater lakes in India and the largest shallow freshwater lake in Asia.

Chapter 19

Climate in India

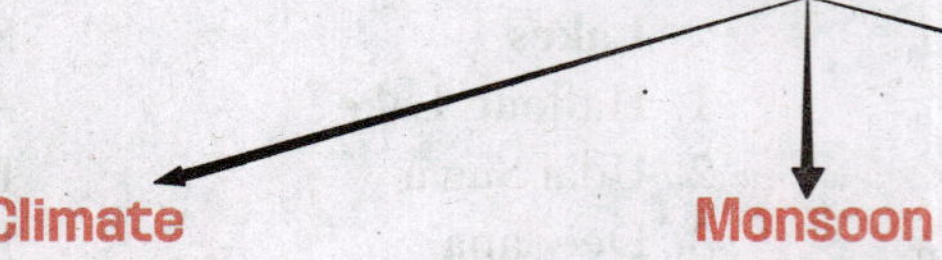

Climate

Introduction

- Indian climate belong to tropical monsoon type indicating the impact of its location in the tropical belt and the monsoon winds
- Salient features of Indian climate are
  - Reversal of winds with the change of seasons in a year
  - Formation of alternatively high and low pressure areas over the land

Climatic Regions of India

- The climate of North India is different from South and of East and West too; So, India is divided into large number of climatic regions of small size They are
- **Monsoon Type with Short Dry Season** Experienced in Western coastal region South of Goa
- **Tropical Savanna Type** Experienced in entire Peninsular region except for coastal areas
- **Semi-arid Steppe Climate** Found in interior parts of Peninsular plateau and parts of Gujarat, Rajasthan, Haryana, etc
- **Hot Desert Type** Found only in Western part of Rajasthan
- **Monsoon Type with Dry Winters** Experienced in largely Northern plains of India
- **Cold Humid Winter Type with Short Summer** Characterised by short summer season and covered North-Eastern part of India
- **Polar Type** Experienced in Jammu and Kashmir and the neighbouring mountain ranges

Monsoon

Introduction

- A complex meteorological phenomenon, usually described as seasonal reversal of winds along the shores of Indian ocean

Salient Features of Indian Monsoon

- Some features of Indian monsoon are as follows

Onset and Advance of Monsoon

- Low pressure at ITCZ becomes intense and pulls the trade winds from Southern Hemisphere Northwards, which thus cross Equator and enter Bay of Bengal with abundant moisture, leading to South-West monsoon to enter in India and burst

Rain Bearing System and Distribution of rainfall

- South-West monsoon splits into two branches, i.e., Arabian sea branch and Bay of Bengal branch, causing rainfall in different parts of India at different points of time

Break in the Monsoon

- During the South-West monsoon period after raining for a few days, if the rain fails to occur for one or more weeks, then it is called break in the monsoon

Retreat of Monsoon

- Monsoon in September starts retreating from North-West part of India; The area under the monsoon influence shrinks slowly and monsoon retreats from all parts of India. While retreating, they pick up moisture and cause rainfall in Tamil Nadu region

Seasons

Winter Season (December to February)

- Temperature decreases with increasing latitude in India to near zero
- The season is characterised by fog and frost in North and North-East India
- There is light rainfall in this region due to Western disturbances

Summer Season (March to May)

- A hot weather season in India from March to May, where central part of India experiences extreme hot weather and an elongated low pressure belt creating monsoon trough
- This season experiences afternoon dust stroms like loo

Rainy Season (June to September)

- This period of South-West monsoon from June to September is known as the rainy season for most part of the country
- Monsoon trough intensifies and these months experience monsoon with violent thunder and lightening

Retreating Monsoon Season (October and November)

- Temperature starts decreasing in North India, monsoon trough becomes weak and is replaced by high pressure system
- South-West monsoon winds weaken and starts withdrawing from North Indian plains

SOURCE *Old NCERT Class VIII* (The Climate), *New NCERT Class IX* (Climate), *Old NCERT Class X* (Climate), *New NCERT Class XI* (Climate)

General Features of Indian Climate

1 **Consider the following statements about Indian climate.** *(Chap 4, Class-IX, New NCERT)*

1. The Indian climate has been described as Monsoon, which is derived from the Arabic word Mausim.
2. Different states of India exhibit only the same type of climate.
3. There are variations in the temperature and rainfall of different regions in India in a year.

Which of the statements given above is/are correct?

(a) Only 1 (b) Only 2 (c) Only 3 (d) 1 and 3

Ans. (d)

Exp. Statements (1) and (3) are correct with reference to Indian climate.

The climate of India is described as the 'Monsoon' type. The word 'Monsoon' is derived from the Arabic word 'Mausim' which literally means season. Monsoon refers to the seasonal reversal in the wind direction during a year. There are variations in temperature and rainfall of different regions in India in a year.

Statement (2) is incorrect because the different states of India exhibit the different type of climate. For instance, the temperature touches 50°C in some parts of Rajasthan in summer. Whereas, it may be around 20°C in Pahalgam in Jammu and Kashmir. Similarly, the rainfall varies from over 400 cm in Meghalaya to less than 10 cm in Ladakh and Western Rajasthan.

2 **With reference to Mawsynram in Meghalay, Consider the following statements.** *(Unit 6, Class-XI, Tamil Nadu Board)*

Statement-I Mawsynram grapples with an acute water shortage after monsoon ends around October.

Statement-II The soil in the limestone plateau doesn't absorb water and also there is barely any forest cover, so a lot a erosion of top soil happens.

Which one of the following is correct in respect of the above statements

(a) Both Statement-I and Statement-II are correct and Statement II is the correct explanation for Statement-I.
(b) Both Statement-I and Statement-II are correct and Statement-II is the correct explanation for Statement-I.
(c) Statement-I is correct, but Statement-II is incorrect.
(d) Statement-I is incorrect, but Statement-II is correct.

Ans. (a)

Exp. Both Statement-I and Statement-II are correct and Statement-II is the correct explanation for Statement-I.

Mawsynram holds the Guinness Record for 'the wettest place on Earth'. The average annual rainfall here is 11,861 mm. However, the soil in the limestone plateau of Mawsynram, Meghalaya doesn't absorb water. There is barely any forest cover, so a lot of erosion of top soil happens. All of the flows down into Bangladesh. The irony is the 'the wettest place on Earth' grapples with an acute water shortage after monsoon ends around October. Hence, world's rainiest place Mawsynram, which is also attributed world's wettest desert.

3 **Consider the following statements with reference to climate of India.** *(Chap 4, Class-XI, New NCERT)*

1. Upper air circulations and jet streams have no effect on the rainfall and climate of India.
2. As India is surrounded by Sea from three sides, the coastal states of India experience moderate climate.

Which of the statements given above is/are correct?

(a) Only 1 (b) Only 2
(c) Both 1 and 2 (d) Neither 1 nor 2

Ans. (b)

Exp. Only statement (2) is correct with reference to climate of India. The coastal states of India experience a moderate climate due to moderating influence of the sea. That's why people of Mumbai and Konkan coast have hardly any idea of extreme temperature and the seasonal rhythm of weather.

Statement (1) is incorrect because upper air circulations and jet streams play a significant role on the rainfall and climate of India.

About 3 km above the surface of Earth, a different pattern of air circulation is observed in the lower troposphere.

4 **Consider the following Assertion (A) and Reason (R) and choose the correct code.** *(Chap 4, Class-XI, New NCERT)*

Assertion (A) The cities such as Delhi and Kanpur, located in the interior of India have higher climatic contrast as compared to coastal cities such as Mumbai.

Reason (R) Coastal regions of India experience more rainfall than the North-Eastern states such as Meghalaya.

Select the correct answer using the codes given below.

(a) Both A and R are true and R is the correct explanation of A.
(b) Both A and R are true, but R is not the correct explanation of A.
(c) A is true, but R is false.
(d) A is false, but R is true.

Ans. (c)

Exp. Assertion (A) is true, but Reason (R) is false.

The cities such as Delhi and Kanpur, located in the interior of India have higher climatic contrast as compared to coastal cities such as Mumbai. It is because the coastal areas have an equable climate i.e., there is not much variation in temperature throughout the year.

North-Eastern states such as Meghalaya experience more rainfall than the coastal regions. In some parts of Khasi and Jaintia hills, the rainfall exceeds 1000 cm. Cherrapunji and Mawsynram in the Khasi hills of Meghalaya receive rainfall over 1080 cm in a year.

5 **Consider the following regions about the dry continental air masses affecting India during the winter season, these air masses originate from** *(Chap 4, Class-XI, New NCERT)*

1. Siberia
2. Central Asia
3. Mongolia
4. China

Codes

(a) Only 1 (b) Only 2
(c) 1, 2 and 4 (d) None of these

Ans. (b)

Exp. Region of Central Asia is the source of the dry continental air mass affecting India. In winter season, the surface winds blowing out of the high pressure centre over Central Asia reach India in the form of a dry continental air mass. These continental winds come in contact with trade winds over North-Western India.

However, the position of this contact zone is not stable. Occasionally, it may shift its position as far as East of the middle Ganga Valley and as a result, whole of the North-Western and Northern India upto middle Ganga Valley come under the influence of dry North-Western winds.

6 **Which of the following statements is/are correct with reference to mechanism of winds in the upper atmosphere during the winter season?** *(Chap 4, Class-XI, New NCERT)*

1. Trade winds blow in the upper atmosphere 3 km above the Earth's surface.
2. Westerly jet streams blow parallel to the Tibetan highlands which results in its bifurcation into two branches.
3. Cyclonic storms bring rainfall in the North-Western parts of India.

Codes

(a) 1 and 2 (b) 2 and 3 (c) 1 and 3 (d) All of these

Ans. (b)

Exp. Statements (2) and (3) are correct with reference to mechanism of winds in the upper atmosphere during the winter season.

Western jet streams blow across the Asian continent at latitudes North of Himalayas roughly parallel to the Tibetan highlands. The highlands act as a barrier in the path of these jet streams. As a result, jet streams get bifurcated. One of its branches blow to the North of the Tibetan highlands, while Southern branch blows in an Eastward direction, South of the Himalayas.

The Western cyclonic disturbances are weather phenomena of the winter months brought in by the Westerly flow from the Mediterranean region. They usually influence the weather of the North and North-Western regions of India. Therefore, cyclonic storms bring rainfall in the North-Western part of India.

Statement (1) is incorrect because the trade winds are air currents closer to Earth's surface that blow from East to West near the Equator.

Indian Monsoon

7 **Which of the following parameters are used by the Indian Meteorological Department (IMD) for the official declaration of the onset of Monsoon in India?** *(Chap 4, Class-XI, New NCERT)*

1. Rainfall reported over various weather stations located in Kerala only.
2. Atmospheric pressure exerted by the Westerlies.
3. Outwave/ Outgoing Longwave Radiation.

Choose the correct answer using the codes given below.

(a) 1 and 2 (b) 2 and 3
(c) 1 and 3 (d) 1, 2 and 3

Ans. (b)

Exp. Statements (2) and (3) are correct. The second guideline relating to the wind field i.e., Depth of westerlies (i.e., Atmospheric pressure exerted by the westerly) should be maintained upto 600 hPa . The source of data can be RSMC wind analysis/satellite derived winds. The third guideline is related to the Outgoing Longwave Radiation (OLR) INSAT derived OLR value should be below 200 wm-2 in the box confined by Lat. 5-10°N and long. 70-75°E. These guidelines are used by IMD, for declaring the onset of monsoon over Kerela.

Statement (1) is incorrect. The first guideline relates to the amount of rainfall received. If after 10th May, 60% of the available 14 stations enlisted, viz. Minicoy, Amini, Thiruvananthapuram, Punalur, Kollam, Allapuzha, Kottayam, Kochi, Thrissur, Kozhikode, Thalassery, Kannur, Kudulu and Mangalore report rainfall of 2.5 mm or more for two consecutive days.

8 **Which of the following are characteristic features of the Indian Monsoons?** *(Chap 4, Class-XI, New NCERT)*

1. Sudden Burst
2. Inter season variability
3. Western disturbances
4. Intra season variability
5. Sudden withdrawal

Codes

(a) 1, 2 and 4 (b) 3, 4 and 5
(c) 1, 2, 3 and 4 (d) 1, 2, 3, 4 and 5

Ans. (a)

Exp. The Monsoonal winds typically burst onto the shores of Kerala in the first week of June. This means that at the time of its arrival, the normal rainfall increases suddenly and continues constantly for several days. Indian Summer Monsoon Rainfall exhibits a prominent inter-annual variability.

A season of deficient June to September monsoon rainfall in India is followed by warm sea surface temperature (SST) anomalies over the tropical Indian Ocean and which generally yields normal or excessive rainfall the following season.

The intra seasonal variability of rainfall during a monsoon season is characterised by the occurrence of active and break phases. During the active phase, the rainfall is above normal over Central India and below normal over Northern India (foothills of the Himalaya) and Southern India. This pattern is reversed during the break phase (also called Monsoon breaks).

9 With reference to Western disturbances, consider the following statements. *(Chap 4, Class-XI, New NCERT)*

1. These are weak tropical cyclones that originate over the Mediterranean Sea.
2. Jet streams play an important role in driving these high-pressure systems into India.
3. The rainfall that occurs due to these disturbances is known to be beneficial for the Rabi crops.

Which of the statements given above is/are incorrect?

(a) Only 1 (b) Only 2 (c) 1 and 2 (d) 1, 2 and 3

Ans. (c)

Exp. Statements (1) and (2) are incorrect. Western disturbances are weak temperate or Extra-Tropical (not tropical) frontal cyclones that originate over the Mediterranean Sea, gain moisture from the Caspian Sea and the Black Sea and cause winter rainfall in the North Western part of India. The Himalayas act as orographic barriers.

The subtropical Westerly jet stream drives this low pressure (cyclones cannot develop in high pressure regions as these regions are characterised bysubsidence of wind) system towards the East of the Mediterranean Sea across Afghanistan, Pakistan and North-West India. These storms are residual frontal cyclones which move at the height of 2000 meters from the mean sea level.

10 Which of the following regions is not affected much by the Arabian Sea branch of monsoon? *(Chap 4, Class-XI, New NCERT) (CGPSC Pre 2016)*

(a) Western Ghats (b) Deccan Plateau
(c) Madhya Pradesh Basin (d) Chhattisgarh Basin

Ans. (d)

Exp. Chhattisgarh basin is not affected much by the Arabian Sea branch of monsoon. Arabian Sea branch monsoon further splits into two branches after being obstructed by the Western Ghats.

First branch moves parallel to Aravalli range causing scanty rainfall which further mingles into Bay of Bengal branch in North India. The second branch after being obstructed by Vindhya mountain causes rainfall in Gujarat and Madhya Pradesh.

11 Consider the following statements. *(Chap 4, Class-XI, New NCERT) (IAS Pre 2015)*

1. The winds which blow between 30°N and 60°S latitudes throughout the year are known as Westerlies.
2. The moist air masses that cause winter rains in the North-Western region of India are part of Westerlies.

Which of the statements given above is/are correct?

(a) Only 1 (b) Only 2
(c) Both 1 and 2 (d) Neither 1 nor 2

Ans. (b)

Exp. Only statement (2) is correct. The moist air masses that cause winter rains in the North-Western region of India are part of Westerlies.

Statement (1) is incorrect because Westerlies flows between 30°N - 60°N and 30°S - 60° S degree latitude. Westerlies are prevailing winds that flow from the West towards the East.

12 The rainfall on the Konkan coast is mainly due to which of the following wind system in the South-West monsoon season? *(Chap 4, Class-XI, New NCERT)*

(a) Bay of Bengal branch of South-West monsoon
(b) Westerly winds originating over Mediterranean
(c) North-East monsoon winds
(d) Arabian Sea branch of South-West monsoon

Ans. (d)

Exp. The rainfall on the Konkan coast is mainly due to Arabian Sea branch of South-West monsoon. South-West monsoon approaches the landmass in two branches, (i) Arabian Sea branch and (ii) Bay of Bengal branch.

The monsoon winds originating over the Arabian Sea is called Arabian Sea branch of South-West monsoon. Arabian Sea branch is obstructed by Western Ghats and the winds climb the slopes of Western Ghats from 900-1200 m. Soon, they become cool and as a result, the windward side of the Sahyadris and Western coastal plain (including Konkan coast) receive rainfall.

13 Which of the following statements is correct with reference to monsoon season in India? *(Chap 4, Class-XI, New NCERT)*

1. The sudden onset of monsoon rainfall in June, which is characterised by thunder and lightning is known as Monsoon burst.
2. Monsoon burst results in the sudden decline of temperature at a rate of 15-20°C over the Northern plains.

Codes

(a) Only 1 (b) Only 2
(c) Both 1 and 2 (d) Neither 1 nor 2

Ans. (a)

Exp. Only statement (1) is correct with reference to monsoon season in India. The sudden onset of the moisture laden winds associated with violent thunder and lightning, is often termed as the 'break' or 'burst' of monsoons. The monsoon may burst in the first week of June in the coastal areas of Kerala, Karnataka, Goa and Maharashtra. While in the interior parts of the country, it may be delayed to the first week of July.

Statement (2) is incorrect. Monsoon bursts bring down the temperature substantially. The day temperature registers a decline of 5° to 8°C between mid-June and mid-July over the Northern plains.

14 Which of the following regions lie in the rainshadow zone of Western Ghats and remains relatively dry during the monsoon? *(Chap 4, Class-XI, New NCERT)*

1. Mumbai
2. Pune
3. Kozhikode
4. Kolkata

Codes

(a) 1 and 3 (b) 2 and 3
(c) 1 and 2 (d) All of these

***Ans.* (b)**

Exp. Pune and Kozhikode lie in the rainshadow zone of Western Ghats and remain relatively dry during the monsoon. Some other rainshadow areas in this region are Mangaluru, Bengaluru etc. Western Ghats is one of the highest rainfall region in India.

After crossing the Western Ghats, Monsoon winds descend and get heated up. This reduces humidity in the winds. As a result, these winds cause little rainfall East of the Western Ghats. This region of low rainfall is known as the 'Rainshadow area.'

15 The Chhota Nagpur plateau region receives majority of its rainfall through which of the following wind system? *(Chap 4, Class-XI, New NCERT)*

(a) Arabian Sea branch of South-West monsoon winds
(b) Bay of Bengal branch of South-West monsoon winds
(c) North-Eastern monsoon winds
(d) None of the above

***Ans.* (a)**

Exp. The Chhota Nagpur plateau region receives a majority of its rainfall through Arabian Sea branch of South-West monsoon winds.

Moving along the Narmada and Tapi river valleys, these winds cause rainfall in extensive areas of Central India. The Chhota Nagpur plateau gets 15 cm rainfall from this branch. Thereafter, they enter the Ganga plains and mingle with the Bay of Bengal branch.

16 Which of the following is the primary reason behind the scanty rainfall caused in the Gujarat and Rajasthan region in the South-West monsoon season of India? *(Chap 2, Class-X, Old NCERT)*

1. The monsoon winds exhaust all of their moisture before reaching this region.
2. The moisture in the monsoon winds is exhausted due to the heat present in the region.
3. The moisture carrying winds generally blow parallel to this region and there is no orographic effect present here.

How many of the statements given above is/are correct?

(a) Only one (b) Only two
(c) All three (d) None of these

***Ans.* (a)**

Exp. Only one Statement i.e., (3) is the primary reason due to, which Gujarat and Rajasthan region in the South-West monsoon season of India experience the scanty rainfall. Monsoonal rainfall is generally governed by relief or topography.

Following are the reasons for the scanty rainfall in these regions

(i) The moisture carrying winds generally blow parallel to this region i.e., Aravallis.
(ii) There is no orographic effect as the moisture laden winds are not obstructed by any mountain or hills.

17 The monsoon winds which are responsible for causing highest rainfall in the Mawsynram region enter Meghalaya from South and South easterly direction. Which of the following physical features is/are responsible for deflection of the South westerly winds towards South- East direction? *(Chap 4, Class-XI, New NCERT)*

(a) Andaman and Nicobar Islands
(b) Eastern Ghats
(c) Arakan Yoma Range (Myanmar)
(d) Chhota Nagpur Plateau

***Ans.* (c)**

Exp. Arakan Yoma Range (Myanmar) is responsible for deflection of the South westerly windy towards South-East direction. It is responsible for highest rainfall in the Mawsynram region in Meghalaya. Meghalaya receives more than 400 cm of rainfall annually. Cherrapunji and Mawsynram in Khasi hills of Meghalaya receive rainfall over 1080 cm in a year.

18 Which of the following regions of India receive high rainfall during the South-West monsoon season? *(Chap 3, Class-VIII, Old NCERT)*

1. Western Ghats
2. Eastern Himalayas
3. Delhi
4. Eastern Ghats

Codes

(a) 1 and 2 (b) 2 and 4
(c) 1 and 4 (d) All of these

***Ans.* (a)**

Exp. Western Ghats and Eastern Himalayas region of India receive high rainfall during the South-West monsoon season. Monsoonal rainfall is largely governed by relief or topography. For instance, the windward side of the Western Ghats register a rainfall of over 250 cm. Again, the heavy rainfall in the North-Eastern states can be attributed to the hill ranges and the Eastern Himalayas.

It is evident that the rainfall received from the South-West monsoon is seasonal in character, which occurs between June and September.

19 **Consider the following statements with reference to the characteristics of rainfall during the South-West monsoon season in India.** *(Chap 4, Class-XI, New NCERT)*

1. The spatial distribution of rainfall varies from 12 cm to 250 cm across various regions.
2. More than 75% of rainfall is received in India during this season.
3. Monsoon breaks occur due to cyclonic depressions formed in Bay of Bengal region.

Which of the statements given above is/are correct?

(a) 1 and 2
(b) 2 and 3
(c) 1 and 3
(d) All of the above

Ans. (d)

Exp. All the given statements are correct with reference to the characteristics of rainfall during the South-West monsoon season in India. The spatial distribution of rainfall varies from 12 cm to 250 cm across the various regions. For example, windward side of Western Ghats receive a rainfall of over 250 cm.

South-West monsoon plays a pivotal role in the agrarian economy of India because over three-fourths (75%) of the total rain in the country is received during this period.

Monsoon breaks occur due to cyclonic depressions formed in Bay of Bengal region and their crossing into the mainland. Besides the frequency and intensity of these depressions, the passage followed by them deform the spatial distribution of rainfall.

20 **Consider the following statements with reference to retreating monsoon season in India.** *(Chap 4, Class-XI, New NCERT)*

1. There is rise in temperature during the retreating monsoon season.
2. This period is characterised by pleasant weather due to the phenomenon of October heat.
3. Coromandel Coast is greatly affected by cyclones during this season.

Which of the statements given above is/are incorrect?

(a) 1 and 2 (b) 2 and 3
(c) Only 2 (d) Only 3

Ans. (c)

Exp. Statement (2) is incorrect with reference to retreating monsoon season in India because this period is not characterised by pleasant weather.

The retreating South-West monsoon season is marked by clear skies and rise in temperature owing to the conditions of high temperature and humidity, the weather becomes rather oppressive. This is commonly known as 'October heat'.

Seasons in India

21 **Consider the following Assertion (A) and Reason (R) and choose the correct code.** *(Chap 4, Class-XI, New NCERT)*

Assertion (A) The mean daily temperature remains below 21°C over most of the parts of Northern India and the night temperature falls below the freezing point during the winter season.

Reason (R) Northern Indian states experience continental climate and there is high amount of snowfall in the Himalayan region during the month of January.

Codes

(a) Both A and R are true and R is the correct explanation of A.
(b) Both A and R are true, but R is not the correct explanation of A.
(c) A is true, but R is false.
(d) A is false, but R is true.

Ans. (a)

Exp. Both Assertion (A) and Reason (R) are true and Reason (R) is the correct explanation of Assertion (A).

The mean daily temperature remains below 21°C over most of the parts of Northern India and the night temperature may be quite low, sometimes going below the freezing point in states like Punjab and Rajasthan. Northern Indian states like Punjab, Haryana and Rajasthan experiences continental climate. Also, there is high amount of snowfall in the Himalayan region during the month of January.

22 **Consider the following statements with reference to cold weather season in India.** *(Chap 4, Class-XI, New NCERT)*

1. The Peninsular region of India do not experience any well-defined cold weather season.
2. Coastal areas experience greatest range of temperature during the cold weather season.
3. Westerly and North-Westerly winds blow over the Gangetic Plains during this season.
4. Shallow cyclonic depressions cause rainfall in some of the North-Western parts of India in this season.

Which of the statements given above is/are incorrect?

(a) 1 and 2 (b) Only 2 (c) 2 and 3 (d) 3 and 4

Ans. (b)

Exp. Statement (2) is incorrect with reference to cold weather season in India.

There is hardly any seasonal change in the distribution pattern of the temperature in coastal areas because of moderating influence of the sea and the proximity Equator to Equator. For example, the mean maximum temperature for January at Thiruvananthapuram is as high as 31°C and for June, it is 29.5°.

23 Which of the following statements is/are correct with reference to Western cyclonic disturbances in India? *(Chap 4, Class-XI, New NCERT)*

1. Rainfall due to Western disturbances is highly beneficial for Rabi crops in India.
2. Southern Andhra Pradesh, Telangana and Tamil Nadu also receive rainfall in winter season due to cyclonic disturbances originating over Mediterranean Sea.

Codes

(a) Only 1 (b) Only 2
(c) Both 1 and 2 (d) Neither 1 nor 2

Ans. (c)

Exp. Both the statements (1) and (2) are correct with reference to Western cyclonic disturbances in India.
In North-Western India the amount of rainfall is less but it is highly beneficial for Rabi crops. Some weak temperate cyclones from Mediterranean Sea cause rainfall in Punjab, Haryana, Delhi and Western Uttar Pradesh.
During October-November, North-East monsoon while crossing over Bay of Bengal, pick up moisture and causes torrential rainfall over the Tamil Nadu Coast, Southern Andhra Pradesh, Telangana, South-East Karnataka and South-East Kerala.

24 Consider the following statements about the distribution of rainfall in India. *(Chap 4, Class-XI, New NCERT)*

1. The Western Ghats act as a barrier to the moisture-laden winds, causing heavy rainfall on the windward side.
2. The Thar Desert experiences the highest rainfall in India due to its proximity to the Arabian Sea.

Which of the statements given above is/are correct?

(a) Only 1 (b) Only 2
(c) Both 1 and 2 (d) None of these

Ans. (a)

Exp. Only statement (1) is correct. The Western Ghats intercept the rain-laden monsoon winds that sweep in from the south-west during late summer. These mountains influence the Indian monsoon weather patterns and are the first to experience the monsoon rains.
Statement (2) is incorrect. The Thar Desert experiences a subtropical desert climate and high pressure. However, the monsoon winds in the South West bring rainfall in the summer seasons. But still, this arid region receives a low annual rainfall (4-20 inches) as compared to the other parts of India. It receives very little rainfall, less than 10 inches per annum.

25 Consider the following statements. *(Chap 4, Class-XI, New NCERT)*

1. The ITCZ shifts at 25° N during this season.
2. Hot winds and dust storms blow in this season in the Northern Plains.
3. Local storms which bring rainfall are common in this season.

Which of the statements given above is/are correct?

(a) Winter season (b) Summer season
(c) South West monsoon season (d) Retreating monsoon season

Ans. (b)

Exp. The given statements characterise the summer season. The summer months are a period of excessive heat and falling air pressure in the Northern half of the country. Due to the heating of the subcontinent, the ITCZ moves Northwards occupying a position centred at 25°N in July.
During this season, hot winds and dust storms blow in the Northern plains. Hot, dry and oppressing winds blowing in Northern plains during season is locally known as 'loo'. Dust storms in the evening are very common during this season in Punjab, Haryana, Eastern Rajasthan and Uttar Pradesh. These temporary storms bring light rain and a pleasant cool breeze. These local storms are associated with violent winds, torrential rainfall and even hailstorms.

Rainfall

26 Consider the following pairs. *(Chap 4, Class-XI, New NCERT)*

Local Storms	Regions
1. Mango Shower	Kerala and Karnataka
2. Bardoli Cheerah	Assam
3. Kal Baisakhi	West Bengal
4. Loo	Telangana

How many of the pairs given above is/are incorrectly matched?

(a) Only one (b) Only two (c) Only three (d) All four

Ans. (a)

Exp. Only one pair i.e., (4) is incorrectly matched. 'Loo' is strong, gusty, hot, dry wind blowing during the day over the North and North-Western India.

27 Which of the following regions is/are characterised by low rainfall in India? *(Chap 4, Class-XI, New NCERT)*

1. Deccan Plateau 2. Khasi Hills
3. Western Uttar Pradesh 4. Ladakh

Codes

(a) 1 and 2 (b) 2, 3 and 4
(c) 1, 3 and 4 (d) All of these

Ans. (c)

Exp. Deccan plateau, Western Uttar Pradesh and Ladakh regions are characterised by low rainfall in India. Deccan plateau and Western Uttar Pradesh come under the areas of low rainfall. These areas receive rainfall between 50-100 cm. Some other areas of low rainfall are Delhi, Haryana, Punjab, Jammu and Kashmir, Eastern Rajasthan etc.
Ladakh comes under the areas of inadequate rainfall. It receives rainfall below 50 cm.
While Khasi Hills experience high amount of rainfall. For examples, Areas like Cherrapunji in Khasi hills receive over 1000 cm rainfall.

28 **Consider the following regions, the rainfall variability is highest as compared to other three?**
(Chap 4, Class-XI, New NCERT)

1. Interior regions of Deccan Plateau
2. Western Ghats
3. North-Eastern Peninsular region
4. Uttarakhand and Himachal Pradesh

Which of the option given above is/are correct?
(a) Only 1
(b) Only 2
(c) Only 3
(d) Only 4

Ans. (a)

Exp. In the given options, interior regions of Deccan plateau has the highest rainfall variability as compared to the other three.

It has the rainfall variability of over 50%. Besides it, Western part of Rajasthan, Northern part of Jammu and Kashmir also have the rainfall variability over 50% on the other hand, a variability of less than 25% exists on the Western coasts, Western Ghats, North-Eastern Peninsula, Eastern plains of Ganga, North-Eastern India, Uttarakhand and Himachal Pradesh.

29 **Which of the following statements is/are correct regarding Western cyclonic disturbances?**
(Chap 4, Class-XI, New NCERT)

1. The Western cyclonic disturbances are brought into India by the Easterly jet stream.
2. An increase in the prevailing night temperature generally indicates an advance in the arrival of these cyclone disturbances.

Select the correct answer using the codes given below.
(a) Only 1
(b) Only 2
(c) Both 1 and 2
(d) Neither 1 nor 2

Ans. (b)

Exp. Only statement (2) is correct. Western disturbances are the cause of the most winter and pre-monsoon season rainfall across North-West India. This phenomenon is usually associated with cloudy sky and unusual rain. Moreover, an increase in the prevailing night temperature generally indicates an advance in the arrival of these cyclone disturbances.

Statement (1) is incorrect. Western Disturbances develop in the mid latitude region (North of the Tropic of Cancer), therefore they are called as mid latitude storms or extra-tropical storms.

The Western cyclonic disturbances are weather phenomena of the winter months brought in by the subtropical westerly jet streams flow from the Mediterranean region.

Climatic Classification

30 **Match the following lists correctly and choose the correct code.**
(Chap 4, Class-XI, New NCERT)

List I (Koeppen's Climatic Region)	List II (Located in)
A. As	1. West Coast of India, South of Goa
B. Bwhw	2. North-Western Gujarat
C. Dfc	3. Arunachal Pradesh
D. Amw	4. Coromandel Coast

Codes

	A	B	C	D		A	B	C	D
(a)	1	2	3	4	(b)	1	4	3	2
(c)	3	1	2	4	(d)	4	2	3	1

Ans. (d)

Exp. The correct matching is A-4, B-2, C-3, D-1.

Koeppen used letter symbols to denote climatic types. Each type is further sub-divided into sub-types on the basis of seasonal variations in the distributional pattern of rainfall and temperature.

As denotes for monsoon with dry summer. It is mainly found in Coromandel Coast of Tamil Nadu.

Bwhw denotes for semi-arid steppe type of climate. It is mainly found in North-Western Gujarat, Some parts of Western Rajasthan and Punjab.

Dfc denotes for cold humid winter with short summer. It in mainly found in Arunachal Pradesh.

Amw denotes the monsoon with short dry season. It is mainly found in West Coast of India, South of Goa.

31 **Which of the following pairs is/are correct vis a vis Koeppen scheme for classification of climate?**
(Chap 4, Class-XI, New NCERT)

1. **Tropical climates** Where the mean monthly temperature throughout the year is over 18°C.
2. **Warm temperate climates** Where mean temperature of the coldest month is between 15°C and minus 4°C.
3. **Ice climates** Where mean temperature of the warmest month is under 0°C to 10 °C.

Select the correct answer from codes given below.
(a) Only 1 (b) 1, 2 and 3 (c) Only 3 (d) 1 and 3

Ans. (a)

Exp. Only statement (1) is correct. Koeppen based his scheme of climatic classification on monthly values of temperature and precipitation. He identified five major climatic types, namely Tropical climates, where the mean monthly temperature throughout the year is over 18°C.

Statements (2) and (3) are incorrect. Dry climates, where precipitation is very low in comparison to temperature, and hence, dry. If dryness is less, it is semiarid (S); if it is more, the climate is arid(W). Warm temperate climates, where the mean temperature of the coldest month is between 18°C and minus 3°C.

Ice climates, where the mean temperature of the warmest month is under 10°C.

32 **According to Koeppen's climate classification, the climate of North Bihar may be explained as**

(Chap 7, Class-XI, New NCERT) (BPSC Pre 2017)

(a) Cwg (b) Aw
(c) CA'w (d) None of these

Ans. (a)

Exp. According to Koeppen's climate classification, the climate of North Bihar may be explained as Cwg. This type of climate is found in most parts of the Northern Ganga Plains.

Most of the rainfalls occur in Summer and Winter are dry. Cwg type climate is also known as 'Monsoon type with dry winters' type climate.

EL-Nino and Southern Oscillations

33 **With reference to the Indian Ocean Dipole (IOD), consider the following statements.**

(Chap 4, Class-XI, New NCERT)

1. It is characterised by an oscillation of sea surface temperatures in which the Western Indian Ocean becomes alternately warmer and colder than the Eastern part of the Pacific Ocean.
2. Unlike an El-Nino, the IOD is a periodically recurring event and can be predicted.
3. It is possible for IOD to cause floods in India and bushfires in Australia in the same year.

Which of the statements given above is/are correct?

(a) 1 and 2 (b) 2 and 3 (c) Only 3 (d) 1, 2 and 3

Ans. (c)

Exp.Only statement (3) is correct. During the 2019-20 Monsoon season, India faced severe floods and Australia witnessed devastating bushfires, attributed to the positive phase of the Indian Ocean Dipole (IOD). Around a million people were displaced in Karnataka and Maharashtra due to the floods.

The warmer Arabian Sea increased moisture for the South Western monsoon winds, causing havoc in Karnataka, Maharashtra, and Kerala. Simultaneously, a cooler Eastern Indian Ocean induced dryness and anticyclonic conditions in Northern Australia, intensifying bushfires.

Statements (1) and (2) are incorrect because the IOD, often termed the 'Indian Nino', involves irregular sea-surface temperature oscillations in the Western and Eastern parts of the Indian Ocean.

Both the IOD and El-Nino can be observed but have limited predictive value, with no consensus on parameters for prediction despite some research claims. This underscores the intricate dynamics shaping regional climate events.

34 **Consider the following statements regarding Indian monsoon.**

(Chap 4, Class-XI, New NCERT)

1. The El-Nino is generally known to suppress monsoon rains in India.
2. The La-Nina has a negative impact on rainfall associated with the North-East monsoon.
3. Heavy snowfall in Tibetan Plateau in the winter season can immensely increase the rainfall received in India during the monsoon season.

Which of the statements given above is/are correct?

(a) Only 1 (b) 1 and 2
(c) 1 and 3 (d) 2 and 3

Ans. (b)

Exp. Statements (1) and (2) are correct. El-Nino and La-Nina (together called the El-Nino Southern Oscillations or ENSO) are phenomena which take place in the Pacific Ocean however, both the processes can have a significant say/impact on India's monsoon and hence economy. In meteorological parlance, these interconnected events are called "TELECONNECTIONS."

- The El-Nino, generally has a negative impact on the Indian monsoon i.e.it suppresses the monsoonal rainfall. This invariably is associated with droughts in many parts of the country which has a ripple effect on various economic indicators such as inflation and prices of commodities.
- While La-Nina conditions enhance the rainfall associated with the Southwest monsoon, it has a negative impact on rainfall associated with the Northeast monsoon.

Statement (3) is incorrect. When there is high snowfall in the Tibetan plateau during the winter season, it is generally seen that the following monsoon in India is considerably weak. The tropical easterly jet stream plays an important role in the manifestation of this phenomenon.

To put it simply, when there is a thick snow cover on the Tibetan plateau, it prevents the development of strong low-pressure conditions (prerequisite for driving the South Western monsoon winds).

Chapter 20

Natural Vegetation and Soils in India

Natural Vegetation and Soils in India

Natural Vegetation

- Refers to a plant community which has grown naturally without human aid and has been left undisturbed by humans for a long time, includes tall trees, shrubs, grasses, bushes, etc

Factors Influencing Natural Vegetation

- **Land** The nature of land influences the type of vegetation e.g. mountainous region has hydrophilus vegetation whereas deserts have xerophytic vegetation
- **Soil** Nature of soil and nutrients present in it provides a basis for different types of vegetation, e.g. sandy soil with few nutrients is not suitable for vegetation however, loamy soil which is nutrient rich is suitable for vegetation
- **Precipitation** Areas with high rainfall support dense and evergreen vegetation whereas with low rainfall support scanty vegetation
- **Temperature** Determines the character and extent of the natural vegetation in a region
- **Photoperiod** Amount of sunlight received by vegetation determines its nature

Classification of Natural Vegetation

- **Moist Tropical Forests** Tropical wet evergreen forests, Tropical semi-evergreen forests, Tropical moist deciduous forests, Littoral swamps
- **Montane Sub-Tropical Forests** Sub-tropical broad leaved hill forests, Sub-tropical moist pine forests , Sub-tropical dry evergreen forests
- **Montane Temperate Forests** Montane wet temperate forests, Himalayan moist temperate forests, Himalayan dry temperate forests

Soils

Alluvial Soil

- Formed due to the silt deposited by Indo-Gangetic-Brahmaputra rivers. They are the largest soil groups
- They also occur in deltas of Mahanadi, Godavari, Krishna, Narmada, Tapi, etc
- They yield crops like rice, sugarcane, wheat, cotton, etc

Saline Soil

- Lacks moisture, humus and living organisms
- Contains large content of NaCl and is infertile
- Found mainly in Haryana, Rajasthan, Punjab, UP, etc

Black Soil

- Black soils are very fertile in valleys and are retentive of moisture. It is rich in lime and iron but deficit in humus, nitrogen and phosphorus content
- Best suited for cotton crops; Other crops grown are wheat, jowar, linseed, etc

Red Soil

- Soil developed on Archaen granite, derives its colour red due to the presence of iron oxides
- Texture ranges from sandy to clay to loamy
- Found mainly in peninsula from Tamil Nadu in South to Bundelkhand in North

Laterite Soil

- Brown in colour composed essentially of a mixture of hydrated oxides of aluminium and iron
- Supports crops like groundnut, cashewnut, coffee, etc

Forest/Mountain Soil

- It is thin layered and the profile is poorly developed
- Rich in organic content
- Supports rubber plantation, tea plantation, coffee, tea, etc

Factors Influencing Soil Formation

- **Desert Soil** Lack moisture content, humus content is also low but rich in iron content
- **Peaty Soil** Rich in organic matter and it supports crops like jute, rice, spices, rubber, etc

SOURCE New NCERT Class IX *(Natural Vegetation and Wildlife)*, Old NCERT Class X *(The Flora, the Fauna and the Soils)*, New NCERT Class XI *(Soils)*, New NCERT Class XI *(Natural Vegetation)*

Natural Vegetation

1 **Which of the following statements is/are correct with reference to Tropical Evergreen forests found in India?** *(Chap 6, Class-XI, New NCERT)*

1. They are found in regions with annual precipitation more than 200 cm.
2. They are widespread in the Malwa Plateau region.
3. Creeper and climber species are found in abundance in these forests.
4. Plantations such as tea, rubber, coffee are generally grown in these regions.

Codes

(a) 1, 2, 3 and 4 (b) 2 and 4 (c) 1, 3 and 4 (d) 2 and 3

Ans. (c)

Exp. Statements (1), (3) and (4) are correct regarding tropical evergreen forest. They are found in warm and humid areas with an annual precipitation of over 200 cm and mean annual temperature above 22° C.

Tropical evergreen forests are well stratified with layers closer to the ground and are covered with shrubs and creepers. Apart from that, the under growing climbers also provide an evergreen character to these forests.

Plantations such as tea, rubber, coffee are generally grown in these regions.

Statement (2) is incorrect because Tropical evergreen forests are found in the Western slope of the Western Ghats, hills of the North-Eastern region and the Andaman and Nicobar Islands.

2 **Consider the following pairs.** *(Chap 5, Class-XI, New NCERT)*

Tree		State
1. Teak	–	Madhya Pradesh
2. Sundari	–	West Bengal
3. Sandalwood	–	Kerala
4. Deodar	–	Madhya Pradesh

How many of the pairs given above are correctly matched?

(a) Only one (b) Only two (c) All four (d) None of these

Ans. (b)

Exp. Only two pairs i.e., (1) and (2) are correctly matched as the Teak is a tropical hardwood tree species in family Lamiaceae. The most Teak forests in India are in Madhya Pradesh, Maharashtra, Kerala, etc. Sundari trees are mainly found in West Bengal. Sundari trees are a type of mangrove tree that are abundant in the Indian subcontinent. The scientific name for the Sundari tree is Heritiera fomes, and it is part of the Malvaceae family.

Pairs (3) and (4) are incorrectly matched because Sandalwood is found in the Deccan plateau mostly in Karnataka and Tamil Nadu. Sandalwood is used for carving and manufacturing in cense. The Deodar forests are widely found in snowfall Himachal Pradesh, Jammu and Kashmir, Uttarakhand, etc.

3 **Consider the following statements with reference to Tropical Deciduous forests in India.** *(Chap 5, Class-XI, New NCERT)*

1. Teak, Sal, Sheesham are found in abundance in the Tropical Moist Deciduous forests.
2. Dry Deciduous forests develop in regions having rainfall between 70-100 cm.

Which of the statements given above is/are correct?

(a) Only 1 (b) Only 2
(c) Both 1 and 2 (d) Neither 1 nor 2

Ans. (c)

Exp. Both the statements (1) and (2) are correct with reference to Tropical Deciduous Forests in India.

Tropical Deciduous forests are the most widespread forests in India. They are also called the monsoon forests They spread over regions which receive rainfall between 70-200 cm. Teak, sal, sheesham, hurra, mahua, amla, semul, kusum and sandalwood, etc. are the main species of these forests.

4 **Consider the following statements about Tropical dry deciduous forest.** *(Chap 5, Class-XI, New NCERT)*

1. These are similar to moist deciduous forests and shed their leaves in the dry season.
2. Tropical dry deciduous forests are found throughout India, except in the Western and the North-Western regions.

Which of the statements given above is/are correct?

(a) Only 1 (b) Only 2
(c) Both 1 and 2 (d) Neither 1 nor 2

Ans. (c)

Exp. Both statements (1) and (2) are correct.

Tropical dry deciduous forests are similar to moist deciduous forests, they shed their leaves in the dry season. This is a survival skill that helps the trees conserve water and ensure there is enough water for photosynthesis.

The Tropical dry deciduous forests are found throughout India, except in the Western and the North-Western regions. They occur in an irregular wide strip running from the foot of the Himalayas to Kanyakumari. The important species found in these forests include, Teak, Axlewood, Rosewood, Common bamboo, Red sanders, Laurel, Satinwood.

5 **Consider the following pairs.** *(Chap 5, Class-XI, New NCERT)*

Altitude		Forests
1. Foothills of Himalayas	–	Wet Temperate Forests
2. 1000-2000 m	–	Deciduous Forests
3. 1500-1750 m	–	Pine Forests
4. 2200-3000 m	–	Temperate Grasslands

How many pairs given above is/are correct?

(a) Only one (b) Only two (c) Only three (d) All four

Ans. (b)

Exp. Only two pairs i.e., (3) and (4) are correct.

Between 1500-1750 m, pine forests are also well-developed in this zone, with Chir pine as a very useful commercial tree.

Blue pine and spruce appear at altitudes of 2225-3048 m along with Temperate grasslands.

While pairs (1) and (2) are incorrect the Himalayan ranges shows a succession of vegetation from the tropical to the tundra, which change in with the altitude.

Deciduous forests are found in the foothills of the Himalayas. Deciduous forest is succeeded by the wet temperate type of forests between an altitude of 1000-2000 m.

6 With reference to various species found in the Himalayan region, consider the following statements. *(Chap 5, Class-XI, New NCERT)*

1. Chir pine species is used for obtaining wood for commercial purpose.
2. Deodar is an endemic species used in construction activities and is common in Western Himalayas.
3. Chinar and walnut are used in the handicrafts industry of Kashmir region.

How many of the statements given above is/are correct?

(a) Only one (b) Only two
(c) All three (d) None of these

***Ans.* (c)**

Exp. All the given statements i.e., (1), (2) and (3) are correct with reference to various species found in Himalayan region. Chir pine is a very useful commercial tree. Pine forests are well-developed between 1,500-1,750 m. In this zone Deodar, a highly valued endemic species grows mainly in the Western part of the Himalayan range.

Deodar is a durable wood mainly used in construction activity. Similarly, the chinar and the walnut, which sustain the famous Kashmir handicrafts, belong to this zone.

7 Consider the following statements with reference to Alpine vegetation found in Himalayas. *(Chap 5, Class-XI, New NCERT)*

1. These forests are found at an altitude of 3000-4000 m in the Himalayas.
2. Tribes such as Gujjars, Bhotiyas and Bakarwals practise transhumance in this region.
3. Rhododendron, juniper and pines are common species of this region.

Which of the statements given above is/are correct?

(a) 1 and 3 (b) 2 and 3 (c) Only 3 (d) All of these

***Ans.* (d)**

Exp. All the given statements (1), (2) and (3) are correct with reference to the Alpine vegetation found in Himalayas. Silver firs, junipers, pines, birch and rhododendrons, etc., occur between 3000-4000 m.

However, these pastures are used extensively for transhumance by tribes like the Gujjars, the Bakarwals, the Bhotiyas and the Gaddis.

In the higher reaches of Himalaya, there are Alpine forests and pastures.

8 Consider the following statements. *(Chap 11, Module-2, NIOS)*

1. Tropical moist deciduous are found in the Eastern part of the country such as in North-Eastern states along the foothills of the Himalayas.
2. Tropical dry deciduous are found in the rainier parts of the Peninsular plateau and the plains of Bihar and Uttar Pradesh.
3. Alpine forest is found in the Western Ghats.

How many of the statements given above are correct?

(a) Only one (b) Only two
(c) Only three (d) None of these

***Ans.* (b)**

Exp. Only two statements i.e. (1) and (2) are correct regarding various forests in India.

Tropical moist deciduous forests are found in the Eastern part of the country such as in North-Eastern states along the foothills of the Himalayas, Jharkhand, West Odisha, and Chhattisgarh, and on the Eastern slopes of the Western Ghats.

Tropical moist deciduous forests are also known as monsoon forests. Tropical dry deciduous are found in the rainier parts of the Peninsular plateau and the plains of Bihar and Uttar Pradesh. The dry deciduous forests are found in areas having rainfall between 100 cm and 70 cm.

Statement (3) is incorrect because Alpine forest is found in Arunachal Pradesh. In India, Alpine forests occur along the Himalayas at altitudes ranging from 2900 to 3500 m above sea level and up to 3800 m.

9 Consider the following statements with reference to Mangrove forests in India. *(Chap 5, Class-XI, New NCERT)*

1. This type of vegetation grows well along the coast in salt marshes, tidal creeks and estuaries.
2. The Sundari tree found in mangrove region cannot survive in soils with high salinity.

Which of the statements given above is/are incorrect?

(a) Only 1
(b) Only 2
(c) Both 1 and 2
(d) Neither 1 nor 2

***Ans.* (b)**

Exp. Only statement (2) is incorrect with reference to Mangrove forests in India.

Sundari is the dominant mangrove tree species of the Sundarbans of India and Bangladesh. Hence, we can conclude that the Sundari tree found in Mangrove region can survive in soils with high salinity.

10 **Consider the following statements regarding Mangroves.** *(Chap 5, Class-XI, New NCERT)*

1. Mangroves are found mainly in tropical and sub-tropical inter-tidal regions of the world.
2. Sundarbans in West Bengal alone account for almost half of the total area that is found under mangroves in India.
3. Gujarat has the maximum mangrove cover in the country, followed by West Bengal and Andaman and Nicobar islands.

How many of the statements given above is/are correct?

(a) Only one (b) Only two
(c) All three (d) None of these

Ans. (b)

Exp. Only two statements i.e., (1) and (2) are correct.

Mangroves are salt-tolerant forest ecosystems found mainly in tropical and sub-tropical inter-tidal regions of the world. They comprise of trees or shrubs that have the common trait of growing in shallow and muddy salt water or brackish waters, especially along quiet shorelines and in estuaries.

Sundarbans in West Bengal alone account for almost half of the total area that is found under mangroves in India.

Statement (3) is incorrect because West Bengal has the maximum mangrove cover in the country, followed by Gujarat and Andaman and Nicobar Islands.West Bengal has a total of 42.45% of India's mangrove cover, followed by Gujarat at 23.66%, and Andaman and Nicobar islands at 12.39%.

11 **Which of the following natural sites is/are included in wetlands of India?** *(Chap 5, Class-XI, New NCERT)*

1. Saline lakes of Rajasthan Gujarat
2. Lagoons located on the East coast of India
3. Freshwater lakes of India
4. Floodplains of Brahmaputra and other marshes

Codes

(a) 1 and 3
(b) 1 and 4
(c) 2 and 3
(d) 1, 2, 3 and 4

Ans. (d)

Exp. All the natural sites given in the question are included in wetlands of India. The country's wetlands have been grouped into following categories i.e.,

The vast saline expanses of Rajasthan, Gujarat and the Gulf of Kachchh.

The delta wetlands and Lagoons of India's East coast (Chilika Lake).

The freshwater marshes of the Gangetic Plain.

The floodplains of the Brahmaputra; the marshes and swamps in the hills of North-East India and the Himalayan foothills.

12 **According to India State of Forests Report, 2019, which of the following statements is/are incorrect with reference to forest and tree cover in India?** *(Chap 5, Class-XI, New NCERT)*

(a) The actual forest cover of India is 21.67% of the total geographical area of the country.
(b) Madhya Pradesh has the highest forest cover among all the states in terms of percentage of geographical area.
(c) Very dense forests constitute 13% of the forest cover of India.
(d) The total recorded forest area of India is about 23%.

Ans. (b)

Exp. Statement (b) is incorrect regarding the State of Forests Report, 2019. Mizoram has the highest area under forest cover in terms of percentage of geographical area covering 85.41%.

13 **Arrange the following Indian States/Union Territories in ascending order based on the reported mangrove cover in square kilometers as per the Forest Report 2021.** *(Chap 5, Class-XI, New NCERT)*

(a) Maharashtra, Andhra Pradesh, Andaman and Nicobar Islands, Gujarat, West Bengal
(b) Maharashtra, Andhra Pradesh, Gujarat, Andaman and Nicobar Islands, West Bengal
(c) Andhra Pradesh, Maharashtra, Gujarat, Andaman and Nicobar Islands, West Bengal
(d) Andhra Pradesh, Maharashtra, Andaman and Nicobar Islands, Gujarat, West Bengal

Ans. (a)

Exp. The ascending order of mangrove cover in square kilometers, based on the Forest Report 2021, is as follows Maharashtra (304 sq km), Andhra Pradesh (404 sq km), Andaman and Nicobar Islands (617 sq km), Gujarat (1140 sq km), and West Bengal (2114 sq km).

14 **Match the given lists correctly and choose the correct code.** *(Chap 5, Class-IX, New NCERT)*

List I (Traditional Medicinal Plants in India)	List II (Uses)
A. Sarpgandha	1. Treats Blood Pressure
B. Neem	2. Cure Eye sores
C. Kachnar	3. Used as Antibiotic
D. Babool	4. Cure Asthma and Ulcers

Codes

	A	B	C	D		A	B	C	D
(a)	4	2	3	1	(b)	1	3	4	2
(c)	2	1	3	4	(d)	3	2	4	3

Ans. (b)

Exp. The correct matching is A-1, B-3, C-4, D-2.

Sarpagandha It is taken from the root of a plant named *Rauvolfia serpentina* or Indian snakeroot, and is a vital drug in Ayurveda used for high blood pressure and insomnia.

Neem Its leaf and its constituents have been demonstrated to exhibit immunomodulatory, anti-inflammatory, anti-hyperglycaemic, antiulcer, anti-malarial, anti-fungal, antibiotic, anti-viral, antioxidant, anti-mutagenic and anti-carcinogenic properties.

Kachnar It is used to cure asthma and ulcers. The roots and buds of the plant are good for digestive issues.

Babool Paste of the leaves of babool on the eyes helps us for reducing redness and sores. It also helps with the pain.

Forest Conservation in India

15 Which of the given statements is/are correct with reference to National Forest Policy of India? *(Chap 5, Class-IX, New NCERT)*

(a) India has a National Forest Policy which was enacted in 1952 and later modified in 1988.
(b) The aim of National Forest Policy of India is to bring 33% of area of the country under forest cover.
(c) The Forest Policy aims to protect forests through social forestry and afforestation.
(d) All of the above

Ans. (d)

Exp. All the given statements are correct regarding the Forest Policy of India. The Government of India has proposed a nation-wide forest conservation policy, and adopted a forest policy in 1952, which was further modified in 1988.

According to the New Forest Policy, the government will emphasise sustainable forest management in order to conserve and expand forest reserve on the one hand, and to meet the needs of local people on the other.

The forest policy aimed at bringing 33% of the geographical areas under forest cover; conserving the natural heritage of the country, its biological diversity and genetic pool; checking soil erosion, extension of the desert lands and reduction of floods and droughts; increasing the forest cover through social forestry and afforestation on degraded land.

16 Consider the following statements with reference to social forestry. *(Chap 5, Class-IX, New NCERT)*

1. It aims to protect forests and promote afforestation on barren lands of the country.
2. It aims to promote agro forestry in rural areas for both tree plantations and agriculture crops.
3. Community forestry, which aims to plant trees on public lands such as village pastures is not included in social forestry.

Which of the statements given above is/are incorrect?

(a) 1 and 3
(b) Only 3
(c) 1 and 2
(d) 2 and 3

Ans. (b)

Exp. Statement (3) is incorrect with reference to social forestry because community forestry is a part of social forestry, it involves the raising of trees on public or community land such as the village pasture and temple land, roadside, canal bank, strips along railway lines, and schools etc. Community forestry programme aims at providing benefits to the community as a whole. Community forestry provides a medium under which the people of landless classes can associate themselves in tree raising and thus, get those benefits, which otherwise are restricted for landowners.

17 Which of the following statements correctly defines farm forestry? *(Chap 5, Class-IX, New NCERT)*

(a) Planting ecologically friendly crops on farms to protect soil moisture.
(b) Protecting soil moisture by covering it with farm residue.
(c) Planting tree belts for commercial purposes on the margins of agriculture fields.
(d) Promoting eco-friendly techniques in exploitation of forest resource.

Ans. (c)

Exp. Statement (c) is correctly defines farm forestry. Farm forestry is the process of planting tree belts for commercial purposes on the margins of agriculture fields. Forest departments of various states distribute seedlings of trees free of cost to small and medium farmers. Several lands such as the margins of agricultural fields, grasslands and pastures, land around homes and cow sheds may be used for raising trees under non-commercial farm forestry.

Soils

18 Consider the following statements regarding the classification of soils in India. *(Chap 6, Class-XI, New NCERT)*

1. The ICAR has classified Indian soils on the basis of United States Department of Agriculture Taxonomy.
2. Soil Survey of India, established in 1956 made elaborate study of Indian soils in the Damodar Valley.
3. The Vertisol group of soils constitutes the largest group of soil in India.
4. The Mollisol is the smallest soil group in India.

How many of the statements given above is/are incorrect?

(a) Only one (b) Only two
(c) Only three (d) None of these

Ans. (a)

Exp. Only one statement i.e. (3) is incorrect regarding the classification of soils in India. Inceptisol group of soils constitute the largest group of soil in India. It covers the area of 130372.90 (in Thousand Hectares) which is 39.74% of the total percentage of soil. While Vertisol group of soil only cover 27960.00 (in Thousand Hectares) which is 8.52 % of the total percentage of soil.

19 With reference to alluvial soils of India, consider the following statements. *(Chap 6, Class-XI, New NCERT)*

1. The alluvial soils vary in nature from sandy loam to clay.
2. These soils are found only in North India and in the Gujarat region.
3. These soils are rich in potash but poor in phosphorous content.
4. These soils are generally coarse at the place of origin and become finer near the deltas.

How many of the statements given above is/are incorrect?

(a) Only one (b) Only two
(c) Only three (d) None of these

Ans. (a)

Exp. Only one statement i.e., (2) is incorrect with reference to the alluvial soils of India. Alluvial soils cover about 40% of the total area of the country. They are depositional soils, transported and deposited by rivers and streams. Through a narrow corridor in Rajasthan, they extend into the plains of Gujarat. In the Peninsular region, they are found in deltas of the East coast and in the river valleys.

20 Arrange the following soil in the ascending order of their availability in India. *(Chap 6, Class-XI, New NCERT)*

1. Alluvial soil 2. Red and yellow soil
3. Black soil 4. Laterite

Select the correct answer using the codes given below.

(a) 4-3-2-1 (b) 2-1-4-3
(c) 1-2-3-4 (d) 2-3-1-4

Ans. (c)

Exp. The ascending order of their availability in India is Alluvial Soil, Red soil, Black soil, Laterite soil.

Alluvial soils are extensively found in the Northern plains and river valleys, constituting the largest soil group, encompassing approximately 40% of India's total land area. The nature of alluvial soils ranges from sandy loam to clay.

Red soil forms on crystalline igneous rocks in regions with low rainfall, predominantly in the Southern and Eastern parts of the Deccan Plateau. This soil type covers about 18% of India's total land area.

Black soil dominates most of the Deccan Plateau, including parts of Maharashtra, Madhya Pradesh, Gujarat, Andhra Pradesh, and certain areas of Tamil Nadu. It accounts for approximately 15% of the country's total land area.

Laterite soils emerge in regions characterised by high temperatures and abundant rainfall, covering around 4.30% of India's total land area. Through the process of leaching with rain, lime and silica are removed, leaving soils enriched with iron oxide and aluminum compounds.

21 Consider the following statements. *(Chap 6, Class-XI, New NCERT)*

1. Red soil covers the second largest area in the country.
2. The laterite soils are more acidic in low-lying areas than the higher areas.
3. In alluvial soils region fertility decreases from East to West.
4. Black soils have high clay content due to which it has high water retention capacity.

How many of the statements given above is/are correct?

(a) Only one (b) Only two
(c) Only three (d) All four

Ans. (c)

Exp. Only three statements i.e., (1), (2) and (4) are correct.

Red soil is the second largest soil group in India, covering about 18% of the country's geographical area. Red soil develops on crystalline igneous rocks in areas of low rainfall in the Southern and Eastern part of the Deccan Plateau.

Alluvial soils are extremely fertile and can be found in the Indus-Ganga-Brahmaputra plain and the Narmada-Tapi plain. The sand content of alluvial soils decreases from West to East. This is because rivers flow from West to East in the alluvial plains.

Black soil is known for its ability to retain moisture due to its high clay content. Clay particles are small and have many small pore spaces that slow the movement of water resulting in a high water-holding capacity.

Statement (2) is incorrect because laterite soils in higher areas are generally more acidic than those in low-lying areas. Laterite soils are formed by the alternation of wet and dry seasons, which causes the siliceous matter of rocks to leach away.

22 Consider the following statements with reference to different types of soils. *(Chap 6, Class-XI, New NCERT*

1. Soils are usually thin on steep slopes and thick over flat upland areas.
2. Tropical soils show shallow profiles than soils in frozen tundra regions.

Which of the statements given above is/are correct?

(a) Only 1 (b) Only 2
(c) Both 1 and 2 (d) Neither 1 nor 2

Ans. (a)

Exp. Statement (1) is correct.

Soils will be thin on steep slopes and thick over flat upland areas. Over gentle slopes where erosion is slow and percolation of water is good, soil formation is very favourable. Soils over flat areas may develop a thick layer of clay with good accumulation of organic matter giving the soil dark colour.

Statement (2) is incorrect. Tropical soils with higher temperatures show deeper profiles and in the frozen tundra regions soils contain largely mechanically broken materials.

Temperature acts in two ways increasing or reducing chemical and biological activity. Chemical activity is increased in higher temperatures, reduced in cooler temperatures (with an exception of carbonation) and stops in freezing conditions.

23 Consider the following statements with reference to black regur soil in India. *(Chap 6, Class-XI, New NCERT) (UPPSC Pre 2018)*

1. It is most abundant in the Deccan Plateau region of India.
2. It develops great depths in the upper reaches of Krishna and Godavari region.
3. It is characterised by wide cracks during the dry season of the year.

Which of the statements given above is/are correct?

(a) 1 and 3 (b) Only 2
(c) Only 3 (d) All of these

Ans. (d)

Exp. All of the given statements are correct regarding to the black regur soil in India.

Black soil covers most abundant in the Deccan Plateau which includes parts of Maharashtra, Madhya Pradesh, Gujarat, Andhra Pradesh and some parts of Tamil Nadu. In the upper reaches of the Godavari and the Krishna and the North-Western part of the Deccan Plateau, the black soil is very deep. It is also known as the 'Regur Soil' or the 'Black Cotton Soil'.

It is generally clayey, deep and impermeable. It swells and becomes sticky when wet and shrinks when dried. So, during the dry season, these soils develop wide cracks. Thus, there occurs a kind of 'self-ploughing'.

24 Assertion (A) Black soils are suitable for cotton cultivation.

Reason (R) They are rich in nitrogen and organic matter. *(Chap 6, Class-XI, New NCERT) (UPPSC Spl. Mains 2004)*

Codes

(a) Both A and R are true and R is the correct explanation of A.
(b) Both A and R are true, but R is incorrect explanation of A.
(c) A is true, but R is false.
(d) A is false, but R is true.

Ans. (c)

Exp. Assertion (A) is true, but Reason (R) is false. Black soils are suitable for cotton cultivation. The Black soil are made up of extremely fine i.e. clayey material. They are well known for their capacity to hold moisture. It is rich in calcium, iron, magnesium but poor in nitrogen and organic matters.

25 Black soil is generally not found in which of the following regions? *(Chap 6, Class-XI, New NCERT)*

1. Maharashtra
2. Andhra Pradesh
3. Madhya Pradesh
4. West Bengal

Codes

(a) 2 and 3 (b) 1, 3 and 4 (c) 1 and 3 (d) Only 4

Ans. (d)

Exp. Black soil is not found in West Bengal. Black soil covers most of the Deccan Plateau which includes parts of Maharashtra, Madhya Pradesh, Gujarat, Andhra Pradesh and some parts of Tamil Nadu.

26 Consider the given statements with reference to red and yellow soils. *(Chap 6, Class-XI, New NCERT)*

1. They are formed by the deposition of rivers which contain high amount of silica.
2. These soils are generally found in the regions of low rainfall.
3. Coarse grained red soils found in upland regions are highly fertile.
4. They are rich in nitrogen, phosphorous and humus content.

How many of the statements given above is/are correct?

(a) Only one (b) Only two (c) Only three (d) All of these

Ans. (a)

Exp. Only one statement i.e., (2) is correct as red soil develops on crystalline igneous rocks in areas of low rainfall in the Eastern and Southern part of the Deccan plateau. Along the piedmont zone of the Western Ghats, long stretch of area is occupied by red loamy soil.

Statements (1), (3) and (4) are incorrect because Alluvial soils are formed by the deposition of rivers which contain high amount of silica.

The fine-grained red and yellow soils are normally fertile whereas coarse-grained soils found in dry upland areas are poor in fertility.

Also red and yellow soils are generally poor in nitrogen, phosphorous and humus.

27 Which of the given statements is/are correct with reference to laterite soil? *(Chap 6, Class-XI, New NCERT)*

1. Laterite soils develop in regions with high humidity and temperature.
2. Laterite soils develop due to intensive leaching due to high rainfall.

Codes

(a) Only 1 (b) Only 2
(c) Both 1 and 2 (d) Neither 1 nor 2

Ans. (c)

Exp. Both the statements (1) and (2) are correct with reference to laterite soil. The laterite soils develop in areas with high temperature and high rainfall. These are the result of intense leaching due to tropical rains. With rain, lime and silica are leached away and soils rich in iron oxide and aluminium compound are left behind.

28 **Laterite soils are rich in which of the following nutrients?** *(Chap 6, Class-XI, New NCERT)*

1. Humus
2. Iron oxide
3. Phosphate
4. Nitrogen

Codes

(a) 1 and 2 (b) Only 2
(c) 1, 3 and 4 (d) 2, 3 and 4

Ans. (b)

Exp. Laterite soil is rich in iron oxide and aluminium compound. These soils are poor in organic matter, nitrogen, phosphate and calcium, while iron oxide and potash are in excess.

29 **Consider the following Assertion(A) and Reason (R) and choose the correct code.** *(Chap 6, Class-XI, New NCERT)*

Assertion (A) Laterite soils are widely developed in the higher regions of Peninsular plateaus of India.

Reason (R) Laterite soils are suitable for cashew cultivation in South India.

Codes

(a) Both A and R are true and R is the correct explanation of A.
(b) Both A and R are true, but R is not the correct explanation of A.
(c) A is true, but R is false.
(d) A is false, but R is true.

Ans. (b)

Exp. Both Assertion (A) and Reason (R) are true, but Reason (R) is not the correct explanation of Assertion (A).

Laterite soils have mainly developed in the higher areas of the Peninsular plateau. Laterite soils are commonly found in Karnataka, Kerala, Tamil Nadu, Madhya Pradesh and the hilly areas of Odisha and Assam.

Laterites are not suitable for cultivation; however, applications of manures and fertilisers are required for making the soils fertile for cultivation. Red laterite soils in Tamil Nadu, Andhra Pradesh and Kerala are more suitable for tree crops like cashew nut.

30 **Consider the following statements regarding the laterite soils of India.** *(Chap 6, Class-XI, New NCERT) (IAS Pre 2013)*

1. They are generally red in colour.
2. They are rich in nitrogen and potash.
3. They are well developed in Rajasthan and Uttar Pradesh.
4. Tapioca and cashewnuts grow well on these soils.

How many of the statements given above is/are correct?

(a) Only one (b) Only two
(c) Only three (d) All Four

Ans. (b)

Exp. Only two statements i.e., (1) and (4) are correct regarding laterite soils of India. Laterite is generally red in colour because it is rich in iron and aluminium and it is present in hot and tropical areas, which causes a bit of rusting in the iron present in the soil. Red laterite soils in Tamil Nadu, Andhra Pradesh, and Kerala are suitable for tree crops like cashew nut and tapioca.

Statements (2) and (3) are incorrect because Red soil is rich in potash but lacks in nitrogen and humus laterite. This soil is well developed in tropical wet areas like Kerala, Tamil Nadu, Andhra Pradesh, Karnataka and hilly areas of Assam.

31 **Consider the following statements with reference to arid soils of India.** *(Chap 6, Class-XI, New NCERT*

1. Arid soils are most suitable for making common salt in dry region of India.
2. They are rich in moisture, humus and organic matter.
3. The bottom horizons restrict infiltration of water in these soils due to Kankar formation.

Which of the statements given above are correct?

(a) 1 and 2 (b) 2 and 3 (c) 1 and 3 (d) 1, 2 and 3

Ans. (c)

Exp. Statements (1) and (3) are correct with reference to arid soils in India.

Arid soils are suitable for making common salt in dry region of India.

Arid soils range from red to brown in colour. They are generally sandy in structure and saline in nature. Lower horizons of the Arid soil are occupied by 'Kankar' layers because of the increasing calcium content downwards. The 'Kankar' layer formation in the bottom horizons restricts the infiltration of water, and as such when irrigation is made available, the soil moisture is readily available for a sustainable plant growth.

Statement (2) is incorrect as due to the dry climate, high temperature and accelerated evaporation, arid soils lack moisture and humus. Nitrogen is insufficient and the phosphate content is normal.

32 **Consider the following statements about the feature of podzol soil.** *(Chap 6, Class-XI, New NCERT)*

1. They are highly leached soils.
2. They support coniferous forests.
3. They lack humus content.

Which of the statements given above are correct?

(a) 1 and 2 (b) 1 and 3
(c) 2 and 3 (d) All of these

Ans. (d)

Exp. All of these statements (1), (2) and (3) are correct regarding Podzols soil.

Podzols are well drained and are leached of clay and organic matter. The lack of calcium and humus in these soils makes them susceptible to erosion and weathering. Podzol soils support coniferous forests.

Podzols are common soils in coniferous and boreal forests. They are also the typical soils of eucalyptus forests and heathlands in Southern Australia.

Podzols are infertile and physically limiting soils for productive use.

33 Consider the following statements with reference to saline soil. *(Chap 6, Class-XI, New NCERT)*

1. Saline soils can be made fertile by treating it with gypsum.
2. Highly fertile alluvial soils become saline soils in regions of over irrigation.
3. Saline soils develop layers of salt on the top layer due to capillary action.

How many of the statements given above is/are correct?

(a) Only one (b) Only two
(c) Only three (d) None of these

Ans. (c)

Exp. All the given statements are correct with reference to saline soil. Saline soil can be treated by using Gypsum. In the areas of intensive cultivation with excessive use of irrigation, especially in areas of green revolution, the fertile alluvial soils are becoming saline.

Excessive irrigation with dry climatic conditions promotes capillary action, which results in the deposition of salt on the top layer of the soil. In such areas, especially in Punjab and Haryana.

35 Consider the following statements with reference to forest soils of India. *(Chap 6, Class-XI, New NCERT)*

1. These soils are characterised by less humus content.
2. In regions with permanent snow, they are acidic and experience high level of denudation.

Which of the statements given above is/are correct?

(a) Only 1
(b) Only 2
(c) Both 1 and 2
(d) Neither 1 nor 2

Ans. (c)

Exp. Both statements (1) and (2) are correct with reference to the forest soil of India.

In the Himalayan snow-covered areas, forest soils are depleted and acidic, with less humus content.

The soil in regions with permanent snow forest is usually acidic. This is because the cold climate and slow decomposition of organic matter limit the availability of base cations such as calcium,magnesium, potassium, and sodium.

In regions with permanent snow forest, soil experiences high level of denudation due to several factors, such as, The cold climate and slow decomposition of organic matter limit the availability of base cations such as calcium, magnesium, potassium, and sodium, which can neutralise the acidity of the soil and make it more resistant to erosion.

36 Which of the following statements is/are correct regarding soil erosion in India? *(Chap 6, Class-XI, New NCERT)*

1. Gully erosion is prevalent in India in the Chambal basin.
2. Sheet erosion leads to removal of the top layers of fertile soil.
3. Construction of check dams is helpful in reducing gully erosion.

Codes

(a) 1 and 2 (b) 2 and 3 (c) 1 and 3 (d) All of these

Ans. (d)

Exp. All the given statements are correct regarding the soil erosion in India.

Gully erosion is common on steep slopes. Gullies deepen with rainfall, cut the agricultural lands into small fragments and make them unfit for cultivation. Ravines are widespread in the Chambal basin. Besides this, they are also found in Tamil Nadu and West Bengal.

Sheet erosion takes place on level lands after a heavy shower and the soil removal is not easily noticeable. But it is harmful since, it removes the finer and more fertile top soil.

Check dams are constructed across the gully bed to stop channel and lateral erosion. By reducing the original gradient of the gully channel, check dams diminish the velocity of water flow and the erosive power of run-off.

37 Which of the following techniques is/are most suitable for reducing degradation of soil? *(Chap 6, Class-XI, New NCERT)*

1. Contour bunding
2. Mixed cropping
3. Gully plugging
4. Agro forestry
5. Shelter plantations

Codes

(a) 1, 2 and 3 (b) 2, 3 and 4
(c) 1, 3 and 5 (d) 1, 2, 3, 4 and 5

Ans. (d)

Exp. All the given techniques are suitable for reducing degradation of soil. Soil conservation is a methodology to maintain soil fertility, prevent soil erosion and exhaustion, and improve the degraded condition of the soil.

Contour bunding is a soil conservation technique for marginal, sloping and hilly land where the soil productivity is very low.

Mixed cropping is a practice of growing two or more crops in the same piece of land.

Gully plugging is a practice of constructing small, temporary dam across a drainage to lower the speed of concentrated flows.

Agro forestry is a land use management system in which trees or shrubs are grown.

Shelter planation is a practice of planting shelter of trees to avoid erosion of soil from wind.

Chapter 21

Natural Resources of India

Natural Resources of India

Land Resource in India

Introduction

- Resources that exist without any action of human kind. They can be of commercial or industrial use, aesthetic value, scientific interest, etc

Classification of Natural Resources

- **On the basis of origin** Biotic and Abiotic
- **On the basis of exhaustability** Non-renewable and Renewable
- **On the basis of ownership** Individual, community, national and international
- **On the basis of status of development** Potential, developed stock and reserves

Land Resource in India

- An important resource as humans live on it and obtain most of their needs from it;
- Utilisation of land depends on physical factors like topography, soil, density of population, etc

Land use Categories

- **Forests** Trees and forest cover are included in this category; It requires massive tree plantations, vigorous restrictions on the reckless felling of trees, reclaiming of forest area, etc
- **Non-agricultural uses** Land under settlements like rural and urban, infrastructure, industries, shops, etc are included in this category
- **Barren and Wastelands** Land maybe classified as wasteland such as barren hilly terrains, desert lands, ravines, etc cannot be brought under cultivation without available technology
- **Area under permanent pastures and grazing lands** Largely owned by Village Panchayats as this land comes under common property resource
- **Area under miscellaneous tree, crops and groves** It includes all cultivable land which is not included under the net sown area but is put to some agricultural use
- **Culturable wasteland** Land available for cultivation but not used for cultivation for one reason or the other
- **Current fallow** Land left fallow for one year; Fallowing is a cultural practice adopted for giving the land rest
- **Fallow other than current fallow** Cultivable land which is left fallow for more than one year but less than five years
- **Net sown area** The physical extent of land on which crops are sown and harvested

Water Resource in India

Surface Water Resource

- There are four major sources, rivers, lakes, ponds and tanks
  - Rivers comprise the most important source of surface water
  - India is blessed with a large number of major, medium and small sized

Groundwater Resource

- India relies excessively on groundwater resources for both irrigation and domestic uses
  - It is very high in the states of Punjab, Haryana, Rajasthan, etc
  - The underground water resource is a function of geological structure, topography, slope, precipitation, run off, soils and hydrological conditions of a region
  - Central Ground Water Authority (CGWA) has been constituted under Environment (Protection) Act, 1986 to regulate and control development and management of groundwater resources in the country

Lagoons and Backwaters

- India has indented coastline in some states causing the formation of lagoons and lakes in states like Kerala, Odisha, etc

SOURCE *Tamil Nadu Board Class XII (Sustainable Development)*

1 **Consider the following pairs.**

(Chap 1, Class-X, New NCERT)

	Natural Resources		Basis of Classification
1.	Biotic and Abiotic resources	–	On the basis of origin
2.	Potential and developed resources	–	On the basis of ownership
3.	Individual and community owned resources	–	On the basis of status of development
4.	Renewable and non-renewable resources	–	On the basis of exhaustibility

How many of the pairs given above is/are correctly matched?

(a) Only one (b) Only two (c) Only three (d) All four

***Ans.* (b)**

Exp. Only two pairs i.e., (1) and (4) are correctly matched. Biotic and Abiotic resources are classified on the basis of origin. Example of Biotic resources are animals, birds, plants, etc and Abiotic resources are water, air, soil, sunlight.

Renewable and non-renewable resources are based on the basis of exhaustibility. Renewable resources are those resources which can be renewed or reproduced by physical, chemical or mechanical processes.

Pairs (2) and (3) are not correctly matched. Potential and developed resources are classified on the basis of status of development. Potential resources are those resources, which are found in a region, but have not been utilised. Developed resources are those resources, which are surveyed and their quality and quantity have been determined for utilisation.

Individual and community owned resources are resources based on ownership. Individual resources are also owned privately by individuals. Community owned resources are resources which are accessible to all the members of the community privately by individuals.

2 **With reference to various landuse categories in India, Consider the following statements.**

(Chap 5, Class-XII, New NCERT)

1. Expansion of secondary and tertiary activities would lead to increase in the 'Land put to Non-agriculture Uses'.
2. Areas under permanent pastures and grazing lands are owned by the Central Government.
3. Any land, which is left fallow for more than 1 year is known as culturable wasteland.

How many of the statements given above is/are correct?

(a) Only one (b) Only two (c) All three (d) None of these

***Ans.* (a)**

Exp. Only one statement i.e., (1) is correct with reference to various landuse categories in India.

Land under rural and urban settlements and for infrastructure such roads, canals, industries, shops, etc., are included in the category of Land put to Non-agricultural Uses.

Thus, it can be concluded that an expansion in the secondary and tertiary activities would lead to an increase in 'Land put to Non-agricultural Uses'.

Statements (2) and (3) are incorrect because areas under permanent pastures and grazing lands are owned by the village 'Panchayat' or the Government. Any land, which is left fallow for more than 5 years is known as culturable wasteland.

3 **Consider the following statements about the land use pattern in India** *(Chap 3, Class-XII, New NCERT)*

1. Net Sown Area is 46% of the total geographic area due to the extensive availability of flat terrain in India.
2. Barren and unculturable wasteland amounts to about 8.5%.
3. About 32% of the country is under forest cover.

How many of the statements given above is/are correct?

(a) Only one (b) Only two
(c) All three (d) None of these

***Ans.* (b)**

Exp. Only two statements i.e., (1) and (2) are correct as Net Sown Area is 46% of the total geographic area because of the extensive availability of flat terrain in India. Barren and unculturable waste land amounts to about 8.5%.

Barren and unculturable wasteland has come down to 8.5%, which is a good indicator that land is being put to productive use.

Statement (3) is incorrect because Forest Area has risen to 24%, which is a good feature, but far lower than the desired 33% forest cover as outlined in the National Forest Policy (1952).

4 **Consider the following statements with reference to Common Property Resources in India.**

(Chap 5, Class-XII, New NCERT)

1. These are the land resources which are owned privately by an individual or a group of special individuals.
2. The land under these resources can be used to obtain fuel, fodder, minor forest produce and rearing livestock.

Which of the statements given above is/are correct?

(a) Only 1 (b) Only 2
(c) Both 1 and 2 (d) Neither 1 nor 2

***Ans.* (c)**

Exp. Both the statements (1) and (2) are correct as common property resources are the land resources which are owned by the state meant for the use of the community.

These resources provide fodder for the livestock and fuel for the households along with other minor forest products like fruits, nuts, fibre, medicinal plants etc.

Common property land is of particular relevance for the livelihood of the landless and marginal farmers and other weaker sections since many of them depend on income from their livestock due to the fact that they have limited access to land.

5 **With reference to pulse production in India, consider the following statements.** *(Chap 5, Class-XII, New NCERT) (IAS Pre 2020)*

1. Black gram can be cultivated as both kharif and rabi crops.
2. Green gram alone accounts for nearly half of pulse production.
3. In the last three decades, while the production of Kharif pulses has increased, the production of rabi pulses has decreased.

Which of the statements given above is/are correct?

(a) Only 1 (b) 2 and 3
(c) Only 2 (d) 1, 2 and 3

Ans. (a)

Exp. Statement (1) is correct with reference to pulse production in India as black gram can be cultivated as both kharif and rabi crops. In India, the important pulse crops grown in winter (rabi) are chickpea, lentil, lathyrus, field pea and kidney bean. However, green gram, black gram and cowpea are grown in both spring and rainy season.

Statements (2) and (3) are incorrect because green gram alone accounts for nearly 8% of pulse production. In the last three decades, both the production of kharif pulses and the production of rabi pulses have increased.

6 **With reference to the cultivation of kharif crops in India in the last five years, consider the following statements.** *(Chap 5, Class-XII, New NCERT) (IAS Pre 2019)*

1. Area under rice cultivation is the highest.
2. Area under the cultivation of jowar is more than that of oilseeds.
3. Area of cotton cultivation is more than that of sugarcane.
4. Area under sugarcane cultivation has steadily decreased.

Which of the statements given above are correct?

(a) 1 and 3 (b) 2, 3 and 4
(c) 2 and 4 (d) 1, 2, 3 and 4

Ans. (a)

Exp. Statements (1) and (3) are correct with reference to the cultivation of kharif crops in India in the last five years. Rice being one of the chief grains of India is the most cultivated crop in last five years.

Cotton and sugarcane being one of the major cash crops in India are produced intensively, but due to good profit margin in cotton it is cultivated more. According to Ministry of Agriculture annual report 2018-19, cotton was cultivated in an area of 124. 29 lakh hectare, which is more than areas under sugarcane cultivation.

Statements (2) and (4) incorrect because area under oil seed cultivation is more than jowar cultivation.

Area under sugarcane has increased in India in last five years.

7 **Consider the following statements.** *(Chap 1, Class-XII, Old NCERT)*

1. Soil erosion and deforestation over a long period may convert an arable land into a wasteland.
2. India has largest land under Plain areas as compared to Mountains and plateaus.
3. The net sown area in India is similar in all the states, excluding the North- Eastern states.

How many of the statements given above is/are correct?

(a) Only one (b) Only two
(c) All three (d) None of these

Ans. (b)

Exp. Only two statements i.e., (1) and (2) are correct as, in the long term, soil erosion by rivers, wind and waves and human deforestation turn arable land into a barren land. In India, 43% of the total land area is covered under plains land, and 30% of the area is covered under mountains.

Statement (3) is incorrect because the total sown area in India is different in all the states except the North-Eastern state.

8 **Which of the following activities is/are responsible for the degradation of land in India?** *(Chap 1, Class-X, New NCERT)*

1. Mining and quarrying 2. Over irrigation
3. Solid waste disposal 4. Shelter belts
5. Mineral extraction and processing

Codes

(a) 2, 3 and 5 (b) 2, 4 and 5 (c) 1, 2, 3 and 5 (d) 1, 2 and 4

Ans. (c)

Exp. Among the given options (1), (2), (3) and (5) are responsible for the degradation of land in India. Human activities have not only brought about degradation of land but have also aggravated the pace of natural forces to cause damage to land.

Some human activities such as deforestation, over grazing, over mineral extraction and processing and quarrying too have contributed significantly in land degradation.

On the other hand shelter belts are used to prevent soil degradation.

9 **Consider the following statements about multi-purpose river projects.** *(Chap 3, Class-XII, New NCERT*

1. Multi-purpose projects bring water to those areas which suffer from water scarcity.
2. Multi-purpose projects by regulating water flow help to control floods.

3. Multi-purpose projects lead to large-scale displacements and loss of livelihood.
4. Multi-purpose projects generate electricity for our industries and our homes.

How many of the arguments given above is/are not in favour of multi-purpose river projects?

(a) Only one (b) Only two
(c) Only three (d) None of these

Ans. (c)

Exp. Only three statements i.e., (1), (2) and (4) are correct arguments in favour of the multi-purpose river project.

Multi-purpose projects, also known as dams, bring water to areas that suffer from water scarcity. These projects create reservoirs that supply water to nearby areas. Multi-purpose projects include a dam which helps us in conserving and managing water.

Floods occur due to heavy rainfall. Building dams in most of our river basins helps in controlling floods as it helps in storing and regulating water resources.

Multi-purpose projects, also known as dams, generate electricity for industries and homes by using the water they impound for multiple purposes.

Statement (3) is incorrect an argument in favour of multi-purpose river projects. Multi-purpose projects cause large-scale displacement, and loss of livelihood is not an argument in favour of multi-purpose river projects.

Dams require a large area of land to be built, and local people living in that area are forced to move to another area, causing loss of livelihood and displacement.

10 With reference to the water on the planet Earth, consider the following statements.

(Chap 4, Class-X, Old NCERT) (IAS Pre 2021)

1. The amount of water in the rivers and lakes is more than amount of groundwater.
2. The amount of water in polar ice caps and glaciers is more than the amount of groundwater.

Which of the statements given above is/are correct?

(a) Only 1 (b) Only 2
(c) Both 1 and 2 (d) Neither 1 nor 2

Ans. (b)

Exp. Statement (2) is correct as 69% of freshwater, resides in glaciers and 30% of is underground. Polar ice caps and glaciers has more water than groundwater.
Statement (1) is incorrect because the out of total freshwater, less than 1% is located in lakes, rivers and swamps. Thus, the amount of water in rivers and lakes is less than amount of groundwater.

11 Consider the following statements with reference to groundwater resources in India.

(Chap 6, Class-XII, New NCERT)

1. The total utilisable groundwater resources in India amount to 433 cubic km.
2. The groundwater utilisation is very high in North-Western states such as Haryana and Punjab.
3. The level of groundwater is highest in Indus river basin.

Which of the statements given above are correct?

(a) 1 and 2 (b) 2 and 3
(c) 1 and 3 (d) All of these

Ans. (d)

Exp. All the given statements are correct with reference to groundwater resources in India. The total replenishable groundwater resource in the country is about 432 cubic km^3.

The groundwater utilisation is very high in the North-Western states of Punjab, Haryana, Rajasthan and Tamil Nadu.

The level of groundwater utilisation is relatively high in the river basins lying in North-Western region.

12 With reference to utilisation of water resources in India, Consider the following statements.

(Chap 6, Class-XII, New NCERT)

1. Industries account for the highest share of groundwater utilisation in India.
2. Agriculture sector accounts for the highest share of surface water utilisation in India.
3. The share of industrial sector is higher in the surface water utilisation as compared to the household sector.

How many of the statements given above is/are incorrect?

(a) Only one (b) Only two
(c) All three (d) None of these

Ans. (b)

Exp. Only two statements i.e., (1) and (3) are incorrect because agriculture sector accounts for most of the surface and groundwater utilisation. Industrial sector is limited to 2% of the surface water utilisation.

The share of industrial sector is lower in the surface water utilisation as compared to the household sector. The share of domestic sector is higher i.e., 9% in surface water utilisation.

13 Match List I with List II. *(Chap 3, Class-XII, New NCERT)*

List I (Multi-purpose River Project)	List II (State)
A. Koyna	1. Karnataka
B. Farakka	2. Bihar
C. Gandak	3. Maharashtra
D. Tungabhadra	4. West Bengal

Codes

	A	B	C	D		A	B	C	D
(a)	3	4	1	3	(b)	2	4	1	3
(c)	4	3	2	1	(d)	3	4	2	1

Ans. (d)

Exp. The correct matching is A-3, B-4, C-2, D-1.

The **Koyna** Hydroelectric Project is located in Koyna Nagar, Satara district, Maharashtra, India.

The **Farakka** Barrage Project is located in the Murshidabad and Malda districts of West Bengal, about 300 km North of Kolkata.

The **Gandak** Project, also known as the Gandak Multipurpose Project, is located in the Indian State of Bihar.

The **Tungabhadra** Hydroelectric Power Project is located in the city of Hospet in the Bellary district of Karnataka.

14 Consider the following statements with reference to degradation of groundwater resources in India. *(Chap 1, Class-XII, Old NCERT)*

1. Intensive irrigation in Punjab and Haryana has led to increase in salinity of soils in these regions.
2. Groundwater is affected by concentration of fluoride in Maharashtra and Rajasthan.
3. The groundwater in West Bengal and Bihar is severely affected by uranium concentration in the groundwater.

Which of the statements given above are correct?

(a) 1 and 2
(b) 2 and 3
(c) 1 and 3
(d) All of the above

Ans. (a)

Exp. Statements (1) and (2) are correct. Western Uttar Pradesh is increasing salinity in the soil and depletion of groundwater irrigation. In Punjab, Haryana and Western Uttar Pradesh, more than 85% of their Net Sown Area (NSA) is under irrigation.

In fact, over withdrawals in some states, like Rajasthan and Maharashtra, has increased fluoride concentration in groundwater. Groundwater is affected by concentration of fluoride in the states like Rajasthan and Maharashtra.

Statement (3) is incorrect because the groundwater in West Bengal and Bihar is severely affected by arsenic concentration in the groundwater.

Water Conservation

15 Consider the following statements regarding watershed development projects in India. *(Unit 7, Class-XII, Tamil Nadu Board)*

1. Watershed development projects in the country have been sponsored and implemented by the Government of India.
2. Watershed development programs primarily focused on soil conservation and rainwater harvesting.

Which of the statements given above is/are correct?

(a) Only 1 (b) Only 2
(c) Both 1 and 2 (d) Neither 1 nor 2

Ans. (c)

Exp. Both the statements (1) and (2) are correct. Watershed development project in the country has been sponsored and implemented by Government of India from early 1970s onwards.

Various watershed development programme like Drought Prone Area Programme (DPAP), Desert Development Programme (DDP), River Valley Project (RVP), etc. were launched subsequently in various hydro-ecological regions.

Watershed development programme primarily focused on soil conservation and rainwater harvesting during the 1980s and before.

16 Consider the following pairs. *(Chap 6, Class-XII, New NCERT)*

Water Conservation Programme		Region
1. Haryali	–	Punjab and Haryana
2. Neeru Meeru	–	Tamil Nadu
3. Arvary Pani Sansad	–	Rajasthan

How many of the pairs given above is/are correctly matched?

(a) Only one (b) Only two
(c) Only three (d) None of these

Ans. (a)

Exp. Only one pair i.e., (3) is correctly matched as Arvary Pani Sansad in Alwar, Rajasthan have taken up constructions of various water-harvesting structures such as percolation tanks; dug out ponds, check dams etc., through people's participation.

Pairs (1) and (2) are incorrect because Haryali is a watershed development project sponsored by the Central Government, which aims at enabling the rural population to conserve water for drinking, irrigation, fisheries and afforestation.

Neeru-Meeru (Water and You) programme is related to Andhra Pradesh.

17 Which of the following techniques is/are mainly used in rainwater harvesting? *(Chap 6, Class-XII, New NCERT)*

1. Storage of rainwater in natural ponds and lakes.
2. Construction of underground tanks and tankas for capturing rainwater.
3. Storing rainwater in lands having depleted coalseams.

Codes

(a) Only 1 (b) Only 3
(c) 2 and 3 (d) 1 and 2

Ans. (d)

Exp. Techniques mentioned in statements (1) and (2) are mainly used in rainwater harvesting as traditional rainwater harvesting in rural areas is done by using surface storage bodies, like lakes, ponds, irrigation tanks, etc. Rainwater harvesting is a method to capture and store rainwater for various uses.

In Rajasthan, rainwater harvesting structures locally known as Kund or Tanka (a covered underground tank) are constructed near or in the house or village to store harvested rainwater. The most common storage devices for harvesting rainwater are tanks.

Statement (3) is incorrect because rainwater harvesting is not stored in coal-deficient lands.

18 Man-made structures locally known as kuls, guls, khadins, etc. are constructed for which of the following purpose in various parts of India? *(Chap 3, Class-X, New NCERT)*

(a) Storage of minor forest produce by the tribal people to protect it from wild animals.
(b) Storage of foodgrains such as wheat and rice in local godowns for using them in times of high inflation.
(c) Capture and storage of rainwater during the monsoon season for the purpose of rainwater harvesting.
(d) Locally developed cold storage for storing recently harvested horticulture produce for a temporary period.

Ans. ***(c)***

Exp. Man-made structures locally known as kuls, guls, khadins, etc are constructed for capture and storage of rainwater during the monsoon season for the purpose of rainwater harvesting. In hill and mountainous regions, people built diversion channels like the guls or kuls during the monsoon season for the purpose of rainwater harvesting in the Western Himalayas.

In arid and semi-arid regions, agricultural fields were converted into rain fed storage structures that allowed the water to stand and moisten the soil like the Khadins in Jaisalmer and 'Johads' in other parts of Rajasthan.

19 Consider the following statements regarding rain water harvesting. *(Unit 7, Class-XII, Tamil Nadu Board)*

1. Rain water harvesting improves the quality of underground water through a process called dilution.
2. The storage of rain water on surface is a modern technique.
3. Rainwater harvesting replenishes the sub soil of the urban area covered with pavements.

How many of the statements given above is/are correct?

(a) Only one (b) Only two
(c) All three (d) None of these

Ans. ***(b)***

Exp. Only two statements i.e., (1) and (3) are correct regarding rain water harvesting.

Rainwater harvesting can improve the quality of groundwater through dilution.

Rainwater harvesting is a method for capturing and storing rainwater for various uses, such as drinking and irrigation.

Rainwater harvesting replenishes the subsoil of the urban area covered with pavements.

Statement (2) is incorrect. The storage of rainwater on surface is a traditional technique and structures used were underground tanks, ponds, check dams, weirs, etc. Recharge of groundwater is a new concept of rainwater harvesting and the structures generally used are: Recharge pits filled with boulders, gravels, and coarse-sand, wells, trenches, etc.

20 Consider the following statements about Common Property Resources (CPRs). *(Chap 5, Class-XII, New NCERT)*

1. There are land resources owned by the state meant for the use of the community.
2. These CPRs are of particular importance to landless and marginal farmers.
3. Owing the their utility, the area under CPRs has registered a consistent increase post-independence.

Which of the statements given above are correct?

(a) 1 and 2 (b) 1 and 3
(c) 2 and 3 (d) 1, 2 and 3

Ans. ***(a)***

Exp. Statements (1) and (2) are correct as CPRs are indeed land resources owned by the state for community use and are crucial for landless and marginal farmers.

Statement (3) is incorrect because the are under CPRs has not increased consistently post-independence.

It has actually faced a decline due to factors like encroachment for agriculture.

21 Which of the given statements is correct with reference to Jal Kranti Abhiyan? *(Chap 6, Class-XII, New NCERT)*

1. It was started by the Central Government in 2015.
2. It involves local bodies, NGOs and local citizens.
3. Under this one water stressed village in every district of the country will be created as a Jal Gram.

Codes

(a) 1 and 3 (b) Only 3
(c) 2 and 3 (d) 1, 2 and 3

Ans. ***(d)***

Exp. All the statements (1), (2) and (3) are correct with reference to the Jal Kranti Abhiyan. It was launched by the Government of India in 2015-16 with an aim to ensure water security through per capita availability of water in the country.

The Jal Kranti Abhiyan aims at involving local bodies, Non-Governmental Organisations (NGOs) and citizens, at large, in creating awareness regarding its objectives. Under the scheme one water stressed village was selected in each 672 districts of the country to create a Jal Gram.

Chapter 22

Agriculture, Irrigation and Animal Husbandary

Agriculture, Irrigation and Animal Husbandary

Agriculture and Irrigation

Agricutlure

- Defined as art, science and business of producing crops and livestock for economic purposes 70% of the labour force is directly or indirectly involved in agricultural sector

Types of Indian Agricultural System

- **Subsistence Farming** When farmers grow food crops to meet their own needs and their families on small holdings. They use primitive tools and don't use high yielding variety of seeds and fertilisers
- **Commercial Farming** Done in areas where irrigation is possible, fertilisers and pesticides are used on a large scale. Machines are also used for mechanisation
- **Sustainable Farming** A system of cultivation with the use of manures, crop rotation and minimum tillage
- **Dryland and Wetland Farming** Dryland farming is practised in regions receiving low rainfall, soil is sandy and has low water retention capacity like parts of Rajasthan, Gujarat and Maharashtra. Wetland farming is practised in regions receiving high rainfall like North-East part of India, Ghats of India, etc

Cropping Seasons of India

There are three distinct cropping seasons in India, namely

- **The Kharif Season** Crops grown require good amount of water thus it coincides with the onset of South-West monsoon in India
- **The Rabi Season** Sowing begins with the onset of October and harvesting is done by April
- **The Zaid Season** A short duration summer cropping season beginning after rabi season and includes the cultivation of watermelon, cucumbers, etc

Types of Crops

- **Beverage Crops Grown In India** Tea and Coffee
- **Food Crops Grown in India** Rice, Wheat, Pulses, Millets
- **Commercial Crops Grown in India** Sugarcane, Cotton, Jute, Oilseeds

Irrigation

- Artificial application of water to the soil or agricultural field. It is a replacement or supplementation of rainwater with other source of water
- **Types of Irrigation System** Well and tubewell irrigation, Canal irrigation, Tank irrigation, Drip irrigation, Sprinkler irrigation, Furrow irrigation
- **Multipurpose Projects** Serving several purposes like flood control, irrigation, hydroelectric generation, navigation, etc. Some of them are – Bhakra Nangal Project, Damodar Valley Project, Hirakud Dam Project, Kosi Project, Narmada Valley Project, Nagarjuna Sagar Project, Tehri Dam Project, Chambal Valley Project

Animal Husbandary

Introduction

Refers to livestock raising and selective breeding. It supports the livelihood of nearly half of the rural population. It includes

- **Buffaloes** Important source of milk supply in India contributing to around half of the country's milk production
- **Goat Rearing** Main source of meat in country
- **Sheep Rearing** Important source of mutton and wool in the country
- **Poultry Farming** Includes domestic fowls like chicken, ducks, geese, etc reared to obtain meat, eggs and feathers
- **Sericulture** Rearing of silkworm for silk production India produces all the five varities of silk
- **Fishing** Important source of food production, nutritional security, employment and income in India. There are two types of fishing
  - **Marine Fishing** It includes the coastal offshore and deep sea fisheries, mainly on the continental shelf upto a depth of 200 m
  - **Inland Fishing** It includes catching of fishes from rivers, lakes, canals, reservoirs, ponds, tanks, etc

SOURCE **New NCERT Class X** *(Water Resources)*, **New NCERT Class X** *(Agriculture)*, **Old NCERT Class X** *(Diversifying Our Agriculture)*, **New NCERT Class XII** *(Primary Activities)*, **Old NCERT Class XII** *(Natural Resources of India)*, **Old NCERT Class XII** *(Main Features of Agriculture)*

Agriculture and Its Types

1 **Consider the following statements with reference to agriculture in India.** *(Chap 5, Class-XII, New NCERT)*

1. Agriculture is the primary source of livelihood for more than 80% of the population of India.
2. Production and yield of food grains have increased manifolds in India since independence.
3. Use of chemical fertilisers and pesticides is steadily declining in India since the past decade.

How many of the statements given above is/are correct?

(a) Only one (b) Only two
(c) All three (d) None of these

Ans. (a)

Exp. Only one statement i.e., (2) is correct with reference to agriculture in India.

After independence, the immediate goal of the government was to increase food grains production by switching over from cash crops to food crops; intensification of cropping over already cultivated land; and increasing cultivated area by bringing cultivable and fallow land under plough. Thus, the production and yield of food grains have increased manifolds in India since, independence.

Statements (1) and (3) are incorrect because agriculture is the primary source of livelihood for more than 58% of the population of India. Use of chemical fertilisers and pesticides is steadily increasing in India since the past ecade.

2 **Consider the following statements with reference to Indian agriculture.** *(Chap 5, Class-XII, New NCERT)*

1. Irrigation covers only 20% of cultivated area in India.
2. Distribution of cultivated land is highly inequitable in India.
3. More than 60% of landholdings in India are below one hectare.

Which of the statements given above are correct?

(a) 1 and 3 (b) 1 and 2 (c) 2 and 3 (d) 1, 2 and 3

Ans. (c)

Exp. Statements (2) and (3) are correct with reference to Indian agriculture. Lack of implementation of land reforms has resulted in continuation of iniquitous distribution of cultivable land which is detrimental to agricultural development.

In India, the landholdings are mostly fragmented. More than 67% of landholdings in India are below 1 hectare.

Statement (1) is incorrect because irrigation covers more than 50% of cultivated area in India.

3 **Consider the following statements with reference to dryland farming in India.** *(Chap 6, Class-X, Old NCERT)*

1. This type of farming is practised in India in regions having annual rainfall more than 100 cm.
2. Rice, jute and sugarcane are commonly grown crops in dryland farming.
3. In this type of farming, the focus is more on rainwater harvesting and conserving soil moisture.

How many of the statements given above is/are correct?

(a) Only one (b) Only two
(c) All three (d) None of these

Ans. (a)

Exp. Only one statement i.e., (3) is correct with reference to dryland farming in India. In India, the dryland farming is largely confined to the regions having annual rainfall less than 75 cm. These regions grow drought resistant crops such as ragi, bajra, moong, gram and guar and practice various measures of soil moisture conservation and rainwater harvesting.

Statements (1) and (2) are incorrect because dry land type of farming is practised in India in regions having annual rainfall more than 75 cm not 100 cm.

These regions grow drought resistant crops such as ragi, bajra, moong, gram and guar; not crops like rice, jute and sugarcane that need more water.

4 **How is permaculture farming different from conventional chemical farming?** *(Chap 4, Class-X, Old NCERT) (IAS Pre 2021)*

1. Permaculture farming discourages monocultural practical but in conventional chemical farming, monoculture practices are pre-dominant.
2. Conventional chemical farming can cause increase in soil salinity but the occurrence of such phenomenon is not observed in permaculture farming.
3. Conventional chemical farming is easily possible in semi-arid regions but permaculture farming is not so easily possible in such regions.
4. Practice of mulching is very important in permaculture farming but not necessarily so in conventional chemical farming.

Select the correct answer using the codes given below.

(a) 1 and 3 (b) 1, 2 and 4 (c) Only 4 (d) 2 and 3

Ans. (b)

Exp. Statements (1), (2) and (4) are correct. Permaculture is a totally integrated design system that's modelled on nature. Permaculture farming promotes multicropping and integrated farming systems. Agroforestry is its example.

Chemical farming is more suitable for monoculture cropping due to use of crop specific inputs like irrigation, chemical fertiliser and harvesting methods. Chemical fertilisers will make the soil less fertile over time, which can lead to serious problems like soil salinisation. But such problems are not seen in permaculture farming as it relies on organic fertilisers.

Mulching is an important component of permaculture systems for promoting maximum efficiency. Chemical farming does not consider it as essential, so farmers in general do not use mulching.

Statement (3) is incorrect as chemical farming is based on intense use of inputs like chemical fertilisers and irrigation that make the soil less fertile over time, thus restricting its practise in semi-arid region. Thus, conventional farming is not suitable for semi-arid regions.

5 The Central Arid Zone Research Institute (CAZRI) is engaged in development of dryland farming techniques to raise the productivity of crops in the drier areas of the country. The headquarters of CAZRI is located at which of the following places?

(Chap 2, Class-XII, New NCERT)

(a) New Delhi (b) Bhopal
(c) Jaipur (d) Jodhpur

Ans. (d)

Exp. The headquarters of CAZRI is located at Jodhpur in Rajasthan. The Central Arid Zone Research Institute is engaged in development of dry land farming techniques to raise the productivity of crops in the drier areas of the country.

6 Consider the following pairs.

(Chap 4, Class-X, New NCERT)

Shifting Cultivation Name		Region
1. Kuruwa	–	Jharkhand
2. Bewar	–	Andhra Pradesh
3. Penda	–	Madhya Pradesh
4. Bringa	–	Odisha

How many og the pairs given above is/are correctly matched?

(a) Only one (b) Only two
(c) Only three (d) All four

Ans. (a)

Exp. Only one pair i.e., (1) is correctly matched.

In India, Kuruwa shifting cultivation is practiced in Jharkhand.

Pairs (2), (3) and (4) are not correctly matched.

The term Bewar is used for shifting cultivation in Madhya Pradesh.

Penda shifting cultivation is practiced in Andhra Pradesh. Koman and Bringa shifting cultivation is practiced in Odisha.

Cropping Seasons

7 Which of the following statements with reference to the main cropping seasons in Indian is/are false?

(Chap 4, Class-X, New NCERT) (HPSC Pre 2023)

1. The terms 'Kharif' and 'Rabi' originate for Arabic language where Kharif means autumn and Rabi means spring.
2. Kharif crops need cold weather for growth and need less water.
3. Rabi crops generally require more water and are called monsoon crops.
4. Zaid is short cropping season during summer months and mostly seasonal fruits and vegetables are grown in this season.

Select the correct answer using the codes given below.

(a) 1 and 2 (b) 1 and 4
(c) 3 and 4 (d) 2 and 3

Ans. (d)

Exp. Statements (2) and (3) are incorrect as Kharif crops are sown in the monsoon season (hot season) and do not need cold weather. They are, however, associated with high water requirements as they are grown during the raining season.

Rabi crops are sown in the winter season and are not dependent on the monsoon. The usually require less irrigation as compared to Kharif crops.

8 Groundnut, ragi, jowar and gram are grown in, which of the following seasons?

(Chap 2, Class-XII, Old NCERT)

(a) Rabi season
(b) Kharif season
(c) Zaid season
(d) Both Rabi and Kharif seasons

Ans. (a)

Exp. Groundnut, wheat, barley, ragi, jowar and gram are grown in rabi season. The rabi season begins with the onset of winter in October-November and ends in March-April.

9 With reference to pulse production in India, consider the following statements.

(Chap 4, Class-X, New NCERT) (IAS Pre 2024)

1. Black gram can be cultivated as both kharif and rabi crops.
2. Green gram alone accounts for nearly half of pulse production.
3. In the last three decades, while the production of kharif pulses has increased, the production of rabi pulses has decreased.

Which of the statements given above is/are correct?

(a) Only 1 (b) 2 and 3 (c) Only 2 (d) All of these

Ans. (a)

Exp. Statement (1) is correct.

Black gram (Urad) is a short-duration crop that can be cultivated as both kharif and rabi crop. Kharif urad is sown in June-July and harvested in October-November, while rabi urad is sown in October-November and harvested in February-March.

Statements (2) and (3) are incorrect. Green gram (Moong) is a major pulse crop in India, but it does not account for nearly half of the total pulse production. In 2022-2023, the production of green gram was estimated to be around 7.2 million metric tonnes, which is about 25% of the total pulse production. Gram (Chana) is the most dominant pulse crop in India, with a production share of around 40%.

The production of both kharif and rabi pulses has increased in the last three decades. According to the Directorate of Economics and Statistics (DES), the production of kharif pulses increased from 10.1 million metric tonnes in 1990-1991 to 14.4 million metric tonnes in 2022-2023, while the production of rabi pulses increased from 10.6 million metric tonnes to 13.6 million metric tonnes during the same period.

Major Crops

10 Which of the following is/are commercial plantation crops in India? *(Chap 4, Class-X, New NCERT)*

1. Coffee
2. Rubber
3. Sugarcane
4. Banana

Codes

(a) 1, 2 and 3
(b) 2, 3 and 4
(c) 1, 3 and 4
(d) 1, 2, 3 and 4

Ans. (d)

Exp. Coffee, rubber, sugarcane and banana are commercial plantation crops in India. The main characteristic of commercial type of farming is the use of higher doses of modern inputs. For example, High Yielding Variety (HYV) seeds, chemical fertilisers, insecticides and pesticides in order to obtain higher productivity. In India, tea, coffee, rubber, sugarcane, banana, etc., are important plantation crops.

11 Consider the following statements with reference to rice cultivation in India. *(Chap 5, Class-XII, New NCERT)*

1. India is the second largest producer of rice in the world.
2. West Bengal is the largest producer of rice in India.
3. Rice is not grown at all in the dry regions of Haryana and Western Uttar Pradesh in India.

Which of the statements given above are correct?

(a) 1 and 3
(b) 2 and 3
(c) 1 and 2
(d) All of the above

Ans. (c)

Exp. Statements (1) and (2) are correct with reference to rice cultivation in India. India is the second largest producer of rice in the world after China.

India produces 24% of the world's total production of rice. West Bengal is the largest producer of rice in India contributing about 14.33% of the total rice production from 12.8% of the rice producing area of the country.

Statement (3) is incorrect because development of dense network of canal irrigation and tubewells has made it possible to grow rice in areas of dry regions of Haryana and Western Uttar Pradesh in India.

12 Consider the following statements. *(Chap 5, Class-XII, New NCERT)*

1. In the Southern states of Tamil Nadu, Andhra Pradesh and Kerala, rice is mainly grown with the help of assured irrigation supply.
2. Punjab is not a traditional rice growing region, and improved varieties of rice were only introduced in Green Revolution.
3. The yield of rice is highest in the regions of Madhya Pradesh.

Which of the statements given above is incorrect?

(a) Only 1 (b) Only 2
(c) Only 3 (d) None of these

Ans. (c)

Exp. Statement (3) is incorrect because the yield of rice crop is very low in rainfed areas of Madhya Pradesh, Chhattisgarh and Odisha. The yield of rice crop is very high in irrigated region of Punjab, Haryana and Western Uttar Pradesh.

13 Consider the following statements with reference to the cultivation of wheat in India. *(Chap 6, Class-X, Old NCERT)*

1. Annual rainfall of 50-75 cm and a cool climate is most suitable for growing wheat in India.
2. Aus, Aman and Boro are the most nutritious varieties of wheat grown in India.
3. India is the largest producer of wheat in the world.

Which of the statements given above is/are correct?

(a) Only 3 (b) 1 and 3 (c) Only 1 (d) None of these

Ans. (c)

Exp. Statement (1) is correct with reference to the cultivation of wheat in India. Wheat is primarily a crop of temperate zone. Hence, its cultivation in India is done during winter i.e. Rabi season. This rabi crop requires a cool growing season and a bright sunshine at the time of ripening. It requires 50 to 75 cm of annual rainfall evenly distributed over the growing season.

Statements (2) and (3) are incorrect because in West Bengal farmers grow three crops of rice called Aus, Aman and Boro. India is not the largest producer of wheat while China is the largest producer.

14 Consider the given statements with reference to wheat cultivation in India. *(Chap 5, Class-XII, New NCERT)*

1. Haryana is the largest producer of wheat in India.
2. It is mainly grown as a rainfed crop in the Malwa plateau and Himalayan region.
3. Bihar has the highest yield of wheat per hectare in the country.
4. High Yielding Varieties (HYVs) of wheat have not yet been developed in India.

Which of the statements given above is correct?

(a) Only 1 (b) Only 2 (c) Only 3 (d) Only 4

Ans. (b)

Exp. Statement (2) is correct with reference to wheat cultivation in India. About 85% of total area under wheat is concentrated in North and Central regions of the country i.e. Indo Gangetic Plain, Malwa Plateau and Himalayas upto 2,700 m altitude.

Statements (1), (3) and (4) are incorrect because Punjab is the largest producer of wheat. Punjab has the highest yield of wheat per hectare in India. High Yielding Varieties (HYVs) of wheat have been developed in India as these varieties were used in region of Green Revolution.

15 Consider the following statements with reference to production of jowar or sorghum in India. *(Chap 5, Class-XII, New NCERT)*

1. Maharashtra is the leading producer of this crop in India.
2. It is sown in both rabi and kharif season in Southern states of India.
3. In the Northern states of India, it is grown as a crop for the fodder.

How many of the statements given above is/are correct?

(a) Only one (b) Only two
(c) All three (d) None of these

Ans. (c)

Exp. All three statements i.e., (1), (2) and (3) are correct with reference to production of jowar in India.

Maharashtra is the largest producer of jowar or sorghum followed by Karnataka, Andhra Pradesh and Madhya Pradesh. It is sown in both kharif and rabi seasons in Southern states. But it is a kharif crop in Northern India where it is mostly grown as a fodder crop.

16 Which of the following statements is/are correct regarding bajra? *(Chap 5, Class-XII, New NCERT)*

1. The largest producer of bajra in India is Rajasthan.
2. Bajra is sown in hot and dry climatic conditions in North-Western and Western parts of the country.

Codes

(a) Only 1 (b) Only 2
(c) Both 1 and 2 (d) Neither 1 nor 2

Ans. (c)

Exp. Both the statements (1) and (2) are correct regarding bajra. The largest producer of bajra in India is Rajasthan which is followed by Uttar Pradesh, Maharashtra, Gujarat and Haryana. Bajra is sown in hot and dry climatic conditions in North-Western and Western parts of the country.

17 Consider the following statements with reference to production of ragi (Finger Millets) in India. *(Chap 4, Class-X, New NCERT)*

1. It is a coarse grain which grows well on sandy soils.
2. Odisha is the largest producer of ragi in India.
3. Ragi can be grown in areas having shallow black soil.
4. Ragi is commonly grown in Tamil Nadu and Karnataka.

Which of the statements given above is incorrect?

(a) Only 1
(b) Only 2
(c) Only 3
(d) Only 4

Ans. (b)

Exp. Statement (2) is incorrect with reference to production of ragi in India.

Karnataka has the largest area under finger millet and is the biggest producer of ragi in India. Other major ragi producing states are Tamil Nadu, Himachal Pradesh, Uttarakhand, etc.

18 Consider the following statements with reference to production of maize in India. *(Chap 4, Class-X, New NCERT)*

1. It requires temperature between 21° to 27 °C.
2. It can be grown in rabi as well as kharif season.
3. It can be used as a food crop as well as a fodder crop.

Which of the statements given above is/are correct?

(a) Only 1 (b) 2 and 3
(c) 1 and 3 (d) All of these

Ans. (d)

Exp. All the given statements are correct with reference to production of maize in India. Maize crop requires temperature between 21°C to 27°C and grows well in old alluvial soil. Maize is a kharif crop. In some states like Bihar, maize is grown in rabi season also.

It is a crop which is used both as food and fodder. Major maize-producing states are Karnataka, Madhya Pradesh and Uttar Pradesh etc.

19 Consider the following statements with reference to pulse farming in India. *(Chap 5, Class-XII, New NCERT)*

1. India is the second largest producer and largest consumer of pulses in the world.
2. Farming of pulses is helpful in improving the quality of soil in India.
3. Pulses cannot be grown in Deccan and Central plateau.

Which of the statements given above is/are incorrect?

(a) 1 and 3 (b) 2 and 3
(c) Only 3 (d) All of these

Ans. (c)

Exp. Statement (3) is incorrect with reference to pulse farming in India because the cultivation of pulses in the country is largely concentrated in the drylands of Deccan and Central plateaus and North-Western parts of the country.

20 Consider the statements with reference to a variety of pulses. *(Chap 5, Class-XII, New NCERT)*

1. Gram is a rainfed crop which is cultivated in Rabi season.
2. Maharashtra is the largest producer of Red Gram in India.
3. The yield of pulse crop is high in the country as compared to wheat.
4. Madhya Pradesh, Uttar Pradesh, Karnataka and Gujarat are important producers of pulses in the country.

Which of the statements given above is incorrect?

(a) Only 1 (b) Only 2 (c) Only 3 (d) Only 4

Ans. (c)

Exp. Statement (3) is incorrect with reference to a variety of pulses as the yield of wheat crop is high in the country as compared to pulses.

The yield of pulses produced in India was over 817 kilograms per hectare. Yield of wheat in India is approximately 3.4 thousand kilograms per hectare.

21 Which of the following groups belong to fibre crop? *(Chap 2, Class-XII, New NCERT) (UPPSC Pre 2017)*

(a) Patsan, Gram, Linseed (b) Lentil, Oat, Dhaincha
(c) Cotton, Jute, Sunhemp (d) Jute, Wheat, Cotton

Ans. (c)

Exp. Cotton, jute and sunhemp belong to the category of fibre crop. Sunhemp is one of the oldest fibre species grown since, 600 BC. Sunhemp is a kharif crop grown in almost all states of India. Cotton is the most important fibre crop of the entire world. Gujarat is the largest cotton producing state of India. Jute is the second most important fiber crop of India and West Bengal leads in jute cultivation.

22 With reference to 'palm oil' consider the following statements. *(Chap 5, Class-XII, New NCERT) (IAS Pre 2021)*

1. The palm oil tree is native to South-East Asia.
2. The palm oil is a raw material for some industries producing lipstick and perfumes.
3. The palm oil can be used to produce bio-diesel.

Which of the statements given above are correct?

(a) 1 and 2 (b) 2 and 3 (c) 1 and 3 (d) 1, 2 and 3

Ans. (b)

Exp. Statement (2) and (3) are correct with reference to Palm oil. It is used in cosmetics products like lipstick and perfumes and cleaning products. Palm oil is one of the best options and most cost-effective cosmetics ingredients. It is versatile. Due to its high fatty acid content, it can be used to make surfactants, emulsifiers and emollients.

The palm oil can be used to produce bio-diesel. It can be used in compression ignition engines, i.e., diesel engines without any modifications. It refers to methyl esters derived from palm oil through a process known as 'Transesterification'.

Statement (1) is incorrect as palm oil is derived from the oil palm tree which is native to West Africa (and not South-East Asia) and grows best in tropical climates with abundant water.

23 Consider the following states. *(Chap 4, Class-XI, Old NCERT) (IAS Pre 2022)*

1. Andhra Pradesh 2. Kerala
3. Himachal Pradesh 4. Tripura

How many of the states given above is/are generally known as tea-producing states?

(a) Only one (b) Only two (c) Only three (d) All four

Ans. (c)

Exp. Only three states are correct regarding tea-producing states. According to the Tea Board of India Annual Report 2019-2020, generally known tea producing states are Assam, Tripura, West Bengal, Tamil Nadu, Kerala, Himachal Pradesh.

24 Consider the given statements with reference to rapeseed and mustard. *(Chap 2, Class-XII, Old NCERT)*

1. These are cultivated during the rabi season as well as kharif season in Central India.
2. Rajasthan is the largest producer of these crops.
3. These crops show high resistance to frost and they can grow in extremely low temperatures.

Which of the statements given above is correct?

(a) Only 1 (b) Only 2 (c) Only 3 (d) None of these

Ans. (b)

Exp. Statement (2) is correct with reference to rapeseed and mustard. Rajasthan is the largest producer of rapeseed and mustard in India. Haryana is the second largest producer of rapeseed and mustard in India.

Statements (1) and (3) are incorrect because rapeseed and mustard are the main oilseed crop for the rabi season. These are sub-tropical crops cultivated during rabi season in North-Western and Central parts of India. These are frost sensitive crops and their yields fluctuate from year to year. These crops cannot grow in extremely low temperature.

25 Consider the following Assertion (A) and Reason (R) and choose the correct code. *(Chap 5, Class-XII, New NCERT) (UPPSC Pre 2019)*

Assertion (A) Sugarcane and sugar production in UP is more than Maharashtra but productivity is less.

Reason (R) Most of the sugar factories in Maharashtra are in the cooperative sector.

Codes

(a) Both A and R are true and R is the correct explanation of A.
(b) Both A and R are true, but R is not the correct explanation of A.
(c) A is true, but R is false.
(d) A is false, but R is true.

Ans. (b)

Exp. Both Assertion (A) and Reason (R) are true, but Reason (R) is not the correct explanation of Assertion (A). Sugarcane and sugar production in Uttar Pradesh is more than Maharashtra but productivity is less. Uttar Pradesh, Maharashtra and Karnataka together produced 111 million tonnes of sugar. UP and Maharashtra together share 66% of sugar production.

Most of the sugar factories in Maharashtra are in cooperative sector is also a correct statement but this is not the reason for the less productivity in UP.

26 Which of the following statements is/are incorrect with reference to cotton production? *(Chap 5, Class-XII, New NCERT)*

1. India grows long staple as well as short staple crop.
2. Maharashtra is the largest producer of cotton in India.
3. India is the third largest producer of cotton in the world.

Codes

(a) 1 and 2 (b) Only 2
(c) 1 and 3 (d) 2 and 3

Ans. (d)

Exp. Statements (2) and (3) are incorrect with reference to cotton production. Gujarat is the largest producer of cotton in India followed by Maharashtra. India is the largest producer of cotton in the world according for about 22% of world cotton production.

27 Which of the following statements is/are incorrect for production of cotton in India? *(Chap 4, Class-X, New NCERT)*

1. Black cotton soil in the Deccan plateau
2. High amount of rainfall and irrigation
3. 210 frost free days
4. 6 to 8 months of maturity period

Codes

(a) 1 and 2 (b) Only 3
(c) Only 2 (d) 2 and 4

Ans. (c)

Exp. Statement (2) is incorrect for the production of cotton in India. High amount of rainfall and irrigation is not required for the production of cotton in India.

Cotton crop requires high temperature, light rainfall or irrigation, 210 frost-free days and bright sunshine for its growth. It is a kharif crop and requires 6 to 8 months to mature.

28 Silk production takes place in India mainly in which of the following states? *(Chap 6, Class-X, Old NCERT)*

(a) Karnataka and Andhra Pradesh
(b) Gujarat and Rajasthan
(c) Odisha and Jharkhand
(d) Himachal Pradesh and Uttarakhand Cash crops

Ans. (a)

Exp. Silk production takes place in India mainly in Karnataka and Andhra Pradesh. Karnataka is the largest silk producing state in India. Andhra Pradesh is the second largest silk producing state in India.

29 Consider the given statements with reference to sugarcane production in India. *(Chap 6, Class-X, Old NCERT)*

1. Sugarcane is grown in well-drained soil in hot and moist climate.
2. Sugarcane is the most irrigated crop in India.
3. Uttar Pradesh is the largest producer of sugarcane in India.

How many of the statements given above is/are correct?

(a) Only one (b) Only two
(c) All three (d) None of these

Ans. (c)

Exp. All three statements i.e., (1), (2) and (3) are correct with reference to sugarcane production in India. Sugarcane is grown in well-drained soil in hot and moist climate.

It grows well in hot and humid climate with a temperature of 21°C to 27°C and an annual rainfall between 75 cm and 100 cm.

Sugarcane is the most irrigated crops in India.

Uttar Pradesh is the largest producer of sugarcane in India and Maharashtra is the second largest producer of sugarcane.

30 Consider the following statements with reference to fruit production in India. *(Chap 6, Class-X, Old NCERT)*

1. India is the second largest producer of fruits in the world.
2. Himachal Pradesh and Jammu and Kashmir provide favourable climate for production of fruits.
3. Only tropical fruits are produced in India.
4. Fruits account for a substantial share of exports of India Beverages.

Which of the statements given above is incorrect?

(a) Only 1 (b) Only 2 (c) Only 3 (d) Only 4

Ans. (c)

Exp. Statement (3) is incorrect with reference to fruit production in India because it is a producer of both tropical as well as temperate fruits.

The major tropical fruits grown in India include mango, banana, guava, pineapple, papaya and lychee.

Temperate fruits like apple, walnut, pears, peach, apricot and plum are grown in India.

31 Consider the following statements with reference to production of tea in India. *(Chap 5, Class-XII, New NCERT)*

1. Tea is mainly grown in dryland farming areas of India.
2. India is the second largest producer of tea in the world.

Which of the statements given above is/are correct?
(a) Only 1 (b) Only 2
(c) Both 1 and 2 (d) Neither 1 nor 2

Ans. (b)

Exp. Statement (2) is correct with reference to production of tea in India. India is the second largest tea producing country in the world. China is the largest tea producing country with an output of 1.9 million tonnes, accounting for more than 38% of the world total. Tea is a plantation crop used as beverage.

Statement (1) is incorrect because tea is grown over undulating topography of hilly areas and well drained soils in humid and sub-humid tropics and sub-tropics region.

32 With reference to the 'Tea Board' in India, consider the following statements.

(Unit 5, Class-XII, Tamil Nadu Board) (IAS Pre 2022)

1. The Tea Board is a statutory body.
2. It is a regulatory body attached to the Ministry of Agriculture and Farmers Welfare.
3. The Tea Board's Head Office is situated in Bengaluru.
4. The Board has overseas offices at Dubai and Moscow.

Which of the statements given above are correct?
(a) 1 and 3 (b) 2 and 4
(c) 3 and 4 (d) 1 and 4

Ans. (d)

Exp. Statements (1) and (4) are correct. Tea Board is functioning as a statutory body of the Central Government. Currently Tea Board has two overseas offices located at Dubai, and Moscow

Statements (2) and (3) are incorrect. Tea Board comes under the Ministry of Commerce. Its headquarters is situated in Kolkata.

33 Arrange the following states of India in increasing order total production of tea and choose the correct option using the codes given below.

(Chap 5, Class-XII, New NCERT)

1. Tamil Nadu 2. Assam
3. West Bengal

Codes
(a) 2, 3 ,1 (b) 1, 3, 2 (c) 1, 2, 3 (d) 3, 2, 1

Ans. (b)

Exp. The correct increasing order is 1, 3, 2 of tea producing state in India i.e., Tamil Nadu, West Bengal and Assam. Assam is the top tea producer state in India. West Bengal is the second largest tea producer state in India. Tamil Nadu is the third largest tea producer state in India.

Assam accounts for about 53.2% of the total cropped area and contributes more than half of total production of tea in the country.

34 Consider the following statements with reference to production of coffee in India.

(Chap 5, Class-XII, New NCERT)

1. India is the second largest producer of coffee in the world.
2. Arabica variety of coffee is mainly grown in India.
3. Karnataka is the largest producer of coffee in India.

Which of the statements given above is/are correct?
(a) 1 and 3 (b) Only 2
(c) Only 1 (d) 2 and 3

Ans. (d)

Exp. Statements (2) and (3) are correct with reference to production of coffee in India. There are three varieties of coffee i.e. Arabica, Robusta and Liberica. India mostly grows superior quality coffee, Arabica, which is in great demand in international market.

The state of Karnataka is the largest producer of coffee in India. The state contributed about 70% of the total coffee production in India during 2019-20.

Statement (1) is incorrect because Vietnam is the second largest coffee producing country in the world. India is seventh largest coffee producing country in the world.

35 Which of the following statements is/are correct?

(Chap 2, Class-XII, Old NCERT) (BPSC Pre 2017)

1. Rubber is an equatorial crop, but under special conditions, it is also grown in tropical and sub-tropical areas.
2. Rubber is an important industrial raw material. It is mainly grown in Kerala, Tamil Nadu and Karnataka.
3. India is the largest producer of rubber in the world.

Codes
(a) 1 and 2
(b) 2 and 3
(c) Only 3
(d) Only 2

Ans. (a)

Exp. Statements (1) and (2) are correct. Rubber is an equatorial crop, but under special conditions, it is also grown in tropical and sub-tropical areas.

It requires moist and humid climate with rainfall of more than 200 cm and temperature above 25°C. Rubber is an important industrial raw material. It is mainly grown in Kerala, Tamil Nadu, Karnataka and Andaman and Nicobar Islands, Garo hills of Meghalaya.

Statement (3) is incorrect because Thailand is the largest producer of rubber in the world. India was the world's sixth largest producer of natural rubber in 2020 and the fourth largest in South Asia behind Thailand, Indonesia, and Vietnam respectively.

36 **With reference to the circumstances in Indian agriculture, the concept of 'Conservation Agriculture' assumes significance. Which of the following fall under the Conservation Agriculture?**

(Chap 4, Class-X, New NCERT) (IAS Pre 2018)

1. Avoiding the monoculture practices
2. Adopting minimum tillage
3. Avoiding the cultivation of plantation crops
4. Using crop residues to cover soil surface
5. Adopting spatial and temporal crop sequencing/crop rotations

Select the correct answer using the codes given below.

(a) 1, 3 and 4 (b) 2, 3, 4 and 5
(c) 2, 4 and 5 (d) 1, 2, 3 and 5

Ans. (c)

Exp. The correct options are (2), (4) and (5) regarding conservation Agriculture because it has principles of such as adopting the minimum village, using crop residuals to cover soil surface and adopting spatial and temporal crop sequencing/crop rotations.

According to Food and Agricultural Organisation of the United Nations, Conservation Agriculture (CA) can be defined as "as concept for resource-saving agricultural crop production that strives to achieve acceptable profits together with high and sustained production levels while concurrently conserving the environment.

37 **With reference to 'Initiative for Nutritional Security through Intensive Millets Promotion', which of the following statements is/are correct?**

(Chap 2, Module-2, NIOS) (IAS Pre 2016)

1. This initiative aims to demonstrate the improved production and post-harvest technologies, and to demonstrate value addition techniques, in an integrated manner, with a cluster approach.
2. Poor, small, marginal and tribal farmers have a larger stake in this scheme.
3. An important objective of the scheme is to encourage farmers of commercial crops to shift to millet cultivation by offering them free kits of critical inputs of nutrients and micro irrigation equipment.

Select the correct answer using the codes given below.

(a) Only 1 (b) 2 and 3 (c) 1 and 2 (d) 1, 2 and 3

Ans. (c)

Exp. Statements (1) and (2) are correct. 'Initiative for Nutritional security through Intensive Millets Promotion' Scheme aims to demonstrate the improved production and post-harvest technologies in an integrated manner with visible impact to catalyse increased production of millets in the country. Besides increasing production of millets, the scheme, through processing and value addition techniques, is expected to generate consumer demand for millet-based food products.

Technology demonstrations in compact blocks would be organised in selected districts for four categories of millets – sorghum, pearl millet, finger millet and small millets.

Poor, small, marginal and tribal farmers have a larger stake in this scheme.

Statement (3) is incorrect. There is no such provision to encourage farmers of commercial crops to shift to millet cultivation.

Irrigation

38 **Consider the following irrigation project has been developed by India in cooperation with Nepal.**

(Chap 4, Class-X, New NCERT)

1. Gandak Multipurpose Project
2. Tehri Dam Project
3. Kosi Project

How many of the statements given above is/are correct?

(a) Only one (b) Only two
(c) All three (d) None of these

Ans. (b)

Exp. Only two statements i.e. (1) and (3) are correct.

Gandak is a multipurpose project and Kosi project are irrigation project that has been developed by India in cooperation with Nepal.

Statement (2) is incorrect. While Tehri Dam located on Bhagirathi river in India is developed in cooperation with Russia.

39 **Which of the following statements is/are correct with reference to drip irrigation in India?**

(Chap 3, Class-X, New NCERT)

1. It has been practised in Meghalaya region for over 200 years.
2. The traditional drip pipes are made up of bamboo.
3. It supplies water directly near the root of the plants efficiently.
4. Tamil Nadu is the first state in India, which has made drip irrigation compulsory.

Codes

(a) 1, 2 and 3 (b) 2, 3 and 4
(c) 1, 3 and 4 (d) 1, 2, 3 and 4

Ans. (a)

Exp. Statements (1), (2) and (3) are correct with reference to drip irrigation in India.

Drip irrigation has been practised in Meghalaya region for over 200 years.

200 years old system of tapping stream and spring water by using bamboo pipes is prevalent in Meghalaya. The channel sections, made of bamboo divert water to the plant site where it is distributed into branches, again made and laid out with different forms of bamboo pipes. It supplies water directly near the roots of plants.

Statement (4) is incorrect because Tamil Nadu is the first state in India which has made roof-top rainwater harvesting structure compulsory (not drip irrigation) to all the houses across the state.

40 What are the benefits of implementing the 'Integrated Watershed Development Programme'? *(Chap 2, Module-2, NIOS) (IAS Pre 2014)*

1. Prevention of soil runoff
2. Linking the country's perennial rivers with seasonal rivers
3. Rainwater harvesting and recharge of the groundwater table
4. Regeneration of natural vegetation

Select the correct answer using the codes given below.

(a) 1 and 2 (b) 2, 3 and 4
(c) 1, 3 and 4 (d) 1, 2, 3 and 4

Ans. (c)

Exp. The correct answer is (1), (3) and (4) about the Integrated Watershed Management Programme, because it focuses include mitigating soil erosion, implementing rainwater harvesting techniques, bolstering groundwater levels, enhancing crop productivity, diversifying agricultural practices, fostering sustainable livelihoods, and augmenting household incomes.

Its comes under the Department of Land Resources within the Ministry of Rural Development, consolidates three key development initiatives aimed at revitalising rainfed and degraded lands across the nation: The Desert Development Programme (DDP), Drought Prone Areas Programme (DPAP), and Integrated Wastelands Development Programme.

Statement (2) is incorrect because the programme does not encompass initiatives related to interlinking perennial rivers with seasonal rivers.

41 Consider the following was the main aim of Intensive Agriculture Area Programme of the government started during the 1960s. *(Chap 1, Class-XII, New NCERT)*

1. To provide high yielding variety seeds to the farmers.
2. To introduce commercial crops and promote their farming.
3. To develop minor and major irrigation sources and promote the use of fertilisers.
4. To manage the on farm activities with the help of professionals.

Which of the statements given above is most appropriate?

(a) Only 1 (b) Only 2 (c) Only 3 (d) Only 4

Ans. (c)

Exp. Statement (3) is most appropriate because the main aim of Intensive Agriculture Area Programme of the government, started during the 1960s is to develop minor and major irrigation sources and promote the use of fertilisers.

A new programme named as IADP, was formulated which was launched gradually from 1960. The third five years plan (1961-1966) incorporated this program into the planned development process.

Animal Husbandary

42 Consider the following statements with reference to livestock in India. *(Chap 1, Class-XII, New NCERT)*

1. The population of Buffalo is 21% of total livestock population in India.
2. Yaks constitutes the lowest share of livestock in India.
3. Uttar Pradesh accounts for the largest share of livestock in the country.

How many of the statements given above is/are correct?

(a) Only one (b) Only two
(c) All three (d) None of these

Ans. (c)

Exp. All three statements are correct i.e., (1), (2) and (3) with reference to livestock in India. The population of Buffalo is 20.45 % of total livestock population in India. The other livestock including mithun, yak, horses, ponies, mule, donkeys, and camel together contribute around 0.23% of the total livestock. Yaks constitute the lowest share of livestock in India.

Uttar Pradesh accounts for the largest share (67.8 million) of livestock in the country.

43 Which of the given pairs is/are correctly matched? *(Chap 1, Class-XII, New NCERT)*

Livestock Breeds	Belongs to
(a) Nagauri	Goat
(b) Murrah	Buffalo
(c) Surti	Yak
(d) Both a and c	

Ans. (b)

Exp. Pair (b) is correctly matched as the Murrah buffalo is a breed of water buffalo mainly kept for milk production. It originates in Haryana state and some district of Punjab and West Uttar Pradesh of India.

Pairs (a) and (c) are incorrectly matched because Nagauri is a cattle breed from Rajasthan.

It is a draught breed, mainly used for agricultural purposes. The Surti is a breed of water buffalo found in the Kaira and Vadodara districts of Gujarat between the Mahi and Sabarmati rivers.

44 What are the advantages of fertigation in agriculture? *(Chap 4, Class-XI, Old NCERT) (IAS Pre 2018)*

1. Controlling the alkalinity of irrigation water is possible.
2. Efficient application of Rock Phosphate and all other phosphatic fertilisers is possible.
3. Increased availability of nutrients to plants is possible.
4. Reduction in the leaching of chemical nutrients is possible.

Select the correct answer using the codes given below.

(a) 1, 2 and 3 (b) 1, 2 and 4
(c) 1, 3 and 4 (d) 2, 3 and 4

***Ans.* (c)**

Exp. Statements (1), (3), and (4) are correct. Fertigation in agriculture offers several advantages.

It enables the control of irrigation water alkalinity, crucial for managing soil pH effectively.

Statement (2) is incorrect as Rock Phosphate is not soluble and thus not suitable.

The technique enhances nutrient availability to plants by delivering them directly through irrigation systems, promoting optimal growth. Fertigation reduces leaching of chemical nutrients, ensuring nutrients are utilised by plants rather than lost to the environment. These benefits collectively contribute to improved crop health, increased yield, and environmental sustainability.

45 Which of the following statements is/are incorrect with reference to fisheries in India? *(Chap 1, Class-XII, New NCERT)*

1. Largest share of fisheries production is obtained from Inland fishing as compared to deep sea fishing.
2. Fisheries cannot be practised in Brackish water ecosystems in India.
3. India accounts for the largest fish production in the world.

How many of the statements given above is/are incorrect?

(a) Only one (b) Only two
(c) All three (d) None of these

***Ans.* (c)**

Exp. All three statements i.e., (1), (2) and (3) are incorrect with reference to fisheries in India. The largest share of fisheries production is obtained from deep sea fishing as compared to inland fishing.

Fisheries can be practised in Brackish, river, ocean and wetlands water ecosystems in India.

China accounts for the largest fish production in the world.

46 Which of the following factors provide a natural potential advantage to India in the development of fisheries? *(Chap 6, Class-X, Old NCERT)*

1. Wider continental shelf on the East coast.
2. A huge exclusive economic zone of 2 million sq. km.
3. Huge discharge of nutrients by the rivers draining in the Bay of Bengal.

Codes

(a) 2 and 3
(b) Only 2
(c) Only 3
(d) All of the above

***Ans.* (d)**

Exp. All the given factors provide a natural potential advantage to India in the development of fisheries. The wider continental shelf on the East coast. A huge exclusive economic zone of 2 million sq. km and huge discharge of nutrients by the rivers draining in the Bay of Bengal factors provide a natural potential advantage to India in the development of fisheries.

Chapter 23

Energy and Mineral Resources in India

Energy and Mineral Resources in India

Energy Resources

Introduction

- India is endowed with rich variety of mineral resources. They are of two types
  - **Metallic Minerals** These minerals contain metal, can be further classified as ferrous (with iron content) and non-ferrous (without iron content)
  - **Non-metallic Minerals** These minerals do not contain metal

Distribution of Mineral in India

- Most of the metallic minerals in India occur in Peninsular plateau region in old crystalline rocks
- Minerals are generally concentrated in three belts namely,
  - **North-Eastern Plateau Region** Covers Chhota Nagpur, Odisha plateau, West Bengal and parts of Chhattisgarh
  - Minerals available are iron-ore, coal, manganese, bauxite, etc
  - **South-Western Plateau Region** Extends over Karnataka, Goa, parts of Tamil Nadu and Kerala Minerals available are iron-ore, bauxite, manganese, etc
  - **North-Western Region** It Extends along Aravalli in Rajasthan and parts of Gujarat Minerals available are copper, zinc, building stones, etc

Ferrous Minerals

Iron Ore

- India has the largest reserves of iron ore in Asia
- 95% of the deposits are found in states of Odisha, Jharkhand, Chhattisgarh, Karnataka, Goa, etc

Manganese

- Deposits are found in almost all geological formations but mainly associated with Dharwar system
- Leading producer is Odisha, Karnataka, Maharashtra, etc

Non-Ferrous Minerals

- **Bauxite** Ore used for manufacturing of aluminium; Leading producer to be Odisha, Gujarat, Chhattisgarh, etc
- **Copper** Deposits are found in parts of Jharkhand, Madhya Pradesh, Rajasthan, etc

Non-Metallic Minerals

- **Gypsum** Mineral commonly found in Earth crust; Largest producer is Rajasthan
- **Mica** Mainly used in electrical and electronic industries; Leading producers are Jharkhand, Andhra Pradesh, Rajasthan, etc
- **Diamond** Is the Purest form of carbon and hardest element found in nature; Found in Golconda mines of Andhra Pradesh, regions of Madhya

Mineral Resources

Introduction

- They can be categorised as
- **Conventional Sources** Resources which are exhaustible like coal, petroleum, etc
- **Non-conventional Sources** Resources which are not exhaustible like solar energy, wind energy, etc

Conventional Resources

- **Coal** Major constituent of energy production in the country; It is of four types - Anthracite (best quality coal), Bituminous, Lignite, Peat; Distributed in the country as Gondwana coal and Tertiary coal (young coal)
- **Petroleum** Occurs in sedimentary rocks of tertiary period; Some important oil fields are located in Digboi, Ankaleshwar, etc
- **Natural Gas** A naturally occuring hydrocarbon gas mixture consisting primarily of methane; Found in areas like Gulf of Kutch, Gulf of Khambat, Bombay high, etc

Non-Conventional Resources

- **Solar Energy** Sun rays trapped in photovoltaic cells are used of convert it into energy called solar energy
- **Wind Energy** An absolutely pollution free source of energy
- **Tidal And Wave Energy** Ocean currents and waves are storehouse of infinite energy that are used to generate electricity
- **Geothermal Energy** This heat is used to produce electrical energy

SOURCE New NCERT Class X *(Mineral and Energy Resources)*, Old NCERT Class X *(Land Use and Water Resources)*, Old NCERT Class X *(Mineral and Energy Resources)*, New NCERT Class XII *(Mineral and Energy Resources)* NIOS Chap 18, Module 8 *(Mineral and Energy Resource)*

Minerals

1 With reference to mineral belts of India, consider the following statements. *(Chap 7, Class-XII, New NCERT)*

1. The South-Western plateau has the largest occurrence of copper in the country.
2. The Dharwar rocks of North-Western region consists of high grade petroleum.
3. Mica, bauxite and iron ore mostly occur in the North-Eastern plateau region of India.

How many of the statements given above is/are correct?

(a) Only one
(b) Only two
(c) All three
(d) None of the above

***Ans.* (a)**

Exp. Only one statement i.e., (3) is correct with reference to mineral belts of India. The North-Eastern plateau region belt covers Chhota Nagpur (Jharkhand), Odisha plateau, West Bengal and parts of Chhattisgarh. The North-Eastern plateau region belt has variety of minerals *viz.* iron ore, coal, manganese, bauxite and mica.

Statements (1) and (2) are incorrect because the North-Western region has the largest occurrence of copper in the country. High grade crude petroleum occurs in sedimentary rocks of the tertiary period.

2 Consider the following statements with reference to occurrence of minerals in India. *(Chap 5, Class-X, New NCERT)*

1. Metallic minerals are found in veins and lodes of igneous and metamorphic rocks.
2. Minerals occur in distinct beds and layers in the sedimentary rock formations.
3. Alluvial deposits are rich source of minerals known as Placer deposits.

Which of the statements given above is/are correct?

(a) 1 and 2
(b) 2 and 3
(c) Only 3
(d) 1, 2 and 3

***Ans.* (d)**

Exp. All the statements are correct with reference to occurrence of minerals in India. In igneous and metamorphic rocks, minerals may occur in the cracks, crevices, faults or joints. The smaller occurrences are called Veins and the larger are called Lodes.

In sedimentary rocks, a number of minerals occur in beds or layers. They have been formed as a result of deposition, accumulation and concentration in horizontal strata.

Certain minerals may occur as alluvial deposits in sands of valley floors and the base of hills. These deposits are called 'Placer deposits' and generally contain minerals, which are not corroded by water.

Ferrous Minerals

3 Consider the following statements about Iron Ore in India. *(Chap 5, Class-XII, New NCERT)*

1. The two main types of ores found in India are haematite and magnetite.
2. About 95 per cent of the total reserves of iron ore is located in the States of Odisha and Jharkhand.
3. Most of the important mines like Noamundi and Gua are located in Poorbi and Pashchimi Singhbhum districts of Jharkhand.

How many of the statements given above is/are correct?

(a) Only one
(b) Only two
(c) All three
(d) None of these

***Ans.* (b)**

Exp. Only two statements i.e., (1) and (3) are correct regarding Iron Ores in India.

The two main types of ore found in our country are haematite and magnetite. India is endowed with fairly abundant resources of iron ore. It has the largest reserve of iron ore in Asia.

Most of the important mines like Noamundi and Gua are located in Poorbi and Paschimi Singhbhum districts of Jharkhand. This belt further extends to Durg, Dantewara and Bailadila. Dalli and Rajhara in Durg are the important mines of iron ore in the country.

Statement (2) is incorrect because 95 per cent of total reserves of iron ore is located in the States of Odisha, Jharkhand, Chhattisgarh, Karnataka, Goa, Telangana, Andhra Pradesh and Tamil Nadu.

4 Consider the following statements with reference to minerals in India. *(Chap 7, Class-XII, New NCERT)*

1. Himalayan belt of India consists of copper, zinc, cobalt and lead.
2. Most of the building stones such as granite, marble and gypsum are found in Rajasthan.

Which of the statements given above is/are correct?

(a) Only 1
(b) Only 2
(c) Both 1 and 2
(d) Neither 1 nor 2

***Ans.* (c)**

Exp. Both the statements (1) and (2) are correct with reference to minerals in India.

The Himalayan belt is important mineral belt in India, where copper, lead, zinc, cobalt and tungsten are known to occur.

They occur on both the Eastern and Western parts. The North-Western Region belt extends along Aravali region in Rajasthan and part of Gujarat.

Rajasthan is rich in building stones i.e. sandstone, granite, marble. Gypsum and fuller's Eearth deposits are also found in Rajasthan.

5 **With reference to iron ore in India, consider the following statements.** *(Chap 7, Class-XII, New NCERT)*

1. Only the haematite ore of iron occurs in India.
2. In Odisha, iron ore occurs in a series of hill ranges in Sundergarh, Mayurbhanj and Jhar.
3. India consists of the largest reserves of iron ore in Asia.
4. More than 90% of iron ore reserves are found in Jharkhand, Chhattisgarh, Karnataka and Goa.

How many of the statements given above is/are incorrect?

(a) Only one (b) Only two
(c) Only three (d) None of these

Ans. (a)

Exp. Only one statement i.e., (1) incorrect with reference to iron ore in India. India is endowed with fairly abundant resources of iron ore. India has the largest reserve of iron ore in Asia. The two main types of ore found in India are haematite and magnetite. It has great demand in international market due to its superior quality.

6 **Consider the following statements about the hematite type of iron ore in India.** *(Chap 5, Class-XII, New NCERT)*

1. Hematite type of iron-ore has the largest reserve in India.
2. It contains 70 per cent metallic content, mainly found in Dharwar and Cuddapah rock system in India.
3. 80 per cent of hematite reserves are in Odisha, and Madhya Pradesh.

How many of the statements given above is/are correct?

(a) Only one (b) Only two
(c) All three (d) None of these

Ans. (b)

Exp. Only two statements i.e., (1) and (2) are correct regarding the hematite type of iron ore in India.

Hematite type of iron-ore has the largest reserve in India. Hematite is best quality Iron-ore. It contains 70 per cent metallic content, mainly found in Dharwar and Cuddapah rock system in India.

Statement (3) is incorrect because 80 per cent of hematite reserves are in Odisha, Jharkhand, Chhattisgarh, and Andhra Pradesh. In the Western section, Karnataka, Maharashtra and Goa have this kind of ore.

7 **With reference to iron ore production in India, consider the following statements.** *(Chap 7, Class-XII, New NCERT)*

1. The largest reserves of iron ore are found in India.
2. Odisha is the largest producer of iron ore in India.
3. Iron ore mines in India lie in close proximity to the coal fields and Iron and steel plants.

Which of the statements given above are correct?

(a) 1 and 2 (b) 2 and 3
(c) 1 and 3 (d) 1, 2 and 3

Ans. (b)

Exp. Statements (2) and (3) are correct with reference to iron ore production in India. Odisha is the largest producer of iron ore in India. In Odisha, iron ore occurs in a series of hill ranges in Sundergarh, Mayurbhanj and Jhar regions.

The important iron ore mines are Gurumahisani, Sulaipet, Badampahar, Kiruburu and Bonai. The iron ore mines occur in close proximity to the coal fields in the North-Eastern plateau region of the country which adds to their advantage.

Statement (1) is incorrect because the largest reserves of iron ore are found in Australia.

8 **Consider the following pairs.** *(Chap 5, Class-XII, New NCERT)*

Mining regions		State
1. Kendujhar	–	Odisha
2. Ballari	–	Maharashtra
3. Bhandara	–	Madhya Pradesh
4. Balaghat	–	Karnataka

How many pairs given above is/are correctly matched?

(a) Only one (b) Only two
(c) Only three (d) All four

Ans. (a)

Exp. Only one pair i.e., (1) is correctly matched.

Kendujhar is associated with the State of Odisha. Major mines in Odisha are located in the central part of the iron ore belt of India, particularly in Bonai, Kendujhar, Sundergarh, Gangpur, Koraput, Kalahandi, and Bolangir.

Pairs (2), (3) and (4) are not correctly matched. Ballari, a remote district in North-Eastern Karnataka known for lush green landscapes, become popular for iron-ore extraction in the mid – 2000s.

Bhandara is a mining region in the state of Maharashtra. Maharashtra is also an important producer of manganese, which is mined in Nagpur, Bhandara and Ratnagiri districts.

Balaghat is a mining area in the state of Madhya Pradesh. The manganese belt of Madhya Pradesh extends in a belt in the Balaghat-Chhindwara-Nimar-Mandla and Jhabua districts.

9 **Consider the following pairs.** *(Chap 7, Class-XII, New NCERT)*

Iron ore mine		State
1. Badampahar	–	Odisha
2. Gua	–	Chhattisgarh
3. Dantewara	–	Jharkhand
4. Baba Budan Hills	–	Karnataka

How many pairs given above is/are correctly matched?

(a) Only one (b) Only two
(c) Only three (d) All four

Ans. (b)

Exp. Only two pairs i.e., (1) and (4) are correctly matched.

Gurumahisani, Sulaipet, Badampahar (Mayurbhanj), Kiruburu (Kendujhar) and Bonai (Sundergarh) iron ore mines are located in Odisha.

In Karnataka, iron ore deposits occur in Sandur-Hospet area of Ballari district, Baba Budan Hills.

Pairs (2) and (3) are not correctly matched. Noamundi and Gua iron ore mines are located in Poorbi and Pashchimi Singhbhum districts of Jharkhand.

Durg, Dantewara and Bailadila, Dalli and Rajhara in Durg are the important iron ore mines of Chhattisgarh.

10 Consider the following pairs. *(Chap 7, Class-XII, New NCERT)*

Iron ore mines	States
1. Chitradurga	Kerala
2. Mayurbhanj	Jharkhand
3. Kudermukh	Karnataka
4. Tumkur	Tamil Nadu

How many of the pairs given above is/are correctly matched?

(a) Only one (b) Only two (c) Only three (d) All four

Ans. (a)

Exp. Only one pair i.e., (3) is correctly matched. Kudermukh, Sandur -Hospet, Baba Budan hills and Chitradurga region are important iron ore mines of Karnataka.

Pairs (1), (2) and (4) are not correctly matched because Chitradurga iron ore region is located in Karnataka. Mayurbhanj iron ore region is located in Odisha. Tumkur iron ore region is located in Karnataka.

11 Which of the following statements is/are correct with reference to manganese ore? *(Chap 7, Class-XII, New NCERT)*

1. It forms an important component of raw materials used for smelting of iron ore.
2. Manganese deposits are usually associated with Gondwana deposits.

Codes

(a) Only 1 (b) Only 2
(c) Both 1 and 2 (d) Neither 1 nor 2

Ans. (a)

Exp. Statement (1) is correct with reference to manganese ore. Manganese is an important component of raw material for smelting of iron ore and also used for manufacturing Ferro alloys.

Statement (2) is incorrect because manganese deposits are found in almost all geological formations. However, it is mainly associated with Dharwar system.

12 Which of the following minerals are found naturally in the State of Odisha? *(Chap 5, Class-XII, New, NCERT)*

1. Iron ore 2. Manganese
3. Chromium 4. Bauxite

Choose the correct answer using the codes given below.

(a) 1 and 2 (b) 2, 3 and 4
(c) 1, 3 and 4 (d) 1, 2, 3 and 4

Ans. (d)

Exp. All the above given options are correct regarding minerals found in Odisha.

Iron-ore, manganese, chromium, bauxite are naturally found in the State of Odisha. Odisha is home to some of the richest iron ore deposits in India. In Odisha, iron ore occurs in a series of hill ranges in Sundergarh, Mayurbhanj and Jhar. The important mines are Gurumahisani, Sulaipet, Badampahar (Mayurbhaj), Kiruburu (Kendujhar) and Bonai (Sundergarh).

13 Match List I with List II. *(Chap 5, Class-XII, New NCERT)*

List I (Mining regions)	List II (State)
A. Bailadila	1. Odisha
B. Kendujhar	2. Karnataka
C. Balaghat	3. Chhattisgarh
D. Kudremukh	4. Madhya Pradesh

Codes

	A	B	C	D		A	B	C	D
(a)	3	4	2	1	(b)	2	4	3	1
(c)	4	3	2	1	(d)	3	1	4	2

Ans. (d)

Exp. The correct matching is A-3, B-1, C-4, D-2.

Bailadila Iron Ore Mine is located in the Dantewada district of Chhattisgarh, India. The Bailadila Hills are one of the largest deposits with the best quality of iron ore in the country.

Kendujhar is a district in the state of Odisha, India. It is a major mineral-producing district, with major minerals including Iron ore, Manganese ore, Chromate, Quartzite, Bauxite, Gold, Pyrophillite, Lime Stone.

Balaghat mines are located in the Balaghat district of Madhya Pradesh, India.

Kudremukh iron ore mine is located in Karnataka. In Karnataka, Kudremukh mines are in the iron ore belt of Bellary- Chitradurga- Chikmagalur- Tumkur.

14 Consider the following pairs. *(Chap 7, Class-XII, New NCERT)*

Manganese mine		States
1. Bhandara	–	Karnataka
2. Shimoga	–	Maharashtra
3. Sundergarh	–	Odisha
4. Mandla	–	Madhya Pradesh

How many pairs given above is/are correctly matched?

(a) Only one (b) Only two
(c) Only three (d) All four

Ans. (b)

Exp. Only two pairs i.e. (3) and (4) are correctly matched. Major mines in Odisha are located in Bonai, Kendujhar, Sundergarh, Gangpur, Koraput, Kalahandi and Bolangir.

In Madhya Pradesh, the manganese belt extends in Balaghat-Chhindwara-Nimar Mandla and Jhabua districts.

Pairs (1) and (2) are not correctly matched because in Maharashtra, it is mined in Nagpur, Bhandara and Ratnagiri districts.

In Karnataka, it is mined in Dharwar, Ballari, Belagavi, Chikkamagaluru and Shimoga.

Non-Ferrous Minerals

15 **Consider the following statements with reference to production of bauxite in India.** *(Chap 7, Class-XII, New NCERT)*

1. In India, largest deposits of bauxite occurs in the Dharwar rock systems.
2. Jharkhand is the largest producer of bauxite in India.
3. Most of the bauxite is found in the laterite rocks on the plateau or hill ranges of peninsula.

Which of the statements given above is/are incorrect?

(a) Only 1 (b) 2 and 3 (c) 1 and 2 (d) Only 3

Ans. (c)

Exp. Statements (1) and (2) are incorrect with reference to bauxite production in India. In India, largest deposits of bauxite found in Panchpatmali in Koraput district of Odisha.

Odisha is the largest producer of bauxite. Kalahandi and Sambalpur regions are the leading producers in Odisha.

16 **Arrange the following Indian states/regions in ascending order based on their percentage contribution to the total bauxite distribution in India.** *(Chap 5, Class-XII, New NCERT)*

(a) Maharashtra, Gujarat, Andhra Pradesh, Odisha
(b) Maharashtra, Andhra Pradesh, Gujarat, Odisha
(c) Gujarat, Maharashtra, Andhra Pradesh, Odisha
(d) Odisha, Andhra Pradesh, Gujarat, Maharashtra

Ans. (a)

Exp. The correct chronological order is Maharashtra, Gujarat, Andhra Pradesh, Odisha.

Maharashtra has a contribution of 5%, followed by Gujarat with 7%, Andhra Pradesh with 18%, and the highest contribution from Odisha at 52%.

17 **Which of the given pairs is/are correctly matched?** *(Chap 7, Class-XII, New NCERT)*

	Bauxite reserves	States
1.	Amarkantak plateau	Chhattisgarh
2.	Jamnagar	Gujarat
3.	Katni-Jabalpur	Madhya Pradesh

Codes

(a) 1 and 2
(b) 2 and 3
(c) Only 3
(d) 1, 2 and 3

Ans. (d)

Exp. All the given pairs (1), (2) and (3) are correctly matched.

The Maikalu range of Bilaspur and Surguja regions of Amarkantak plateau are bauxite rich deposits of Chhattisgarh.

In Madhya Pradesh, the Katni-Jabalpur Shahdol Mandla, Rewa, district are famous for its bauxite deposits.

Gujarat, the second largest producer of bauxite in India have its bauxite deposits in the district of Jamnagar.

18 **Consider the following pairs.** *(Chap 5, Class-XII, New NCERT)*

	List I		List II
1.	Iron ore	–	Found in the hill ranges of Sundergarh, Mayurbhanj and Jhar of Odisha.
2.	Manganese	–	Particularly found in Bonai, Kendujhar, Koraput, Kalahandi, and Bolangir of Odisha.
3.	Copper	–	Found in Jhunjhunu and Alwar districts of Rajasthan.

How many of the pairs given above is/are correctly matched?

(a) Only one (b) Only two
(c) All three (d) None of these

Ans. (c)

Exp. All three pairs i.e., (1), (2) and (3) are correctly matched.

Odisha is known for its significant deposits of iron ore, iron ore occurs in a series of hill ranges in Sundergarh, Mayurbhanj and Jhar.

Odisha is the leading producer of manganese, and major mines are located in the central part of India's iron ore belt. These mines are located in Bonai, Kendujhar, Sundergarh, Gangpur, Koraput, Kalahandi and Bolangir.

Copper is found in the Jhunjhunu and Alwar districts of Rajasthan. The Khetri-Singhana belt is an 80 km long mountainous belt that runs from the North-East to the South-West.

19 **Consider the following statements about Bauxite in India.** *(Chap 5, Class-XII, New NCERT)*

1. Bauxite is the ore used in the manufacturing of aluminum.
2. Odisha is the largest producer of bauxite.
3. Lohardaga in Jharkhand has rich deposits of bauxite.
4. The major deposits of bauxite in Gujarat are in Surat and Vadodara.

How many of the statements given above is/are correct?

(a) Only one (b) Only two
(c) Only three (d) All four

Ans. (c)

Exp. Only three statements i.e., (1), (2) and (3) are correct regarding bauxite in India.

Bauxite is the ore, which is used in the manufacturing of aluminium. It is a clay mineral found in tropical and sub-tropical areas such as Australia and the West Asia.

Odisha is India's largest bauxite producer accounting for about 49% of the total production followed by Gujarat (24%). Lohardaga district is known as Bauxite Mineral. This bauxite extends to Pakhar, Hisari, Rudhali Pat, Khamar Pat, Gumla and Latehar district also, which goes to the North-West.

Statement (4) is incorrect. The most important bauxite deposits in Gujarat are in a belt between the Gulf of Kutch and the Arabian Sea, through Bhavnagar, Junagadh and Amreli districts.

20 **Consider the following statements about mica.**

(Chap 5, Class-XII, New NCERT)

1. Koderma located in the State of Odisha is famous for its rich deposits of mica.
2. Mica is known for its heat-resistant and insulating properties, making it an important component in the production of electrical equipment.

Which of the statements given above is/are correct?

(a) Only 1 (b) Only 2
(c) Both 1 and 2 (d) Neither 1 nor 2

Ans. (b)

Exp. Statement (2) is correct as Mica is particularly valued for its heat-resistant and insulating properties, making it a crucial component in the production of electrical equipment. Cosmetics and other materials. It is also used in toothpaste and cosmetics because of its glittery.

India is the leading producer of mica in the world. It accounts for over 80% of the world's mica production.

Statement (1) incorrect. Koderma located in the State of Jharkhand is renowned for its rich deposits of mica, a mineral widely used in various industries.

21 **With reference to limestone production in India, consider the following statements.**

(Chap 5, Class-X, New NCERT)

1. Limestone occurs in association with rocks composed of calcium carbonates.
2. It is used in iron ore smelting and cement industry.
3. It occurs in the sedimentary rock formations.

How many of the statements given above is/are correct?

(a) Only one (b) Only two
(c) All three (d) None of these

Ans. (c)

Exp. All three statements i.e., (1), (2) and (3) are correct with reference to limestone production in India.

Limestone is found in association with rocks composed of calcium carbonates or calcium and magnesium carbonates.

Limestone is the basic raw material for the cement industry and essential for smelting iron ore in the blast furnace.

It is found in sedimentary rocks of geological formations.

22 **Match the following lists correctly and choose the correct code.**

(Chap 7, Class-XII, New NCERT) (UPPSC Pre 2019)

List I (Coalfields)	List II (Location)
A. Talcher	1. Damodar valley
B. Karanpura	2. Son valley
C. Singrauli	3. Godavari valley
D. Singareni	4. Mahanadi valley

Codes

	A	B	C	D		A	B	C	D
(a)	4	1	2	3	(b)	3	2	1	4
(c)	2	4	3	1	(d)	1	3	2	4

Ans. (a)

Exp. The correct matching is A-4, B-1, C-2, D-3.

Talcher coalfield is the largest repository of power grade coal in India. It occupies a basin in the South-Eastern part of Mahanadi valley belt of Gondwana basin. It is mainly located in Anguly district of Odisha.

North Karanpura coalfield is located in Chatra, Ranchi, Hazaribagh and Chatra district in Jharkhand. Damodar valley region consists of Gondwana coal.

Singrauli coalfied is spread across the districts of Singrauli and Sonbhadra in Madhya Pradesh and Uttar Pradesh. It is mostly located in basin of Son valley (Son river).

Singareni coalfield is located in the Godavari valley of Telangana. It is jointly owned by Telangana Government and Union Government.

23 **Tertiary coalfields are generally not found in India in which of the following regions?**

(Chap 7, Class-XII, New NCERT

1. Assam
2. Nagaland
3. Odisha
4. Meghalaya
5. Kerala

Codes

(a) 1, 2 and 5 (b) 2, 3 and 4
(c) 3 and 5 (d) 1, 3 and 4

Ans. (c)

Exp. Tertiary coalfields are generally not found in Odisha and Kerala. Tertiary coal is the lignite coal, Tertiary coals occur in Assam, Arunachal Pradesh, Meghalaya and Nagaland. Gondwana coal is found in Odisha.

24 **Which of the given pairs is/are correctly matched?** *(Chap 7, Class-XII, New NCERT)*

	Tertiary coalfields		State
(a)	Langrin	–	Meghalaya
(b)	Nazira	–	Gujarat
(c)	Kalakot	–	Uttarakhand
(d)	Namchik-Namphuk	–	Assam

Ans. (a)

Exp. Pair (a) is correctly matched. Tertiary coals occur in Assam, Arunachal Pradesh, Meghalaya and Nagaland. Tertiary coals are extracted from Darangiri, Cherrapunji, Mewlong and Langrin region in Meghalaya.

Pairs (b), (c) and (d) are incorrectly matched because Nazira tertiary coal mine is located in Assam. Kalakot tertiary coal mine is located in Jammu and Kashmir. Namchik-Namphuk tertiary coal mine is located in Arunachal Pradesh.

25 **Match the given lists correctly and choose the correct code.** *(Chap 7, Class-XII, New NCERT)*

List I (Thermal Power Plant)	List II (State)
A. Panki Power Plant	1. Bihar
B. Barauni Power Plant	2. Assam
C. Namrup Power Plant	3. Maharashtra
D. Uran Power Plant	4. Uttar Pradesh

Codes

	A	B	C	D		A	B	C	D
(a)	4	1	2	3	(b)	1	3	2	4
(c)	1	2	3	4	(c)	2	4	1	3

Ans. (a)

Exp. The correct matching is A-4, B-1, C-2, D-3.

Thermal Power Plant generate electricity by using heat from a fuel source.

Panki Thermal Power Station is located at Panki in Kanpur district in the Indian State of Uttar Pradesh. It was commissioned in 1967.

Barauni and Patratu Thermal Power Station are located in Bihar state.

Namrup Thermal Power Plant is located 12 km from Namrup, which is situated in Dibrugarh district in Assam.

Uran Gas Turbine Power Station is a gas-based thermal power plant located at Uran in Raigad district, Maharashtra.

26 **Consider the following pairs.** *(Chap 5, Class-X, New NCERT)*

1. Ukai Power Plant – Gujarat
2. Rihand Power Plant – Uttar Pradesh
3. Korba Power Plant – Jharkhand

How many of the pairs given above is/are correctly matched?

(a) Only one
(b) Only two
(c) All three
(d) None of these

Ans. (b)

Exp. Only two pairs i.e., (1) and (2) are correctly matched as Ukai Thermal Power Station is located in Gujarat. It is one of Gujarat's major coal-fired power plants, located on the bank of the Tapi river.

Rihand Super Thermal Power Plant is located at Renukut in Sonbhadra district in Indian State of Uttar Pradesh. The power plant is one of the coal based power plants of NTPC Limited.

Pair (3) is not correctly matched because Korba Power plant is located in Chhattisgarh.

27 **Consider the following pairs.** *(Chap 5, Class-XII, New NCERT)*

	Oilfields		Locations
1.	Naharkatiya	–	Gujarat
2.	Mehsana	–	Rajasthan
3.	Mangala	–	Assam
4.	Aliabet	–	Gulf of Khambhat

How many of the pairs given above is/are correctly matched?

(a) Only one
(b) Only two
(c) Only three
(d) All four

Ans. (a)

Exp. Only one pair i.e., (4) is correctly matched.

The Aliabet oilfield is located on Aliabet Island in the Gulf of Khambhat, which is about 45 kilometres off the coast of Bhavnagar in Gujarat, India.

Pairs (1), (2) and (3) are not correctly matched.

The Naharkatiya oilfield is located in the State of Assam. It is located in the Dibrugarh district, on the left bank of the Burhi Dibing river.

The Mehsana oilfield is located in the State of Gujarat.

The Mangala oilfield is located in the Barmer district of Rajasthan. It is part of the Mangala Bhagyam Aishwarya (MBA) trinity, which is a major oil field in the Rajasthan block.

28 **With reference to mineral oil exploration in India, consider the following statements.** *(Chap 7, Class-XII, New NCERT)*

1. Mineral oil exploration and production was systematically started after the establishment of Oil and Natural Gas Commission in 1956.
2. Crude petroleum reserves in India primarily occur in the sedimentary rocks of tertiary period.
3. Most of the oil reserves of India can be located in the Ganga-Brahmaputra valley and offshore continental shelf.
4. Till independence, Gujarat was the only state where mineral oil was drilled and refined.

How many of the statements given above is/are incorrect?

(a) Only one (b) Only two (c) Only three (d) All four

Ans. (a)

Exp. Only one statement i.e., (4) is incorrect with reference to mineral oil exploration in India. Till independence Assam was the only state where mineral oil was drilled and refined. During pre-independence, the Assam Oil Company in the North-Eastern and Attock Oil Company in North-Western part of undivided India were the only oil companies producing oil in the country.

29 Consider the following pairs. *(Chap 7, Class-XII, New NCERT)*

Oil Refinery		State
1. Bina	–	Madhya Pradesh
2. Koyali	–	Andhra Pradesh
3. Tatipaka	–	Gujarat
4. Bongaigaon	–	Assam

How many of the pairs given above is/are correctly matched?

(a) Only one (b) Only two (c) Only three (d) All four

Ans. (b)

Exp. Only two pairs i.e., (1) and (4) are correctly matched. Bina Refinery is an Indian oil refinery located at Bina in the Sagar district of Madhya Pradesh. The Bina Refinery was commissioned in May 2011.

Bongaigaon Refinery is a petroleum refinery located in Assam. It was incorporated in 1974 by the Government of India.

Pairs (2) and (3) are incorrectly matched.

Koyali Refinery is an oil refinery located at Koyali, Vadodara district in Gujarat, Western India. It is the second largest refinery owned by Indian Oil Corporation.

Tatipaka Oil Refinery is located in the East Godavari district in Andhra Pradesh. It was set up in 2001. It is ONGCs first ever oil refinery to produce petro-products.

30 Consider the following statements with reference to mineral oil production in India. *(Chap 7, Class-XII, New NCERT)*

1. Ankleshwar, Kalol, Mehsana and Kosamba are the important mineral oil producing regions of Maharashtra.
2. Mineral oil deposits have been found in Krishna-Godavari-Kaveri basin in South India.

Which of the statements given above is/are correct?

(a) Only
(b) Only 2
(c) Both 1 and 2
(d) Neither 1 nor 2

Ans. (b)

Exp. Statement (2) is correct with reference to mineral oil production in India.

Mineral deposit have been found in Krishna-Godavari-Kaveri basin in South India. Oil and gas along with coal, iron ore are found in Godavari basin.

Statement (1) is incorrect because Ankleshwar, Kalol, Mehsana and Kosamba are the important mineral oil producing regions of Gujarat.

31 Consider the following statements about coal in India. *(Chap 5, Class-XII, New NCERT)*

1. About 80 percent of the coal deposits in India are of bituminous type and non-coking grade.
2. The most important Gondwana coal fields in India are located in the Damodar valley.
3. Raniganj is the largest coal field followed by Jharia.

How many of the statements given above is/are correct?

(a) Only one (b) Only two
(c) All three (d) None of these

Ans. (b)

Exp. Only two statements i.e., (1) and (2) are correct regarding coal in India.

About 80 percent of the coal deposits in India are of a bituminous type and are of non-coking grade.

Bituminous coal is soft and has a carbon content of 60–80%. Most of India's coal is bituminous.

The most important Gondwana coal fields in India are located in Damodar valley. These fields include Raniganj, Jharia, Bokaro, Giridih, and Karanpura.

Statement (3) is incorrect. Jharia is the largest coal field followed by Raniganj. Jharia is located in the East of Jharkhand. The most important coal mining centres are Singrauli in Madhya Pradesh (part of Singrauli coal field lies in Uttar Pradesh), Korba in Chhattisgarh, Talcher and Rampur in Odisha, Chanda–Wardha, Kamptee and Bander in Maharashtra and Singareni in Telangana and Pandur in Andhra Pradesh.

Non-conventional Resources

32 Which of the given statement(s) is/are correct with reference to uranium exploration in India? *(Chap 7, Class-XII, New NCERT)*

1. Most of the uranium deposits of India occur in the Dharwar deposits.
2. Uranium mines are located along the Singhbhum copper belt.
3. Uranium can be obtained from the monazite sands which occur in the coastal regions of India.

Codes

(a) 2 and 3 (b) 1 and 2
(c) 1 and 3 (d) 1, 2 and 3

Ans. (b)

Exp. Statements (1) and (2) are correct with reference to uranium exploration in India. Uranium mineral deposits are occur in the Dharwar rocks. Uranium occurs naturally in low concentrations in soil, rock and water. It is a hard, dense, malleable, ductile, silver-white, radioactive metal. Geographically, uranium ores are known to occur in several locations along the Singhbhum copper belt.

Statement (3) is incorrect as thorium can be obtained from the monazite sands, which occur in the coastal regions of India.

33 **Which of the given pairs of Nuclear Power Plant and States is/are matched incorrectly?**
(Chap 7, Class-XII, New NCERT)

	Nuclear Plant		States
1.	Tarapur Atomic Plant	–	Maharashtra
2.	Rawatbhata Atomic Plant	–	Chhattisgarh
3.	Narora Atomic Plant	–	Uttar Pradesh
4.	Kakrapara Atomic Plant	–	Karnataka

Codes
(a) 1, 2 and 3 (b) Only 2 (c) 1 and 4 (d) Only 3

***Ans.* (b)**

Exp. Pair (2) is incorrectly matched because the Rawatbhata Atomic Plant is located in Rajasthan. It was the first facility in India to operate pressurised heavy water reactors. A Nuclear Power Plant is a Thermal Power station in which the heat source is a nuclear reactor.

34 **Which of the following statements is/are correct with reference to solar power production?**
(Chap 7, Class-XII, New NCERT)

1. Production of solar power is more efficient than coal and nuclear energy.
2. Kamuthi Solar Power Project is the largest solar project in India.

Codes
(a) Both 1 and 2 (b) Only 1
(c) Only 2 (d) Neither 1 nor 2

***Ans.* (a)**

Exp. Both the statements (1) and (2) are correct with reference to solar power production. Solar energy is 7% more effective than coal or oil based plants and 10% more effective than nuclear plants. Solar thermal technology has some relative advantages over all other non-renewable energy sources like coal and nuclear energy. The Kamuthi Solar Power Project is the largest solar power plant spread over 2,500 acres in Kamuthi in Tamil Nadu.

35 **With reference to wind energy in India, consider the following statements.** *(Chap 7, Class-XII, New NCERT)*

1. Westerly winds in winter season can be utilised to generate wind energy in India.
2. Periodic monsoon winds are not suitable for production of wind energy in India.
3. India's wind energy potential is more than 50,000 MW.
4. Tamil Nadu leads in the production of wind power in India.

How many of the statements given above is/are incorrect?
(a) Only one (b) Only two (c) Only three (d) All four

***Ans.* (a)**

Exp. Only one statement i.e., (2) is incorrect with reference to wind energy in India as periodic monsoon wind are suitable for production of wind energy in India. The permanent wind systems such as trade winds, Westerlies and seasonal wind like monsoon are used for the production of wind energy in India. The mechanism of energy conversion from blowing wind is simple, the kinetic energy of wind, through turbines is converted into electrical energy.

36 **Which of the following regions of India has very high potential for tidal energy production in India?**
(Chap 7, Class-XII, New NCERT)

1. Gulf of Khambhat 2. Palk Bay
3. Gulf of Kuchchh

Codes
(a) 1 and 2 (b) 2 and 3
(c) 1 and 3 (d) 1, 2 and 3

***Ans.* (d)**

Exp. In India, the Gulf of Khambhat, Gulf of Kuchchh in Gujarat on the Western coast, Palk Bay in Southern India have high potential for tidal energy production in India. Gangetic delta in Sunderban regions of West Bengal also provide ideal conditions for utilising tidal energy.

37 **Geothermal energy is generally produced with the help of which of the following techniques?**
(Chap 7, Class-XII, New NCERT)

(a) Trapping the heat energy from the atmosphere.
(b) Producing energy with the help of burning charcoal.
(c) Energy production with the help of magma inside the Earth.
(d) Energy production by thermal heating of coal.

***Ans.* (c)**

Exp. Statement (c) is correct with reference to geo-thermal energy. Geothermal energy is generally produced with the help of magma inside the Earth. When the magma from the interior of Earth, comes out on the surface, tremendous heat is released. This heat energy can successfully be tapped and converted to electrical energy.

38 **Which of the given statements is not one of the advantages of using bioenergy?**
(Chap 7, Class-XII, New NCERT)

(a) Improving economic and social life in rural areas.
(b) Reducing pressure on forests for fuel wood.
(c) Improving groundwater recharge in hilly areas.
(d) Reducing land pollution in rural and urban areas.

***Ans.* (c)**

Exp. Improving groundwater recharge in hilly areas is not the advantage of using bioenergy. Bioenergy refers to energy derived from biological products which includes agricultural residues, municipal, industrial and other wastes.

39 **Match the given lists correctly and choose the correct code.** *(Chap 4, Class-X, Old NCERT)*

List I (Hydel Project)	List II (River)
A. Bhakra Nangal Project	1. Krishna
B. Hirakud Dam	2. Sutlej
C. Nagarjuna Sagar Dam	3. Chambal
D. Gandhi Sagar Dam	4. Mahanadi

Codes

	A	B	C	D
(a)	3	4	2	1
(b)	1	3	2	4
(c)	4	2	3	1
(d)	2	4	1	3

***Ans.* (d)**

Exp. The correct matching is A-2, B-4, C-1, D-3.

Bhakra Dam It is a concrete gravity dam and second tallest dam on the Sutlej river in Bilaspur, Himachal Pradesh in Northern India.

Hirakud Dam It is built across the Mahanadi river, about 15 kilometres from Sambalpur in the State of Odisha. It is the longest dam in the world.

Nagarjuna Sagar Dam It is a masonry dam across the Krishna river at Nagarjuna Sagar which straddles the border between Nalgonda district in Telangana and Guntur district in Andhra Pradesh.

Gandhi Sagar Dam It is one of the four major dams built on India's Chambal river. The dam is located in the Mandsaur, districts of the State of Madhya Pradesh.

40 **Match List-I with List-II.** *(Chap 5, Class-XII, New NCERT)*

List I (Power plants)	List II (Type of energies)
A. Chamera	1. Nuclear Power
B. Gwal Pahari	2. Thermal Power
C. Kudankulam	3. Hydro Power
D. Patratu	4. Solar Power

Codes

	A	B	C	D
(a)	3	4	1	2
(b)	2	4	1	3
(c)	4	3	2	1
(d)	3	1	2	4

***Ans.* (a)**

Exp. The correct matching is A-3, B-4, C-1, D-2.

Chamera Hydroelectric Power Plant in India is located at Chamera village of Chamba district in Himachal Pradesh.

Gwal Pahari Solar Power Plant is located in Gurugram, Haryana.

Kudankulam Nuclear Power Plant is located in Tamil Nadu.

Patratu Thermal Power Station is in the State of Jharkhand. It has 840 MW capacity.

41 **Which of the following statements is/are correct with reference to Tehri Hydropower Project?** *(Chap 4, Class-X, Old NCERT)*

1. Tehri Hydro Development Corporation was set up in 1988 for implementation of this project.
2. It is the highest gravity dam in India and it has been constructed on river Son.

Codes

(a) Only 1 (b) Only 2
(c) Both 1 and 2 (d) Neither 1 nor 2

***Ans.* (a)**

Exp. Statement (1) is correct with reference to Tehri Hydropower Project. Tehri Hydro Development Corporation India Limited is under the ownership of National Thermal Power Corporation Limited, Ministry of Power and Government of India. It was incorporated in July 1988 to develop, operate and maintain the Tehri Hydro Power Complex and other Hydro Projects.

Statement (2) is incorrect because it is the tallest dam in India and it has been constructed on Bhagirathi river.

42 **Which of the given pairs of Hydro Power Project and states is/are correctly matched?** *(Chap 4, Class-X, Old NCERT)*

(a) Rihand Project – Rajasthan
(b) Koyna Project – Madhya Pradesh
(c) Sharavathi Project – Karnataka
(d) Salal hydel Project – Tamil Nadu

***Ans.* (c)**

Exp. Pair (c) is correctly matched as Sharavathi Hydro Power Plant is located at Karnataka. Sharavathi Hydro Power Plant is constructed on Sharavathi river.

Pairs (a), (b) and (d) are not correctly matched because Rihand Hydro Power Plant is located in Uttar Pradesh.

Koyna Hydro Power Plant is located in Maharashtra.

Salal Hydro Power Plant is located in Jammu and Kashmir.

Chapter 24

Transport and Communication in India

Transport and Communication in India

Road and Rail Transport

Road Transport in India

- Most popular mode of transportation
- India has one of the largest road networks in the world
- Roads are classified as National highways, State highways, major district roads and rural roads
- Factors that influence the construction of roads include Nature of terrain and level of economic development, presence of industries, climatic factors favourable in plains than hilly areas, etc

Rail Transport in India

- Indian railways is among the world's largest rail networks
- It provides both passenger and freight mode of transportation
- Some of the important railways are Konkan railways , Metro rail
- Factors affecting the railways include topography like plains, plateau regions hilly areas, etc; economically advanced areas where there is more need of railways, connecting the hinterlands, maintaining of military supremacy, movement of goods, etc

Water and Air Transport

Waterways

- Water transport is the cheapest and oldest mode of transport
- Operates on a natural track and does not require huge capital investment in construction and maintenance of tracks
- A fuel-efficient and environment friendly mode of transport and can carry large quantities of heavy and bulky goods
- It is of two types namely,
  (a) **Inland Waterways** Transport by rivers, canals, lakes
  (b) **Ocean Transport** Important for foreign trade
- Major ports in India in this regard include Vishakhapatnam port, Kolkata port, Kandla port, Mumbai port, Paradip port, etc

Pipelines

- Most convenient and suitable mode of transportation for petroleum products and gases in bulk for longer distances
- Consume very little energy in comparison to other mode of transportation

Airways

- A modern means of transportation, important for the growth of trade and commerce-Rapid speed is a peculiar feature
- Capable of making their way everywhere since they face no physical barriers

Communication

Introduction

- It is an act of exchanging information. Personal communication and Mass communication are the major means of communication in the country

Personal Communication

- Process of transferring and transmitting a message between two peoples
- **Indian Post** Handles parcels as well as written personal communications
- **Telecom Network** Made possible due to integration of developments in space technology with communication technology
- **Mail Channel** To facilitate quick delivery of mail in large towns and cities

Mass Communication

- Process of transferring or transmitting a message to large group of people, provides entertainment and creates awareness among people
- **Radio** To broadcast a variety of programmes related to information, education and entertainment
- **Television** Most effective audio-visual medium for disseminating information and educating masses
- **Films** India is the largest producer of feature films in the world, produces short films, video feature films, etc
- **Satellite Communication** Can be used for weather forecast, monitoring of natural calamities, surveillance of border areas, etc

SOURCE *Old NCERT Class VIII* (*Trade, Transport and Communication*), **New NCERT Class X** (*Lifelines of National Economy*), **Old NCERT Class X** (*Transport, Communication and International Trade*), **New NCERT Class XII** (*Transport and Communication*), **Old NCERT Class XII** (*Transport Systems*)

Road Transport

1 Consider the following statements with reference to road transport in India. *(Chap 10, Class-XII, New NCERT)*

1. Metalled roads have been in use since ancient times in India.
2. More than 95% of passenger traffic is carried by roads in India.
3. Bombay plan was drafted in 1943 for development of roads in India.
4. Twenty-year Road Plan was introduced by the government for development of roadways in 1961.

Which of the statements given above is correct?

(a) Only 1 (b) Only 2 (c) Only 3 (d) Only 4

***Ans.* (d)**

Exp. Statement (4) is correct with reference to road transport in India. After independence, Twenty-year Road Plan was introduced in 1961 to improve the conditions of roadways in India.

Statements (1), (2) and (3) are incorrect. The pathways and unmetalled roads have been used for transportation in India since ancient times.

More than 85% of passenger traffic is carried by roads in India.

Nagpur plan was drafted in 1943 for development of roads in India.

2 Which of the following statements is/are incorrect with reference to Golden Quadrilateral Project? *(Chap 10, Class-XII, New NCERT) (BPSC Pre 2016)*

(a) It aims to connect Delhi-Mumbai-Chennai-Kolkata.
(b) It is a project under the Indian Railways.
(c) It consists of construction of over 5,800 km of transport corridor.
(d) It has been subsumed under the Bharatmala Project.

***Ans.* (b)**

Exp. Statement (b) is incorrect with reference to Golden Quadrilateral because Golden Quadrilateral Project is under the National Highway Authority of India.

Golden Quadrilateral Project comprises construction of 5,846 km long high density traffic corridor, to connect India's four big metro cities of Delhi-Mumbai-Chennai-Kolkata. This project has reduced time, cost and distance of transit between megacities.

3 Consider the following statements with reference to North-South-East-West Corridor. *(Chap 10, Class-XII, New NCERT) (MPPSC Pre 2019)*

1. The North-South Corridor will connect Delhi to Kanyakumari with a road length of 4076 km.
2. The East-West Corridor will connect Porbandar to Silchar with a road length of 3,640 km.

Which of the statements given above is/are correct?

(a) Only 1 (b) Only 2
(c) Both 1 and 2 (d) Neither 1 nor 2

***Ans.* (b)**

Exp. Statement (2) is correct as the North-South-East-West Corridor is the largest ongoing highway project in India. The East-West corridor has been planned to connect Silchar in Assam with the port town of Porbandar in Gujarat with 3,640 km of road length.

Statement (1) is incorrect because North-South Corridor aims at connecting Srinagar in Jammu and Kashmir with Kanyakumari in Tamil Nadu with 4,076 km long road.

4 Arrange the following types of roads in India in increasing order, according to their proportion of the road length. *(Chap 10, Class-XII, New NCERT)*

1. Major District Roads
2. State Highways
3. National Highways

Codes

(a) 2-3-1 (b) 3-2-1 (c) 1-2-3 (d) 3-1-2

***Ans.* (b)**

Exp. The correct increasing order of roads in India, according to their proportion of strength is 3-2-1 i.e., National Highways, State Highways and Major District Roads. The main roads which are constructed and maintained by the Central Government are known as the National Highways. The National Highways constitute only about 2% of the total road length.

State Highways are constructed and maintained by State Government.

District roads are the connecting link between District Headquarters and the other places of the district. These roads are maintained by Zila Parishad.

5 Which of the given statements is/are correct with reference to Border Roads Organisation (BRO)? *(Chap 10, Class-XII, New NCERT)*

1. BRO was established in 1960 with an aim to accelerate economic development and strengthening defence preparedness along Northern border of India.
2. Border Roads Organisation is also responsible for maintenance of strategic roads in the coastal area of India.

Codes

(a) Only 1 (b) Only 2
(c) Both 1 and 2 (d) Neither 1 nor 2

***Ans.* (a)**

Exp. Statement (1) is correct as the Border Road Organisation was established in May, 1960 for accelerating economic development and strengthening defence preparedness through rapid and coordinated improvement of strategically important roads along the Northern and North-Eastern boundary of the country.

Statement (2) is incorrect because Border Roads Organisation is responsible for maintenance of strategic roads in the border areas (not coastal areas) of India.

6 **Consider the following statements with reference to density of roads in India.** *(Chap 10, Class-XII, New NCERT)*

1. Level of economic development and terrain are the determinants of road density in a region.
2. Road density is high in North-Eastern states as compared to the Southern states of India.
3. Road density of Kerala is higher than the average national road density.

Which of the statements given above is incorrect?

(a) Only 1 (b) Only 2 (c) Only 3 (d) Only 4

Ans. (b)

Exp. Statement (2) is incorrect because due to hilly and forested areas, high rainfall and annual floods in the North-Eastern states, the density of roads is less as compared to the Southern states of India.

7 **Which of the following states have high density of road network in India?** *(Chap 9, Class-X, New NCERT)*

1. Bihar
2. Arunachal Pradesh
3. Kerala
4. Goa

Codes

(a) 1 and 3 (b) 1 and 2 (c) 3 and 4 (d) 1 and 4

Ans. (c)

Exp. Among the given options, Kerala and Goa have high density of road network in India because they are coastal states. Bihar is affected by the annual floods that's why, it is difficult task to build a road here. Thus, the density of roads in Bihar is low. Also the Arunachal Pradesh is a hilly state, that's why the construction of roads is difficult.

Railways

8 **Consider the following statements with reference to development of railways in India.** *(Chap 10, Class-XII, New NCERT)*

1. The first railway line was started in 1853 from Bombay to Pune.
2. The broad gauge covers the highest proportion of tracks of Indian railways.

Which of the statements given above is/are incorrect?

(a) Only 1 (b) Only 2
(c) Both 1 and 2 (d) Neither 1 nor 2

Ans. (a)

Exp. Statement (1) is incorrect with reference to development of railways in India as Indian Railway was introduced in 1853, when a line was constructed from Bombay to Thane (not Pune) covering a distance of 34 km.

9 **Which of the given statements is/are not correct with reference to Konkan Railways?** *(Chap 10, Class-XII, New NCERT) (IAS Pre 1999)*

1. Konkan Railways was constructed in 1998.
2. It connects Goa and Kerala.
3. The total length of this route is 760 km.
4. It lies on the Arabian sea coast.

Codes

(a) Only 2 (b) 1 and 3 (c) 3 and 4 (d) Only 1

Ans. (a)

Exp. Statement (2) is not correct about Konkan Railways because these are 760-km long rail route connecting Roha in Maharashtra to Mangalore in Karnataka. Konkan Railway was constructed in 1998. It lies on Arabian sea coast; with its headquarters at CBD Belapur in Navi Mumbai, Maharashtra.

10 **Consider the following pairs.** *(Chap 10, Class-XII, New NCERT)*

List I (Railway Zones)	List II (Headquarters)
1. Eastern Railways	– Delhi
2. Northern Railways	– Kolkata
3. South Central Railways	– Secunderabad
4. South Western Railways	– Hubli

How many pairs given above is/are correctly matched?

(a) Only one (b) Only two (c) Only three (d) All four

Ans. (c)

Exp. Only two pairs i.e., (3) and (4) are correctly matched.

The Headquarters of South Central Railway Zone is Secunderabad. The Headquarters of South Western Railway Zone is Hubli.

Pairs (1) and (2) are not correctly matched.

The Headquarters of Eastern Railway Zone is Kolkata.

The Headquarters of Northern Railway Zone is Delhi.

11 **Consider the following statements with reference to density of railway network in India.** *(Chap 4, Class-XII, Old NCERT)*

1. Railways network is well developed in the Peninsular and plateau regions of India.
2. Railways are more continuous on the Eastern coast of India as compared to the Western coast.
3. Railway network is sparse in Himalayan region as well as Brahmaputra Valley.

How many of the statements given above is/are correct?

(a) Only one (b) Only two (c) All three (d) None

Ans. (c)

Exp. All three statements i.e., (1), (2) and (3) are correct with reference to density of railway network in India as availability of raw materials in the Peninsular and plateau regions of India and being a productive area, the railway network here is well developed.

The East coast is less elevated than the West coast and has more resources. For this reason, the railway network is more on the East coast than on the West coast.

Due to high altitute and rugged region, it get difficult to establish railway network in Himalayas. In the Brahmaputra Valley, it is due to flooding caused by river Brahmaputra.

Inland Waterways

12 Which of the following is/are included in inland water transport in India? *(Chap 10, Class-XII, New NCERT)*

1. Creeks
2. Rivers
3. Canals
4. Backwaters

Codes

(a) 1, 2 and 4 (b) 2, 3 and 4
(c) 1, 2, 3 and 4 (d) 1 and 3

Ans. (c)

Exp. All the options (1), (2), (3) and (4) correct with reference to inland water transport.

Inland water transport includes creeks, rivers, canals and backwaters. India has 14,500 km of navigable waterways, contributing about 1% to the country's transportation. At present, 5,685 km of major rivers are navigable by mechanised flat bottom vessels.

13 Which of the following statements is/are incorrect with reference to inland waterways in India? *(Chap 10, Class-XII, New NCERT)*

1. The National Waterways Authority of India is the nodal body for regulation of waterways in India.
2. National Waterways are mainly used for foreign trade with neighbouring countries.

Codes

(a) Only 1 (b) Only 2
(c) Both 1 and 2 (d) Neither 1 nor 2

Ans. (b)

Exp. Statement (2) is incorrect with reference to inland waterways in India because oceanic routes are mainly used for foreign trade with neighbouring countries.

14 Consider the following statements with reference to National Waterway I. *(Chap 10, Class-XII, New NCERT)*

1. The Patna-Allahabad stretch is the longest stretch of this waterway.
2. It connects Uttar Pradesh with West Bengal.
3. It is on river Ganga and it is the longest waterway in India.

How many of the statements given above is/are correct?

(a) Only one (b) Only two
(c) All three (d) None of these

Ans. (c)

Exp. All three statements i.e., (1), (2) and (3) are correct with reference to National Waterway I as the Patna-Allahabad stretch (600 km) is the longest stretch of this waterway.

National Waterway I is one of the most important waterways in India, which is navigable by mechanical boats upto Patna and by ordinary boats upto Haridwar.

National Waterway I connects Uttar Pradesh with West Bengal. It is on the river Ganga and it is the longest waterway (1,600 km) in India.

15 Which of the given statements is/are incorrect with reference to National Waterways II? *(Chap 10, Class-XII, New NCERT)*

1. The total length of this stretch is 891 km.
2. It is located on the Indus river.
3. It connects Sadiya to Dhubri.
4. It is regulated by National Waterways Authority of India.

Codes

(a) 1 and 3 (b) Only 2
(c) 3 and 4 (d) All of these

Ans. (b)

Exp. Statement (2) is incorrect with reference to National Waterway II (NW-2) because this waterway is located on Brahmaputra river having a length of 891 km is between the Bangladesh border near Dhubri and Sadiya in Assam.

16 Consider the following stretch of navigable canals is included in National Waterways III. *(Chap 10, Class-XII, New NCERT)*

1. Kakinada – Puducherry
2. Kollam – Kottapuram
3. Kalyan – Thane waterway
4. Wainganga – Pranhita

Which of the pairs given above is/are correctly matched?

(a) 1 and 2 (b) 1 and 3 (c) Only 2 (d) 1, 2 and 3

Ans. (b)

Exp. Pairs (1) and (3) are correctly matched.

Kakinada-Puducherry Cannals stretch between Godavari and Krishna river. It was declared a National Waterway on 24th November, 2008. It is being developed by the Inland Waterways Authority of India (IWAI).

Kalyan-Thane-Mumbai Waterway stretch between Vasai Creek and Ulhas river. It comes under National Waterway-53.

Air Transport

17 Consider the following statements with reference to development of air transport in India. *(Chap 17, Class-VIII, Old NCERT)*

1. First airmail operation was started in 1931 between Allahabad and Naini.
2. Air transport was nationalised in 1975.
3. Pawan Hans Ltd. was started in India for providing tourist services in hilly areas.
4. Open Sky Policy has been adopted by India for helping Indian Defence Services.

Codes

(a) 1 and 3
(b) Only 2
(c) Only 3
(d) All of the above

Ans. (c)

Exp. Statement (3) is correct as Pawan Hans is the helicopter service operating in hilly areas and is widely used by tourists in North-Eastern region.
Statements (1), (2) and (4) are incorrect because air transport in India made a beginning in 1911 when airmail operation commenced over a little distance of 10 km between Allahabad and Naini. Air transport was nationalised in 1953. Open Sky Policy has been adopted by India for helping Indian Cargo Services.

Pipelines

18 'This pipeline runs through the states of Gujarat, Madhya Pradesh and Uttar Pradesh. It has been constructed by the Gas Authority of India Limited and is 1750 kilometres long. It connects the Bombay High with Northern India.'
Which of the following pipelines in India is best described by the above excerpt?
(Chap 10, Class-XII, NCERT)
(a) Salaya-Koyali-Mathura Pipeline
(b) Hajira-Bijapur-Jagdishpur Gas Pipeline
(c) Jamnagar-Loni LPG Pipeline
(d) Kandla-Bhatinda Pipeline
Ans. (b)

Exp. Hajira-Bijapur-Jagdishpur Gas Pipeline (HVJ Pipeline) is best describes the above excerpt. The project was started in 1986 after the incorporation of GAIL (India) Limited to supply gas to the fertiliser plants located in the state of Uttar Pradesh. The first phase of the project consisting of a non-branched 1,750-kilometer grid was commissioned in 1987. Later on, the system was expanded with additional branches to supply gas for industrial and domestic use in the states of Rajasthan, Haryana and NCT, which increased the total grid length to 3,474 km.

19 Consider the following statements with reference to pipelines in India. *(Chap 10, Class-XII, New NCERT)*
1. Pipelines are used for transport of only liquid and gases over long distances.
2. The first cross country pipeline of Asia was started from Assam to Bihar.
3. Numaligarh-Siliguri Pipeline is constructed by ONGC Ltd.

How many of the statements given above is/are correct?
(a) Only one
(b) Only two
(c) All three
(d) None of the above
Ans. (a)

Exp. Only one statement i.e., (2) is correct as Asia's first cross country pipeline covering a distance of 1,157 km was constructed by Oil India Limited (OIL) from Naharkatiya oilfield in Assam to Barauni refinery in Bihar. It was further extended up to Kanpur in 1966.
Statements (1) and (3) are incorrect because pipelines are the most convenient and efficient mode of transporting liquids and gases over long distances. Even solids can also be transported by pipelines after converting them into slurry. Numaligarh-Siliguri pipeline is constructed by OIL Ltd.

Ports

20 Consider the following statements with reference to development of ports in India.
(Chap 10, Class-XII, New NCERT)
1. The policies of major ports is decided by the Central Government whereas the policy of minor ports is decided by State Government.
2. Major ports handle more than 75% of country's total port traffic.
3. The Major ports are used to handle only international cargo.
4. Many ports of India went to Pakistan after partition.

Which of the statements given above is/are incorrect?
(a) Only 1 (b) 2 and 3
(c) Only 3 (d) 3 and 4
Ans. (c)

Exp. Statement (3) is incorrect with reference to development of ports in India because today, major port in Indian handling large volumes of domestic, as well as, overseas trade. Most of the ports are equipped with modern infrastructure.
Kandla, Mumbai, Chennai New Mangalore Port, etc., are major ports of India. Major ports handle more than 75% of country's total port traffic.

21 Which of the following statements is/are correct?
(Chap 10, Class-XII, New NCERT) (Chap 3, Module-2, NIOS)
1. Mumbai port is the largest port of India.
2. Kandla port was developed to reduce pressure on Mumbai port.

Codes
(a) Only 1
(b) Only 2
(c) Both 1 and 2
(d) None of the above
Ans. (c)

Exp. Both the statements (1) and (2) are correct.
Mumbai port is a natural harbour and the biggest port of the country. The port is situated closer to the general routes from the countries of Middle East, Mediterranean countries, North Africa, North America and Europe.
Kandla port was developed to reduce the pressure at Mumbai port and in wake of loss of Karachi Port to Pakistan after the partition.
Kandla Port is situated at the head of Gulf of Kuchchh. It has been developed as a major port to cater to the needs of Western and North-Western parts of the country.

22 **Consider the following statements about the Mumbai Port.** *(Chap 10, Class-XII, NCERT)*

1. It is the largest port in India.
2. It is located on the mainland of West Mumbai.
3. It handles about one-fifth of India's foreign trade.
4. It is also known as the Gateway of India.

How many of the statements given above is/are correct?

(a) Only one (b) Only two
(c) Only three (d) Only four

Ans. (a)

Exp. Only one statement i.e., (2) is correct as it is located on the mainland of West Mumbai.

Statement (1), (3) and (4) are incorrect because it is not the largest port in India. The Jawaharlal Nehru Port at Nhava Sheva, developed as a satellite port to relieve the pressure at the Mumbai port, is the largest container port in India.

The specific proportion of India's foreign trade handled by the Mumbai Port is not as 1/5th specific volume of trade it's one of the busiest port in India. The term 'Gateway of India' is actually a monument located in Mumbai and is not a nickname for the Mumbai Port.

23 **With reference to waterway transport, consider the following statements.** *(Chap 10, Class-XII, NCERT)* *(Chap 3, Module-2, NIOS)*

1. India has 14,500 km of navigable waterways, contributing about 1% to the country's transportation comprising rivers, canals, backwaters, creeks, etc.
2. Approximately 95% of India's foreign trade by volume and 70% by value moves through ocean routes.

Which of the statements given above is/are correct?

(a) Only 1 (b) Only 2
(c) Both 1 and 2 (d) Neither 1 nor 2

Ans. (c)

Exp. Both the statements (1) and (2) are correct with reference to waterway transport.

India has 14,500 km of navigable waterways, contributing about 1% to the country's transportation. It comprises rivers, canals, backwaters, creeks, etc. Approximately 95% of India's foreign trade by volume and 70% by value moves through ocean routes.

Waterways is an important mode of transport for both passenger and cargo traffic in India. It is the cheapest means of transport and is most suitable for carrying heavy and bulky material.

24 **Consider the following statements about the Paradip and Mormugao Ports.** *(Chap 10, Class-XII, NCERT)*

1. Paradip port is located in the Jagatsinghpur district of Odisha, at the confluence of the Mahanadi river and the Bay of Bengal.
2. Mormugao port, a natural harbour in Goa, is the leading iron ore exporting port of India.
3. Paradip port was opened on 12th March, 1996.
4. Mormugao port has been a Major Port since 1963.

How many of the statements given above is/are correct?

(a) Only one (b) Only two
(c) Only three (d) All four

Ans. (d)

Exp. All four statements i.e., (1), (2), (3) and (4) are correct about the Paradip and Mormugao ports are correct. Paradip Port is located in Jagatsinghpur district of Odisha at the confluence of the Mahanadi river and the Bay of Bengal.

Mormugao port, a natural harbour in Goa, is the leading iron ore exporting port of India. Mormugao port handles a significant portion of India's iron ore exports.While Paradip port existed before 1996, it wasn't officially inaugurated until 12th March of that year. Mormugao Port was designated as a Major Port in 1963.

25 **Which of the following constitute the main hinterland of New Mangalore port in India?**

1. Karnataka *(Chap 10, Class-XII, New NCERT)*
2. Goa
3. Maharashtra

Codes

(a) Only 3 (b) Only 1
(c) 1 and 2 (d) 1, 2 and 3

Ans. (b)

Exp. Option (1) is correct with reference to main hinterland of New Mangalore. Karnataka is the major hinterland of New Mangalore Port. This port is located in the state of Karnataka and caters to the needs of the export of iron-ore and iron-concentrates. Karnataka, Goa and Southern Maharashtra also constitute Mormugao port hinterland.

26 **Which of the given statements is/are correct with reference to Kochi port?** *(Chap 10, Class-XII, New NCERT)*

1. It is an artificial harbour.
2. It is located closer to Suez-Colombo route.
3. It is located at the head of Vembanad Kayal.

Codes

(a) 1 and 3 (b) 2 and 3
(c) 1 and 2 (d) Only 1

Ans. (b)

Exp. Statements (2) and (3) are correct with reference to Kochi port.

Kochi port has an advantageous location being close to the Suez-Colombo route. It caters to the needs of Kerala Southern Karnataka and South-Western Tamil Nadu. It is situated at the head of Vembanad Kayal.

Statement (1) is incorrect because Kochi port is a natural harbour port.

27 Consider the following statements with reference to Kolkata port. *(Chap 10, Class-XII, New NCERT)*

1. It is located on the Ganga delta river.
2. Uttar Pradesh, Bihar and Jharkhand constitute the hinterland of this port.

Which of the statements given above is/are correct?

(a) Only 1 (b) Only 2
(c) Both 1 and 2 (d) Neither 1 nor 2

Ans. (b)

Exp. Statement (2) is correct as Kolkata port hinterland covers Uttar Pradesh, Bihar, Jharkhand, West Bengal, Sikkim and the North-Eastern states. Apart from this, it also extends ports facilities to our neighbouring landlocked countries such as Nepal and Bhutan.

Statement (1) is incorrect with reference to Kolkata port because, Kolkata port is located on the Hooghly River, 128 km inland from the Bay of Bengal.

28 With reference to India's projects on connectivity, consider the following statements. *(Chap 3, Module-2, NIOS) (IAS Pre 2023)*

1. East-West Corridor under Golden Quadrilateral Project connects Dibrugarh and Surat.
2. Trilateral Highway connects Moreh in Manipur and Chiang Mai in Thailand via Myanmar.
3. Bangladesh - China - India - Myanmar Economic Corridor connects Varanasi in Uttar Pradesh with Kunming in China.

How many of the statements given above is/are correct?

(a) Only one (b) Only two
(c) All three (d) None of these

Ans. (d)

Exp. None of the statement is correct.

The East-West Corridor is a part of Golden Quadrilateral project and connects Silchar in Assam to Porbandar in Gujarat.

The IMT Trilateral Highway connects Moreh in the Indian state of Manipur with Mae Sot in Thailand, passing through Myanmar. It is an ambitious infrastructure project aimed at enhancing connectivity and trade between India, Myanmar and Thailand.

The Bangladesh-China-India-Myanmar Economic Corridor (BCIM) is a proposed connectivity project that aims to enhance economic cooperation and trade between Bangladesh, China, India, and Myanmar.

The Golden Quadrilateral Project is a major highway development project in India that aims to connect the four major metropolitan cities: Delhi, Mumbai, Chennai, and Kolkata.

29 Consider the given statements with reference to Paradwip Port. *(Chap 10, Class-XII, New NCERT)*

1. It is situated on the Krishna-Godavari delta.
2. It is the deepest harbour in India.
3. It was developed mainly for petroleum exports.
4. The main hinterland of this port is Andhra Pradesh.

How many of the statements given above is/are correct?

(a) One only (b) Only two (c) Only three (d) All four

Ans. (a)

Exp. Only one statement i.e., (2) is correct with reference to Paradwip port as it is the deepest harbour especially suited to handle very large vessels.

Statements (1), (3) and (4) are incorrect because Paradwip port is situated in the Mahanadi delta, about 100 km from Cuttack. It has been developed mainly to handle large-scale export of iron-ore. Odisha, Chhattisgarh and Jharkhand are the parts of its hinterland.

30 Consider the following statements about the Visakhapatnam Port. *(Chap 10, Class-XII, NCERT)*

1. It is the deepest natural harbour in India.
2. It is located on the East coast of India in Andhra Pradesh.
3. The port primarily handles thermal coal and petroleum products.
4. It was commissioned in 1894, making it one of the oldest operational ports in India.

How many of the statements given above is/are correct?

(a) Only one (b) Only two
(c) Only three (d) All four

Ans. (c)

Exp. Only three statements, i.e., (1), (2) and (3) are correct regarding to Visakhapatnam port. It is known for being the deepest natural harbour in India, which allows it to handle large vessels and cargo.

Visakhapatnam port is situated on the east coast of India in the state of Andhra Pradesh, making it a strategic location for maritime trade.The port is a major hub for handling various types of cargo, including thermal coal and petroleum products.

Its diverse handling capabilities contribute to its significance in trade and commerce.

Statement (4) is incorrect because Visakhapatnam port was actually commissioned in 1933, and while it is one of the oldest ports.

31 Match the following lists correctly and choose the correct code. *(Chap 10, Class-XII, New NCERT)*

List I (Port)	List II (State)
A. Tuticorin port	1. Odisha
B. Paradwip port	2. Tamil Nadu
C. New Mangalore port	3. Karnataka
D. Kandla port	4. Gujarat

Codes

	A	B	C	D
(a)	1	2	3	4
(b)	2	1	3	4
(c)	2	1	4	3
(d)	3	1	2	4

Ans. (b)

Exp. The correct matching is A-2, B-1, C-3, D-4.

Tuticorin port was also developed to relieve the pressure of Chennai port. Tuticorin port is located in Tamil Nadu. It deals with a variety of cargo, including coal, salt, food grains, edible oils, sugar, chemicals and petroleum products.

Paradwip port is located in Odisha. Paradwip Port is situated on the Mahanadi delta, Cuttack. It has the deepest harbour especially suited to handle very large vessels.

New Mangalore port is located in the state of Karnataka and caters to the needs of the export of iron-ore and iron-concentrates.

Kandla port situated at the head of Gulf of Kuchchh in Gujarat.

32 Consider the following pairs.

(Chap 10, Class-XII, New NCERT) (IAS Pre 2023)

	Port		Well knows as
1.	Kamarajar port	–	First major port in India registered as a company
2.	Mudra port	–	Larget privtely owned poart in India
3.	Visakhapatnam	–	Largest container port in India

How many of the pairs given above is/are correctly matched?

(a) Only one (b) Only two (c) All three (d) None

Ans. (b)

Exp. Only two pairs i.e., (1) and (2) are correctly matched. Kamarajar port is the first port in India which is a public company. The Kamarajar Port Limited is the only corporatized major port and is registered as a company.

Mundra port is the largest private port in India. The port of Mundra is located on the North shores of the Gulf of Kutch near Mundra, Kutch district in the state of Gujarat.

Pair (3) is incorrect because Jawaharlal Nehru Port Trust-Nhava Sheva (JNPT) is the largest container port in India and one of the most essential subcontients harbours on the Western coast.

Communication

33 Which of the given statements is/are incorrect with reference to development of communications in India?

(Chap 8, Class-X, Old NCERT)

1. Radio broadcasting was started in India with the establishment of Radio Club of Bombay in 1923.
2. Akashwani was established in 1936 by the Government of India.

Codes

(a) Only 1 (b) Only 2
(c) Both 1 and 2 (d) Neither 1 nor 2

Ans. (b)

Exp. Statement (2) is incorrect with reference to development of communications in India because radio broadcasting was changed to All India Radio in 1936 and Akashwani in 1957.

34 Consider the following statements with reference to satellite communications of India.

(Chap 10, Class-XII, New NCERT)

1. INSAT satellite system was established in 1983.
2. All India Radio and Television were separated in 1967 with the development of Doordarshan.
3. Indian Remote Sensing satellite was used for broadcast of Doordarshan.

Which of the statements given above are correct?

(a) 2 and 3 (b) 1 and 2
(c) 1 and 3 (d) 1, 2 and 3

Ans. (b)

Exp. Statements (1) and (2) are correct with reference to satellite communication of India. INSAT satellite was established in 1983, it is a multi-purpose satellite system. It was used for telecommunication, meteorological observation and for various other data and programmes. In 1976, TV was delinked from All India Radio and got a separate identity as Doordarshan.

Statement (3) is incorrect because INSAT-IA satellite was used for broadcast of Doordarshan.

Chapter 25

Industries in India

Industries in India

Iron and Steel Industry

Iron and Steel Industry

- Basic industry for other industries and provides raw material for development of other industries
- Largely located near the source of raw materials Indian iron and steel industry consists of large integrated steel plants and many mini steel plants. Some of them are

TISCO

- The full form of TISCO is Tata Iron and Steel Company. It lies very close to Mumbai-Kolkata railway line with nearest port Kolkata
- Rivers Subarnarekha and Kharkai provide water to the plant
- Iron ore is obtained from Noamundi and coal from Joda mines

IISCO

- The full form of IISCO is Indian Iron and Steel Company. It is located near to Damodar valley coalfields
- Iron ore comes from Singhbhum in Jharkhand; Barakar river provides water to the plant

Bhilai Steel Plant

- Established in Durg district of Chhattisgarh
- Iron ore comes from Dalli-Rajhara mine and coal from Korba fields
- Lies on Mumbai-Kolkata railway link line

Rourkela Steel Plant

- Located in Sundargarh district of Odisha, location chosen on the close proximity to the raw materials

Textile and Sugar Industry

Textile Industry

- **Cotton Textiles Industry** One of the traditional industries of India; Factors responsible for its flourishment include favourable climatic conditions for the growth of cotton abundant skilled labour
- **Silk Industry** India is second largest producer of silk in the world; It is the only country in the world which produces all five known varieties of silk
- **Woollen Textiles Industry** A rapidly developing industry and mainly an export oriented industry; Largely divided into cottage and factory industry
- **Jute Textiles Industry** India is the largest producer of raw jute and jute goods; Most of the mills are located in West Bengal, along with banks of Hugli river

Sugar Industries

- It is the second most important agro-based industry of India
- India is largest producer of sugarcane
- A seasonal industry due to seasonality of raw materials
- It is a weight losing crop since its sucrose content decreases with time, so industry is located in close proximity to raw material source
- Leading producer is Maharashtra followed by Uttar Pradesh

Petrochemical and Other Industries

Petrochemical Industry

- A fast growing industry in India
- Many items are derived from crude petroleum which provides raw materials for many new industries
- This group of industries include polymers synthetic fibers, elastomers and surfactant intermediate
- Leading industrial centers and Mumbai, Ratnagiri, Jamnagar, Hajira, Haldia, Vishakhapatnam, etc

Other Industries

Automobile Industry

- Provides vehicles for quick transport of goods, services and passengers
- Includes trucks, buses, cars, motorcycles, etc

Cement Industry

- Essential for construction acitivity like buildings, towers, bridges, roads, etc
- Requires heavy and bulky raw materials like limestone, gypsum, etc

Fertilisers Industry

- Centered around the production of nitrogenous fertilisers mainly urea, DAP and combination of NPK
- Located around Gujarat, Tamil Nadu, Uttar Pradesh, Punjab, etc

Paper Industry

- A vital and core industry
- Raw material includes salai and sabai grasses, bamboo, wood pulp, etc
- Located around Maharashtra, West Bengal, Andhra Pradesh, etc

Industrial Regions of India

Mumbai-Pune Industrial Region It Extends from Mumbai-Thane to Pune and in adjoining districts of Nasik and Solapur

Hugli Industrial Region It is Located along Hugli river, Kolkata-Haora has become the nucleus for this industrial region

Bengaluru-Chennai Industrial Region Cotton textile was first industry to take roots here

Chhotanagpur Industrial Region This region known for heavy metallurgical industries and owes its development

Gurugram-Delhi-Meerut Industrial Region Industries here are light and market oriented including electronics and electrical goods

SOURCE *New NCERT Class VIII (Industries), New NCERT Class X (Manufacturing Industries), Old NCERT Class X (Progress of Industries), New NCERT Class XII (Manufacturing Industries)*

Types of Industries

1 Consider the following pairs.

(Chap 5, Class-X, New NCERT)

	Industries		Basis of Classification
1.	Metallurgical industries	–	On the basis of ownership
2.	Public and Private industries	–	On the basis of nature of manufactured products
3.	Agro based industry	–	On the basis of nature of raw material used
4.	Intermediate goods industry	–	On the basis of use of products

How many of the pairs given above is/are correctly matched?

(a) Only one (b) Only two (c) Only three (d) All four

***Ans.* (b)**

Exp. Only two pairs i.e., (3) and (4) are correctly matched.

Agro based industries are based on the basis of nature of raw material used. These industries consist of processing, preservation and preparation of agricultural produce for the intermediate and final consumption.

Intermediate goods industry is based on the basis of use of products. Intermediate goods are the partly finished goods, used as inputs for the production of other goods including final goods.

Pairs (1) and (2) are not correctly matched.

Metallurgical industries are based on the nature of the manufactured products. Metallurgical industries generate vast quantities of different types of wastes such as the flue dust of secondary copper smelting.

Public and private industries are based on the basis of ownership. The private sector comprises businesses, which are owned, managed and controlled by individuals.

2 Consider the following statements with reference to factors affecting the location of industries.

(Chap 8, Class-XII, New NCERT)

1. Industries which use weight losing raw materials are located closer to the sources of raw materials.
2. Iron and steel industry mainly uses weight-losing raw materials.
3. Industries which are based on perishable raw materials are located closer to the markets.

Which of the statements given above is/are correct?

(a) 1 and 2 (b) 2 and 3 (c) 1 and 3 (d) 1, 2 and 3

***Ans.* (a)**

Exp. Statements (1) and (2) are correct with reference to factors affecting the location of industries. Industries using weight losing raw materials are located in the regions where raw materials are located. Like pulp industry, copper smelting and big iron industries are located near their raw materials.

In iron and steel industries, iron ore and coal both are weight-losing raw materials. Therefore, an optimum location for iron and steel industries should be near raw material sources.

Statement (3) is incorrect because industries based on perishable raw materials are also located close to raw material sources.

3 In India, which of the following industries is most likely to be located closer to the sources of power?

(Chap 8, Class-XII, New NCERT)

1. Aluminium manufacturing industry
2. Machine tools industry
3. Plastics manufacturing industry
4. Petroleum refining industry

Select the correct answer using the codes given below

(a) Only 1 (b) Only 2 (c) Only 3 (d) Only 4

***Ans.* (a)**

Exp. Aluminium manufacturing industry tends to be located near sources of power because they are power intensive and require huge quantum of electricity. Power provides the motive force for machines and therefore, its supply has to be ensured before the location of any industry.

4 Consider the following statements with reference to iron and steel industries in India.

(Chap 5, Class-VIII, New NCERT)

1. Bhilai and Rourkela steel plants were started in India for the purpose of balanced regional development.
2. Iron and steel is a basic industry on which most of the sectors of Indian industries depend.
3. Fireclay, limestone and coking coal are common raw materials used in this industry.

Which of the statements given above are correct?

(a) 1 and 2

(b) 2 and 3

(c) 1 and 3

(d) 1, 2 and 3

***Ans.* (d)**

Exp. All the given statements (1), (2) and (3) are correct with reference to iron and steel industries in India.

Bhilai and Rourkela steel plants were started in India for the purpose of balanced regional development in tribal region.

Iron and steel industry is a basic industry on which most of the sectors of Indian industries depend.

The other raw materials besides iron ore and coking coal, essential for iron and steel industry are limestone, dolomite, manganese and fireclay. The Bhilai Steel Plant was established with Russian collaboration in Chhattisgarh and started production in 1959. The Rourkela Steel Plant was set up in 1959 in Odisha in collaboration with Germany.

5 Consider the given statements with reference to iron and steel industry in India. *(Chap 8, Class-XII, New NCERT)*

1. Indian iron and steel industry only consists of large integrated steel plants and no mini steel mills have been established.
2. Iron and steel industry uses non-weight losing raw materials.
3. Most of the iron and steel plants of India are located closer to their markets.
4. Iron and steel industry is mainly concentrated in Northern Odisha, Chhattisgarh, Jharkhand and West Bengal.

How many of the statements given above is/are correct?

(a) Only one (b) Only two
(c) Only three (d) All four

Ans. (a)

Exp. Only one statement i.e., (4) is correct with reference to iron and steel industry in India. There is a crescent-shaped region in India, comprising parts of Chhattisgarh, Northern Odisha, Jharkhand and Western West Bengal, that are extremely rich in high grade iron ore, good quality coking coal and other supplementing raw materials.

Statements (1), (2) and (3) are incorrect because the Indian iron and steel industry consists of large integrated steel plants as well as mini steel mills.

Iron and steel industry uses weight losing raw materials.

Most of the iron and steel plants of India are not located near their raw materials.

6 Which of the following statements are correct with reference to Tata Iron and Steel Company Limited (TISCO)? *(Chap 8, Class-XII, New NCERT)*

1. It was established on the confluence of Yamuna and Chambal.
2. The iron ore is obtained from Noamundi and Badam Pahar.
3. It lies very close to Mumbai-Kolkata railway line.

Codes

(a) 1 and 3 (b) 2 and 3
(c) 1 and 2 (d) 1, 2 and 3

Ans. (b)

Exp. Statements (2) and (3) are correct with reference to TISCO. The iron ore for the TISCO plant is obtained from Noamundi and Badam Pahar and coal is brought from Joda mines in Odisha.

Coking coal comes from Jharia and West Bokaro coal fields. The Tata Iron and Steel Company Limited lies very close to the Mumbai-Kolkata railway line.

Statement (1) is incorrect because TISCO was established on the confluence of Subarnarekha and Kharkai river.

7 Consider the following statements with reference to IISCO. *(Chap 8, Class-XII, New NCERT)*

1. The Indian Iron and Steel Company (IISCO) consists of three integrated steel plants.
2. The steel plants of IISCO are located on Kolkata-Asansol railway line.
3. Barakar river supplies water to this steel plant.
4. Coal is obtained in these plants from the Neyveli coal fields.

Which of the statements given above is incorrect?

(a) Only 1 (b) Only 2 (c) Only 3 (d) Only 4

Ans. (d)

Exp. Statement (4) is incorrect with reference to IISCO. Coal is obtained in these plants from the Damodar valley coal fields. The company established its first factory at Hirapur and later on another at Kulti. The Indian Iron and Steel Company's (IISCO's) plants are located very close to Damodar valley coal fields (Raniganj, Jharia and Ramgarh).

8 Consider the following statements with reference to Vishvesvaraiya Iron and Steel Works. *(Chap 8, Class-XII, New NCERT)*

1. It is located near Kemmangundi in the Baba Budan Hills.
2. Coal is abundantly available locally near this power plant.
3. Bhadravati river supplies water to this plant.

Which of the statements given above are correct?

(a) 2 and 3 (b) 1 and 3 (c) 1 and 2 (d) 1, 2 and 3

Ans. (b)

Exp. Statements (1) and (3) are correct with reference to the Vishvesvaraiya Iron and Steel Works. It was initially called the Mysore Iron and Steel Works. It is located close to an iron ore producing area of Kemmangundi in the Baba Budan hills. The Bhadravati river supplies water to this plant. This plant produces specialised steels and alloys.

Statement (2) is incorrect because coal is abundantly not available locally near this power plant.

9 Match the following lists correctly and choose the correct code. *(Chap 7, Class-X, Old NCERT)*

List I (Iron and Steel Plant)	List II (State)
A. Durgapur Steel Plant	1. Odisha
B. Rourkela Steel Plant	2. Chhattisgarh
C. Bhilai Steel Plant	3. West Bengal
D. Vizag Steel Plant	4. Andhra Pradesh

Codes

	A	B	C	D		A	B	C	D
(a)	2	1	3	4	(b)	1	3	4	2
(c)	2	1	4	3	(d)	3	1	2	4

Ans. (d)

Exp. The correct matching is A-3, B-1, C-2, D-4.
Durgapur Steel Plant in West Bengal was set up in collaboration with the government of the United Kingdom and started production in 1962.
Rourkela Steel Plant was set up in 1959 in the Sundargarh district of Odisha in collaboration with Germany.
Bhilai Steel Plant was established with Russian collaboration in Durg district of Chhattisgarh and started production in 1959.
Vizag Steel Plant in Visakhapatnam in Andhra Pradesh is the first port-based plant which started operating in 1992.

10 **Consider the following.** *(Chap 13, Module-2, NIOS)*
1. B-heavy Molasses
2. C-heavy Molasses
3. Surplus rice with Food Corporation of India (FCI)
4. Damaged food grain
5. Maize
6. Sugarcane juice

Which of the above categories of feed stock can be used for production of Ethanol under the Ethanol Blending Programme of the Ministry of Petroleum and Natural Gas?
(a) 1, 2, 4 and 6 (b) 1, 3, 4, 5 and 6
(c) 2, 3 and 5 (d) 1, 2, 3, 4, 5 and 6
Ans. (d)
Exp. With a view to support sugar and in the interest of sugarcane farmers, the Government has allowed production of ethanol from B-Heavy molasses, C-heavy molasses, sugarcane juice to divert excess sugarcane to ethanol. To increase production of fuel ethonal grade and to achieve blending targets, Government has allowed use of maize, rice surplus rice with FCI, damaged food grain for production of ethanol.

11 **Which of the following industries can be categorised as Footloose industries?** *(Chap 6, Class-XII, NCERT)*
1. Mobile and Computer manufacturing
2. Diamond Cutting
3. Aluminium Smelting
4. Fertilisers Industry
5. Automobile Manufacturing

Codes
(a) 1, 2 and 5 (b) 1, 3 and 4
(c) 2, 3 and 4 (d) All of these
Ans. (a)
Exp. Statements (1), (2) and (5) are correct with reference to Footloose industry. Mobile and computer manufacturing, diamond cutting and automobile manufacturing are some examples of footloose industries. These are generally non-polluting industries.
It is a general term for an industry that can be placed and located at any location without effect from factors of production such as resources, land, labour and capital.

12 **Consider the following Assertion (A) and Reason (R) and choose the correct code.**
(Chap 7, Class-X, Old NCERT) (UPPSC Pre 2019)
Assertion (A) Ahmedabad is the largest centre of cotton textile industry in India.
Reason (R) Ahmedabad is located in major cotton growing region of India, so it has no problem of raw materials.
Codes
(a) Both A and R are true and R is the correct explanation of A.
(b) Both A and R are true, but R is not the correct explanation of A.
(c) A is true, but R is false.
(d) A is false, but R is true.
Ans. (d)
Exp. Assertion (A) is false, but Reason (R) is true. Mumbai, Maharashtra is the largest centre of cotton textile industry, which is followed by Ahmedabad. Ahmedabad being located in India's major cotton production area, it does not face any raw material problem.

13 **Consider the following statements.**
(Chap 8, Class-XII, New NCERT)
1. Shahpur and Calico cotton mills were established in Ahmedabad in Gujarat.
2. Ahmedabad is known as the 'Manchester of India' due to its textile production.
3. Powerloom sector produces more cotton than the organised handloom sector of India.

How many of the statements given above is/are incorrect?
(a) Only one (b) Only two
(c) All three (d) None of these
Ans. (c)
Exp. All three statements i.e., (1), (2) and (3) are correct. The Shahpur Mill and the Calico Mill were established in Ahmedabad. It soon became the second largest textile city of India, after Mumbai.
Ahmedabad was therefore often referred to as the 'Manchester of India' due to textile production.
Powerloom sector produces more cotton in less time than the organised handloom sector of India.

14 **Consider the following statements with reference to location of cotton industries in India.**
(Chap 8, Class-XII, New NCERT
1. Cotton is a pure raw material which does not lose weight.
2. Cotton industries tend to locate closer to the source of raw materials.

Which of the statements given above is/are incorrect?
(a) Only 1 (b) Only 2
(c) Both 1 and 2 (d) Neither 1 nor 2
Ans. (b)

Exp. Statement (2) is incorrect with reference to location of cotton industries in India because at present, the tend is to locate the industry at or close to markets, as it is the market that decides, what kind of cloth is to be produced.

15 **Consider the following statements is not correct with reference to factors determining setting up of cotton textile industries in various regions.** *(Chap 8, Class-XII, New NCERT)*

1. Cotton textile mills have been set up in Kolkata due to its port facilities.
2. Rapid development of cotton textile industry in Tamil Nadu is attributed to cheap availability of cotton import.
3. Nagpur, Indore, Sholapur and Vadodara are important cotton textile centres in the Central India.
4. Lower labour costs has led to development of this industry in Ujjain, Bharuch, Agra and Hathras.

How many of the statements given above is/are incorrect?

(a) Only one (b) Only two (c) Only three (d) All four

Ans. (a)

Exp. Only one statement i.e., (2) is incorrect because the rapid development of this industry in Tamil Nadu is the result of the abundant availability of hydro power for the mills. Lower labour costs at centres like Coimbatore and Tirunelveli also caused industries to be located away from cotton-producing areas.

16 **Match the following lists correctly and choose the correct code.** *(Chap 8, Class-XII, New NCERT)*

List I (Cotton Textile centre)	List II (State)
A. Murshidabad	1. West Bengal
B. Wardha	2. Tamil Nadu
C. Devangere	3. Maharashtra
D. Salem	4. Karnataka

Codes

	A	B	C	D		A	B	C	D
(a)	2	1	3	4	(b)	1	3	4	2
(c)	2	1	4	3	(d)	3	1	2	4

Ans. (b)

Exp. The correct matching is A-1, B-3, C-4, D-2.

In West Bengal, the cotton mills are located in the Hugli region. Howrah, Serampur, Murshidabad, Kolkata and Shyamnagar are the important centres.

Maharashtra is the important state for cotton production. Wardha, Kolhapur, Sholapur, Nagpur, Mumbai, Pune etc., cotton textile regions.

In Karnataka, the cotton textile regions are located in Mysuru, Hubli, Ballari, Devangere, etc.

In Tamil Nadu, the centres of cotton located in Chennai, Madurai, Salem and Coimbatore.

17 **Tamil Nadu is the leading producer of mill-made cotton yarn in India. What could be the reason?** *(Chap 8, Class-XII, New NCERT) (UPPSC Pre 2010)*

1. Black cotton soil is the predominant type of soil in the state.
2. Rich pool of skilled labours is available.

Codes

(a) Only 1 (b) Only 2
(c) Both 1 and 2 (d) Neither 1 nor 2

Ans. (b)

Exp. Tamil Nadu is a leading producer of mill-made cotton yarn in the country due to presence of numerous spinning mills, skilled labour forces, cheap electricity availability, etc.

18 **Which of the given statements is/are correct with reference to sugar industry of India?** *(Chap 8, Class-XII, New NCERT)*

1. The first modern sugar mill was started in India in Bihar in 1903.
2. It uses weight losing raw material and sugarcane has to be crushed within 24 hours of its harvesting.

Codes

(a) Only 1 (b) Only 2
(c) Both 1 and 2 (d) Neither 1 nor 2

Ans. (c)

Exp. Both the statements (1) and (2) are correct with reference to sugar industry of India.

Development of the sugar industry on modern lines dates back to 1903, when a sugar mill was started in Bihar. Subsequently, sugar mills were started in other parts of Bihar and Uttar Pradesh. It uses weight losing raw material. Better recovery of sugar is dependent upon its being crushed within 24 hours of its harvesting. Thus, sugar factories are located within the cane producing regions.

19 **Consider the following statements with reference to sugar production in India.** *(Chap 8, Class-XII, New NCERT)*

1. Andhra Pradesh is the largest sugar producing state in India.
2. Highest number of sugar mills are located in Gujarat.
3. Most of the sugar is produced in India in the states of Uttar Pradesh, Maharashtra and Karnataka.

How many of the statements given above is/are correct?

(a) Only one (b) Only two
(c) All three (d) None of these

Ans. (a)

Exp. Only one statement i.e., (3) is correct with reference to sugar production in India. Most of the sugar is produced in India in the states of Uttar Pradesh, Maharashtra and Karnataka. Uttar Pradesh is leading/largest sugar producer in the country.

Statements (1) and (2) are incorrect because Karnataka is the major producer of sugar in India. Belagavi, Bellary,

Mandya, Shivmoga and Chitradurga districts are the major producers in Karnataka. The sugar industry is distributed in the coastal regions.

Highest number of sugar mills are located in Maharashtra.

20 **The petrochemical industry in India constitutes, which of the following?** *(Chap 8, Class-XII, New NCERT)*

1. Polymers
2. Synthetic fibres
3. Elastomers
4. Surfactant intermediates

Codes

(a) 1, 2 and 3
(b) 2, 3 and 4
(c) 1, 3 and 4
(d) 1, 2, 3 and 4

Ans. (d)

Exp. All the given options are correct with reference to petrochemical industry. The petrochemical group of industries is divided into four sub-groups, polymers, synthetic fibres; elastomers and surfactant intermediates. Petrochemical industries are the major source of organic and inorganic toxic pollutants.

21 **Consider the following statements with reference to polymer and synthetic fibre industry in India.** *(Chap 8, Class-XII, New NCERT)*

1. More than 75% polymer units are found in the small scale sector of India.
2. Acrylic staple fibre industry is located in Kota and Vadodara in Gujarat.
3. Production of plastic polymers started in India in 1960s in Mumbai.

How many of the statements given above is/are incorrect?

(a) Only one
(b) Only two
(c) All three
(d) None of these

Ans. (d)

Exp. None of the above given statements are incorrect with reference to polymer and synthetic fibre industry in India. About 75% of these units are in small scale sector. The industry also uses recycled plastics, which constitutes about 30% of the total production.

Acrylic staple fibre is manufactured at Kota in Rajasthan and Vadodara in Gujarat.

Production of plastic polymers started in India in 1960s in Mumbai. Polymers are made up of ethylene and propylene. These materials are obtained in the process of refining crude oil.

22 **Consider the following statements with reference to knowledge based industries in India.** *(Chap 8, Class-XII, New NCERT)*

1. The IT software and IT enabled services are growing at a robust rate in India and contribute to more than 25% in GDP.
2. The IT sector provides employment to a large number of people which has almost doubled every year.
3. Software technology industry has surpassed the electronics manufacturing industry in India.
4. India's IT sector has been accorded international recognition.

Which of the statements given above is incorrect?

(a) Only 1
(b) Only 2
(c) Only 3
(d) Only 4

Ans. (a)

Exp. Statement (1) is incorrect with reference to knowledge based industries in India because the IT software and IT enabled services are growing at a robust rate in India and contribute to more than 8% in GDP in 2019.

Indian software industry has emerged as one of the fastest growing sectors in the economy.

23 **With reference to Sugar industry in India, consider the following statements.** *(Chap 6, Class-XII, NCERT)*

1. While sugar mills are generally located close to sugarcane growing areas, sugar refineries can be set up at relatively distant locations.
2. In India, the pricing of sugarcane is governed by the statutory provisions of the Sugarcane (Control Order, 1966 issued under the Essential Commodities Act, 1955.

Which of the statements given above is/are incorrect?

(a) Only 1
(b) Only 2
(c) Both 1 and 2
(d) Neither (1) nor (2)

Ans. (d)

Exp. Neither statement (1) nor (2) is incorrect with reference to sugar industry.

While sugar mills are generally located close to sugarcane growing areas, sugar refineries can be setup at relatively distant locations.

Sugar refining can therefore be done throughout the year and hence a sugar refinery can be set up near or relatively distant location from a sugar mill - preferably near ports for ease of exporting.

In India, the pricing of sugarcane is governed by the statutory provisions of the Sugarcane (Control) Order, 1966 issue under the Essential Commodities Act (ECA), 1955. While on the other hand, the state governments fix State Advised Prices (SAP) citing differences in cost of production, productivity levels and also as a result of pressure from farmer groups.

24 **Which one of the following industries uses limestone as a principal raw material?** *(Chap 8, Class-XII, New NCERT) (CGPSC Pre 2017)*

(a) Aluminium
(b) Cement
(c) Fertiliser
(d) Ferromaganese

Ans. (b)

Exp. Cement industry uses limestone as a principal raw material. Due to this, cement industry is mainly located in the areas having an abundance of limestone.

Limestone is used as a building material and to purify iron in blast furnaces. Beside, manufacturing of cement, it is also used in the manufacture of glass.

25 **Consider the following Assertion (A) and Reason (R) and choose the correct code.**
(Chap 8, Class-XII, New NCERT) (UPPSC Pre 2017)

Assertion (A) Sugar industry is more developed in South India.

Reason (R) Per hectare production and quantity of juice of sugarcane is higher in the Southern states.

Codes

(a) Both A and R are true, and R is the correct explanation of A.
(b) Both A and R are true, but R is not the correct explanation of A.
(c) A is true, but R is false.
(d A is false, but R is true.

Ans. (a)

Exp. Both Assertion (A) and Reason (R) are correct and Reason (R) is the correct explanation of Assertion (A). Sugar industry is more developed in South India because Peninsular India has a tropical climate which gives higher yield per unit area as compared to North India. Per hectare production and quantity of juice of sugarcane are higher in the Southern states.

26 **Which of the following statements is/are correct?**
(Chap 6, Class-X, New NCERT)

1. The first cement plant of India was established in Chennai.
2. India's cement factory is the second largest in the world after China.

Codes

(a) Only 1 (b) Only 2
(c) Both 1 and 2 (d) Neither 1 nor 2

Ans. (c)

Exp. Both the statements (1) and (2) are correct.
The first cement plant was set up in 1904 in Madras/Chennai. It was set up by a company called South India Industrial Ltd. India's cement factory is the second largest in the world after China.

27 **Which of the given statements is/are correct with reference to fertiliser industry in India?**
(Chap 6, Class-X, New NCERT)

1. India does not have any reserves of commercially usable potassium.
2. Gujarat, Tamil Nadu, Punjab and Kerala are the important states which produce most of the fertiliser of India.
3. Fertiliser units can be found in private as well as cooperative sector of India.

Which of the statements given above is incorrect?

(a) Only 1 (b) Only 3 (c) Only 2 (d) None of these

Ans. (d)

Exp. None of the given statement is incorrect with reference to fertiliser industry in India. India does not have any reserves of commercially usable potassium.
Gujarat, Tamil Nadu, Uttar Pradesh, Punjab and Kerala contribute towards half of the fertiliser production.
Fertiliser units can be found in private as well as cooperative sector of India.
Potash is entirely imported as the country does not have any reserves of commercially usable potash or potassium compounds in any form.
After the Green Revolution, the industry expanded to several other parts of the country.

Industrial Regions of India

28 **Which of the following is not a major industrial region in India?** *(Chap 8, Class-XII, New NCERT)*

1. Hooghly region
2. Kolhapur-South Kannada region
3. Gujarat region
4. Vishakhapatnam-Guntur region
5. Durg-Raipur region

Codes

(a) 1, 2 and 4 (b) 2 and 5
(c) 1, 4 and 5 (d) 3 and 5

Ans. (b)

Exp. Options (2) and (5) are incorrect with reference to major industrial region. Kolhapur-South Kannada and Durg-Raipur region are not major industrial regions in India.
Mumbai-Pune, Hooghly, Bengaluru-Tamil Nadu, Gujarat, Chhota Nagpur, Vishakhapatnam- Guntur, Gurugram-Delhi-Meerut and Kollam- Thiruvananthapuram region are major industrial regions in India.

29 **Consider the following statements with reference to Mumbai-Pune industrial region.**
(Chap 8, Class-XII, New NCERT)

1. The establishment of jute textiles industry led to development of this region.
2. Opening of Suez Canal aided in the development of this region.
3. Engineering goods, petrochemical refining, leather and synthetic plastic goods are the major industries in this region.
4. Mumbai High oil refinery and establishment of Nuclear power plant have provided a pull to this region.

Which of the statements given above is incorrect?

(a) Only 1 (b) Only 3 (c) Only 2 (d) Only 4

Ans. (a)

Exp. Statement (1) is incorrect about Mumbai-Pune industrial region because the establishment of cotton textiles industry led to development of this region.
Development of this region started with the location of cotton textile industry in Mumbai.
Mumbai, with cotton hinterland and moist climate favoured the location of cotton textile industry.

30 **Which of the following statements with reference to Hooghly industrial region?** *(Chap 8, Class-XII, New NCERT)*

1. Kolkata-Howrah forms the core of this industrial region.
2. Development of tea plantations in Assam has led to rapid development of this region.
3. Establishment of jute mill at Rishra in 1855 led to the development of this region in the initial period.

Which of the statements given above is/are correct?

(a) 1 and 3 (b) 2 and 3 (c) 1 and 2 (d) 1, 2 and 3

Ans. (d)

Exp. All the given statements (1), (2) and (3) are correct with reference to Hooghly industrial region. This region is located along the Hooghly river.

Kolkata-Howrah region is forms the core of the Hooghly industrial region.

Development of tea plantation in Assam and Northern hills of West Bengal, contributed to the industrial development of the region.

The establishment of first jute mill at Rishra in 1855 ushered in the era of modern industrial clustering in this region.

31 **Which of the following factors has not played a key role in the development of Hooghly industrial region?** *(Chap 8, Class-XII, New NCERT)*

1. Availability of cheap labour from Bihar and Uttar Pradesh.
2. Presence of Haldia refinery and opening of coalfields of Damodar valley.
3. Cultivation of indigo plantations and jute cultivations.
4. Establishment of a nuclear reactor in close proximity in the region.

Codes

(a) Only 1 (b) Only 3 (c) Only 2 (d) Only 4

Ans. (d)

Exp. The establishment of a nuclear reactor has not played a key role in the development of Hooghly industrial region. Establishment of a nuclear reactor factor has played a key role in the development of Mumbai-Pune industrial region.

Hooghly industrial region is located along the Hooghly river, this region extends from Bansberia in the North to Birla Nagar in the South for a distance of about 100 km.

32 **The industrial centres such as Bansberia, Budge-Budge, Kakinara, Shamnagar, Titagarh, Belur etc., are important industrial centres of which of the following industrial region?** *(Chap 8, Class-XII, New NCERT)*

(a) Gujarat Industrial Region
(b) Chhotanagpur Industrial Region
(c) Vishakhapatnam Guntur Region
(d) Hooghly Industrial Region

Ans. (d)

Exp. The industrial region such as Kakinara, Shamnagar, Titagarh, Sodepur, Budge-Budge, Birla Nagar, Bansberia, Belur, etc., are important centres of Hooghly industrial region. The first jute mill of the country was established in this region. This is the main industry of jute.

33 **Consider the following statements with reference to Bengaluru-Chennai industrial region.** *(Chap 8, Class-XII, New NCERT)*

1. The primary factor for the growth of this industrial region was the coal obtained from nearby coalfields.
2. Cotton growing areas are mostly developed around this region.
3. The development of Pykara Hydroelectric Plant in 1932 has provided an impetus to this region.

Which of the statements given above is/are correct?

(a) 1 and 3 (b) 1 and 2 (c) 2 and 3 (d) 1, 2 and 3

Ans. (c)

Exp. Statements (2) and (3) are correct with reference to Bengaluru-Chennai industrial region as cotton textile industry was the first to take roots due to the presence of cotton growing areas in Bengaluru-Chennai industrial region. Along with cotton mills, loom industry spread very rapidly.

Its development is dependent on the Pykara Hydroelectric Plant, which was built in 1932.

Statement (1) is incorrect because the primary factor for the growth of Bengaluru-Chennai industrial region was the development is dependent on the Pykara Hydroelectric Plant.

34 **Consider the following statements with reference to Gujarat industrial region.** *(Chap 8, Class-XII, New NCERT)*

1. Development of this region is associated with the development of cotton textile industry.
2. Petrochemicals industry is well developed around Gujarat industrial region due to the discovery of oil fields.
3. It has the advantage of both market as well as nearness to raw materials.
4. The establishment of Nhava Sheva port has aided in the development of Gujarat industrial region.

How many of the statements given above is/are incorrect?

(a) Only one (b) Only two
(c) Only three (d) All Four

Ans. (a)

Exp. Only one statement i.e., (4) is incorrect with reference to Gujarat industrial region because the establishment of Kandla Port has aided in the development of Gujarat industrial region. Development of this region is also associated with the location of the cotton textile industry since 1860s. Located in cotton growing area, this region has double advantage of the proximity of raw materials as well as of market.

35 **Consider the following statements with reference to Chhota Nagpur industrial region.**

(Chap 8, Class-XII, New NCERT)

1. It extends over Jharkhand, Odisha and West Bengal.
2. It is known for the presence of heavy metallurgical industries.
3. The main source of power in this region is the energy generated from nearby nuclear power plants.

Which of the statements given above is/are incorrect?

(a) 1 and 2 (b) 2 and 3 (c) Only 3 (d) 1 and 3

Ans. (c)

Exp. Statement (3) is incorrect with reference to Chhota Nagpur industrial region because Chhota Nagpur industrial region owes its development to the discovery of coal in the Damodar Valley. To meet the power requirement, thermal and hydroelectric plants have been constructed in the Damodar Valley.

The main source of power in this region is the energy generated from nearby thermal and hydroelectric plants.

36 **Consider the following statements with reference to Visakhapatnam-Guntur industrial region.**

(Chap 8, Class-XII, New NCERT)

1. Petrochemicals industry and ship building industry are well developed in this industrial region.
2. The main source of energy in this industrial region is coalfields of Godavari basin.

Which of the statements given above is/are correct?

(a) Only 1 (b) Only 2
(c) Both 1 and 2 (d) Neither 1 nor 2

Ans. (c)

Exp. Both the statements (1) and (2) are correct with reference to Visakhapatnam-Guntur industrial region. Petrochemicals industry and ship building industry are well developed in Visakhapatnam-Guntur industrial region. Ship building industry was started at Visakhapatnam in 1941. Petroleum refinery based on imported petroleum facilitated the growth of several petrochemical industries. The main source of energy in this industrial region is coalfields of Godavari basin.

37 **Consider the following statements with reference to Kollam-Thiruvananthapuram industrial region.**

(Chap 8, Class-XII, New NCERT)

1. Establishment of petroleum refinery at Kochi hasprovided an impetus to this industrial region.
2. It is located near the coal and mineral belts of the country.
3. Plantations and hydropower has provided an industrial base to this region.
4. Food processing, paper, coconut and coir products are well developed in this region.

Which of the statements given above is/are incorrect?

(a) 1 and 2 (b) Only 2
(c) 3 and 4 (d) Only 4

Ans. (b)

Exp. Statement (2) is incorrect with reference to Kollam-Thiruvananthapuram industrial region because it is spread over Thiruvananthapuram, Kollam, Aluva, Ernakulam and Alappuzha districts.

Kollam-Thiruvananthapuram industrial region is located far from the mineral belt of the country. Hydropower energy provides industrial base to this industrial region.

38 **Match the following lists correctly and choose the correct code.**

(Chap 8, Class-XII, New NCERT)

List I (Industrial region)	List II (Industrial Centres)
A. Mumbai-Pune industrial region	1. Vijayawada, Kurnool, Rajahmundry
B. Vishakhapatnam-Guntur region	2. Kolaba, Kalyan, Trombay
C. Bengaluru-Chennai Industrial region	3. Salem, Madurai
D. Chhota Nagpur region	4. Durgapur, Bokaro, Kulti

Codes

	A	B	C	D
(a)	2	1	3	4
(b)	1	3	4	2
(c)	2	1	4	3
(d)	3	1	2	4

Ans. (a)

Exp. The correct matching is A-2, B-1, C-3, D-4.

Mumbai-Pune industrial region is extends from Mumbai-Thane to Pune and in adjoining districts of Nashik and Solapur. Besides, industrial development has been rapid in Kolaba, Kalyan and Trombay.

Visakhapatnam-Guntur industrial region extends from Visakhapatnam district to Kurnool, Vijayawada and Rajahmundry are important industrial centres.

Bengaluru-Chennai industrial region has witnessed most rapid industrial growth in post-Independence period. Salem and Madurai are the major industrial hubs of Tamil Nadu now.

Chhota Nagpur industrial region is extends over Jharkhand, Durgapur, Bokaro, Kulti are major industrial centre.

Chapter 26

Population and Human Settlement

Population and Human Settlement

Population

Introduction
- It refers to the demography of a region or the related statistical data
- Growth rate of population is the population increase by difference between births and deaths in a particular region between two points of time
- India's population has grown significantly in the last century due to variations in annual birth rate, death rate, migration, etc

Demographic Composition
- **Density of Population** Defined as number of persons per sq km area, showing the concentration of population in a particular area
- **Sex Composition** Distribution pattern of male and female in the population of a given area at a given point of time. A widely used tool for cross-sectional analysis to measure gender balance
- **Literacy** A key variable in improving quality of life, directly related to life expectancy, infant mortality, learning levels, nutritional levels, etc
- **Ethnic Composition** Composition of racial and ethnic groups in a population of a given area
- **Linguistic Composition** Composition of different language speaking communities or people in a population of a given area

Tribes of India

India is home to large number of indigenous people who are still untouched to modern lifestyles. They are also known as Adivasis. Major tribal groups in India are
- **North Zone** Tribes like Gujjars, Tharu, Bhutias, etc
- **North-Eastern Zone** Tribes like Nagas, Garo, Khasi, Mishmi, etc
- **Central Zone** This region has maximum tribal concentration like Ho, Mundas, etc
- **Southern Zone** Tribes like Toda, Koyas, Chenchus, etc
- **Eastern Zone** Tribes like Parajas, Kondhs, Bondas, Bhutias, etc
- **Western zone** Tribes like Bhils, Garasiya, Meenas, etc
- **Island groups** Tribes like great Andamanese, Sentinelese, Onges, Jarawas, etc

Human Settlement

Introduction

Defined as a place which is inhabited permanently. There are certain types of settlement namely,
- Temporary Settlement – Permanent Settlement
- Rural Settlement – Urban Settlement

Rural Settlement

Most closely and directly related to land, primarily dominated by primary activities such as agriculture, animal husbandry, etc

Types of Rural Settlement
- Clustered settlement, a compact or closely built up area of houses
- Semi-clustered settlement, due to segmentation or fragmentation of a large compact village
- Hamleted settlement, locally called as panna, palli, nagla, etc
- Dispersed settlement, in the forms of isolated huts or hamlets of few huts

Patterns of Rural Settlement

Linear pattern, rectangular pattern, circular pattern, star-like pattern, T-shaped pattern, etc

Urban Settlement
- Generally compact and are larger in size, engaged in a variety of non-agricultural, economic and commercial activities
- Towns have flourished since pre-historic times, have developed ancient towns, medieval towns and modern towns

SOURCE New NCERT Class XII *(Human Settlements)*

1 With reference to clustered settlements in India, consider the following statements. *(Chap 4, Class-XII, New NCERT)*

1. Living area is distinct and separated from the farms.
2. It forms various patterns such as rectangular, linear radial, etc.
3. These settlements develop for defence purposes or for conservation of water resources.

How many of the statements given above is/are correct?

(a) Only one (b) Only two
(c) All three (d) None of these

Ans. (c)

Exp. All three statements i.e., (1), (2) and (3) are correct with reference to clustered settlements in India. In this type of village, the general living area is distinct and separated from the surrounding farms, barns and pastures. The closely built-up area and its intervening streets present some recognisable pattern or geometric shape, such as rectangular, radial, linear, etc. Such settlements are generally found in fertile alluvial plains and in the North-Eastern states.

These settlements develop for defence purposes or for conservation of water resources. The clustered rural settlement is a compact or closely built up area of houses.

2 Consider the following statements with reference to semi-clustered settlements in India. *(Chap 4, Class-XII, New NCERT)*

1. These settlements are developed due to fragmentation of large compact villages.
2. These settlements are mainly found in Southern India.

Which of the statements given above is/are incorrect?

(a) Only 1 (b) Only 2
(c) Both 1 and 2 (d) Neither 1 nor 2

Ans. (b)

Exp. Statement (2) is incorrect with reference to semi-clustered settlements in India as semi-clustered settlements are widespread in the Gujarat plain and some parts of Rajasthan.

3 Consider the following pairs. *(Chap 2, Class-XII, New NCERT)* *(Unit 2, Class-XII, Tamil Nadu Board)*

1. Clustered Settlements– Compact or closely built up area with recognisable geometric patterns.
2. Semi-Clustered Settlements – Result of segregation or fragmentation of a large compact village.
3. Hamleted Settlements – Physically separated units bearing a common name, motivated by social and ethnic factors.
4. Dispersed Settlements – Appears as isolated huts or hamlets in remote areas, caused by fragmented terrain.

How many of the pairs given above is/are correctly matched?

(a) Only one (b) Only two
(c) Only three (d) All of these

Ans. (d)

Exp. All the pairs i.e., (1), (2), (3) and (4) are correctly matched. The clustered rural settlements is a compact or closely built-up area of houses. In this type of village, built-up area and its intervening streets present some recognisable pattern or geometric shape, such as rectangular, radial, linear, etc.

Semi-clustered or fragmented settlements may result from tendency of clustering in a restricted area of dispersed settlement.

Hamleted settlements are fragmented into several units physically separated from each other bearing a common name. These units are locally called Panna, Para, Palli, Nagla, Dhani, etc. in various parts of the country.

Dispersed or isolated settlements pattern in India appears in the form of isolated huts or hamlets of few huts in remote jungles, or on small hills with farms or pasture on the slopes.

4 Consider the following statements about Human Settlements. *(Chap 2, Class -XII, New NCERT)* *(Unit 2, Class-XII, Tamil Nadu Board)*

1. Human Settlement means a cluster of dwellings of any type or size where human beings live.
2. The process of settlement inherently involves grouping of people and apportioning of territory as their resource base.
3. Settlements may also be classified by their shape and pattern types.

How many of the statements given above is/are correct?

(a) Only one (b) Only two
(c) All three (d) None of these

Ans. (c)

Exp. All three statements i.e., (1), (2) and (3) are correct regarding human settlements.

A human settlement is a group of dwellings of any size or type where people live. Settlements can range in size from a hamlet to a metropolitan city.

The process of settlement involves people grouping and allocating territory as their resource base.

Settlements can be classified by their shape and pattern types. The shape of a settlement refers to the outline of its built-up area. Settlements can be linear, rectangular, circular, or star-shaped.

5 Match List I with List II. *(Chap 2, Class-VII, New NCERT)*

	List I (Town)		List II (Function)
A.	Industrial towns	1.	Raniganj
B.	Transport cities	2.	Kolkata
C.	Commercial towns	3.	Coimbatore
D.	Mining towns	4.	Kochchi

Codes

	A	B	C	D		A	B	C	D
(a)	3	4	2	1	(b)	2	4	1	3
(c)	4	3	2	1	(d)	3	1	2	4

Ans. (a)

Exp. The correct matching is A-3, B-4, C-2, D-1.

Industrial towns Industries constitute prime motive force of these cities, such as Mumbai, Salem, Coimbatore, Modinagar, Jamshedpur, Hugli, Bhilai, etc.

Transport cities They may be ports primarily engaged in export and import activities such as Kandla, Kochchi, Kozhikode, Vishakhapatnam, etc.

Commercial towns Towns and cities specialising in trade and commerce are kept in this category such as Kolkata, Saharanpur, Satna, etc.

Mining towns These towns have developed in mineral rich areas such as Raniganj, Jharia, Digboi, Ankaleshwar, Singrauli, etc.

6 **Consider the following pairs.** *(Chap 2, Class-XII, New NCERT)*

Towns	Examples
1. Educational towns	Roorki, Varanasi, Aligarh, Pilani
2. Religious and cultural towns	Varanasi, Mathura, Amritsar, Madurai
3. Tourist towns	Nainital, Mussoorie, Shimla, Pachmarhi

How many of the pairs given above is/are correctly matched?

(a) Only one
(b) Only two
(c) All three
(d) None of these

Ans. (c)

Exp. All three pairs i.e., (1), (2) and (3) are correctly matched. Educational towns like Roorki, Varanasi, Aligarh, and Pilani have grown into major campus towns due to educational institutions.

Religious and cultural towns such as Varanasi, Mathura, Amritsar and Madurai are prominent because of their religious and cultural significance.

Tourist towns like Nainital, Mussoorie, Shimla and Pachmarhi attract visitors due to their scenic beauty and tourist attractions.

7 **Which of the following statements is/are incorrect with reference to urbanisation in India?** *(Chap 4, Class-XII, New NCERT)*

1. More than 31.16% of population of India resides in urban areas.
2. The rate of urban growth has increased rapidly in the past two decades.
3. There are only two mega cities in India.

Codes

(a) 1 and 2
(b) 2 and 3
(c) 1 and 3
(d) 1, 2 and 3

Ans. (b)

Exp. Statements (2) and (3) are incorrect with reference to urbanisation in India.

The growth rate of urbanisation has slowed down during last two decades.

There are six mega cities with population over five million each in India.

8 **Which of the following can be classified as an urban agglomeration?** *(Chap 4, Class-XII, New NCERT)*

1. University Campus
2. Railways Colony
3. A Military Cantonment

Codes

(a) 1 and 3
(b) Only 3
(c) 1 and 2
(d) 1, 2 and 3

Ans. (d)

Exp. University campus, railway colony and military cantonment can be classified as an urban agglomeration.

An urban agglomeration may consist of any one of the following three combinations

A town and its adjoining urban outgrowths.

Two or more contiguous towns with or without their outgrowths.

A city and one or more adjoining towns with their outgrowths together forming a contiguous spread.

Environment

Environment

Introduction
- The place, people, things and nature that surround any living organism is called Environment
- It is a combination of both natural and man-made

Types of Environment
- **Natural Environment** The non-human made surroundings and conditions in which all living and non-living organisms exist e.g., water, air, etc
- **Man-made Environment** The surroundings created by humans to provide facilities for satisfying its needs e.g., buildings, roads, bridges, etc
- **Socio-cultural Environment** Humans interact with their surroundings and adapt them to suit their needs e.g., community, religion, etc

Components of Environment
- **Abiotic Environment** Includes all the physical and chemical aspects of an ecosystem. Abiotic factors include rainfall, temperature, sunlight, etc
- **Biotic Environment** Known as world of living organisms, including producers, consumers and decomposers

Human Impact On Environment

Direct Impact
- Preplanned or premediated since man is aware of the consequences beforehand
- Includes land use changes, constructions, nuclear programs, etc
- The direct impacts are noticeable within short period and may continue to affect the environment for long time. These effects are reversible

Indirect Impact
- Not preplanned or premediated and are experienced after a long time
- Includes the activities which are directed to accelerate the pace of economic growth. e.g., industrial revolution
- Majority of the indirect impacts of human activities on the environment are related to pollution and environmental degradation

Parts Of Environment

1. Biosphere
- A narrow zone where we find water and air together and it contains all forms of life
- Organisms in biosphere are roughly divided into plant and animal kingdom
- All living organisms included humans are linked to each other and biosphere for survival

2. Lithosphere
- Solid portion of the earth on which we live
- Comprises the rocks of earth's crust and thin layers of soils

3. Hydrosphere
- Comprises water in all its forms ice, water and water vapour
- Oceans are a major part of hydrosphere, that are interconnected and always moving

4. Atmosphere
- Earth is surrounded by a layer of gas
- Density of atmosphere varies with height, is maximum at sea levels and decreases as we go up

SOURCE *New NCERT Class VII* (Environment), *Old NCERT Class IX* (Biosphere)

1 **Environment is a composite state of**

(Chap 1, Class-VII, New NCERT) (BPSC Pre 2011)

(a) biotic factors (b) physiographic factors
(c) abiotic factors (d) All of these

Ans. (d)

Exp. Environment is a composite state of biotic factors, physiographic factors and abiotic factors.

Biotic factors are living organism in the ecosystem. These are obtained from the biosphere and are capable of reproduction. Physiographic factors are those associated with the physical nature of the area.

Abiotic factors are non-living part of an ecosystem that shapes its environment.

2 **Environment refers to**

(Chap 1, Class-VII, New NCERT) (UPPSC Pre 2006)

1. the natural world of land, water, air, plants and animals that exists around it.
2. the sum total of conditions, which surround human beings at a given point of time.
3. the interacting system of physical, biological and cultural elements, which are interlinked.

How many of the statements given above is/are correct?

(a) Only one (b) Only two
(c) All three (d) None of these

Ans. (c)

Exp. All three statements i.e., (1), (2) and (3) are correct.

Environment refers to an aggregate of conditions or surroundings in which living beings (such as humans, animals and plants live or survive) and non-living things exists.

Environment is the sum total of conditional, which surround human beings at a given point of time. It is the natural world of land, water, air, plants and animals that exists around it.

Also, it refers to the interacting system of physical, biological and cultural elements, which are interlinked.

3 **Generally, environment can be classified as following categories, which among the following is not a part of such category?**

(Chap 5, Class-IX, Old NCERT) (UPPSC Pre 2020)

(a) Operational environment
(b) Physical environment
(c) Cultural environment
(d) Biological environment

Ans. (a)

Exp. Operational environment is not a classification of environment. On the basis of the extent of intimacy, environmental factors are classified into physical, biological and cultural environment.

Environment is a basic life support system and provides better ecosystem to the human beings to survive and make their life better.

4 **Consider the following Assertion (A) and Reason (R) and choose the correct code.**

(Chap 1, Class-VII, New NCERT) (IAS Pre 1999)

Assertion (A) Environment is the store of immense force.

Reason (R) Environmental elements are created as a result of environmental forces and process.

Codes

(a) Both A and R are true and R is the correct explanation of A.
(b) Both A and R are true, but R is not the correct explanation of A.
(c) A is true, but R is false.
(d) A is false, but R is true.

Ans. (a)

Exp. Both Assertion (A) and Reason (R) are true and Reason (R) is the correct explanation of Assertion (A).

Environment comprises various types of forces.

Environment is constituted by the interacting systems of physical, biological and cultural elements inter-related in various ways, individually as well as collectively. These elements are created as the result of environmental forces and processes.

5 **Consider the following statements with regarding environment.** ***(Chap 5, Class-IX, Old NCERT)***

1. Every green plants can decompose their dead bodies.
2. Decomposers cannot make their own food.
3. Biosphere is fundamental unit of the study of environment.
4. In biosphere physical as well as biological elements are present.

How many of the statements given above is/are incorrect?

(a) Only one (b) Only two (c) Only three (d) All four

Ans. (a)

Exp. Only one statement i.e., (1) is incorrect regarding environment because green plants cannot decompose their dead bodies. Fungi are important decomposers of plants in the forest.

Decomposers are organisms that break down dead or decaying organisms. They are also responsible for carrying out decomposition process.

Biosphere indicates the realm of living organisms and their interactions with environment. In biosphere, both physical and biological elements exists.

6 **Which among the following statements is incorrect?**

(Chap 5, Class-IX, Old NCERT) (IAS Pre 1997)

(a) The working system of environment is governed by natural laws.
(b) Terrestrial unity is present in the environment elements.
(c) Environment is the reserve of physical resource not the biological resource.
(d) Self-enrichment capacity is inherent in environment.

Ans. (c)

Exp. Statement (c) is incorrect because environment is the reserve of physical and biological resources. Physical reserves are space, land forms, water bodies, climate, soils, rocks and minerals. They determine the variable character of human habitat. Biological elements plants, animals, micro-organism are the biological resources of our environment.

7 **Consider the following Assertion (A) and Reason (R) and choose the correct code.** *(Chap 1, Class-VII, New NCERT)*

Assertion (A) Environment is a combination of natural and human made phenomena.

Reason (R) Natural environment refers to both biotic and abiotic conditions existing on the Earth.

Codes

(a) Both A and R are true and R is the correct explanation of A.
(b) Both A and R are true, but R is not the correct explanation of A.
(c) A is true, but R is false.
(d) A is false, but R is true.

Ans. (a)

Exp. Both Assertion (A) and Reason (R) are true and Reason (R) is the correct explanation of Assertion (A).
The place, people, things and nature that surround any living organism is called environment.
It is a combination of natural and human-made phenomena. While the natural environment refers to both biotic and abiotic conditions existing on the Earth. Human environment reveals the activities, creations and interactions among human beings.

8 **Consider the following statements.** *(Chap 1, Class-IX, Old NCERT)*

1. The environment interact with human life and its economic activities.
2. Species adapt their environment through natural selection in successive generation.
3. More complex living organisms can communicate through various means.

Which of the statements given above are correct?

(a) 1 and 2
(b) 1 and 3
(c) 2 and 3
(d) All of the above

Ans. (d)

Exp. All the given statements (1), (2) and (3) are correct. The environment encompasses the interaction of all living species, climate, weather and natural resources that affect human survival and economic activities.
Living organisms under go to grow and reproduce through natural selection, adapt to their environment in successive generations.
More complex living organisms can communicate through various means.

9 **Consider the following.** *(Chap 1, Class-VII, New NCERT)*

1. Photosynthesis
2. Respiration
3. Decay of organic matter
4. Volcanic action

Which of the above add carbon dioxide to the carbon cycle on the Earth?

(a) 1 and 4 (b) 2 and 3
(c) 2, 3 and 4 (d) 1, 2, 3 and 4

Ans. (c)

Exp. The decay of organic matter, volcanic action, respiration and burning of fossil fuel, etc, contributes carbon dioxide to the carbon cycle, whereas plants use carbon dioxide in the process of photosynthesis. Thus, plants do not add carbon dioxide to the carbon cycle rather they release oxygen and consumes carbon dioxide.
Three natural allotropes of elemental carbon are; fullerene, graphite and diamond. Besides, as a compound, it is found as carbon dioxide, carbonate and hydrogen carbonate.

10 **Consider the following statements.** *(Chap 1, Class-IX, Old NCERT)*

1. Some micro-organisms can grow in environments with temperature above the boiling point of water.
2. Some micro-organisms can grow in environments with temperature below the freezing point of water.
3. Some micro-organisms can grow in highly acidic environment with a pH below 3.

Select the correct answer by using the codes given below.

(a) Only 1 (b) Only 2
(c) All of these (d) None of these

Ans. (c)

Exp. All the given statements are correct as some micro-organisms, known as thermophiles, can grow in environments with temperature above the boiling point of water.
They are adapted to thrive in extreme heat, such as hot springs or hydrothermal vents. Some micro-organisms, known as psychrophiles or cryophiles, can grow in environments with temperature below the freezing point of water.
They are adapted to cold environments, such as polar regions or deep-sea-ice. Some micro-organisms known as acidophiles can grow in highly acidic environment with a pH below 3.

Chapter 28

Ecology, Ecosystem and Biome

Ecology, Ecosystem and Biome

Ecology

Introduction
- Study of the Earth as a household of plants, human beings, animals and micro-organisms.
- Also termed as study of interactions between life forms and physical environment

Ecological Factors
- **Climatic Factors** Include light, temperature, rainfall, wind, humidity and pH
- **Biotic Factors** Derived from interactions between different species of living organisms
- **Topographic Factors** Include altitude, slope and direction of mountains, valleys, etc
- **Edaphic Factors** Includes structure, formation and characteristics of different types of soils

Levels of Organisation in Ecology
- **Organism** Group of genetically linked individuals that can breed to generate fruitful offspring. Individuals are not considered members of same species if they are unable to generate offspring
- **Population** Consists of all organisms of plants and species inhabiting a given area e.g. all individuals of lion and tiger in an area constitute their population
- **Community** A collection of plant, animal, bacterial and fungal populations that reside in a certain area and interact with one other

Ecosystem

Introduction
- System formed by the interaction of all living organisms with the physical and chemical factors of environment
- There are 2 components of ecosystem, Biotic (living) and Abiotic (non-living)
- Factors affecting ecosystem are temperature, water, sunlight and soil

Terrestrial Ecosystem

Broadly classified into three types
- **Forest Ecosystem** Most ecologically complex ecosystem, home to a large variety of trees, plants, animals, etc
- **Desert Ecosystem** Found in water deficit areas where flora and fauna are scarce and portly developed due to high temperature, low water availability and intense sunlight
- **Grassland Ecosystem** Unaltered areas of land where grass is dominant plant life

Aquatic Ecosystem
- Ecosystem consisting of water as the main habitat, broadly divided into two parts
- **Marine Ecosystem** Biggest ecosystem covering around 71% of the Earth surface, consisting of oceans, inter-tidal zones, coral reefs, salt marshes, etc
- **Lakes Ecosystem** Bodies of non-marine standing water connected by water flow

Biome

Introduction
- Total assemblage of plant and animal species interacting within specific conditions

Types of Biomes
- **Tropical Forest**
  - Equatorial, having multi-layered canopy, tall and large trees
  - Deciduous, less dense having trees of medium height
  - Temperate, have moderately dense broad leaved trees
  - Boreal, having evergreen conifers like pine, fur, spruce, etc
- **Desert**
  - Hot and dry, have scanty vegetation like Kalahari desert
  - Semi-arid, marginal areas of hot deserts
  - Coastal, like Atacama desert
  - Cold, found in Tundra climatic regions
- **Grassland**
  - Tropical, have grasses, trees and large shrubs are absent
  - Temperate, have grasses with occasional trees such as cottonwood, oaks, willows, etc
- **Aquatic**
  - Freshwater, have algae and other aquatic and marine plant communities
  - Marine, found in oceans, coral reefs, lagoons, estuaries
- **Altitudinal**
  - Consists of deciduous to tundra vegetation varying according to the altitude

SOURCE *New NCERT Class VI* (*Major Domains of the Earth*), *Old NCERT Class VI* (*Realms of the Earth*), *New NCERT Class VII* (*Environment*), *Old NCERT Class IX* (*Biosphere*), *New NCERT Class XI* (*Biodiversity and Conservation 'Biology'*), *New NCERT Class XI* (*Life on the Earth*), *New NCERT Class XII* (*Ecosystem 'Biology'*)

1 **Consider the following statements about an ecosystem.** *(Chap 1, Class-VII, New NCERT)*

1. It is a system formed by the interaction of all living organisms with their physical and chemical factors.
2. Transfer of energy and material takes place through the ecosystem.
3. Ecosystem involves the interdependence among the organisms and dependence on their environment.

How many of the statements given above is/are not correct?

(a) Only one (b) Only two
(c) All three (d) None of these

Ans. (d)

Exp. None of the given statements are not correct about an ecosystem. Ecosystem is a system formed by living beings interacting with each other and their non-living surroundings in a wide geographical area.

Ecosystem functions include exchange of energy and nutrients in the food chain. It is important for ecological processes and regulation of the energy flow, supporting life systems and providing stability.

It involves the interdependence among the organisms and dependence on their environment.

2 **'R2 Code of Practices' constitutes a tool available for promoting the adoption of** *(Class-XI, Old NCERT) (IAS Pre 2021)*

(a) environmentally responsible practices in electronics recycling industry.
(b) ecological management of Wetlands of International Importance under the Ramsar Convention.
(c) sustainable practices in the cultivation of agricultural crops in degraded lands.
(d) 'Environmental Impact Assessment' in the exploitation of natural resources.

Ans. (a)

Exp. The R2 Code of Practices serves as a valuable tool for promoting the adoption of environmentally responsible practices in the electronics recycling industry. It also known as the Responsible Recycling (R2) Practices, ensures that electronics are recycled with a high level of environmental responsibility. It sets voluntary principles and guidelines for electronics recyclers to follow.

3 **In the context of ecosystem productivity, marine upwelling zones are important as they increase the marine productivity by bringing the** *(Chap 5, Class-VI, Old NCERT) (IAS Pre 2011)*

1. decomposer microorganisms to the surface.
2. nutrients to the surface.
3. bottom-dwelling organisms to the surface.

Which of the statements given above is/are correct?

(a) 1 and 2 (b) Only 2 (c) 2 and 3 (d) Only 3

Ans. (b)

Exp. Statement (2) is correct. In the context of ecosystem productivity, marine upwelling zones are important as they increase the marine productivity by bringing the nutrient-rich waters from deeper layers to the surface. These nutrients, such as nitrogen and phosphorus, support the growth of phytoplankton and other marine organisms.

4 **Which of the following can be considered as a biotic component of the ecosystem?** *(Chap 5, Class-IX, Old NCERT)*

1. Climate
2. Temperature
3. Phytoplankton
4. Carbon dioxide
5. Primary producers

Codes

(a) 2 and 5 (b) 1, 2 and 4
(c) 3 and 5 (d) All of these

Ans. (c)

Exp. Phytoplankton and primary producers can be considered as biotic components of ecosystem. The term 'biotic' describes a living component of an ecosystem. e.g., plants and animals. Phytoplankton, also known as microalgae, are similar to terrestrial plants as they contain chlorophyll and require sunlight in order to live and grow. Autotrophs or primary producers are organisms that acquire their energy from sunlight and materials from non-living sources. Climate, temperature and carbon dioxide are abiotic components.

5 **With reference to food chains in ecosystems, consider the following statements.** *(Chap 12, Class-XII, New NCERT, Biology) (IAS Pre 2013)*

1. A food chain illustrates the order in which a chain of organisms feed upon each other.
2. Food chains are found within the populations of a species.
3. A food chain illustrates the numbers of each organism which are eaten by others.

Which of the statements given above is/are correct?

(a) Only 1 (c) 1, 2 and 3
(b) 1 and 2 (d) None of these

Ans. (a)

Exp. Statement (1) is correct regarding the food chain in ecosystem.

A food chain represents the linear sequence of who eats whom in an ecosystem. It shows the transfer of energy from one organism to another.

Statements (2) and (3) are incorrect.

Food chains are not found within the populations of a species (man will not eat man).

A food web illustrates the numbers of each organism which are eaten by others.

6 Consider the following statements about food chain. *(Chap 5, Class-IX, Old NCERT)*

1. Only 10% of energy is transferred from one trophic level to another trophic level.
2. The autotrophs are located at the bottom most trophic level.
3. The ecosystem has the highest capacity to support the organisms at the higher trophic levels.
4. The lowest amount of energy is transferred to the highest trophic level.

How many of the statements given above is/are not correct?

(a) Only one (b) Only two
(c) Only three (d) All four

Ans. (a)

Exp. Only one statement i.e., (3) is not correct about food chain because the ecosystem has the highest capacity to support the organisms at the lowest trophic levels. Lowest trophic level has the highest species population and thus possess highest carrying capacity.

7 Consider the following statements regarding saprophytes. *(Chap 5, Class-IX, Old NCERT)*

1. Saprophytes are not a part of decaying food chain.
2. Saprophytes are organisms who feed and live on dead organic material.
3. They obtain nutrition for their growth through dead organic material.

How many of the statements given above is/are correct?

(a) Only one (c) Only two
(b) All three (d) None of these

Ans. (b)

Exp. Only two statements i.e., (2) and (3) are correct regarding saprophytes.
Saprophytes feed and live on dead organic material. Saprophytes cannot make their own food.
They obtain nutrition for their growth through dead organic material. Saprophytes have no leaves, stem or roots, they produce spores and cannot perform photosynthesis. Mushrooms, molds, fungi are some of the examples of saprophytes.
Statement (1) is incorrect because Saprophyte are a part of decaying food chain.

8 Consider the following statements. *(Class-XI, Old NCERT)*

1. The Chemical Oxygen Demand (COD) is the total measurement of all chemicals (organics and in-organics) in the water.
2. The Biochemical Oxygen Demand (BOD) is a measure of, the amount of oxygen that requires for the bacteria to degrade the organic components present in water.

Which of the above-mentioned statements is/are correct?

(a) Only 1
(b) Only 2
(c) Both 1 and 2
(d) Neither 1 nor 2

Ans. (c)

Exp. Both the statements (1) and (2) are correct.
COD represents the amount of oxygen required to chemically oxidize both organic and inorganic substances in water. It provides an overall measure of water pollution.
BOD specifically measures the amount of oxygen consumed by microorganisms (bacteria) during the biological degradation of organic matter in water. It reflects the organic pollution level.

9 Consider the following Assertion (A) and Reason (R) and choose the correct code. *(Chap 5, Class-IX, Old NCERT)*

Assertion (A) Estuaries are characterised by low salinity.

Reason (R) Estuaries are formed by mixing salt and freshwater.

Codes

(a) Both A and R are true and R is the correct explanation of A.
(b) Both A and R are true, but R is not the correct explanation of A.
(c) A is true, but R is false.
(d) A is false, but R is true.

Ans. (a)

Exp. Both Assertion (A) and Reason (R) are true and Reason (R) is the correct explanation of Assertion (A).
Estuaries are formed by mixing salt and freshwater. That is why, they are characterised by low salinity.
The salinity in an estuary varies according to its location in the estuary. An estuary is a partially enclosed coastal water body where freshwater from rivers and streams mixes with salt water from the ocean. The mixture of seawater and fresh water in estuaries is called brackish water and its salinity can range from 0.5 to 35 ppt.

10 Which among the following is the major coral reef located in India? *(Chap 16, Module-6, NIOS)*

1. Gulf of Kuchchh
2. Andaman and Nicobar Islands
3. Lakshadweep
4. Gulf of Mannar

Codes

(a) 1 and 2
(b) 1, 3 and 4
(c) 2, 3 and 4
(d) All of these

Ans. (d)

Exp. All the options are correct as Major Coral reefs of India are located in Gulf of Kuchchh, Andaman and Nicobar Islands, Lakshadweep and Gulf of Mannar. India is home to several stunning coral reefs that play a crucial role in marine ecosystems. The Gulf of Kuchchh boasts some of the most northerly reefs in the world. In Andaman and Nicobar Islands all three coral reefs are found atolls, fringing reefs, and barrier reefs. The warm tropical waters around Lakshadweep provide an ideal environment for coral growth.

11 Which of the following factors is/are responsible for the efficient growth of terrestrial ecosystems? *(Chap 5, Class-IX, Old NCERT)*

1. Rainfall
2. Temperature
3. Sunlight
4. Soil

Codes

(a) 1, 2 and 3 (b) 2, 3 and 4
(c) 1, 2, 3 and 4 (d) 1 and 2

Ans. (c)

Exp. Rainfall, temperature, sunlight and soil are the factors responsible for the efficient growth of terrestrial ecosystem. Terrestrial ecosystem dependent on the temperature range, the average amount of precipitation received, the soil type and amount of light received by it.

12 Which of the following is/are decomposers in an ecosystem? *(Chap 14, Class-XII, New NCERT)*

1. Zooplankton 2. Bacteria
3. Flagella

Codes

(a) 1 and 2 (b) 1 and 3
(c) 2 and 3 (d) All of these

Ans. (c)

Exp. Bacteria and flagella are the decomposers in an ecosystem. Decomposers are the organisms that are involved in the process of decomposition of the dead, both animal as well as plant matter, in the ecosystem. Major decomposers in the ecosystem include bacteria and fungi.

However, zooplankton are small, aquatic microorganisms which are present in water bodies.

13 With reference to the food chains in ecosystems, which of the following kinds of organism is/are known as decomposer organism/organisms? *(Chap 12, Class-XII, New NCERT, Biology)*

1. Virus 2. Fungi
3. Bacteria

Codes

(a) Only 1 (b) 2 and 3
(c) 1 and 3 (d) 1, 2 and 3

Ans. (b)

Exp. Fungi and Bacteria are known as decomposer organism.

Fungi breakdown dead organic matter, such as fallen leaves and wood, into simpler nutrients. Without fungi, forest floors would be covered in plant debris and animal carcasses, leading to nutrient accumulation.

Bacteria are also essential decomposers. They actively break down organic material, releasing nutrients back into the ecosystem. Soil bacteria, for instance, play a vital role in nutrient cycling.

However, viruses are not typically considered decomposers. They are not part of the decomposition process.

14 With reference to an initiative called 'The Economics of Ecosystems and Biodiversity (TEEB)', which of the following statements is/are correct? *(Chap 13, Class-XII, Biology, New NCERT) (IAS Pre 2016)*

1. It is an initiative hosted by UNEP, IMF and World Economic Forum.
2. It is a global initiative that focuses on drawing attention to the economic benefits of biodiversity.
3. It presents an approach that can help decision-makers recognise, demonstrate and capture the value of ecosystems and biodiversity.

Select the correct answer using the codes given below.

(a) 1 and 2 (b) Only 3
(c) 2 and 3 (d) 1, 2 and 3

Ans. (c)

Exp. Statements (2) and (3) are correct regarding 'The Economics of Ecosystems and Biodiversity (TEEB)'. The Economics of Ecosystems and Biodiversity (TEEB) is a global initiative focused on "making nature's values visible". Its principal objective is to mainstream the values of biodiversity and ecosystem services into decision-making at all levels.

It aims to achieve this goal by following a structured approach to valuation that helps decision-makers recognise the wide range of benefits provided by ecosystems and biodiversity, demonstrate their values in economic terms and, where appropriate, capture those values in decision-making.

Statement (1) is incorrect. In 2007, Germany and the European Commission launched the Economics of Ecosystems and Biodiversity (TEEB).

15 Consider the following pairs. *(Chap 5, Class-IX, Old NCERT)*

1. Xerophyte – Plant that can survive in dry regions
2. Hydrophyte – Plant surviving in excessive water
3. Tropophyte – Plant adapting to seasonal variations

How many of the pairs given above is/are correctly matched?

(a) Only one (b) Only two
(c) All three (d) None of these

Ans. (c)

Exp. All the given pairs i.e., (1), (2) and (3) are correctly matched. A xerophyte is a plant, which is able to survive in an environment with low availability of water or moisture such as deserts etc.

Hydrophyte is a plants that live in water and adjust with its surroundings. e.g., water lilies and lotus.

Tropophyte is a plant adapted to seasonal variations in which periods of heavy rainfall alternate with periods of drought.

16 Consider the following statements about decomposition. *(Chap 14, Class-XII, New NCERT)*

1. The degradation of detritus into simpler inorganic substances is known as catabolism.
2. The breakdown of humus into inorganic substances leads to mineralisation.

Which of the statements given above is/are correct?

(a) Only 1
(b) Only 2
(c) Both 1 and 2
(d) Neither 1 nor 2

Ans. (c)

Exp. Both the statements (1) and (2) are correct about decomposition. The degradation of detritus into simpler inorganic substances is known as catabolism. It is the process of breaking down complex molecules into simpler molecules. Mineralisation is the process of degradation of the humus to release inorganic nutrients.

17 Which of the following factors aid the process of aerobic decomposition? *(Chap 14, Class-XII, New NCERT)*

1. Anaerobiosis
2. High temperature
3. Humidity

Codes

(a) 1, 2 and 3 (b) 1 and 2
(c) 2 and 3 (d) Only 1

Ans. (c)

Exp. Among the given factors, humidity and high temperature aid the process of aerobic decomposition. Aerobic decomposition is the process by, which the complex organic substances breakdown into simpler substances by the action of microorganisms in presence of oxygen. Anaerobiosis means the process, which is held in absence of oxygen.

18 Consider the following statements about the phosphorus cycle. *(Chap 15, Class-XI, New NCERT)*

1. Phosphorus plays a central role in aquatic ecosystems and water quality.
2. On land, phosphorus is usually found in the form of phosphates.
3. In the ocean, phosphorus accumulates on continental shelves in the form of insoluble deposits.

How many of the statements given above is/are correct?

(a) Only one
(b) Only two
(c) All three
(d) None of the above

Ans. (c)

Exp. All three statements i.e., (1), (2) and (3) are correct regarding the phosphorus cycle.

Phosphorus plays a central role in aquatic ecosystems and influences water quality. It is an essential nutrient for both aquatic plants and animals.

The phosphorus cycle is a vital biogeochemical process that describes the movement of phosphorus through the lithosphere, hydrosphere and biosphere.

On land, phosphorus primarily exists in the form of phosphates. These compounds are crucial for plant growth and are found in soil and rocks.

In the ocean, phosphorus accumulates on continental shelves in the form of insoluble deposits.

19 Consider the following kinds of organisms. *(Chap 15, Class-XI, New NCERT) (IAS Pre 2021)*

1. Copepods
2. Cyanobacteria
3. Diatoms
4. Foraminifera

Which of the above are primary producers in the food chains of oceans?

(a) 1 and 2 (b) 2 and 3
(c) 3 and 4 (d) 1 and 4

Ans. (b)

Exp. Cyanobacteria and Diatoms are the primary producers in the food chain of oceans.

Cyanobacteria, also called blue-green algae, are microscopic organisms found naturally in all types of water. These organisms are primary producers who use Sunlight to make their own food.

Diatoms are photosynthesising algae. They are primary producers in oceanic food chain.

Copepods are found in nearly every freshwater and saltwater habitats. They are major primary consumers in the World Ocean.

Foraminifera are single-celled organisms that are found in most marine environments. These are heterotrophic organisms, which consume smaller organisms and organic matter.

20 With reference to the food chain, consider the following statements. *(Chap 12, Class-XII, New NCERT, Biology)*

1. Only 10 percent of the energy is transferred to each trophic level from the lower trophic level.
2. The flow of energy takes place in both directions in the food chain.
3. The natural interconnection of food chains makes it a food web.

How many of the statements given above is/are correct?

(a) Only one (b) Only two
(c) All three (d) None of these

Ans. (b)

Exp. Only two statements i.e., (1) and (3) are correct regarding the food chain.

The amount of energy at each trophic level decreases as it moves through an ecosystem. As little as 10 percent of the energy at any trophic level is transferred to the next level; the rest is lost largely through metabolic processes such as heat. The natural interconnection of food chains is called the food web.

Statement (2) is incorrect. In a food chain, the flow of energy occurs unidirectionally-from one trophic level to another. Energy enters the system through producers (such as plants) that convert sunlight into chemical energy through photosynthesis.

21 Consider the following statements about ecological pyramids. ***(Chap 14, Class-XII, New NCERT)***

1. A trophic level in an ecological pyramid represents a particular species.
2. A given species may occupy one or more trophic level in an ecological pyramid.
3. The pyramid of biomass in a sea is generally inverted.

Which of the statements given above are correct?

(a) 1 and 2 (b) 2 and 3 (c) 1 and 3 (d) 1, 2 and 3

Ans. (b)

Exp. Statements (2) and (3) are correct. The pyramid of biomass in the sea is inverted because the amount of biomass is least at the base of the pyramid and the amount of biomass is maximum at the apex of the pyramid.

In aquatic ecosystem, the producers are small organisms with least biomass and the biomass gradually increase towards the apex of the pyramid. Thus, the pyramid of biomass of aquatic ecosystems is inverted in shape.

Statement (1) is incorrect about ecological pyramids because in ecology. A tropic level in an ecological pyramid represents a group of organisms.

22 With reference to ecological succession consider the following statements. ***(Chap 14, Class-XII, New NCERT)***

1. The climax community is innear equilibrium with the environment.
2. Succession results in changes in the composition of various ecosystems.
3. The process of succession and evolution are not parallel with each other.

How many of the statements given above is/are not correct?

(a) Only one (b) Only two (c) All three (d) None of these

Ans. (a)

Exp. Only one statement i.e., (3) is incorrect with respect to ecological succession because the process of succession and evolution are parallel with respect to time.

Succession is a process which starts in an area where no living organism are present.

Ecological succession is the process of change in the species structure of an ecological community over time.

23 Consider the following statements. ***(Chap 14, Class-XII, New NCERT)***

1. Secondary options is often faster than primary succession.
2. Primary succession can take place over barren and rocky surface.
3. Hydrarch succession of plants takes place in wetter areas.

How many of the statements given above is/are correct?

(a) Only one (b) Only two
(c) All three (d) None of these

Ans. (c)

Exp. All three statements i.e., (1), (2) and (3) are correct. In primary succession, newly exposed or newly formed rock is colonised by living things for the first time.

Secondary succession, an area that was previously occupied by living things is disturbed, then re-colonised following the disturbance.

A hydrarch succession is a form of plant succession that starts out in shallow water and eventually culminates in a forest.

24 With reference to food chains in ecosystems, consider the following statements. ***(Chap 15, Class-XI, New NCERT) (IAS Pre 2013)***

1. A food chain illustrates the order in which a chain of organisms feeds upon each other.
2. Food chains are found within the populations of a species.
3. A food chain illustrates the numbers of each organism which are eaten by others.

Which of the statements given above is/are incorrect?

(a) Only 1 (b) 1 and 2
(c) 1, 2 and 3 (d) 2 and 3

Ans. (d)

Exp. Statements (2) and (3) are incorrect with reference to food chains in ecosystems.

Food chains are not found within the populations of a species, because technically, food chain is the sequence of organisms through which the energy flows. If the species starts eating itself, then flow of energy will not proceed.

A food web illustrates the numbers of each organism, which are eaten by others.

25 **In nature, which of the following is/are most likely to be found surviving on a surface without soil?**

(Chap 12, Class-XII, New NCERT Biology)
(Chap 14, Class-XII, New NCERT)

1. Fern
2. Lichen
3. Mosses
4. Mushroom

Codes

(a) 1 and 4 (b) Only 2
(c) 2 and 3 (d) 1, 3 and 4

Ans. (c)

Exp. Lichens and mosses can survive on surfaces without soil. Lichens are fascinating organisms that can indeed survive on surfaces without soil. They are a symbiotic combination of fungi and algae or cyanobacteria. Lichens can grow on rocks, tree bark, and other non-soil surfaces, using the nutrients available in the air and rainwater. Mosses are another example of organisms that can thrive without soil. They have specialised structures called rhizoids that allow them to attach to various surfaces, including rocks, tree trunks, and even concrete. Mosses obtain nutrients and water directly from the environment, making them well-suited for soil-less habitats.

26 **Consider the following statements.**

(Chap 5, Class-VI, New NCERT)

1. A zone of mixing of all the species on Earth and having life.
2. A zone of intermixing of living and non-living organisms where human habitations exists.
3. A bio zone of humans and animals which consists of living organisms.
4. A zone of contact between land, water and air, where life exists on Earth.

Which of the statements given above is most appropriately defines a biosphere?

(a) Only 1 (b) Only 2 (c) Only 3 (d) Only 4

Ans. (d)

Exp. Statement (4) most appropriately defines a biosphere. The portion of the universe where all life is found is called the biosphere. The biosphere is made of three parts, called the lithosphere (land), atmosphere (air) and hydrosphere (water).

27 **Which of the following processes results in release of carbon dioxide in the atmosphere?**

(Chap 14, Class-XII, New NCERT)

1. Combustion of organic material
2. Burning of forests
3. Photosynthesis

Codes

(a) Only 3 (b) 2 and 3
(c) 1 and 2 (d) All of these

Ans. (c)

Exp. Combustion of organic material and burning of forests can result in release of carbon dioxide in the atmosphere.

Combustion is the process of burning an organic compound in oxygen to produce energy, carbon dioxide and water vapour. When trees catch fire during burning of forest fires, the carbon in their timber combines with oxygen to release energy and carbon dioxide.

However, photosynthesis is the process by which plants use sunlight, water and Carbon dioxide to create oxygen and energy in the form of sugar.

28 **Which one of the following terms describes not only the physical space occupied by an organism but also its functional role in the community of organisms?**

(Chap 13, Class-XI, New NCERT) (IAS Pre 2013)

(a) Ecotone (b) Ecological niche
(c) Habitat (d) Home range

Ans. (b)

Exp. Among the given options, ecological niche describes not only the physical space occupied by an organism but also its functional role in the community of organisms.

An ecotone is a zone of transition between two biological communities when the two collide and merge. Habitat can be defined as the natural environment of an organism, the type of place in which it is natural for it to live and grow.

29 **Which of the following adds/add carbon dioxide to the carbon cycle on the planet Earth?**

(Chap 15, Class-XI, New NCERT) (IAS Pre 2014

1. Volcanic action
2. Respiration
3. Photosynthesis
4. Decay of organic matter

Codes

(a) 1 and 3 (b) Only 2
(c) 1, 2 and 4 (d) 1, 2, 3 and 4

Ans. (c)

Exp. Volcanic action, respiration and decay of organic matter adds carbon dioxide to the carbon cycle on the planet Earth.

However, photosynthesis uses carbon dioxide to produce food, that is why does not add carbon dioxide to the carbon cycle on the planet Earth.

30 **Consider the following statements about nitrification.**

(Chap 15, Class-XI, New NCERT

1. Nitrification is the process that converts ammonia to nitrite and then to nitrate.
2. Most nitrification occurs aerobically and there are two distinct steps of nitrification that are carried out by distinct types of microorganisms.

Which of the statements given above is/are correct?
(a) Only 1
(b) Only 2
(c) Both 1 and 2
(d) Neither 1 nor 2

Ans. (c)

Exp. Both the statements (1) are (2) correct as the conversion of ammonia into nitrite and subsequently into nitrate is known as nitrification. The majority of nitrification processes occur in aerobic conditions and entail two distinct stages facilitated by different microorganisms. Initially, ammonia is oxidised to nitrite by specialised microbes called ammonia-oxidisers. Subsequently, nitrite (NO_2^-) is further oxidised to nitrate (NO_3^-) by a separate group of prokaryotes, specifically nitrite-oxidising bacteria, in the second stage of nitrification.

31 Consider the following statements with respect to biochemical cycle. ***(Chap 15, Class-XI, New NCERT)***

1. It is the way in which an element or compound moves between its several biotic and abiotic forms and locations in the biosphere.
2. It starts by absorbing the chemical elements of the organism and is returned to the air, water and soil through decomposition.

Which of the statements given above is/are correct?
(a) Only 1
(b) Only 2
(c) Both 1 and 2
(d) Neither 1 nor 2

Ans. (c)

Exp. Both the statements (1) and (2) are correct with respect to biochemical cycle. A biogeochemical cycle refers to the natural pathways by which essential elements of living matter circulate between the non-living (abiotic) components of the biosphere (such as air, water, and soil) and the living (biotic) components. These cycles involve the biological, geological and chemical aspects of each element. Biogeochemical cycles start by absorbing chemical elements from the environment. For instance, plants take up nutrients from the soil, animals consume these nutrients, and eventually, through processes like decomposition, these elements are returned to the air, water and soil.

32 Consider the following statements about phosphate cycle. ***(Chap 14, Class-XII, New NCERT)***

1. Gaseous exchange between organisms and environment is almost negligible.
2. Weathering of rocks releases phosphate into soil.
3. Dead organisms are decomposed by the phosphate solubilising bacteria.

How many of the statements given above is/are correct?
(a) Only one
(b) Only two
(c) All three
(d) None of these

Ans. (c)

Exp. All three given statements i.e., (1), (2) and (3) are correct about phosphate cycle. Gaseous exchange between organisms and environment is almost negligible. Much of the phosphorus on Earth is tied up in rock and sedimentary deposits, from which it is released by weathering, leaching and mining.

Phosphate Solubilising Bacteria (PSB) are beneficial bacteria capable of solubilising inorganic phosphorus from insoluble compounds.

Some of the most common examples are the species of Pseudomonas, Bacillus and Micrococcus.

33 With reference of ecological niche, which of the following statement(s) is/are correct? ***(Unit 3, Module-1, NIOS)***

1. It represents the range of conditions that it can tolerate the resources it utilises and its functional role in ecological system.
2. Each species has a distinct niche.

Select the correct answer by using the codes given below.
(a) Only 1
(b) Both 1 and 2
(c) Only 2
(d) Neither 1 nor 2

Ans. (c)

Exp. Only statement (2) is correct with reference to ecological niche as each species has a distinct niche. An ecological niche is the role of a species in its environment, including the physical and environmental conditions it requires and the interactions it has with other species. It is important to note that a niche is not simply a physical location, but also encompasses the organism's behaviour, diet and interactions with other organisms.

Chapter 29

Biodiversity

Biodiversity

Introduction

- Number and variety of various organisms found within a specified geographic region
- It refers to varieties of plants, animals and microorganisms, the genes they contain and the ecosystem they form

Types of Biodiversity

- **Genetic Biodiversity** Variation of genes within species. Genetic diversity is essential for healthy breeding of population of species
- **Species Biodiversity** Refers to variety of species, i.e., number of species in a defined area. The diversity of species can be measured though its richness, abundance and types
- **Ecosystem Biodiversity** Refers to variety of ecosystems both in terms of nature and number, where living organisms interact with their environment

Measurement of Biodiversity

- **Alpha Diversity** Mean diversity of species in different sites or habitats within a local scale
- **Beta Diversity** Comparison of diversity ecosystems i.e., change in number of species in ecosystem
- **Gamma Diversity** Measure of total species diversity in a landscape

Biodiversity Hotspots

A biogeographic region with a significant reservoir of biodiversity that is under threat from humans

- India has 2 biodiversity hotspots
- **Eastern Himalayan Biodiversity Hotspot** Comprises of Nepal, Bhutan and states of East and North-East India with an estimated 9000 plant species, of which 3500 are endemic
- **Western Ghats Biodiversity Hotspot** Spread to 6 states of India, one of the richest centres of endemism

Biodiversity Conservation

- **In-situ** Conservation meaning conservation of natural habitats and maintenance and recovery of viable populations in their natural surroundings.
  e.g., national parks, Sanctuaries, etc
- **Ex-situ** Conservation meaning threatened animals and plants are taken out from their natural habitat and placed in a special setting where they can be protected. e.g., zoological parks, botanical gardens, etc

Geological Biodiversity

1. **Regions of Excess Biodiversity**
   There are regions where growth of plants and animals is greater than other parts of world due to favourable climatic conditions, such as
   a) **Tropical Rainforest** Found in warm and humid areas with annual precipitation above 200cm favouring excess biodiversity
   b) **Coral Reefs** Large underwater structures composed of calcium carbonate skeletons favouring excess growth
   c) **Tropical Oceanic Region** High precipitation and high temperature favours excess biodiversity
   d) **Wetlands** Support high concentrations of animals including mammals, birds, fish etc
2. **Regions of High Biodiversity** Some regions support high biodiversity due to geomorphological structure and climate of that area, e.g., monsoon regions, grasslands etc
3. **Regions of Normal Biodiversity** Some parts lack biodiversity due to lack of favourable conditions for growth of plants and animals
4. **Regions of Least Biodiversity** e.g., Polar ice and Arctic Tundra

SOURCE **New NCERT Class VIII** *(Resources)*, **New NCERT Class VIII** *(Soil, Water, Natural Vegetation and Wildlife Resources)*, **New NCERT Class X** *(New Resources and Development)*, **New NCERT Class XI** *(Forest and Wildlife Resources)*, **New NCERT Class XI** *(Biodiversity and Conservation)*, **New NCERT Class XI** *(Natural Vegetation)*, **New NCERT Class XII** *(Biodiversity and Conservation (Biology)*, **New NCERT Class XII** *(Planning and Sustainable Development in Indian Context)*

1 **Consider the following statements about biodiversity.** *(Chap 14, Class-XI, New NCERT)*

1. Genetic diversity refers to the variety of species in a defined area.
2. Species diversity relates to the variation of genes within species.
3. Ecosystem diversity encompasses differences in habitats and ecological processes.

How many of the statements given above is/are correct?

(a) Only one (b) Only two
(c) All three (d) None of these

Ans. (a)

Exp. Only one statement i.e., (3) is correct regarding biodiversity.

Ecosystem diversity encompasses differences in habitats and ecological processes occurring within various ecosystem types. Ecosystems vary significantly based on factors such as climate, soil type, vegetation, and geographical features. The boundaries of ecosystems (such as forests, wetlands, grasslands, etc.) are not rigidly defined, making their demarcation complex.

Statements (1) and (2) are incorrect because genetic diversity does not refer to the variety of species in a defined area. Instead, it pertains to the variation of genes within a single species. Species diversity does not relate to the variation of genes within species. Instead, it refers to the variety of species present in a defined area.

2 **Consider the following statements regarding the ecological role of biodiversity.** *(Chap 14, Class-XI, New NCERT)*

1. Every organism in an ecosystem contributes something useful to other organisms.
2. Species in an ecosystem help water cycle and nutrients throughout the system.
3. The loss of species increases the ability of the ecosystem to maintain itself.
4. An ecosystem with high biodiversity is more stable and productive.

How many of the statements given above is/are correct?

(a) Only one (b) Only two (c) Only three (d) All four

Ans. (c)

Exp. Only three statements i.e., (1), (2) and (4) are correct regarding the ecological role of biodiversity.

Organisms within an ecosystem play various roles, such as capturing and storing energy, producing and decomposing organic materials, and participating in nutrient cycles. These functions benefit other organisms and contribute to the overall ecosystem.

Species play a crucial role in nutrient cycling. For example, decomposers breakdown organic matter, releasing nutrients back into the soil. Plants take up water and nutrients, which are then transferred through the food web.

Ecosystems with greater species diversity tend to be more stable and productive. High biodiversity ensures that ecological niches are filled and reducing the impact of disturbances.

Statement (3) is incorrect becasue the loss of species actually decreases the ecosystem's ability to maintain itself. Biodiversity provides resilience and stability to ecosystems. When species are lost, critical ecological functions may be disrupted, affecting the overall health of the ecosystem.

3 **Consider the following statements with reference to biodiversity.** *(Chap 15, Class-XII, New NCERT)*

1. Species diversity is the diversity at the species level.
2. The species diversity of Western ghats region is more than the Eastern ghats region.
3. The global species diversity can be estimated at about 70 million species.

Which of the statements given above is/are correct?

(a) Only 1 (b) Only 3
(c) 1 and 2 (d) All of these

Ans. (c)

Exp. Statements (1) and (2) are correct with reference to biodiversity. Species diversity is the diversity at the species level. The number of species per unit area is called as species richness.

Western ghats have more species diversity as compared to Eastern ghats.

Statement (3) is incorrect because according to some scientists, global species diversity range from 20 to 50 millions.

4 **With reference to 'Agenda 21', consider the following statements.** *(Chap 16, Class-XI, New NCERT) (IAS Pre 2016)*

1. It is a global action plan for sustainable development.
2. It originated in the World Summit on sustainable development held in Johannesburg in 2002.

Which of the statements given above is/are correct?

(a) Only 1 (b) Only 2
(c) Both 1 and 2 (d) Neither 1 nor 2

Ans. (a)

Exp. Statement (1) is correct with reference to 'Agenda 21'. It is a global action plan for sustainable development. It is a comprehensive plan of action to be taken globally, nationally and locally by organisations of the United Nations System, Governments and major groups in every area in which human impacts on the environment.

Statement (2) is incorrect because 'Agenda 21' is a product of the Earth Summit (UN Conference on Environment and Development) held in Rio de Janeiro, Brazil, in 1992.

5 **Consider the following statements about the distribution of biodiversity.**

(Chap 15, Class-XII, New NCERT)

1. The biodiversity of tropical regions is more as they had a long evolutionary period of species.
2. Higher solar insolation in the tropical regions has led to higher productivity of the ecosystem.

Which of the statements given above is/are correct?

(a) Only 1 (b) Only 2
(c) Both 1 and 2 (d) Neither 1 nor 2

Ans. (c)

Exp. Both the statements (1) and (2) are correct regarding the distribution of biodiversity.

Tropical environments unlike temperate ones are less seasonal, relatively more constant and predictable. Such constant environments promote niche specialisation and lead to a greater species diversity.

There is more solar energy available in the tropics, which contributes to higher productivity; this in turn might contribute indirectly to greater diversity.

6 **Consider the following statements.**

(Chap 15, Class-XII, New NCERT)

1. A stable community of species has more biodiversity than an unstable community.
2. Increase in biodiversity contributes to higher productivity in the ecosystem.
3. Species richness in an ecosystem leads to higher biodiversity.

How many of the statements given above is/are correct?

(a) Only one (b) Only two
(c) All three (d) None of these

Ans. (c)

Exp. All three statements i.e., (1), (2) and (3) are correct. A stable community of species has more biodiversity than an unstable community. David Tilman's long-term ecosystem experiments showed increased diversity.

Increase in biodiversity contributes to higher productivity in the ecosystem.

Larger numbers of species and more even abundances of s_cies lead to higher biodiversity.

7 **Consider the following statements with reference to the importance of biodiversity.**

(Chap 16, Class-XI, New NCERT)

1. Increase in the biodiversity of a region improves the cycling of nutrients and energy.
2. Species diversity on Earth is uniformly distributed.
3. An ecosystem with greater biodiversity will adapt quickly to climate change.

Which of the statements given above is/are correct?

(a) 1 and 2 (b) 2 and 3 (c) 1 and 3 (d) 1, 2 and 3.

Ans. (c)

Exp. Statements (1) and (3) are correct with reference t importance of biodiversity. Increase in the biodiversity of a region improves the cycling of nutrients and energy because of greater stability.

For example, species with high genetic diversity and many populations that are adapted to a wide variety of conditions are more likely to be able to weather disturbances, disease and climate change.

Statement (2) is incorrect because species diversity on Earth is distributed variably.

8 **Which of the following committees is/are set up to study the ecological sensitivity of the Western ghat**

(Chap 14, Class-XI, New NCER

1. Kasturirangan Committee
2. Gadgil Committee
3. TSR Subramanian Committee

Codes

(a) 1 and 2
(b) 2 and 3
(c) Only 1
(d) 1, 2 and 3

Ans. (a)

Exp. The Gadgil Committee Report and the Kasturirangan Committee Report are set up study the ecological sensitivity of the Western ghats.

In 2010, the Ministry of Environment established the Gadgil Committee to examine the effects of population pressure, climate change, and development activities or the Western ghats.

The Kasturirangan Committee, formed in 2012, aimed devise a comprehensive approach to safeguard the biodiversity of the Western ghats.

Statement (3) is incorrect because TSR Subramanian Committee was set up by the Government of India in 2017. It reviewed the National Policy on Education (NPE) of 1986 and the Right of Children to Free and Compulsory Education Act (RTE) of 2009. The Committee submitted its report in 2019.

9 **Consider the following statements.**

(Chap 14, Class-XI, New NCE

1. Species diversity increases from the Equator towards the poles.
2. Tropics harbour more species than temperate areas.
3. The greatest biodiversity occurs in the Amazon rainforest.
4. Species diversity decreases from temperate are toward the poles.

How many of the statements given above is/are correct?

(a) Only one (b) Only two
(c) Only three (d) All four

Ans. (c)

Exp. Only three statements i.e., (2), (3) and (4) are correct. The tropical zone has greater biodiversity than the temperate zone, the first is the constant temperatures and climate.

The temperate zone has a severe climate which makes it very difficult for animals to survive in such extreme climatic conditions.

The Amazonian rainforest is a tropical rainforest in Brazil. It is known to have the greatest biodiversity on Earth. Species diversity decreases as we move away from the equator towards the poles.

Statement (1) is incorrect because the species diversity decreases as well as we move away from the Equator towards the poles.

10 Which of the following factors will lead to decline of the biodiversity in a region? *(Chap 15, Class-XII, New NCERT)*

1. Forest fires and loss of habitat
2. Over use of natural resources
3. Introduction of alien species
4. Mutual co-extinctions

Codes

(a) 1 and 2 (b) 2 and 3
(c) 1 and 3 (d) All of these

Ans. (d)

Exp. All the given factors i.e., (1), (2), (3) and (4) will lead to decline of the biodiversity in a region. These are Forest fires and loss of habitat, Over use of natural resources, Introduction of alien species, Mutual co-extinctions, Pollution, Climate change associated with global warming and Anthropogencal activities

11 Which of the following is/are invasive/exotic species which can lead to a decline in biodiversity of a region? *(Chap 15, Class-XII, New NCERT)*

1. Water hyacinth
2. Nile perch
3. Lantana
4. Carrot grass

Codes

(a) 1, 2 and 3 (b) 2, 3 and 4
(c) 1, 3 and 4 (d) All of these

Ans. (d)

Exp. Water hyacinth, Nile perch, Lantana and Carrot grass are the invasive/exotic species that can lead to a decline in biodiversity of a region.

Invasive species is a living organism, that is not native to an ecosystem and cassrss hasm.

Invasive weed species like Carrot grass (Parthenium), Lantana and Water hyacinth (Eicchornia) cause environmental damage.

12 With reference to the loss of biodiversity, consider the following statements. *(Chap 16, Class-XI, New NCERT)*

1. Pesticides and insecticides are helpful in preserving the biodiversity of a region.
2. Introduction of alien species promotes the growth and development of indigenous species by providing them nutrition.
3. Loss of biodiversity has resulted in increase in floods and droughts on Earth.

How many of the statements given above is/are correct?

(a) Only one (b) Only two
(c) Only three (d) None of these

Ans. (a)

Exp. Only one statement i.e., (3) is correct with reference to the loss of biodiversity. Loss of biodiversity has resulted in increase in floods and droughts on Earth as climate change is one of the consequences.

Statements (1) and (2) are incorrect because introduction of pesticides, insecticides and alien species harm the biodiversity of a region. It deteriotes the growth and development of native species.

13 Match the following lists correctly and choose the correct codes. *(Chap 16, Class-XI, New NCERT)*

List I (Type of Species)	List II (Name)
A. Endangered Species	1. Gangetic Dolphin
B. Critically Endangered	2. Sangai
C. Endemic Species	3. Asiatic Cheetah
D. Vulnerable Species	4. Mithun

Codes

	A	B	C	D
(a)	3	2	1	4
(b)	1	2	3	4
(c)	2	3	4	1
(d)	1	3	2	4

Ans. (c)

Exp. The correct matching is A-2, B-3, C-4, D-1.

Sangai is listed as endangered in the IUCN Red List of Threatened Species and Schedule I of the Indian Wildlife (Protection) Act, 1972.

Asiatic Cheetah (*Acinonyx jubatus venaticus*) is a critically endangered cheetah sub-species surviving today only in Iran.

Mithun is a semi-wild animal which is highly priced among the tribal people of Arunachal Pradesh. It is an endemic species.

Gangetic Dolphin is an example of vulnerable species.

14 **Consider the following statements.**
(Chap 2, Class-X, New NCERT)

1. The Global Red Data list of endangered species is published by UNICEF.
2. Some species are classified as extinct if they are only found in man-made habitats.
3. Asiatic buffalo is an example of extinct species.

How many of the statements given above is/are correct?

(a) Only one (b) Only two
(c) All three (d) None of these

Ans. (d)

Exp. None of the statements are correct.

The organisation, which publishes the Global Red Data Book is the International Union for Conservation of Nature and Natural Resources (IUCN).

Red Data Book includes a Red List in which the names of all endangered plants and animals are provided for public information.

Species of animals or organisms are considered extinct when there are no more of them alive. Asiatic buffalo is an example of rare species.

15 **Arrange the following events in chronological order of their commencement and select the correct answer from the codes given below.**
(Chap 14, Class-XI, New NCERT)

1. Wildlife (Protection) Act
2. Biological Diversity Act
3. Project Tiger
4. Project Elephant

Codes

(a) 1, 2, 3, 4 (b) 1, 3, 4, 2
(c) 2, 3, 4, 1 (d) 2, 3, 1, 4

Ans. (b)

Exp. The correct chronological order is 1, 3, 4, 2.

The Wildlife (Protection) Act, 1972 provides a legal framework for the protection of various species of wild animals and plants, management of their habitats, regulation, and control of trade in wild animals, plants, and products made from them.

Project Tiger is a Wildlife Conservation Initiative in India that was launched in 1973. Its primary objective is to ensure the survival and maintenance of the tiger population in their natural habitats by creating dedicated Tiger Reserves.

Project Elephant was launched in 1992 to protect elephants and their habitats. It focuses on conservation measures, research, and management of elephant populations.

The Biological Diversity Act was enacted in 2002 to conserve biological diversity, promote sustainable use of its components, and ensure equitable sharing of benefits arising from the use of biological resources.

16 **Consider the following statements with reference to Chiru.**
(Chap 7, Class-X, New NCERT)

1. Chiru is hunted for shahtoosh in the Tibet region.
2. It is an endangered species of antelope.
3. It is used for the purpose of transportation in the high altitude regions.

How many of the statements given above is/are correct?

(a) Only one (b) Only two
(c) All three (d) None of these

Ans. (b)

Exp. All three statements i.e., (1), (2) and (3) are correct with reference to Chiru.

Chiru goat, which is also known as the Tibetan antelope, has long been hunted for its underfur (Shahtoosh). It is renowned for its quality. It has traditionally been transported to Srinagar where it is woven into an extremely fine fabric used to make shawls. In 1980s and 1990s, they had become endangered due to massive illegal poaching.

It is used for the purpose of transportation in the high altitude regions

17 **Which of the following have species that can establish symbiotic relationships with other organisms?**
(Chap 13, Class-XII, New NCERT, Biolog

1. Cnidarians
2. Fungi
3. Protozoa

Codes

(a) 1 and 2 (b) 2 and 3 (c) 1 and 3 (d) 1, 2 and 3

Ans. (d)

Exp. All species establish symbiotic relationships with other organisms.

Many Cnidarians (such as corals) establish symbiotic relationships with algae (such as zooxanthellae).

Fungi are involved in various symbiotic relationships: Fungi help plants absorb nutrients (especially phosphorus) from the soil, and in return, they receive sugars produced by the plant through photosynthesis.

Protozoa can also establish symbiotic relationships with other organisms. Protozoa are single-celled organisms. Although they were once classified in the kingdom Animalia, they are now considered a subkingdom of the kingdom Protista.

18 **Consider the following statements with reference to biodiversity hotspots.**
(Chap 15, Class-XII, New NCE

1. Western ghats and Himalayas are global biodiversity hotspots in India.
2. India has the largest area under biodiversity hotspot in the world.

Which of the statements given above is/are correct?

(a) Only 1 (b) Only 2
(c) Both 1 and 2 (d) Neither 1 nor 2

Ans. (a)

Exp. Statement (1) is correct with reference to biodiversity hotspots. Western ghats and Himalayas are global biodiversity hotspots in India. India hosts four biodiversity hotspots i.e., the Himalayas, the Western ghats, the Indo-Burma region and the Sundaland (includes Nicobar group of islands).

Statement (2) is incorrect because Brazil has the largest area under biodiversity hotspot in the world.

19 Which of the given countries hosts a Global Biodiversity Hotspot in their territory?

(Chap 16, Class-XI, New NCERT)

1. Tanzania
2. Australia
3. Indonesia
4. Brazil

Codes

(a) 1, 2 and 3 (b) 2, 3 and 4
(c) 1 and 3 (d) 1, 2, 3 and 4

***Ans.* (d)**

Exp. All the given countries in the question hosts a Global Biodiversity Hotspot in their territory. Eastern Afro-Montane hotspot is in Tanzania. South-Western Australian region hotspot is in Australia. Western Sunda is (Indonesia, Malas and Brunei) a global hotspot region. Brazil's Cerrado is also a global biodiversity hotspot region of the world.

20 Consider the following statements regarding the Convention on International Trade in Endangered Species of Wild Fauna and Flora (CITES).

(Chap 13, Class-XII, New NCERT, Biology)

1. It serves as a global intergovernmental agreement aimed at overseeing the global commerce of wild animal and plant species.
2. It is legally binding on parties.
3. The trade of species listed in Appendix I of CITES is subject to regulation through permits.

Which of the statements given above is/are correct?

(a) 1 and 2 (b) 2 and 3
(c) 1 and 3 (d) 1, 2 and 3

***Ans.* (a)**

Exp. Statements (1) and (2) are correct regarding CITES. CITES is an international agreement that aims to ensure that international trade in specimens of wild animals and plants does not threaten the survival of the species.

As an international agreement, CITES is legally binding on the states parties. It establishes common minimum standards for international trade in the specimens of species regulated by it.

Statement (3) is incorrect because the trade of species listed in Appendix I of CITES is prohibited except in extraordinary situations for scientific or educational reasons.

21 Which of the following statements is/are correct regarding the Convention on Biological Diversity (CBD)?

(Chap 14, Class-XI, New NCERT)

1. The convention was opened for signature at the Earth Summit in Rio de Janeiro on 5th June, 1992 and entered into force on 29th December, 1993.
2. The Secretariat of the Convention on Biological Diversity (SCBD) is located in Montreal, Canada.
3. Russia is the only UN member state which has not ratified the convention.

Codes

(a) 1 and 2 (b) 2 and 3 (c) 1 and 3 (d) 1, 2 and 3

***Ans.* (a)**

Exp. Statements (1) and (2) are correct.

The Convention on Biological Diversity (CBD) officially entered into force on 29th December, 1993. It was adopted during the Earth Summit (United Nations Conference on Environment and Development) held in Rio de Janeiro, Brazil in 1993.

The Secretariat of the Convention on Biological Diversity (SCBD) is based in Montreal, Canada. It serves as the administrative body responsible for supporting the implementation of the Convention and facilitating communication among the parties.

Statement (3) is incorrect because it has been ratified by 196 nations. The United States is the only UN member state which has not ratified the convention.

22 Consider the following statements in respect of Trade Related Analysis of Fauna and Flora in Commerce (TRAFFIC).

(Chap 13, Class-XII, New NCERT, Biology) (UPSC Pre 2017)

1. TRAFFIC is a bureau under United Nations Environment Programme (UNEP).
2. The mission of TRAFFIC is to ensure that trade in wild plants and animals is not a threat to the conservation of nature.

Which of the statements given above is/are correct?

(a) Only 1 (b) Only 2
(c) Both 1 and 2 (d) Neither 1 nor 2

***Ans.* (b)**

Exp. Statement (2) is correct in respect of Trade Related Analysis of Fauna and Flora in Commerce (TRAFFIC). Its primary focus is on monitoring and analysing wildlife trade patterns to ensure that trade in wild fauna and flora does not endanger their conservation.

TRAFFIC is not a bureau under UNEP. Instead, it is an independent organisation with its own mission and focus. TRAFFIC is a leading non-governmental organisation specialising in biodiversity conservation and sustainable development.

Chapter 30

Biosphere Reserves, National Parks and Wildlife Sanctuaries

Biosphere Reserves, National Parks and Wildlife Sanctuaries

Biosphere Reserves

Biosphere Reserves

- A unique and representative ecosystem of terrestrial and coastal areas which are internationally recognised within UNESCO's MAB programme
- Main objectives are conservation, development research and monitoring. For example, Nilgiri Biosphere Reserve, Nokrek Biosphere Reserve, Panchmarhi Biosphere Reserve and Gulf of Mannar Biosphere Reserve

Institutes Associated With Biodiversity Conservation in India

- **Botanical Survey of India** An apex research organisation to explore the plant resources of the country and identify the plant species with economic virtues
- **Zoological Survey of India** Aims to promote the survey, exploration, research and documentation leading to advancement in our knowledge about animal taxonomy
- **Forest Survey of India** Goal is to conduct forest surveys, studies and research on regular basis to monitor the changing situation of land and forest resources

National Parks/ Wildlife Sanctuaries

National Parks

- Area designated by national government to preserve the natural environment and are declared in areas of adequate ecological, geomorphological and natural significance
  - First National park was established in 1936 as Jim Corbett National Park in Uttarakhand
  - Hemis National park is largest National park with an area of 4400 sq km, situated in Ladakh.
  - There are 106 existing national park in India covering an area of 44,402. 95 sq km

Wildlife Sanctuary

- A place where animals and their habitats are protected. Animal capture, slaughter and poaching are severely prohibited here. For example, Bhindawas Wildlife Sanctuary, Manas Wildlife Sanctuary, Sathyamanglam Wildlife Sanctuary band Similipal Wildlife Sanctuary

Wildlife Conservation Schemes

Wildlife Conservation Schemes

- **Project Tiger** Launched in 1973, main objective was to ensure the maintenance of viable population of tigers in India for scientific, cultural, aesthetic and ecological values
- **Project Snow Leopard** Started in 2006 on the lines of Project elephant, Project rhino and Project tiger to conserve and protect the highly endangered species in its natural habitat
- **Project Elephant** Launched in 1992 to assist states having free ranging population of wild elephants
- **Project Rhino** Aimed to protect the greater one-horned rhino, native to Indian subcontinent
- **Project Manipur Thamin** Found in Loktak lake of Manipur, project was aimed to conserve and increase the population of this species
- **Project Red Panda** Project started in 1966 to conserve the dwindling population of the species
- **Project Olive Ridley Turtles** Project started by Government of Odisha to conserve the dwindling population of olive ridly turtles, launched at Bhitarkanika in Cuttack
- **Project Hangul** To protect and Conserve the Kashmir Red Stag and its habitat. This initiative was dubbed project Hangul. The Hangul, also known as Kashmir Red stag

SOURCE **New NCERT Class VIII** *(Land, Soil, Water, Natural Vegetation and Wildlife Resources)*, **New NCERT Class X** *(Forest and Wildlife Resources)*, **New NCERT Class XI** *(Biodiversity and Conservation)*, **New NCERT Class XI** *(Natural Vegetation)*, **New NCERT Class XII** *(Biodiversity and Conservation 'Biology')*

1 **Consider the following statements.**
Once the Central Government notifies an area as a 'Community Reserve' *(Chap 2, Class-X, New NCERT) (IAS Pre 2023)*

1. the Chief Wildlife Warden of the State becomes the governing authority of such forest.
2. hunting is not allowed in such areas.
3. people in such areas are allowed to collect non-timber forest produce.
4. people of such area are allowed traditional agricultural practices.

How many of the statements given above is/are correct?

(a) Only one (b) Only two
(c) Only three (d) All four

Ans. (c)

Exp. Only three statements i.e., (1), (2) and (3) are correct. As per the Section 33 of the Wildlife Protection Act (WLPA), once the Centre notifies an area as a community reserve, the Chief Wildlife Warden of the state becomes the governing authority of the forest, whose consent is required for all decisions pertaining to the area. After a forest has been made into a community reserve, people are not allowed to hunt there, thus hunting is prohibited in community reserves. The people of community reserves are allowed to collect non-timber forest produce.

Statement (4) is incorrect because the people of community reserves are not allowed to use community reserves for traditional agricultural practices such as shifting (jhum) cultivation.

2 **Consider the given statements with reference to Wildlife Protection Act, 1972.** *(Chap 2, Class-X, New NCERT)*

1. It includes the species of endangered animals and plants.
2. It consists of list of protected species at all-India level.
3. Projects for conservation of specific species have been started under this Act.

How many of the statements given above is/are correct?

(a) Only one (b) Only two
(c) All three (d) None of these

Ans. (d)

Exp. All three statements i.e., (1), (2) and (3) are correct with reference to Wildlife Protection Act, 1972. This Act has divided the protection status of various plants and animals under the six schedules.

Schedule I to VI contain list of animals and plants from endangered to regulated. The Act provides for the protection of wild animals, birds and plants. All the animals in Schedule I of the Wildlife Protection Act are granted protection from poaching, killing, trade etc. Some of the projects for specific species are Project Snow Leopard, Project Tiger and Project Elephant.

3 **The most important strategy for the conservation of biodiversity together with traditional human life is the establishment of** *(Chap 2, Class-X, New NCERT) (IAS Pre 2014)*

(a) biosphere reserves (b) botanical gardens
(c) national parks (d) wildlife sanctuaries

Ans. (a)

Exp. The most important strategy for the conservation of biodiversity together with traditional human life is the establishment of biosphere reserves. The biosphere reserves help to maintain the biodiversity and culture of that area. Botanical garden is a collection of living plants designed chiefly to illustrate relationships within plant groups. A national park is a natural park that is used for conservation purposes. It is created and protected by national governments. A wildlife sanctuary is an area where animals and birds can live protected and safe in their natural habitats, away from poaching or trafficking.

4 **If a particular plant species is placed under Schedule VI of the Wildlife Protection Act 1972, what is the implication?** *(Chap 2, Class-X, New NCERT) (IAS Pre 2020)*

(a) A license is required to cultivate that plant
(b) Such a plant cannot be cultivated under any circumstances.
(c) It is a genetically modified crop plant.
(d) Such a plant is invasive and harmful to the ecosystem

Ans. (a)

Exp. If a particular plant species is placed under Schedule VI of the Wildlife Protection Act 1972, a licence is required to cultivate that plant. The Indian Parliament enacted the Wildlife (Protection) Act in 1972, which provides for the safeguard and protection of the wildlife (flora and fauna) in the country. The Act created six schedules which gave varying degrees of protection to classes of flora and fauna.

5 **Consider the following statements.** *(Chap 5, Class-XI, New NCERT)*

1. Keystone species perform a check and balance over the population of other species in an ecosystem.
2. Keystone species are also called Ecosystem Engineers.
3. Keystone species have high functional redundancy.

Which of the statements given above is/are correct?

(a) Only 1 (b) 2 and 3
(c) 1 and 3 (d) None of these

Ans. (a)

Exp. Only statement (1) is correct. Keystone species perform a check and balance over the population of other species in an ecosystem. Keystone species is a species whose addition to or loss from an ecosystem leads to major changes in the occurrence of at least one other species. All top predators are considered as keystone species because they regulate all other animals' population indirectly.

Statements (2) and (3) are incorrect. Keystone species are not Ecosystem Engineers. Ecosystem engineers modify, create and maintain habitats. They modify their habitats through their own biology or by physically changing biotic and abiotic factors in the environment.

Keystone species have low functional redundancy. This means that if the species were to disappear from the ecosystem, no other species would be able to fill its ecological niche. The ecosystem would be forced to radically change, allowing new and possibly invasive species to populate the habitat.

6 It is a series of protected areas, which are linked through a global network, which aims to demonstrate the relationship between conservation and development. *(Chap 2, Class-VIII, New NCERT)*

The statement given above describes which of the following?

(a) National Park (b) Wildlife Sanctuary
(c) Biosphere Reserve (d) World Heritage Site

Ans. (c)

Exp. Biosphere Reserve is a series of protected areas, which are linked through a global network, which aims to demonstrate the relationship between conservation and development. It includes terrestrial, marine and coastal ecosystems. Each site promotes solutions reconciling the conservation of biodiversity with its sustainable use. The main aim of biosphere reserve is to preserve genetic diversity in representative ecosystems. It is done by protecting wild animals, traditional life style of inhabitant and domesticated plant/animal genetic resources.

7 Which of the following statements is/are correct about Project Tiger? *(Chap 2, Class-X, New NCERT)*

1. Project Tiger was started in 1973 in India by IUCN.
2. Tiger conservation reserves have been established under Project Tiger in many states.
3. It has not improved the population of tigers even after a long period of its implementation.

Codes

(a) Only one (b) Only two
(c) All three (d) None of these

Ans. (a)

Exp. Only one statement i.e., (2) is correct with reference to Project Tiger. Project Tiger is a Tiger Conservation Programme launched in April 1973 by the Government of India. The various tiger reserves were created in the country under Project Tiger.

Shivalik-Terai Conservation Unit, North-East Conservation Unit and Sunderbans Conservation Unit are some of the tiger conservation reserves. Project Tiger has been successful in increasing the population of the tigers. As per 2023 Census report, there are 3167 tigers in India.

8 Consider the given statements with reference to Man and Biosphere (MAB) Programme. *(Chap 5, Class-XI, New NCERT)*

1. This programme is an international programme started by UNESCO.
2. India has also taken conservation measures under this programme.
3. Nilgiri Biosphere Reserve has been recognised under the World Network of Biosphere Reserves under this programme.

How many of the statements given above is/are correct?

(a) Only one (b) Only two
(c) All three (d) None of the above

Ans. (c)

Exp. All statements i.e., (1), (2) and (3) are correct with reference to Man and the Biosphere (MAB) Programme. It is an intergovernmental scientific programme, launched in 1971 by United Nations Educational, Scientific and Cultural Organisation (UNESCO). It aims to establish a scientific basis for the improvement of relationships between people and their environments.

India has also taken conservation measures under this programme. There are total 18 biosphere reserves in India from which 12 are also part of UNESCO's Man and Biosphere Programme.

Hill ranges of Nilgiris and its surrounding environment were constituted as Nilgiris Biosphere Reserve by UNESCO in September 1986 under the MAB Programme.

9 If you visit the famous Kaziranga National Park, which of the following wildlife you may see? *(Chap 5, Class-XI, New NCERT)*

1. One horned rhino
2. Bengal tiger
3. Golden Langur
4. Swamp deer
5. Feral horse
6. Wild water buffalo

Codes

(a) 1, 2, 3, 4 and 5 (b) 1, 3, 4, 5 and 6
(c) 1, 2, 4 and 6 (d) 1, 2, 3 and 4

Ans. (c)

Exp. Option (c) is correct. The KazirangaNational Park hosts two-thirds of the world's greater one horned rhinoceros. Kaziranga has the largest population of the Wild water buffalo anywhere, accounting for about 57% of the world population. Kaziranga has one of the highest densities of tigers in the world (1 per 5 km^2). There are 118 Royal Bengal Tigers, according to the latest census. It is also an important breeding ground of Swamp Deer. The one horned rhinoceros, Royal Bengal Tiger, Asian elephant, wild water buffalo and swamp deer are collectively known as the 'Big Five' of Kaziranga.

Feral or wild horses are found only in the Dibru-Saikhowa National Park in India. Golden Langur endemic to Western Assam, India, and Southern Bhutan. It is not found in Kaziranga National Park.

10 **Match the following lists correctly and choose the correct codes.** *(Chap 2, Class-X, New NCERT)*

List I (Protected Areas)	List II (Located in)
A. Bandipur National Park	1. Madhya Pradesh
B. Manas Tiger Reserve	2. Assam
C. Bandhavgarh National Park	3. Karnataka
D. Corbett National Park	3. Uttarakhand

Codes

	A	B	C	D		A	B	C	D
(a)	3	2	1	4	(b)	1	2	3	4
(c)	2	3	1	4	(d)	1	3	2	4

***Ans.* (a)**

Exp. The correct matching is A-3, B-2, C-1, D-4.

Bandipur National Park It has the second highest tiger population in India. It is located in Karnataka.

Manas National Park It is a national park, UNESCO Natural World Heritage site, a Project Tiger reserve, an elephant reserve and a biosphere reserve in Assam.

Bandhavgarh National Park It is spread at Vindhya hills in Madhya Pradesh.

Corbett National Park It is located in Nainital, Uttarakhand. It is regarded as first national park of India established in 1936.

11 **Consider the following is not recognised by UNESCO under its world network of biosphere reserves.** *(Chap 5, Class-XI, New NCERT)*

1. Simlipal Biosphere Reserve
2. Jim Corbett National Park
3. Sunderban National Park
4. Nokrek Biosphere Reserve

Codes

(a) 1 and 2 (b) Only 2 (c) 1, 2 and 3 (d) 4 and 3

***Ans.* (b)**

Exp. Jim Corbett National Park is not recognised by UNESCO under its world network of biosphere reserves. Simlipal Biosphere Reserve is a national park and a Tiger Reserve situated in the Northern part of Odisha's, Mayurbhanj district. It is under MAB programme of UNESCO since 2009. Sundarban Biosphere Reserve received the recognition of UNESCO under its Man and Biosphere (MAB) Programme in November, 2001.

The Nokrek Biosphere Reserve is located in the North-East of India on the Tura Range, which forms part of the Meghalaya Plateau.

12 **Consider the following statements with reference to biosphere reserves in India.** *(Chap 5, Class-XI, New NCERT)*

1. Sunderbans was the first biosphere reserve to be established in India.
2. Nokrek Biosphere Reserve is located in Manipur.
3. The Gulf of Mannar Biosphere Reserve is a marine biosphere reserve located in the Indian Ocean.
4. Biosphere Reserves can be established in India under the Wildlife Protection Act.

How many of the statements given above is/are correct?

(a) Only one (b) Only two (c) Only three (d) All four

***Ans.* (b)**

Exp. Only two statements i.e., (3) and (4) are correct with reference to biosphere reserves in India. The Gulf of Mannar, the first marine biosphere reserve is located in the South and South-East Asia of Indian Ocean. In India, the Gulf of Mannar region in Tamil Nadu is one of the four major coral reef areas. The Gulf of Mannar is one of the biologically richest coastal regions in all of mainland of India.

Biosphere Reserves can be established in India under the Wildlife Protection Act.

Statement (1) and (2) are incorrect. The Nilgiri Biosphere Reserve is India's first biosphere reserve. Nokrek Biosphere Reserve is located in Meghalaya not in Manipur.

13 **Consider the following statements with reference to Nilgiri Biosphere Reserve.** *(Chap 5, Class-XI, New NCERT)*

1. The biosphere reserve consists of evergreen forests known as Shola forests.
2. It has a large population of lion tailed Macaque and Tahr.
3. More than 50% of flowering plant species in Western Ghats are located in this region.

Which of the statements given above is/are correct?

(a) Only 1 (b) Only 2 (c) 1 and 3 (d) 1, 2 and 3

***Ans.* (d)**

Exp. All the given statements are correct with reference to Nilgiri Biosphere Reserve. The Shola montane temperate grasslands of the Nilgiri reserve are a treasure house of rare plant species. The Nilgiri Biosphere Reserve is very rich in plant diversity.

About 3,300 species of flowering plants can be seen here which is more than 50% of species in Western Ghats. The reserve hosts largest population of endangered lion tailed Macaque, Nilgiri Tahr and vulnerable Nilgiri langur.

14 **"This national park is located in the Chambal region, that forms part of Sheopur-Shivpurideciduous open forest landscape and is estimated to have a capacity to sustain cheetahs. It offers the prospect of housing four big cats of India - tiger, lion, leopard and cheetah and allowing them to coexist. It is also a part of the Khathiar- Gir dry deciduous forests ecoregion".** *(Chap 5, Class-XI, New NCERT)*

Which of the following is referred to in the above lines?

(a) Kuno National Park
(b) Bandhavgarh National Park
(c) Gir National Park
(d) Nauradehi Wildlife Sanctuary

***Ans.* (a)**

Exp. Kuno National Park (KNP) in Madhya Pradesh is 748 sq. km. in area forming part of Sheopur-Shivpuri (Khathiar-Gir dry deciduous forests ecoregion) deciduous open forest landscape. Kuno offers the prospect of housing four big cats of India - tiger, lion, leopard and cheetahs. In 2018, it was given the status of a national park. In the 1990s, it was selected as a possible site to implement the Asiatic Lion Reintroduction Project, which aimed at establishing a second lion population in India. Most of the inhabitants were Saharia tribal people. In January 2022, environment ministry launched the action plan for reintroducing cheetahs in India, starting with Kuno National Park.

15 Consider the following statements with reference to Sundarban National Park. *(Chap 5, Class-XI, New NCERT)*

1. It is known for the Asiatic lion.
2. It consists of mangrove type of vegetation.
3. The Mangroves of Sunderbans are known for *Heritiera fomes*, used for timber.

Which of the statements given above is/are incorrect?

(a) 1 and 2 (b) 1 and 3
(c) Only 1 (d) All of these

Ans. (c)

Exp. Statement (1) is incorrect with reference to Sunderban National Park because it known as the house of numerous Bengal tigers (not Asiatic Lion).

White tigers are also spotted in the dense woods of Sundarbans. It is the largest delta and mangrove forest in the world. *Heritiera fomes* is the dominant mangrove species in the area. Its local name, sundari, gives the Sunderban region its name.

16 Consider the following pairs. *(Chap 5, Class-IX, NCERT)*

Tiger Reserves Region		States
1. Dudhwa	–	Uttar Pradesh
2. Dampa	–	Arunachal Pradesh
3. Sitanadi-Udanti	–	Odisha
4. Kawal	–	Andhra Pradesh

How many of the pairs given above is/are incorrectly matched?

(a) Only one (b) Only two (c) Only three (d) All four

Ans. (a)

Exp. Only one pair i.e., (1) is correctly matched. The Dudhwa Tiger Reserve is a protected area in Uttar Pradesh. It shares the North-Eastern boundary with Nepal, which is defined to a large extent by the Mohana river. The area is a vast alluvial floodplain traversed by numerous rivers and streams flowing in South-Easterly direction.

Pairs (2), (3) and (4) are incorrectly matched. Dampa Tiger Reserve or Dampha Tiger Reserve is a tiger reserve of Western Mizoram. Sitanadi-Udanti Tiger Reserve came into existence in the year 2008-09, are two separate reserves (Udanti and Sitanadi Wildlife Sanctuaries) combined together. It is located in the Gariaband district, Chhattisgarh.Kawal Tiger Reserve is located at Jannaram mandal of Mancherial district (Old Adilabad district) in Telangana.

17 Which of the given pairs is/are correctly matched? *(Chap 5, Class-XI, New NCERT)*

Biosphere Reserve		States
1. Dehang-Debang	–	Sikkim
2. Dibru-Saikhowa	–	Assam
3. Khangchendzonga	–	Arunachal Pradesh

Codes

(a) Only 1 (b) Only 2 (c) Only 3 (d) None of these

Ans. (b)

Exp. Pair (2) is correctly matched.
Dibru-Saikhowa National Park is a national park located in Dibrugarh and Tinsukia districts of Assam.

Pairs (1) and (3) are incorrectly matched. Dihang-Dibang or Dehang-Debang is a biosphere reserve constituted in 1998. It is located in the Indian state of Arunachal Pradesh.

Khangchendzonga National Park also known as Kanchenjunga Biosphere Reserve is a national park and a biosphere reserve located in Sikkim.

18 Consider the following pairs regarding Ramsar sites. *(Chap 5, Class-IX, NCERT)*

Wetlands		States/Regions
1. Bakhira	–	Rajasthan
2. Khijadia	–	Gujarat
3. Shallabugh	–	Himachal
4. Haigam	–	Jammu and Kashmir

How many of the pairs given above is/are correctly matched?

(a) Only one (b) Only two
(c) Only three (d) All the four

Ans. (b)

Exp. Pairs (2) and (4) are correctly matched.
Khijadia Wildlife Sanctuary is a bird sanctuary located in Jamnagar district of Gujarat.

Haigam Wetland Conservation Reserve is located in Baramulla district of Jammu and Kashmir.

Pairs (1) and (3) are incorrectly matched because the Bakhira Bird Sanctuary is the largest natural flood plain wetland of India in Sant Kabir Nagar district of Eastern Uttar Pradesh.

Shallabugh Wetland Conservation Reserve is located in the district Srinagar, Union Territory of Jammu and Kashmir.

19 The Cold Desert Biosphere Reserve in Himachal Pradesh, consists of which of the following regions? *(Chap 5, Class-XI, New NCERT*

1. Pin Valley National Park
2. Kibber Wildlife Sanctuary
3. Chandratal Wildlife Sanctuary

How many of the options given above is/are correct?
(a) Only one (b) Only two
(c) All three (d) None of these

Ans. (d)

Exp. All the three options i.e., (1), (2) and (3) are correct about the Cold Desert Biosphere Reserve. It is a biosphere reserve located in the Western Himalayas region, within Himachal Pradesh state in North India. Cold Desert has an area of 7,770 sq. km (1,920,000 acres). It includes Pin Valley National Park, Chandratal, Sarchu and Kibber Wildlife Sanctuary.

20 Arrange the given biosphere reserves in North to South and choose the correct answer using the codes given below. *(Chap 5, Class-XI, New NCERT)*

1. Panchmarhi 2. Nokrek 3. Nilgiri 4. Nanda Devi

Codes
(a) 1-2-3-4 (b) 3-4-2-1 (c) 4-2-1-3 (d) 3-4-1-2

Ans. (c)

Exp. The correct sequence is 4-2-1-3. North to South arrangement of biosphere reserves given in question is Nanda Devi (Uttarakhand), Nokrek (Meghalaya), Panchmarhi (Madhya Pradesh) and Nilgiri (Kerala).

21 Which of the given pairs is/are not correctly matched? *(Chap 5, Class-XI, New NCERT)*

Biosphere Reserve		States
(a) Kachchh Biosphere Reserve	–	Gujarat
(b) Panna Biosphere Reserve	–	Madhya Pradesh
(c) Achanakmar-Amarkantak Reserve	–	Odisha
(d) Sesachalam Biosphere Reserve	–	Andhra Pradesh

Ans. (c)

Exp. Pair (c) is not correctly matched. Achanakmar-Amarkantak Biosphere Reserve is a part of Annupur and Dindori districts of Madhya Pradesh and Bilaspur district of Chhattisgarh.

22 Which one of the following National Parks lies completely in the temperate alpine zone? *(Chap 2, Class-X, New NCERT) (IAS Pre 2019)*

(a) Manas National Park
(b) Namdapha National Park
(c) Neora Valley National Park
(d) Valley of Flowers National Park

Ans. (d)

Exp. Among the given options, Valley of Flowers National Park (Uttarakhand) lies completely in the temperate alpine zone.

The Alpine forests are found all along the Himalaya at altitude ranging between 2500 m to 3500 m. Valley of Flowers National Park is located at 3352 to 3658 m above sea level.

23 Which of the following statements is/are correct regarding Dachigam National Park? *(Chap 16, Class-XI, New NCERT)*

1. It is located in Jammu and Kashmir.
2. Dachigam National Park is known for the conservation of Hangul, a rare and critically endangered species.

Codes
(a) Only 1
(b) Only 2
(c) Both 1 and 2
(d) Neither 1 nor 2

Ans. (c)

Exp. Both the statements (1) and (2) are correct regarding Dachigam National Park. The Dachigam National Park is located in Jammu and Kashmir. The park is best known as the home of the rare and critically endangered Hangul or Kashmir stag located high among its interiors is the Marsar lake. Dagwan river is also flows here.

24 Which of the given pairs is/are correctly matched? *(Chap 16, Class-XI, New NCERT)*

(a) Salim Ali Bird Sanctuary	–	Bihar
(b) Bharatpur Bird Sanctuary	–	Rajasthan
(c) Sultanpur Bird Area	–	Punjab

(d) All of the above

Ans. (b)

Exp. Pair (b) is correctly matched as Bharatpur Bird Sanctuary or Keoladeo Ghana National Park, is home to the finest birds and faunal species. It is located in the state of Rajasthan.

Pairs (a) and (c) are incorrectly matched because Salim Ali Bird Sanctuary is located in Goa. Sultanpur Bird Area is located in the state of Haryana.

Chapter 31

Climate Change, Greenhouse Effect and Ozone Depletion

Climate Change, Greenhouse Effect and Ozone Depletion

Climate Change

Climate Change

- Significant variation of average weather conditions observed over a period of time.

Causes of Climate Change

- **Natural Causes** Continental drift, decrease in sunspots raising the global temperature, volcanic activity etc
- **Anthropogenic Causes** Deforestation, burning of fossil fuels, industrialisation and urbanisation, modern agricultural practices etc
- **Global Warming**
  - Increased amount of carbon dioxide in the air causes global warming
  - Impacts of global warming melting of ice, rise in sea levels, change in ocean currents
  - Impacting biodiversity leading to habitat

Missions Related to Climate Change

- National action plan on climate change
- National solar mission
- National mission on sustainable habitat
- National water mission
- National mission for sustainable Agriculture, etc

Climate Change Mitigation Methods

- Carbon dioxide capture and sequestration
- Carbon tax is levied on carbon content of fuels
- Carbon footprint, a measure of impact that human activities have on environment

Greenhouse Effect

Greenhouse Effect

A naturally occurring phenomenon that blankets the Earth's lower atmosphere and warms it thereby maintaining a suitable temperature for living conditions

Greenhouse Gases

- **Carbon Dioxide** absorbs infrared radiations and affects stratospheric ozone
- **Methane** Absorbs infrared radiations, affects tropospheric ozone, produces carbon dioxide
- **Nitrous Oxide** absorbs infrared radiations and affects stratospheric ozone
- **Ozone** (ground layer) absorbs ultraviolet and infrared radiations
- **Carbon Monoxide** affects stratospheric ozone and hydrogen cycles, produces carbon dioxide
- **Chlorofluorocarbons** absorbs ultraviolet and infrared radiations
- **Water vapours** forms a part of hydrological cycle
- **Sulphur dioxide** forms aerosols which scatter solar radiation

Ozone Depletion

Ozone Layer Depletion

- Ozone is a higly reactive gas made up of three oxygen atoms
- It influences life on Earth
- Compounds like CFCs destroy the ozone and cause its depletion
- **Causes** CFCs used in refrigerants, Halogens used in fire extinguishers, etc

Consequences

- Depletion causes UV rays to enter the troposphere which damages the DNA and causes mutation
- Causes ageing of skin, damage to skin cells and also skin cancers
- Inflammation of cornea, cataract, etc
- Increases evaporation of surface water through stomata and decreases the moisture content of soil

Acid Rain

- Acid from the atmosphere is deposited on scatter solar radiation at the Earth's surface
- **Causes**
  Burning of fossil fuels
  Vehicular emissions
  Natural sources like lightening strikes, volcanic eruptions, etc
- **Impacts**
  - Harmful for agriculture, trees and plants as it dissolves and washes away the nutrients
  - Causes respiratory ailments in humans
  - Corrodes water pipes leading to leaching of heavy metals in drinking water
  - Damages structures and buildings made of stone and metal

SOURCE New NCERT Class XI *(World Climate and Climate Change)*
New NCERT Class XII *(Geographical Perspective on Selected Issues and Problems)*

Climate Change

1 Consider the following statements with reference to climate change. *(Chap 12, Class-XI, New NCERT)*

1. Climate change is a natural as well as man-made process.
2. Climate change can result in improving the fertility and productivity of soil.
3. Climate change is responsible for melting of polar ice caps.

Which of the statements given above is/are correct?

(a) 1 and 2
(b) 2 and 3
(c) Only 3
(d) All of the above

Ans. (d)

Exp. All the given statements (1), (2) and (3) are correct with reference to climate change. Climate change is the long-term alteration of temperature and typical weather patterns in a place.

It can result in improving the fertility and productivity of soil. The cause of current climate change is largely human activity, like burning fossil fuels, natural gas, oil, and coal. Polar ice caps are melting as global warming causes climate change. Planet as a whole is affected by changes in these polar regions as ice melts.

2 Which of the following natural factors is/are responsible for causing climate change? *(Chap 12, Class-XI, New NCERT)*

1. Sunspots and solar flares
2. Changes in the Earth's axial tilt (Milankovitch cycle)
3. Volcanic eruptions

Codes

(a) Only one (b) Only two
(c) All three (d) None of these

Ans. (c)

Exp. All the given options i.e., (1), (2) and (3) are natural factors responsible for causing climate change.

Climate change has been caused by many natural factors. It includes changes in the sunspot and solar flares, emissions from volcanoes, variations in Earth's orbit and levels of Carbon dioxide (CO_2). Global climate change has typically occurred very slowly, over thousands or millions of years.

3 Which of the following can be considered as most probable effects of climate change on humans? *(Chap 12, Class-XI, New NCERT)*

1. Crop failure
2. Severe drought
3. Severe flood

Codes

(a) 1 and 3 (b) 1 and 2 (c) Only 2 (d) 1, 2 and 3

Ans. (d)

Exp. Crop failure, severe drought and severe flood are the most probable effects of climate change on humans. The warmer temperatures associated with climate change are projected to significantly reduce yields of the world's staple food crops. Climate change induced by increasing greenhouse gases is likely to affect crops differently from region to region.

Climate change is increasing the levels of water vapour in the atmosphere and is making water availability less predictable. This can lead to more intense rain storms in some areas, while other regions may face more severe drought conditions, especially during the summer months.

4 Consider the following statements regarding Dissolved Oxygen (DO). *(Chap 13, Class-XII, NCERT Biology)*

1. Decomposition of organic matter increases the Dissolved Oxygen (DO) of the water.
2. Chemical Oxygen Demand (COD) lowers the concentration of DO in water.
3. The concentration of DO is varied by respiration and photosynthesis only.

Which of the statements given above is/are correct?

(a) 1 and 3 (b) 1 and 2
(c) Only 2 (d) Only 1

Ans. (b)

Exp. Statements (1) and (2) are correct.

Decomposition of organic matter increase the dissolve oxygen into the water as dissolved oxygen levels drop in water body that contains a lot of dead decomposing material.

Chemical Oxygen Demand (COD) lowers the concentration of Dissolve Oxygen (DO) into water. A reduction in DO can lead to anaerobic conditions.

Statement (3) is incorrect because dissolved oxygen concentrations are constantly affected by diffusion and aeration, photosynthesis, respiration and decomposition.

5 Which of the given statements is/are correct with reference to climate change and global warming? *(Chap 12, Class-XI, New NCERT)*

1. The rate of increase in temperature of the Earth has slowed down after 1940.
2. Extreme variability in climate has resulted in devastating droughts in the Sahara region during 1967.

Codes

(a) Only 1 (b) Only 2
(c) Both 1 and 2 (d) Neither 1 nor 2

Ans. (c)

Exp. Both the statements (1) and (2) are correct with reference to climate change and global warming.

Global average temperatures got down by about 0.2°C after 1940 and remained low until 1970, after which they began to climb rapidly again.

Thus, it shows that the rate of increase in temperature of the Earth has slowed down after 1940.

Climate variability refers to the climatic parameter of a region varying from its long-term mean. It has resulted in devastating droughts in the Sahara region during 1967.

6 In the context of mitigating the impending global warming due to anthropogenic emissions of carbon dioxide, which of the following can be potential sites for carbon sequestration?

(Chap 12, Class-XI, New NCERT) (IAS Pre 2017)

1. Abandoned and uneconomic coal seams
2. Depleted oil and gas reservoirs
3. Subterranean deep saline formalities

Codes

(a) 1 and 2 (b) Only 3 (c) 1 and 3 (d) 1, 2 and 3

Ans. (d)

Exp. Carbon sequestration is the process of storing atmospheric carbon dioxide. The potential sites for carbon sequestration are abandoned and uneconomic coal seams, depleted oil and gas reservoirs and subterranean deep saline formalities.

7 Consider the following pairs. *(Chap 34, Module-1, NIOS)*

Waste treatment process		Feature
1. Sanitary landfills	–	Leaching
2. Vermiculture	–	Fungi and bacteria
3. Pyrolysis	–	Burning without oxygen
4. Incineration	–	Burning under controlled oxygen

How many pairs given above is/are correctly matched?

(a) Only one (b) Only two
(c) Only three (d) All four pairs

Ans. (d)

Exp. All the four pairs i.e., (1), (2), (3) and (4) given are correctly matched.

Sanitary landfills involve the disposal of waste in a manner that minimises environmental hazards, one of which is leaching.

Vermiculture involves the use of worms to decompose organic waste. During this process, fungi and bacteria play a crucial role.

Pyrolysis is a process that involves the thermal decomposition of materials at elevated temperatures in an inert atmosphere, i.e., without oxygen.

Incineration is the process of burning waste, biomass, or other inorganic and organic materials under controlled conditions, in the presence of oxygen.

Greenhouse Effect

8 Which of the following greenhouse gases is/are responsible for global warming?

(Chap 16, Class-XII, New NCERT)

1. Carbon dioxide
2. Water vapour
3. Methane
4. Chlorofluorocarbons

Codes

(a) 1 and 3 (b) 1, 2 and 3
(c) 1, 2 and 4 (d) All of these

Ans. (d)

Exp. Carbon dioxide, water vapour, methane and chlorofluorocarbons are responsible for global warming. Greenhouse gases include water vapour, carbon dioxide, methane, nitrous oxide, ozone and some artificial chemicals such as chlorofluorocarbons (CFCs). The absorbed energy warms the atmosphere and the surface of the Earth leading to global warming.

9 Consider the following statements with reference to global warming. *(Chap 16, Class-XII, New NCERT)*

1. Increase in greenhouse gases results in erratic changes in the climate.
2. Global warming results in increase in sea level over a period of time.
3. Ozone depletion is caused mainly due to global warming.
4. Carbon dioxide is the largest contributor to global warming among all other gases.

Which of the statements given above is/are incorrect?

(a) 1 and 3 (b) 3 and 4 (c) Only 3 (d) 1 and 4

Ans. (c)

Exp. Statement (3) is incorrect with reference to global warming because the main cause of ozone depletion and the ozone hole is manufactured chemicals, especially manufactured halocarbon refrigerants, solvents, propellants and foam-blowing agents (CFCs, HCFCs, halons).

Ozone Depletion

10 Consider the following statements.

(Chap 12, Class-XI, New NCERT

1. Chlorofluorocarbons are responsible for depletion of ozone layer, which results in melting of glaciers
2. Chlorofluorocarbons are mainly emitted by natural sources.
3. Carbon dioxide is a major CFC gas.

How many of the statements given above is/are correct?

(a) Only one (b) Only two
(c) All three (d) None of these

Ans. (a)

Exp. Only one statement i.e., (1) is correct. Chlorofluorocarbons (CFCs) are mainly responsible for ozone depletion in the stratosphere. CFC in the stratosphere are broken down by UV rays and release chlorine atom. The faster melting of glacier is a result of temperature increase brought on by global warming. Statements (2) and (3) are incorrect because CFCs are not emitted by natural resources it is an anthropogenic compounds that have been released into the atmosphere Carbon dioxide is greenhouse gas not CFC gas.

11 **Consider the following statements.**

(Chap 12, Class-XI, New NCERT)

1. Kyoto Protocol is an international agreement which came into force in 2005.
2. The Nagoya Protocol aims to reduce the harmful effects of chlorofluorocarbons on the ozone layer.

Which of the statements given above is/are incorrect?

(a) Only 1 (b) Only 2
(c) Both 1 and 2 (d) Neither 1 nor 2

Ans. (b)

Exp. Statement (2) is incorrect because the Nagoya Protocol is a global agreement that implements the access and benefit-sharing obligations of the Convention on Biological Diversity (CBD).

12 **Consider the following Assertion (A) and Reason (R) and choose the correct code.**

(Chap 16, Class-XII, New NCERT)

Assertion (A) Ozone layer is formed by continuous action of Ultraviolet rays over molecular oxygen.

Reason (R) The Montreal Protocol, signed in 1987 aims to reduce the emission of ozone depléting substances in the atmosphere.

Codes

(a) Both A and R are true and R is the correct explanation of A.
(b) Both A and R are true, but R is not the correct explanation of A.
(c) A is true, but R is false.
(d) A is false, but R is true.

Ans. (b)

Exp. Both Assertion (A) and Reason (R) are true, but Reason (R) is not the correct explanation of Assertion (A). Ozone is formed naturally through the interaction of solar Ultraviolet (UV) radiation with molecular oxygen (O_2).

The Montreal Protocol on substances that deplete the ozone layer (the Montreal Protocol) is an international agreement made in 1987.

It was designed to stop the production and import of ozone depleting substances and reduce their concentration in the atmosphere to help protect the Earth's ozone layer.

13 **Ozone depleting substances such as CFCs are usually used in the refrigeration and air-conditioning industries. If the amount of these substances increases, the thickness of ozone layer decreases. Which of the following can be the possible effects of decline in thickness of ozone layer?**

(Chap 16, Class-XII, New NCERT)

(a) Premature ageing of skin and skin cancer
(b) Snow blindness and cataract
(c) Inflammation in the lungs
(d) Both a and b

Ans. (d)

Exp. Premature ageing of skin, skin cancer, snow blindness and cataract can be possible effects of decline in thickness of ozone layer. Ozone layer depletion causes increased ultraviolet radiation levels at the Earth's surface, which is damaging to human health. Negative effects include increases in certain types of skin cancers, eye cataracts and immune deficiency disorders.

Chapter 32

Environmental Issues

Environmental Issues

Environmental Pollution

Effect of undesirable changes in our surroundings that have harmful effects on plants, animals and human beings. Substances which cause pollution are called pollutants

Other Environmental Issues

- Soil erosion
- Desertification
- Deforestation

Air Pollution

- Occurs due to undesirable solid or gaseous particles, particulate matter in the air in quantities that are harmful to human health
- Air pollutants are gaseous pollutants (oxides of sulphur, nitrogen, carbon, ozone) and particulate matter (dust, mist, fumes)
- **Effects**
  - Irritation of eyes, nose, throat, respiratory ailments like asthama, bronchities, etc
  - Hamrful to vegetation, animals, cattle, etc
  - Acid deposition and acid rain
- **Measures to Control Air Pollution**
  - Electrostatic precipitator to be used in thermal power plants Scrubber to remove harmful gases
  - Catalytic convertors to be fitted in automobiles to remove harmful gases; Catalytic convertors to be fitted in automobiles to remove harmful gases
  - Proper maintenance of automobiles along with the use of lead free petrol or diesel

Noise Pollution

- State of unbearable and uncomfort to humans caused by noise from different sources
- Main sources are factories, mechanised construction, demolition works etc
- **Measures to Prevent Noise Pollution**
  - Turning off appliances at home and office
  - Close the door when using noisy machines
  - Obey the noise level

Soil Pollution

- Addition of substances to the soil which adversely affect the physical, chemical and biological properties of soil and reduces its productivity
- **Measures to Prevent Soil Pollution**
  - Reducing the use of chemical fertilsers and pesticide
  - Use of biofertilisers and biopesticides
  - Organic farming
  - Soil waste treatment
  - Afforestation and reforestation

Water Pollution

- Generating from human activities, when pollutants through different ways reaches surface or ground water
- Point sources are municipal wastes and industrial discharge, etc; Non-point sources are agricultural runoff, acid rain, etc
- **Meaures to Control Water Pollution**
  - Clean Water Act and other such acts to regulate the processing of released water from industries
  - Preventing soil erosion to reduce the amount of sediment buildup in water bodies

Other Types of Pollution

- **Radioactive Pollution**
  - Generated as a byproduct of nuclear reactors, fuel processing plants, hospitals and research units
  - It can be prevented by safe disposal of nuclear waste, regular monitoring and taking safety measures
- **Solid Waste Pollution**
  - Solid waste is everything that goes out in trash. It can be biodegradable waste, non-biodegradable waste and recyclable waste
  - It can be prevented by creating lanfills, open dumps, incineration plants, pyrolysis techniques, etc
- **E-waste Pollution**
  - E-wastes are the irreparable electronic goods that are buried or dumped.
  - It can be prevented by recycling, generating awareness, etc

Wildlife Conservation Schemes

Government Initiatives

- The Air (Prevention and Control of Pollution) Act
- National Air Quality Index
- National Air Quality Monitoring Programme
- National Ambient Air Quality Standards, etc

SOURCE Old NCERT Class IX *(Human Impact on Environment)*, New NCERT Class XI *(World Climate and World Climate Change)*, New NCERT Class XII *(Environmental Issues 'Biology')*, New NCERT Class XII *(Geographical Perspective on Selected Issues and Problems)*

Pollution

1 **Consider the following statements regarding atmospheric gases.** *(Chap 16, Class-XI, New NCERT)*

1. Carbon monoxide and nitrogen oxide gases are mainly emitted from the exhaust of automobiles.
2. Motor vehicle exhaust emissions are known to contain carbon monoxide and nitrogen oxides.
3. Hydrofluorocarbons are man-made organic compounds.

How many statements given above is/are correct?

(a) Only one (b) Only two
(c) All three (d) None of these

Ans. (c)

Exp. All three statements i.e., (1), (2) and (3) are correct regarding atmospheric gases. Carbon monoxide and nitrogen oxide gases are mainly emitted from the exhaust of automobiles.

Motor vehicle exhaust emissions are known to contain carbon monoxide, nitrogen oxides, hydrocarbons, suspended particulate matter and a small amount of sulphur dioxide. It is the major cause of global warming. Hydrofluorocarbons are man-made organic compounds, They are frequently used in air conditioning and refrigerator.

2 **Among the following crops, which one is the most important anthropogenic source of both methane and nitrous oxide?** *(Chap 11, Class-XI, NCERT)(IAS Pre 2022)*

(a) Cotton (b) Rice (c) Sugarcane (d) Wheat

Ans. (b)

Exp. The most important anthropogenic source of both methane and nitrous oxide among the crops listed is rice. Agriculture is estimated to account for 10%–20% of anthropogenic Greenhouse Gas (GHG) emissions worldwide. In 2005, it accounted for 50% and 60% of the total anthropogenic methane (CH_4) and nitrous oxide (N_2O) emissions, respectively. Rice paddies are considered one of the most important sources of methane and nitrous oxide emissions, which have attracted considerable attention due to their contribution to global warming.

3 **Which of the following gases/particles is mainly responsible for causing air pollution?** *(Chap 16, Class-XII, New NCERT)*

1. Hydrocarbons 2. PM 2.5
3. Carbon dioxide 4. Nitrogen

Codes

(a) 1 and 3 (b) 1 and 4 (c) 2 and 4 (d) 1 and 2

Ans. (d)

Exp. Hydrocarbons and PM 2.5 (Particulate Matters) are mainly responsible for causing air pollution.

A hydrocarbon is any compound that consists of carbon and hydrogen atoms. They are organic compounds.

60% of air pollution is caused due to automobiles that run on hydrocarbon-based fuels.

Fine particulate matter, PM 2.5 is an air pollutant. PM 2.5 are tiny particles in the air that reduce visibility and cause the air to appear hazy when levels are elevated.

4 **Burning of fuel in coal powered plants and factories releases from which of the following air pollutant?** *(Chap 11, Class-IX, Old NCERT)*

1. Lead 2. Sulphur dioxide
3. Nitrogen oxides

Codes

(a) Only 1 (b) 1 and 3
(c) 2 and 3 (d) 1, 2 and 3

Ans. (d)

Exp. Lead, sulphur dioxide and nitrogen oxides are air pollutants that release due to burning of fuel in coal powered plants. Sulphur dioxide (SO_2), which contributes to respiratory illnesses. Nitrogen oxides (NOx), which contribute to smog and respiratory illnesses.

Lead is the most toxic metal considered as a priority pollutant as an industrial pollutant, which enters in an environment *via* soil, air and water/wastewater.

5 **Consider the following statements with reference to acid rain.** *(Chap 11, Class-IX, Old NCERT)*

1. Carbon monoxide in the atmosphere is the main constituent of acid rain.
2. Acid rain damages the agriculture crops due to the reaction of hydrogen sulphate with water vapour.
3. Sulphur dioxides and nitrogen oxides are mixed in rainwater to form acid rain.
4. Ozone is a primary pollutants which is responsible for formation of acid rain.

How many statements given above is/are correct?

(a) Only one (b) Only two
(c) Only three (d) All four

Ans. (b)

Exp. Only two statements i.e., (2) and (3) are is correct with reference to acid rain. Acid rain results when sulphur dioxide (SO_2) and nitrogen oxides (NOx) are emitted into the atmosphere and transported by wind and air currents. The SO_2 and NOx react with water, oxygen and other chemicals to form sulphuric and nitric acids.

Both of these mix with water and other materials before falling to the ground. Acid rain is very harmful to agriculture, plants and animals. it damages the root system of plant.

Statement (1) and (4) are incorrect. Pollution from burning of fossil fuels is the main constituent of acid rain not carbon monoxide.

Sulphur dioxide is a primary pollutants that is responsible for formation of acid rain.

6 **Which of the following is/are the most probable effects of acid rain on human and natural ecosystem?** *(Chap 11, Class-IX, Old NCERT)*

1. Damage to rainforests
2. Decline in productivity of fishes
3. Respiratory diseases

Codes

(a) Only 1 (b) 1 and 2 (c) 2 and 3 (d) None of these

Ans. (b)

Exp. Damage to rainforests and decline in productivity of fishes are the most probable effects of acid rain on human and natural ecosystem. Acid rain can be extremely harmful to forests. Acid rain also causes aluminium to be released into the soil, which makes it difficult for trees to take up water. High concentrations of dissolved aluminium released from soils often enter streams and lakes damaging fish gills and impair respiration.

7 **Which of the following steps will be the most helpful in reducing the harmful effects of air pollution in the urban areas?** *(Chap 16, Class-XII, New NCERT)*

1. Promoting the use of leaded petrol in automobiles.
2. Using CNG as a fuel in public transport.
3. Promoting Bharat Stage VI standards.
4. Promoting use of electrostatic precipitator.

Codes

(a) 1, 2, 3 and 4 (b) 2, 3 and 4
(c) 1, 3 and 4 (d) 1, 2 and 4

Ans. (d)

Exp. All the given options will be the most helpful steps in reducing the harmful effects of air pollution in the urban areas. Proper maintenance of automobiles along with use of lead-free petrol or diesel can reduce the pollutants they emit. CNG burns most efficiently, unlike petrol or diesel, in the automobiles and very little of it is left unburnt.

As per Bharat Stage-VI norms, the emission of carbon monoxide is to be reduced by 30% and (NOx) by 80%. The BS-VI norms also set limits for hydrocarbon and particulate emissions, which were not specified in earlier norms. Electrostatic precipitators are important tools in the process of cleaning up flue gases. They are used in industries kike steel plants and thermal energy plants.

8 **Consider the following statements with reference to Air (Prevention and Control of Pollution) Act.** *(Chap 16, Class-XII, New NCERT)*

1. It was enacted by the Government of India in 1987.
2. Noise has been categorised as an air pollutant under this Act.

Which of the statements given above is/are incorrect?

(a) Only 1 (b) Only 2
(c) Both 1 and 2 (d) Neither 1 nor 2

Ans. (a)

Exp. Statement (1) is incorrect with reference to the Air (Prevention and Control of Pollution) Act because the act was enacted by Government of India in 1981 and it was amended in 1987 to include noise as an air pollutant. Noise is undesired high level of sound. Noise causes sleeplessness, increased heartbeat, altered breathing pattern, thus considerably stressing humans.

9 **Magnetite particles suspected to cause neurodegenerative problems are generated as environmental pollutants from which of the following?** *(Chap 16, Class-XII, New NCERT) (IAS Pre 2021)*

1. Brakes of motor vehicles
2. Engines of motor vehicles
3. Microwave stoves within homes
4. Power plants
5. Telephone lines

Codes

(a) 1, 2, 3 and 5 (b) 1, 2 and 4
(c) 3, 4 and 5 (d) 1, 2, 3, 4 and 5

Ans. (b)

Exp. Among the given factors (1), (2) and (4) are correct with reference to magnetic particles suspected to cause neurodegenerative problems.

They are fine dust emitted by metallurgical industry, brakes of motor vehicles are the major source of airborne magnetite at the roadside petrol and diesel-engine exhaust and power plants.

Magnetic nanoparticles are a class of nanoparticle that can be manipulated using magnetic fields. Such particles commonly consist of two components, a magnetic material, often iron, nickel and cobalt, and a chemical component that has functionality.

Water and Noise Pollution

10 **Which of the following pollutants of water is/are considered most difficult to remove from water among others?** *(Chap 16, Class-XII, New NCERT)*

(a) Small plastic material (b) Toxic metals
(c) Inorganic solid particles (d) Large metal pieces

Ans. (b)

Exp. Among the given options, toxic metals are most difficult to remove from water.

Toxic metals, including 'heavy metals,' are individual metals and metal compounds that negatively affect people's health. After release from both natural and anthropogenic sources, heavy metals contaminate natural water bodies, sediments and soils.

11 **Which of the following constitutes a colloidal pollutant in water?** *(Chap 16, Class-XII, New NCERT)*

1. Sand and silt
2. Ammonia and phosphate
3. Bacteria and faecal matter
4. Calcium and nitrate

Select the correct answer from the codes given below.
(a) Only 1 (b) Only 2 (c) Only 3 (d) Only 4

Ans. (c)

Exp. Bacteria and faecal matter constitute a colloidal pollutant in water. Colloidal particles are small solid particles that are suspended in a fluid phase. Colloids are very low diameter particles which are responsible for the turbidity or the colour of surface water.

12 Which of the following is/are can be considered as a source of water pollution? *(Chap 12, Class-XII, New NCERT)*

1. Landslides 2. Plant and animal decay
3. Agriculture 4. Power plants

Codes
(a) Only 1 (b) Only 2
(c) 2 and 3 (d) All of these

Ans. (d)

Exp. All the given options can be considered as a source of water pollution. Large silt deposits as a result of landslides that can pollute the freshwater system mainly by increasing a freshwater systems' turbidity.

Agriculture, which accounts for 70% of water withdrawals worldwide, plays a major role in water pollution. Too much decaying plant and animal i.e., organic matter in water is a pollutant because it removes oxygen from water which can kill fish, shellfish and aquatic insects.

Power plants dump millions of tonnes of toxic pollutants into nation's waterways. Coal-fired power plants alone account for 72% of all toxic water pollution in the country.

13 Which of the following are some important pollutants released by steel industry in India? *(Chap 16, Class-XII, New NCERT) (UPSC Pre 2014)*

I. Oxides of sulphur 2. Oxides of nitrogen
3. Carbon monoxide 4. Carbon dioxide

Codes
(a) 1, 3 and 4 (b) 2 and 3
(c) 1 and 4 (d) 1, 2, 3 and 4

Ans. (d)

Exp. Important pollutants released by steel industry in India are oxides of sulphur, oxides of nitrogen, carbon monoxide and carbon dioxide. In steel furnace, coke reacts with iron ore, releasing iron and generating CO and CO_2 gases. Due to use of coal, pollutants such as SOx and NOx are released.

14 Contaminated water, due to water pollution of rivers and lakes, may have consider the following pollutants. *(Chap 12, Class-XII, New NCERT)*

1. Urea 2. Coliform 3. Arsenic

How many of the above is/are correct?
(a) Only one (b) Only two
(c) All three (d) None of these

Ans. (c)

Exp. Contaminated water, due to water pollution of rivers and lakes, may contain urea, coliform and arsenic. Urea contributes to the eutrophication of inland and coastal waters.

Coliform group is a large collection of different kinds of bacteria which have adverse effect on health.

Arsenic contamination of groundwater is a form of groundwater pollution which is often due to naturally occurring high concentrations of arsenic in deeper levels of groundwater.

15 Considered the following statements regarding dissolved oxygen *(Chap 11, Class-XI, NCERT)*

1. Biological Oxygen Demand (BO(D)is a better indicator to measure the concentration of required oxygen as compared to Chemical Oxygen Demand (COD).
2. COD measures the concentration of oxygen required for the oxidation of non-biodegradable matters while BOD measures the same for the degradable matter.
3. The dissolved oxygen is inversely proportional to the dissolved organic wastes in the water body.

Which of the statements given above is/are incorrect?
(a) 1 and 2 (b) Only 3
(c) Only 2 (d) 2 and 3

Ans. (a)

Exp. Statements (1) and (2) are incorrect with reference to dissolved oxygen as Chemical Oxygen Demand is better indicator to measure the concentration of dissolved oxygen. COD is the amount of oxygen required to chemically breakdown the pollutants. Whereas BOD is the amount of oxygen required to do this biologically through micro-organisms. There is a strong correlation between COD and BOD, however COD analysis is a much faster and more accurate method.

BOD measures the amount of oxygen utilised by aerobic microorganisms to breakdown organic matter in water. In contrast, COD measures the amount of oxygen needed to oxidise total organic and inorganic pollutants in water chemically without the involvement of microbes.

16 Which of the following statements is/are correct with reference to algal bloom? *(Chap 16, Class-XII, New NCERT)*

1. It is caused due to presence of large amount of nutrients in the water.
2. It involves rapid growth of planktonic algae in the water bodies.

Codes
(a) Only 1
(b) Only 2
(c) Both 1 and 2
(d) Neither 1 nor 2

Ans. (c)

Exp. Both the statements (1) and (2) are correct with reference to algal bloom.

An algal bloom is the overgrowth of microscopic algae or algae like bacteria in fresh, salt or brackish water. Higher concentrations of these nutrients in water cause increased growth of planktonic algae and green plants. Algal blooms are the result of an excess of nutrients (particularly phosphorus and nitrogen) into water.

17 Consider the following statements defines biomagnification in an aquatic ecosystem such as lakes and rivers. *(Chap 16, Class-XII, New NCERT)*

1. The natural ageing of a lake due to large amount of nutrient.
2. Increase in concentration of toxic substances with the increase in trophic levels.
3. Accumulation of waste water in the oceans.

Which of the statements given above is/are correct?

(a) Only 1 (b) Only 2 (c) 1 and 3 (d) 2 and 3

Ans. (b)

Exp. Only statement (2) is correctly defines biomagnification in an aquatic ecosystem.

Biomagnification occurs when the concentration of a pollutant increases from one link in the food chain to another.

It is the method of accruing toxic elements by different organisms within a food chain. For example, polluted fish will contaminate the next consumer and continues up a tropic food web as each level consumes another.

Statements (1) and (3) are incorrect. Eutrophication is the natural ageing of a lake due to large amount of nutrients. Accumulation of waste water in the oceans does not define biomagnification.

18 Which of the following statements is/are correct with reference to water hyacinth? *(Chap 16, Class-XII, New NCERT)*

1. It grows rapidly in water bodies where there is high level of eutrophication.
2. It causes imbalance in the water bodies.
3. It is an aquatic weed, which is commonly referred to as 'Terror of Bengal'.

Codes

(a) 1 and 2
(b) 2 and 3
(c) 1 and 3
(d) All of the above

Ans. (d)

Exp. All three statements i.e., (1), (2) and (3) are correct with reference to water hyacinth.

Water hyacinth grows rapidly in water bodies where there is high level of euthrophication. Euthrophication is the process in which a water body becomes overthy rich with nutrients, leading to the plentiful growth of simple plant life. Like algae, water hyacinth, etc.

It is a free-floating perennial aquatic plant. Water hyacinth has a strong capacity to absorb nutrients, heavy metals and organic pollutants. That is why it causes imbalance in the water bodies.

It is commonly referred to as 'Terror of Bengal'. This is because it hampers the growth of fish and other aquatic organisms by cutting down the supply of sunlight and dissolved oxygen in the water bodies.

19 Consider of the given factors is responsible for causing accelerated eutrophication. *(Chap 16, Class-XII, New NCERT)*

1. Increasing use of fertilisers in agriculture fields.
2. Discharging industrial waste into water bodies.
3. Use of phosphates for increasing plant growth.

How many statements given above is/are correct?

(a) Only one (b) Only two
(c) All three (d) None of these

Ans. (c)

Exp. All three statements i.e., (1), (2) and (3) are the responsible factors for causing accelerated eutrophication. Runoff of fertilisers from nearby field to the water body causes algal bloom which leads to eutrophication.

Sewage and industrial effluents increase the temperature and BOD of the water body, thereby causing increased biological activity, leading to algal blooms. Too much use of phosphorus can cause increased growth of algae and large aquatic plants, which can result in decreased levels of dissolved oxygen. This process is called eutrophication.

20 Which the following statements is/are correct with reference to water pollution in lakes? *(Chap 16, Class-XII, New NCERT)*

1. Thermal wastewater flowing out of electricity generation units causes damage to indigenous flora and fauna in a water body.
2. Cultural eutrophication is the radical acceleration in the ageing process of lakes due to human activities.

Codes

(a) Only 1
(b) Only 2
(c) Both 1 and 2
(d) Neither 1 nor 2

Ans. (c)

Exp. Both the statements (1) and (2) are correct with reference to water pollution in lakes. Thermal wastewater eliminates or reduces the number of organisms sensitive to high temperature.

Cultural or accelerated eutrophication is the phenomenon in which pollutants from man's activities like effluents from industries and homes can radically accelerate the ageing process of lake.

21 Which of the given methods cannot reduce the pollution of water in certain water bodies?

(Chap 16, Class-XII, New NCERT)

1. Treatment of land with the help of natural bacteria and fungi.
2. Chlorine treatment and filtering.
3. Using dry compost toilets.
4. Using Portland cement in construction.

Codes

(a) 1 and 2 (b) 2 and 4 (c) Only 4 (d) Only 3

Ans. (c)

Exp. Use of Portland cement in construction cannot reduce the pollution of water in certain water bodies. Ecological sanitation is a sustainable system for handling human excreta, using dry composting toilets. This is a practical, hygienic, efficient and cost-effective solution to human waste disposal. Appropriate plants, algae, fungi and bacteria neutralise, absorb and assimilate the pollutants. Hence, as the water flows through the marshes, it gets purified naturally.

22 Which of the statements given below is/are correct?

(Chap 16, Class-XII, New NCERT)

1. The Water (Prevention and Control of Pollution) Act was enacted in 1974.
2. EcoSan toilets in various parts of Kerala have been constructed under this Act.

Codes

(a) Only 1
(b) Only 2
(c) Both 1 and 2
(d) Neither 1 nor 2

Ans. (a)

Exp. Statement (1) is correct as Government of India has passed the Water (Prevention and Control of Pollution) Act, 1974 to safeguard our water resources.
Statement (2) is incorrect because EcoSan toilets have not been constructed under this Act. EcoSan toilet is a closed system that does not need water. When the pit of an EcoSan toilet fills up, it is closed and sealed.

23 Which of the given statements is/are incorrect with reference to noise pollution?

(Chap 12, Class-XII, New NCERT)

1. Sounds produced from only high intensity sources can cause psychological distress in humans.
2. Noise pollution can also cause stress, poor concentration and communication difficulties.

Codes

(a) Only 1 (b) Only 2
(c) Both 1 and 2 (d) Neither 1 nor 2

Ans. (a)

Exp. Statement (1) is incorrect because noise pollution can be caused from various sources and not only from high intensity sources.
There can be various sources of noise pollution such as sounds of vehicles, Bursting of crackers, loudspeakers at high volume, Air traffic noise, concentration sites and all sources can contribute to psychological distress.

Solid Waste

24 Consider the following with respect to Municipal solid waste generated from households.

(Chap 16, Class-XII, New NCERT)

1. Glass and metal 2. Organic food waste
3. Radium and molybdenum 4. Leather and textiles

Which of the above is/are not correct?

(a) Only 1 (b) Only 2 (c) Only 3 (4) Only 4

Ans. (c)

Exp. Municipal solid waste generated from households does not include **radium and molybdenum.** Municipal Solid Waste (MSW) includes all items from homes and businesses that people no longer have any use for. These wastes are commonly called trash or garbage and include items such as food, paper, plastics, textiles, leather, wood, glass, metals, sanitary waste in septic tanks and other wastes. Radium and molybdenum are examples of radioactive waste.

25 Which of the following techniques can be used to reduce the generation of harmful municipal solid waste in a region? *(Chap 16, Class-XII, New NCERT)*

1. Using polythene and plastic packaging.
2. Transporting solid waste to landfills outside the city.
3. Recycling and reuse of solid material generated by households.

Codes

(a) 1 and 2 (b) 1 and 3 (c) Only 3 (d) All of these

Ans. (c)

Exp. 'Recycling and reuse of solid material generated by households' can be used to reduce the generation of harmful municipal solid waste in a region. Separating, recovering and reusing components of solid waste that may still have economic value is called recycling.
The essence of reuse is that it preserves some or all of the energy and materials that went into making an item. Landfills are sites designated for dumping rubbish, garbage or other sorts of solid wastes.

26 Consider the following statements with reference to e-waste generated by households.

(Chap 16, Class-XII, New NCERT)

1. It is buried in landfills in huge quantities in the developing countries.
2. Recycling of e-waste involves exposure to toxic substances.

Which of the statements given above is/are correct?

(a) Only 1 (b) Only 2
(c) Both 1 and 2 (d) Neither 1 nor 2

Ans. (c)

Exp. Both the statements (1) and (2) are correct with reference to e-waste generated by households.

E-waste buried in landfills in huge quantities in the developing countries. Also the recycling of e-waste involves exposure to toxic substances.

Electronic waste or e-waste describes discarded electrical or electronic devices. It also contain chemicals that are harmful to people and the environment. For example mercury, lead, beryllium, brominated flame retardants and cadmium.

27 Consider the following statements with reference to polyblend. *(Chap 16, Class-XII, New NCERT)*

1. It is made up of recycled plastic substances.
2. It can be used for construction of roads by mixing it with bitumen.
3. It has been developed by Government of India in partnership with UNEP.

Which of the statements given above is/are correct?

(a) 1 and 3 (b) 1 and 2
(c) 2 and 3 (d) All of these

Ans. (b)

Exp. Statements (1) and (2) are correct with reference to polyblend. It is a colloidal mixture of two or more polymers, particularly man-made fibres or modified recycled plastic. Plastic manufacturers made it for recycling plastic waste.

Polybends can be used for construction of road by mixing it with bitumen. When blended which bitumen, polyblend can be used to lay roads which have increased road life.

Statement (3) is incorrect because polyblend has been developed in collaboration with RV College of Engineering and the Bengaluru City Corporation.

28 Consider the following statements regarding solid waste management. *(Chap 12, Class-XII, New NCERT)*

1. Untreated municipal waste will lead to release of toxic biogas over a period of time.
2. Municipal waste can be converted to energy and compost with the help of suitable technologies.
3. Solid waste in urban areas can be reduced with the help of organic farming.
4. Municipal waste may lead to diseases such as diarrhoea and malaria.

How many statements given above is/are incorrect?

(a) Only one (b) Only two
(c) Only three (d) None of these

Ans. (a)

Exp. Only one statement i.e., (3) is incorrect because solid waste management may be defined as the discipline associated with the control of generation, collection, storage, transfer and transport, processing and disposal of solid wastes. Most cities and towns in India dispose of their waste by depositing it in low-lying areas outside the city, without taking adequate precautions.

Land Degradation and Desertification

29 Consider the following statements with reference to land degradation. *(Chap 16, Class-XII, New NCERT)*

1. Over cultivation and soil erosion results in land degradation in rural areas.
2. Persistent land degradation over a period of time results in desertification of land.
3. Cartagena Protocol is an international agreement which aims at reducing land degradation.

How many statements given above is/are correct?

(a) One only (b) Two only
(c) All three (d) None of these

Ans. (b)

Exp. Only two statements i.e., (1) and (2) are correct with reference to land degradation. Rural land degradation basically means soil deterioration. Soil is said to be deteriorated if it cannot support the vegetation cover that it previously supported.

Degradation occurs when the soil is exposed to erosion. Desertification is a form of land degradation by which fertile land becomes desert.

Statement (3) is incorrect because Cartagena Protocol on Biosafety to the Convention on Biological Diversity is an International Agreement on Biosafety. It is a supplementary agreement to the United Nations Convention on Biological Diversity (CBD).

30 Consider the following statements regarding landslides. *(Chap 11, Class-XI, NCERT)*

1. Landslides are a type of mass wasting, which denotes any down-slope movement of soil and rock under the direct influence of gravity.
2. About 12.6% of the land area of our country is prone to landslide hazards.
3. The National Disaster Management Authority and is undertaking a 'National Landslide Susceptibility Mapping' in country

Which of the statements given above are correct?

(a) 1 and 2 (b) 2 and 3
(c) 1 and 3 (d) 1, 2 and 3

Ans. (a)

Exp. Statements (1) and (2) are correct. Landslides are a type of 'mass wasting,' which denotes any down-slope movement of soil and rock under the direct influence of gravity. The term 'landslide' encompases five modes of slope movement: falls, topples, slides, spreads and flows. According to Geological Survey of India, about 0.42 million sq. km or 12.6% of land area, excluding snow covered area, is prone to landslide hazard. Out of this, 42% falls in North East Himalaya, including Darjeeling and Sikkim Himalaya.

Statement (3) is incorrect because National Landslide susceptibility mapping is undertaken by Geological Survey of India since 2014-15.

31 **Which of the given programs is/are associated with conservation of land and forest resources?**

(Chap 16, Class-XII, New NCERT)

1. Chipko Movement
2. Joint Forest Management (JFM)
3. Beej Bachao Andolan

Codes

(a) 1 and 2
(b) 2 and 3
(c) 1 and 3
(d) All of the above

Ans. (d)

Exp. All the programs given above are associated with conservation of land and forest resources.

Chipko Movement was a non-violent social and ecological movement by rural villagers particularly women in India in the 1970s. It aimed at protecting trees and forests slated for government-backed logging.

Joint Forest Management is a concept of developing relationships between fringe forest groups and forest department on the basis of mutual trust and jointly defined roles and responsibilities for forest protection and development.

Beej Bachao Andolan was a people's movement to conserve indigenous seeds and promote traditional agricultural practices.

32 **Consider the following.**

(Chap 11, Class-XI, NCERT) (IAS Pre 2022)

1. Carbon monoxide
2. Nitrogen oxide
3. Ozone
4. Sulphur dioxide

Excess of which of the above in the environment is/are causes of acid rain?

(a) 1, 2 and 3 (b) 2 and 4
(c) Only 4 (d) 1, 3 and 4

Ans. (b)

Exp. Option (b) is correct with respect to acid rain. Acid rain is primarily caused by the emissions of nitrogen oxide (NOx) and sulphur dioxide (SO_2). These compounds react with water molecules in the atmosphere to produce acids. Therefore, among the options given, nitrogen oxide and sulphur dioxide are the causes of acid rain.

33 **Assertion** (A) Soil pollution is more dangerous as compared to industrial pollution.

Reason (R) Fertiliser and pesticide enter into food cycle. *(Chap 16, Class-XII, New NCERT)*

Codes

(a) Both A and R are true and R is the correct explanation of A.
(b) Both A and R are true, but R is not the correct explanation of A.
(c) (A) is true, but R is false.
(d) (A) is false, but R is true.

Ans. (a)

Exp. Both A and R are true and R is the correct explanation of A.

Soil pollution is more dangerous as compared to industrial pollution as fertilisers and pesticides used on crops enter into food cycle, which effects human health.

One of the main danger of soil pollution is that it can enter the food cycle, when crops are grown in polluted soil.

Chapter 33

Sustainable Development

Sustainable Development

Sustainable Development

- Concept was emphasised by United Nations Conference on Environment and Development (UNCED) which was also known as Earth Summit (1992)
- Development that meets the needs of present generation without compromising the ability of future generation to meet their own needs
- A multi-dimensional concept signifying the positive, irreversible transformation of the society, economy and environment
- United Nations has approved 17 Sustainable Development goals (SDGs) as a universal call of action for sustainable development

Objectives of Sustainable Development

- Aims at decreasing the absolute poverty of poor; Minimise resource depletion, environment degradation, cultural disruption and social instability

Parameters of Sustainable Development

- **Inter-generational Equity** Use of Earth's resources in a manner that the present generation does not consume it completely
- **Intra-generational Equity** Being fair in utilisation of resources among human members of present generation
- **Carrying Capacity** Number of individuals who can be supported in a given area within the natural resource limits
- **Gender Inequality** Due to unequal responsibilities over man and woman

Measures for Promotion of Sustainable Development

- Revamped cropping patterns
- Measures to reduce water loss
- Achieving social sustainability
- Achieving economic sustainability
- Solar power through photovoltaic cells
- CNG in urban areas
- Wind power
- Traditional knowledge and practices

Fundamental Ideas of Sustainable Development

- **Adaptability** Ability to adapt to changing environment
- **Renewability** Rate of utilisation of renewable resources should be lower than or equal to rate of regeneration
- **Interdependence** Neither imports resources due to deprivation and nor exports its wastes
- **Substitution** Ensuring substitution of non-renewable resources by use of renewable natural resources

Strategies for Achieving Sustainable Development

- **Lifestyle** Including the food we eat, how we interact with others, etc
- **Population** Population growth, population ageing and decline, migration and urbanisation needs to be addressed
- **Conservation** Maintenance and sustainability of resources in a rational manner

SOURCE *New NCERT Class X (Resources and Development), New NCERT Class XII (Planning and Sustainable Development in Indian Context)*

1 **Which of the following statements is/are correct about sustainable development?**

(Chap 1, Class-X, New NCERT)

1. The concept of sustainable development was introduced by Brundtland Commission Report in 1987.
2. The report 'Our Common Future' promoted the concept of sustainable development for the conservation of our resources.
3. Sustainable development advocates the use of resources keeping in mind the needs of future generation.

Codes

(a) 1 and 2 (b) 2 and 3 (c) Only 1 (d) 1, 2 and 3

Ans. (d)

Exp. All the statements (1), (2) and (3) are correct about sustainable development. The modern concept of sustainable development is derived mostly from the 1987 Brundtland Commission Report of 1987.

Our Common Future, also known as the Brundtland Report, was published on October 1987 by the United Nations through the Oxford University Press. Brundtland Commission defined sustainability as 'meeting the needs of the present without compromising the ability of future generations to meet their own needs'.

2 **Consider the following with reference to sustainable development.** *(Chap 9, Class-XII, New NCERT)*

1. Only social and economic aspects
2. Both ecological and economic aspects
3. Social, economic and ecological aspects
4. Only ecological aspects

Select the most appropriate answer using the codes given below.

(a) Only 1 (b) Only 2 (c) Only 3 (d) Only 4

Ans. (c)

Exp. Sustainable development takes social, economic and ecological aspects into account for development. The three main pillars of sustainable development include economic growth, environmental protection and social equality.

Economic growth is the pillar that most groups focus on when attempting to attain more sustainable efforts and development. Social equality and equity are pillars of sustainable development that focus on the social well-being of people.

3 **Consider the following statements with reference to 'Agenda 21' for sustainable development.**

(Chap 1, Class-X, New NCERT)

1. It was signed in the Rio Earth Summit in 1992.
2. It aims to combat environmental damage by global cooperation.
3. It involves local agendas that are to be drawn by local governments.

How many of the statements given above is/are correct?

(a) Only one (b) Only two
(c) Only three (d) None of these

Ans. (c)

Exp. All three statements i.e., (1), (2) and (3) are correct with reference to 'Agenda 21' for sustainable development. Agenda 21 is a non-binding action plan of the United Nations with regard to sustainable development. It was signed in the Rio Earth Summit in 1992.

The implementation of Agenda 21 was intended to involve action at international, national, regional and local levels. One major objective of the Agenda 21 initiative is that every local government should draw its own local Agenda 21. Its aim initially was to achieve global sustainable development by 2000. Agenda 21 is referring to the original target of the 21st century.

4 **Consider the following statements about sustainable development and its principles.**

(Chap 6, Class-XII, New NCERT)

1. According to the United Nations Conference on Environment and Development (UNCED), sustainable development is defined as development that meets the needs of the present generation without compromising the ability of future generations to meet their own needs.
2. The concept of 'needs' in the definition of sustainable development is primarily linked to the equitable distribution of resources.
3. Edward Barbier's perspective on sustainable development emphasises increasing the material standard of living of the poor at the grassroots level, measured quantitatively through factors like income, education, healthcare, sanitation and water supply.
4. The Brundtland Commission highlights the moral obligation to protect the future generation by handing over a well-maintained planet Earth.

How many of the statements given above is/are correct?

(a) Only one (b) Only two (c) Only three (d) All four

Ans. (d)

Exp. All four statements i.e., (1), (2), (3) and (4) are correct.

The United Nations Conference on Environment and Development (UNCED) indeed defines sustainable development as development that meets the needs of the present generation without compromising the ability of future generations to meet their own needs.

The concept of 'needs' in the definition of sustainable development is primarily linked to the essential needs of the world's poor, to which overriding priority should be given. Edward Barbier's perspective on sustainable development emphasises that per capita welfare should not decline over time. The minimum condition is ensuring that any depletion of natural capital is compensated by reproducible and human capital, so that the value of the aggregate stock does not decrease.

The Brundtland Commission, chaired by Norwegian Prime Minister Gro Harlem Brundtland, explored the causes of environmental degradation, attempted to understand the interconnections between social equity, economic growth, and environmental problems, and developed policy solutions that integrated all three areas. This indeed highlights the moral obligation to protect future generations by handing over a well-maintained planet Earth.

5 **Consider the following statements.**

(Chap 9, Class-XII, New NCERT) (IAS Pre 2016)

1. The Sustainable Development Goals were first proposed in 1972 by a global think tank called the 'Club of Rome'.
2. The Sustainable Development Goals have to be achieved by 2030

Which of the statements given above is/are correct?

(a) Only 1 (b) Only 2
(c) Both 1 and 2 (d) Neither 1 nor 2

Ans. (b)

Exp. Only statement (2) is correct as the Sustainable Development Goals have to be achieved by 2030. Statement (1) is incorrect because the Sustainable Development Goals (SDG) were adopted by all United Nations member states in 2015 to end poverty, reduce inequality and build more peaceful prosperous societies by 2030.

6 **Given below are two statements, one is labelled as Assertion (A) and the other as Reason (R).**

Assertion (A) There is a positive relation between Human Development Index (HDI) and Sustainable Develoment Goals (SDGs) ranking of Indian state.

Reason (R) The underlying dimension of SDG targets are closely related to education and health aspect.

(Chap 9, Class-VII, New NCERT) (UPPSC Pre 2019)

Select the correct answer from the codes given below.

(a) Both A and R are true and R is the correct explanation of A.
(b) Both A and R are true, but R is not the correct explanation of A.
(c) A is true, but R is false.
(d) A is false, but R is true.

Ans. (a)

Exp. Both Assertion (A) and Reason (R) are true and Reason (R) is the correct explanation of Assertion (A). Indian states with higher HDIs also tend to have higher SDG rankings. For example, Kerala, which has the highest HDI in India, also has the highest SDG ranking. Conversely, Indian states with lower HDIs also tend to have lower SDG rankings. For example, Bihar, which has the lowest HDI in India, also has the lowest SDG ranking.

Education and health are two of the most important underlying dimensions of the SDGs. Education is essential for breaking the cycle of poverty and inequality. It also empowers people to make informed decisions about their lives and to contribute to their communities. Health is essential for a productive and fulfilling life. It is also essential for sustainable development, as healthy people are more likely to be economically active and to protect the environment.

7 **Arrange the following events in chronological order.**

(Chap 6, Class-XII, New NCERT) (UPPSC Pre 2020)

1. Rio Earth Summit
2. Publication of Brundtland Commission Report
3. Enforcement of Montreal Protocol
4. Publication of 'The Limit to Growth' Report

Select the correct answer from the codes given below

(a) 1, 4, 3, 2 (b) 4, 2, 3, 1
(c) 4, 3, 2, 1 (d) 4, 1, 3, 2

Ans. (b)

Exp. The correct chronological order is 4, 2, 3, 1. The Limits to Growth is a 1972 report that discussed the possibility of exponential economic and population growth with finite supply of resources, studied by computer simulation.

In 1987, the United Nations Brundtland Commission defined sustainablitliy as "meeting the needs of the present without compromising that ability of future generations to meet their own needs."

The Montreal Protocol is an international treaty designed to protect the ozone layer by phasing out the production of numberous substances that are responsible for ozone depletion. It was agreed on 16th September, 1987 and entered into force on 1st January, 1989. The United Nations Conference on Environment and Development also known as the Rio Conference or the Earth Summit, was a major United Nations Conference held in Rio de Janeiro from 3rd June to 14th June, 1992.

8 **What is Rio+20 Conference, often mentioned in the news?**

(Chap 6, Class-XII, New NCERT) (IAS Pre 2015)

(a) It is the United Nations Conference on Sustainable Development.
(b) It is Ministerial Meeting of the World Trade Organisation.
(c) It is a Conference of the Inter-Governmental Panel on Climate Change.
(d) It is Conference of Member Countries of the Convention on Biological Diversity.

Ans. (a)

Exp. Rio +20 Conference, often mentioned in the news because it is the United Nations Conference on Sustainable Development (UNCDS). The United Nations Conference on Sustainable Development, also known as Rio 2012, Rio +20 or Earth Summit, 2012 was the third International Conference on Sustainable Development.

Chapter 34

Disaster Management

Disaster Management

Natural Disasters

Introduction

- A result of natural or man-made causes leading to sudden disruption of normal life and causing severe damage to life and property

Earthquake

- Most unpredictable and highly destructive. There can be tectonic earthquakes (due to Earth movements) as well as volcanic earthquakes (due to volcanic activities)
- **Earthquake Zones**
  - Zone-I-Very high damage risk zone
  - Zone-II-High damage risk zone
  - Zone-III-Moderate damage risk zone
  - Zone-IV-Low damage risk zone
  - Zone-V-Very low damage risk zone
- **Hazard Mitigation**
  - Establishing earthquake monitoring centers for regular monitoring and dissemination of information
  - Use of Geographical Positioning System (GPS) for monitoring the movement of tectonic plates
  - Preparing a vulnerability map of the country
  - Modifying the house types and building designs

Tsunami

- Known as seismic sea waves, the sudden displacement of ocean channel blocking due to rock falls, floods due to diversion of river water caused by earthquakes or volcanic eruptions
- **Causes** Earthquakes generated in subduction zone, sudden motion of ocean floor due to earthquake, volcanic eruption or underwater landslide

Tropical Cyclones

- Intense low pressure areas in the atmosphere aroud which high velocity wind blows. Center of cyclone is warm and low pressure with a cloudless core known as eye
- **Tropical Cyclones In India** The extensive coastal belt of India is very vulnerable to the dadlay storms known as tropical cyclones. Some of the devastating cyclones that have hit India so far are, Cyclone Thane in 2001, Odisha Super Cyclone in 1999, Cyclone Nilofar in 2014, etc Cyclone Biparjoy made landfall in Gujarat on 15th June, 2023

Floods

- Inundation of land and human settlements caused by the rise of water in the channels and its spill over
- This occur when water as surface run off exceeds the carrying capacity of the streams and river channels
- **Causes** Heavy rainfall, sediment deposition, deforestation, cyclones, tsunamis, change in course of rivers, etc
- **Flood Mitigation**
  - Mapping of flood prone areas. Warning systems
  - Land use control to reduce the danger of loss of life and property

Landslides

- Rapid sliding of large mass of bedrocks, largely controlled by macro, regional or highly localised factors
- **Mitigation**
  - Construction of bunds to reduce the flow of water. Terrace farming
  - Restricting the construction and development activities like compared to other natural hazards roads, dams, etc in highly vulnerable areas

Man-made Disasters and Disaster Management in India

Droughts

- A prolonged time of scarcity of water due to insufficient precipitation, excessive rate of evaporation and over-utilisation of water from reservoirs or other storages
- **Man-made Disaster** Chemical spills, hazardous material spills, explosive, chemical or biological attacks, nuclear blasts are all instances of man-made disasters
- **Mitigation** Drought monitoring i.e., continuous observation of rainfall, storage reservoirs water levels, etc Rain water harvesting

Disaster Management in India

- Involves planning and responding to natural disasters to mitigate damage
- Three stage
  - **Pre Disaster Management** Generating data and spread awareness
  - **During Disaster** Conducting rescue and relief operations Construction of shelters and camps
  - **Post Disaster** Rehabilitation and recovery of victims. Capacity building for future disaster

SOURCE New NCERT Class XI *(Natural Hazards and Disasters)*

Earthquake and Tsunami

1 Which of the following statements is/are correct with respect to earthquake zones in India?

(Chap 7, Class-XI, New NCERT)

1. National Institute of Disaster Management is formed with collaboration of National Geophysical Laboratory and Geological Survey of India.
2. India is divided into five earthquake zones.

Codes

(a) Only 1 (b) Only 2
(c) Both 1 and 2 (d) Neither 1 nor 2

Ans. (c)

Exp. Both statements (1) and (2) are correct with respect to earthquake zones in India. National Institute of Disaster Management is formed with collaboration of National Geophysical Laboratory and Geological Survey of India, Department of Meteorology and Government of India. India is divided into five earthquake zones i.e.,

(i) Very high damage risk zone
(ii) High damage risk zone
(iii) Moderate damage risk zone
(iv) Low damage risk zone
(v) Very low damage risk zone.

2 Consider the following statements regarding National Disaster Response Force (NDRF).

(Chap 7, Class-XI, New NCERT)

1. It is a statutory body created under Disaster Management Act, 2005.
2. It works directly under the Prime Minister's Office.
3. It comes to the rescue during situations of natural disasters only.

Which of the statements given above is/ are true?

(a) 1 and 2
(b) Only 1
(c) 1 and 3
(d) 2 and 3

Ans. (b)

Exp. Only statement (1) is correct regarding the National Disaster Response Force (NDRF).

The NDRF was constituted under the Disaster Management Act, of 2005. Its purpose is to provide specialised response to both natural and man-made disasters. The Act mandates the establishment of the NDRF as a statutory body.

Statements (2) and (3) are incorrect.

The NDRF does not work directly under the Prime Minister's Office. Instead, it operates under the unified command of the Director-General (DG) of NDRF.

The NDRF responds to a wide range of disasters, including both natural and man-made emergencies. It is not limited to natural disasters alone.

3 Consider the following statements about Tsunami waves.

(Chap 7, Class-XI, New NCERT)

1. Tsunami waves are generated by the force produced by Moon on the Earth.
2. Tsunami waves move at a faster rate near the coast than in the deep ocean.
3. Tsunami waves are generally known as shallow water waves.

How many of the statements given above is/are not correct?

(a) Only one (b) Only two
(c) Only three (d) None of these

Ans. (a)

Exp. Only one statement i.e., (2) is not correct about Tsunami waves. Tsunamis are giant waves caused by earthquakes or volcanic eruptions under the sea.

The speed of a tsunami depends on the depth of the water it is travelling through. Therefore, Tsunami waves move at a faster rate in the deep ocean than near the coast.

4 Consider the following natural calamities.

(Chap 7, Class-XI, New NCERT)

1. Urban Floods
2. Landslides
3. Nuclear and Radiological Disaster
4. Tsunamis

How many of the above is/are included in the National Disaster Management Authority's 'Disaster' list?

(a) Only one (b) Only two
(c) Only three (d) All four

Ans. (d)

Exp. All four options i.e., (1), (2), (3) and (4) are correct.

The National Disaster Management Authority (NDMA), headed by the Prime Minister of India, is the apex body for Disaster Management in India. Setting up of NDMA and the creation of an enabling environment for institutional mechanisms at the State and District levels is mandated by the Disaster Management Act, 2005. NDMA is mandated to lay down the policies, plans and guidelines for Disaster Management. It involves the following disasters.

Natural Disaster : Earthquakes, Floods, Landslides, Cyclones, Tsunamis, Urban Floods, Heat Wave, Man-Made Disasters, Nuclear and Radiological Disaster, Chemical Disaster and Biological Disaster.

5 Consider the following statements about Tsunami.

(Chap 7, Class-XI, New NCERT)

1. It occurs due to lunar and solar gravitational forces.
2. The Indian Tsunami Early Warning System (ITEWS) established in 2007 is an integrated network of seismic stations and tide gauges.

Which of the statements given above is/are correct?
(a) Only 1
(b) Only 2
(c) Both 1 and 2
(d) Neither 1 nor 2
Ans. (b)

Exp. Only statement (2) is correct about Tsunami. The Indian Tsunami Early Warning System (ITEWS) established in 2007 is an integrated network of seismic stations and tide gauges.

Statement (1) is incorrect because it do not occurs due to lunar and solar gravitational forces. Tsunamis are usually caused by underwater earthquakes, but they can also result from volcanic eruptions, landslides, rapid changes in atmospheric pressure, or even meteorite impacts.

The Indian Tsunami Early Warning System comprises a real-time network of seismic stations, Bottom Pressure Recorders (BPR).

Landslides

6 Consider the following statements reference to landslides. *(Chap 7, Class-XI, New NCERT)*

1. Landslides are caused mainly due to localised factors rather than macro factors.
2. Geology and geomorphic agents play an important role in the occurrence of a landslide in a region.
3. Due to the localised occurrence of landslides, it has not been possible to make landslide vulnerability zones.
4. Forecasting and monitoring landslides is highly costly.

How many of the statements given above is/are not correct?
(a) Only one (b) Only two
(c) Only three (d) None of these
Ans. (a)

Exp. Only one statement i.e., (3) is not correct with reference to landslides. A landslide is the movement of rock, earth, or debris down a sloped section of land. Landslide-zone maps depict areas with a higher probability of landsliding.

The major landslide prone areas in India include the Western Ghats and Konkan Hills (Tamil Nadu, Kerala, Karnataka, Goa and Maharashtra), Eastern Ghats (Araku region in Andhra Pradesh), North-East Himalayas (Darjeeling and Sikkim) and North-West Himalayas (Uttarakhand, Himachal Pradesh, Jammu and Kashmir).

7 Consider the following pairs. *(Chap 7, Class-XI, New NCERT)*

Landslide Vulnerability Region	Zone
1. Very high	– Nilgiri hills
2. High	– Himachal Pradesh
3. Moderate and low	– Aravalli hills

How many of the pairs given above is/are correctly matched?
(a) Only one (b) Only two
(c) All three (d) None of these
Ans. (c)

Exp. All three pairs i.e., (1), (2) and (3) are correctly matched. Rainfall is the major triggering factor for landslides in Nilgiris and is under very high landslide vulnerable zones. Hilly areas of Himachal Pradesh are vulnerable to High landslides due to geological meteorological and anthropogenic factors. Aravallis hills are old mountains and thus having moderate and low landslides vulnerability.

8 In which of the following region, mining and subsidence largely contribute to landslides? *(Chap 7, Class-XI, New NCERT)*

1. Chhattisgarh 2. Karnataka
3. Jharkhand 4. Assam Plains

Codes
(a) 1 and 3 (b) 2, 3 and 4
(c) 1, 2 and 3 (d) All of these
Ans. (c)

Exp. Landslides due to mining and subsidence are most common in states like Jharkhand, Odisha, Chhattisgarh, Madhya Pradesh, Maharashtra, Andhra Pradesh, Karnataka, Tamil Nadu, Goa and Kerala. These are mineral rich states where lot of illegal and unscientific mining takes place which leads to landslides.

9 Which of the following steps, if taken, can mitigate the occurrence of landslides in a region? *(Chap 7, Class-XI, New NCERT)*

(a) Practising agriculture on steep slopes
(b) Encouraging terrace cultivation
(c) Promoting Jhumming
(d) All of the above
Ans. (b)

Exp. Encouraging terrace cultivation can mitigate the occurrence of landslides in a region. It is a common agriculture practice followed in mountain regions by creating terraces.

Terraces are horizontal human-made spaces created for the cultivation of crops on the slopes of hills and mountains. It should be encouraged in the North-Eastern hill states where Jhumming (Slash and Burn/Shifting Cultivation) is still prevalent .

Tropical Cyclones

10 Consider the following statements with reference to Tropical cyclones. *(Chap 7, Class-XI, New NCERT)*

1. Tropical cyclones are usually confined between 5° North and 5° South of the Equator.
2. The vertical extent of tropical cyclone is about 12-15 km.

3. A tropical cyclone lasts for 2-3 weeks.

Which of the statements given above is/are correct?

(a) 1 and 3 (b) Only 2 (c) Only 3 (d) All of these

Ans. (b)

Exp. Statement (2) is correct with reference to tropical cyclones. Tropical cyclones are intense low-pressure areas. The vertical extent of tropical cyclone is about 12-15 km.

Absence of strong vertical wind wedge, which disturbs the vertical transport of latent heat, is a pre-requisite for development of tropical cyclone.

Statements (1) and (3) are not correct because Tropical cyclones are confined to 10° North and 30° South of Equator. A tropical cyclone doesn't lasts for more than a week. Temperate cyclones lasts for 2-3 weeks.

11 With reference to Tropical cyclones in India, consider the following statements. *(Chap 7, Class-XI, New NCERT)*

1. Tropical cyclones develop in the months of October and November.
2. Tropical cyclones mainly occur in the Arabian Sea and Bay of Bengal.
3. Cyclonic circulations often result in Storm surge in the coastal areas.

How many of the statements given above is/are correct?

(a) Only one (b) Only two
(c) All three (d) None of these

Ans. (c)

Exp. All three statements i.e., (1), (2) and (3) are correct with reference to tropical cyclones in India. In case of the Bay of Bengal, cyclones mostly develop during the months of October and November.

Owing to its peninsular shape surrounded by the Bay of Bengal in the East and the Arabian Sea in the West, the tropical cyclones in India originate in these two important locations. Storm surges are oscillations in the period range of a few minutes to a few days in water levels in a coastal or inland body of water.

Floods and Droughts

12 With reference to flood, consider the following statements. *(Chap 7, Class-XI, New NCERT)*

1. Floods are slow in occurrence as compared to other disasters.
2. Floods do not occur at all in coastal regions of India.
3. Floods can be predicted easily as they occur during a particular period of time.

How many of the statements given above is/are correct?

(a) Only one (b) Only two
(c) Only three (d) None of these

Ans. (b)

Exp. Only two statements i.e., (1) and (3) are correct with reference to flood. Floods are relatively slow in occurrence and often, occur in well-identified regions and within expected time in a year.

Statement (2) is not correct as floods occur commonly when water in the form of surface run-off exceeds the carrying capacity of the river channels and streams and flows into the neighbouring low-lying flood plains.

13 Which of the following factors is/are responsible for causing floods? *(Chap 7, Class-XI, New NCERT)*

1. Deforestation
2. Storm surges
3. Rapid melting of glaciers
4. Colonisation of flood-plains

Codes

(a) 1 and 3 (b) 2, 3 and 4
(c) 1, 3 and 4 (d) All of these

Ans. (d)

Exp. All the given options are responsible for causing floods. Indiscriminate deforestation, storm surges, Rapid melting of glaciers, unscientific agricultural practices, Disturbances along the natural drainage channels and colonisation of flood-plains and River-beds are some of the human activities that play an important role in increasing the intensity, magnitude and gravity of floods.

Human beings play an important role in the genesis as well as spread of floods. Floods can also be caused due to a storm surge in the coastal regions.

14 Consider the following statements. *(Chap 7, Class-XI, New NCERT)*

1. Bihar and West Bengal are highly flood prone regions of India.
2. Some parts of Tamil Nadu experience floods during retreating monsoon season.
3. Flash floods are responsible for flooding in Gujarat, Haryana and Punjab.

How many of the statements given above is/are correct?

(a) Only one (b) Only two
(c) All three (d) None of these

Ans. (c)

Exp. All three statements i.e., (1), (2) and (3) are correct. Various states of India face heavy loss of lives and property due to recurrent floods. West Bengal and Bihar are among the high flood-prone states of India due to perennial rivers flowing from the Himalayas.

A flood caused by heavy or excessive rainfall in a short period of time, generally less than 6 hours. Tamil Nadu experiences flooding during November - January due to the retreating monsoon. Gujarat, Haryana and Punjab are also getting inundated in recent decades due to flash floods.

Disaster Mitigation

15 Consider the following statements.

(Chap 7, Class-XI, New NCERT)

1. UN has declared 1990-2000 as the decade of Natural Disaster Reduction.
2. The National Institute of Disaster Management was established in 1995.
3. The first World Conference on Disaster Management was held in Yokohama, Japan.

How many of the statements given above is/are correct?

(a) Only one (b) Only two
(c) All three (d) None of these

Ans. (c)

Exp. All three statements i.e., (1), (2) and (3) are correct. The United Nations General Assembly designated the 1990s as the International Decade for Natural Disaster Reduction (IDNDR).

National Institute of Disaster Management (NIDM) is a premier institute for training and capacity development programs for managing natural disasters in India, on a national as well as regional basis. It was established in 1995.

The First World Conference on Natural Disasters in Yokohama, Japan from 23rd to 27th May, 1994, adopted the Yokohama Strategy for a Safer world. Yokohama strategy provides guidelines for natural disaster prevention, preparedness and mitigation.

16 Consider the following statements.

(Chap 7, Class-XI, New NCERT)

1. Intensification of human activities results in increasing vulnerabilities to disasters.
2. The management of disasters is dependent upon socio-environmental conditions of different regions.
3. Unscientific land use and man-made pollution have increased the intensity of disaster.

How many of the statements given above is/are correct?

(a) Only one (b) Only two
(c) All three (d) None of these

Ans. (c)

Exp. All three statements i.e., (1), (2) and (3) are correct.
Intensification of human activities results in increasing vulnerabilities to disasters.

The management of disasters is dependent upon socio-environmental conditions of different regions.

Unscientific land use and man-made pollution have increased the intensity of disaster.

Vulnerability is the human dimension of disasters and is the result of the range of economic, social, cultural, institutional, political and psychological factors that shape people's lives and the environment that they live in poverty and inequality.

17 Which of the following is/are not the aims of Yokohama Strategy and Plan of action for a safer World?

(Chap 7, Class-XI, New NCERT)

1. Giving priority to developing countries in disaster management.
2. Strengthening national capacities and capabilities for preventing and mitigating disasters.
3. Providing $100 billion for disaster management to poor countries.

Codes

(a) Only 1 (b) Only 2
(c) Only 3 (d) 2 and 3

Ans. (c)

Exp. Statement (3) is not the aim of Yokohama strategy and Plan of action for a safer world. Yokohama strategy provides guidelines for natural disaster prevention, preparedness and mitigation.

There are ten principles of the Yokohama strategy for a safer world. The international community should provide financial, scientific and technological means, in the field of natural disaster reduction, to the developing countries, particularly the least developed countries. The development and strengthening of capacities to prevent, reduce and mitigate disasters is a top priority area to be addressed during the decade so as to provide a strong basis for follow-up activities to the decade.

18 Consider the following statements with reference to disaster mitigation in India.

(Chap 7, Class-XI, New NCERT)

1. Geological Survey of India and National Institute of Disaster Management are responsible for carrying out disaster mitigation in India.
2. The Disaster Management Bill was passed by the Government of India in 2005 with an aim to improve the capabilities of India in Disaster Management.

Which of the statements given above is/are correct?

(a) Only 1 (b) Only 2
(c) Both 1 and 2 (d) Neither 1 nor 2

Ans. (c)

Exp. Both the statements (1) and (2) are correct with reference to disaster mitigation in India.

Geological Survey of India (GSI) relate to creation and updation of national geo-scientific data and mineral resource assessment, air-borne and marine surveys.

And it is responsible for carrying out disaster mitigation in India.

The Disaster Management Bill was passed by the Government of India in 2005 with an aim to improve the capabilities of India in disaster management.

It aims for planning and implementation of disaster plans to prevent or mitigate people from disaster-affected areas, to respond and recover from disaster events.

NCERT MCQ

Practice Set (1-3)

India & World Geography

Scan the QR Code given below to get the PDF of these Practice Sets.